Ancient Jewish Diaspora

Supplements to the Journal for the Study of Judaism

Editor

René Bloch (*Institut für Judaistik, Universität Bern*)
Karina Martin Hogan (*Department of Theology, Fordham University*)

Associate Editors

Hindy Najman (*Theology & Religion Faculty, University of Oxford*)
Eibert J.C. Tigchelaar (*Faculty of Theology and Religious Studies, KU Leuven*)
Benjamin G. Wright, III (*Department of Religion Studies, Lehigh University*)

Advisory Board

A.M. Berlin – K. Berthelot – J.J. Collins – B. Eckhardt – Y. Furstenberg
S. Kattan Gribetz – G. Anthony Keddie – L. Lehmhaus – O. Malka
A. Manekin – S. Mason – F. Mirguet – J.H. Newman – A.K. Petersen
M. Popović – P. Pouchelle – I. Rosen-Zvi – J.T.A.G.M. van Ruiten – M. Segal
J. Sievers – L.T. Stuckenbruck – L. Teugels – J.C. de Vos – Sharon Weisser

VOLUME 206

The titles published in this series are listed at *brill.com/jsjs*

Ancient Jewish Diaspora

Essays on Hellenism

By

René Bloch

BRILL

LEIDEN | BOSTON

Library of Congress Cataloging-in-Publication Data

Names: Bloch, René S., author.
Title: Ancient Jewish diaspora : essays on Hellenism / by René Bloch.
Description: Leiden ; Boston : Brill, [2022] | Series: Supplements to the Journal for the study of Judaism, 1384-2161 ; vol 206 | Includes bibliographical references and index.
Identifiers: LCCN 2022024913 (print) | LCCN 2022024914 (ebook) | ISBN 9789004521889 (hardback) | ISBN 9789004521896 (ebook)
Subjects: LCSH: Jewish diaspora. | Jews–History–To 70 A.D. | Jews–Identity. | Civilization, Ancient.
Classification: LCC DS134 .B58 2022 (print) | LCC DS134 (ebook) | DDC 909/.04924–dc23/eng/20220607
LC record available at https://lccn.loc.gov/2022024913
LC ebook record available at https://lccn.loc.gov/2022024914

Typeface for the Latin, Greek, and Cyrillic scripts: "Brill". See and download: brill.com/brill-typeface.

ISSN 1384-2161
ISBN 978-90-04-52188-9 (hardback)
ISBN 978-90-04-52189-6 (e-book)

Copyright 2022 by René Bloch. Published by Koninklijke Brill NV, Leiden, The Netherlands.
Koninklijke Brill NV incorporates the imprints Brill, Brill Nijhoff, Brill Hotei, Brill Schöningh, Brill Fink, Brill mentis, Vandenhoeck & Ruprecht, Böhlau and V&R unipress.
Koninklijke Brill NV reserves the right to protect this publication against unauthorized use. Requests for re-use and/or translations must be addressed to Koninklijke Brill NV via brill.com or copyright.com.

This book is printed on acid-free paper and produced in a sustainable manner.

PRINTED BY DRUKKERIJ WILCO B.V. - AMERSFOORT, THE NETHERLANDS

In memory of my grandmother Gitta Schmeidler-Strausz (1913–2013):
Wer war Turnus?

∵

Contents

Acknowledgments IX

Introduction 1

PART 1
Moses and Exodus

1   Alexandria in Pharaonic Egypt: Projections in *De vita Mosis*   21

2   Moses and the Charlatans: On the Charge of γόης καὶ ἀπατεών in *Contra Apionem* 2.145, 161   39

3   Moses: Motherless with Two Mothers   55

4   Leaving Home: Philo of Alexandria on the Exodus   69

PART 2
Places and Ruins

5   Geography without Territory: Tacitus's Digression on the Jews and its Ethnographic Context   83

6   Show and Tell: Myth, Tourism, and Jewish Hellenism   101

7   What If the Temple of Jerusalem Had Not Been Destroyed by the Romans?   128

PART 3
Theater and Myth

8   Philo's Struggle with Jewish Myth   153

9   Part of the Scene: Jewish Theater in Antiquity   173

VIII

10   Take Your Time: Conversion, Confidence and Tranquility in *Joseph and Aseneth*   200

PART 4
Antisemitism and Reception

11   Antisemitism and Early Scholarship on Ancient Antisemitism   223

12   A Leap into the Void: The *Philo-Lexikon* and Jewish-German Hellenism   245

13   Tacitus's Excursus on the Jews through the Ages: An Overview of the History of its Reception History   257

14   Polytheism and Monotheism in Antiquity: On Jan Assmann's Critique of Monotheism   293

15   *Testa incognita*: The History of the Pseudo-Josephus Bust in Copenhagen   314

Index of Cited Passages   339
Index of Names and Places   353
Index of Subjects   359

Acknowledgments

All chapters of this book (with the exception of the introduction) have been published previously elsewhere, some of them in places not easily accessible. Four chapters, originally written in German, appear here for the first time in English translation (chapters 2, 6, 12, and 14). I would like to thank Dr. Carson Bay, University of Bern, for having translated these chapters and for having provided helpful advice throughout the production of this book. Chapters 9 and 13 have been translated at an earlier stage from the German into English and are here reprinted in their English version (see the acknowledgments at the beginning of these two articles). These essays were written over the course of 25 years. I have left them unchanged, even in cases where I might see matters a bit differently today (and look back with a smile). Obvious mistakes have been corrected, the language slightly adjusted here and there. I wish to thank Judith Göppinger and Sarah-Maria Hebeisen who patiently prepared the indices.

I would like to thank the publishers of the journals and volumes in which the articles originally appeared for allowing me to reprint them here. The original places of publication are as follows:

"Alexandria in Pharaonic Egypt: Projections in *De Vita Mosis*." *SPhiloA* 24 (2012): 69–84.

"Moses and the Charlatans: On the Charge of γόης καὶ ἀπατεών in *Contra Apionem* 2.145.161." Pages 142–157 in *Internationales Josephus-Kolloquium Bruxelles 1998*. Münsteraner Judaistische Studien 4. Edited by Folker Siegert and Jürgen U. Kalms. Münster: LIT, 1999 (originally published in German as: "Mose und die Scharlatane: Zum Vorwurf γόης καὶ ἀπατεών in *Contra Apionem* 2.145.161").

"Moses: Motherless with Two Mothers." Pages 237–250 in *Missing Mothers: Maternal Absence in Antiquity*. Edited by Sabine Hübner and David Ratzan. Peeters: Louvain 2021.

"Leaving Home: Philo of Alexandria on the Exodus." Pages 357–364 in *Israel's Exodus in Transdisciplinary Perspective: Text, Archaeology, Culture, and Geoscience*. Edited by Thomas E. Levy, Thomas Schneider, and William H.C. Propp. Cham: Springer, 2015.

"Geography without Territory: Tacitus' Digression on the Jews and its Ethnographic Context." Pages 38–54 in *Internationales Josephus-Kolloquium Aarhus*

1999. Münsteraner Judaistische Studien 5. Edited by Jürgen U. Kalms. Münster: LIT, 2000.

Show and Tell: Myth, Tourism, and Jewish Hellenism. Franz Delitzsch-Vorlesung 2015. Münster: Franz-Delitzsch-Gesellschaft and Institutum Judaicum Delitzschianum at the Westfälische Wilhelms-Universität, 2017 (originally published in German as: "Andromeda in Jaffa. Mythische Orte als Reiseziele in der jüdischen Antike").

"What if the Temple of Jerusalem Had not Been Destroyed by the Romans?" Pages 43–57 in *"If Only We Had Died in Egypt!" What Ifs? of Jewish History from Abraham to Zionism*. Edited by Gavriel D. Rosenfeld. Cambridge: Cambridge University Press, 2016.

"Philo's Struggle with Jewish Myth." Pages 107–126 in *Philo of Alexandria and Greek Myth: Narratives, Allegories, and Arguments*. Studies in Philo of Alexandria 10. Edited by Francesca Calabi and Ludovica De Luca. Leiden: Brill, 2019.

"Part of the Scene: Jewish Theater in Antiquity." *Journal of Ancient Judaism* 8 (2017 [2018]): 150–169.

"Take Your Time: Conversion, Cofidence and Tranquility in *Joseph and Aseneth*." Pages 77–96 in *Anthropologie und Ethik. Frühjüdische Literatur und Neues Testament. Wechselseitige Wahrnehmungen*. Edited by Matthias Konradt and Esther Schläpfer. Tübingen: Mohr Siebeck, 2014.

"Antisemitism and Early Scholarship on Ancient Antisemitism." Pages 41–62 in *Protestant Bible Scholarship: Antisemitism, Philosemitism, and Anti-Judaism*. Edited by Arjen Bakker et al. Leiden: Brill, 2022.

"A Leap into the Void: The *Philo-Lexikon* and Jewish-German Hellenism." Pages 410–419 in *Lebenskunst. Erkundungen zu Biographie, Lebenswelt und Erinnerungen: Festschrift für Jacques Picard*. Edited by Konrad J. Kuhn et al. Köln: Böhlau, 2017 (originally published in German as: "Ein Sprung ins Leere: Das *Philo-Lexikon* und der jüdisch-deutsche Hellenismus").

"Tacitus' Excursus on the Jews through the Ages: An Overview of its Reception History." Pages 377–409 in *Oxford Readings in Tacitus*. Edited by Rhiannon Ash. Oxford: Oxford University Press, 2012.

ACKNOWLEDGMENTS

"Polytheism and Monotheism in Antiquity: On Jan Assmann's Critique of Monotheism." Pages 5–24 in *Fremdbilder-Selbstbilder. Imaginationen des Judentums von der Antike bis in die Neuzeit*. Edited by René Bloch, Simone Haeberli, and Rainer C. Schwinges. Basel: Schwabe, 2010 (originally published in German as "Polytheismus und Monotheismus in der paganen Antike: Zu Jan Assmanns Monotheismus-Kritik").

"*Testa incognita:* The History of the Pseudo-Josephus Bust in Copenhagen." In "*A Vision for/of the Days": Studies in Early Jewish History and Historiography in Honor of Daniel R. Schwartz*. Edited by Robert Brody et al. Leiden: Brill, 2023.

I am grateful that this book can appear in the Supplements to the Journal for the Study of Judaism (JSJS) with Brill. I would like to thank the anonymous reviewers for their helpful comments and especially my colleague and co-editor Karina Martin Hogan for the always inspiring and productive cooperation we have as fellow JSJS editors. I would also like to thank Marjolein van Zuylen, our liaison at Brill, for her extraordinary support and Madelon Janse for all her help during the production of this book.

I dedicate this book to the memory of my grandmother Gitta Schmeidler-Strausz. Well educated in classical texts in pre-war Hungary, she had the talent to remind others of their imperfections in a charming, yet demanding way, always pushing for more, and insisting that the other side be considered. When as a young student I proudly mentioned Aeneas in a conversation with her, my grandmother responded: "Do you also know who Turnus was?" I didn't know. Then I learned: in Roman myth, Turnus is king of the Rutulians and the inferior counter-part to Aeneas, the mythical ancestor of ancient Rome. I came to understand her reproach as an encouragement not only to learn more, but always try to see the whole picture, to include the other side(s) and to bear in mind the relations of power. As this book shows, the study of the Jews in the Hellenistic and Roman periods is much more than simply the reflection of a minority finding its place in the large context of the ancient Mediterranean. But it is that, too.

Introduction

> When the high-priest learned that Alexander was not far from the city, he went out with the priests and the body of citizens, and, making the reception sacred in character and different from that of other nations, met him at a certain place called Saphein. This name, translated into the Greek tongue, means "Lookout." For, as it happened, Jerusalem and the temple could be seen from there. Now the Phoenicians and the Chaldaeans who followed along thought to themselves that the king in his anger would naturally permit them to plunder the city and put the high priest to a shameful death, but the reverse of this happened. For when Alexander while still far off saw the multitude in white garments, the priests at their head clothed in linen, and the high priest in a robe of hyacinth-blue and gold, wearing on his head the mitre with the golden plate on it on which was inscribed the name of God, he approached alone and prostrated himself before the Name and first greeted the high priest. Then all the Jews together greeted Alexander with one voice and surrounded him, but the kings of Syria and the others were struck with amazement at his action and supposed that the king's mind was deranged.
>
> JOSEPHUS, *AJ* 11.329–332 [trans. LCL]

Josephus's description of a summit between Alexander the Great and the Jewish high priest (Jaddus) in Jerusalem is full of drama and replete with symbolism. It is a meeting of two leaders who are very keen to approach each other. The get-together takes place on Mount Scopus (Saphein), whence Jerusalem with its Jewish temple can be seen. Alexander prostrates himself before the Jewish god and the high priest. His greeting is immediately echoed by a unanimous and enthusiastic welcome from the Jews. The Jewish-Hellenistic summit then turns into a love-feast. There are also other people, from different ethnic backgrounds, on the stage: Phoenicians, Chaldeans, Syrians (and others) and they cannot believe their eyes. Instead of giving the order to plunder Jerusalem and kill the high priest, Alexander shows the utmost respect for Judaism: their god, their religious leadership, their temple and their city. In Josephus's report of the summit on Mount Scopus, Judaism and Hellenic culture merge into one. Later, we hear how Alexander and the high priest shake hands and, accompanied by the other Jewish priests who "run alongside," hurry to the Jerusalem temple where Alexander makes a sacrifice under the guidance of the high priest. There he is shown the biblical book of Daniel, from whose prophecies Alexander concludes that he is predestined to destroy the empire of the Persians. Alexander's

© RENÉ BLOCH, 2022 | DOI:10.1163/9789004521896_002

decision to attack the Persians thus matures in the course of his reading of Daniel in the Jewish temple in Jerusalem. In gratitude, Alexander guarantees the Jews the right to live according to their customs.[1]

The story of Alexander's visit to Jerusalem is exactly that: a story. In all likelihood, Alexander was never in Jerusalem: after the conquest of Phoenicia and the capture of Tyre (332 BCE), Alexander travelled along the Mediterranean coast to Gaza and from there to Egypt. There was no obvious reason for a detour inland to Jerusalem. With the claim that Alexander had visited Jerusalem and the temple, however, a symbolic link is created between the Jewish and the Hellenic realms. At the same time, this legend, which circulated among Jews up to the Middle Ages and for which Josephus is our earliest source,[2] also assumes Jewish sovereignty: Alexander the Great prostrates himself before the high priest, not the other way around, and the Book of Daniel is the catalyst for Alexander's political decisions. Jerusalem becomes the decisive hinge for Alexander's great victory over the Persians (331 BCE). This twofold strategy of trying to connect with the greater political power while claiming sovereignty is a common feature of Jewish Hellenism.[3] Jewish Hellenism is characterized by the processing of Jewish topics with Hellenistic features, but simultaneously by an almost absolute adherence to basic Jewish values (such as monotheism, lack of images) that did not agree with those of the majority culture. The Jewish priests make the reception of Alexander the Great "different from that of other nations."[4] Jewish-Hellenistic literature developed within these parameters, at times embracing and at other times resisting acculturation with the larger culture.[5] Jewish Hellenism was not simply a love-feast, and Josephus was very well

---

1 Josephus, *AJ* 11.336–339.

2 See Shaye J.D. Cohen, "Alexander the Great and Jaddus the High Priest According to Josephus," *AJS Review* 7/8 (1982/83): 41–68; René Bloch, "Alexandre le Grand et le judaïsme: La double stratégie d'auteurs juifs de l'antiquité et du Moyen Âge," in *Le voyage d'Alexandre au Paradis terrestre: Orient et Occident, regards croisés*, ed. Catherine Gaullier-Bougassas and Margaret Bridges (Turnhout: Brepols, 2012), 145–162; Ory Amitay, "Alexander in Jerusalem: The Extra-Josephan Traditions," in Paul Spilsbury and Chris Seeman, *Judean Antiquities 11: Translation and Commentary*. Vol. 6a of *Flavius Josephus: Translation and Commentary*, ed. Steve Mason (Leiden: Brill, 2017), 128–147.

3 On this see the groundbreaking work of Erich S. Gruen, especially *Heritage and Hellenism: The Reinvention of Jewish Tradition* (Berkeley: University of California Press, 1998). In Josephus the meeting between Alexander and the high priest is preceded by divine reassurance: God speaks to the high priest (who earlier had been loyal to the Persian king Darius) in his sleep and tells him to adorn Jerusalem and welcome Alexander and his followers (*AJ* 11.327–328).

4 Josephus, *AJ* 11.329: διαφέρουσαν τῶν ἄλλων ἐθνῶν ποιούμενος τὴν ὑπάντησιν.

5 See John M.G. Barclay, *Jews in the Mediterranean Diaspora. From Alexander to Trajan* (323 BCE–

INTRODUCTION 3

aware of this: his last work, *Contra Apionem*, is one long defense of Judaism against pagan attacks (see below chapters 2, 11, and 14).

The legend of Alexander in Jerusalem as told by Josephus (written down in Rome towards the end of the first century CE) is a complex narrative. Politically, it can be read as a legitimization of the privileges (*privilegia*) that the Jews were receiving in Roman times (Alexander had already granted them![6]). Culturally, the story also tells us something about the continuing importance of Jerusalem in the diaspora, even after the loss of the city. But Alexander the Great was also a reference for the Jewish diaspora. It is once more Josephus, the man who spent one half of his life in Jerusalem and the other in the Roman diaspora, who is our source. According to Josephus, it was indeed Alexander himself who settled the Jews in the newly founded city of Alexandria. Before Alexander decided in favor of the Jews as the first settlers, he did a thorough casting of all other candidates:

> For it was not lack of inhabitants to people the city, whose foundation he had so much at heart, that led Alexander to assemble in it a colony of our nation. This privilege he conferred on our people, after careful and thorough scrutiny, as a reward of valour and fidelity.
>
> JOSEPHUS, *CA* 2.42 [trans. LCL]

This passage is part of a literary counter-attack against the Egyptian author Apion, who questioned the citizenship of the Jews of Alexandria. Here too, then, the reference to Alexander serves as evidence and legitimation: the Jews have been residents of this city since its foundation by Alexander (331 BCE). Early Jewish settlement in Egypt is well documented, but Josephus's claim here is as legendary as in the case of Alexander's visit to Jerusalem. Hellenism represented an epoch in which Jews reinvented themselves, looked for coalitions, and stood in conflict with others. In this, they did not really differ from other peoples of the Hellenistic age, least of all from the Greeks. Hellenism stands for a number of new characteristics in Greek society: with regard to language (e.g. the development of Koine Greek), literature (e.g. small-scale poetry as represented by Callimachus), and politics (e.g. the increasing importance of the individual). Greeks (and Romans) of the Hellenistic period, too, created coalitions based on legends.[7] Jewish Hellenism is very much a part of Hellenism—it

---

117 CE) (Berkeley: University of California Press, 1996) and John J. Collins, *Between Athens and Jerusalem: Jewish Identity in the Hellenistic Diaspora* (Grand Rapids: Eerdmans, 1999).

6 Josephus, *AJ* 11.338.

7 See Erich S. Gruen, "Greek and Non-Greeks," in *The Cambridge Companion to the Hellenis-*

is a specific example of it. After all, it is Ezekiel's *Exagoge*, a Jewish play on the exodus in Greek iambic trimeters (see chapter 9), that is the longest specimen of Hellenistic drama.[8] In the same vein, *Joseph and Aseneth*, the love story of the daughter of an Egyptian priest and the Jewish governor of Egypt, is one of the few Hellenistic novels that have come down to us (see chapter 10). Judaism and Hellenism are hardly two entirely separate concepts.

The 15 chapters of this book all in one way or another tackle the manifold aspects of Jewish Hellenism. The book covers a wide range of topics, divided into four clusters: Moses and Exodus, Places and Ruins, Theater and Myth, Antisemitism and Reception (see the summaries of each chapter below). The fourth subdivision goes beyond antiquity, reaching all the way to contemporary history. In Classics, Hellenism was for a long time an *agnatus* of sorts, the child born when a will was already written, an afterthought to 'Classical Antiquity' proper. But Hellenism, and in particular Jewish Hellenism, was also a recurrent point of orientation and self-understanding (see chapter 12). In recent years, scholarship on Hellenism, including Jewish Hellenism, has grown enormously. The age of Hellenism as the step-child of Classics has long passed.[9]

With the exception of 'Essays' (literally 'attempts'—and that is indeed what is being proposed here), all the words in this book's title—*Ancient Jewish Diaspora: Essays on Hellenism*—have been the subject of much discussion in recent scholarship. What does 'ancient' mean with regard to Judaism and,

---

    tic World, ed. Glenn R. Bugh (Cambridge: Cambridge University Press, 2006), 295–314; Irad Malkin, *A Small Greek World: Networks in the Ancient Mediterranean* (Oxford: Oxford University Press, 2011), 119–142.

8   See Agnieszka Kotlińska-Toma, *Hellenistic Tragedy: Texts, Translations and a Critical Survey* (London: Bloomsbury, 2015).

9   For good surveys on the Hellenistic age see Peter Green, *The Hellenistic Age: A Short History* (New York: Modern Library, 2008); Klaus Meister, *Der Hellenismus: Kultur- und Geistesgeschichte* (Stuttgart: J.B. Metzler, 2016); Angelos Chaniotis, *Age of Conquests: the Greek World from Alexander to Hadrian (336 BC–AD 138)* (London: Profile Books, 2018). Among the many innovative studies on Jewish Hellenism in recent times see, e.g. Maren R. Niehoff, *Jewish Exegesis and Homeric Scholarship in Alexandria* (Cambridge: Cambridge University Press, 2011); Françoise Mirguet, *An Early History of Compassion: Emotion and Imagination in Hellenistic Judaism* (Cambridge: Cambridge University Press, 2017); Jonathan R. Trotter, *The Jerusalem Temple in Diaspora: Jewish Practice and Thought During the Second Temple Period* (Leiden: Brill, 2019); Ashley L. Bacchi, *Uncovering Jewish Creativity in Book III of the Sibylline Oracles: Gender, Intertextuality, and Politics* (Leiden: Brill, 2020). For a recent good survey on the Jews in the Hellenistic age see Lester L. Grabbe, *A History of the Jews and Judaism in the Second Temple Period*. Volume 2: *The Coming of the Greeks: The Early Hellenistic Period (335–175 BCE)* (London: T&T Clark, 2008), id. *A History of the Jews and Judaism in the Second Temple Period*. Volume 3: *The Maccabean Revolt, Hasmonean Rule, and Herod the Great (175–174 BCE)* (London: T&T Clark, 2020).

INTRODUCTION

related to this: is 'Jewish' even the appropriate term, or should one not rather speak of 'Judean'? I prefer 'ancient' Judaism to the common alternative (especially among German scholars) 'early Judaism' ('Frühjudentum'). The latter has replaced the highly problematic term 'late Judaism' ('Spätjudentum'), but in its use as a parallel epoch to 'early Christianity' ('Frühchristentum'), it is not free of an agenda either. With the admittedly imprecise adjective 'ancient,' one places Judaism in the larger context of the study of antiquity.[10] As for the hotly debated question of 'Jew' and 'Judean' I have elsewhere, in a recent article, explained why in my view in most cases there is no reason to adjust the "traditional" translation 'Jew'/'Jewish' for Greek *Ioudaios* or Latin *Iudaeus*. A chronological distinction between an ethnic and geographic meaning of *Ioudaios/Iudaeus* on the one hand, and a religious one on the other, seems to me a rather artificial construct for the ancient world.[11] As for 'diaspora', this term is first used in the Septuagint in theologically-loaded language denoting divine punishment.[12] As John Barclay rightly notes, the "first and most obvious feature" of diaspora "is its formation of *both local and translocal identities*. Diaspora communities are, by definition, 'not-here to stay'. They retain a sense of belonging elsewhere ...."[13] Yet this is hardly what Jewish-Hellenistic authors such as Philo of Alexandria would have understood by their living outside the land of Israel (see chapter 4). As Erich Gruen rightly notes: "It is striking and significant that Jews in the Second Temple period omitted to contrive a theory or philosophy of diaspora. Although the issue seems gripping in retrospect, it does not appear to have

---

10   On the question of the beginning of Judaism in scholarship see Steven Weitzman, *The Origin of the Jews: The Quest for Roots in a Rootless Age* (Princeton: Princeton University Press, 2017).

11   *Pace* Shaye J.D. Cohen, *The Beginnings of Jewishness: Boundaries, Varieties, Uncertainties* (Berkeley: University of California Press, 1999); see René Bloch, "Jew or Judean: The Latin Evidence," in *Torah, Temple, Land: Constructions of Judaism in Antiquity*, ed. Markus Witte, Jens Schröter, and Vera M. Lepper (Tübingen: Mohr Siebeck, 2021), 231–242. As for the term 'Judaism' it has been declared an anachronistic term for the ancient world by Daniel Boyarin, *Judaism: The Genealogy of a Modern Notion* (New Brunswick: Rugters University Press, 2019). For a good critique on Boyarin see Adele Reinhartz, "Was the Word in the Beginning? On the Relationship between Language and Concepts," *Marginalia: Los Angeles Review of Books*. 5 July 2019, https://marginalia.lareviewofbooks.org/word-beginning -relationship-language-concepts. That at times 'Judean' is indeed the preferable translation for *Ioudaios/Iudaeus* is not to be doubted: see on this also chapter 5 in this volume.

12   Deut 28:64 LXX: "and the Lord your God will disperse (διασπερεῖ) you to all nations;" 30:4: "If your dispersion (ἡ διασπορά σου) be from an end of the sky to an end of the sky" (NETS).

13   John M.G. Barclay, "Introduction: Diaspora Negotiations," in *Negotiating Diaspora: Jewish Strategies in the Roman Empire*, ed. John M.G. Barclay (London: T&T Clark, 2004), 1–6, at 2.

been compelling at the time."[14] Nevertheless, in spite of the misleading and anachronistic assumptions 'diaspora' may convey, it remains the commonly used umbrella term for the Jews (and other peoples) living outside their original "home." Moreover, the exchange between Egypt and Israel—or even more generally between Jews in the West and those in the East—may have been more intense than is often assumed (with the linguistic implications that come along with it).[15]

And, finally, 'Hellenism': this term for the period between Alexander the Great and the emergence of the Roman empire was introduced by the ancient historian Johann Gustav Droysen whose three volumes of *Geschichte des Hellenismus* appeared in two editions between 1836 and 1878. Droysen, the son of an army chaplain, understood by 'Hellenism' primarily the rapid and extensive spread of the Greek idea: of Greek language and Greek culture.[16] Moreover, Droysen conceived of Hellenism as a preparation for Christianity. In the introduction to the third volume of his grand history, Droysen stresses that Hellenism was not "a dead spot in the history of mankind," but "a living link in the chain of human development" and "bearer of greater determinations that should mature in her lap."[17] Droysen needs to be credited for having placed the spotlight on a period that until then had been neglected, but his understanding of Hellenism is indeed problematic and dated.[18] Incidentally, in his *Geschichte des Hellenismus* Droysen has practically nothing to say about Judea and the Jews. Since Droysen, the scholarly use of the term 'Hellenism' has developed quite a bit. More recently, not least in the context of postcolonial approaches, scholars have questioned the extent to which the spread of Greek language and culture was simply the result of a top-down policy. Was Hellenism the result of

---

14   Erich S. Gruen, *Diaspora: Jews amidst Greeks and Romans* (Cambridge: Harvard University Press, 2002, 6); see also chapter 5 in this volume.

15   See René Bloch, "How much Hebrew in Jewish Alexandria?," in *Alexandria—Hub of the Hellenistic World*, ed. Benjamin Schliesser et al. (Tübingen: Mohr Siebeck, 2021), 261–278.

16   On Droysen see Wilfried Nippel, *Johann Gustav Droysen: Ein Leben zwischen Wissenschaft und Politik* (München: C.H. Beck, 2008).

17   Johann Gustav Droysen, *Geschichte des Hellenismus* III: *Geschichte der Epigonen* (Darmstadt: Wissenschaftliche Buchgesellschaft 2008), x ("toter Fleck in der Geschichte der Menschheit", "ein lebendiges Glied in der Kette menschlicher Entwicklung", "Trägerin größerer Bestimmungen, die in ihrem Schoß heranreifen sollten").

18   See Reinhold Bichler, *"Hellenismus": Geschichte und Problematik eines Epochenbegriffs* (Darmstadt: Wissenschaftliche Buchgesellschaft, 1983); Edouard Will and Claude Orrieux, *Ioudaïsmos-Hellènismos: essai sur le judaïsme judéen à l'époque hellénistique* (Nancy: Presses Universitaires de Nancy, 1986), 9–35; Philipp S. Alexander, "Hellenism and Hellenization as Problematic Historiographical Categories," in *Paul beyond the Judaism/Hellenism Divide*, ed. Troels Engberg-Pedersen (Louisville: Westminster 2001), 63–80.

INTRODUCTION

a more natural confrontation and exchange with Greek culture? The question finds exemplary expression in the case of Judea, where in the second century BCE the conflict between the Seleucids and Maccabees arose. In the modern understanding of the term, 'Hellenism' is no longer simply a term for "cultural fusion" in the sense of Droysen. At the same time, the emergence of new forms of culture and religion as the result of exchange with Hellenistic culture continues to be an important aspect of the study of Hellenism and in particular of Jewish Hellenism. Several articles collected in this volume discuss Jewish responses to aspects of pagan culture (such as theater, myth, the novel).

Epochs are, of course, always to some extent simply heuristic constructs helping us navigate through history. If in Droysen it is the Prussian monarchy that shines through his presentation of the Hellenistic age,[19] for modern interpreters other fixations come to the surface. As Angelos Chaniotis writes in his recent history of Hellenism: "This period is truly the cosmopolitan era of the Greeks in a way that no preceding period of Greek history was. Many of the phenomena that one observes in the 'long Hellenistic age' find parallels in the modern world, and the 'modernity' of this historical period adds to its attractiveness for both historians and alert observers of our own day and age." Chaniotis then refers to four parallels: globalization (multiculturalism), megacities, new religions and governance.[20] These are indeed fundamental themes of the Hellenistic age, including the Jewish experience: one may think of the way Moses is imagined as a cosmopolitan citizen in Philo (see chapters 3 and 4) or the importance of the city of Alexandria in Hellenistic Judaism (including the question of political rights for Jews).[21] Jewish Hellenism is a significant element in the general study of Hellenism, prominent because of the large number of available sources, among other things. In a way, Jewish Hellenism epitomizes Hellenism at large containing all the characteristics by which we have come to understand that term. It is in that sense, as suggested by the subtitle of the book, that the articles collected in this volume are simply meant as essays on Hellenism.

---

19   See Albert B. Bosworth, "Alexander the Great and the Creation of the Hellenistic Age," in *The Cambridge Companion to the Hellenistic World*, ed. Glenn R. Bugh (Cambridge: Cambridge University Press, 2006), 9–27 at 9: "His vision of the Macedonia of Philip and Alexander was not intended as a political manifesto for the present, but it was eagerly seized upon as foreshadowing what could be achieved by the German states united under the leadership of the Prussian monarchy."

20   Chaniotis, *Age of the Conquests*, 6.

21   On Alexandria see most recently Benjamin Schliesser et al., eds., *Alexandria—Hub of the Hellenistic World* (Tübingen: Mohr Siebeck, 2021).

8   INTRODUCTION

1   Moses and Exodus

Moses and Philo of Alexandria are the two figures who stand in the center
of the first section and thus at the beginning of this volume. The two share a
number of biographical features. They both hail from Egypt and become interpreters (ἑρμηνεῖς) of the Jewish law. Rather hesitantly, they both act as political
leaders (at least temporarily): they defend Jewish rights at the courts of the
authorities in power, the Pharaoh and the Roman emperor Caligula respectively. In "Alexandria in Pharaonic Egypt: Projections in *De vita Mosis*," I argue
that Philo made use of such parallels and that, in a way, he slipped autobiographically into the world of Moses. About Philo's life very little is known,
and Moses of course remains to us more a mythical than a historical person.
However, through Philo's Moses we can, I suggest, grasp a little more about the
former's biography. In his fundamental tractate on Moses's life, *De vita Mosis*,
there is some sort of *Tagespolitik* tangible: the dire straits of Jewish Alexandria
during the time of the anti-Jewish riot (38 CE) come to resemble the oppression
of the Israelites as reported in the book of Exodus.

The chapter on "Moses and the Charlatans: On the Charge of γόης καὶ ἀπατεών in *Contra Apionem* 2.145, 161" asks a seemingly simple question: What
exactly is meant by the charge brought forward, according to Josephus, by
the Hellenistic authors "Apollonius Molon, Lysimachus, and others"? Here I
question the common assumption of a widespread pagan accusation of Jews
as magicians. Greco-Roman mockery of Jewish magic is in fact quite rare,
and Josephus hardly appears to react to such a stereotype. Much more of
a concern to Josephus are the political and religious charlatans of the kind
of John of Gischala, as he describes them in the *Jewish War* as well as in
the *Jewish Antiquities*. This philological study shows just how difficult it is
to understand and contextualize particular citations and references in Josephus's tractate *Against Apion*, a major source for the study of ancient antisemitism.[22]

The next chapter is all about Moses—and his two mothers, the Hebrew
Yochebed and the daughter of the Pharaoh who found him among the reeds of
the Nile and named him Moses (and thus is introduced in the story as at least
as important as his biological mother). The biblical Moses myth very much follows the ancient paradigm of mythological heroes. Like Odysseus or Aeneas,
Moses depends heavily on feminine support. That Moses had two mothers—
one "Jewish," one "pagan"—on the one hand obscured Moses's origins and, in a

---

22   On the applicability of this modern term for the ancient world see below and chapter 11.

INTRODUCTION 9

way, his hybrid roots made him motherless (ἀμήτωρ: incidentally a surprisingly common word in Philo). On the other hand, the doubling of Moses's mother allowed for hybrid readings, particularly attractive to Jewish Hellenism. This becomes most conspicuous in Philo and Ezekiel the Tragedian, who both send Moses to both Jewish and Hellenistic schools.

In "Leaving Home: Philo of Alexandria on the Exodus" I ask how Jewish-Hellenistic authors writing in Egypt came to terms with the exodus story of liberation from Egyptian slavery and longing for the promised land. After all, to authors such as Philo, Egypt was their fatherland. Remarkably, in Philo's rewriting of the exodus the destination of the journey through the wilderness is barely mentioned. Contrary to the biblical narrative, in the scene of the burning bush, as retold by Philo, God does not tell Moses where to go. Philo's main concern is what happens in Egypt, both in biblical times and in his own days. The exodus is nevertheless important to Philo: he reads the story allegorically as a journey from the land of the body to the realms of the mind. Yet such a symbolic reading also permitted him to control the meaning of the exodus and to stay, literally and figuratively, in Egypt. The chapter focuses on Philo, but also briefly looks into the *Wisdom of Solomon* and Ezekiel's *Exagoge* (two texts for which Egyptian origin can be assumed). As I show, in these cases too the destination of the exodus lies anywhere but at the center of the tale.

2   Places and Ruins

The second cluster of the book includes three chapters, written over a span of twenty years. "Geography without Territory: Tacitus's Digression on the Jews and its Ethnographic Context" grew out of my University of Basel dissertation in Classics.[23] Tacitus's fairly detailed excursus on the Jews and Judea is rarely placed into the larger ethnographic tradition of Greeks and Romans or into relation with Tacitus's other ethnographic texts (especially his *Germania* and the digression on Britannia in the *Agricola*). In this chapter, I argue that the fact that the Jews were scattered across the Mediterranean (and beyond) had an impact on the way they were described by Greek and Roman authors. Diaspora by definition transcends geographical territory and boundaries. While hardly a phenomenon of the Jews alone, their Diasporic "condition" led, I argue, to

---

23   René Bloch, *Antike Vorstellungen vom Judentum. Der Judenexkurs des Tacitus im Rahmen der griechisch-römischen Ethnographie* (Stuttgart: Franz Steiner, 2002).

a variety of specifics in the way they were viewed by others—specifics that made pagan ethnography on the Jews different from that on other peoples such as the Germani or Britanni. I highlight three differences: 1) There are hardly any anthropogeographical arguments about the Jews. Judea does not explain the Jews (while, e.g., the geographic features of Germania and Britannia are brought into relation with the character of the inhabitants). 2) Some other topoi of the ethnographic codex such as clothing and housing are missing in Greco-Roman descriptions of the Jews. 3) Jews apparently did not fit into the "dualistic" scheme Greeks/Romans vs. barbarians. They are hardly ever called barbarians in Greco-Roman literature. I suggest that these exceptions are connected to the fact that while Jews inhabited a characteristic region, namely Judea or Palestine, they mostly lived in various places outside their home country, i.e. in the diaspora. Diversity and cosmopolitanism within ancient Judaism led to its being something of an *aporia* for Greco-Roman ethnography.

In "Show and Tell: Myth, Tourism, and Jewish Hellenism" I am interested in a phenomenon which is well known from pagan and Christian antiquity: the tangible connection of material remains to mythical stories. I show that Jews, too, had their own showcases where objects from mythical times could be visited. Going beyond the biblical descriptions, Jewish-Hellenistic authors describe or at least hint at a tourism of sorts to Jewish sites: in Hebron the bones of the biblical giants were on show. People visited the ashes from the destroyed city of Sodom. In the Hellenistic period, Jews went on sightseeing trips just like non-Jews. This placed them on equal footing with Greeks and Romans who pursued a similar strategy of making mythical objects and events real and visible. A particularly striking example of this shared interest in mythical "tourism" is the show-casing of Andromeda, who according to the myth was chained to the rocks of Joppa/Jaffa until she was freed by the Greek hero Perseus. Andromeda's chains were shown in situ, but other traces of the same myth (bones of the monster that was killed by Perseus) were on display in Rome. Romans and Jews shared the Greek myth of Andromeda. There are no indications that visits to Jewish sites involved any kind of ritual performance (contrary to what rabbinic sources say about encounters with biblical sites). Moreover, the texts suggest informal and occasional visits rather than prescribed itineraries (in this respect, our sources differ from later Christian pilgrimage reports). Nevertheless, "tourism" to Jewish sites, a practice which developed in the Hellenistic period, marks a remarkable phenomenon of Jewish Hellenism.

The third chapter of the "Places and Ruins" section delves into a counterfactual question: What would have happened if the temple of Jerusalem had not been destroyed by the Romans in the year 70 CE? The fall of Judaism's only sacrificial center is generally believed to be a watershed in Jewish history. If

INTRODUCTION

Jerusalem had not fallen, what would this have meant for the Jews in the land of Israel and in the diaspora, and what would have been the consequences for the development of nascent Christianity? While there is always a playful element in counterfactual history, the "fact" behind this particular question—the destruction of the temple—was not the result of absolute necessity. Whether or not the Romans intended to destroy the temple was already debated in antiquity, and it continues to be a question until today. In this chapter, I argue, partly following up on work by J.Z. Smith, that Jews would have stopped sacrificing even if the temple had not been destroyed in the Jewish-Roman War. As for the Jews living in the diaspora outside of Judea, the destruction must have been a massive shock, but it would not have substantially affected their daily religious practice. More fundamental is the counterfactual question for the development of rabbinic Judaism, and that of early Christianity. Rabbinic culture and literature stands in direct relation to the temple's destruction. Detailed descriptions of the temple service preserve the memory of the Second Temple Period and simultaneously prepare Judaism for a messianic age. The rabbis filled the void that resulted from the destruction of the temple with new meaning—and so did early Christians. For the latter, the destruction of the temple was a sign of divine punishment of the Jews, and Jesus was the consummation of all sacrifices. It is difficult to imagine Christianity having taken flight as a world religion like it did had not the temple been destroyed.

3   Theater and Myth

The third cluster of chapters is on "Theater and Myth," two areas of essential importance in the ancient world. Jews too, I argue here, had their part in these domains. In my 2011 book *Moses und der Mythos*, I focused to a large extent on Josephus's dealings with Greek myth, with brief sections on other Jewish-Hellenistic authors.[24] "Philo's Struggle with Jewish Myth" asks how the Alexandrian theologian and philosopher came to terms with the parallels between Greek and Jewish mythology, of which Philo, in spite of his anti-pagan polemics, was very much aware. While Jewish myth is hardly ever named as such in Philo, from a number of comments on biblical stories, such as the metamorphosis of Lot's wife into a pillar of salt or the creation of Eve out of the side

---

24   René Bloch, *Moses und der Mythos: Die Auseinandersetzung mit der griechischen Mythologie bei jüdisch-hellenistischen Autoren* (Leiden: Brill, 2011).

of Adam, it becomes obvious that for him, Jewish 'myth' is not simply an oxymoron. Some had declared the story of the tower of Babel straightforwardly as a myth in line with Greek mythology. Philo, who reports on this, barely distances himself from those radical critics of myth. Moreover, Philo does not shy away from recourse to Greek myth within theological reflections on biblical passages: he uses the myths of Pasiphae and Scylla in order to support Bible exegesis. Surprisingly, in Philo the Bible and myth can at times convene. As a consequence, I suggest that the assumption that, for Philo, myths "neither are literally true nor have an underlying meaning"[25] (Harry A. Wolfson), needs qualification.

In Greek culture, theater is genuinely connected with myth. And it comes as no surprise that the Jewish rejection of Greek myth goes along with the condemnation of theater (as in Philo and Josephus). However, here too things are more complicated. In "Part of the Scene: Jewish Theater in Antiquity," I show that in Greco-Roman antiquity Jews were indeed part of the (theater) scene. Jews had an ambivalent and complex relationship with theater and spectacles (as did Christians). Theater was associated with idolatry, immorality, and a departure from truth in favor of illusion and hypocrisy. Moreover, the theater was at times a place where people mocked Jews or, worse, where Jews were tortured and killed. At the same time, the literary evidence from both rabbinic and Jewish-Hellenistic sources suggests that many Jews did not avoid the spectacles. Throughout antiquity, the theater remained an important place not just of entertainment, but also of communication and exchange. Contrary to what one can still find written in handbooks on theater, and in handbooks on Judaism, Jews did not necessarily look the other way. They attended the theater; some even acted on stage or wrote theater plays. Ancient Jewish theater may exemplify best what Jewish Hellenism was.

The next chapter looks into another genre of Hellenistic culture: the novel. In "Take Your Time: Conversion, Confidence and Tranquility in *Joseph and Aseneth*," I aim at contextualizing this narrative, which grew out of a brief passage in the Book of Genesis. I interpret *JosAs* as a theater-like piece of popular fiction which seeks more to entertain than to convey a theological message. It is best understood as an example of the idealistic novel (with chastity of the protagonists typically being upheld until the end of the plot). The conversion of Aseneth is central to the narrative, but *JosAs* is by no means a missionary text. An important characteristic of the ancient novel is the overcoming of obsta-

---

25   Harry A. Wolfson, *Philo: Foundations of Religious Philosophy in Judaism, Christianity, and Islam*. 2 vols. (Cambridge: Harvard University Press, 1947), 1.36.

INTRODUCTION   13

cles that stand in the way of the prospective union of the starring couple. Here the obstacle is Aseneth's Egyptian origin, which is removed by her conversion. Once converted, Aseneth becomes a different person, not just with regard to religion. Before her conversion to Judaism, in the first part of the novel, Aseneth is presented as restless and insecure. She is constantly on the move. Only as a Jewish woman is she able to exhibit self-sovereignty similar to what Joseph has possessed from the beginning. The novel consistently has Jews act in a confident, almost stoic manner. An exact dating of *JosAs* is impossible. I suggest that this playful Jewish novel originated in the Ptolemaic period, a rather peaceful time for Jews in Egypt.

4   Antisemitism and Reception

The five chapters of the last cluster all tackle themes of ancient Judaism discussed earlier in the volume: antisemitism, Philo of Alexandria, Tacitus on the Jews, monotheism, Flavius Josephus. But here I am interested in how these topics have been viewed and interpreted over time, thus in the reception of ancient Judaism and of Jewish Hellenism. The first article tracks early scholarship on ancient antisemitism. That the use of the term "antisemitism" is not unproblematic for the study of the ancient world is granted, but the alternatives, including "anti-Judaism," are not without issues either. It is legitimate, I believe, to use the term "antisemitism" as the general denominator for any kind of hostility or agitation against the Jews. Adjectives such as "religious," "racist," as well as "ancient," "Christian," "medieval," and "modern" help clarify further what kind of antisemitism is meant. For there are indeed substantial differences between, e.g., pagan antisemitism and that of Christian tradition. In this chapter I show how in early scholarship on ancient antisemitism, from the late nineteenth century onward, antisemitism is regularly understood as a reaction to some kind of deterioration (whether religious or political) within Judaism. Pagan sources describing an earlier, pious form of Judaism and a later, superstitious, ritually overladen one (Posidonius/Strabo, Tacitus) came to be pressed into service in support of the Christian conviction that Hellenistic and rabbinic Judaism was a religion and culture in decline. Christian classicists who published on ancient antisemitism (such as Zacher, Stähelin and Mommsen) followed the Wellhausian model of a deteriorating Judaism in the ancient world so common among theologians (exemplified by Johannes Leipoldt).

With "A Leap into the Void: The *Philo-Lexikon* and Jewish-German Hellenism" we move towards the Jewish reception of ancient Judaism. The *Philo-Lexikon* was a one-volume dictionary of Judaism which first appeared in 1935

14   INTRODUCTION

and grew to extraordinary popularity among Jews in Germany until its pub-lisher, the Philo Verlag, was forbidden by the Nazis in 1938. The name of both lexicon and publisher hints at the presence of Philo of Alexandria, and more generally of Jewish Hellenism, among German Jews at the time. While the lexicon as such does not focus on Philo (or on the ancient world in general), some of the features of Jewish-Hellenistic literature, such as the urge to show the Jewish contribution to culture, are also tangible in the *Philo-Lexikon*. Philo and Hellenistic Judaism generally could and did function as both a starting point and a topic of contention for articulating Jewish self-understanding in Germany in the 1920s and 1930s. To German Jews, Hellenism could be understood as a "springboard" ("Sprungbrett"), but by November 1938, when Jewish publications in Germany were no longer allowed, it turned out to be a "leap into the void."

With the next chapter we return to Tacitus. The twelve chapters on Jews and Judea in the *Histories* wielded an enormous influence beginning in the late classical period. They are consistently referred to and have even had something of a collateral effect on the reception of the entire Tacitean *oeuvre*. In "Tacitus's Excursus on the Jews through the Ages: An Overview of its Reception History" I trace these reactions and their background in intellectual history. The early Christian reception of Tacitus (Sulpicius Severus, Orosius, Pseudo-Hegesippus) is in large part a reception of the Jewish excursus. Throughout the ages, Tacitus's ethnographic digression with its invidious comments on the Jews led to fierce critique (Tertullian, Budé) as well as sophisticated defenses (Bodin, Muret). In the many commentaries published following the editio princeps (1470) one notes a great effort to comment soberly on Tacitus's notes on the Jews. Firm rebuttals came from more theologically oriented authors (Worm, Kirchmaier in the second half of the seventeenth century). Notably, neither in late antiquity nor in the Renaissance (after the rediscovery of Tacitus) did the Jewish excursus serve as a source for antisemitic statements. Jewish authors have struggled with Tacitus's erroneous description of Judaism. Particularly interesting are the seventeenth century reactions by the Venetian rabbi Simone Luzzatto and the Dutch philosopher Baruch de Spinoza. Luzzatto wrote an actual apology in response to Tacitus's ethnography on the Jews; Spinoza, on the other hand, uses Tacitus as a source for his own critical understanding of religion. Yet Luzzatto too shows great appreciation of Tacitus as a historian. Jews thus participated in the discourse on Tacitus, which had received an additional twist with the phenomenon of Tacitism. Rather different is the reception of Tacitus's comments on the Jews during the Enlightenment when the Roman historian became a fellow 'esprit critique'. At a time when Judaism was often the target of freethinking and anti-clerical polemics,

Voltaire happily endorsed some of Tacitus's sneers. In the nineteenth century, at a time when the role of Jews in society was the subject of heated debate and in which broader studies on the Jews in Greco-Roman antiquity appeared, Tacitus's excursus became an important point of reference (Leo, Mommsen). Some saw their own understanding of Judaism as a depraved religion confirmed in Tacitus. Then again, the nineteenth-century commentary editions of Tacitus's *Histories* (by Kiessling, Orellius and others) do not launch or justify anti-Jewish rhetoric. This changes in the National Socialist period, when antisemitic authors sought backing for their own ideological purposes from Tacitus.

"Polytheism and Monotheism in Antiquity: On Jan Assmann's Critique of Monotheism" is a response to Jan Assmann's theory of monotheism as presented in a number of publications since his 1998 monograph *Moses the Egyptian*. In this chapter I criticize Assmann's simplistic dichotomy of a non-violent (because non-exclusive) polytheism on the one hand and an essentially violent monotheism (because exclusive) on the other. Assmann's discussion of monotheism often reads like an Egyptological apology for Egyptian culture. He interprets Egyptian antisemitism as a reaction against Jewish monotheism, which in Egyptian memory (Akhenaten's monotheistic revolution), according to Assmann, felt like anti-cosmotheism. Overall, Assmann erects too great a theoretical construct of monotheism and does not sufficiently account for the power relations in the Greco-Roman world. Monotheism remained mostly a quiet idea in antiquity. Finally, I criticize Assmann's tendency to apply World War II imagery (forced labor, concentration camps, Auschwitz) to the context of Greco-Roman antiquity, where it does not easily fit.

The last chapter of the book, "*Testa incognita:* The History of the Pseudo-Josephus Bust in Copenhagen," brings together several things introduced earlier in the book in a convoluted way: Josephus, ethnography, and antisemitism. At the Ny Carlsberg Glyptotek in Copenhagen there is an impressive group of busts from the time of Vespasian to Trajan on show. Among the portraits is a small head of an unnamed man with a beard and a crooked nose. The portrait became notorious when in 1930 the Austrian art historian and polymath Robert Eisler identified it as depicting the head of the Jewish-Roman general and author Flavius Josephus. The identification by Eisler, who was of Jewish origin but converted to Catholicism as a young man, was based on racist stereotypes and followed up on the general attribution of the bust to a "young Jew" by the Danish art historian Frederik Poulsen five years before. In this chapter, I track the history of this portrait. I am particularly interested in racist assumptions that surfaced during the 1920s and 1930s which transformed this bust, hitherto known as a beautiful head, into an ugly face. I focus here also on the tragic role of Robert Eisler, who throughout his life wavered between strong attachment to, and maintaining the greatest possible distance from, Judaism.

Bibliography

Alexander, Philipp S., "Hellenism and Hellenization as Problematic Historiographical Categories." Pages 63–80 in *Paul beyond the Judaism/Hellenism Divide*. Edited by Troels Engberg-Pedersen. Louisville: Westminster 2001.

Amitay, Ory, "Alexander in Jerusalem: The Extra-Josephan Traditions." Pages 128–147 in Paul Spilsbury and Chris Seeman, *Judean Antiquities 11: Translation and Commentary*. Vol. 6a of *Flavius Josephus: Translation and Commentary*, ed. Steve Mason (Leiden: Brill, 2017).

Bacchi, Ashley L., *Uncovering Jewish Creativity in Book III of the Sibylline Oracles: Gender, Intertextuality, and* Politics. Leiden: Brill, 2020.

Barclay, John M.G., "Introduction: Diaspora Negotiations." Pages 1–6 in *Negotiating Diaspora: Jewish Strategies in the Roman Empire*. Edited by John M.G. Barclay. London: T&T Clark, 2004. Bichler, Reinhold, *"Hellenismus": Geschichte und Problematik eines Epochenbegriffs*. Darmstadt: Wissenschaftliche Buchgesellschaft, 1983.

Barclay, John M.G., *Jews in the Mediterranean Diaspora. From Alexander to Trajan (323 BCE–117 CE)*. Berkeley: University of California Press, 1996.

Bloch, René, *Antike Vorstellungen vom Judentum. Der Judenexkurs des Tacitus im Rahmen der griechisch-römischen Ethnographie*. Franz Steiner: Stuttgart, 2002.

Bloch, René, *Moses und der Mythos: Die Auseinandersetzung mit der griechischen Mythologie bei jüdisch-hellenistischen Autoren*. Leiden: Brill, 2011.

Bloch, René, "Alexandre le Grand et le judaïsme: La double stratégie d'auteurs juifs de l'antiquité et du Moyen Âge." Pages 145–162 in *Le voyage d'Alexandre au Paradis terrestre: Orient et Occident, regards croisés*. Edited by Catherine Gaullier-Bougassas and Margaret Bridges. Turnhout: Brepols, 2012.

Bloch, René, "Jew or Judean: The Latin Evidence." Pages 231–242 in *Torah, Temple, Land: Constructions of Judaism in Antiquity*. Edited by Markus Witte, Jens Schröter, and Vera M. Lepper. Tübingen: Mohr Siebeck, 2021.

Bloch, René, "How much Hebrew in Jewish Alexandria?" Pages 261–278 in *Alexandria: Hub of the Hellenistic World*. Edited by Benjamin Schliesser et al. Tübingen: Mohr Siebeck, 2021.

Bosworth, Albert B., "Alexander the Great and the Creation of the Hellenistic Age." Pages 9–27 in *The Cambridge Companion to the Hellenistic World*. Edited by Glenn R. Bugh. Cambridge: Cambridge University Press, 2006.

INTRODUCTION   17

Boyarin, Daniel, *Judaism: The Genealogy of a Modern Notion*. New Brunswick: Rugters University Press, 2019.

Chaniotis, Angelos, *Age of Conquests: The Greek World from Alexander to Hadrian (336 BC–AD 138)*. London: Profile Books, 2018.

Cohen, Shaye J.D., "Alexander the Great and Jaddus the High Priest According to Josephus." *AJS Review* 7/8 (1982/83): 41–68.

Cohen, Shaye J.D., *The Beginnings of Jewishness: Boundaries, Varieties, Uncertainties*. Berkeley: University of California Press, 1999.

Collins, John J., *Between Athens and Jerusalem: Jewish Identity in the Hellenistic Diaspora*. Grand Rapids: Eerdmans, 1999.

Droysen, Johann Gustav, *Geschichte des Hellenismus* III: *Geschichte der Epigonen*. Darmstadt: Wissenschaftliche Buchgesellschaft 2008.

Grabbe, Lester L., *A History of the Jews and Judaism in the Second Temple Period. Volume 2: The Coming of the Greeks: The Early Hellenistic Period (335–175 BCE)*. London: T&T Clark, 2008.

Grabbe, Lester L., *A History of the Jews and Judaism in the Second Temple Period. Volume 3: The Maccabean Revolt, Hasmonean Rule, and Herod the Great (175–174 BCE)*. London: T&T Clark, 2020.

Green, Peter, *The Hellenistic Age: A Short History*. New York: Modern Library, 2008.

Gruen, Erich S., *Heritage and Hellenism: The Reinvention of Jewish Tradition*. Berkeley: University of California Press, 1998.

Gruen, Erich S., *Diaspora: Jews amidst Greeks and Romans*. Cambridge: Harvard University Press, 2002.

Gruen, Erich S., "Greek and Non-Greeks." Pages 295–314 in *The Cambridge Companion to the Hellenistic World*. Edited by Glenn R. Bugh. Cambridge: Cambridge University Press, 2006.

Kotlińska-Toma, Agnieszka, *Hellenistic Tragedy: Texts, Translations and a Critical Survey*. London: Bloomsbury, 2015.

Malkin, Irad, *A Small Greek World: Networks in the Ancient Mediterranean*. Oxford: Oxford University Press, 2011.

Meister, Klaus, *Der Hellenismus: Kultur- und Geistesgeschichte*. Stuttgart: J.B. Metzler, 2016.

Mirguet, Françoise, *An Early History of Compassion: Emotion and Imagination in Hellenistic Judaism*. Cambridge: Cambridge University Press, 2017.

Niehoff, Maren R., *Jewish Exegesis and Homeric Scholarship in Alexandria*. Cambridge: Cambridge University Press, 2011.

Nippel, Wilfried, *Johann Gustav Droysen: Ein Leben zwischen Wissenschaft und Politik*. München: C.H. Beck, 2008.

Reinhartz, Adele, "Was the Word in the Beginning? On the Relationship between Language and Concepts." *Marginalia: Los Angeles Review of Books*. July 5, 2019 (https:

//marginalia.lareviewofbooks.org/word-beginning-relationship-language-concepts /).

Schliesser, Benjamin et al., eds., *Alexandria: Hub of the Hellenistic World*. Tübingen: Mohr Siebeck, 2021.

Trotter, Jonathan R., *The Jerusalem Temple in Diaspora: Jewish Practice and Thought During the Second Temple Period*. Leiden: Brill, 2019.

Weitzman, Steven, *The Origin of the Jews: The Quest for Roots in a Rootless Age*. Princeton: Princeton University Press, 2017.

Will, Edouard and Orrieux, Claude, *Ioudaïsmos-Hellènismos: essai sur le judaïsme judéen à l'époque hellénistique*. Nancy: Presses Universitaires de Nancy, 1986.

Wolfson, Harry A. *Philo: Foundations of Religious Philosophy in Judaism, Christianity, and Islam*. 2 vols. Cambridge: Harvard University Press, 1947.

PART 1

Moses and Exodus

∵

CHAPTER 1

Alexandria in Pharaonic Egypt: Projections in *De vita Mosis*

Who was Philo of Alexandria? A short, but honest answer to this question would be: we don't really know.[1] In spite of the impressively large oeuvre of Philo of Alexandria, there is very little one can say for sure about his life and his activities. While Philo's extensive philosophical work allows for a fairly good assessment of his philosophical and theological ways of understanding Judaism, his biography—in a simple chronological, but also in an intellectual sense—is very difficult to grasp. Philo only rarely speaks of himself.

We do not even know the exact dates of Philo's life. He was probably, or so it is stated in the encyclopedias, born around 20 BCE and died around 50 CE. However, it is telling that much of the dating of Philo's life depends on when one wants to imagine a man of the ancient world turning gray. As is well known, at the beginning of his tractate *Legatio ad Gaium*, which deals with the Jewish embassy to the emperor Caligula in the late 30s of the first century CE, Philo refers to himself as an old man (γέρων) who had turned gray (πολιός).[2] Philo's hair in *Legatio ad Gaium* is part of the very spurious DNA which might help us define Philo's life span more accurately.

Fortunately, Josephus in his *Jewish Antiquities* approximately one generation after Philo has a few lines on our Alexandrian philosopher.[3] The context of Josephus's remarks is again the Jewish embassy to the Roman emperor Caius Caligula. However, there are some inconsistencies between Philo's and Josephus's line-up of the Jewish team sent to Rome. According to Josephus, the embassy consisted of three men, according to Philo of five.[4] And while Philo nowhere explicitly confirms that he was the head of the Jewish delegation to Rome, Josephus does.[5] Josephus also tells us that his brother Alexander, the

---

1 This paper was presented to the Philo of Alexandria Group at the Annual meeting of the Society of Biblical Literature in San Francisco, November 21, 2011. A German version of this paper appeared as a chapter in my book *Jüdische Drehbühnen: Biblische Variationen im antiken Judentum*, Tria corda 7. Jenaer Vorlesungen zu Judentum, Antike und Christentum (Tübingen: Mohr Siebeck, 2013), 29–52.
2 Philo, *Legat.* 1.
3 Josephus, *AJ* 18.257–260.
4 Josephus, *AJ* 18.257; Philo, *Legat.* 370.
5 Josephus, *AJ* 18.259.

© RENÉ BLOCH, 2022 | DOI:10.1163/9789004521896_003

father of Tiberius Julius Alexander whom we know from both Jewish and pagan sources, was an alabarch.[6] What this title exactly stands for is a matter of controversy. It certainly was the title of a senior official, perhaps one working in the area of tax collection.[7] Even if it is sometimes stated too quickly that Philo came out of one of the very wealthy Jewish families of Alexandria, it is safe to state that Philo grew up in an established family in Alexandria. The very existence of his vast oeuvre indicates that he must have enjoyed financial independence.

Philo probably lived all his life in Alexandria, the intellectual center of Greek-speaking Judaism at the time. Occasionally he may have travelled—and thus lived up to what he states in the context of Abraham's departure from Ur: men who have never travelled are like blind people.[8] At least once Philo visited the temple in Jerusalem.[9] That he was "very knowledgeable in the field of philosophy," as Josephus states, is the least one can say about Philo on the basis of his work.[10]

Thus far the familiar, barren *Curriculum vitae* of our author, as we know it.[11] However, it seems to me that we can learn more about Philo by taking a closer look at the representation of the most important figure in his work: Moses. I would like to argue that when writing about Moses, Philo has his autobiographic moments. We will start by looking at passages concerning Moses and/or Philo as "politicians," and then as philosophers.

1   Moses and Philo as Politicians

It seems to me that between Philo's *De vita Mosis* and his "political" tractate on the embassy to Caligula, the *Legatio ad Gaium*, there are thematic and linguis-

---

6   Josephus, *AJ* 20.100; Tacitus, *Hist.* 2.74, 79. Cf. Gregory E. Sterling, "Tiberius Julius Alexander," in *The Eerdmans Dictionary of Early Judaism*, ed. John J. Collins and Daniel C. Harlow (Grand Rapids: Eerdmans Publishing Company, 2010), 1309–1310.

7   Daniel R. Schwartz, "Philo, His Family, and His Times," in *The Cambridge Companion to Philo*, ed. Adam Kamesar (Cambridge: Cambridge University Press, 2009), 12.

8   Philo, *Abr.* 65.

9   As he mentions briefly in *Prov.* 2.64 (2.107 in the Armenian version).

10   As stated by Josephus, *AJ* 18.259; οὐκ ἄπειρος ("not inexperienced") is a litotes and is meant to underline Philo's great knowledge. Josephus uses the same phrase—with much less sympathy!—referring to his rival Justus of Tiberias (*Vita* 40).

11   For a more detailed evaluation of the scarce sources on Philo's life cf. Schwartz, "Philo, His Family, and His Times," and also the detailed attempt by Louis Massebieau and Emile Bréhier, "Essai sur la chronologie de la vie et des œuvres de Philon," *RHR* 53 (1906): 25–64; 164–185; 267–289.

tic parallels which allow us to draw conclusions about Philo's understanding of his role in the delegation, about his understanding of the figure of Moses, and not least about the place of *De vita Mosis* in Philo's oeuvre. As far as I can tell, these matters have not yet been studied in depth.[12]

Philo was probably not politically active for a long time. In *De specialibus legibus* 3.3 Philo mentions "a vast ocean of civic worries" which began to distract him from his philosophical studies. In that passage he is probably referring to the political turmoil in Alexandria in the late 30s.[13] It was then, in light of the suffering of his fellow Jews in Egypt that Philo felt obliged to get involved in politics and to speak up on behalf of the Jews at the court of the emperor. To some extent, then, Philo slipped into the role of Moses, who according to the biblical story only reluctantly, seeing the oppression of the Israelites and urged on by God, stepped forward and talked to the emperor of *his* time, the Pharaoh. In a small delegation, together with his brother Aaron, Moses argued with the Emperor and fought for justice for his people.[14] Moses, too, would have preferred to stay out of it. According to Philo, when still in Midian and before his political involvement, Moses was very much committed to the study of philosophy.[15]

To prevent any misunderstandings: I am not trying to suggest that Philo was presenting himself as a *Moses redivivus*. Such an equation would surely have been perceived as outrageous—by his readers and by Philo himself—and certainly was not Philo's intention. In Philo's presentation, Moses is the unattainable ideal of piety and wisdom.[16] Moses is the "most pious" man who has ever lived,[17] the "perfect wise man," the only one to have tasted pure and "undi-

---

12   On *De vita Mosis* cf. Sarah J.K. Pearce, "King Moses: Notes on Philo's Portrait of Moses as an Ideal Leader in the *Life of Moses*," in *The Greek Strand in Islamic Political Thought*, ed. Emma Gannagé et al. (Beirut: Imprimerie catholique, 2004), 37–74; Brian McGing, "Philo's Adaptation of the Bible in his Life of Moses," in *The Limits of Ancient Biography*, ed. Brian McGing and Judith Mossman (Swansea: Classical Press of Wales, 2006), 117–140; Louis H. Feldman, *Philo's Portrayal of Moses in the Context of Ancient Judaism* (Notre Dame: University of Notre Dame Press, 2007).

13   For a different reading of *Spec.* 3.3 cf. Erwin R. Goodenough, *The Politics of Philo of Judaeus: Practice and Theory* (New Haven: Yale University Press, 1938), 66–68.

14   Exod 3–4.

15   Philo, *Mos.* 1.48. Feldman, *Philo's Portrayal of Moses*, 74, also notes this parallel between Philo and his Moses.

16   See David Winston, "Sage and Supersage in Philo of Alexandria," in *The Ancestral Philosophy: Hellenistic Philosophy in Second Temple Judaism. Essays of David Winston*, ed. Gregory E. Sterling (Providence: Brown University, 2001), 171–180.

17   Philo, *Mos.* 2.192: ὁσιώτατον τῶν πώποτε γενομένων.

luted wisdom."[18] Moses's wisdom begins where Abraham's reached its peak.[19] Philo was not so presumptuous as to equate himself with Moses. But Philo does admire Moses.[20] While he realizes that Moses is inaccessible due to his unique proximity to God, he is also—because of this very proximity—a landmark to be followed. As Philo writes in his *Life of Moses*: Moses is "a role model for those who want to imitate him" (παράδειγμα τοῖς ἐθέλουσι μιμεῖσθαι). "Happy," Philo continues, "are all those who imprint or strive to imprint that image in their souls."[21]

Now, Philo's Moses is obviously what he is: *Philo's* Moses. Philo is, as I will show below, mirroring his philosophical ideals in his presentation of Moses. He felt tempted, it seems to me, to connect Moses's biography, as presented in the Torah, with his own. I would like to argue that *De vita Mosis* can be read as a tractate in which Philo ponders over his own life and, especially, on what happened during the anti-Jewish riot in Alexandria.

In fact, there are some striking parallels between the description of the Jews' suffering in *Legatio ad Gaium* and *De vita Mosis*: in both cases the Jews are treated as prisoners of war. In *De vita Mosis* Philo describes the suppression of the Israelites as follows:

> So, then, these strangers, who had left their own country and come to Egypt hoping to live there in safety as in a second fatherland (ἐν δευτέρᾳ πατρίδι), were made slaves by the ruler of the country and reduced to the condition of captives taken by the custom of war (τούτους ... ὁ τῆς χώρας ἡγεμὼν ἠνδραποδίζετο καὶ ὡς πολέμου νόμῳ λαβὼν αἰχμαλώτους), or persons purchased from the masters in whose household they have been bred.[22]

And in the context of the anti-Jewish riot in Alexandria Philo writes:

> For treating us as persons, given over by the emperor to suffer the extremity of calamity undisguised or as overpowered in war (πολέμῳ κατακρα-

---

18   Philo, *Mos.* 2.204: πάνσοφε, μόνος ἀμιγοῦς ἠκρατίσω σοφίας.

19   Philo, *Post.* 174.

20   Philo, *Sacr.* 50. Cf. Feldman, *Philo's Portrayal of Moses*, 74 who notes that this is one of the rare instances where Philo speaks in the first person singular.

21   Philo, *Mos.* 1.158–159 (trans. LCL, slightly adjusted); cf. also *Virt.* 51 (Moses's "own life" as an "archetypal model"). Cf. Alan Mendelson, *Secular Education in Philo of Alexandria* (Cincinnati: Hebrew Union College Press, 1982), 63–64.

22   Philo, *Mos.* 1.36 (trans. LCL).

τηθέντας), they worked our ruin with insane and most brutal rage. They overran our houses, expelling the owners with their wives and children, and left them uninhabited.[23]

In *De vita Mosis*, Philo in his paraphrase of the biblical events in Egypt seems to plead on behalf of his fellow Jews in Alexandria. Biblical Egypt is described as the (second) fatherland of the Israelites, where the Israelites wanted to live in security. As is well known, in Philo's understanding Jerusalem is the *metropolis* or "mother city" of all the Jews, while their "fatherland" (πατρίς) is the place where they actually live.[24] Thus to Philo, Alexandria and Egypt was certainly his fatherland.[25] Philo and the Israelites share the same fatherland.

The overseers of Egypt—at the time of Philo as well as at the time of Moses—were brutal, inhumane, even bestial: the overseers of the Israelites are "animals in human shape" (ἀνθρωποειδῆ θηρία).[26] In the *Legatio* we hear how the Egyptians with "animal rage" (θηριωδεστάταις ὀργαῖς) went off on the Jews.[27] Thus, the Egyptian overseers—in Roman as well as in Pharaonic Egypt—were both of "beastly furor." Philo describes the maltreatment of the Jews in both his own and in biblical times in identical terms: they were "subjected to every kind of ill-treatment."[28]

There are also parallels between the villains Pharaoh and Caligula: both emperors share a tendency towards rage and injustice.[29] Both succeeded rulers who had some sympathies towards the Jews: Augustus and Tiberius on the one hand, and the previous Pharaoh of Joseph's time on the other.[30] Both Caligula and the Pharaoh of Moses's time are in their blindness unable to understand

---

23 Philo, *Legat.* 121 (trans. LCL). Roger Arnaldez et al. in their French edition of *De vita Mosis* (Paris: Éditions du Cerf, 1967), 42 n. 4, also suspect an "allusion à la situation de sa propre communauté à Alexandrie," but do not elaborate this observation.

24 Philo, *Flacc.* 46.

25 Cf. Carlos Lévy, "Mais que faisait donc Philon en Égypte?: A propos de l'identité diasporique de Philon," in *La rivelazione in Filone di Alessandria, natura, legge, storia: atti del VII Convegno di Studi del Gruppo italiano di ricerca su Origene e la tradizione alessandrina (Bologna 29–30 settembre 2003)*, ed. Angela Maria Mazzanti and Francesca Calabi (Verruchio: Pazzini, 2004), 295–312.

26 Philo, *Mos.* 1.43.

27 Philo, *Legat.* 121.

28 Philo, *Mos.* 1.44: πάσας αἰκιζόμενος αἰκίας; *Legat.* 128: αἰκιζόμενοι πάσαις αἰκίαις.

29 Philo, *Mos.* 1.45; *Legat.* 190.

30 Tiberius always "acted with profound prudence" (*Legat.* 33: φρονήσει βαθείᾳ χρώμενος) and no one "was a greater master of thought or of language among those who were in the prime of life in his time" (142; trans. LCL). In his eulogy on Augustus (*Legat.* 143–147), Philo does not hesitate to praise him for having hellenized the barbarians (147). In the biblical story,

the aniconic regulations of the Jews: Caligula's insistence on the importance of visual representations of gods and himself is at the very core of the treatise *Legatio ad Gaium*. Similarly, for Philo's Pharaoh in *De vita Mosis*, it is unthinkable, that a God could be thought of without anything visual (ἔξω τῶν ὁρατῶν).[31]

These parallels may suggest, then, that *De vita Mosis* should be read in the context of the anti-Jewish riot in 38 CE and the subsequent Jewish embassy to Rome. And one may indeed even speculate that Philo was aware of the parallels between Moses's pleading with Pharaoh on behalf of the Israelites in Egypt and his own efforts on behalf of the Jews in Egypt at the palace of the Roman Emperor. The parallels—in content and in language—between Pharaonic and Roman Alexandria bring Philo's *Legatio ad Gaium* into the vicinity of Moses's "Legatio ad Pharaonem." In fact, in the *Legatio ad Gaium* there is a passage where Philo brings his own time, the suppression in 38 and the difficulties surrounding the embassy to Rome, into connection with the Bible: "Perhaps these things are sent to try the present generation, to test the state of their virtue and whether they are schooled to bear dire misfortunes?"[32] In his answer to this question, Philo refers to earlier difficult times when God saved the people from hopeless and desperate situations.[33] Philo does not mention a specific biblical parallel, but for him the exodus story would certainly be the most important reference for divine help and reliability.

As already mentioned, Philo nowhere explicitly states that he was the head of the Jewish delegation to Rome. This is only reported by Josephus. In the *Legatio*, Philo, who is rarely explicit about himself, mentions that because of his age and his good education he "seemed to have greater prudence."[34] Philo tries to be modest: the differences between him and his colleagues are due to his age, his education, and his experience. Nevertheless, the two keywords mentioned in this brief self-presentation—prudence (φρόνησις) and education (παιδεία)—are also, and especially, characteristics of Moses—as we will see shortly in the context of the descriptions of Moses's and Philo's education.[35]

Philo slips into the role of Moses. This is also true for the accidental nature of his assumption of the role of leader of a political movement. As already men-

---

too, the depiction of the "bad" pharaoh is built up on the positive image of his predecessor (Exod 1:8–10). In *Mos.* Philo does not refer to the earlier, "good" pharaoh (mentioned, in a positive light, in *Ios.* 119–121).

31 Philo, *Mos.* 1.88.

32 Philo, *Legat.* 196 (trans. LCL).

33 ibid.: πολλάκις ἐξ ἀμηχάνων καὶ ἀπόρων περιέσωσε τὸ ἔθνος.

34 Philo, *Legat.* 182: φρονεῖν τι δοκῶν περιττότερον.

35 Philo, *Mos.* 1.23, 180.

tioned, we can safely assume that Philo was not eager to leave his philosophical studies behind in order to take over a political role—just as the biblical and Philonic Moses was reticent with respect to his calling. Philo's Moses is aware of how unstable Fortune is and therefore remains modest in successful moments without seeking a leadership position.[36] Only the suffering of the Jews in Egypt forced him to do so. Philo may have seen his political role in a very similar light. The very fact that he does not mention that he was the leader of the Jewish delegation may point in this direction. Philo is not simply projecting himself onto Moses, he also seems simply to notice certain parallels between his life and Moses's life as described in the Torah.

The observations made so far, especially regarding the strong echoes of the political tensions in Alexandria in *De vita Mosis*, also have implications for the difficult question of the dating of this treatise. Among the numerous works by Philo of Alexandria, *De vita Mosis* is perhaps the tractate most difficult to categorize, and its intentions have been a matter of great dispute. It certainly does not belong to the "Allegorical Commentary." Some have understood it as part of or an introduction to the "Exposition of the Law."[37] *De vita Mosis* has been understood by some scholars as an introductory tractate with an agenda of making Moses known to a larger audience.[38] Recent scholarship places *De vita Mosis* among the apologetic and historical works—more or less *e negativo*, though, because the tractate does not seem really to be part of the "Exposition."[39]

I believe that the parallels between *De vita Mosis* and *Legatio ad Gaium* could very well help us better understand the place and the role of *De vita Mosis* in Philo's oeuvre. In light of our discussion so far, I would like to suggest that Philo's *De vita Mosis* and *Legatio ad Gaium* were written around the same time. If Philo was already an old man, as he claims, when he wrote the *Legatio*, *De vita Mosis* cannot have been what it is often understood to be: an early introduc-

---

36   Philo, *Mos.* 1.30–31.
37   Cf. Erwin R. Goodenough, "Philo's Exposition of the Law and His De Vita Mosis," *HTR* 26 (1933): 109–125 and more recently Gregory E. Sterling, "How Do You Introduce Philo of Alexandria? The Cambridge Companion to Philo," *SPhiloA* 21 (2009): 67–68 ("an introduction to the Exposition in particular"); James R. Royse, "The Works of Philo," in *The Cambridge Companion to Philo*, ed. Adam Kamesar (Cambridge: Cambridge University Press, 2009), 47 ("there seems to be some relationship between the 'Exposition' and the *De vita Mosis*. It seems clear, on the one hand, that *De vita Mosis* is not properly part of the 'Exposition', but on the other hand, it may have been intended as a kind of introduction to it").
38   David T. Runia, "Philon von Alexandreia," *DNP* 9:852.
39   Royse, "The Works of Philo," 47, 50.

28   CHAPTER 1

tory tractate to the Philonic oeuvre. *De vita Mosis* is probably a late and mature work of Philo.[40] It is true that in this tractate Philo makes important general statements (e.g., on the Septuagint), but one does not have to be young to write what one might call an introduction to Judaism. Philo could also have written a work functioning as a general introduction at a later stage.

In addition to the parallels with the *Legatio*, there may be other signs in *De vita Mosis* indicating that this tractate was written around the time of the political turmoil in 38 CE. Philo's allegorical reading of the burning bush episode— the burning bush is a "symbol of those who suffered wrong"—may not only refer to the biblical suffering of the Israelites in Egypt, but also to the suppression in Philo's Alexandria.[41] Elsewhere in *De vita Mosis* and in a more contemporary context Philo describes the Jews as a people "which has not flourished for a long time."[42]

I am not the first scholar to suggest a late dating of *De vita Mosis*. In fact, Leopold Cohn had already done so more than a hundred years ago. Cohn suspected that the tractate originated from the "period of the political fights." Cohn's argument is rather different from mine, though. He reads the tractate as an apologetic text which was trying to defend Judaism in the light of these fights.[43] More recently, Louis Feldman took a similar approach.[44] However, I see very little apologetic in *De vita Mosis*. This is, as so often in Jewish-Hellenistic literature, much more of an inner-Jewish dialogue (which may still reflect non-Jewish discourses on Judaism) than some sort of counterattack.

---

40   If so, this would obviously mean that tractates where Philo refers to *Mos.* (*Virt.* 52; *Praem.* 53: cf. Sterling, "How Do You Introduce Philo of Alexandria?," 67) were written later.

41   Philo, *Mos.* 1.65–70 (67: σύμβολον … τῶν ἀδικουμένων).

42   Philo, *Mos.* 2.43 (ἐκ πολλῶν χρόνων τοῦ ἔθνους οὐκ εὐτυχοῦντες/μὴ ἐν ἀκμαῖς).

43   Leopold Cohn, "Einteilung und Chronologie der Schriften Philos," *Phil Suppl.* 7 (1899): 434: "In diese Zeit der politischen Kämpfe gehören wohl auch die Bücher *de vita Mosis*. Die für einen griechischen Leserkreis bestimmte Lebensbeschreibung des jüdischen Gesetzgebers war vermutlich die erste in der Reihe der apologetischen Schriften, zu deren Abfassung Philo zum Zwecke litterarischer Abwehr der Angriffe der Gegner gegen das Judentum sich entschloß."

44   Feldman, *Philo's Portrait of Moses*, 61. Cf. also the classification by Royse, "The Works of Philo," 51: "The current consensus is that *De vita Mosis* belongs among the apologetic and historical works, although it certainly differs from the other works included here in its concentration on events of the distant past."

2 Moses and Philo as Philosophers

I suggest, then, that in addition to his explicitly historical tractates *Legatio ad Gaium* and *In Flaccum*, in *De vita Mosis* Philo is also addressing the painful times in Alexandria during which he became the leader of the Jews. His role as leader of the Jewish delegation to Rome opened up an opportunity to follow in the steps of Moses, who at least to some extent seems to have been his *paradeigma*. Philo sees in Moses a mirror image of himself. Moses is an ideal that cannot be attained, but it remains Philo's goal. Let us take a look at another theme where one can observe a similar process: Philo's identity as a philosopher. In this short paper I can only hint at a few aspects.

The biblical Moses can hardly be called a philosopher (even if he does have his moments of intense reflection). The image of Moses as philosopher is not one which Philo invented, on the other hand. It goes back to earlier Jewish-Hellenistic authors such as Pseudo-Eupolemus, Artapanus and Aristobulus. From the second century BCE on, in Jewish-Hellenistic literature there was an opinion circulating that Moses was the first sage[45] or even the inventor of philosophy[46] *tout court*. Artapanus, in a catalog of Mosaic inventions which recalls a list of inventions connected with Prometheus,[47] adds philosophy to Moses's list of innovations. Moses had brought many useful things to humanity: "boats and devices for stone construction and the Egyptian arms and the implements for drawing water and for warfare, and philosophy."[48] Probably around the same time, Aristobulus, the first Jewish philosopher of whom we know, linked the Greek philosophers Pythagoras, Socrates, and Plato to Moses.[49] At the time of Philo, then, the connection of Moses with philosophy was something of a cliché. However, as we are going to see, in Philo Moses the philosopher is quite a bit more complex a figure than in these earlier texts (of which we obviously have only excerpts).

Philo speaks through Moses. He profits from the old cliché of Moses as the philosopher and projects his own philosophical agenda onto Moses. *De vita Mosis* is again a key text for this project. Moses's teaching stands for "true philosophy" (τῷ ὄντι φιλοσοφεῖν), which consists of the three elements "deliberation" (βούλευμα), "reason" (λόγος), and "fact" (πρᾶξις) and leads to a happy life (εὐδαι-

---

45 Pseudo-Eupolemus *apud* Eusebius, *Praep. ev.* 9.26.1.
46 Clement, *Strom.* 1.23.150.4.
47 Cf. Aeschylus, *Prom.* 442–506.
48 Artapanus *apud* Eusebius, *Praep. ev.* 9.27.4 (trans. J.J. Collins, OTP).
49 Aristobulus *apud* Eusebius, *Praep. ev.* 13.12.3–4.

μονία).[50] For this form of philosophy, Philo writes, the Sabbath is especially suited. As a matter of fact, Moses taught philosophy on the Sabbath.[51] And Philo sees himself very much in this tradition: "Even now this practice is retained, and the Jews every seventh day occupy themselves with the philosophy of their fathers, dedicating that time to the acquiring of knowledge and the study of the truths of nature."[52]

That Philo found himself walking in Moses's footsteps can also be seen in connection with his presentation of Moses's early years. Philo sends Moses to school.[53] He describes in some detail the *paideia*, the education and training that Moses underwent. Moses, in Philo's presentation, enjoys a first class education, a "royal upbringing" (τροφὴ βασιλική).[54] Philo imagines an international education for Moses:

> Teachers at once arrived from different parts, some unbidden from the neighbouring countries and the provinces of Egypt, others summoned from Greece under promise of high reward. But in a short time he advanced beyond their capacities; his gifted nature forestalled their instruction, so that his seemed a case rather of recollection than of learning, and indeed he himself devised and propounded problems which they could not easily solve. For great natures carve out much that is new in the way of knowledge; and, just as bodies, robust and agile in every part, free their trainers from care, and receive little or none of their usual attention, and in the same way well-grown and naturally healthy trees, which improve of themselves, give the husbandmen no trouble, so the gifted soul takes the lead in meeting the lessons given by itself rather than the teacher and is profited thereby, and as soon as it has a grasp of some of the first principles of knowledge presses forward like the horse to the meadow, as the proverb goes. Arithmetic, geometry, the lore of metre, rhythm and harmony, and the whole subject of music as shown by the use of instruments or in textbooks and treatises of a more special character, were imparted to

---

50   Philo, *Mos.* 2.212.

51   Philo, *Mos.* 2.215: "for it was customary on every day when opportunity offered, and preeminently on the seventh day ... to pursue the study of wisdom with the ruler expounding and instructing the people what they should say and do, while they received edification and betterment in moral principles and conduct" (trans. LCL).

52   Philo, *Mos.* 2.216: ἀφ' οὗ καὶ εἰσέτι νῦν φιλοσοφοῦσι ταῖς ἑβδόμαις Ἰουδαῖοι τὴν πάτριον φιλοσοφίαν τὸν χρόνον ἐκεῖνον ἀναθέντες ἐπιστήμῃ καὶ θεωρίᾳ τῶν περὶ φύσιν (trans. LCL). Philo speaks about the Jews in general, but he clearly shares this understanding of the Sabbath.

53   Philo, *Mos.* 1.20–26.

54   Philo, *Mos.* 1.20.

him by learned Egyptians. These further instructed him in the philosophy conveyed in symbols, as displayed in the so-called holy inscriptions and in the regard paid to animals, to which they even pay divine honours. He had Greeks to teach him the rest of the regular school courses, and the inhabitants of the neighbouring countries for Assyrian letters and the Chaldean science of the heavenly bodies. This he also acquired from Egyptians, who give special attention to astrology. And, when he had mastered the lore of both nations, both where they agree and where they differ, he eschewed all strife and contention and sought only for truth.[55]

This is a remarkable description of Moses's education. Arithmetic and geometry, rhythm, harmony, metrics, music, and astronomy: these subjects are part of the ancient educational canon, as described in particular by Plato. From the first century BCE on, such a *Bildungskanon* was known as the *enkyklios paideia* (ἐγκύκλιος παιδεία) and this is the term which Philo uses here.[56] Philo's list of subjects is indeed reminiscent of those in Plato's *Republic*,[57] but above all it is probably based on Philo's own school days. We know that Philo, probably like most Jewish children of noble families in Alexandria, traversed a thorough curriculum, as explained in his tractate *De congressu eruditionis gratia* (*On the Preliminary Studies*).[58] There Philo looks back on his school days and lists three areas of study, two of which—geometry and music—were also part of Moses's education, as he has it in *De vita Mosis*:

> For instance when first I was incited by the goads of philosophy to desire her I consorted in early youth with one of her handmaids, Grammar, and all that I begat by her, writing, reading and study of the writings of the poets, I dedicated to her mistress. And again I kept company with another, namely Geometry, and was charmed with her beauty, for she showed symmetry and proportion in every part. Yet I took none of her children for my private use, but brought them as a gift to the lawful wife. Again my ardour moved me to keep company with a third; rich in rhythm, harmony and melody was she, and her name was Music, and from her I begat diatonics, chromatics and enharmonics, conjunct and disjunct melodies, conforming with the consonance of the fourth, fifth or octave intervals. And again

---

55   Philo, *Mos.* 1.21–24 (trans. LCL).
56   Philo, *Mos.* 1.23.
57   Plato, *Resp.* 526–530d.
58   Cf. Mendelson, *Secular Education in Philo of Alexandria*, 26–27.

of none of these did I make a secret hoard, wishing to see the lawful wife a lady of wealth with a host of servants ministering to her.[59]

Philo's personal canon of subjects does not entirely agree with that of Moses. But Philo generally does not evince a conclusive definition of the *enkyklios paideia*,[60] and one can safely say that Moses and Philo are introduced into the same *kind* of education. Alan Mendelson, who has written an important book on Philo's secular education, explains Moses's Hellenistic education in *De vita Mosis* with the apologetic intent of that work. According to Mendelson, Philo wanted to build a bridge for his pagan readers by giving Moses a "classical" training.[61] This seems unlikely. Once more, the apologetic intent of this text has been overestimated. What is more important in Philo's parallel readings on Moses's and his own education is, again, his endeavor to present himself as a close follower of Moses and possibly also to convey a message to his Jewish readers: even Moses enjoyed a secular education!

In the center of Philo's *De congressu eruditionis gratia* one finds his interpretation of Abraham's relationship with the slave Hagar, who at the time of Sarai's infertility gives birth to a son (Gen 16). In Philo's allegorical reading Hagar stands for basic education, for the *enkyklios paideia*, which ideally only prepares one for occupation with philosophical work:

> When Abraham is about to wed the handmaid of wisdom, the school culture, he does not forget, so the text implies, his faith plighted to her mistress, but knows that the one is his wife by law and deliberate choice, the other only by necessity and the force of occasion. And this is what happens to every lover of learning. ... For philosophy is the practice or study of wisdom, and wisdom is the knowledge of things divine and human and their causes. And therefore just as the culture of the schools is the bond-servant of philosophy, so must philosophy be the servant of wisdom.[62]

In his allegorical reading of Genesis 16, Philo describes in a Jewish context the pagan model of a philosophy which is introduced by means of a basic educa-

---

59   Philo, *Congr.* 74–76 (trans. LCL).

60   Cf. Monique Alexandre, *Philon d'Alexandrie. De Congressu Eruditionis Gratia* (Paris: Éditions du Cerf, 1967), 34–35; Mendelson, *Secular Education in Philo of Alexandria*, 4.

61   Mendelson, *Secular Education in Philo of Alexandria*, 64: "Especially if we assume that De Vita Mosis is an apologetic work, there is every reason for Philo to elaborate any points of contact between the experience of his audience and that of his protagonist. One of these points would be encyclical education."

62   Philo, *Congr.* 73, 79 (trans. LCL).

tion, the *enkyklios paideia*. The ultimate goal, though, is always philosophy and by means of philosophy the achievement of wisdom (σοφία).[63] In the words of Plato, all other sciences are "only the overtures to the melody, which should actually be learned."[64] Philo's allegorical interpretation—Hagar being the stepping stone to philosophy—seems to follow a similar pagan allegory according to which a restriction to the subjects of the *enkyklios paideia* would render one equivalent to the suitors of Penelope, who only want to amuse themselves with Penelope's maids.[65] As we have already seen, Philo describes this ideal form of a curriculum with respect to his own youth: the basic subjects are merely servants of philosophy.[66] And as for Moses, his training—as imagined by Philo—follows these very same lines: Moses, too, first passes through the *enkyklios paideia*,[67] and only then devotes himself to the study of wisdom (φρόνησις).[68] Certainly: Moses is a student of a first rate "university," he attracts international elite teachers, and this only in order subsequently to leave them behind.[69] Again: Philo cannot and does not claim to be Moses. But he has Moses agree with his education policy. As young men they were both taken by an enormous desire for education. Such a desire for education (παιδείας ἵμερον),[70] Philo says, had always been deep in his soul. The same goes for Moses: he was, as a young man, zealous for education and culture (ἐζήλωσε παιδείαν)[71] and for "what was sure to profit his soul" (ἃ τὴν ψυχὴν ἔμελλεν ὠφελήσειν).[72] This is how Philo presents his Moses, and this is how he sees himself.

Philo's Moses learned the *enkyklios paideia* from his Greek teachers. But he also had Egyptian teachers: he learned hieroglyphs, astronomy, and mathematics from local teachers.[73] Interestingly, Philo mentions that Moses was introduced by Egyptian teachers into the symbols of the hieroglyphs. Philo goes so far as to refer in this context to the Egyptian veneration of animals—which otherwise is a very common topic of intellectual critique in Jewish Hellenistic (and also pagan) literature.[74] Here, however, the symbolic, that is, allegorical

---

63   Philo, *Congr.* 79.
64   Plato, *Resp.* 531d: προοίμιά ἐστιν αὐτοῦ τοῦ νόμου ὃν δεῖ μαθεῖν.
65   On this metaphor cf. Harald Fuchs, "Enkyklios Paideia," *RAC* 5:382 and Alexandre, *De congressu*, 62–64.
66   Philo, *Congr.* 74–76.
67   Philo, *Mos.* 1.23: τὴν δ'ἄλλην ἐγκύκλιον παιδείαν Ἕλληνες ἐδίδασκον.
68   Philo, *Mos.* 1.25.
69   Philo, *Mos.* 1.21.
70   Philo, *Spec.* 3.4.
71   Philo, *Mos.* 1.32.
72   Philo, *Mos.* 1.20.
73   Philo, *Mos.* 1.23–24.
74   Philo, *Mos.* 1.23. On Philo's presentation of Egypt cf. Maren Niehoff, *Philo on Jewish Identity*

philosophy, taught by Egyptians, is important enough to make it part of Moses's curriculum. This Egyptian kind of philosophy, together with the Greek *enkyklios paideia*, is Moses's basic curriculum, his first degree, so to speak. It is true that for Moses this degree involves more memorizing than actual study,[75] but this is more of a Platonic stereotype than a negation of Egyptian learning. Philo after all was not obliged to include Egyptian teachers in Moses's curriculum, but he did. Very much like the Israelites who later took their pagan education with them when they left Egypt,[76] Moses already does this in his youth.

Recently Ekaterina Matusova has shown in an article in the *Studia Philonica Annual* that in Philo's time Egyptian allegorical interpretation played a certain role in the intellectual discourse in Alexandria. Matusova writes: "By Philo's time Egyptian culture became in Egypt highly significant as a symbolical culture and the barbarian culture par excellence. This locates Philo in a special set of circumstances in which, when using the tradition of allegorical interpretation of *hieroi logoi*, he could not avoid clear allusions to the Egyptian context as paradigmatic for his approach."[77] If this is so, we see again to what extent Moses's education in Philo's *De vita Mosis* is aligned with the intellectual education in Philo's own time.[78]

Philo's Moses passes—as fast as a "horse in the field," as Philo has it[79]—the best possible curriculum of his time. He studies with both Egyptian and Greek professors; in the end, however, in his search for truth he finds his own way, leaving both behind.[80] This is very much Philo's understanding of Judaism: it surpasses the teachings of others, but it is, at the same time, very much dependent on foreign impulses.

---

    and Culture (Tübingen: Mohr Siebeck, 2001), 45–74 and Sarah J.K. Pearce, *The Land of the Body: Studies in Philo's Representation of Egypt* (Tübingen: Mohr Siebeck, 2007), esp. 241–308, for a treatment of animal worship.

75   Philo, *Mos.* 1.21.

76   Philo, *Her.* 272–274.

77   Ekaterina Matusova, "Allegorical Interpretation of the Pentateuch in Alexandria: Inscribing Aristobulus and Philo in a Wider Literary Context," *SPhiloA* 22 (2010): 34–35.

78   However, Philo does not state that he himself studied the Egyptian tradition of allegorical interpretation.

79   Philo, *Mos.* 1.22. For this proverbial expression cf. Plato, *Theaet.* 183d: calling Socrates to an argument is like calling cavalry into an open plain. Thus the proverb is on people who are invited to do something in which they excel. In *Mos.* 1.22 it is on people, like Moses, who as soon as they have "a grasp of some of the first principles of knowledge press forward like the horse to the meadow."

80   Philo, *Mos.* 1.24: "He surpasses them, without contention" (ἀφιλονείκως τὰς ἔριδας ὑπερβάς, τὴν ἀλήθειαν ἐζήτει).

Philo's Moses does not simply adhere to the traditional, biblical role, nor does he merely adapt to the dominant Hellenistic (Egyptian-Roman) culture. Rather, Philo creates for Moses—and for himself—a third way, a new approach.[81] Philo and his Moses take advantage of the education of their times, but in the end they go their own ways. Philo is consistently trying to situate Jewish tradition in the context of contemporary philosophy and science: he attempts to make sense of the paradoxes in Jewish tradition, while at the same time participating in Jewish and non-Jewish discourses.

The biblical plot of Moses growing up at Pharaoh's palace before returning to his Israelite parents' home invited an updated reading of such a double course of education.[82] The Book of Exodus does not give us any information on Moses's education; but according to the Bible Moses's mother brought him to Pharaoh's daughter, and he became her son. To Jewish-Hellenistic authors the biblical story of Moses's exposure offered an attractive platform for a more detailed description of an ideal Jewish-Hellenistic education. In fact, Philo was not the first Jewish-Hellenistic author to stage such a double education. In Ezekiel's *Exagoge* Moses more explicitly than in the Bible enjoys two kinds of education: first, through his mother, he receives a Jewish education;[83] second, at the Egyptian court the Egyptian princess introduces Moses into Egyptian (or Hellenistic) *paideumata*.[84] In both examples, Ezekiel and Philo, the conviction, typical of Jewish Hellenism, that Judaism and Hellenism are not two separate entities, becomes fairly explicit. Philo is obviously much more detailed and concrete. And Philo adds philosophy to the mix. According to Philo, Moses did not invent philosophy, contrary to Artapanus who, as we have seen, had stated just that.[85] It is true that Philo, too, at times stresses the antiquity and originality of Jewish philosophy: Philo argues, for example, that the philosophical statement that virtue equals happiness is not an invention of pagan philosophy but of Moses.[86] Similarly, the Greek philosophers Heraclitus and Zeno did not come up with "new inventions" (εὕρεσις καινή), but simply used "old findings of

---

81   John M.G. Barclay's postcolonial reading of Josephus (*Against Apion* [Flavius Josephus, Translation and Commentary 10; Leiden: Brill, 2006]) could also be fruitfully applied with regard to Philo.

82   While Philo says very little about Moses's Jewish upbringing, there is no doubt that he took it for a given; cf. Mendelson, *Secular Education in Philo of Alexandria*, 26.

83   Ezekiel, *Exagoge*, v. 35: γένος πατρῷον καὶ θεοῦ δωρήματα.

84   Ezekiel, *Exagoge*, v. 37. Cf. on this passage René Bloch, "'Meine Mutter erzählte mir alles': Ezechiel *Exagoge* 34–35 und der Mythos," *Judaica* 61 (2005): 97–109.

85   Cf. above p. 29.

86   Philo, *Mut.* 167–168 (Philo refers to Exod 4:14).

Moses" (παλαιὸν εὕρεμα Μωυσέως)[87] or (in the case of Zeno) the "source of Jewish law" (ἀπὸ πηγῆς τῆς Ἰουδαίων νομοθεσίας).[88] But still: Philo nowhere claims absolute originality of Jewish philosophy. On the contrary, he is very open about his own philosophical predecessors, especially Plato. But in the end, Philo, too, chooses his own path. Philo pursues the very same dialectics as his Moses does. He addresses different opinions of the philosophical schools of his time, but in the end he formulates his own philosophy.

We have looked now at very different aspects of Philo's projecting his opinions onto Moses. It is, of course, not unusual that an author has his main protagonist represent his main theses. In the case of Philo, it seems to me, one has so far underestimated how much this is the case with regard to Moses. Such a projection or even parallelization was to some extent offered up to Philo as an accidental gift of history, because of biographic parallels between Moses and his own life: their Egyptian origins, their political roles in favour of the Jewish people against foreign, pagan powers, their roles as philosophers (in the case of Moses present early on in Jewish-Hellenistic literature)—there were several reasons why Philo could feel tempted to blend his presentation of Moses with autobiographical elements. I leave it an open question whether this should be read as a sign of Philo's modest admiration for Moses or rather as some sort of preposterous hubris. Maybe a little bit of both. Philo's portrait of Moses in *De vita Mosis* should in any case be taken into account in our search for the historical Philo. There is some sort of *Tagespolitik* in *De vita Mosis*, which makes this treatise a late rather than an early text. And there are some autobiographic moments in *De vita Mosis*. Both observations can help us grasp Philo a little better.

Bibliography

Alexandre, Monique, *Philon d'Alexandrie. De Congressu Eruditionis Gratia*. Paris: Éditions du Cerf, 1967.
Arnaldez, Roger, et al., eds., *De Vita Mosis*. Paris: Éditions du Cerf, 1967.
Barclay, John M.G., *Against Apion*. Flavius Josephus, Translation and Commentary 10. Leiden: Brill, 2006.
Bloch, René, "'Meine Mutter erzählte mir alles': Ezechiel Exagoge 34–35 und der Mythos," *Judaica* 61 (2005): 97–109.

---

87 Philo, *Her.* 214.
88 Philo, *Prob.* 57.

Bloch, René, *Jüdische Drehbühnen: Biblische Variationen im antiken Judentum*. Tübingen: Mohr Siebeck, 2013.

Cohn, Leopold, "Einteilung und Chronologie der Schriften Philos," *Phil Suppl.* 7 (1899): 387–435.

Feldman, Louis H., *Philo's Portrayal of Moses in the Context of Ancient Judaism*. Notre Dame: University of Notre Dame Press, 2007.

Fuchs, Harald, "Enkyklios Paideia," *RAC* 5: 365–398.

Goodenough, Erwin R., "Philo's Exposition of the Law and His De Vita Mosis," *HTR* 26 (1933): 109–125.

Goodenough, Erwin R., *The Politics of Philo of Judaeus: Practice and* Theory. New Haven: Yale University Press, 1938.

Lévy, Carlos, "Mais que faisait donc Philon en Égypte?: A propos de l'identité diasporique de Philon." Pages 295–312 in *La rivelazione in Filone di Alessandria, natura, legge, storia: atti del VII Convegno di Studi del Gruppo italiano di ricerca su Origene e la tradizione alessandrina* (Bologna 29–30 settembre 2003). Edited by Angela Maria Mazzanti and Francesca Calabi. Verruchio: Pazzini, 2004.

Massebieau, Louis and Bréhier, Emile, "Essai sur la chronologie de la vie et des œuvres de Philon," *RHR* 53 (1906): 1–91.

Matusova, Ekaterina, "Allegorical Interpretation of the Pentateuch in Alexandria: Inscribing Aristobulus and Philo in a Wider Literary Context," *SPhiloA* 22 (2010): 1–52.

McGing, Brian, "Philo's Adaptation of the Bible in his Life of Moses." Pages 117–140 in *The Limits of Ancient Biography*. Edited by Brian McGing and Judith Mossman. Swansea: Classical Press of Wales, 2006.

Mendelson, Alan, *Secular Education in Philo of Alexandria*. Cincinnati: Hebrew Union College Press, 1982.

Niehoff, Maren, *Philo on Jewish Identity and Culture*. Tübingen: Mohr Siebeck, 2001.

Pearce, Sarah J.K., "King Moses: Notes on Philo's Portrait of Moses as an Ideal Leader in the Life of Moses." Pages 37–74 in *The Greek Strand in Islamic Political Thought*. Mélanges de l'Université Saint-Joseph LVII. Edited by Emma Gannagé et al. Beirut: Imprimerie catholique, 2004.

Pearce, Sarah J.K., *The Land of the Body: Studies in Philo's Representation of Egypt*. Tübingen: Mohr Siebeck, 2007.

Royse, James R., "The Works of Philo." Pages 32–64 in *The Cambridge Companion to Philo*. Edited by Adam Kamesar. Cambridge: Cambridge University Press, 2009.

Runia, David T., "Philon von Alexandreia," *DNP* 9: 852.

Schwartz, Daniel R., "Philo, His Family, and His Times." Pages 9–31 in *The Cambridge Companion to Philo*. Edited by Adam Kamesar. Cambridge: Cambridge University Press, 2009.

Sterling, Gregory E., "How Do You Introduce Philo of Alexandria? The Cambridge Companion to Philo," *SPhiloA* 21 (2009): 63–72.

Sterling, Gregory E., "Tiberius Julius Alexander." Pages 1309–1310 in *The Eerdmans Dictionary of Early Judaism*. Edited by John J. Collins and Daniel C. Harlow. Grand Rapids: Eerdmans Publishing Company, 2010.

Winston, David, "Sage and Supersage in Philo of Alexandria." Pages 171–180 in *The Ancestral Philosophy: Hellenistic Philosophy in Second Temple Judaism. Essays of David Winston*. Edited by Gregory E. Sterling. Providence: Brown University, 2001.

CHAPTER 2

Moses and the Charlatans: On the Charge of γόης καὶ ἀπατεών in *Contra Apionem* 2.145, 161

For my father ז״ל

∴

1   Introduction

At the beginning of his presentation of the Jewish constitution and laws, introducing the final segment of his apologetic tractate *Contra Apionem* (2.145–286), Flavius Josephus cites the accusation circulated by "Apollonius Molon, Lysimachus, and others," to the effect that Moses was a γόης καὶ ἀπατεών.[1] Josephus rebuts this allegation in no uncertain terms shortly thereafter (*CA* 2.161).[2] What is the meaning of this charge, whose authorship Josephus so imprecisely relates?

Ἀπατεών (from ἀπατάω: "to defraud," "to cheat") carries the meaning of "cheat" or "beguiler." Γόης, a term which will be discussed in greater detail further below, can refer to a "magician" or "sorcerer." Figuratively, the term can also signify a "cheat" or "swindler."[3] In the translations of *CA* 2.145 and 2.161,

---

1   I would like to thank my teacher, Professor Fritz Graf, for his valuable advice during the development of this article.

2   The texts are as follows: (a) *CA* 2.145: Ἐπεὶ δὲ καὶ Ἀπολλώνιος ὁ Μόλων καὶ Λυσίμαχος καί τινες ἄλλοι τὰ μὲν ὑπ' ἀγνοίας, τὸ πλεῖστον δὲ κατὰ δυσμένειαν, περί τε τοῦ νομοθετήσαντος ἡμῖν Μωυσέως καὶ περὶ τῶν νόμων πεποίηνται λόγους οὔτε δικαίους οὔτε ἀληθεῖς, τὸν μὲν ὡς γόητα καὶ ἀπατεῶνα διαβάλλοντες .... / "But since Apollonios Molon and Lysimachus and certain others, partly out of ignorance, but mostly from ill-will, have made statements about our legislator Moses and the laws that are neither just nor true—libeling Moses a charlatan and fraudster." (b) *CA* 2.161: Τοιοῦτος μὲν δή τις [αὐτὸς] ἡμῶν ὁ νομοθέτης, οὐ γόης οὐδ' ἀπατεών, ἅπερ λοιδοροῦντες λέγουσιν ἀδίκως, ἀλλ' οἷον παρὰ τοῖς Ἕλλησιν αὐχοῦσιν τὸν Μίνω γεγονέναι καὶ μετ' αὐτὸν τοὺς ἄλλους νομοθέτας. / "Such was the character of our legislator, not a charlatan or fraudster as they say, insulting him unjustly, but of such a kind that Greeks boast Minos to have been, and the other subsequent legislators" (trans. Barclay, Brill).

3   See Karl H. Rengstorf, ed., *A Complete Concordance to Flavius Josephus.* 4 vols. (Leiden: Brill, 1973–1983), 1:390: "rogue, cheat, swindler, fraud, magician, wizard, fraudulent miracle-worker."

© RENÉ BLOCH, 2022 | DOI:10.1163/9789004521896_004

40   CHAPTER 2

one encounters both of these possible renditions: for Blum, γόης here should
be taken as "sorcier,"[4] and Gerber accordingly translates it with "Zauberer,"[5]
and likewise Troiani with "mago."[6] On the other hand, the old translation by
Clementz had "Gaukler,"[7] and finally the Loeb translation by Thackeray reads
"charlatan."[8] Moses the magician or Moses the swindler?

Change of scene: In *Antiquitates Judaicae* 20.167 we find again the exact
same phrase, γόης καὶ ἀπατεών (albeit in the plural). But here Josephus is not
quoting an anti-Jewish author like Apollonius Molon or Lysimachus; rather,
Josephus himself is speaking. And in any case, the rather unflattering description of γόης καὶ ἀπατεών here does not describe Moses, but rather an unspeci-
fied number of men living in Judea under the governorship of Felix who were
seeking to persuade the crowds (τὸν ὄχλον ἔπειθον) to follow them into the
desert where they would see signs and wonders according to the πρόνοια of
God. Many were indeed persuaded, for which reason Felix later executed these
men.[9] The immediately following episode[10] tells the story of an Egyptian who
claimed to be a prophet—yet who was not, in the eyes of Josephus. This pseudo-
prophet acts exactly like the γόητες καὶ ἀπατεῶνες, whom Josephus had just
mentioned: he led astray the common people (τῷ δημοτικῷ πλήθει) and led
them to a remote location. This time it is not a desert, but the Mount of Olives,

---

4   Léon Blum, ed., *Flavius Josèphe: Contre Apion* (Paris: Les Belles-Lettres, 1972): (a) "accusant
        l'un de sorcellerie et d'imposture;" (b) "ce n'est pas un sorcier ni un imposteur."

5   Christine Gerber, *Ein Bild des Judentums für Nichtjuden von Flavius Josephus: Untersuchun-
        gen zu seiner Schrift Contra Apionem* (Leiden: Brill, 1997): (a) "indem sie jenen als einen
        Zauberer und Betrüger verleumdeten" (although see p. 134 ["mikrostrukturelle Analyse"]:
        "Mose ist ein Schwindler und Scharlatan"); (b) "Ein solcher Mann ist also unser Gesetzge-
        ber, weder ein Zauberer noch ein Betrüger."

6   Lucio Troiani, *Commento storico al "Contro Apione" di Giuseppe* (Pisa: Giardini, 1977): (a)
        "calunniando l'uno come mago ed impostore" (b) "non un mago nè un impostore."

7   Heinrich Clementz, ed., *Flavius Josephus: Kleinere Schriften* (Wiesbaden: Fourier, 1993): (a)
        "indem sie jenen verleumderisch als Gaukler und Betrüger bezeichnen;" (b) "Ein solcher
        Mann eben war unser Gesetzgeber, kein Gaukler, auch kein Betrüger."

8   Henry St. J. Thackeray, trans. and ed., *Josephus: The Life—Against Apion* (Cambridge: Har-
        vard University Press, 1926): (a) "maligning the one as a charlatan and an impostor;" (b)
        "Such was our legislator; no charlatan or impostor."

9   *AJ* 20.167–168: οἱ δὲ γόητες καὶ ἀπατεῶνες ἄνθρωποι τὸν ὄχλον ἔπειθον αὐτοῖς εἰς τὴν ἐρημίαν
        ἕπεσθαι· δείξειν γὰρ ἔφασαν ἐναργῆ τέρατα καὶ σημεῖα κατὰ τὴν τοῦ θεοῦ πρόνοιαν γινόμενα. καὶ
        πολλοὶ πεισθέντες τῆς ἀφροσύνης τιμωρίας ὑπέσχον· ἀναχθέντας γὰρ αὐτοὺς Φῆλιξ ἐκόλασεν.
        Slightly earlier, at *AJ* 20.160, Josephus summarizes that, during the time of the Procurator
        Felix, the land was full of λῃστηρίων ... καὶ γοήτων ἀνθρώπων who swayed the masses (οἳ τὸν
        ὄχλον ἠπάτων).

10   *AJ* 20.169–172.

MOSES AND THE CHARLATANS

which lies directly across from the city.[11] There he was to show them how at his command the walls of Jerusalem would fall down. In the skirmish that follows, the Egyptian prophet escapes unnoticed.

At the corresponding place in the narrative in the *Bellum Judaicum*[12] Josephus reports, in the form of a climax, first of the *sicarii* and then of other criminals—in the *Antiquitates* he calls them γόητες καὶ ἀπατεῶνες, while here they are called πλάνοι ... ἄνθρωποι καὶ ἀπατεῶνες—, who, under the pretense of divine inspiration, moved the crowds to a demonic enthusiasm (δαιμονᾶν). The false prophet from Egypt represented a greater evil still: here he is called a ἄνθρωπος γόης who presented himself as a prophet. Finally, the γόητες and the gangs of brigands joined forces and in this way pulled many to ruin.

The modern translations agree concerning the above passages in the *Antiquitates* and *Bellum*: the very fact that Josephus can call the γόητες in a parallel passage πλάνοι ("cheats," "enticers"), indicates that the term γόης—as in the respective translations—refers to an "impostor"[13] or "betrügerischer Wundertäter"[14] and "charlatan."[15]

I would like to take these two passages at CA 2.145 and 2.161 and their parallels in the *Antiquitates* and *Bellum* as a starting point to address two further issues:

1. What did Josephus mean by the terms γόης and γοητεία? What is meant at CA 2.145, 161?

2. How is it possible that Josephus could take a polemic which—according to himself—was directed against Moses (that of his being a γόης καὶ ἀπατεών) by anti-Jewish authors and apply it in the context of his own inner-Jewish critique?

While I do not wish to provide a detailed overview of the semantic range of the term "sorcerer" (or "Zauberer")—this has already been performed within a larger context by Fritz Graf[16]—it is still appropriate here to outline the main

---

11   AJ 20.169: τῆς πόλεως ἄντικρυς.

12   BJ 2.254–265. The two accounts, to be sure, do not agree completely. See Martin Hengel, *Die Zeloten: Untersuchungen zur jüdischen Freiheitsbewegung in der Zeit von Herodes I. bis 70 n. Chr.* (Leiden: Brill, 1961), 237.

13   Louis H. Feldman, trans. and ed., *Josephus: Jewish Antiquities—Book 20, General Index* (Cambridge: Harvard University Press, 1965), AJ 20.167.

14   Otto Michel and Otto Bauernfeind, eds., *Flavius Josephus: De bello Judaico, Der jüdische Krieg—griechisch und deutsch, eingeleitet und mit Anmerkungen versehen.* Vols. 1–3 (Darmstadt: Wissenschaftliche Buchgesellschaft, 1959–1969), BJ 2.261.

15   André Pelletier, *Flavius Josèphe: Guerre des Juifs* (Paris: Les Belles-Lettres, 1975–1982), BJ 2.261.

16   Fritz Graf, *Gottesnähe und Schadenzauber: Die Magie in der griechisch-römischen Antike*

points before examining how Josephus used the terms γόης and γοητεία in his collected works (the terms appear in all four of his extant works). Γόης, stemming originally from the term γόος ("lament for the dead"),[17] is an old term for "sorcerer" with predominantly negative connotations. Early on, the γόης acquired a reputation for unpredictability and the ability to transform,[18] so that soon one could also signify a "fraudulent sorcerer" with this term. Plato calls those who terrify other people by means of tricks γόητες.[19] From here it is a small step to a common swear word: γόης can mean "liar" and "cheat," without necessarily denoting anything that we might call sorcery. As Walter Burkert once put it, "The sorcerer was disenchanted and thus became a charlatan and a cheat."[20] The breadth of semantic possibilities for γόης ranges from "sorcerer" to "fraudulent sorcerer" and all the way to simply "fraud" as such, where it has almost completely lost its function as a technical term. Still, the term applies mostly to the religious realm, and thus means something like "charlatan in religious matters" (and γόης (or γοητεία) can still refer to a "sorcerer" down into late antiquity[21]). Likewise the term μάγος, a well-known word for "sorcerer" borrowed from Old Persian, which Fritz Graf has shown to have gradually displaced γόης over the course of the fifth century CE, can also carry negative connotations.[22]

2 Magic and Trickery: An Anti-Jewish Accusation?

Ancient descriptions (and not only these) of magicians and Jews were sometimes quite similar: both worlds, that of the magicians and that of the Jews,

---

(Munich: C.H. Beck, 1996), 24–36. See also Walter Burkert, "ΓΟΗΣ: Zum griechischen Schamanismus," *Rheinisches Museum für Philologie* [Neue Folge] 105 (1962): 36–55; Gerhard Delling, "γόης," *TWNT* 1.737–738.

17   Burkert, "ΓΟΗΣ," 44.

18   Herodotus, *Hist.* 4.105 (regarding the Scythian Neuroi, who annually transform themselves into wolves); Plato, *Resp.* 380d, 383a (regarding the transformative abilities of the gods).

19   Plato, *Nom.* 649a; *Resp.* 413b–d; *Men.* 80a–b.

20   "Der Zauberer wurde entzaubert und damit zum Scharlatan und Betrüger." Burkert, "ΓΟΗΣ," 51. See *Sudas* s.v. γόης: κόλαξ, πλάνος, ἀπατεών.

21   See Augustine, *Civ.* 10.9 (*goetia*).

22   So already in Plato, *Resp.* 572e. The transition of the usage of γόης to μάγος led to a paradigm shift: "Magie, bisher integraler Teil der religiösen Tradition, wird ausgeschieden und negativ bewertet" (Graf, *Gottesnähe*, 31). See also Gerhard Delling, "μάγος," *TWNT* 4.360–363. Μάγος in Josephus refers to a "Babylonian dream-interpreter" (*AJ* 10.195–238 *passim*) and in *AJ* 20.141–144 to one who performs a love-spell. See p. 47 below.

MOSES AND THE CHARLATANS 43

were regularly viewed as being inherently different; sorcerers and Jews were described as marginal figures, and the same accusations are sometimes made against both groups: for example, impiety and the misleading of others.[23]

Given this background, it is not surprising that the Jews in antiquity, as a kind of extrapolation of their marginalization, were characterized as sorcerers or sorceresses. Thus, for example, Juvenal in his tirade against women could speak thus of an old Jewish woman: "the shaking Jewess, having left her basket of hay, whispers secretly into your ear that she is the interpreter of the laws of Jerusalem, high priestess of the tree, and a reliable messenger of highest heaven."[24]

In an isolated pericope, Posidonius reports of Jewish γόητες who with the help of feigned incantations attempt to extract the asphalt from the Dead Sea.[25] Lucian of Samosata has only scorn for the fool who lets himself be tricked by the spells of the Jews;[26] finally, the philosopher Celsus is said to have indicted the Jews for having given themselves over to γοητεία and to the one who taught it, Moses.[27]

Nevertheless, the collocation of 'Judaism (or Moses) and sorcery' in Greco-Roman literature is not so widespread as it has sometimes been claimed to be in research: for example, Marcel Simon's statement—that "for the ancients, magic is, one might say, congenital to Israel"—goes too far.[28] The 'Jewish sorcerer'

---

23   Plato accuses sorcerers of impiety and of leading others astray (*Leg.* 909b; *Resp.* 364b). For the anti-Jewish accusation of impiety see, e.g., Josephus, *CA* 2.148; for the accusation that Jews lead others astray see Tacitus, *Hist.* 5.5.2. (Menahem Stern, *Greek and Latin Authors on Jews and Judaism.* 3 vols. [Jerusalem: The Israel Academy of Sciences and Humanities, 1974–1984], § 281). On the marginality of sorcerers, see Graf, *Gottesnähe,* 28, 81–82, 203–204.

24   Juvenal 6.542–546 (Stern § 299): *cophino fenoque relicto / arcanam Iudaea tremens mendicat in aurem, / interpres legum Solymarum et magna sacerdos / arboris ac summi fida internuntia caeli.* Here the marginalization is reinforced by indications of sex and age.

25   Strabo, *Geogr.* 16.2.43 (Stern § 45): Γόητας δὲ ὄντας σκήπτεσθαί φησιν ἐπῳδὰς ὁ Ποσειδώνιος τοὺς ἀνθρώπους.

26   Lucian, *Trag.* 171–173 (Stern § 374), 173: Ἰουδαῖος ἕτερον μωρὸν ἐξᾴδει λαβών. See also *Alex.* 13 (Stern § 373) and *Philops.* 16 (Stern § 372; also Graf, *Gottesnähe,* 73).

27   Origen, *Cels.* 1.26 (Stern § 375): Κέλσος λέγων αὐτοὺς σέβειν ἀγγέλους καὶ γοητείᾳ προσκεῖσθαι, ἧς ὁ Μωϋσῆς αὐτοῖς γέγονεν ἐξηγητής. According to Diogenes Laertius, some claimed that the Jews were descended from the Magi (*Lives* 1.9 Prologue [Stern § 397]). Numenius of Apamea places the Jews in line with the Brahmins and Magi (Eusebius, *Hist. eccl.* 9.7.1 [Stern § 364 a]).

28   Marcel Simon, *Verus Israel: Etude sur les relations entre chrétiens et juifs dans l'empire romain (132–245)* (Paris: E. de Boccard, 1948), 136: "Pour les anciens, la magie est, peut-on dire, congénitale à Israël."

is not an ethnographic *idion* in describing the Jews. The frequent mention of Moses in the Magical Papyri apparently had no influence on ethnographic descriptions of the Jews, which had already solidified in earlier times.[29] It is significant that precisely in the polemical chapters on the Jews in Cicero and especially in Tacitus, for whom magicians were a constant thorn in the side,[30] one finds no mention of Jewish sorcery.

Also, the above-mentioned negatively-colored statements about Jewish sorcery seem on the whole to be rather isolated. Other comments on 'Jewish sorcery' are generally neutral.[31] Moses, the lawgiver of the Jews, is listed as a magician several times in the literature and yet, with the exception of the late passage of Celsus (or Origen), never in a polemical tone: Strabo names Moses in a list of prophets, magicians, and soothsayers and explicitly places Moses at a remove from his depraved followers.[32] According to Pompeius Trogus, Joseph, thanks to his attentive spirit (*sollerti ingenio*), acquired *artes magicae* in Egypt and then passed them on to his son Moses, who was in no way inferior to him.[33] Finally, Moses appears in the magician catalogues of both Pliny and Apuleius, neither of which contain any particular polemic against Moses.[34] However one would like to translate *CA* 2.145 and 2.161, "Moses the magician" or "Moses the charlatan," the accusation of "Apollonius Molon, Lysimachus, and others" against which Josephus defends himself appears to have practically no parallels.[35]

---

29   Vice-versa, in the Magical Papyri Moses is not associated with the *topoi*, as they are known from Greek and Roman digressions on the Jews; see John G. Gager, *Moses in Greco-Roman Paganism* (New York: Abingdon, 1972), 159: "he [Moses] is nowhere called the lawgiver of the Jews. In this respect the Moses of the magical and alchemical documents is largely independent of the Moses in the Greek and Roman literary tradition, although some of the literary authors were familiar with Moses' reputation as a magician."

30   See, for example, Tacitus, *Hist.* 1.22.1.

31   Incidentally, Hellenistic Jewish circles also associated Jewish figures with "sorcery". The Greco-Jewish historians Artapanus (Eusebius, *Hist. eccl.* 9.18.1) and Pseudo-Eupolemus (*Hist. eccl.* 9.17.8) do not hesitate to call Abraham an astrologer. According to Jubilees 10.10–15 Noah learned the healing arts of the angels and passed this on to his son Shem. See also Acts 7:22 (Moses's familiarity with Egyptian wisdom).

32   Strabo, *Geogr.* 16.2.39 (Stern § 115).

33   Justin, *Ep.* 36.2.7.11 (Stern § 137).

34   Pliny, *Nat.* 30.11 (Stern § 221): *est et alia magices factio a Mose et Ianne et Lotape ac Iudaeis pendens, sed multis milibus annorum post Zoroastren.* Apuleius, *Apol.* 90 (Stern § 361): *ego ille sim Carmendas vel Damigeron vel *his* Moses vel Iohannes vel Apollobex vel ipse Dardanus vel quicumque alius post Zoroastren et Hostanen inter magos celebratus est.*

35   A passage from Philo's poorly preserved *Hypothetica*, which has come down to us through Eusebius, addresses the accusation that Moses is a γόης (Eusebius, *Praep. Ev.* 8.6.2: ἐλοιδό-

MOSES AND THE CHARLATANS   45

3   Moses Before Pharaoh

One of the central passages for dealing with the issues at hand is *AJ* 2.284–287, where the 'magical competition' between Moses and the Egyptian magicians of Pharaoh is recorded (Exod 7:8–15). First, the rendition in Josephus: when Moses, as if for a warning, reports to Pharaoh of all the signs (σημεῖα) that God had revealed to the Israelites on Mount Sinai, Pharaoh shows nothing but disdain for such wonder-working and sorcery (τερατουργίαι καὶ μαγείαι). Moses had earlier escaped from Egyptian servitude, Pharaoh says, and now he comes back with plans for deception (ἐξ ἀπάτης). Thereafter Pharaoh calls on his priests to perform the same wonders (ὄψεις), from which it should become clear that the Egyptians are also adept at this science (ἐπιστήμη): they throw down their staffs, which are then turned into serpents. Moses is not surprised: by no means does he despise the Egyptian σοφία; but what he, Moses, has done (τὰ ὑπ' ἐμοῦ πραττόμενα) transcends the magical arts (μαγεία and τέχνη) of the Egyptians—that is to say, as much as divine things (τὰ θεῖα) are different from human things (τὰ ἀνθρώπινα): "And I will show that it is from no witchcraft (γοη-τεία) or deception (πλάνη) of true judgement, but from God's providence and power (κατὰ δὲ θεοῦ πρόνοιαν καὶ δύναμιν) that my miracles proceed."[36] Moses throws his staff: it becomes a serpent and right away eats the serpents created by the staffs of the Egyptians.

A comparison with the underlying biblical episode shows that Josephus's rendition distances itself from the much more condensed episode as it appears in the Bible, where the Egyptian priests do essentially the same thing as Mo-ses.[37] However, in *AJ* 2.284–287 there is nothing to suggest that Josephus is

---

ρουν γόητα καὶ κέρκωπα λόγων); but it is not entirely clear here whether Philo is referring to the grumbling of the Israelites (as the use of the imperfect tense may indicate) or an accusation he knows from the literature. On the usage of the word γόης in Philo, see *Spec.* 1.315, where the terms γόης and προφήτης are juxtaposed.

36   *AJ* 2.286 (trans. LCL).

37   After Aaron has accomplished the staff miracle before Pharaoh, Exod 7:11 reads: "And Pharaoh also (גם) called his wise-men and sorcerers (מכשפים) and they, the Egyptian magicians (חרטמי מצרים), also (גם) did the same with their secret arts." The Masoretic Text has no problem with this parallelism (which is even clearer in the LXX 7:11: ἐποίη-σαν καὶ οἱ ἐπαοιδοὶ τῶν Αἰγυπτίων ταῖς φαρμακείαις αὐτῶν ὡσαύτως). Neither is the power of the magicians for the Egyptian domain questioned. The important difference seems to be what power stands behind the sorcery: "Während Mose und Aaron, wie ausdrücklich bestätigt wird, auf göttlichen Auftrag hin handeln, verrichten die ägyptischen Zauber-priester ihr Wunder—zumindest ohne ausdrücklichen Befehl—auf Grund ihrer magis-chen Fähigkeiten, ihrer Geheimkünste" (Werner H. Schmidt, *Exodus* [Neukirchen: Neu-kirchener Verlag, 1974], ad loc.).

implicitly responding to a charge of magic whether against the Jews in general or Moses in particular. It is true that the word order is clearly delineated: in the debate with Moses, the Egyptians operate with μαγεία καὶ τέχνη, while the actions of Moses are simply referred to as πραττόμενα and φαινόμενα. But, first of all, Josephus deviates from the biblical text insofar as he has not Aaron but Moses accomplish the staff miracle; he thus only could have encouraged any potential charge of Moses being a magician;[38] second, in Josephus's account Moses does not consider it necessary to respond at all to Pharaoh's charge that the signs at Sinai were wonder-working and magic (τερατουργίαι καὶ μαγεῖαι). He implicitly distances himself from μαγεία καὶ τέχνη, which belong fundamentally to τὰ ἀνθρώπινα and stand no chance against τὰ θεῖα (divine acts are the norm, while magic is just marginal).[39] He only explicitly defends himself against the charges of γοητεία and πλάνη, by which here, too, is meant "dishonesty and trickery."

A few paragraphs later this becomes even clearer: In *AJ* 2.320 Josephus reports that after the ten plagues the Egyptians regretted that they let the Hebrews go; Pharaoh was angry that this had come about through the γοητεία of Moses. Pharaoh did not mind that Moses had practiced sorcery—his priests had done the same thing. It is not about *what*, but *with what purpose* it transpired. Pharaoh is bothered by the fact that he has been deceived by Moses.[40] With this Pharaoh picks back up the above-mentioned accusation regarding Moses's escape from Egyptian slavery and his returning with fraudulent intent (ἐξ ἀπάτης). It thus also becomes clear that in Josephus's rendition of Exod 7:8–15 there is not so much a connotation of the accusation of sorcery as an accusation of fraud and deception.[41] The passage serves more to illustrate the discrepancy between "human trickery and divine power"[42] than to attempt to

---

38   Moses plays the role of the protagonist overall in the *Antiquitates*, while Aaron remains in the background; so also Louis H. Feldman, "Josephus' Portrait of Moses," *JQR* 82 (1991): 285–328, at 306: "in Josephus ... it is Moses rather than Aaron who performs the miracles."

39   *AJ* 2.286: τοσῷδε μέντοι κρείττονα τὰ ὑπ᾽ ἐμοῦ πραττόμενα τῆς τούτων μαγείας καὶ τέχνης φημί, ὅσῳ τὰ θεῖα τῶν ἀνθρωπίνων διαφέρει.

40   The biblical account knows no such reflection on Pharaoh's part. Exod 14:5 only has the Egyptians say: "When the king of Egypt was told that the people had fled, the minds of Pharaoh and his officials were changed toward the people, they said: 'What have we done, letting Israel leave our service?'" (NRSV).

41   *Pace* Feldman, "Portrait," 308 and John G. Gager, "Moses the Magician: Hero of an Ancient Counter-Culture?" *Helios* 21 (1994): 179–188, both of whom suspect behind Josephus's argument a conscious dissociation from Jewish magic.

42   Feldman, "Portrait," 307.

MOSES AND THE CHARLATANS

'disenchant' Moses. And it comes as no surprise that in the *Antiquities* Josephus never goes into the prohibitions of any magical practices that the Torah proffers in no uncertain terms (Exod 22:17; Deut 18:10–11).[43]

Another example: In *AJ* 20.141–144 Josephus gives a summary report of a case of a commercial love-spell. When the procurator Felix desires a married woman named Drusilla, in order to win her over he sends for a Cypriot Jew who pretended to be a magician (μάγον εἶναι σκηπτόμενον)[44] in an effort to convince Drusilla to leave her husband for Felix. We are not told the specifics of this love-spell. In any case, Drusilla does leave her husband, something for which Josephus, of course, offers rather prosaic reasons: she wanted to escape the influence of her sister Berenice. Josephus incorporates the entertaining episode into his narrative without reservation—without any apology he accepts that here we are talking about a Jewish μάγος.[45]

To be sure, one finds in Josephus's rewriting of biblical miracle stories a tendency to rationalize, but ultimately the impetus of the Hellenistic historiographical tradition which was open to the miraculous prevailed.[46] We find just this kind of literary imprint in Josephus's version of Ex 7:8–15. Josephus even goes so far as to attribute unreservedly to King Solomon the ability to wield power over demons;[47] not only this, but Josephus also assures the reader that such exorcism is still practiced "among us" (παρ' ἡμῖν) to this day, whereupon he provides the example of a certain Eleazar.[48]

---

43   Exod 22:17: "You shall not permit a female sorcerer to live!"; Deut 18:10–11: "No one shall be found among you who makes a son or a daughter pass through fire, or who practices divination, or is a soothsayer, or an augur, or a sorcerer, or one who casts spells, or who consults ghosts and spirits, or who seeks oracles from the dead." (NRSV).

44   *AJ* 20.142. Acts 13:4–12 and Pliny *Nat.* 30.2 also know of Jewish magicians from Cyprus.

45   On μάγος see above p. 42 with n. 22.

46   Wolfgang Fauth, "'Zeichen und Wunder' im Alten Testament und bei Josephus," in *Memoria Rerum Veterum: Neue Beiträge zur antiken Historiographie und Alten Geschichte— Festschrift für C.J. Classen zum 60. Geburtstag*, ed. Wolfram Ax (Stuttgart: Franz Steiner Verlag, 1990), 9–31, at 16; Otto Betz, "Das Problem des Wunders bei Flavius Josephus im Vergleich zum Wunderproblem bei den Rabbinen und im Johannesevangelium," in *Josephus-Studien: Untersuchungen zu Josephus, dem antiken Judentum und dem Neuen Testament*, ed. Otto Betz, Klaus Haacker, and Martin Hengel (Göttingen: Vandenhoeck & Ruprecht, 1974), 23–44, at 25–27.

47   *AJ* 8.45: Παρέσχε δ' αὐτῷ μαθεῖν ὁ θεὸς καὶ τὴν κατὰ τῶν δαιμόνων τέχνην εἰς ὠφέλειαν καὶ θεραπείαν τοῖς ἀνθρώποις· ἐπῳδάς τε συνταξάμενος αἷς παρηγορεῖται τὰ νοσήματα καὶ τρόπους ἐξορκώσεων κατέλιπεν, οἷς οἱ ἐνδούμενοι τὰ δαιμόνια ὡς μηκέτ' ἐπανελθεῖν ἐκδιώκουσι.

48   *AJ* 8.46: καὶ αὕτη μέχρι νῦν παρ' ἡμῖν ἡ θεραπεία πλεῖστον ἰσχύει.

48   CHAPTER 2

4   The γόητες in the *Bellum* and *Antiquitates*

The impostors which we hear about at AJ 20.167–172 and BJ 2.254–265 are known to be no isolated case. On the contrary, Josephus repeatedly reports on such fraudulent men, who take advantage of the gullibility of the crowds:[49]

– In BJ 4.84–120 Josephus tells of how the entire Galilee lay in the hands of the Romans, save for the small farming town of Gischala. A band of robbers, says Josephus, had established themselves in the otherwise peaceful Gischala. Their leader is John, whom Josephus describes as a γόης ἀνὴρ καὶ ποικιλώτατος τὸ ἦθος.[50] When Titus proposes to negotiate for peace, John refuses under the pretext of a Sabbath rest and flees the following night. "With such words he tricked Titus," comments Josephus (4.103: τοιούτοις ἐσοφίζετο τὸν Τίτον). John is no sorcerer, but rather—in the eyes of Josephus—simply a deceiver.

– In BJ 5.317–330 (with Jerusalem lying under siege and Titus himself approaching a tower wall with a battering ram) we find the episode of a man named Castor, who is lying behind the North Wall in ambush. Josephus also calls this man an ἀνὴρ γόης. Michel and Bauernfeind translate this here with "Zauberer," but the ensuing narrative shows that here too γόης is meant to signify a deceiver: Castor stretches out his hands to Titus as if he is begging for mercy (5.318: ὡς ἱκετεύων) and is ready to give himself up. Shortly thereafter a Roman soldier shoots at Castor, whereupon he complains to Titus. Titus then sends Josephus, who is standing right next to him, to give his right hand to Castor. But Josephus refuses, an authorial reference to Josephus's personal valuation of such γόητες. Another Roman soldier, enticed by Castor's promise of money, finally goes over, whereupon Castor throws a rock at him and thus wounds a Roman soldier. Then at last Titus recognizes Castor's deceptive game (5.329: συννοήσας ... τὴν ἀπάτην). The tower is finally brought down, but Castor and his people escape through a secret passage. Like John of Gischala, Castor also escapes by means of deception.

---

49   A compilation of 'γόητες sections' in *Bellum* and *Antiquitates* (without an account of CA 2.146, 161, but with New Testament parallels) is provided by Klaus-Stefan Krieger, *Geschichtsschreibung als Apologetik bei Flavius Josephus* (Tübingen: Francke, 1994), 145–148; see also idem, "Die Zeichenpropheten—eine Hilfe zum Verständnis des Wirkens Jesu?" in *Von Jesus zum Christus: Christologische Studien—Festgabe für Paul Hoffmann zum 65. Geburtstag*, ed. Rudolf Hoppe and Ulrich Busse (Berlin: de Gruyter, 1998), 175–188.

50   BJ 4.85 (Michel and Bauernfeind, *Flavius Josephus*): "ein Verführer von schillerndem Charakter."

MOSES AND THE CHARLATANS

– We have already mentioned the account of the γόητες under the procuratorship of Felix. But already under his predecessor Fadus one finds a certain Theudas who is said to have been a γόης. In *AJ* 20.97–99 we again find the by now well-known pattern: Theudas persuades a large crowd to follow him to the Jordan River. Calling himself a prophet, he promises to divide the Jordan. With these words, says Josephus, he deceived many. In the end, however, he is killed by Fadus's soldiers.[51]

– In very similar terms, at *AJ* 20.188 Josephus once again provides an account of such a *Volksverführer*. This time the procurator Felix is responsible for putting down another ἄνθρωπος γόης who has promised salvation to the people if they will follow him into the wilderness. The swindler and his entourage are killed.[52]

Sorcery is not discussed explicitly in any of these passages. They are concerned with fraudulent actions, in both of the last two cases (and those mentioned above) concerning promised yet unfulfilled delusions. We are faced with two types of γόητες:

– The first group negotiates with the occupying Roman troops under pseudo-religious pretexts (John of Gischala) or the use of other tricks (Castor) and escapes.

– The second group convinces the people to follow them to an out-of-the-way district (wilderness, mountain) where they will see miracles (e.g., the parting of the Jordan). These γόητες (fraudulent wonder-workers) are tracked down and killed by their respective Roman procurators.

Both groups have in common certain demagogic 'abilities;' likewise Castor and (especially) John prey on the people.

5   A Projection of Josephus?

I have shown that neither an accusation of magic in general nor a polemical construction of 'Moses as magician' were a part of 'classical' anti-Jewish argumentation. It is therefore not surprising that Josephus makes no particular

---

51   *AJ* 20.97–98: Φάδου δὲ τῆς Ἰουδαίας ἐπιτροπεύοντος γόης τις ἀνὴρ Θευδᾶς ὀνόματι πείθει τὸν πλεῖστον ὄχλον ἀναλαβόντα τὰς κτήσεις ἕπεσθαι πρὸς τὸν Ἰορδάνην ποταμὸν αὐτῷ· προφήτης γὰρ ἔλεγεν εἶναι ... καὶ ταῦτα λέγων πολλοὺς ἠπάτησεν.

52   *AJ* 20.188: πέμπει δὲ Φῆστος δύναμιν ἱππικήν τε καὶ πεζικὴν ἐπὶ τοὺς ἀπατηθέντας ὑπό τινος ἀνθρώπου γόητος σωτηρίαν αὐτοῖς ἐπαγγελλομένου καὶ παῦλαν κακῶν, εἰ βουληθεῖεν ἕπεσθαι μέχρι τῆς ἐρημίας αὐτῷ, καὶ αὐτόν τε ἐκεῖνον τὸν ἀπατήσαντα καὶ τοὺς ἀκολουθήσαντας διέφθειραν οἱ πεμφθέντες.

effort to respond to such an accusation.[53] But he defends heartily against the idea that Moses was a charlatan and a fraud: this is what he wants to emphasize in his rendition of Exod 7:8–15. This is also what he argues against in his later work *Contra Apionem*, which contains the two passages from which we began: in *CA* 2.145 and 2.161 γόης means something like "charlatan" and not "magician."

If one examines the passage that comes between the report of Apollonius Molon's and Lysimachus's accusation (that Moses was a γόης καὶ ἀπατεών) and Josephus's defiant rebuttal ("such was our lawgiver, no γόης καὶ ἀπατεών"), one finds that here Josephus defends Moses against the very accusations which he himself makes in the *AJ* and *BJ* against the charlatans. Josephus employs the same vocabulary (in part) in speaking about Moses as appears in the passages about the charlatans: πείθειν and πλῆθος occur several times—just as the γόητες persuade the common folk, so too does Moses. But Josephus attaches great importance to differentiating between them. Although Moses did bid the entire people follow him on a difficult road through the wilderness, he made no personal gain from this[54]—Moses is no John of Gischala. And Josephus emphasizes: before Moses attempts to convince others, he must convince himself that he really was acting according to divine will[55]—Moses is no Theudas, but, as Josephus highlights, "the best leader and guide of the people,"[56] and no simple γόης καὶ ἀπατεών (*CA* 2.161).

The *Vorlage* for *AJ* 2.284–287 was the biblical account, and the new emphasis within this episode as presented by Josephus is relatively easy to establish. More complicated is the situation of Apollonius Molon and Lysimachus, whose statements about the Jews are only fragmentary and preserved for the most part only by Josephus: did both of these authors really accuse Moses of being a γόης καὶ ἀπατεών, as Josephus claims in *CA* 2.145 and 2.161?

It seems to me that in both passages Josephus is projecting his own *inner-Jewish criticism* onto extra-Jewish engagement with the Jewish lawgiver Moses. When he defends Moses against the charge of γοητεία he is thinking primarily

---

53 Something which Josephus otherwise does. The anti-Jewish charge of misanthropy, e.g., shows through Josephus's usage of the terms κοινωνία and φιλανθρωπία again and again; see Katell Berthelot, "Koinonia et Philanthropia: dans le *Contre Apion* de Flavius Josèphe," in *Internationales Josephus-Kolloquium, Brüssel 1998*, ed. Jürgen U. Kalms and Folker Siegert (Münster: LIT Verlag, 1998), 94–123.

54 *CA* 2.158: εἰς οὐδεμίαν οἰκείαν ἔλαβεν ταῦτα πλεονεξίαν.

55 *CA* 2.160: καὶ πείσας πρότερον ἑαυτὸν ὅτι κατὰ τὴν ἐκείνου βούλησιν ἅπαντα πράττει καὶ διανοεῖται.

56 *CA* 2.156: ἑαυτόν τε παρέσχεν ἄριστον τοῖς πλήθεσιν ἡγεμόνα καὶ σύμβουλον.

MOSES AND THE CHARLATANS

of the charlatans of his own time![57] Lysimachus at least had indeed produced a polemic on the exodus,[58] but there Moses is not presented as a *Volksverführer*. In the context of his digression on the Jews, Tacitus, who uses the same source as Lysimachus (or Lysimachus himself) in his sixth and longest origins-hypothesis, portrays a proactive Moses. In this he follows his ethnographic predecessors Hecataeus of Abdera and Posidonius/Strabo. This Moses leads an anxious Jewish people to Judea with a strong hand, but he does not *mis*lead: Tacitus reports that Moses, after the expulsion from Egypt, encouraged the Jews not to ask for help either from gods or from men, since they had been abandoned by both; rather, they should trust in themselves and in the messenger sent from heaven, by means of which they would cope with their present misery.[59]

Moses promises in this Tacitean version of exodus—similar to the γόητες in Josephus!—a heavenly sign in this difficult situation. This sign actually materializes, and takes the form of a herd of donkeys, which leads the Israelites to streams of water. Tacitus identifies Moses here as neither a sorcerer nor a fraud, and it is also unlikely for his sources to have done so. However, the exodus story as we can glean it from Tacitus, and as Josephus will have known it from Tacitus's sources, must have contained what were to Josephus's sensibilities the features of a charlatan. Behind the formula γόης καὶ ἀπατεών there is much more likely to stand an interpretation of Josephus's rather than a precise reproduction of a polemical statement.[60] It seems to me, therefore, that in CA 2.145 and 2.161 Josephus is ultimately unlikely to have been responding to a real accusation; rather, it appears more probable that he is using such an accusation as a basis upon which to present the integrity of Moses all the more clearly: 'Moses is the true prophet and has nothing in common with these modern pseudo-prophets.'

---

57 This has also been emphasized regarding the Pharaoh scene (AJ 2.284–287) by Betz, "Problem," 30: "Die Auslegung von Exod 7:1–13 und die darin zutage tretende Bedeutung des Begriffs σημεῖον ist m. E. stark *von eigenen Erfahrungen des Josephus* mitbestimmt; sie reflektieren aktuelle Geschichte. Josephus kannte aus seiner Zeit Männer, die sich durch das Versprechen wunderbarer Zeichen als Werkzeuge der von Gott geschenkten Befreiung legitimieren wollten."

58 We do not learn from Josephus what Apollonius Molon exactly had reported about the Jewish exodus. Of Lysimachus Josephus says that, in his version of Exodus, Moses had called his followers to be well-disposed toward no one and only to advise bad things (CA 1.309).

59 Tacitus, *Hist.* 5.3.1 (Stern § 281).

60 Also speaking against the idea of an exact reproduction is the improbability of the implication that Apollonius Molon, Lysimachus, and others (!) had used the exact same phrasing.

6 Γόης—An Argument from a Literary Dispute?

There is still one more dimension to consider here: γόης can also signify, without any religious implications, a "rhetorical beguiler." This has already become clear in our examination above (esp. in the case of John of Gischala and Castor). In his *Vita*, Josephus himself accuses his historiographical rival Justus of Tiberias of γοητεία καὶ ἀπάτη in this sense, where the wording and reasoning are remarkably similar to that of the descriptions discussed above.[61] The passage in the *Vita* is about a literary dispute, which is why it resembles to a certain extent our passages in *Contra Apionem*: When "Apollonius Molon, Lysimachus, and others" call Moses a γόης καὶ ἀπατεών (according to Josephus's report), they brand him as a 'Sophist' in the platonic sense.[62]

But Josephus portrays Moses as a true philosopher, with regard to whom any 'sophistic' associations are foreign: he works not for any personal gain (πλεονεξία), but for the truth. The 'antisemitic' authors are therefore scolded explicitly by Josephus as "sophists and deceivers of youth" (σοφισταί, μειρακίων ἀπατεῶνες).[63] We encounter here a 'literary feud' of sorts,[64] about which we cannot know to what extent it was staged by Josephus.

7 Conclusion

We set out from CA 2.145, the beginning of the final segment of *Contra Apionem* and the accusation against Moses of being a γόης καὶ ἀπατεών. It has been shown that in this passage γόης means "charlatan," not "sorcerer."[65] This con-

---

61   *Vita* 40: Ταῦτα λέγων προετρέψατο τὸ πλῆθος· ἦν γὰρ ἱκανὸς δημαγωγεῖν καὶ τῶν ἀντιλεγόντων τὰ βελτίω περιεῖναι γοητείᾳ καὶ ἀπάτῃ τῇ διὰ λόγων. In *BJ* 2.565 Josephus reports that Eleazar, the son of Simon, brought the people to accept him as the leader of their city through rhetorical beguilement (γοητεύων). See also 2 Macc 12:24 regarding Timothy, who attempts to free himself from the captivity of Dositheus and Sosipater μετὰ πολλῆς γοητείας. Otherwise, γόης and γοητεία do not appear in the LXX.

62   See Plato, *Symp.* 203d: δεινὸς γόης καὶ φαρμακεὺς καὶ σοφιστής. See Burkert, "ΓΟΗΣ," 55: "Merkwürdig oft wird γόης mit σοφιστής verbunden …. Ist nicht wirklich der Sophist weithin Nachfolger des wandernden Wundermanns? Heimatlos, auf eigenes Können vertrauend, tritt er im Purpurgewand vor das Volk hin und sucht es durch seinen Vortrag in seinen Bann zu ziehen."

63   CA 2.236: Εἶτα Λυσίμαχοι καὶ Μόλωνες καὶ τοιοῦτοί τινες ἄλλοι συγγραφεῖς, ἀδόκιμοι σοφισταί, μειρακίων ἀπατεῶνες, ὡς πάνυ ἡμᾶς φαυλοτάτους ἀνθρώπων λοιδοροῦσιν.

64   Hans Dieter Betz, *Der Apostel Paulus und die sokratische Tradition: Eine exegetische Untersuchung zu seiner 'Apologie' 2 Korinter 10–13* (Tübingen: Mohr Siebeck, 1972), 30.

65   In connection, γόης and ἀπατεών form then a hendiadys.

MOSES AND THE CHARLATANS

clusion comes, on the one hand, from an examination of the other passages in which the terms γόης or γοητεία appear: namely, the accounts of the Jewish pseudo-prophets and Josephus's account of the staff-miracle before Pharaoh. On the other hand, an excursus on the alleged literary accusation of 'Moses as magician' has shown that such an accusation was only ever marginal at best and that Josephus does not aim any apologetic argument at such a charge. It has also been suggested that the report of the accusation that Moses is a γόης καὶ ἀπατεών is a projection or interpretation on the part of Josephus. In *CA* 2.145 and 2.161 Josephus is thinking mostly of the Jewish pseudo-prophets (projection). Anti-Jewish versions of exodus, such as that of Lysimachus, must have given Josephus the impression that in them Moses was denigrated as a γόης καὶ ἀπατεών (interpretation). Josephus's Moses has nothing in common with the religious charlatans of his own time. Finally, the rhetorical aspect of the γοητεία-accusation has been addressed. This accusation becomes, in the argument of *CA* 2.145 and 2.161, an attack in the context of a literary dispute.

Bibliography

Berthelot, Katell, "Koinonia et Philanthropia: dans le *Contre Apion* de Flavius Josèphe." Pages 94–123 in *Internationales Josephus-Kolloquium, Brüssel 1998*. Edited by Jürgen U. Kalms and Folker Siegert. Münster: LIT Verlag, 1998.

Betz, Hans Dieter, *Der Apostel Paulus und die sokratische Tradition: Eine exegetische Untersuchung zu seiner 'Apologie' 2 Korinter 10–13*. Tübingen: Mohr Siebeck, 1972.

Betz, Otto, "Das Problem des Wunders bei Flavius Josephus im Vergleich zum Wunderproblem bei den Rabbinen und im Johannesevangelium." Pages 23–44 in *Josephus-Studien: Untersuchungen zu Josephus, dem antiken Judentum und dem Neuen Testament*. Edited by Otto Betz, Klaus Haacker, and Martin Hengel. Göttingen: Vandenhoeck & Ruprecht, 1974.

Blum, Léon, ed., *Flavius Josèphe: Contre Apion*. Paris: Les Belles-Lettres, 1972.

Burkert, Walter, "ΓΟΗΣ: Zum griechischen Schamanismus." *Rheinisches Museum für Philologie* [Neue Folge] 105 (1962): 36–55.

Clementz, Heinrich, ed., *Flavius Josephus: Kleinere Schriften*. Wiesbaden: Fourier, 1993.

Delling, Gerhard, "γόης." *TWNT* 1.737–739.

Delling, Gerhard, "μάγος." *TWNT* 4.360–363.

Fauth, Wolfgang, "'Zeichen und Wunder' im Alten Testament und bei Josephus." Pages 9–31 in *Memoria Rerum Veterum: Neue Beiträge zur antiken Historiographie und Alten Geschichte—Festschrift für C.J. Classen zum 60. Geburtstag*. Edited by Wolfram Ax. Stuttgart: Franz Steiner Verlag, 1990.

54   CHAPTER 2

Feldman, Louis H., trans. and ed., *Josephus: Jewish Antiquities. Book 20, General Index.* Cambridge: Harvard University Press, 1965.

Feldman, Louis H., "Josephus' Portrait of Moses." *JQR* 82 (1991): 285–328.

Gager, John G., *Moses in Greco-Roman Paganism.* New York: Abingdon, 1972.

Gerber, Christine, *Ein Bild des Judentums für Nichtjuden von Flavius Josephus: Untersuchungen zu seiner Schrift Contra Apionem.* Leiden: Brill, 1997.

Graf, Fritz, *Gottesnähe und Schadenzauber: Die Magie in der griechisch-römischen Antike.* Munich: C.H. Beck, 1996.

Krieger, Klaus-Stefan, *Geschichtsschreibung als Apologetik bei Flavius Josephus.* Tübingen: Francke, 1994.

Krieger, Klaus-Stefan, "Die Zeichenpropheten—eine Hilfe zum Verständnis des Wirkens Jesu?" Pages 175–188 in *Von Jesus zum Christus: Christologische Studien—Festgabe für Paul Hoffmann zum 65. Geburtstag.* Edited by Rudolf Hoppe and Ulrich Busse. Berlin: de Gruyter, 1998.

Michel, Otto and Otto Bauernfeind, eds., *Flavius Josephus: De bello Judaico, Der jüdische Krieg—griechisch und deutsch, eingeleitet und mit Anmerkungen versehen. 3 vol.* Darmstadt: Wissenschaftliche Buchgesellschaft, 1959–1969.

Pelletier, André, *Flavius Josèphe: Guerre des Juifs.* Paris: Les Belles-Lettres, 1975–1982.

Rengstorf, Karl H., ed., *A Complete Concordance to Flavius Josephus.* Leiden: Brill, 1973–1983.

Schmidt, Werner H., *Exodus.* Neukirchen: Neukirchener Verlag, 1974.

Simon, Marcel, *Verus Israel: Etude sur les relations entre chrétiens et juifs dans l'empire romain (132–245).* Paris: E. de Boccard, 1948.

Stern, Menaham, *Greek and Latin Authors on Jews and Judaism.* 3 vols. Jerusalem: The Israel Academy of Sciences and Humanities, 1974–1984.

Thackeray, Henry St. J., trans. and ed., *Josephus: The Life—Against Apion.* Cambridge: Harvard University Press, 1926.

Troiani, Lucio, *Commento storico al "Contro Apione" di Giuseppe.* Pisa: Giardini, 1977.

CHAPTER 3

Moses: Motherless with Two Mothers

In Judaism there is no other figure like Moses. The Torah, which is to some extent also simply a biography of Moses, closes by stating that: "Never since has there arisen a prophet in Israel like Moses, whom the Lord knew face to face" (Deut 34:10). The very same sentence is repeated in synagogues in the daily prayer *Yigdal*. In Judaism of antiquity, but also of later periods, Moses goes beyond the imaginable. It is hardly a coincidence that, a few exceptions aside, until the end of late antiquity naming a child "Moses" remained a taboo in Jewish communities both in Palestine and in the diaspora. In Judaism Moses is big—even in a literal sense: When the Bible, in Exod 2:10–11, states that Moses had "grown up," the rabbis explained this apparently unnecessary piece of information as follows: "And Moses had grown up—does not every child grow up? In order to tell you that Moses did not grow up just like everybody else."[1] According to the rabbis, but also, as we will see later, to Jewish-Hellenistic authors, Moses grew to an unimaginable size. The biblical story of Moses is told along the lines of that of an ancient mythological hero: as a young child he is exposed, later he commits murder (Exod 2:11–12), and becomes the leader of his people. If there is no explicit apotheosis at the end of his life, there is certainly a tendency to divinization (Exod 4:16; 7:1).[2]

Yet what is particularly remarkable in the Moses myth, as it is told in the Bible, is Moses's heavy dependence on the help of women. In Moses's birth story of Exod 2 all protagonists, besides Moses himself, are female:

> The woman conceived and bore a son; and when she saw that he was a fine baby, she hid him three months. When she could hide him no longer she got a papyrus basket for him, and plastered it with bitumen and pitch; she put the child in it and placed it among the reeds on the bank of the river. His sister stood at a distance, to see what would happen to him. The daughter of Pharaoh came down to bathe at the river, while her attendants walked beside the river. She saw the basket among the reeds and sent her maid to bring it. When she opened it, she saw the child. He was

---

1 *Ex. Rab.* 1.26.
2 René Bloch, "D'une grandeur sans pareil et d'une humanité profonde: Moïse dans le judaïsme ancien," in *Figures de Moïse* (Le Monde la Bible [E-book: https://www.mondedelabible.com/figures-de-moise-en-numerique/], November 10, 2015), 29–47.

© RENÉ BLOCH, 2022 | DOI:10.1163/9789004521896_005

crying, and she took pity on him. "This must be one of the Hebrews' children," she said. Then his sister said to Pharaoh's daughter, "Shall I go and get you a nurse from the Hebrew women to nurse the child for you?" Pharaoh's daughter said to her, "Yes." So the girl went and called the child's mother. Pharaoh's daughter said to her, "Take this child away and nurse it for me, and I will give you your wages." So the woman took the child and nursed it. When the child grew up, she brought him to Pharaoh's daughter, and she took him as her son. She named him Moses, "because," she said, "I drew him out of the water."

Exod 2:2–10 EXOD 4:24--26 NRSV

In Hebrew where feminine verb forms differ from masculine ones in most cases, it becomes even more obvious than in the English translation how much the biblical story of Moses's birth is directed by women. In the Hebrew original there are no less than thirty-four female verb forms in these eight biblical verses. Indeed, the action around Moses's birth is steered by women only. Who is on stage? There is "the woman" in verse 2: this is Yochebed, Moses's mother, followed by "his sister" Miriam in verse 4, and "the daughter of Pharaoh" and her "attendants" in verse 5. Then, in verse 7, there is mention of a possible "nurse from the Hebrew women" (מִן הָעִבְרִיֹּת אִשָּׁה מֵינִקֶת). That nurse will later turn out to be Moses's mother Yochebed. In this short passage there is thus mention of four female individuals (Moses's mother, his sister, Pharaoh's daughter, the nurse) and of two female groups: the princess's attendants and the Hebrew women. This abundantly female passage in Exod 2:2–10 is remarkable and taken by itself does not easily fit into the otherwise rather patriarchal world of the Hebrew Bible. Moses's life lies in the hands of women. To the female figures already mentioned we should add the Hebrew midwives Shiphrah and Puah (Exod 1:15–21), who ignore Pharaoh's decree to kill all Hebrew boys.

A little later in the book of Exodus, Exod 4:24–26, this aspect of the biblical Moses biography reaches its peak. In a brief, fascinating, and rather enigmatic passage, Moses is confronted by God at some lodging place; there God tries to kill Moses. And there, again, it is a woman, this time Moses's wife Zipporah, who saves his life:

> On the way, at a place where they spent the night, the LORD met him and tried to kill him. But Zipporah took a flint and cut off her son's foreskin, and touched Moses's feet with it, and said, "Truly you are a bridegroom of blood to me!" So he let him alone. It was then she said, "A bridegroom of blood by circumcision."
>
> Exod 4:24--26 NRSV

MOSES: MOTHERLESS WITH TWO MOTHERS 57

The meaning of this passage is intensely debated among biblical scholars.[3] It seems that the episode wishes to underline the importance of the circumcision of newborn sons—by circumcising their son, Zipporah saves Moses from God's attack—, but it also simply continues the story of Moses relying on women.

Feminine support for male heroic figures is not an unusual feature of ancient mythologies. Here, too, the biblical Moses myth follows the ancient paradigm of mythological heroes. One may think of Aeneas who in Virgil's *Aeneid* counts on the continuing aid and protection by his mother Venus.[4] In the parallel myth of Romulus and Remus it is a she-wolf who guarantees the survival of the twin boys. And in Homer's *Odyssey* Athena consistently stands by Odysseus's side. Had Moses in the divine attack of Exod 4 been Odysseus, he would have been saved by Athena. Heroic figures who are guarded by women—humans, goddesses, female animals—are thus nothing extraordinary per se. What is rather unusual in the Moses myth is the double mothering that is bestowed on Moses and which, as we will see, led to different readings in rabbinic and Jewish-Hellenistic literature. One of the consequences of the doubling of Moses's mother, I would like to argue, is that it obscures Moses's origins. Because it remains unclear who his actual mother is, Moses becomes motherless. At the same time, it is this very ambivalence of Moses's ancestry that makes him an attractive motive for hybrid interpretations of the biblical story. I will first discuss some rabbinic comments on Moses's mother(s) and then focus on Jewish-Hellenistic readings.

Let us first take a look at the Moses-Yochebed story in rabbinic sources. A key passage is Sotah 12a–13a in the Babylonian Talmud, but one could also refer to very similar passages in the midrash *Exodus Rabbah* and in the *Chronicle of Moses* (*Divre ha-yamim shel Moshe*).[5] The rabbis take up Exod 2:1: "Now a man from the house of Levi went and married a Levite woman." This is the verse preceding the passage that we cited before. As in the following verses here, too, no names are mentioned. Only eventually does the Torah disclose the names of Moses's family members: Amram is his father and Yochebed his mother (Exod 6:20), Miriam his sister.[6] But this is not what the rabbis are interested in here. Instead they are trying to clarify the pre-history of Moses's birth:

---

3   Among recent commentaries cf. Rainer Albertz, *Exodus*. Vol. 1. *Ex 1–18* (Zürich: Theologischer Verlag, 2012), 94–98.

4   Cf. Elina Pyy, "Maternal Absence and Heroic Identity in Virgil's *Aeneid*", in *Missing Mothers: Maternal Absence in Antiquity*, ed. Sabine Hübner and David M. Ratzan (Leuven: Peeters 2021), 187–208.

5   Cf. Günter Stemberger, *Mose in der rabbinischen Tradition* (Freiburg im Breisgau: Herder, 2016), 17, 48.

6   The whole family is mentioned in Num 26:59.

And there went a man of the house of Levi (Exod 2:1). Where did he go? Rabbi Judah ben Zebina said that he went in the counsel of his daughter. It is taught: Amram was the greatest man of his generation; when he saw that the wicked Pharaoh had decreed *Every boy that is born to the Hebrews you shall throw into the Nile* (Exod 1:22), he said, "In vain do we labour." He arose and divorced his wife. All (the Israelites) thereupon arose and divorced their wives. His daughter said to him, "Father, your decree is more severe than Pharaoh's; because Pharaoh decreed only against the males whereas you have decreed against the males and females. Pharaoh only decreed concerning this world whereas you have decreed concerning this world and the World to Come (unborn children cannot be resurrected). In the case of the wicked Pharaoh there is a doubt whether his decree will be fulfilled or not, whereas in your case, since you are righteous, it is certain that your decree will be fulfilled, as it is said, *You will decide on a matter, and it will be established for you!* (Job 22:28)." He arose and took his wife back; and they all arose and took their wives back. *And took to wife* (Exod 2:1): it should have read "and took back!" Rabbi Judah ben Zebina said: He acted towards her as though it had been the first marriage; he seated her in a palanquin, Aaron and Miriam danced before her, and the Ministering Angels proclaimed, *A joyful mother of children* (Ps 113:9: אם־הבנים שמחה).

> Babylonian Talmud, Sotah 12a, trans. SONCINO, slightly adjusted

This is an intriguing passage. It extends what we have observed already in the biblical text: women play an important role in Moses's birth story. It is again Miriam who intervenes on Moses's behalf. While in the Bible she is advising the Egyptian princess as well as her mother, here she now also counsels her father Amram. And he, too, listens to her. In the light of Pharaoh's decree to kill all newborn Hebrew children, Amram had divorced his wife Yochebed in order to prevent the children "who are asking to be born" (to use a phrase from the late songwriter Leonard Cohen).[7] Amram, of course, wanted to prevent the murder of newborn Hebrew boys, but thereby turns into Pharaoh's accomplice and Miriam's adversary.[8] In this rabbinic version, the biblical story of the Pharaoh

---

7   In another rabbinic version of the story, Amram divorced his wife when she was already three months pregnant with Moses: *Ex. Rab.* 1.13.

8   In Pseudo-Philo (a first- or second-century CE author who wrote in Hebrew, but whose work has been transmitted only in Latin) 9.2–9 it is "the elders of the people" who resolve "that a man should not approach his wife lest the fruit of their wombs be defiled and our offspring serve idols" (trans. Howard Jacobson) and Amram who successfully fights this decree.

MOSES: MOTHERLESS WITH TWO MOTHERS

trying to kill the Hebrew newborns and Miriam contributing to Moses's survival is thus expanded to include a suggestive prehistory.

Miriam's argument that Amram's order that the Hebrew men divorce their wives was worse than Pharaoh's is also interesting from a gender perspective. What Miriam is saying, or at least implying, is that Pharaoh was wrong in thinking that it is enough to kill only the boys in order to prevent the Hebrews from becoming a stronger people. Amram's decree went further than Pharaoh's, Miriam argues, because it would also prevent the birth of girls and would thus truly lead to the end of the Hebrew people. Ultimately, Amram is convinced by his perceptive daughter and takes Yochebed back. *This*—in the brilliant reading of the rabbis—is the true meaning of the "went and took" a woman in Exod 2:1: Amram "went in the counsel of his daughter" and took his wife back again, that is, remarried her.

If one includes other midrashic material on the biblical report on Moses's birth, such as *Exodus Rabbah*, in which it is said that Amram divorced his wife when she was already three months pregnant with Moses, the ambiguity of Moses's mother becomes even more pronounced. In this version of the narrative, Moses for some time loses his mother before he is born. Taken together, Bible and midrash tell a story which maneuvers between a Moses who has no mother and a Moses who has two mothers. First Yochebed is not supposed to give birth to Moses (because of her husband's decree and his divorcing her); then she gives birth anyway only to expose the child, who in turn is taken up by Pharaoh's daughter, but only briefly: the Egyptian princess returns the baby to Yochebed to nurse the child. But again only for a limited time: when the child is grown up, the Egyptian princess takes him back. Young Moses was thus repeatedly passed back and forth between his two mothers (Sigmund Freud discusses the twofold origins of Moses at the beginning of his study *Der Mann Moses und die monotheistische Religion*[9]).

Exod 2:2 seems to be explicit about the identity of Moses's mother: "The woman" (this is the Levite woman mentioned in Exod 2:1, thus Yochebed) "conceived and bore a son." But only a few verses later, in Exod 2:10, the text states: "she took him as her son." Pharaoh's daughter is not only an adoptive mother: it is she who gives the child his name, and in that respect—after all, in the Hebrew Bible children are regularly named by their mothers[10]—she *is* his real mother. And so, at birth Moses is betwixt and between: he has, at the same time, two

---

9   Sigmund Freud, *Der Mann Moses und die monotheistische Religion. Schriften über die Religion* (Frankfurt am Main: Fischer 1975 [1941]), 25–32.

10   Cf. Edward J. Bridge, "A Mother's Influence: Mothers naming Children in the Hebrew Bible," *VT* 64 (2014): 389–400.

mothers and no mother. In the version of Pseudo-Philo, which is parallel to later midrashim, the correspondence between doubling mothers and being therefore motherless is even more obvious:

> When she [Pharaoh's daughter] saw the boy and noticed that he was covenantal (that is, he was in the covenant of the flesh), she said, "He is one of the Hebrew children." She took him and nursed him. And he became her own son (*et factus est ei filius*), and she called him by the name Moses. But his mother called him Melchiel (*mater autem eius vocavit eum Melchiel*). The child grew up and became glorious above all other men, and through him God freed the sons of Israel as he had said.
>
> PSEUDO-PHILO, *Liber Antiquitatum Biblicarum* 9.15–16, trans. H. JACOBSON

Here Yochebed also names the child, who then has two names: Moses and Melchiel. Pseudo-Philo thus reflects a problem that is evident already in the biblical version: Moses is an Egyptian name. The Egyptian root that lies behind the name of Moses (*ms/msj*), known from several Pharaonic names, means to "give birth." Moses is "the one who was born," or simply "the son." In the biblical story the naming by the Egyptian princess explains and justifies the Egyptian name of the boy.[11] But also in the biblical version Moses has, in a way, two names. While Moses may be an Egyptian name, the etymology offered in Exod 2 is a Hebrew one: the name Moshe stems from Hebrew *mashah*, to pull out (of the water). This double identity of the young Moses, represented by his two mothers, became an important topic in Jewish-Hellenistic literature. Jewish-Hellenistic authors reinvented Moses in the image of a hero who certainly has a good deal in common with the biblical character, but transcends it and exceeds the demands of a typical heroic curriculum vitae. In Jewish-Hellenistic literature Moses is a far more convincing hero and he is heavily embedded both in Jewish and Greek (Egyptian) culture. For instance, in the Exodus drama *Exagoge* by the tragic poet Ezekiel (fr. 1–2), to whom we will return shortly, Moses enters the stage right away with a prologue in Greek and shows no rhetorical weakness. Authors such as Artapanus (second century BCE) and Josephus

---

11 Ina Willi-Plein, "Ort und literarische Funktion der Geburtsgeschichte des Mose," *VT* 41 (1991): 110–118. Cf. also Jaques T.A.G.M van Ruiten, "The Birth of Moses in Egypt According to the Book of Jubilees (Jub 47.1–9)," in *The Wisdom of Egypt: Jewish, Early Christian, and Gnostic Essays in Honour of Gerard P. Luttikhuizen*, ed. Anthony Hilhorst and George H. van Kooten (Leiden: Brill, 2005), 43–65 and Athalya Brenner, "Female Social Behaviour: Two Descriptive Patterns Within the "Birth of the Hero" Paradigm," *VT* 36 (1986): 257–273.

MOSES: MOTHERLESS WITH TWO MOTHERS

portray Moses as a successful military leader. Several Jewish authors from the second century BCE onwards make Moses the *prōtos heuretēs*, the author of a whole series of achievements (such as the invention of scripture, weapons, and philosophy), and Plato is said to have plagiarized Moses.[12]

A particularly interesting case is the Jewish theologian and philosopher Philo of Alexandria, writing in the first half of the first century CE. Philo presents Moses as the ideal legislator and philosopher, addressing not only the Jews, but in fact all nations. Philo has much more to say about Moses's youth than the Bible. But before discussing Moses's mothers in Philo, let me expand briefly on Philo's use of the term "motherless" in general. Remarkably, in Philo's *oeuvre* the Greek word for "motherless," ἀμήτωρ, appears no less than eleven times. There is no other ancient author from the classical period who uses the word "motherless" more frequently than Philo.[13] This, however, is not because Philo had a particular interest in family, mothers, or orphans; rather, most of Philo's references to "being motherless" are linked to his strong interest in the symbolic meaning of numbers. A number of particular importance to Philo is the number seven, which is immanent and omnipresent in the world: the creation of the world came to an end on the seventh day and the holy Sabbath is a continuing reminder of this. The Menora, "the sacred candlestick," has seven branches, "symbols of the planets."[14] According to Philo, the human body is organized in clusters of seven pieces.[15] Most important, however, is the deeper meaning of the seventh day of the week, the Sabbath, which, in Philo's reading of biblical legislation, was introduced by Moses:

> The prophet magnified the holy seventh day, seeing with his keener vision its marvelous beauty stamped upon heaven and the whole world and enshrined in nature itself. For he found that she [the number seven] was in the first place motherless (ἀμήτορα), exempt from female parentage, begotten by the Father alone, without begetting, brought to the birth, yet not carried in the womb. Secondly, he saw not only these, that she was all lovely and motherless (ἀμήτωρ), but that she was also ever virgin, neither born of a mother nor a mother herself (οὔτ' ἐκ μητρὸς οὔτε μήτηρ), neither bred from corruption nor doomed to suffer corruption.[16]

---

12   Eusebius, *Praep. Ev.* 9.27.4 (Artapanus); Josephus, *CA.* 2.257.

13   More frequently is the use in John Chrysostom (twenty-nine times, often referring to Jesus).

14   Philo, *Her.* 216; *Mos.* 2.103.

15   Philo, *Opif.* 118.

16   Philo, *Mos.* 2.209–210 (all translations of Philo are taken from the Loeb Classical Library).

In Philo's reading, which is heavily influenced by Pythagorean thinking (as he states himself[17]), seven is a prime number that stands for consistency, which cannot produce nor be produced, and in that sense it is symbol of the Lord of the universe.[18] Philo does not hesitate, again openly referring to earlier sources, to relate this insight to Greek myth. Other philosophers, Philo states, have compared the number seven to the "motherless Nike" (ἀμήτορι Νίχῃ), who had sprung from the head of Zeus. Nike is here an epithet of the goddess Athena, who "was born without a mother," "as not generated by any other," and "will not generate any other."[19] In Greek myth Athena is motherless and never becomes a mother. Philo calls her also "always-maidenly" (ἀειπάρθε-νος).[20]

But in Philo there is also a *Jewish* equivalent to Athena: Sarah, Abraham's wife. Taking up Genesis 20:12, where Abraham explains to Abimelech (to whom he had presented his wife Sarah as his sister) that "she is indeed my sister, the daughter of my father but not the daughter of my mother," Philo concludes that Sarah grew up motherless:

> (Sarah) is declared, too, to be without a mother (ἀμήτωρ), and to have inherited her kinship only on the father's side and not on the mother's (οὐ πρὸς μητρός), and thus to have no part in female parentage. For we find it said, "Indeed she is my sister, the daughter of my father but not of my mother" (ἀλλ' οὐκ ἐκ μητρός: Gen 20:12). She is not born of that material substance perceptible to our senses, ever in a state of formation and dissolution, the material which is called mother or foster-mother or nurse of created things (μητέρα καὶ τροφὸν καὶ τιθήνην τῶν ποιητῶν) by those in whom first the young plant of wisdom grew; she is born of the Father and Cause of all things.[21]

---

17   Philo, *Opif.* 100; *Leg.* 1.15.

18   Philo, *Opif.* 100.

19   Philo, *Leg.* 1.15.

20   Philo, *Mos.* 2.210. Cf. Karl Staehle, *Die Zahlenmystik bei Philon von Alexandrien* (Leipzig: Teubner, 1931), 34–50; David T. Runia, *Philo of Alexandria. On the Creation of the Cosmos according to Moses. Introduction, Translation and Commentary* (Leiden: Brill, 2001), 273–274.

21   Philo, *Ebr.* 61. Cf. also *Her.* 62 where Philo more briefly makes the very same point: "for male descent is the sole claim of her, who is the motherless ruling principle (ἡ ἀμήτωρ ἀρχή) of things, begotten of her father alone, even God the Father of all. For 'indeed,' it runs, 'she is my sister from the father, not from the mother.' 'For truly,' says the scripture, 'she is my sister by my father's side, but not by my mother's.'"

MOSES: MOTHERLESS WITH TWO MOTHERS   63

Although Philo does not explicitly compare Sarah with the Greek goddess Athena, the reasoning is strikingly similar: like Athena, Sarah is born out of the highest God alone and has no mother. Philo uses Gen 20:12 to make this point (although it actually only says that Abraham and Sarah had the same father, but not the same mother, adding no further comment). Since to Philo the female stands for the body with its passions, he thus points to Sarah's virtuous life, a life free of passions, as evidence of her divine parentage.[22] In Philo's reading Sarah is thus characterized as the immediate daughter of God, without any traceable genealogy.

What about Philo's Moses? Philo's description of Moses's birth shares with the biblical story its focus on the figure of Moses himself. The names of the other protagonists—his father, mother, and sister—are similarly elided. But Philo has quite a bit more to say about Moses than the book of Exodus. Moses "had for his father and mother," Philo writes, "the best of their contemporaries, members of the same tribe, though with them mutual affection was a stronger tie than family connections."[23] Typically, Philo is less interested in the fact, reported in the Bible, that both of his parents belonged to the tribe of Levi. In his telling, Amram and Yochebed married not because of genealogical ties, but rather because they shared the same values. As in the biblical version, so in Philo Moses first was hidden by his mother for three months: "he was kept at home and fed from his mother's breast for three successive months."[24] But then, Philo adds dramatic color to Moses's exposure, casting it as a family tragedy. Thus, both parents commit Moses to the Nile and then immediately accuse themselves of being child murderers (αὐτοὺς ... τεκνοκτόνους ἀποκαλοῦν-τες) and reproach themselves for not having exposed the child immediately after birth, when he would have suffered less. When Miriam then comes to help, she does so because she is "moved by family affection" (ὑπὸ φιλοικείου πάθους).[25]

The Egyptian princess in Philo's narrative is also given a deeper psychological motivation: she had been hoping in vain for a child, especially a son, for a very long time. On the day of Moses's exposure she was particularly sad:

> Depressed and loud in lamentation she always was, but on this particular day she broke down under the weight of cares; and, though her custom

---

22   This is a point Philo also makes in *Cher.* 50.
23   Philo, *Mos.* 1.7.
24   Philo, *Mos.* 1.9.
25   Philo, *Mos.* 1.10–12.

was to remain at home and never even cross the threshold, she set off with her maids to the river, where the child was exposed. Then, as she was preparing to make her ablutions in the purifying water, she saw him lying where the marshland growth was thickest, and bade him be brought to her. Thereupon, surveying him from head to foot, she approved of his beauty and fine condition, and seeing him weeping took pity on him, for her heart was now moved to feel for him as a mother for her own child (ἤδη τῆς ψυχῆς τετραμμένης αὐτῇ πρὸς μητρῷον πάθος ὡς ἐπὶ γνησίῳ παιδί).[26]

As in the biblical version, also here it is Pharaoh's daughter who names the child Moses. But the etymology presented for this name is here an Egyptian one: Then she "gave him a name derived from this, and called him Moses, for *Möu* is the Egyptian word for water."[27] This Egyptian instead of a Hebrew etymology may be at first sight surprising, but it fits into Philo's complex relationship to Egypt quite nicely. While the picture of Egypt in Philo is often rather negative (mainly, though, in the context of allegorical interpretations), one should not ignore those passages in which a different, perhaps a more realistic view of Egypt shines through. Indeed, in Philo's *Life of Moses* there are also attempts to stress some sort of an Egyptian-Jewish cultural "symbiosis." Thus Philo imagines for Moses an international, elite formation in Egypt: wise teachers from different parts of the world come to the royal palace to assure a first-class education, starting with the *enkyklios paideia* and leading to the most important field of study, philosophy. Among Moses's many teachers Egyptian scholars are mentioned with praise: "Teachers at once arrived from different parts, some unbidden from the neighboring countries and the provinces of Egypt." And a little later: "Arithmetic, geometry, the lore of the meter, rhythm and harmony, and the whole subject of music as shown by the use of instruments or in textbooks and treatises of a more special character, were imparted to him by learned Egyptians (Αἰγυπτίων οἱ λόγιοι)."[28] It should, then, come as no surprise that in Philo's telling, Moses's Egyptian mother plays a more prominent role than in the biblical version of the story. The Egyptian princess:

conceived for him an even greater fondness than before, and took him for her son (υἱὸν ποιεῖται), having at an earlier time artificially enlarged the fig-

---

26   Philo, *Mos.* 1.14–15.

27   Philo, *Mos.* 1.17.

28   Philo, *Mos.* 1.21–23. Cf. chapter 1 in this volume.

ure of her womb to make him pass as her real and not a suppositious child (ἵνα γνήσιος ἀλλὰ μὴ ὑποβολιμαῖος νομισθῇ).[29]

Philo, who explicitly calls Alexandria his hometown,[30] thus strengthens the role of Moses's Egyptian mother and does not hesitate to send him to both a Jewish and an Egyptian school. Yes, Moses was, as Philo states, "zealous for the discipline and culture of his kinsmen and ancestors,"[31] but not only:

> and so, estimating the claims of his real and his adopted parents (τῶν γεν-νησάντων καὶ τῶν εἰσποιησαμένων) like an impartial judge, he requited the former with good feeling and profound affection, the latter with gratitude for their kind treatment of him.[32]

Philo of Alexandria thus imagines a double education of Moses, with both mothers competing in their care for their young son and each introducing him to her respective culture and history.

The biblical plot in Exod 2 proved to be an attractive subject matter for Jewish-Hellenistic authors writing in Egypt. Another example is Ezekiel the Tragedian, who probably wrote in the second century BCE. Ezekiel's Moses also receives two kinds of education: first a Jewish education through his mother, then a pagan one at the Egyptian court. In the prologue to his *Exagoge* Ezekiel has Moses tell the audience that, before returning to the Egyptian court, his mother had revealed everything to him about his origins:

> When my infancy had passed,
> my mother brought me to the princess' palace,
> after telling me all about
> my lineage and God's gifts.
> Accordingly, for the period of my youth, the princess
> gave me a royal upbringing and education,
> as if I were her own son.
>
> ἐπεὶ δὲ καιρὸς νηπίων παρῆλθέ μοι,
> ἦγέν με μήτηρ βασιλίδος πρὸς δώματα,
> ἅπαντα μυθεύσασα καὶ λέξασά μοι

---

29   Philo, *Mos.* 1.19.
30   Philo, *Leg.* 150: "our Alexandria."
31   Philo, *Mos.* 1.32.
32   Philo, *Mos.* 1.33.

γένος πατρῷον καὶ θεοῦ δωρήματα.
ἕως μὲν οὖν τὸν παιδὸς εἴχομεν χρόνον,
τροφαῖσι βασιλικαῖσι καὶ παιδεύμασιν
ἅπανθ' ὑπισχνεῖθ', ὡς ἀπὸ σπλάγχνων ἑῶν·[33]

Both mothers teach what they consider their own son and introduce him to their culture and history. Moses's education, as described in Ezekiel's *Exagoge*, reflects the cultural "hybridity" of the author and Jewish-Hellenistic Alexandria in general. That in Ezekiel it is the Egyptian princess herself, and not one of her slaves as in Exod 2, who rescues Moses strengthens the Egyptian connection from the beginning.[34]

That foundlings and future heroes have two mothers (or two sets of parents) is nothing unusual in ancient mythologies. Oedipus, for example, was born to Jocasta and Laios, exposed, and later raised by another royal couple, Polybus and Merope. But the extensive meandering in the myth of Moses is rather unusual, and it turned out to be appealing to Jewish-Hellenistic authors. To the rabbis, this is not what is important. If anything, they make the Egyptian princess Jewish and give her a Hebrew name: Bitjah. The rabbis took this name from the first book of Chronicles, where there is mention of a "Bitjah daughter of Pharaoh,"[35] and interpret the name as "daughter of YHWH." Bitjah is called "the Jewess" (היהודיה), "because she repudiated idolatry, as it is written, 'And the daughter of Pharaoh went down to bathe in the river'; and R. Johanan (commenting on this) said that she went down to cleanse herself from the idols of her father's house." In this reading the Egyptian princess converts, so to speak, to Judaism just in time to become one of Moses's mothers.[36]

What all texts—biblical, Jewish-Hellenistic as well as rabbinic—have in common is that both of Moses's mothers, his birth mother and his adoptive mother, play an important role around his birth, but soon after they disappear from the scene. We have seen that in some rabbinic versions this occurs, in a way, even before Moses's birth. Moses is no Aeneas whose relationship to Venus may be complicated, but who nevertheless counts on his mother's

---

33   Ezekiel, *Exagoge* v. 32–38 (trans. H. Jacobson). Cf. René Bloch, "Meine Mutter erzählte mir alles: Ezechiel Exagoge 34–35 und der Mythos," *Judaica* 61 (2005): 97–109.

34   Lorena Miralles Maciá, "Judaizing a Gentile Biblical Character through Fictive Biographical Reports: The Case of Bityah, Pharao's Daughter, Moses's Mother, according to Rabbinic Interpretation," in *Narratology, Hermeneutics, and Midrash. Jewish, Christian, and Muslim Narratives from Late Antiquity through to Modern Times*, ed. Constanza Cordoni, Gerhard Langer (Göttingen: Vandenhoeck & Ruprecht, 2014), 145–175, 153.

35   1 Chr 4:18.

36   b. Meg. 13a (trans. Soncino). Cf. Stemberger, *Mose*, 35.

"divine guidance and support."[37] Instead, Moses quickly leaves his mother—or rather his two mothers—behind. According to some spare rabbinic tradition, Yochebed shows up one more time, when Moses has difficulty finding the bones of Joseph before leaving Egypt (the Israelites were only supposed to leave Egypt if they brought Joseph's bones with them, as he had wished).[38] Usually it is, though, another woman who comes to Moses's aid in this task: Serah bat Asher shows Moses where Joseph was buried.[39] Otherwise, Moses acts on his own and in cooperation with God. Moses's actual parent is God. For Philo, Moses comes very close to being divine: "For he was named god and king of the whole nation."[40] This is reminiscent of Philo's Sarah, who is "motherless" (ἀμή-τωρ), because she is directly "born of the Father and Cause of all things" and of the number seven, "begotten by the Father alone" (*Ebr.* 61 and *Mos.* 2.210, see above). According to the Talmud, Yochebed suffered no pain during her pregnancy with Moses or at the delivery, thus exempted from the punishment for all women according to Gen 3:16 ("in pain shall you bear children").[41] It is not only the stories about Moses's death, but also about his birth, that show a tendency to divinization.[42] In both Jewish-Hellenistic and rabbinic literature, Moses transcends human family ties. A large group of women, starting with the midwives, make the birth of this hero happen. As for Moses's mothers, it is not least the very doubling of the image of the mother that erases the figure of Moses's mother.

Bibliography

Albertz, Rainer, *Exodus, Band 1: Ex 1–18*. Zürich: Theologischer Verlag, 2012.

Bloch, René, "Meine Mutter erzählte mir alles: Ezechiel Exagoge 34–35 und der Mythos." *Judaica* 61 (2005): 97–109.

Bloch, René, "D'une grandeur sans pareil et d'une humanité profonde: Moïse dans le judaïsme ancien." Pages 29–47 in *Figures de Moïsee. Le Monde la Bible* [E-book:

---

37 Cf. Pyy, "*Maternal Absence*," 187–208.

38 Sabba, *Zeror Ha-Mor, Beshallah*: ויוכבד אמו אמרה אני אראך את האיש אשר אתה מבקש ("And his mother Yochebed said: 'I will show you the man for whom you are searching.'"). Cf. Ginzberg, *The Legends of the Jews*, 5.

39 b. Sota 13a; Bet Ha-Midrash 6, 112–113. Cf. Moshe Reiss, "Serah bat Asher in Rabbinic Literature," *JBQ* 42 (2014): 45–51.

40 Phil, *Mos.* 1.158.

41 b. Sota 12a.

42 Cf. Stemberger, *Mose*, 29–30, who refers to parallels in the Maria-Jesus story.

https://www.mondedelabible.com/figures-de-moise-en-numerique/], November 10, 2015.

Brenner, Athalya, "Female Social Behaviour: Two Descriptive Patterns Within the "Birth of the Hero" Paradigm." *VT* 36 (1986): 257–273.

Bridge, Edward J., "A Mother's Influence: Mothers naming Children in the Hebrew Bible." *VT* 64 (2014): 389–400.

Freud, Sigmund, *Der Mann Moses und die monotheistische Religion. Schriften über die Religion*. Frankfurt am Main: Fischer 1975 [1941].

Ginzberg, Louis, *The Legends of the Jews*. Vol. 3. Philadelphia: The Jewish Publication Society of America, 1968.

Miralles Maciá, Lorena, "Judaizing a Gentile Biblical Character through Fictive Biographical Reports: The Case of Bityah, Pharao's Daughter, Moses's Mother, according to Rabbinic Interpretation." Pages 145–175 in *Narratology, Hermeneutics, and Midrash. Jewish, Christian, and Muslim Narratives from Late Antiquity through to Modern Times*. Edited by Constanza Cordoni and Gerhard Langer. Göttingen: Vandenhoeck & Ruprecht, 2014.

Pyy, Elina, "Maternal Absence and Heroic Identity in Virgil's *Aeneid*." Pages 187–208 in *Missing Mothers: Maternal Absence in Antiquity*. Edited by Sabine Hübner and David M. Ratzan. Leuven: Peeters 2021.

Reiss, Moshe, "Serah bat Asher in Rabbinic Literature." *JBQ* 42 (2014): 45–51.

Runia, David T., *Philo of Alexandria. On the Creation of the Cosmos according to Moses. Introduction, Translation and* Commentary. Leiden: Brill, 2001.

Staehle, Karl, *Die Zahlenmystik bei Philon von Alexandrien*. Leipzig: Teubner, 1931.

Stemberger, Günter, *Mose in der rabbinischen Tradition*. Freiburg im Breisgau: Herder, 2016.

Willi-Plein, Ina, "Ort und literarische Funktion der Geburtsgeschichte des Mose." *VT* 41 (1991): 110–118.

van Ruiten, Jaques T.A.G.M., "The Birth of Moses in Egypt According to the Book of Jubilees (Jub 47.1–9)." Pages 43–65 in *The Wisdom of Egypt: Jewish, Early Christian, and Gnostic Essays in Honour of Gerard P. Luttikhuizen*. Edited by Anthony Hilhorst and George H. van Kooten. Leiden: Brill, 2005.

CHAPTER 4

Leaving Home: Philo of Alexandria on the Exodus

Moses at the burning bush in chapter 3 of the Exodus book is one of the most dramatic scenes in the Hebrew Bible. All necessary ingredients for a dramatic epiphany are at play: Moses, who is watching the flock of his father-in-law Jethro near the mountain Horeb, the "mountain of God," becomes aware of a paradoxical scene of nature: there is a flame of fire coming out of a bush, but the bush is not consumed by the fire. Moses hears a divine voice calling him by name and telling him to keep away from the site. The scene of the burning bush is a classic example of how sacred space is created: "Remove the sandals from your feet, for the place on which you are standing is holy ground."[1] This is the site where Moses is informed by God about the land where the Israelites will dwell in the future. It is here, on sacred ground, that the territory of Israel's future home is described and announced to Moses. In this fiery and, one can imagine, smoky scene of Exodus 3, the destination of the journey becomes clear:

> and I have come down to deliver them from the Egyptians, and to bring them up out of that land to a good and broad land, a land flowing with milk and honey, to the country of the Canaanites, the Hittites, the Amorites, the Perizzites, the Hivites, and the Jebusites.[2]

This is the ticket. To leave no doubt where the journey is going the destination is repeated a little later: "I declare that I will bring you up out of the misery of Egypt, to the land of the Canaanites, the Hittites, the Amorites, the Perizzites, the Hivites, and the Jebusites, a land flowing with milk and honey."[3]

Among the several ancient Jewish authors who comment on and make use of this scene, the Jewish philosopher Philo of Alexandria is particularly interesting. In his vast oeuvre, Philo comes to talk most prominently about the Exodus in his *Life of Moses*, a fascinating Jewish-Hellenistic rewriting of the biblical Moses-narrative, and in his *Questions and Answers on Exodus*. In the former tractate the biblical scene of the burning bush is treated in detail and with quite

---

1   Exod 3:5 NRSV.
2   Exod 3:8 NRSV.
3   Exod 3:17 NRSV.

© RENÉ BLOCH, 2022 | DOI:10.1163/9789004521896_006

a few additions. Philo reads the burning bush which is not consumed by fire allegorically as a symbol for the resistance of the Jewish people:

> For the burning bramble was a symbol of those who suffered wrong, as the flaming fire of those who did it. Yet that which burned was not burnt up, and this was a sign that the sufferers would not be destroyed by their aggressors, who would find that the aggression was vain and profitless while the victims of malice escaped unharmed.[4]

Philo imagines that the biblical bush had thorns: it "is a very weakly plant, yet it is prickly and will wound if one should but touch it."[5] The miracle that the bush was not devoured by fire refers in Philo's reading to the nation's condition and to Israel's strength in difficult times. God tells Moses: "Do not lose heart; your weakness is your strength, which can prick, and thousands will suffer from its wounds."[6] As in the biblical version, God then strengthens Moses's limited self-confidence by showing him additional miracles and by assuring him that he would support Moses when it comes to rhetorics. To the Jewish people, Moses would not just be "an assistant to their liberation," but a "leader" of their "migration" (*apoikias*).[7]

In comparison to the biblical report there is something crucial missing in God's speech to Moses and in the lengthy passage on the biblical scene of the burning bush:[8] Where is Moses supposed to go? There is no mention of any destination. Philo's God tells Moses that he would soon become the leader of their migration from Egypt but forgets to tell Moses where to take his people. All he is told is to "make a three-days' journey beyond the bounds of the country" and to sacrifice there.[9]

In this chapter I would like to ask what it meant for an author such as Philo of Alexandria, who lived in Egypt, to write on the exodus, the biblical story of Israel's migration from Egypt to a better place. For Jewish-Hellenistic authors writing in Egypt, the exodus story posed unique challenges. After all, to them Egypt was, as Philo of Alexandria states, their fatherland (*patris*).[10] How does Philo come to terms with the biblical story of liberation from Egyptian slav-

---

4   Philo, *Mos.* 1.67. All translations of Philo are, if not stated otherwise, from the LCL editions.

5   Philo, *Mos.* 1.68.

6   Philo, *Mos.* 1.69.

7   Philo, *Mos.* 1.71.

8   The passage comprises some twenty paragraphs: *Mos.* 1.65–84.

9   Philo, *Mos.* 1.73.

10   Philo, *Flacc.* 49, see below.

LEAVING HOME: PHILO OF ALEXANDRIA ON THE EXODUS 71

ery and the longing for the promised land? And while I focus on Philo for the majority of this chapter, towards the end I add two more examples from Jewish-Hellenistic literature: the *Wisdom of Solomon* and Ezekiel's exodus tragedy *Exagoge*.

Perhaps a few biographical remarks on Philo of Alexandria are in order. As a matter of fact, there is not much one can say for sure about his life: in spite of his impressively large oeuvre (thirty-seven tractates have survived, but Philo wrote quite a few more), very little can be said with certainty about his life and activities.[11] Contrary to the other major literary figures of Diaspora Judaism, Josephus and Paul, Philo very rarely speaks of himself and provided no autobiography. Even the dates of his life are debated. Philo was probably born around 20 BCE and died around 50 CE. Even when Philo discusses the Jewish embassy to the Roman emperor Caligula (39/40 CE), of which he was most probably the leader, we learn very little about the author himself.[12] Josephus has a few lines on Philo and his family which indicate that Philo grew up in an upper class Jewish family in Alexandria.[13] Philo probably lived his whole life in Alexandria, which at the time was the intellectual center of Greek-speaking Judaism. He surely left the city for travelling: in the context of the biblical account on Abraham's departure from Ur, Philo makes the point that "the stay-at-home is to the travelled as the blind are to the keen-sighted." One reason which makes people travel is, "the chance of benefiting their country, when occasion offers, in its most vital and important interests."[14] Philo certainly lived up to this ideal when he participated in the Jewish embassy to Rome in response to the Jews of Alexandria coming under attack. We will come back to this later.

Philo was at least once in Jerusalem and he visited the temple while there.[15] In Philo's understanding Jerusalem is the *mētropolis* or "mother city" of all the Jews, while their "fatherland" (*patris*) is the place where they actually live. The *locus classicus* for this is *In Flaccum* 46:

> it is the holy city where the sacred temple of the Most High God stands, that they (the Jews) regard as their mother city, but the regions they obtained from their fathers, grandfathers, great-grandfathers, and even

---

11 Cf. Daniel R. Schwartz, "Philo, His Family, and His Times," in *The Cambridge Companion to Philo*, ed. Adam Kamesar (Cambridge: Cambridge University Press, 2009), 9–31.
12 Philo *Legat.*; *Flacc.*
13 Josephus, *AJ* 18.257–260.
14 Philo, *Abr.* 65.
15 Philo, *Prov.* 2.64.

more remote ancestors, to live in, (they regard) as their fatherland where they were born and brought up.[16]

To Philo, Egypt, or at least the city of Alexandria, was his fatherland. He refers to the city as "our Alexandria."[17] Philo repeatedly, as with the scene of the burning bush, uses the Greek term *apoikia*, "migration," when writing about the Exodus. *Apoikia* literally means "settlement far from home."[18]

Let us return to Philo's Moses: according to Philo, Moses who grew up in the royal family of the Pharaoh, had the opportunity to make a political career in Egypt.[19] But being the prototype of the ideal wise man, Moses showed no interest in the superficial symbols of power. In Philo's reading, it is at the scene of the burning bush that Moses is rewarded for his wise behavior and becomes the leader of the Jewish people. But again: What is the destination? Instead of making Moses explicitly the leader who would bring the Israelites to Canaan, Philo states that God gave Moses "the whole world:"

> And that is but natural, for he is a world citizen (*kosmopolitēs*), and therefore not on the role of any city of men's habitation, rightly so because he has received no mere piece of land but the whole world as his portion.[20]

While the biblical text makes it very clear that Moses would lead the Israelites out of Egypt to the land of Canaan, Philo's Moses, right after he has been made the leader and savior of the Jews, is presented as a cosmopolitan citizen. Philo uses the term *kosmopolitēs*, "citizen of the world," only eight times in his oeuvre, but his understanding of the term is of great importance for his concept of the world and the law. According to Philo, as he states at the beginning of his tractate on the creation of the world, "the world is in harmony with the Law,

---

16 Philo, *Flacc.* 46 (trans. Pieter W. van der Horst, *Philo's Flaccus: The First Pogrom: Introduction, Translation and Commentary* [Atlanta: SBL, 2005]).

17 Philo, *Legat.* 150. See Erich S. Gruen, *Diaspora: Jews Amidst Greeks and Romans* (Cambridge: Harvard University Press, 2002), 74.

18 LSJ, s.v. On the other hand, by calling Jerusalem *mētropolis* Philo uses a term which is regularly used for "*the mother-state*, in relation to colonies" (LSJ, s.v.). Jerusalem can thus be both the origin of the Jewish colony and its destination. Cf. on this Sarah Pearce, "Jerusalem as 'Mother-City' in the Writings of Philo of Alexandria," in *Negotiating Diaspora. Jewish Strategies in the Roman Empire*, ed. John M.G. Barclay (New York: T&T Clark, 2004), 19–36.

19 Philo, *Mos*, 1.150–154. For a detailed study on Philo's Moses in comparison with the biblical narrative, see Louis H. Feldman, *Philo's Portrayal of Moses in the Context of Ancient Judaism* (Notre Dame: University of Notre Dame Press, 1997).

20 Philo, *Mos.* 1.157.

and the Law with the world" and "a man who observes the law is constituted thereby a loyal citizen of the world." For Philo there is no difference between the law of nature and the law of Moses.[21] Therefore, Moses must be a citizen of the world and not just of a specific city or land. The biblical narrative of a Moses who would not live to arrive in the promised land suited Philo's understanding of Moses as a cosmopolitan citizen (and more generally of a 'cosmic' Judaism). Moses reaches out beyond a limited territory. And it comes as no surprise when Philo at the end of his tractate on Moses does not stick to the biblical description of Moses's death. According to Philo, Moses is not buried in the valley in the land of Moab (as stated in Deut 34:6), but rather he migrates to heaven. Here, as in the passage on the burning bush, Philo uses the word *apoikia* for Moses's migration. But here it is clear where this migration was to lead: "the migration from there ... to heaven."[22] God resolved Moses's "twofold nature of soul and body into a single unity, transforming his whole being into mind, pure as the sunlight."[23] Moses becomes immortal and joins God. This is Moses's Exodus in Philo: it is a spiritual journey towards God.

It is not that the destination of the journey of the Israelites is not mentioned at all in Philo's *Life of Moses*. Eventually, more as an aside, Philo mentions the destination of the Exodus by name: Moses was to lead the Israelites to "Phoenicia and Coelesyria and Palestine, then called the land of the Canaanites."[24] But the narrative in Philo's *Life of Moses* does not focus on the promised land. Rather, it focuses on the point of departure: it focuses on Egypt.

In Philo, Egypt is repeatedly described as a country to be avoided and to be left behind—not in a geographic sense, though, or with a specific destination in mind, but from a philosophical point of view: for Philo Egypt is the "symbol" of the body and of passion.[25] Egypt is a "bodily land" (*sōmatikē chōra*).[26] In her thorough study *The Land of the Body* Sarah Pearce has shown how for Philo Egypt consistently symbolizes the material sphere, the land of the body.[27] In Philo's *Life of Moses* there are certainly also attempts to stress some sort of an Egyptian-Jewish "symbiosis." Thus Philo imagines for Moses an international

---

21   Philo, *Opif.* 3. Cf. on this John W. Martens, *One God, One Law: Philo of Alexandria on the Mosaic and Greco-Roman Law* (Leiden: Brill, 2003).

22   Philo, *Mos.* 2.288; the phrasing (τὴν ἐνθένδε ἀποικίαν) is identical with that in 1.71 on the Exodus.

23   Philo, *Mos.* 2.288.

24   Philo, *Mos.* 1.163.

25   Philo, *Migr.* 77.

26   Philo, *Migr.* 151, 154; *Mut.* 90.

27   Sarah Pearce, *The Land of the Body: Studies in Philo's Representation of Egypt* (Tübingen: Mohr Siebeck, 2007), 89 on the phrase "bodily land."

education in Egypt: wise teachers from different parts of the world come to the royal palace to assure a first class education, starting with the *enkyklios paideia* and leading to the most important field of study, philosophy. Among Moses's many teachers, Egyptian scholars are mentioned with praise.[28] Nevertheless, Pearce is right in stressing the overall negative image of Egypt in Philo. Egypt stands for the body, and the exodus stands for the migration of the soul from the body. When the Israelites departed from Egypt, they thus approached a higher stage of understanding. In his comment on Gen 26:2 ("The Lord appeared to Isaac, and said, 'Do not go down to Egypt'"), Philo explains the etymology of Egypt:

> Egypt is to be translated as "oppressing," for nothing else so constrains and oppresses the mind as do desire for sensual pleasures and grief and fear. But to the perfected man (Isaac), who by nature enjoys the happiness of virtue, the sacred and divine word recommends all perfection and not to go down into the passions but to accept impassivity with joy, bidding (the passions) a fond farewell.[29]

To avoid Egypt or to leave Egypt behind, as in the exodus, is in Philo's mind an allegorical way of saying fare well to the body and its passions.

Philo's understanding of Egypt is ambivalent: on the one hand, he understands Egypt as his home. Philo clearly participated in the cultural life of Alexandria—as becomes obvious, e.g. when he describes his visits to the theater[30]—and time and again he demonstrates a very thorough knowledge of Greco-Roman culture.[31] On the other hand, Egypt is negatively understood as a symbol for the body and passion. These are two different ways of understanding Egypt, but they are not mutually exclusive. The journey of the soul towards the world of God is a central theme in Philo and the exodus was *the* obvious example for a symbolic reading of an actual journey. For Philo, it seems to me,

---

28 Philo, *Mos.* 1.21–24. Cf. René Bloch, "Alexandria in Pharaonic Egypt: Projections in *De vita Mosis*," *SPhiloA* 24 (2012): 73–88, at 80–83 (chapter 1, pp. 30–34, in this volume).

29 Philo, *QG* 4.177. Philo seems to connect the Hebrew word for Egypt, *mizrayim*, with the Hebrew verb *zarar* ("to bind, tie up"; "to show hostility"). In this passage, Philo interprets the physical oppression, as related in the book of Exodus, allegorically, as an oppression of the mind: on this etymology cf. Pearce, *Land of the Body*, 82–85.

30 Philo, *Ebr.* 177. Cf. René Bloch, "Part of the Scene: Jewish Theater in Antiquity," *Journal of Ancient Judaism* 8 (2017 [2018]): 150–169 (chapter 9 in this volume).

31 Cf. René Bloch, *Moses und der Mythos: Die Auseinandersetzung mit der griechischen Mythologie bei jüdisch-hellenistischen Autoren* (Leiden: Brill, 2011), 173–189 and chapter 8 in this volume.

LEAVING HOME: PHILO OF ALEXANDRIA ON THE EXODUS

such a symbolic (instead of a literal) reading of the exodus also permitted him to keep the exodus under control, so to speak, and to stay in Egypt.

God's curious silence on the destination of Moses's migration in the scene of the burning bush is no exception. Philo generally shows very little interest in Canaan/Palestine.[32] His discussion of the biblical narrative focuses on the books of Genesis (mainly) and exodus, not on the books of Joshua and Judges. When Philo comes to talk about Gen 15:18, God's promise to Abram that his offspring would receive the land "from the river of Egypt to the great river, the river Euphrates," he prefers an allegorical over a geographical reading.[33] Only rarely is the conquest of Canaan a topic.[34] In his treatise *Questions and Answers on Exodus*, of which only a fraction survives (covering Exodus 12–28), Philo asks and answers one hundred twenty-four questions on the Book of Exodus. But nowhere is the final aim of the exodus mentioned. When he comments on Exod 23:20 ("I am going to send an angel in front of you, to guard you on the way and to bring you to the place that I have prepared"), Philo interprets the "place," once more, allegorically:

> … the entry into the land, (that is) an entry into philosophy, (which is), as it were, a good land and fertile in the production of fruits, which the divine plants, the virtues, bear.[35]

This is where the philosopher Philo wants to go and this is the ideal destination of the Israelites.

The exodus is important to Philo: in part because of the allegorical message which he sees behind the story, but also in part because of certain parallels

---

32   On Philo and Palestine cf. Berndt Schaller, "Philon von Alexandreia und das 'Heilige Land,'" in *Fundamenta Judaica: Studien zum antiken Judentum und zum Neuen Testament* (Göttingen: Vandenhoeck & Ruprecht, 2001), 13–27 and Jacobus C. de Vos, *Heiliges Land und Nähe Gottes: Wandlungen alttestamentlicher Landvorstellungen in frühjüdischen und neutestamentlichen Schriften* (Göttingen: Vandenhoeck & Ruprecht, 2012), 87–100. Feldman, *Philo's Portrayal*, 78 suspects an apologetic reason behind Philo's reluctance to mention the destination of the Exodus: he could thus avoid the charge of dual allegiance. But this seems unlikely. The apologetic agenda of the *Life of Moses* has been overstated.

33   Philo, *Som.* 2.255: "Again God promises wise Abraham a portion of land 'from the river of Egypt to the great river Euphrates,' not mentioning a section of country, but rather the better part in ourselves. For our body and the passions engendered in it or by it are likened to the river of Egypt, but the soul and what the soul loves to the Euphrates." Cf. Pearce, *Land of the Body*, 104–105.

34   Cf. Katell Berthelot, "Philo of Alexandria and the Conquest of Canaan," *Journal for the Study of Judaism* 38 (2007): 39–56.

35   Philo, *QE* 2.13.

between the Egypt of biblical tradition and that of his own days. It seems to me that Philo's way of talking about Egypt is heavily colored by personal impressions. I have recently argued that Philo's *Life of Moses*, or at least parts of this tractate, can be read as a text in which Philo ponders on his own life, not least his response to the anti-Jewish riot in Alexandria in 38 CE. As a matter of fact, Philo's description of the suffering of the Israelites under the cruel Egyptian despots in *Life of Moses* is very similar to his report on the suppression of the Jews at the time of the riot in the tractate *Embassy to Caligula* (*Legatio ad Gaium*). Moreover, by going to Rome and pleading at the emperor's palace on behalf of the Jews, Philo slips into the role of Moses, who did the same at Pharaoh's palace. Moses is obviously out of reach, but he is Philo's *paradeigma*, his constant point of orientation.[36] When Philo writes about Moses and the exodus he is very much in Egypt. At times Moses and Philo even merge into one person. They enjoyed the same kind of education[37] and were both confronted with animosity in Egypt. And Philo's main concern is Egypt.

How did other Jewish-Hellenistic authors conceptualize the exodus? In the remainder of this chapter, I will briefly hint at two other takes on the issue from Jewish-Hellenistic literature: the *Wisdom of Solomon* and Ezekiel's tragic play *Exagoge* on the exodus.

Wisdom of Solomon is a pseudepigraphic text which became part of the Septuagint. The author, most likely writing in Alexandria and possibly a contemporary of Philo, takes up the identity of king Solomon.[38] The book, written in a Greek which shows both Hebrew and pagan influences, belongs to Jewish Wisdom literature. It falls into three sections, of which the first compares the life of the righteous, who pursues wisdom, to that of the wicked, who first ridicules the values of Jewish wisdom but then realizes that in the end righteousness wins over injustice. The middle section of the book is an intense praise of wisdom in the name of King Solomon. The third and last section (chapters 10–19) contrasts, like the first, righteous and wicked approaches to life, but this time the author presents examples from Israel's "history:" in the center of the discussion is the biblical story of the exodus and the respective destinies of the Israelites and the Egyptians. The author is eager to show that the Egyptians are punished by the same means through which the Israelites are delivered:[39] the

---

36   Bloch, "Alexandria in Pharaonic Egypt," 69–84 (chapter 1 in this volume).

37   Philo, *Mos.* 1.21–24 (on Moses's education); Philo, *Congr.* 74–76 (on Philo's education).

38   On content, structure, and authorship of *Wisdom of Solomon*, cf. the concise introduction by Randall D. Chestnutt, "Solomon, Wisdom of," in *The Eerdmans Dictionary of Early Judaism*, ed. John J. Collins and Daniel Harlow (Grand Rapids: Eerdmans, 2010), 1242–1244.

39   Chestnutt, "Solomon, Wisdom of," 1243.

LEAVING HOME: PHILO OF ALEXANDRIA ON THE EXODUS   77

Egyptians try to kill Moses in the Nile, but in the end their men drown in the water of the Sea of Reeds (i.e., the "Red Sea"). God shows the Israelites the path to water in the desert but makes the water of the Egyptians undrinkable. In the words of the author:

> For by those very things through which their enemies were punished, they in their want were benefited.[40]

A major critique in *Wisdom of Solomon* is, as in Philo, the Egyptian worship of animals. For this, too, the Egyptians are punished adequately by the plagues:

> In repayment for their wicked and witless reasoning, by which they were misled into worshiping brute reptiles and worthless beasts, you sent against them a swarm of creatures devoid of reasoning; that they might know that by those things through which a man sins, through them he is punished.[41]

Another parallel with Philo—and this brings us back to our earlier argument—is the remarkable fact that in *Wisdom of Solomon*, after a detailed description of the suffering of the Israelites and the punishment of the Egyptians, the exodus does not really happen anyway. The Israelites do not get further than the Sea of Reeds. One might say that they remain in Egypt. *Wisdom of Solomon* ends somewhat abruptly with a statement about God's constant help for Israel "in every time and place."[42] Some scholars have wondered about the rather abrupt end of the book. Why does the author make no mention of Israel's subsequent arrival in the promised land?[43] The reason for our author's silence on this issue seems to be the same as in the case of Philo: his main concern is Egypt.

Let me add a third example of such a reluctance to really leave Egypt: the drama *Exagoge* by the Jewish-Hellenistic poet Ezekiel. The play—probably also written in Alexandria, maybe in the second century BCE—has only survived in fragments.[44] However, the extant 269 Greek verses allow for more than a brief

---

40   Wis 11:5. I follow the translation of David Winston, *The Wisdom of Solomon* (New York: Doubleday, 1979).

41   Wis 11:15–16.

42   Wis 19:22.

43   Cf. the discussion in Joseph Reider, *The Book of Wisdom: An English Translation with Introduction and Commentary* (New York: Harper & Bros., 1957), 224–225.

44   On Ezekiel cf. the excellent editions by Howard Jacobson, *The Exagoge of Ezekiel* (Cambridge: Cambridge University Press, 1983) and Pierluigi Lanfranchi, *L'Exagoge d'Ezéchiel le Tragique: Introduction, texte, traduction et commentaire* (Leiden: Brill, 2006).

78   CHAPTER 4

insight. The play starts out with a typical prologue of the kind familiar from many Greek tragedies: it is Moses himself who dares to enter the stage all alone (something the rhetorically challenged Moses of the Torah would never have done) and tells the audience of the beginnings of the Jewish people as well as his own origins. This is the beginning of the first fragment:

> When Jacob left Canaan
> he came to Egypt with seventy
> souls and fathered a great
> people that has suffered and been oppressed.
> Till this day we have been ill-treated
> by evil men and a powerful regime.[45]

We do not know whether this was the actual beginning of the play. It might very well have been. In any case, Moses early on in the drama explains the Israelites' presence in Egypt: Jacob had left Canaan and migrated to Egypt, and Moses is a descendent of Jacob. Moses then reports how he was saved by the Egyptian princess and how, after having killed an Egyptian, he had to flee, and how he met the daughters of Raguel (Jethro). The fragmentary nature of the transmission of the text leaves many questions open. But of Ezekiel's version of the biblical scene of the burning bush a substantial part has survived. Strikingly, here, too, God does not tell Moses where to go:

> Now go, and report in my words
> to all the Hebrews and
> then to the king my instructions to you,
> that you lead my people from the land.[46]

A little later, God speaks of the destination as "your own land" (*idion chōron*).[47] But the name of the land is not mentioned, neither here nor anywhere else in the surviving fragments. In the drama, there is certainly a movement out of Egypt and towards the end there is mention of reports by scouts who visited the land. But to Ezekiel, what happened in Egypt appears to be of greater importance. In what seems to have been the fourth act of the play there is a long speech by an Egyptian soldier who returns home, apparently the only sur-

---

45   Ezekiel, *Exagoge* 1–6. I follow the translation by Jacobson, *Exagoge*.
46   Ezekiel, *Exagoge* 109–112.
47   Ezekiel, *Exagoge* 167.

vivor of the Egyptian disaster at the Sea of Reeds. The Egyptian messenger tells the probably mostly Jewish audience—which must have enjoyed this scene— how the armed forces of the Pharaoh had no chance against the Israelites. Too late did the Egyptians realize "that God was helping them."[48] As in *Wisdom of Solomon*, this is a central message of the text: wrong-doers are punished for their unjust behavior and the righteous prevail. And here too, as in Philo, the author's main interest is Egypt. Shortly after the Israelites leave Egypt, the Egyptian messenger returns (to Alexandria, one can assume) and continues the dialogue with the Jews in Egypt.

We have looked at three Jewish-Hellenistic ways of rewriting the exodus: Philo's *Life of Moses*, and, very briefly, *Wisdom of Solomon* and Ezekiel's *Exagoge*. In many ways these three examples could not be more different from each other: Philo's *Life of Moses* is a philosophical biography, *Wisdom of Solomon* is a piece of Wisdom literature, and Ezekiel's drama is a Hellenistic tragedy. But the three authors, who probably all wrote in Egypt, all have in common that in their rewritings of the exodus they remain very much in Egypt and barely ever leave home.

Bibliography

Berthelot, Katell, "Philo of Alexandria and the Conquest of Canaan." *Journal for the Study of Judaism* 38 (2007): 39–56.

Bloch, René, *Moses und der Mythos: Die Auseinandersetzung mit der griechischen Mythologie bei jüdisch-hellenistischen Autoren.* Leiden: Brill, 2011.

Bloch, René, "Alexandria in Pharaonic Egypt: Projections in *De vita Mosis*." *SphiloA* 24 (2012): 73–88.

Bloch, René, "Part of the Scene: Jewish Theater in Antiquity." in *Journal of Ancient Judaism* 8 (2017 [2018]): 150–169.

Chestnutt, Randall D., "Solomon, Wisdom of." Pages 1242–1244 in *The Eerdmans Dictionary of Early Judaism.* Edited by John J. Collins and Daniel Harlow. Grand Rapids: Eerdmans, 2010.

Feldman, Louis H., *Philo's Portrayal of Moses in the Context of Ancient Judaism.* Notre Dame: University of Notre Dame Press, 1997.

Gruen, Erich S., *Diaspora: Jews Amidst Greeks and Romans.* Cambridge: Harvard University Press, 2002.

---

48   Ezekiel, *Exagoge* 236.

van der Horst, Pieter W., *Philo's Flaccus: The First Pogrom: Introduction, Translation and Commentary*. Atlanta: SBL, 2005.

Jacobson, Howard, *The Exagoge of Ezekiel*. Cambridge: Cambridge University Press, 1983.

Lanfranchi, Pierluigi, *L'Exagoge d'Ezéchiel le Tragique: Introduction, texte, traduction et commentaire*. Leiden: Brill, 2006.

Martens, John W., *One God, One Law: Philo of Alexandria on the Mosaic and Greco-Roman Law*. Leiden: Brill, 2003.

Pearce, Sarah, "Jerusalem as 'Mother-City' in the Writings of Philo of Alexandria." Pages 19–36 in *Negotiating Diaspora. Jewish Strategies in the Roman Empire*. Edited by John M.G. Barclay. New York: T&T Clark, 2004.

Pearce, Sarah, *The Land of the Body: Studies in Philo's Representation of Egypt*. Tübingen: Mohr Siebeck, 2007.

Reider, Joseph, *The Book of Wisdom: An English Translation with Introduction and Commentary*. New York: Harper & Bros., 1957.

Schaller, Berndt, "Philon von Alexandreia und das 'Heilige Land.'" Pages 13–27 in *Fundamenta Judaica: Studien zum antiken Judentum und zum Neuen Testament*. Edited by Berndt Schaller. Göttingen: Vandenhoeck & Ruprecht, 2001.

Schwartz, Daniel R., "Philo, His Family, and His Times." Pages 9–31 in *The Cambridge Companion to Philo*. Edited by Adam Kamesar. Cambridge: Cambridge University Press, 2009.

de Vos, Jacobus C., *Heiliges Land und Nähe Gottes: Wandlungen alttestamentlicher Landvorstellungen in frühjüdischen und neutestamentlichen Schriften*. Göttingen: Vandenhoeck & Ruprecht, 2012.

Winston, David, *The Wisdom of Solomon*. New York: Doubleday, 1979.

PART 2

Places and Ruins

CHAPTER 5

Geography without Territory: Tacitus's Digression on the Jews and its Ethnographic Context

1   Introduction

A distinguished scholar of modern ethnography, Marcel Mauss, defined in his "manuel d'éthnographie" the duties of scientific ethnography: an ethnographer has to be accurate and complete; the ethnographer is not supposed to believe ("ne pas croire"), but to know. The ethnographer is not allowed to be surprised ("ne pas s'étonner") or to pass moral judgments on a people ("ne porter aucun jugement moral"), and finally the ethnographer is obliged to live for a certain time within the community of the people which is supposed to be described. Only then, says Mauss, is it possible not only to describe, but also to understand a people's character and customs and to overcome the danger inherent in every ethnographic description: the temptation of subjectivity ("difficultés subjectives").[1]

Ancient ethnography, to be sure, is so different from Mauss's approach that for this reason alone one might hesitate to use the term "ethnography" in the context of ancient literature at all. Ancient ethnographers often do not want to be complete, and they love to be subjective and judgmental. Because the approach and paradigms of ancient ethnography are markedly different from its modern namesake and also because it cannot be construed as a specific genre but permeates all ancient literature (because of its unrestraint, one might say), we may pay even more attention to what is *not* said about a people than to what is said. This search for ethnographic silence is indeed most productive when we try to understand how the Jews are described in Greco-Roman literature.

In recent years the study of Judaism in Greco-Roman times, especially that of Diaspora Judaism, has increasingly attracted the interest of historians, theologians, and philologists. From different perspectives scholars have attempted to reconstruct the historical reality of the ancient Jewish diaspora.[2] In this paper I

---

1   Marcel Mauss, *Manuel d'éthnographie* (Paris: Payot, 1947), 7–9.

2   Cf. e.g. Shaye J.D. Cohen and Ernest S. Frerichs, eds., *Diasporas in Antiquity* (Atlanta: Scholars, 1993); John M.G. Barclay, *Jews in the Mediterranean Diaspora: From Alexander to Trajan (323 BCE–117 CE)* (Edinburgh: Edinburgh University Press, 1996); Leonard V. Rutgers, *The Hid-*

© RENÉ BLOCH, 2022 | DOI:10.1163/9789004521896_007

shall read Greek and Roman depictions of Judaism not so much to understand the actual conditions of the diaspora as to understand the perspective of the pagan authors. I shall, therefore, focus on how the Jews were viewed by outsiders and not on how they viewed themselves or how one group of Jews was viewed by another.

My thesis is that the fact that the Jews were scattered across the Mediterranean (and beyond) had a very important impact on the way they were described by Greek and Roman authors. I shall argue that the ethnographic portraits of the Jews are in several respects different from representations of other peoples because of the fact that Jews lived not only in one specific place, namely in Judea or Palestine, but also in many places outside their home country, i.e. in the diaspora, which by definition transcends geographical territory and boundaries. In this paper I intend to focus on three aspects of ancient ethnography: the "anthropogeographical approach," certain *topoi* of the ethnographic codex, and the distinction Greeks/Romans vs. "Barbarians." I shall put a special emphasis on Tacitus's famous ethnographic digression on the Jews.

2 Anthropogeography

In Greek and Roman ethnography a very popular and at the same time thoroughly serious approach in explaining the character, the ἦθος of a people, was anthropogeography. By anthropogeography we understand the idea that the geographical environment affects the character of its inhabitants. The character, but also the physical body, τὸ εἶδος, of a people can be explained by the nature of the surrounding region. The theory that place creates man's εἶδος and ἦθος survived in a remarkably persistent manner through many centuries.[3] The opposite approach, the theory that the human creates place and not place the human, has been formulated more recently by humanistic geographers and theoretically explained by scholars such as Jonathan Z. Smith.[4]

---

    den Heritage of Diaspora Judaism (Leuven: Peeters 1998); cf. also the good review essay on ancient Jewish diaspora by Jonathan J. Price, "The Jewish Diaspora of the Graeco-Roman Period," *Scripta Classica Israelica* 13 (1994): 169–186.

3   Cf. Clarence J. Glacken, *Traces on the Rhodian Shore: Nature and Culture in Western Thought from Ancient Times to the End of the Eighteenth Century* (Berkeley: University of California Press, 1976), and the short historical introduction on anthropogeography by Eckart Olshausen, "Anthropogeographie," in *Mensch und Landschaft in der Antike: Lexikon der Historischen Geographie*, ed. Holger Sonnabend (Stuttgart: Metzler, 1999), 31–32.

4   Jonathan Z. Smith, "Father Place," in *To Take Place: Toward Theory in Ritual* (Chicago: The University of Chicago Press, 1987), 24–46, at 30–31: "The approach taken by present-day human-

GEOGRAPHY WITHOUT TERRITORY

In Greco-Roman literature we find anthropogeographical arguments from the fifth century on: Herodotus lets Cyrus state that "soft lands breed soft men; wondrous fruits of the earth and valiant warriors grow not from the same soil." In a possibly Hippocratic book entitled "Airs, Waters, Places" (περὶ ἀέρων ὑδάτων, τόπων), dating from the fifth or fourth century BCE, the author contrasts the mellow character of Asian peoples with European strength and explains it by means of the opposite climatic conditions in Asia and Europe.[5] Similarly, Strabo (or his source) brings the *physis* of the Indians into relationship with the strong humidity of India: "For on account of the humidity of the air their hair does not curl."[6] Likewise, the infertile ground of the Ligurians corresponds with their physical conditions: "The Ligurians who dwell in this land possess a soil which is stony and altogether wretched, and, in return for the labours and exceedingly great hardships of the natives, produces only scanty crops which are wrung from it. Consequently (διὸ) the inhabitants are of small bulk and are kept vigorous by their constant exercise."[7] Herodotus explains the strange customs of the Egyptians by their strange geography.[8] According to Polybius the austerity of the Arcadians results from the cold and gloomy atmospheric conditions in Arcadia.[9]

This anthropogeographical approach was adopted and adapted by many Greek and Roman authors. And, irrespective of any theoretical background, it was something of a *communis opinio* that the customs and character of a people were related to their geographic surrounding. The number of examples is endless. In the second century CE the Roman historian Curtius Rufus could still write: "The character of the people (the Indians) has been formed, *as everywhere*, by the nature of the geography they lived in."[10]

---

istic geographers stands in sharp contrast to the mainstream of geographic theories of place in most of Western history.... the traditional theories held that it is place that creates man and his culture as well as his character, rather than the other way round. *Topos* or *physis* is what shapes, what gives form and content to *nomos* and *ethos*. This is the dominant European intellectual tradition often oversimplified under the rubric 'environmental determinism' (since the Enlightenment, perhaps better labeled 'environmental relativism')."

5   Herodotus 9.122. Translations of Greek and Latin texts follow LCL (where available). On the Hippocratic text cf. Karl Trüdinger, *Studien zur Geschichte der griechisch-römischen Ethnographie* (Basel: Birkhäuser, 1918), 37–43.
6   Strabo 15.1.13.
7   Diodorus Siculus 4.20.1.
8   Herodotus 2.35.
9   Polybius 4.21.1.
10   Curtius 8.9.20: *Ingenia hominum sicut ubique, apud illos locorum quoque situs format.* Ancient criticism of anthropogeography is rare. Most explicit is Philo, who argues against

86   CHAPTER 5

There is, I should like to argue, an exception to the dominant pattern: the Jews. From the beginning of the third century BCE many Greek and Roman authors described the customs of the Jews and the land of Judea, but none of them tried to explain Jewish customs or Jewish character by their geography.[11] The character of the Jews stays, it seems, unrelated to their territory; ethnographic aspects related to space are missing from the numerous descriptions of the Jews, such as the ones written by Hecataeus of Abdera, Posidonius, Strabo, Cicero, Pompeius Trogus, Juvenal, and many others. Judea does not seem to explain the Jews.[12]

I should like, though, to challenge my own argument by focusing for a few moments on a central text of ancient ethnography on the Jews: Tacitus's excursus on the Jews in the fifth book of the *Histories*, which introduces his report on the destruction of Jerusalem by the Flavians.[13] This relatively long digression is well known, but has rarely been placed within a larger context. Previous studies of this text have focused on Tacitus's sources and his ethnographic reliability. In my book *Antike Vorstellungen vom Judentum* I try to contextualize this text within the history of Greco-Roman ethnography and relate it to other *Ethnographica* in Tacitus's oeuvre.[14] Tacitus deals extensively with the origin, customs, geography, and history of the Jews. His comments on Judean geog-

---

the environmental explanations of certain authors: "And then we find them alleging causes for this (i.e. the fact that different peoples have different customs) which are no real causes, such as unfavourable seasons, want of fertility, poverty of soil or how the state is situated, whether it is maritime or inland or whether it is on an island or on the mainland and the like" (Philo, *Ios.* 30).

11   One might argue that the well-known fact that Jews were not autochthonous but immigrated to Judea did not invite anthropogeographical explanations. But immigration did not exclude the possibility of an environmental argument: the Scythians, whose character and customs were often explained by environmental factors, were, according to some sources at least, also regarded as immigrants (cf. Herodotus 4.11).

12   The late Alexandrian astronomer Ptolemy (second century CE), who also thought that national characteristics were conditioned by the geographical (and astrological) situation, indeed connected the deplorable character of Near Eastern peoples with the astrological location of their territory (Ptolemy, *Apotelesmatica* 2.3.65–66 [29–31]). Ptolemy does not explicitly mention the Jews, however, but speaks more generally about a huge geographic space reaching from Phoenicia in the West to Babylonian Chaldaea in the East.

13   Tacitus, *Hist.* 5.2–13.

14   René Bloch, *Antike Vorstellungen vom Judentum. Der Judenexkurs des Tacitus im Rahmen der griechisch-römischen Ethnographie* (Stuttgart: Franz Steiner, 2002), with full bibliography. Most important are still Hans (Yohanan) Lewy, "Tacitus on the Origin and Manners of the Jews," *Zion* 8 (1943): 1–23, 61–83 (Hebr.), and the commentary by Menahem Stern, *Greek and Latin Authors on Jews and Judaism.* 3 vols. (Jerusalem: The Israel Academy of Sciences and Humanities, 1974–1984), §281.

GEOGRAPHY WITHOUT TERRITORY   87

raphy are surprisingly lengthy if one considers Tacitus's usually very limited
interest in geography. To come back to our original question: Does Tacitus connect the features of Judean geography with the εἶδος or the ἦθος of the Jews? This
is a legitimate question when one considers Tacitus's description of the Britons
and the Germans. In the *Agricola*, considering the physique of the Britons, Tacitus takes a possible anthropogeographic explanation seriously (although he
finally rejects it): Was it the climatic condition (*positio caeli*) which stamped a
certain physique on the human body?[15] The German Mattiaci, Tacitus writes
in the *Germania*, closely resemble the Batavi, "except that among other things
both the soil and climate of their land of themselves stimulate to greater ani-
mation."[16]

What, then, about Tacitus's description of Judea? There is indeed no explicit
link between Judean geography and Jewish customs in Tacitus's description
of Judean geography. But nevertheless, Bezalel Bar-Kochva is only partly right
when he writes in a short survey of Greek and Roman digressions on the Jews
that Tacitus "was obviously unable to connect the pleasant features of the land
and its climate with his hostile characterization of its inhabitants."[17] This does
not hold completely and I intend to take a closer look at Tacitus's description
of Judean geography.

It is curious that, contrary to the traditional order of such ethnographic
excursuses, Tacitus does not treat the geography part (*situs*) at the very beginning of his digression—as he does in his monograph on the Germans as well
as in his digression on the Britons. His description of Judean geography is surrounded by chapters on the customs (*mores*) and history (*historia*) of the Jews.
Eduard Norden explained this odd structure by arguing that the topography
of Judea and Jerusalem would lead logically to the report of the decisive days
before the fall of Jerusalem: "der Schriftsteller hat weiterhin von Jerusalems

---

15   Tacitus, *Agr.* 11.2: *positio caeli corporibus habitum dedit.*
16   Tacitus, *Germ.* 29.3. The wild chorography of Germany (Tacitus, *Germ.* 5.1: *terra* [...] *aut
     silvis horrida aut paludibus foeda*) goes well with the ethnography of the Germans, whose
     northern home made them receptive to 'classical' northern characteristics such as wild-
     ness. Cf. Klaus E. Müller, *Geschichte der antiken Ethnographie und ethnologischen The-
     oriebildung.* Vol. 2 (Wiesbaden: Franz Steiner, 1980), 84: "der passende Hintergrund für
     ein ungestüm-wildes Barbarenvolk;" similarly Beatrix Günnewig, *Das Bild der Germanen
     und Britannier: Untersuchungen zur Sichtweise von fremden Völkern in antiker Literatur
     und moderner wissenschaftlicher Forschung* (Frankfurt am Main: Peter Lang, 1998), 117. For
     another example of (nonexplicit) anthropogeography cf. Tacitus *Ann.* 6.34.2 on the Iberi-
     ans and Albanians: *Nam Hiberi Albanique saltuosos locos incolentes duritiae patientiaeque
     magis insuevere.*
17   Bezalel Bar-Kochva, *Pseudo-Hecataeus, On the Jews: Legitimizing the Jewish Diaspora* (Ber-
     keley: University of California Press, 1996), 215–216.

Schicksal zu erzählen und strebt daher über das Volks- und Besiedelungs-geschichtliche hinweg zu der Topographie von Land und Stadt."[18] But this does not really solve the problem: in fact, the topographic chapters (chapters 6–7) do not lead directly to the report of the fall of Jerusalem, but only to a long digression on Judean-Roman history (chapters 8–10). The structure, then, has other reasons.

In the first place, we have to correct Bar-Kochva's view that Tacitus described Judean geography as having "pleasant features." In fact, this geography is not pleasant at all. It is on the contrary a gloomy and frightening land. In Taci-tus's description the Dead Sea has more and more uncomfortable features: "It is a lake of great size, like the sea, but its water has a nauseous taste and its offensive odor is injurious (*pestifer*) to those who live near it." The descrip-tion culminates in the strong adjective *pestifer*, a *hapax* in Tacitus's oeuvre.[19] Using Virgilian style and vocabulary Tacitus then draws a very dark picture of the wasteland around the Dead Sea: "In fact, all the plants there, whether wild or cultivated, turn black, become sterile, and seem to wither into dust, either in leaf or in flower or after they have reached their usual mature form."[20] It is not by coincidence that Tacitus's description of the destroyed area around Sodom and Gomorrah follows very closely a formulation of the Virgilian description of the gloomy *lugentes campi* in the sixth book of the *Aeneid*.[21] In fact, this *ekphrasis* of the inhospitable Dead Sea and surrounding region goes beyond similar descriptions by earlier authors.[22] Moreover it is striking that Tacitus does not enter into the nice features of Judean geography mentioned by other authors: he leaves out the pleasant perfume of the Judean balsam, for exam-

---

18   Eduard Norden, *Die germanische Urgeschichte in Tacitus' Germania* (Leipzig: Teubner, 1921 [1998]), 41.

19   Tacitus, *Hist.* 5.6.2: *lacus immenso ambitu, specie maris, sapore corruptior, gravitate odoris accolis pestifer.*

20   Tacitus, *Hist.* 5.7.1: *nam cuncta sponte edita aut manu sata, sive herba tenus aut flore seu solidam in speciem adolevere, atra et inania velut in cinerem vanescunt.*

21   *Haud procul inde campi, quos ferunt olim uberes magnisque urbibus habitatos fulminum iactu arsisse; et manere vestigia* (Tacitus, *Hist.* 5.7.1) clearly follows *nec procul hinc partem fusi monstrantur in omnem / lugentes campi* (Virgil, *Aen.* 6.440–441). Cf. Eduard Nor-den, "Josephus und Tacitus über Jesus Christus und eine messianische Prophetie," *Neue Jahrbücher für das klassische Altertum* 31 (1913): 636–666, reprinted in Eduard Norden, *Kleine Schriften zum klassischen Altertum*, ed. Bernhard Kytzler (Berlin: de Gruyter, 1966), 241–275, at 271: "Diese Verse lagen Tacitus im Ohr, als er seine Vorlage stilisierte: das Gefilde am Toten Meer, das Grab der Städte, waren auch 'Trauergefilde'."

22   Also Diodorus and Pliny comment on the odious smell of the Dead Sea. Cf. Diodorus 2.48.7; 19.98; Pliny, *Nat.* 5.71.

GEOGRAPHY WITHOUT TERRITORY   89

ple.[23] This is, I think, not so much because of Tacitus's alleged antisemitism. Rather, Tacitus strengthens the ominous and sad features of Judean geography in the central chapters of his digression, for two reasons: first, these features of a dead geography anticipate the geography of the destroyed city of Jerusalem. The city of Jerusalem will be as desolate as Sodom and Gomorrah: the temple will be as empty and vain as the burnt surroundings of the Dead Sea. In both cases Tacitus uses the same strong adjective *inanis*.[24] Second, these unpleasant features mirror the unpleasant features of the Jewish customs which Tacitus describes in the preceding chapters. The inhospitable nature of the Dead Sea, which is unfavorable to any living creature, corresponds with the traditional misanthropy of the Jews. The inertness of the heavy water of the Dead Sea mirrors the similarly lazy institution of the Sabbath. It might not be a coincidence that Tacitus uses the adjective *iners* (*inertes undae*) in this context: previously, Tacitus polemically commented on Jewish *inertia* with regard to the Sabbath and the Sabbatical year.[25] Furthermore, the asphalt which the natives of Judea collect from the Dead Sea, Tacitus reports, is so hard that it can only be split "like timber or stone with axes and wedges."[26] This amazing cohesion of Judean asphalt automatically reminds the attentive reader of the strong *concordia* of the Jews so heavily stressed in the previous chapters on Jewish customs.[27]

---

23   Cf. Theophrastus, *HP* 9.6.1–4; Pliny, *Nat.* 12.111 with Tacitus, *Hist.*5.6.l.
24   Tacitus, *Hist.* 5.7.1: *nam cuncta sponte edita aut manu sata, sive herba tenus aut flore seu solidam in speciem adolevere, atra et **inania** velut in cinerem vanescunt.* 9.1: *inde volgatum nulla intus deum effigie vacuam sedem et **inania** arcana.*
25   Cf. Tacitus, *Hist.* 5.4.3: *Septimo die otium placuisse ferunt, quia is finem laborum tulerit; dein blandiente inertia septimum quoque· annum ignaviae datum.* The description of the sluggish and breathless Dead Sea (6.2: *neque vento impellitur ... inertes undae*) is similar to the description of the Ocean in the digression on the Britons (Tacitus, *Agr.*10.5: *mare pigrum et grave remigantibus ... ne ventis quidem perinde adtolli*) as well as to that of the sea to the North of the *Suiones* (Tacitus, *Germ.* 45.1: *mare pigrum ac prope immotum*). A *mare pigrum* apparently could be understood as an ethnographic θαυμάσιον. But it is noteworthy that only with respect to the Dead Sea does Tacitus use the adjective *iners*. *Iners/inertia* are often used as negative characteristics in Tacitus: cf. e.g. *Germ.* 36.1 and *Hist.* 1.46.3. For a similar formulation to that on the Dead Sea, cf. Lucan 6.107: (*hostis*) *aere non pigro nec inertibus angitur undis.*
26   Tacitus, *Hist.* 5.6.4.
27   That Tacitus's geography of Judea reflects more than what it seems to be has been noted, in general terms, by a few Italian scholars; cf. Concetto Marchesi, "Le genti straniere. Germani, Parti e Britanni. Ebrei e Cristiani," in *Tacito* (Milan: Principato, 1942), 2.155–170, at 2.167: "di questo popolo lugubre è lugubre pure il territorio ... l'impressione di un paesaggio maledetto per una gente maledetta." Pierpaolo Fornaro, *Flavio Giuseppe, Tacito e l'impero (Bellum Judaicum 6,248–315; Historiae V 13)* (Torino: Giappichelli, 1980), 70: "ma tutta l'archeologica giudaica e la stessa geografia palestinese sono insigni per eccezion-

I should like to argue that Tacitus's technique of reflecting his argument, both backwards (to the chapters on the Jewish customs), and forward (to the report on the fall of Jerusalem), has mainly literary goals: his description of Judean geography draws a gloomy picture which, by mirroring the vain customs and institutions of the Jews, anticipates the fall of Jerusalem and the destruction of the Jewish temple. The *situs*-section, written in a more exquisite style than the rest of the excursus, is therefore of great importance for the whole digression. This, finally, is why Tacitus moved these chapters on Judean geography, contrary to the ethnographic tradition, to the center of his excursus on the Jews.[28]

Is this passage then a real challenge to my thesis that there was no anthropogeography on the Jews in Greco-Roman ethnography? To some extent, it is: in Tacitus's excursus on the Jews, geography does indeed reflect the character of the people described, but it is, contrary to the anthropogeographical passages on other peoples I mentioned before, not intended to *explain* their character and can hardly be called anthropogeographical. Tacitus's links between Jewish customs and Judean geography, which he most probably invented himself, follow, I believe, only the literary intentions I mentioned.

3   **Missing Ethnographic *Topoi* in Ancient Ethnography on the Jews**

Another striking aspect of Greco-Roman ethnography on the Jews is the fact that certain important *topoi* of the ancient ethnographic *topoi*-codex are missing in Greek and Latin texts dealing with Jews. It is, I think, once more worth listening to the silence of ethnography. Karl Trüdinger, the author of a still very valuable history of ancient ethnography entitled *Studien zur griechisch-*

---

alità, per difforme e quasi mostruosa stranezza di cose e di eventi; con la descrizione del balsamo, del bitume, del Libano, delle città incinerite fanno unica tonalità parole rubricate come *diversitas, pravitas, odium, superstitio*." Maria Antonietta Giua, "Paesaggio, natura, ambiente, come elementi strutturali nella storiografia di Tacito," in *ANRW* 2.33.4, 2879–2902, at 2895n87: "Attraverso il paesaggio si esprime irrazionalmente la ripugnanza per un popolo che, pur all'intemo del 'nostro' *orbis*, si mostrava assolutamente impermeabile ad influssi esterni."

28   In the central chapters of the excursus (chapters 5–8) Tacitus indeed uses more unusual formulations (ἅπαξ εἰρημένα in Latin literature) than elsewhere in the excursus (cf. the comments of Heinz Heubner and Wolfgang Fauth, *P. Cornelius Tacitus: Die Historien: Kommentar, Buch V* [Heidelberg: Winter, 1982]): 13 in chapter 5, 7 in chapter 6, 6 in chapter 7, 8 in chapter 8. It seems that Tacitus intends to emphasize the strangeness of Jewish customs and Judean geography by making use of exquisite language.

Ethnographical *topoi*	Tacitus's excursus on the Jews
Origin	six *origo*-versions (*Hist.* 5.2–3)
Name	*Idaeos aucto in barbarum cognomento Iudaeos vocitari* (2.1)
Number of population	*sexcenta milia fuisse* (13.3) [fighters in Jerusalem]
Physical appearance	*corpora hominum salubria et ferentia laborum* (6.1)
Nutrition	*sue abstinent* (4.2)
	crebris adhuc ieiuniis/panis Iudaicus (4.3)
	separati epulis (5.2)
Governance, political institutions	*honor sacerdotii firmamentum potentiae* (8.3)
Deities	*unumque numen intellegunt* etc. (5.4)
Sacrifices	*caeso ariete/bos quoque immolatur* (4.2)
Marriage, sexual behavior	*discreti cubilibus/proiectissima ad libidinem*
	gens/alienarum concubitu abstinent/
	inter se nihil inlicitum/circumcidere genitalia (5.2)
	augendae tamen multitudini consulitur (5.3)
Hospitality[29]	*quia apud ipsos fides obstinata, misericordia in promptu, sed adversus omnes alios hostile odium* (5.1)
Funeral customs	*corpora condere quam cremare* (5.3)
National character	*despectissima pars servientium/taeterrimam gentem* (8.2)
	gens superstitioni obnoxia, religionibus adversa (13.1)
Exceptional customs	*novos ritus contrariosque ceteris mortalibus/profana illic omnia quae apud nos sacra, rursum concessa apud illos quae nobis incesta* (4.1)
	cetera instituta sinistra foeda (5.1)
	Iudaeorum, mos absurdus sordidusque (5.5)
Paradoxa	*Libanum … fidumque nivibus / inertes undae superiacta ut solido ferunt* (6.2)
Divination	*evenerant prodigia/pluribus persuasio inerat antiquis sacerdotum litteris contineri, eo ipso tempore fore ut valesceret Oriens profectique Judaea rerum potirentur* (5.13)

---

29   This *topos* does not appear in Trüdinger's list, but Trüdinger mentions its importance elsewhere in his study: "War nicht eine der wichtigsten Fragen für den fahrenden Jonier die nach der Gastfreundschaft eines Volkes?" (Trüdinger, *Studien*, 42, with examples in the footnote).

römischen Ethnographie (Basel 1918), lists at the end of his study twenty ethnographic *topoi* which he believes to be the most important, after having surveyed the development of ancient ethnography from Homer to the early Roman empire.[30] If I may continue to focus on Tacitus for a moment, one notices that fifteen out of twenty *topoi* Trüdinger mentions in his list surface in Tacitus's excursus on the Jews. In other words, Tacitus presents his ethnography on the Jews in very traditional clothing.

To be sure, the *topoi* codex of the ethnographic discourse allows for exceptions, and certain *topoi* are sometimes of greater or lesser interest. But the missing *topoi* in Tacitus's excursus on the Jews are striking: armour and customs of war, clothing, housing, climatic theories, and the somewhat less important *topos* of oaths and alliances. This is not, as some have argued, because Tacitus was not interested in these things:[31] in fact, he deals with the housing and clothing of the Germans,[32] writes about the Britons' hair color,[33] and the battle tactics of the Germans.[34] But when he comes to write about the Jews, he does not give any information about any of this.

This observation remains true even when we expand our perspective and look at all the Greek and Roman texts dealing with the Jews. That climatic theories were not applied with regard to the Jews we have already mentioned. But the other silent *topoi* in Tacitus's digression are also missing in every ancient ethnography on the Jews. Shaye Cohen addressed this phenomenon in an article entitled, "'Those Who Say They Are Jews and Are Not': How Do You Know a Jew in Antiquity When You See One?" Cohen's answer is that you do not: "Not a single ancient author says that Jews are distinctive because of their looks, clothing, speech, names or occupations."[35] Although it is obvious that Jews *could* be recognized because of their religious activity and abstentions, Cohen's general observation is accurate.[36] One may argue that Tacitus, in a short note of his

---

30   Trüdinger, *Studien*, 175.

31   Cf. Wilhelm Capelle, "Zu Tacitus' Archäologien," *Philologus* 84 (1929): 201–208, 349–367, 464–493 (491: "Wie wenig ihn im Grunde Ethnologisches interessiert, geht schon daraus hervor, dass er ... von dem anthropologischen Habitus der Juden, der doch auffällig genug ist [sic!], kein Wort sagt.").

32   Tacitus, *Germ.* 16–17.

33   Tacitus, *Agr.* 11.2.

34   Tacitus, *Germ.* 29.1, 30.2–3 (*Chatti*); 32 (*Tencteri*).

35   Shaye J.D. Cohen, "'Those Who Say They Are Jews and Are Not': How Do You Know a Jew in Antiquity When You See One?" in *Diasporas in Antiquity*, ed. Shaye J.D. Cohen and Ernest S. Frerichs (Atlanta: Scholars, 1993), 1–45, at 3. Reprinted in Shaye J.D. Cohen, *The Beginnings of Jewishness: Boundaries, Varieties, Uncertainties* (Berkeley: University of California Press, 1999), 25–68.

36   For a critique of Cohen's argument, cf. Barclay, *Jews*, 429.

GEOGRAPHY WITHOUT TERRITORY

digression on the Jews, mentions "the bodies of the people:" they are healthy and tenacious, but this description is practically a literal copy of a note on the Africans by Sallust and not an authentic qualification.[37]

Scholarship has often raised the question whether Jews in antiquity were described overall in a positive or in a negative way. Just how problematic this question is has been shown convincingly and on several levels by Erich Gruen in his book *Heritage and Hellenism*.[38] But I do think that ancient ethnography on the Jews differed in very important respects from that on other peoples. So far I have noticed that the common usage of an anthropogeographical understanding of a people's character did not apply to the Jews and that certain other important *topoi* are missing in ancient ethnography on the Jews. I would like to add a third point.

4   Jews and Barbarians

Zvi Yavetz has recently argued that "though Jews were in many respects barbarians like all others, they were in some respects a little more so."[39] Yavetz shows that Greek and Roman authors "dealt with Jews in a manner very similar to the way in which they dealt with other peoples, but that in a few important respects the Jews were described more negatively." We do not have to summarize Yavetz's argument here, but I should like to question not so much the contents of his study as the formulation of his conclusion. Were the Jews really considered barbarians?

---

37   Cf. Tacitus, *Hist.* 5.6.1 *corpora hominum salubria et ferentia laborum* with Sallust, *Jug.* 17.6 *genus hominum salubri corpore, velox, patiens laborum*. Both authors apparently want to emphasize the physical strength (and danger) of the enemy they describe. The Jewish ritual of circumcision, of course, was widely known, but more as a cultic phenomenon than as an obvious physical distinction. On this problem cf. Cohen, "Those Who Say," 12–22. I leave aside a discussion of the *IUDAEA CAPTA* coins issued by Vespasian and Titus showing a mourning Judean at the foot of a palm-tree. The Judean prisoner on these coins does not seem to have any specific features. For a good discussion of these coins cf. Annalina C. Levi, *Barbarians on Roman Imperial Coins and Sculpture* (New York: American Numismatic Society, 1952), 9–12.

38   Erich S. Gruen, *Heritage and Hellenism: The Reinvention of Jewish Tradition* (Berkeley: University of California Press, 1998).

39   Zvi Yavetz, "Judeophobia in Classical Antiquity: A Different Approach," *Journal of Jewish Studies* 44 (1993): 1–22, at 13. Yavetz exemplifies his argument in a comparison of Latin statements on Jews and Dacians: cf. idem, "Latin Authors on Jews and Dacians," *Historia* 47 (1998): 77–107.

94   CHAPTER 5

The Greeks, and to a certain degree the Romans, used the term βάρβαρος or *barbarus* to distinguish themselves from the "other," the non-Greek or the non-Roman. The etymology of the word is not absolutely clear, but most probably βάρβαρος/*barbarus* is an onomatopoetic term for somebody who speaks a foreign, and thus unintelligible, language.[40] Given that this distinction was made on a linguistic basis, the Greek and Latin term was by no means restricted to language usage, but meant the non-Greek or non-Roman in general. It was often used as an aggressive term (as it is in modern languages), but its use is equally often relatively harmless.[41]

A list of all the peoples called "barbarians" in ancient literature would be endless. It seems, though, that the Jews never really entered that list. Tacitus, for example, calls the following peoples *barbari*: the Germans, the Britons, the Spaniards, the Thracians, the Celts, the Armenians, the Parthians, the peoples of the *Pontos* region, the Numidians, and Pannonians, but not the Jews.[42] Tacitus does not seem to be an exception in this respect, either: in fact, there is no direct evidence of any pagan author calling the Jews "barbarians." Cicero once calls Judaism a *barbara superstitio*, but he does not denote the Jews as *barbari*.[43] I am unaware of any Roman reference to them which uses that term. Diodorus speaks about the peoples living around the Dead Sea as βάρβαροι, but does not denote the Jews specifically in doing so.[44]

---

40   Strabo already explained the term κατ' ὀνοματοποιίαν (Strabo 14.2.28). For a good survey of literature on the problematic etymology of βάρβαρος cf. David M. Goldenberg, "Geographia Rabbinica: The Toponym Barbaria," *Journal of Jewish Studies* 50 (1999): 53–73, at 53–54n1.

41   The connotations of the term βάρβαρος and *barbarus* did not always stay the same. For a thorough survey of this development cf. Karl Christ, "Römer und Barbaren in der hohen Kaiserzeit," *Saeculum* 10 (1959): 273–288. Reprinted in idem, *Römische Geschichte und Wissenschaftsgeschichte* (Darmstadt: C.H. Beck, 1983). Vol. 2,28–43.

42   Cf. Gerold Walser, *Rom, das Reich und die fremden Völker in der Geschichtsschreibung der frühen Kaiserzeit: Studien zur Glaubwürdigkeit des Tacitus* (Basel: Helbing & Lichtenhahn, 1951), 73n328.

43   Cicero, *Flacc.* 67. In Pompeius Trogus' *Historiae Philippicae* the Illyrians, Persians, Scythians and others are called *barbari*, but not the Jews (with whom Trogus deals extensively in a digression: Iust. 36.2.1–3.9).

44   Diodorus 2.48.7 (οἱ περιοικοῦντες βάρβαροι); cf. also Diodorus 19.99.3. According to Josephus, *AJ* 2.148, Apollonius Molon called the Jews "the most unproductive of the barbarians" (λέγει δὲ καὶ ἀφυεστάτους εἶναι τῶν βαρβάρων); but how exact is Josephus's citation? Plutarch, in his treatment of the Jewish religion (Plutarch, *Quaest. conv.* 4.5.3), does not call the Jews βάρβαροι, but seems in some way to imagine them as part of the barbarians. The text, though, is not very clear. Similarly open is Plutarch *Quaest. conv.* 4.6.2.

GEOGRAPHY WITHOUT TERRITORY   95

It is interesting that the Jews themselves used the expression βάρβαροι with reference to others.[45] And they frequently employed the same contrast between Greeks and Barbarians that appears regularly in Greek literature.[46] Philo even includes the Jews among the "barbarians" himself.[47] In rabbinic literature the word "barbarian" is found with a similar range of meaning as that which we know from Greek and Roman authors.[48] But as far as external sources are concerned, the Jews, it seems, are always and only Jews ('Ιουδαῖοι, *Iudaei*) and not "barbarians." Although ancient descriptions of the Jews are very similar to those of other peoples, the Jews apparently did not fit into the "dualistic" scheme Greeks/Romans vs. barbarians.[49]

5 Jewish Diaspora: Transcending Geography

Why do classical authors not give us any information about the clothing, language, living conditions, appearance, and occupations of the Jews, some of the most fundamental ethnographic *topoi*? Why do Jews not fit into the utterly common dichotomy Greeks/Romans vs. barbarians? And why are their customs and character not put into relationship with the geographical conditions of Judea as the anthropogeographical tradition did in so many cases?

My suggestion is that all these exceptions are connected to the fact that Jews not only lived in a specific place, namely in Judea or Palestine, but in many places outside their home country, hence in the diaspora. One person cannot

---

45   2 Macc 2:21.

46   Philo, *Mos.* 2.18–20; Josephus, *BJ* 5.17; *AJ* 4.12; *CA* 2.282; cf. Romans 1:14.

47   Philo, *Mos.* 2.27; *Prob.* 73–75. I am very grateful to Erich Gruen, who drew my attention to these passages. Cf. also Josephus, *BJ* 4.45, where, in Josephus's words, Vespasian reminds the Roman soldiers that "incautiousness in war and mad impetuosity are alien to us Romans, who owe all our success to skill and discipline: they are a barbarian fault (βαρβαρικόν) and one to which the Jews mainly owe their defeats."

48   For a discussion of the frequent toponym "Barbaria" in rabbinic literature, cf. Goldenberg, "Geographia Rabbinica."

49   For a different view cf. Yves-Albert Dauge, *Le Barbare: Recherches sur la conception romaine de la barbarie et de la civilisation* (Bruxelles: Revue d'Études latines Latomus, 1981), 476 who argues that the Jews were "l' exemple même" of what the Romans understood by *barbarus*. But Dauge does not take into account the fact that Jews are not called *barbari* in Latin literature. In his long report on possible origins of the Jews Tacitus mentions the argument that *Iudaei* were originally called *Idaei: aucto in barbarum cognomento Iudaeos vocitari* (Tacitus, *Hist.* 5.2.1). But by this Tacitus does not mean that the Jews become barbarians (as Dauge, *Le barbare*, 652 wrongly argues); it is the change of name itself which is "barbarian." Cf. Heubner, *Tacitus* ad loc.: "*in barbarum* eigentlich 'zum Barbarischen hin', d.h. mit dem Ergebnis barbarischer Entstellung."

96   CHAPTER 5

be at two different places at the same time. Similarly, as Jonathan Z. Smith puts it: "Simply as a function of its specific location mapped on a system of spatial and temporal coordinates, any place is, by definition, individual."[50] Both human and place are individual. The dichotomy Greeks/Romans vs. "barbarians" is only possible, if it can occur in a particular place. Jews in Rome, for example, behaved differently from other Romans, but differently in the same, Roman space: therefore they could hardly have been called *barbari*. Diaspora goes beyond this dichotomy.[51]

The religious customs in both Judea and the diaspora were probably more or less the same. Customs like circumcision, abstinence from eating pork, observation of the Sabbath, etc. were all noticed and described by Greek as well by Roman authors. But how to describe elements which were most probably different in Judea and in the diaspora, such as clothing and living conditions? And how to make a link between the geography of Judea and the character of the Jews, when the Jews were not living in one specific place, but in many?

John Barclay's thorough study of the *Jews in the Mediterranean Diaspora* illustrates the variety of ways in which Jews responded to their diverse diasporic conditions in Egypt, Cyrenaica, Syria, Asia, and Rome. Barclay rightly argues that "there were no 'typical' diaspora conditions. Understanding the social milieu of diaspora Jews requires attention to each individual site and period as well as the peculiar circumstances of Jewish individuals and communities in each environment."[52] Ancient ethnography could not do justice to this phenomenon.

Tacitus, in his digression preceding the decisive moments of the Jewish-Roman war, speaks about the customs of the Judeans in a manner similar to that which Cicero and Juvenal use in discussing the Jews in Rome.[53] In fact, Tacitus certainly thought about the Jewish communities in Rome when he wrote his chapters on the customs and institutions of the Judeans. It is not a coincidence, I think, that at the beginning of his chapters on Judean geography,

---

50   Smith, "Father Place," 34.
51   This dichotomy was, of course, not always as polar as it seems, especially in Roman times, cf. Christ, "Römer und Barbaren," 282: "Wenn im 5. und 4. Jahrhundert v. Chr. die Begriffe Hellenen und Barbaren sich gegenseitig abgrenzten, so ist demgegenüber für das Imperium Romanum wesentlich, dass es schon auf römischer Seite zunächst keine parallele Gleichung gab, dass vielmehr die graduelle juristische Abstufung des Reiches im Innern alle ethnischen und kulturellen Merkmale und Wertungen überlagerte." But as far as the Jews are concerned, there was no change: neither Greek nor Roman sources call the Jews "barbarians."
52   Barclay, *Jews*, 399.
53   Cicero, *Flacc.* 66–69; Juvenal, *Sat.* 14.96–106.

GEOGRAPHY WITHOUT TERRITORY

and right after the chapters on Jewish customs, Tacitus does not explicitly say what country he is writing about: *Terra finesque* he simply says, "land and borders." But land and borders of what? In his digression on the Britons, when Tacitus comes to mention the British geography he repeatedly (four times in a row) puts the word *Britannia* at the beginning of the sentence.[54] When Tacitus comes to talk about the bodies of the Judean population (we mentioned this passage before),[55] he simply says *habitus corporum*. But the body of whom? It is quite unimaginable, I think, that Tacitus would have written *habitus corporum Iudaeorum*. Jews in pagan Greek and Roman literature, it seems, have no body.

Greek and Roman ethnography on the Jews, then, differs in quite a few important respects from that on other peoples, because the Jews were not only a *longinqua provincia*, not only a population living far away from, let's say, Rome, but they also, and perhaps more than any other people, constituted an important part of the city's population. *Iudaeus* can mean both a Jew in the diaspora as well as a Jew in Judea.[56] This "double identity," the fact that Jews could be both internal and external strangers, goes beyond any territory.[57] Their geography is one without territory, without a specific clothing or housing conditions.

Greek and Roman authors were well aware that Jews lived dispersed throughout the Mediterranean. Strabo, to mention just one famous example, states (according to Josephus), "This people (sc. the Jews) has already made its way into every city, and it is not easy to find any place in the habitable world which has not received this nation and in which it has made its power

---

54   Tacitus, *Agr.* 10.1, 2, 3; 11.1.

55   Cf. above n. 37.

56   When Tacitus speaks of the *bellum Iudaicum* (Tacitus, *Hist.* 1.10.3) he apparently means the "war in Judea;" by *Iudaicus exercitus* (*Hist.* 2.79) he understands the "army which is stationed in Judea," while *de ... Iudaicis ... pellendis* in a passage in the *Annals* dealing with the expulsion of the Jews from Rome obviously means the Jews in the Roman diaspora (*Ann.* 2.85.4). Cohen, *The Beginnings of Judaism*, 70, argues "that all occurrences of the term *Ioudaios* before the middle or end of the second century B.C.E. should be translated not as 'Jew', a religious term, but as 'Judean', an ethnic-geographic term." Cohen further argues that *Iudaeus* was understood in the same way even as late as in the first century CE (95), but I would doubt whether e.g. Juvenal in his mocking comments on the *Iudaei* (Juvenal, *Sat.* 14) understood them as a geographic community.

57   For the term "internal stranger" cf. Meinhard Schuster, ed., *Die Begegnung mit dem Fremden: Wertungen und Wirkungen in Hochkulturen vom Altertum bis zur Gegenwart* (Stuttgart: Teubner, 1996), 3. There were obviously other diaspora populations in antiquity such as the Egyptian or Phoenician diaspora, and one would have to compare the impact of the Jewish diaspora with that of others. It seems, though, that as far as my argument is concerned the reading of the Jewish diaspora by outsiders differed also from that of other diasporas.

98 CHAPTER 5

felt."[58] Cicero notes that Jews in Rome were ready to help Jews in Asia.[59] At the same time, it seems that the Jewish diaspora as a phenomenon was never fully conceptualized and never became an ethnographic *idion* of the Jews. In the numerous digressions and commentaries on the Jews in Greek and Roman historiography, the Jewish diaspora as such is usually not a topic.[60] We have seen that Tacitus does not clearly distinguish between diaspora Jews and Judeans. The diaspora is rarely a subject and yet it seems to be the ferment which made ancient ethnography on the Jews different from that on other peoples.

Bibliography

Barclay, John M.G., *Jews in the Mediterranean Diaspora: From Alexander to Trajan (323 BCE–117 CE)*. Edinburgh: Edinburgh University Press, 1996.

Bar-Kochva, Bezalel, *Pseudo-Hecataeus, On the Jews: Legitimizing the Jewish Diaspora*. Berkeley: University of California Press, 1996.

Bloch, René, *Antike Vorstellungen vom Judentum. Der Judenexkurs des Tacitus im Rahmen der griechisch-römischen Ethnographie*. Stuttgart: Franz Steiner, 2002.

Capelle, Wilhelm, "Zu Tacitus' Archäologien." *Philologus* 84 (1929): 201–208, 349–367, 464–493.

Fornaro, Pierpaolo, *Flavio Giuseppe, Tacito e l'impero (Bellum Judaicum 6,248–315; Historiae V 13)*. Torino: Giappichelli, 1980.

Christ, Karl, "Römer und Barbaren in der hohen Kaiserzeit." *Saeculum* 10 (1959): 273–288.

Christ, Karl, *Römische Geschichte und Wissenschaftsgeschichte*. Darmstadt: C.H. Beck, 1983.

Cohen, Shaye J.D., Frerichs, Ernest S., eds., *Diasporas in Antiquity*. Atlanta: Scholars, 1993.

Cohen, Shaye J.D., "'Those Who Say They Are Jews and Are Not': How Do You Know a

---

58 Josephus, *AJ* 14.115. Other examples of references for a big dispersion of the Jewish population are: Seneca, *De Superst. apud* Augustine, *Civ.* 6.11; Arrian, *Epict.* 2.9.19–20; Plutarch, *Superst.* 3.166 A and, of course, Josephus, *CA* 2.123, 282.

59 Cicero, *Pro Flacco* 66.

60 This is also true for the Jewish sources; cf. Price, "Jewish Diaspora," 170: "One would be hard pressed to find either a concrete definition among ancient Jewish authors of the borders of the land from which Israel was dispersed—that is, who exactly was a "Diaspora Jew," although many identified themselves as such—or a conventional, universal understanding of the world-wide dispersion. Moreover, evidence for any ancient notion of "Diaspora," factual or theoretical, actually affected behavior is just as sparse. Neither the word διασπορά nor any other general expression was used by Jewish authors writing in Greek."

Jew in Antiquity When You See One?" Pages 1–45 in *Diasporas in Antiquity*. Edited by Shaye J.D. Cohen and Ernest S. Frerichs. Atlanta: Scholars, 1993.

Cohen, Shaye J.D., *The Beginnings of Jewishness: Boundaries, Varieties, Uncertainties*. Berkeley: University of California Press, 1999.

Dauge, Yves-Albert, *Le Barbare: Recherches sur la conception romaine de la barbarie et de la civilisation*. Bruxelles: Revue d'Études latines Latomus, 1981.

Giua, Maria Antonietta, "Paesaggio, natura, ambiente, come elementi strutturali nella storiografia di Tacito." *ANRW* II 33.4 (1991): 2879–2902.

Glacken, Clarence J., *Traces on the Rhodian Shore: Nature and Culture in Western Thought from Ancient Times to the End of the Eighteenth Century*. Berkeley: University of California Press, 1976.

Goldenberg, David M., "Geographia Rabbinica: The Toponym Barbaria." *Journal of Jewish Studies* 50 (1999): 53–73.

Gruen, Erich S., *Heritage and Hellenism: The Reinvention of Jewish Tradition*. Berkeley: University of California Press, 1998.

Günnewig, Beatrix, *Das Bild der Germanen und Britannier: Untersuchungen zur Sichtweise von fremden Völkern in antiker Literatur und moderner wissenschaftlicher Forschung*. Frankfurt am Main: Peter Lang, 1998.

Heubner, Heinz; Fauth, Wolfgang, *P. Cornelius Tacitus: Die Historien: Kommentar, Buch V*. Heidelberg: Winter, 1982.

Levi, Annalina C., *Barbarians on Roman Imperial Coins and Sculpture*. New York: American Numismatic Society, 1952.

Lewy, Hans (Yohanan), "Tacitus on the Origin and Manners of the Jews." *Zion* 8 (1943): 1–23, 61–83 (Hebr.).

Marchesi, Concetto, "Le genti straniere. Germani, Parti e Britanni. Ebrei e Cristiani," in *Tacito*. Milan: Principato, 1942, 2.155–170.

Mauss, Marcel, *Manuel d'éthnographie*. Paris: Payot, 1947.

Müller, Klaus E., *Geschichte der antiken Ethnographie und ethnologischen Theoriebildung*. Vol. 2. Wiesbaden: Franz Steiner, 1980.

Norden, Eduard, "Josephus und Tacitus über Jesus Christus und eine messianische Prophetie." *Neue Jahrbücher für das klassische Altertum* 31 (1913): 636–666.

Norden, Eduard, *Die germanische Urgeschichte in Tacitus' Germania*. Leipzig: Teubner, 1921 (1998).

Norden, Eduard, *Kleine Schriften zum klassischen Altertum*. Edited by Bernhard Kytzler. Berlin: De Gruyter, 1966.

Olshausen, Eckart, "Anthropogeographie." Pages 31–32 in *Mensch und Landschaft in der Antike: Lexikon der Historischen Geographie*. Edited by Holger Sonnabend. Stuttgart: Metzler, 1999.

Price, Jonathan J., "The Jewish Diaspora of the Graeco-Roman Period." *Scripta Classica Israelica* 13 (1994): 169–186.

Rutgers, Leonard V., *The Hidden Heritage of Diaspora Judaism*. Leuven: Peeters 1998.

Schuster, Meinhard, ed., *Die Begegnung mit dem Fremden: Wertungen und Wirkungen in Hochkulturen vom Altertum bis zur Gegenwart*. Stuttgart: Teubner, 1996.

Smith, Jonathan Z., "Father Place." Pages 24–46 in *To Take Place: Toward Theory in Ritual*. The University of Chicago Press, 1987.

Stern, Menahem, *Greek and Latin Authors on Jews and Judaism*, 3 vols. Jerusalem: The Israel Academy of Sciences and Humanities, 1974–1984.

Trüdinger, Karl, *Studien zur Geschichte der griechisch-römischen Ethnographie*. Basel: Birkhäuser, 1918.

Walser, Gerold, *Rom, das Reich und die fremden Volker in der Geschichtsschreibung der frühen Kaiserzeit: Studien zur Glaubwürdigkeit des Tacitus*. Basel: Helbing & Lichtenhahn, 1951.

Yavetz, Zvi, "Judeophobia in Classical Antiquity: A Different Approach." *Journal of Jewish Studies* 44 (1993): 1–22.

Yavetz, Zvi, "Latin Authors on Jews and Dacians." *Historia* 47 (1998): 77–107.

CHAPTER 6

Show and Tell: Myth, Tourism, and Jewish Hellenism

In the biblical narrative of the destruction of Sodom and Gomorrah in chapter 19 of the book of Genesis, one very brief scene stands out as especially dramatic: right before the sinful towns are about to be destroyed, two divine messengers help Lot, Abraham's nephew, and his wife escape. They bring the couple outside of town and tell Lot to hide in the hills. He should not look back or stop anywhere (Gen 19:17). But Lot's wife *did* look back and turned into a pillar of salt (Gen 19:26).[1] The biblical text has nothing more to say on this unexpected metamorphosis. When the first-century CE Jewish-Roman historian Flavius Josephus, in his paraphrase of the Torah in the first book of his *Jewish Antiquities*, arrives at the destruction of Sodom, he adds an interesting piece of information: the pillar of salt is still there; it can still be seen *in situ*:

> But Lot's wife, who during the flight was continually turning round towards the city, curious to observe its fate, notwithstanding God's prohibition of such action, was changed into a pillar of salt: I have seen it, for it even now remains.
>
> ἡ δὲ Λώτου γυνὴ παρὰ τὴν ἀναχώρησιν συνεχῶς εἰς τὴν πόλιν ἀναστρεφομένη καὶ πολυπραγμονοῦσα τὰ περὶ αὐτήν, ἀπηγορευκότος τοῦ θεοῦ τοῦτο μὴ ποιεῖν, εἰς στήλην ἁλῶν μετέβαλεν· ἱστόρησα δ᾽ αὐτήν, ἔτι γὰρ καὶ νῦν διαμένει.[2]

Josephus refers to himself as an eyewitness: he has seen the pillar of salt with his own eyes. Josephus was there. The Greek verb used in this passage is ἱστορέω, "to examine by looking," an expression which is best known from Herodotus's *Histories*. But it is also quite common in Josephus where it usu-

---

1 Gen 19:26: ‏ותהי נציב מלח‎. See ‏ותבט אשתו מאחריו‎ Gen 19:17–26 for the whole episode. In a similar way Orpheus lost his wife Eurydice on the way out of Hades, because he looked back in violation of the prohibition of the ruler of the underworld (Virgil, *Georg.* 4.490–491). Lot's wife remains nameless both in Gen 19 and within Hellenistic Jewish literature. She is one time called Edith in the Midrashim (‏עדית‎: Pirqe R. El. 25; Yalqut Parashat Wayera).
2 Josephus, *AJ* 1.203 (trans. LCL).

© RENÉ BLOCH, 2022 | DOI:10.1163/9789004521896_008

ally means "to see with one's own eyes."[3] In the New Testament the verb shows up once in the context of Paul's journey to Jerusalem, where he intended to see—that is, to get to know—the high priest Caiaphas.[4] What Josephus is saying in this passage from the first book of *AJ* is that he actually was there, at the site where Lot's wife turned into a pillar of salt. He went to see her with his own eyes.[5] Josephus did what Herodotus calls *theōria* (θεωρία), "sightseeing."[6]

Josephus at the site of the pillar of salt is one of a number of passages in Jewish-Hellenistic literature where we hear that people visited the sites of biblical miracles in order to see them or to have them shown by others. The beginning of some kind of 'sight-seeing' at places of biblical miracle and wonder is, I would like to argue, a phenomenon of Jewish Hellenism. In the Hellenistic period some sort of "biblical" travelling developed. Its exact circumstances remain unknown to us, but as we will see, there are striking parallels both to the pagan search for relics and later Christian pilgrimage. Pausanias (1.21.3) reports on his autopsy of the petrified Niobe in similar words to those of Josephus in his visual examination of the salt pillar at Sodom:

> This Niobe I myself saw when I had gone up to Mount Sipylus. When you are near it is a beetling crag, with not the slightest resemblance to a

---

3 LSJ s.v. The verb ἱστορέω is related to the Greek οἶδα (to know in terms of understanding) and the Latin *video*; see Pierre Chantraine, *Dictionnaire étymologique de la langue grecque*, vol. 1 (Paris: Klincksieck, 1968), 779–780. The verb is used 45 times in Josephus. In the same form as used here (ἱστόρησα: "I have seen") and in the same kind of affirming context the verb appears at *AJ* 8.46, where Josephus says that he saw a certain Eleazar exorcise evil spirits from people in the presence of Vespasian.

4 Gal 1:18: ἀνῆλθον εἰς Ἱεροσόλυμα ἱστορῆσαι Κηφᾶν.

5 This becomes even clearer in the parallel passage in his *Jewish War*, to which *AJ* 1.203 explicitly refers: *BJ* 4.483–485, see below pp. 109–110. Wis 10:7 speaks of the pillar of salt as a thereafter ever-present monument reminiscent of Lot's wife, who had not trusted God (ἀπιστούσης ψυχῆς μνημεῖον ἑστηκυῖα στήλη ἁλός). Very similar is the formulation of Philo in *Mos.* 2.56 (see below pp. 105–106). Rabbinic literature will also note that the pillar of salt still remains standing: Pirqe R. El. 25 (where oxen lick continually on the salt, but the column will then regrow anew the next day). For the blessing which one should pronounce next to the pillar of salt according to b. Ber. 54a, see below (pp. 115–116). Egeria mentions in her travelogue that she was only shown the location of the salt pillar–the pillar itself was no longer there (*Egeria Itin.* 12.7 [CCL 175: 53.37–38]: *columna ipsa iam non paret, locus autem ipse tantum ostenditur*). To this day tourists in the region of modern-day Sodom will be shown a salt-rich rock formation identified as Lot's wife; see Michel Rauch, *Reisehandbuch (Dumont) Israel, Palästina, Sinai* (Ostfildern: Dumont, 2015), 203.

6 See Herodotus 1.30 and James Redfield, "Herodotus the Tourist," *CP* 80 (1985): 97–118 (see p. 98 for *theōria*).

SHOW AND TELL: MYTH, TOURISM, AND JEWISH HELLENISM 103

woman, mourning or otherwise; but if you go further away you will think
you see a woman in tears, with head bowed down.[7]

The following presents a closer look at the phenomenon of "tourism" at biblical sites in Judea/Palestine in the Hellenistic and Roman period.[8] I concentrate
on places where the traces of wondrous events of former times were visited
or displayed.[9] As in the case of the metamorphosis of Lot's wife, we will be
dealing with traces of Jewish myths: ashes of cities destroyed by divine fire,
bones of giants, or a tree going back to the beginning of the world. Whether
one would like to define myth with regard to its content (e.g. stories of gods
and heroes from primordial times) or, better, with regard to the function of
these stories (e.g., a narrative of cultural relevance and authority for a group of
people) the biblical stories of the beginnings of the world are myths.[10] Jewish-
Hellenistic authors would not have agreed: they often attacked Greek mythol-

---

7   Pausanias 1.21.3 (trans. LCL): ταύτην τὴν Νιόβην καὶ αὐτὸς εἶδον ἀνελθὼν ἐς τὸν Σίπυλον τὸ
     ὄρος. On Pausanias see John Elsner, "Pausanias: A Greek Pilgrim in the Roman World," *Past
     & Present* 135 (1992): 3–29.
8   "Tourism" is obviously a modern term and cannot be applied to the ancient world with-
     out caution. However, even if what we are looking at concerns the travelling of only a
     few people, and although the economic implications and the forms of this travelling must
     remain open, I believe that the use of the term "tourism" for antiquity is justified. See Karl-
     Wilhelm Weeber, "Reisen," *DNP* 10 (2001): 856–866; Andreas Hartmann, *Zwischen Relikt
     und Reliquie: Objektbezogene Erinnerungspraktiken in antiken Gesellschaften* (Berlin: Ver-
     lag Antike, 2010), 192–246; Redfield, "Herodotus the Tourist," as well as the relevant articles
     in Alex Norman and Carole M. Cusack, eds., *Religion, Pilgrimage, and Tourism*. 2 vols. (Lon-
     don: Routledge, 2015); see also Robert Turcan, *L'Archéologie dans l'Antiquité: Tourisme,
     lucre et découvertes* (Paris: Les Belles-Lettres, 2014).
9   I will leave aside Jewish pilgrimage to the temple in Jerusalem (for rabbinic accounts
     of travel to the treasures of the destroyed temple held at Rome, see below pp. 115–118).
     On Jewish temple pilgrimage see Catherine Hezser, *Jewish Travel in Antiquity* (Tübingen:
     Mohr Siebeck, 2011), 365–388; Allen Kerkeslager, "Jewish Pilgrimage and Jewish Identity in
     Hellenistic and Early Roman Egypt," in *Pilgrimage and Holy Space in Late Antique Egypt*,
     ed. David Frankfurter (Leiden: Brill, 1998), 99–225. On the fluidity between pilgrimage and
     tourism, see, e.g., George Williamson, "Mucianus and a Touch of the Miraculous: Pilgrim-
     age and Tourism in Roman Asia Minor," in *Pilgrimage in Graeco-Roman & Early Christian
     Antiquity: Seeing the Gods*, ed. Jas Elsner and Ian Rutherford (Oxford: Oxford University
     Press, 2007), 219–252. On visits to the graves of the prophets (in some cases difficult to
     trace), see Pieter van der Horst, "Die Prophetengräber im antiken Judentum," in *Interesse
     am Judentum: Die Franz-Delitzsch-Vorlesungen 1989–2008*, ed. J. Cornelis de Vos and Folker
     Siegert (Münster: LIT, 2008), 55–71 (with earlier literature).
10   See René Bloch, *Moses und der Mythos: Die Auseinandersetzung mit der griechischen
     Mythologie bei jüdisch-hellenistischen Autoren* (Leiden: Brill, 2010), 55–70.

ogy and denied any form of Jewish myth.[11] One of our earliest sources of Jewish-Hellenistic literature, the philosopher Aristobulus, warns his readers "not to fall into the mythical … way of thinking about God."[12] However, the reactions to what one might call the "mythical challenge" were by no means uniform, but ranged from outright rejection of anything remotely mythical—whether Jewish or pagan—to endorsement of Greek myth within Jewish myth: Jewish-Hellenistic authors could and did connect biblical motifs with Greek myths and thus devise mythological affinities.[13] As we will see shortly in the case of the myth of Andromeda (often located in Joppa), in some cases Jews and pagans could literally share a myth.

Josephus is not the first Jewish-Hellenistic author to discuss the metamorphosis of Lot's wife and the burnt region of Sodom. Philo of Alexandria, the other great Jewish diaspora author in the Hellenistic period, living two generations before Josephus, repeatedly mentions the drama of Gen 19. On the one hand, Philo—the theologian and philosopher whose main philosophical tool is allegory—is interested in the deeper meaning of the metamorphosis. On the other hand, he, too, already refers to the local interest in the visual remnants at the site. In his tractate *De fuga et inventione* (121–122), Philo reads the story of Lot's wife's flight as an example of someone

> who is led by innate and habitual laziness to pay no attention to his teacher and neglects what lies in front of him, which would enable him to see and hear and use his other faculties for the observation of nature's facts. Instead he twists his neck and turns his face backwards, and his thoughts are all for the dark and hidden side—of life, that is, not of the body and its parts, and so he turns into a pillar and becomes like a deaf and lifeless stone.

> ὃς γὰρ ἂν ὀλιγωρήσας τοῦ διδάσκοντος ὑπὸ ῥαθυμίας ἐμφύτου τε ὁμοῦ καὶ συνήθους τὰ μὲν πρόσω καταλίπῃ, δι᾽ ὧν ὁρᾶν καὶ ἀκούειν καὶ ταῖς ἄλλαις δυνάμεσιν ἔστι χρῆσθαι πρὸς τὴν τῶν φύσεως πραγμάτων ἐπίκρισιν, ἐκτραχηλίσας

---

11 Josephus, *AJ* 1.15–23; *CA* 236–256; Philo, *Opif.* 1–2. The Jewish-Hellenistic critique of mythology stands not least within the realm of pagan philosophical thinking (as Josephus himself maintained: *CA* 2.239).

12 Aristobulus *apud* Eusebius, *Praep. ev.* 8.10.2: μὴ ἐκπίπτειν εἰς τὸ μυθῶδες.

13 Thus was Heracles, the most important hero within Greek mythology, briefly connected with Abraham: Heracles married a granddaughter of Abraham (Josephus, *AJ* 1.240). Not negotiable, however, was the great antiquity of Judaism (note that Abraham did not marry *Heracles's* granddaughter). On this passage and on the general appropriation of Greek mythology within Josephus see Bloch, *Moses und der Mythos*, 191–229.

δ' αὐτὸν εἰς τοὐπίσω περιαγάγῃ, τὰ τυφλὰ τῶν ἐν τῷ βίῳ πραγμάτων μᾶλλον ἢ τῶν τοῦ σώματος μερῶν ἐζηλωκώς, ἀψύχου καὶ κωφῆς λίθου τρόπον στηλιτεύεται.[14]

Philo's allegorical interpretation of the metamorphosis begins with a critique of pagan myth: Moses did not invent a myth (οὐ μυθοπλαστῶν), but indicated a real fact.[15] For Philo, allegory is a particularly helpful tool when dealing with myth, as it allows him to search for a deeper meaning.[16] While the historian Josephus examines the very existence of the pillar of salt at the Dead Sea, Philo brings the story to a higher level: Philo's text is also about investigating and discovering (as a matter of fact, in one place Philo interprets Sodom simply as "blindness"),[17] but Philo himself, unlike Josephus, shows no interest in the visual artifact of the salt pillar. Most likely Philo had not visited the site; Judea/Syria is generally less present in Philo's thought than that of Josephus, who grew up in Jerusalem.[18] But Philo, too, knows that the violent end of Sodom left very real traces and he mentions that these are still shown to passers-by in the area. In his *Life of Moses* (*De vita Mosis*), Philo refers explicitly to memorial displays at the site of Sodom current in his own time:

> Then, as the oracles declare, the lightning poured from heaven and consumed the impious and their cities, and to the present day the memorials to the awful disaster are shown in Syria, ruins and cinders and brimstone and smoke, and the dusky flame still arises as though fire were smoldering within.

> τότ' οὖν, ὡς μηνύει τὰ λόγια, κεραυνοὶ ῥυέντες ἐξ οὐρανοῦ τούς τε ἀσεβεῖς κατέπρησαν καὶ τὰς πόλεις αὐτῶν· καὶ μέχρι τοῦ νῦν μνημεῖα τοῦ συμβεβηκότος ἀλέκτου πάθους δείκνυται κατὰ Συρίαν, ἐρείπια καὶ τέφρα καὶ θεῖον καὶ καπνὸς καὶ ἡ ἔτι ἀναδιδομένη φλὸξ ἀμαυρὰ καθάπερ διασμυχομένου πυρός.[19]

---

14 Philo, *Fug.* 122 (trans. LCL). Philo is here playing with the verb στηλιτεύω, which otherwise means "inscribed on [a] stone;" elsewhere, at *Leg.* 3.213, Philo uses the more classical formulation: λιθουμένη.

15 Philo, *Fug.* 121.

16 On Philo's treatment of Jewish myth, see chapter 8 in this volume.

17 Philo, *Ebr.* 122.

18 Philo speaks only once about a trip to Jerusalem, at *Prov.* 2.64 (= 2.107 in the Armenian version).

19 Philo, *Mos.* 2.56. By "oracles" (τὰ λόγια) Philo means the divine revelation proclaimed by Moses. In *Abr.* 134–141 Philo writes in similar terms of the burnt region of Sodom.

When Philo wrote his tractate on Moses (likely in the late 30s or early 40s of the first century CE), the remains (μνημεῖα) of the destroyed cities at the Dead Sea could still be seen ("to the present day").[20] Long before Eusebius's *Onomastikon* of biblical sites (or its translation into Latin by Jerome) already here we encounter the phrase familiar from Eusebius and Jerome: δείκνυται (*perhibetur*).[21] It is well known that from the fourth century CE onward, in the context of the first Christian pilgrimage trips, biblical sites of Palestine were shown to visitors.[22] But as becomes obvious from passages in Josephus and Philo, people traveled to biblical sites much earlier than this; that is, in the Hellenistic and Roman periods. As we will see, local tour guides led visitors to various locations throughout Judea-Palestine.[23]

Such hints of visual evidence or concrete proof of miraculous events are absent from the Hebrew Bible. There are, of course, numerous examples of etiological explanations of names and places. One may think of the book of Joshua, where a later redactor seems to have added the phrase "until this day" (עד היום הזה) in several places, creating a connection between the Israelites' capture of the land and the topography of his own time. Consider Joshua 7:26: "They raised over him (that is Achan, who was stoned for the crimes he had committed) a great heap of stones that stands to this day."[24] Similarly, Deuteronomy 3:11 refers to the iron bed of the gigantic king Og: "For only Og king of Bashan remained of the remnant of the giants. Indeed his bedstead was an iron bedstead. (Is it not in Rabbah of the people of Ammon?) Nine cubits is its length and four cubits its width, according to the standard cubit."[25] But the biblical text goes no further:

---

20 By μνημεῖα Philo can also mean actual monuments (*Mos.* 2.29: those of Ptolemy II Philadelphus) or textual sources (*Mos.* 1.4: the 'holy books' of Moses). Here he is referring to material traces or evidence. On the dating of *Mos.* see chap. 1 in this volume.

21 In Jerome already in the first entry on Ararat: *On.* (ed. Klostermann, GCS 11.2.22).

22 On this, see Katharina Heyden, *Orientierung: Die westliche Christenheit und das Heilige Land in der Antike* (Munich: Aschendorff, 2014), 183–248.

23 Thus far there has been rather little research on this topic. In his study, Hartmann does point to some relevant passages within Jewish Hellenistic literature, but without discussing them in much detail. See Hartmann, *Zwischen Relikt und Reliquie*, as well as the respective entries in the handbook by Othmar Keel and Max Küchler, eds., *Orte und Landschaften der Bibel: Ein Handbuch und Studien-Reiseführer zum Heiligen Land*. Vol. 2: *Der Süden* (Göttingen: Vandenhoeck & Ruprecht, 1982); for Sodom, see 250–253.

24 Or Josh 4:9, where it is said of the stones which Joshua is said to have erected in the middle of the Jordan: "they are still there to this day" (ויהיו שם עד היום הזה). See Klaus Bieberstein, *Josua—Jordan—Jericho: Archäologie, Geschichte und Theologie der Landnahmeerzählungen Josua 1–6* (Göttingen: Vandenhoeck & Ruprecht, 1995), 418–421.

25 Deut 3:11 (trans. NKJ, slightly adjusted): הנה ערשו ערש ברזל הלה הוא ברבת בני עמון תשע אמות ארכה וארבע אמות רכבה באמת-איש.

we do not hear that traces of key events are currently showcased on location. In the Hebrew Bible, as far as I can tell, there are no explicit references to places of sight-seeing (*theōria*), where miraculous things have happened. Only—or from the perspective of late antiquity: already—in the Hellenistic period does biblical tourism become a topic.

Philo in his passage on Sodom does not say who visited the site or who gave the tour. Our sources generally do not say anything about the structure of this tourism. We can assume, though, that it was knowledge about the biblical myth (whether through a written source or indirectly) that led some to visit sites such as Sodom. It was the biblical myth about the divine punishment of Sodom which made the area a place of sight-seeing. People wanted to see where it all happened. We can further assume that it was locals who guided the visitors on the site. As a matter of fact, the Augustan geographer Strabo, who also reports about the burnt region of Sodom, explicitly refers to the "talk of the locals (ἐγχώριοι)."[26] In the Hellenistic-Roman period, guides (περιηγη- ταί, ἐξηγηταί) who led visitors through the ancient site, and who were already then considered by some more of an annoyance than anything, are well documented.[27] The second century satirist Lucian, in a passage where he pokes fun at the mythical hype of tourists in Greece, writes that "if these fabulous tales should be taken away from Greece, there would be nothing to prevent the guides there from starving to death, as the foreigners would not care to hear the truth, even gratis!"[28] The assumption here clearly is that these guides are getting paid. No site in pre-Christian Judea had become a tourist attraction which could have competed with the famous and popular sites in Greece, Italy, and not least in Egypt. But, as becomes clear from Philo, Strabo, and Josephus, in the Hellenistic-Roman period tourists visited sites in Judea, both before and after the destruction of the temple in 70 CE. One might read the fictional account of Aristeas's trip to Jerusalem in the *Letter of Aristeas* (second century BCE) as early evidence for the presence of guided tourism in Judea: Aristeas allows the high priest Eleazar to show him around Jerusalem and the surrounding region.[29] In any case, one can assume that diaspora Jews visiting the Jerusalem

---

26   Strabo 16.2.44 (in the region of Masada there are to be seen [δεικνύουσι] a burnt and largely destroyed region).

27   See Plutarch, *De Pyth.* 2 (uninspired tour-guides!); Pausanias 5.10.7; Cicero, *Verr.* 2.4.132 (*ii qui hospites ad ea quae visenda sunt solent ducere et unum quidque ostendere*). See Lionel Casson, *Travel in the Ancient World* (Baltimore: The Johns Hopkins University Press, 1974), 261–291.

28   Lucian, *Phil.* 4 (trans. LCL); Casson, *Travel*, 267.

29   Arist. 83–120 (112: παρεξέβημεν δὲ ταῦτα διὰ τὸ καλῶς ἡμῖν τὸν Ἐλεάζαρον ὑποδειχέναι τὰ προ- ειρημένα). See Daniel Barbu, "Aristeas the Tourist," *Bulletin der Schweizerischen Gesellschaft*

temple in the context of pilgrimage also visited the city as tourists.[30] In what follows, however, we will continue to focus only on visits to places that were supposed to have been sites of mythical events.

In the wider context of ancient presentation of myth the spectacular geography of Sodom is just one (Jewish) example among many. In Greco-Roman antiquity, people were looking for traces of mythical stories and for people to show them to them: often this was about artifacts such as weapons once used by heroes or landmarks where parts of a myth took place.[31] A pagan example which is comparable to the burnt city of Sodom with its malodorous river is the equally malodorous spring of water which according to Strabo was shown to visitors in Leuca, south of Tarent, and was understood as evidence (δείχνυται) for the giants who were buried there.[32]

The dramatic story about the end of Sodom was also known to non-Jews. I have already mentioned Strabo's knowledge of this legend. More famous is the passage in Tacitus's *Histories*, written at the beginning of the second century CE:

> Not far from this lake is a plain which, according to report, was once fertile and the site of great cities, but which was later devastated by lightning; and it is said that traces of this disaster still exist there, and that the very ground looks burnt and has lost its fertility. In fact, all the plants there, whether wild or cultivated, turn black, become sterile, and seem to wither into dust, either in leaf or in flower or after they have reached their usual mature form.

> *Haud procul inde campi quos ferunt olim uberes magnisque urbibus habitatos fulminum iactu arsisse; et manere vestigia, terramque ipsam, specie*

---

    für Judaistische Forschung 23 (2014): 5–12. Priests as tour-guides is a theme attested elsewhere also: Strabo 17.1.29; Tacitus, *Ann.* 2.60.

30   Moreover, it is by no means impossible that, in the context of Jewish pilgrimage while the temple was still standing, visitors were already much earlier coming as tourists to biblical site of wonder, something of which we only have record beginning in the Hellenistic-Roman era. Perhaps such visits did not begin in those later times, but rather only then became literary topics.

31   See the comprehensive studies of Friedrich Pfister, *Der Reliquienkult im Altertum* (Berlin: De Gruyter, 1974 [1909–1912]) and Hartmann, *Zwischen Relikt und Reliquie*, along with John Boardman, *The Archaeology of Nostalgia: How the Greeks Re-Created their Mythical Past* (London: Thames & Hudson, 2002).

32   Strabo 6.3.5; see Hartmann, *Zwischen Relikt und Reliquie*, 87. Strabo's description of the region of Sodom (16.2.44) is very similar to this.

SHOW AND TELL: MYTH, TOURISM, AND JEWISH HELLENISM

*torridam, vim frugiferam perdidisse. Nam cuncta sponte edita aut manu
sata, sive herba tenus aut flore seu solidam in speciem adolevere, atra et inania velut in cinerem vanescunt.*[33]

Tacitus had not examined the miraculous geography of Sodom and the Dead
Sea himself. He is relying either on Josephus or on a common source. But from
Tacitus it also becomes clear, although in a less explicit way than in Philo, that
the region of Sodom was an attraction (and hardly only for Jews).

But the most detailed description of the Dead Sea and its morbid environment comes from Josephus's *Jewish War*. In addition to the passage already
cited from Josephus's *Jewish Antiquities* on the metamorphosis of Lot's wife,
Josephus reports the following in the fourth book of the *Jewish War*:

> Adjacent to it (the Dead Sea) is the land of Sodom, in days of old a country
> blest in its produce and in the wealth of its various cities, but now all burnt
> up. It is said that, owing to the impiety of its inhabitants, it was consumed
> by thunderbolts; and in fact vestiges of the divine fire and faint traces of
> five cities are still visible. Still, too, may one see ashes reproduced in the
> fruits, which from their outward appearance would be thought edible, but
> on being plucked with the hand dissolve into smoke and ashes. So far are
> the legends about the land of Sodom borne out by ocular evidence.
>
> γειτνιᾷ δ' ἡ Σοδομῖτις αὐτῇ, πάλαι μὲν εὐδαίμων γῆ καρπῶν τε ἕνεκεν καὶ τῆς
> κατὰ πόλιν περιουσίας, νῦν δὲ κεκαυμένη πᾶσα. φασὶ δ' ὡς δι' ἀσέβειαν οἰκη-
> τόρων κεραυνοῖς καταφλεγῆναι· ἔστι γοῦν ἔτι λείψανα τοῦ θείου πυρός, καὶ
> πέντε μὲν πόλεων ἰδεῖν σκιάς, ἔτι δὲ κἀν τοῖς καρποῖς σποδιὰν ἀναγεννωμένην,
> οἳ χροιὰν μὲν ἔχουσι τῶν ἐδωδίμων ὁμοίαν, δρεψαμένων δὲ χερσὶν εἰς καπνὸν
> διαλύονται καὶ τέφραν. τὰ μὲν δὴ περὶ τὴν Σοδομῖτιν μυθευόμενα τοιαύτην ἔχει
> πίστιν ἀπὸ τῆς ὄψεως.[34]

This is in many respects a remarkable passage. Here too, as in the passage in the
Jewish Antiquities Josephus stresses the fact that the traces of the destruction
are still visible (ἰδεῖν, ὄψις). The Greek equivalent to the Latin *vestigia* in Tacitus
is λείψανα, "remains."[35] The burnt fruits and the ashes are the "relics" (the "left-

---

33   Tacitus, *Hist.* 5.7 (trans. LCL). Although Tacitus may thereafter concede that "famous cities
were once destroyed by fire from heaven," he prefers a geological explanation for the infertility of the area: the evaporation of the Dead Sea had poisoned the earth.

34   Josephus, *BJ* 4.483–485 (trans. adapted from LCL).

35   With the term *vestigia* Tacitus can also refer to the remains and debris of a destroyed city;
see Tacitus, *Hist.* 3.54 on the destroyed city of Cremona (*Cremonae vestigia*).

overs") of Sodom. This is what visitors at the site like Josephus are looking for. In pagan Greek literature λείψανα can mean the corporeal remains of a human being, and Christian authors later use the word in the context of relics of holy men.[36]

Like Tacitus Josephus describes a morbid region.[37] The dead territory of Sodom is scrutinized, as if by a pathologist: some traces, literally "shadows," are immediately visible, but to become aware of the full dimension of the evidence, one must look closely. The fruits in this region may look edible from afar; but once you hold them in your hand, they disintegrate into smoke and ashes: *quod erat demonstrandum*. The ashes and the inedible fruits help Josephus read the story as an authentic one. Josephus does not arrive at this conclusion with ease: he is wavering between what people say and what can be plausibly stated. This combination of rejecting and accepting myth is typical of the intellectual discourse on myth during the Hellenistic-Roman period.[38] Remarkably Josephus, when referring to this legend, uses the Greek verb μυθεύω (τὰ μυθευόμενα), one of several verbs related to the noun μῦθος and which here means "to relate fabulously." To Josephus the story of the divine destruction of Sodom was a "fabulous story"—but then the truth claim of the myth is validated by the visual evidence in his conclusion.[39]

---

36   See LSJ s.v.; *PGL* s.v.; see also David Bouvier, "Reliques héroïques en Grèce archaïque: l'exemple de la lance d'Achille," in *Les objets de la mémoire: Pour une approche comparatiste des reliques et de leur culte*, ed. Philippe Borgeaud and Youri Volokhine (Bern: Peter Lang, 2005), 73–93, at 75.

37   Tacitus leans linguistically upon Virgil's description of the underworld (*Aen.* 6.440–441); see Eduard Norden, *Josephus und Tacitus über Jesus Christus und eine messianische Prophetie* (Leipzig: Teubner, 1913), 27 and René Bloch, *Antike Vorstellungen vom Judentum: Der Judenexkurs des Tacitus im Rahmen der griechisch-römischen Ethnographie* (Stuttgart: Steiner, 2002), 100. Josephus's description also recalls pagan underworld scenes: destroyed cities are only 'shadows' of their former selves.

38   See Paul Veyne, *Les Grecs ont-ils cru à leurs mythes? Essai sur l'imagination constituante* (Paris: Seuil, 1983), 64: "Quand ils détaillent quelque légende, les écrivains de l'époque hellénistique et romaine semblent hésitants; souvent ils refusent à s'exprimer en leur propre nom; "on dit que …", écrivent-ils, ou "d'après le mythe;" mais, dans la phrase suivante, ils seront très affirmatifs sur un autre point de la même légende. Ces alternances d'audace et de réserve ne doivent rien au hasard; elles suivent trois règles: ne pas se prononcer sur le merveilleux et le surnaturel, admettre un fond d'historicité, et se récuser sur les détails."

39   On the use of μυθεύω and other words in the semantic field of μῦθος in Josephus see Bloch, *Moses und der Mythos*, 94–97. Strabo uses the verb regularly when speaking about traces of myths and so also in reference to the odorous springs of Leuca (Strabo 6.3.5; see above p. 108).

SHOW AND TELL: MYTH, TOURISM, AND JEWISH HELLENISM 111

1   Hebron

Very similar to Josephus's report on the destruction of Sodom is his comment on the antiquity of the city of Hebron. The passage is again from the fourth book of the *Jewish War*:

> According to the statements of its inhabitants, Hebron is a town of greater antiquity not only than any other in the country, but even than Memphis in Egypt, being reckoned to be two thousand three hundred years old. They further relate (μυθεύουσι) that it was there that Abraham, the progenitor of the Jews, took up his abode after his migration from Mesopotamia, and from there that his posterity went down into Egypt. Their tombs are shown in this little town to this day, of really fine marble and of exquisite workmanship. At a distance of six furlongs from the town there is also shown a huge terebinth-tree, which is said to have stood there ever since the creation.

> ὡς δέ φασιν οἱ ἐπιχώριοι τὴν Χεβρὼν οὐ μόνον τῶν τῇδε πόλεων ἀλλὰ καὶ τῆς ἐν Αἰγύπτῳ Μέμφεως ἀρχαιοτέραν· δισχίλια γοῦν αὐτῇ καὶ τριακόσια ἔτη συναριθμεῖται. μυθεύουσι δὲ αὐτὴν καὶ οἰκητήριον Ἀβράμου τοῦ Ἰουδαίων προγόνου γεγονέναι μετὰ τὴν ἐκ τῆς Μεσοποταμίας ἀπανάστασιν, τούς τε παῖδας αὐτοῦ λέγουσι καταβῆναι εἰς Αἴγυπτον ἔνθεν· ὧν καὶ τὰ μνημεῖα μέχρι νῦν ἐν τῇδε τῇ πολίχνῃ δείκνυται, πάνυ καλῆς μαρμάρου καὶ φιλοτίμως εἰργασμένα. δείκνυται δ' ἀπὸ σταδίων ἓξ τοῦ ἄστεος τερέβινθος μεγίστη, καὶ φασὶ τὸ δένδρον ἀπὸ τῆς κτίσεως μέχρι νῦν διαμένειν.[40]

As is to be expected from a historian of the time, here too Josephus hesitates to lend credibility to this story: the people of Hebron relate (Josephus uses again the verb μυθεύω) that Abraham lived there after he had left Mesopotamia. But here too the visual evidence is striking: Abraham's and his family's tombs, crafted by experts, are still to be seen (twice the keyword δείκνυται is used). Close by is a tree which is said to have always been there and is older than the city itself.[41] Both the tombs of the patriarchs and matriarchs as well as the old

---

40   Josephus, *BJ* 4.530–533 (trans. LCL). The great antiquity of Hebron is also a theme in Num 13:22.

41   In *AJ* 1.186 Josephus dubs the same tree in the region of Hebron "Ogyges." The name is probably a play on ὠγύγιος ("ancient"), which underscores the tree's great antiquity; see Cristiano Grottanelli, "The Ogygian Oak at Mamre and the Holy Town of Hebron," *Vicino Oriente* 2 (1979): 39–63. On Mamre in Greco-Roman times see Keel and Küchler, *Orte*

112   CHAPTER 6

tree (the terebinth of Mamre) are already mentioned in the Bible.[42] But again, it is only here in Jewish-Hellenistic literature that there is mention of these sites being visited and 'on display.' As in the case of Sodom, we can assume that it was locals who guided visitors at the sites of Hebron. As a matter of fact, the ἐπιχώριοι are explicitly mentioned by Josephus. Here too, though, we cannot say who the visitors were. Jewish tourists were certainly interested in visiting the tombs of Abraham, Sarah, and their descendants.[43] And here too we need to keep in mind the wider cultural context: tombs of pagan heroes constituted an important point of reference in the Greco-Roman memorial landscape.[44] And Hebron had a Jewish pendant on show. The same is true for mythical trees: trees served as local marks of pagan myth. Athena's olive tree on the Acropolis in Athens is just one example among many.[45]

In Josephus's comments on the region surrounding Sodom and on Hebron we have seen just how central the aspects of antiquity, authenticity, and myth are. Let me add another example of mythical footprints to be found in Josephus, this time almost literally: those of the giants.

2   Giants

Giants play an important role in both Jewish and Greco-Roman mythology. In both cases, giants are the monstrous result of transgression and sexual violation. According to Genesis 6:1–4 they were the children of the "sons of God" and

---

      und Landschaften, 2.701–705; for late antiquity, see Katharina Heyden, "Hain der Religionen: Das Abrahamsheiligtum von Mamre als Begegnungsort und locus theologicus," in *Fremdenliebe—Fremdenangst: Zwei akademische Reden zur interreligiösen Begegnung in Spätantike und Gegenwart* (Zurich: Theologischer Verlag, 2016), 17–69.

42   The cave of Machpelah: Gen 23:19; 25:9; 49:29–32; 50:12–13; the terebinth near Hebron: Gen 13:18.

43   On the Mausoleum in Hebron, probably built by Herod, see Ehud Netzer, *The Architecture of Herod, the Great Builder* (Tübingen: Mohr Siebeck, 2006), 228–229. Jack N. Lightstone, *The Commerce of the Sacred: Mediation of the Divine among Jews in the Graeco-Roman Diaspora* (Chico: Scholars Press, 1984), 71 and van der Horst, "Die Prophetengräber im antiken Judentum," 63 both read the building as an indication of Jewish pilgrimage to Hebron in the late first-century BCE.

44   See Pfister, *Der Reliquienkult im Altertum* and Hartmann, *Zwischen Relikt und Reliquie*, 264–286.

45   Herodotus 8.55; see Pfister, *Der Reliquienkult im Altertum*, 361–363. Very similar to Josephus's account of the oak of Mamre as Abraham's dwelling place is an oak mentioned by Plutarch near which Alexander is said to have pitched his tent and which is still on display (Plutarch, *Alex.* 9: ἔτι δὲ καὶ καθ' ἡμᾶς ἐδείκνυτο παλαιὰ παρὰ τὸν Κηφισὸν Ἀλεξάνδρου καλουμένη δρῦς).

SHOW AND TELL: MYTH, TOURISM, AND JEWISH HELLENISM

the "daughters of men" and thus resulted from a union of the divine and human spheres. The giants of Greek myth originate, as do the furies, from the blood of the castrated Uranos. The dramatic passage on the giants in the Hebrew Bible is short and invited a number of sequels.[46] Unlike the Greek myth, the Hebrew Bible has no gigantomachy, no battle between God and the giants. Jewish-Hellenistic authors, however, extended the biblical story. In Josephus Nimrod, mentioned only briefly in the Bible as "the first strong man (גבור) on earth" (Gen 10:8), becomes a real threat to God and the leader of a revolutionary group. Jewish authors created their own, extra-biblical gigantomachy (most conspicuously in the so-called Sibylline Oracles).[47] When Josephus, in his paraphrase of Genesis 6 in the *Jewish Antiquities*, characterizes the giants, he openly states: "in fact the deeds that tradition ascribes to them resemble the audacious exploits told by the Greeks of the giants (*AJ* 1.73)."[48]

What happened to the giants after those events? They did not disappear entirely. The Hebrew Bible knows of descendants of the giants who continued to be a threat to the Israelites,[49] and Josephus follows up on this. Very much as in Greco-Roman culture, for Josephus the giants remain a welcome chiffre for the opposite of a civilized and orderly world. The Bible, again, does not allude to any visual remnants of the giants. Josephus, however, describes traces of giants which can still be seen. According to him the ancient town of Hebron is once more the site of ancient traces. In his paraphrase of the Israelites' conquest of Canaan Josephus writes

> So they (Judah and Simeon) moved their camp to Hebron, took that town and massacred all therein. Howbeit there remained a race of giants, who, by reason of their huge frames and figures in no wise like to the rest of mankind, were an amazing spectacle and a tale of terror to the ear. Their bones are shown to this day, bearing no resemblance to any that have come within men's ken.

---

46 See Bloch, *Moses und der Mythos*, 204–214 and Matthew Goff, Loren T. Stuckenbruck, and Enrico Morano, eds., *Ancient Tales of Giants from Qumran and Turfan* (Tübingen: Mohr Siebeck, 2016).

47 Josephus, *AJ* 1.113–114; Jane L. Lightfoot, *The Sibylline Oracles: with introduction, translation, and commentary on the first and second books* (Oxford: Oxford University Press, 2008), 207–219.

48 Josephus, *AJ* 1.73 (trans. LCL).

49 Giants appear repeatedly in the Tanakh under various names: see Num 13:28, 33; 2 Sam 21:16. See Lothar Perlitt, *Riesen im Alten Testament: Ein literarisches Motiv im Wirkungsfeld des Deutoronomiums* (Göttingen: Vandenhoeck & Ruprecht, 1990).

Ὅθεν μετεστρατοπέδευσαν εἰς Χεβρῶνα καὶ ταύτην ἑλόντες κτείνουσι πάντας· ὑπελείπετο δὲ τῶν γιγάντων ἔτι γένος, οἳ διὰ σωμάτων μεγέθη καὶ μορφὰς οὐδὲν τοῖς ἄλλοις ἀνθρώποις παραπλησίας παράδοξον ἦσαν θέαμα καὶ δεινὸν ἄκουσμα. δείκνυται δὲ καὶ νῦν ἔτι τούτων ὀστᾶ μηδὲν τοῖς ὑπὸ πύστιν ἐρχομένοις ἐοικότα.[50]

Thus, when Josephus wrote his *Jewish Antiquities* towards the end of the first century CE, bones of giants were on display in Hebron (δείκνυται).[51] Next to the old terebinth and the beautiful tombs of the biblical ancestors visitors there could enjoy the very special spectacle of the giants: "an unbelievable show" (παράδοξον θέαμα). The local tourist guides at Hebron clearly knew how to impress their visitors. And they were not alone with this: numerous sources from the Greco-Roman period report discoveries of giant bones that were subsequently exhibited.[52] The Roman biographer Suetonius mentions that Augustus in his villa on the island of Capri collected "objects noteworthy for their antiquity and rarity;" for example, at Capri "the monstrous bones of huge sea monsters and wild beasts, called the 'bones of the giants,' and the weapons of the heroes."[53] Greeks, Romans, and Jews had their showcases where objects from mythical times could be visited, seen, and, one can only assume, also touched: in Hebron or on the island of Capri. And an author like Josephus, who composed his entire oeuvre in Rome, was aware that this "show and tell" was very much in vogue in Rome and elsewhere. Showing bones of biblical giants or ashes from the destroyed city of Sodom provided Jews with vivid evidence of biblical narratives and helped make them tangible. But, at least as significantly, it also placed them on equal footing with Greeks and Romans who pursued a similar strategy of making mythical objects and events real and visible. As did Philo, so too Josephus denies any form of Jewish myth. But 'archaeological' traces of primordial times in Judaism are important to him and he does not shy away from presenting them very much like Greco-Roman authors discuss traces of pagan myth.

---

50   Josephus, *AJ* 5.125 (trans. LCL). Josephus also describes these giants at *AJ* 3.305.

51   Christopher T. Begg, *Flavius Josephus, Judean Antiquities 5–7: Translation & Commentary* (Leiden: Brill, 2005), translates this quite appropriately: "even now their bones ... are displayed."

52   Pfister, *Der Reliquienkult im Altertum*, 425–426. At the beginning of the third century CE, Philostratus provides an entire list of such 'giant sites': *Her.* 8.14–17. On the search for and display of bones, see Peter Mayor, *The First Fossil Hunters: Paleontology in Greek and Roman Times* (Princeton: Princeton University Press, 2000) and Boardman, *The Archaeology of Nostalgia*, 33–34.

53   Suetonius, *Aug.* 72: *immanium beluarum ferarumque membra praegrandia, quae dicuntur gigantum ossa, et arma heroum* (trans. LCL).

SHOW AND TELL: MYTH, TOURISM, AND JEWISH HELLENISM   115

Josephus's manner of negotiating myth mirrors the cultural sensibilities of the time. But there is more to it. As Susan Stewart reminds us in her insightful reading of the meanings of souvenirs, a souvenir "may be seen as emblematic of the nostalgia that all narrative reveals—the longing for its place of origin .... The souvenir seeks distance (the exotic in time and space), but it does so in order to transform and collapse distance into proximity to, or approximation with, the self."[54] While giants, pillars of salt, and weapons of heroes are not exactly souvenirs, here, too, distance is collapsed into proximity. The mythical past is brought closer through visual representations. But whereas the raison d'être of the souvenir lies, finally, in its removal from its original location, in the case of the pillar of salt or bones of giants, 'being there' is the defining experience ensuring authenticity. Seeing the sights in their original context simultaneously confirms the completely wondrous quality of the mythical events while collapsing that very difference and transporting the mythical to real time. The phrase "still today"—already present in the Hebrew Bible (עד היום הזה) and amplified in Jewish Hellenistic literature (καὶ νῦν ἔτι)—suggest a seamless continuity between myth and living reality. As with late antique Christian pilgrimage, biblical report could be verified by on-site visit.[55]

3   Rabbinic *Mirabilia* and Journeys to Rome

Neither Josephus nor any other Jewish-Hellenistic author reporting on such visual proofs of biblical narratives mentions any ritual performance. There is no indication of sacrifice or prayer performed at the sites where something miraculous took place. According to the rabbis, on the other hand, one should say a blessing at such sites. For they, too, at least in theory, knew of the actual locations of some biblical miracles. The Mishna states:[56]

---

54   Susan Stewart, *On Longing: Narratives of the Miniature, the Gigantic, the Souvenir, the Collection* (Durham, NC: Duke University Press, 1993 [1984]), xii, 135.

55   Raymond van Dam, "Relics," in *Late Antiquity: A Guide to the Postclassical World*, ed. G.W. Bowersock, Peter Brown, and Oleg Grabar (Cambridge: Harvard University Press, 1999), 667–668: "Actually seeing the sacred topography provided historical verification for the biblical narratives and effectively transformed distant events into compellingly present realities. The inverse of pilgrimages was the circulation of relics. One particularly attractive relic was dirt from Palestine, since it allowed people to recreate, literally, the Holy Land in their homeland."

56   m. Ber. 9:1 (trans. Soncino). This is followed by a prescription for the blessing for places at which idolatry had been eradicated.

116   CHAPTER 6

> If one sees a place where miracles have been wrought for Israel, he should
> say: Blessed be he who wrought miracles for our ancestors in this place.

הרואה מקום שנעשו בו נסים לישראל אומר ברוך שעשה נסים לאבותינו במקום הזה.

And the Gemara of the Babylonian Talmud, commenting on this Mishna, gives
a list of such places:[57]

> Our Rabbis taught: If one sees the place of the crossing of the Red Sea, or
> the fords of the Jordan, ... or the stone on which Moses sat when Joshua
> fought with Amalek, or (the pillar of salt of) Lot's wife, or the wall of Jeri-
> cho which sank into the ground—for all of these he should give thanks-
> giving and praise to the Almighty.

תנו רבנן הרואה מעברות הים ומעברות הירדן ... ואבן שישב עליה משה בשעה שעשה
יהושע מלחמה בעמלק ואשתו של לוט וחומת יריחו שנבלעה במקומה על כולן צריך
שיתן הודאה ושבח לפני המקום.

The veracity of these places is not questioned: God is omnipresent and he performed miracles at particular places. Appropriately, a form of the divine name
is used here which means "place" or "site" (מקום). Seeing these sites does not
trigger some procedure of verification, but a blessing. In both the Mishna and
Gemara there is reference to the process of seeing (הרואה: "one who sees"), but
this serves the purpose of establishing ritual rather than verifying knowledge.
In the case of Lot's wife the Gemara does not even mention that she was transformed into mineral. When the rabbis see the pillar of salt, they recognize it
as the site of a biblical miracle and say a prayer. When Josephus sees it, he
gains confidence in the veracity of the myth. In this respect Josephus is closer
to the pagan way of dealing with mythical vestiges than he is to the rabbinic
approach. On the other hand, the rabbinic list of biblical places of wonder certainly has parallels in the pagan reception of myth: thus, the stone on which
Moses sat is very much comparable to the stone on which the Greek hero Telamon sat (when he watched how his sons Ajax and Teucer sailed off to Troy)
and which, according to Pausanias, was showcased in Salamis.[58] Moreover, we
cannot exclude that the Talmudic list of sites does not only refer to incidental

---

57   m. Ber. 54a (trans. Soncino). This passage concludes with an explanation of the individual
      sites (54a–b).

58   Pausanias 1.35.3.

SHOW AND TELL: MYTH, TOURISM, AND JEWISH HELLENISM 117

visits, but also planned ones. This would bring the Talmudic passage closer to contemporary sources on Christian pilgrimage.

There are more explicit traces of rabbinic sightseeing with regard to the diaspora: several rabbinic texts mention that rabbis went to Rome and saw there the remains of the temple of Jerusalem.[59] In the halakhic midrash *Sifre Zuta* Rabbi Simeon is cited for having seen the Menorah in Rome: "When I went to Rome and saw there the Menorah" (כשהלכתי לרומי וראיתי שם את המנורה), all the lamps were directed toward the center lamp."[60] Similarly, the Tosefta mentions that Rabbi Eleazar ben Rabbi Jose has seen the temple curtain in Rome (אני ראיתיה ברומי; "I saw it in Rome").[61] The historical value of these sources (late antique or even early medieval) is difficult to evaluate. It is certainly very possible that rabbis who came to Rome showed an interest in the relics of the temple of Jerusalem or even went there for the purpose of seeing them. Parts of the temple treasure could be seen in Rome (and not only on the Arch of Titus). Josephus reports that in the newly built temple of Pax, the goddess of Peace, the golden vessels and instruments of the Jewish temple were put on display. And the Torah scroll, "the law," as well as the purple curtains were stored, at Vespasian's insistence, in his palace.[62] Exactly how and when such rabbinic visits to Rome took place (the temple of Peace burnt down in 192 CE)[63] is impossible to say. But the passage in Josephus on how "Jerusalem" was put on display in Rome is also relevant for the wider context of tourism in the Hellenistic-Roman period: according to Josephus the newly built *Templum Pacis* was something like a museum. Vespasian, Josephus writes, put on display in the temple ancient paintings as well as sculptures from around the world: "Indeed, into that shrine

---

59 See Steven Fine, "'When I went to Rome ... There I saw the Menorah ...': The Jerusalem Temple Implements during the Second Century C.E.," in *Art, History, and the Historiography of Judaism in Roman Antiquity* (Leiden: Brill, 2014), 63–86; Ra'anan Boustan, "The Spoils of the Jerusalem Temple at Rome and Constantinople: Jewish Counter-Geography in a Christianizing Empire," in *Antiquity in Antiquity: Jewish and Christians Pasts in the Greco-Roman World*, ed. Gregg Gardner and Kevin Osterloh (Tübingen: Mohr Siebeck, 2008), 327–372; David Noy, "Rabbi Aqiba Comes to Rome: A Jewish Pilgrimage in Reverse?," in *Pilgrimage in Graeco-Roman and Early Christian Antiquity*, eds. Elsner and Rutherford, 373–385.

60 *Sifre Zuta, be-haalotekha* 8.2 (Horovitz). On the difficulty of dating this fragmentary midrash, see Günter Stemberger, *Einleitung in Talmud und Midrasch* (Munich: C.H. Beck, 2011), 298–299.

61 t. Kippurim 2:16 (Lieberman), as also at b. Joma 57a. According to b. Šabb. 63b and b. Sukkah 5a Rabbi Eleazar also saw the breastplate of the high priest in Rome. See further passages listed in Fine, "Jerusalem Temple Implements," 64–66.

62 Josephus, *BJ* 7.158–162.

63 Cassius Dio 73.24.1–2. See Noy, "Rabbi Aqiba Comes to Rome," 383–384.

118   CHAPTER 6

were accumulated and stored all objects for the sight of which (δι' ὧν τὴν θέαν) men had once wandered over the whole world, eager to see them severally while they lay in various countries."[64]

4   Noah's Ark

There is no doubt that the presentation of relics in situ—as was the case in Sodom and Hebron—made an especially authentic impression. But it is also true that visual presentations of the mythical past gain additional importance when the objects are shown abroad and by others; that is when, so to speak, a local exhibition becomes a success abroad. This is the case with another example of a mythical footprint in Josephus: the remains of Noah's ark. Twice in his *Jewish Antiquities* (in the first and the last book) Josephus refers to the place where "remains" of the ark were still available for viewing in his time. They can be observed on location in Armenia.[65] The Hebrew Bible knows of a similar location: according to Genesis 8:4, "the ark came to rest on the mountain of Ararat." But again, in the biblical version this place is not specifically pointed out or said to be visited. Josephus, on the other hand, refers to a non-Jewish author, the Babylonian priest Berossus, according to whom the remains (τὰ λείψανα) of Noah's ark are still displayed in Armenia. There the locals, at least according to Josephus, show them (ἐπιδείκνυται) to "those who want to see them" (τοῖς ἰδεῖν βουλομένοις).[66] That another people, the Armenians, showcase the remains of Noah's ark and that a foreign author wrote about this makes this biblical myth all the more important. Herodotus reports in the fourth book of his *Histories* that in Scythia the locals "show a footprint of Heracles by the river Tyras stamped on the rock, like the mark of a man's foot, but two cubits in length."[67] The Scythians, not a Greek people, were thus able to claim that Heracles, the greatest hero of Greek myth, had passed by their territory. And for Herodotus the footprint proved that Greek culture had literally touched ground also in Scythia.[68] Josephus's report on Noah's footprint in Armenia follows a similar line.

---

64   Josephus, *BJ* 7.160 (trans. LCL).

65   Josephus, *AJ* 1.93; 20.25.

66   Josephus, *AJ* 20.25. According to the parallel passage in *AJ* 1.93, visitors also chipped pieces of bitumen from the ark (which Noah had used in its construction) and carried them off to be used as talismans.

67   Herodotus 4.82 (trans. LCL).

68   Sarolta A. Takács, "Divine and Human Feet: Records of Pilgrims Honouring Isis," in *Pilgrimage in Graeco-Roman and Early Christian Antiquity*, ed. Elsner and Rutherford, 353–369 (358).

5 Andromeda

Jewish myth could thus be tracked abroad. But pagan myth from abroad also left its mark in Palestine. An important figure of Greek myth, Andromeda, left her footprints at the harbor of Joppa, modern Jaffa. Our source for this is, once more, Flavius Josephus:

> Nature has not provided Joppa with a port. It terminates in a rugged shore, which runs for nearly its whole length in a straight line, but is slightly curved at its two extremities in crescent fashion; these horns consist of steep cliffs and reefs jutting far out into the deep; here are still shown the impressions of Andromeda's chains, to attest the antiquity of that legend.

> Ἀλιμένου δ' οὔσης φύσει τῆς Ἰόππης, αἰγιαλῷ γὰρ ἐπιλήγει τραχεῖ καὶ τὸ μὲν ἄλλο πᾶν ὀρθίῳ, βραχὺ δὲ συννεύοντι κατὰ τὰς κεραίας ἑκατέρωθεν· αἱ δέ εἰσιν κρημνοὶ βαθεῖς καὶ προύχουσαι σπιλάδες εἰς τὸ πέλαγος, ἔνθα καὶ τῶν Ἀνδρο-μέδας δεσμῶν ἔτι δεικνύμενοι τύποι πιστοῦνται τὴν ἀρχαιότητα τοῦ μύθου.[69]

The context of this geographic vignette is the capture of Joppa by the Romans during the Jewish-Roman war. Josephus briefly describes the port of Joppa with its steep cliffs. It was there, Josephus reports, that Andromeda was once chained to the rock. And these chains are still being shown. Josephus's language is strikingly similar to his mention of the traces of Sodom and of the biblical giants. In the case of Sodom, it was seeing the ashes and the smoke that made the myth credible. So here, too: locating the remnants of the chains of Andromeda in one of the rocks of Jaffa gives this myth—μῦθος—credibility (πιστοῦνται; in the case of Sodom Josephus used the word πίστις).[70]

Andromeda was the daughter of the Ethiopian king Cepheus and Cassiopeia. Cassiopeia was competing with the beauty of the sea-nymphs (the Nereids). They complained to Poseidon, who then sent a flood over the land. An oracle revealed that only the sacrifice of the royal daughter, Andromeda, would prevent the land's destruction. This is why she was chained to a rock and exposed to a monster; this occurred, according to one version of the myth, probably the older one, in Ethiopia. According to another, more common version, one also widely held in pagan sources, this happened in Joppa. There was probably also an etymological pun involved: the city of Joppa could eas-

---

69   Josephus, *BJ* 3.419–420 (trans. LCL).
70   See Bloch, *Moses und der Mythos*, 89–91.

120 CHAPTER 6

ily be recognized in Eth-*iopi*-a, the land of Andromeda's origins.[71] In the end it was Perseus who, with his flying sandals, flew by the rock, slew the monster, and freed the princess.[72] And this not without profit: he immediately took Andromeda as his wife. The myth of Andromeda and Perseus was important (their son Perses became the ancestor of the Persians),[73] well known in antiquity and a popular scene in Greek and Roman art.[74] And the stage of the crucial scene of the myth was, at least according to some, the harbor of Joppa in Palestine. Josephus underlines the importance of the myth by mentioning it—in spite of his severe critique of pagan myth in other contexts. The impressions of Andromeda's chains and the fact that they are still pointed out to visitors attest to the antiquity of that myth. Josephus does not explain the myth of Andromeda, he assumes that his readers (both Jews and non-Jews) knew it.

Next to Josephus a number of pagan authors also report on the myth of Andromeda at Joppa. And, as in the case of Josephus, so also in the other sources it is not totally clear who owns this Greek myth which is set in Palestine. Strabo connects the site where Andromeda was chained to Jerusalem:

> Then one comes to Joppa, where the seaboard from Egypt, though at first stretching towards the east, makes a significant bend towards the north. Here it was, according to certain writers of myths, that Andromeda was exposed to the sea-monster; for the place is situated at a rather high elevation—so high, it is said, that Jerusalem, the metropolis of the Jews, is visible from it; and indeed the Jews have used this place as a seaport when they have gone down as far as the sea.

> Εἶτα Ἰόπη, καθ᾽ ἣν ἡ ἀπὸ τῆς Αἰγύπτου παραλία σημειωδῶς ἐπὶ τὴν ἄρκτον κάμπτεται, πρότερον ἐπὶ τὴν ἕω τεταμένη. ἐνταῦθα δὲ μυθεύουσί τινες τὴν Ἀνδρομέδαν ἐκτεθῆναι τῷ κήτει· ἐν ὕψει γάρ ἐστιν ἱκανῶς τὸ χωρίον, ὥστ᾽ ἀφο-

---

71   See Stephan of Byzantium, s.v. "Iope" (ed. Meineke, 333). See also Strabo 1.35.

72   Ruth E. Harder, "Andromeda," *BNP* 1.692. On the myth of Andromeda in Joppa, see Michael Avi-Yonah, "Perseus and Andromeda in Japho," *Yediot* 31 (1967): 213–210 (Hebr.); Heinrich Heubner and Wolfgang Fauth, *P. Cornelius Tacitus: Die Historien: Kommentar. Vol. V* (Heidelberg: C. Winter, 1982), 25–26 (there also the Ancient Near Eastern parallels to the Andromeda myth); Keel and Küchler, *Orte und Landschaften der Bibel* 2.13–14; Paul B. Harvey, Jr., "The Death of Mythology: The Case of Joppa," *JECS* 2 (1994): 1–14; Ted Kaizer, "Interpretations of the Myth of Andromeda at Iope," *Syria* 88 (2011): 323–339.

73   Herodotus 7.61.

74   See K. Schauenburg, "Andromeda," *LIMC* 1.1, 774–790.

ρᾶσθαί φασιν ἀπ' αὐτοῦ τὰ Ἱεροσόλυμα, τὴν τῶν Ἰουδαίων μητρόπολιν· καὶ δὴ καὶ ἐπινείῳ τούτῳ κέχρηνται καταβάντες μέχρι θαλάττης οἱ Ἰουδαῖοι·[75]

Similarly, Pausanias refers to red water at the harbor of Joppa "in the land of the Hebrews" (Ἐβραίων ἡ γῆ) and the talk of the people saying that the water was red from the blood which Perseus washed off after he had killed the sea-monster.[76] A Greek myth was thus displayed in Jewish territory (and maybe it was Jewish locals who displayed it).[77]

At Joppa tourists were not only shown the traces of Andromeda's chains but also—according to Pomponius Mela (writing in the first century CE)—the "huge bones" of that monster which Perseus finally managed to kill.[78] But other bones of the very same sea-monster (or so it was claimed) were put on display in Rome! Pliny the Elder, a contemporary of Josephus, reports the following:

> The skeleton of the monster to which Andromeda in the story was exposed was brought by Marcus Scaurus from the town of Joppa in Judaea and shown at Rome among the rest of the marvels during his aedileship [58 BCE]; it was 40 feet long, the height of the ribs exceeding the elephants of India, and the spine 1 foot 6 inches thick.

> *beluae cui dicebatur exposita fuisse Andromeda ossa Romae apportata ex oppido Iudaeae Ioppe ostendit inter reliqua miracula in aedilitate sua M. Scaurus longitudine pedum xl, altitudine costarum Indicos elephantos excedente, spinae crassitudine sesquipedali.*[79]

Thus the Romans shipped vestiges of the Andromeda myth back again to "pagan" territory. The same myth—Andromeda chained to the rocks of Joppa—could be shown in Rome as well as in Palestine. The Romans recovered what they thought were the bones of the monster killed by Perseus and brought them home. But other traces of the myth remained in situ and were shown there. In both places, in Rome as well as in Judea, the material remains of the mythical episode could be used to "transform distant events into com-

---

75 Strabo 16.2.28 (trans. LCL, adapted). See Menahem Stern, *Greek and Latin Authors on Jews and Judaism*. 3 vols. (Jerusalem: Israel Academy of Sciences and Humanities, 1974), ad loc.

76 Pausanias 4.35.9.

77 On the Jewish population of Joppa over time, see Harvey, *The Death of Mythology*, 9–11.

78 Mela 1.64: *marinae beluae ossa immania ostentant.* Pomponius Mela also referred to vestiges of a cult of Cepheus and his brother Phineas at Joppa; see also Pliny, *Nat.* 5.69.

79 Pliny, *Nat.* 9.5.11 (trans. LCL).

pellingly present" reality.[80] Just how similar the needs for such visual markers were in Rome and Palestine can be seen in their mutual use of this very same myth.

But the myth of Andromeda in Joppa does not end there. Three hundred years after Josephus Jerome reports in a very similar way about the rock of Andromeda at Joppa, which he says is still on display "until today" (*usque hodie saxa monstrantur*).[81] The context in Jerome is not the Jewish-Roman war, but the biblical book of Jonah, according to which Jonah sailed off from Japho (Jon 1:3).[82] It seems likely that already in Hellenistic-Roman times locals combined the Andromeda myth with the Jonah story, with which it shares structural and linguistic parallels.[83] Both myths remained present far beyond the bounds of late antiquity: the first *Baedeker-Reiseführer* to Palestine and Syria from 1875 refers, after a long forward, on its first pages to the vestiges of Andromeda before Jappo (the western point-of-arrival for modern tourists):

> Not only till the end of Roman times, but until well into the late 16th century, the place where Andromeda was tied to the harbor boulders, or at least the chains and the iron rings recalling the old tale, were shown. Similarly, the bone remains of a monstrous fish were displayed for a long time.[84]

Of course, Andromeda-tourism in Joppa by no means came to an end in the sixteenth century. Indeed, the Andromeda myth is still visible today: a rock at Jaffa

---

80 van Dam, "Relics," 667.

81 Jerome, *In Ion.* 1.3b (*Fontes Christiani* 60.104); *Ep.* 108.8.2 (CSEL 55.314); see Karsten C. Ronnenberg, *Mythos bei Hieronymus: Zur christlichen Transformation paganer Erzählungen in der Spätantike* (Stuttgart: Franz Steiner, 2015), 102–109.

82 That the Jonah story could have played a role in the Jewish-Hellenistic reception of the Andromeda myth has been suspected, probably rightly by Ronnenberg, *Mythos bei Hieronymus*, 106; Harvey, *Death of Mythology*, 6. See also Martin Mulzer, "Andromeda und Jona in Jafo," *ZDPV* 122 (2006): 46–60.

83 Mulzer, "Andromeda und Jona in Jafo," 49. Jonah was also confronted with something gigantic: the "great fish," by which Jonah was swallowed (Jon 2:1), is translated in the Septuagint with the same word that was used to designate the (sea-) creature in the Andromeda myth: κῆτος (Euripides fr. 115 Nauck). See Harvey, *Death of Mythology*, 6; Ronnenberg, *Mythos bei Hieronymus*, 106.

84 Karl Baedeker, ed., *Palästina und Syrien: Handbuch für Reisende* (Leipzig: Baedeker, 1875), 113: "Nicht nur bis ans Ende der römischen Zeit, sondern noch bis spät ins 16. Jahrhundert hinein wurde die Stelle gezeigt, wo Andromeda an den Hafenfelsen gebunden war, oder wenigstens Ketten und eiserne Ringe, die an die alte Sage erinnerten. Ebenso wurden lange noch Knochenüberreste eines ungeheuren Fisches daselbst vorgewiesen." The author of this volume was the Orientalist Albert Socin.

SHOW AND TELL: MYTH, TOURISM, AND JEWISH HELLENISM 123

port is known as the Andromeda Rock (סלע אנדרומדה). Local guides (the "*exege-tai*" of today) as well as Israeli websites report about the myth of Andromeda in Israel:

> Now an integrated component in the sprawling Tel Aviv–Jaffa complex, Jaffa has a long and colorful history, dating from biblical times. This is the port, the Bible tells us, where King Solomon's ally, the Phoenician King Hiram of Tyre, landed cedars of Lebanon for the construction of Solomon's Temple. From here Jonah embarked for his adventure with the whale. The Greeks were here too, and they fostered the legend that a poor maiden named Andromeda, chained to a rock and on the verge of being sacrificed to a sea monster, was rescued by Perseus on his winged white horse. Today, visitors are shown this rock, a tourist attraction since ancient times.[85]

On *Trip Advisor* some of today's tourists are rather disappointed about what they see at the site.[86] Someone writes:

> Unless you have someone (like a guide) to tell you the myth, then don't go out of your way to see a small rock ... well a few of them, but nothing special.

Other tourists proudly report what they have learned from their guides and even try to contribute something to the ongoing research:

> A rock off the old port of Jaffa has been known as 'Andromeda's Rock' since antiquity, identified with the myth of Andromeda and the Sea Monster by Pausanias, Strabo, and Josephus. Modern guides point to the small rock in the picture; I suspect that the ancient writers were referring to a larger rock that, though still visible, has been incorporated in modern

---

85   "Things to See in Tel Aviv": https://www.frommers.com/destinations/tel-aviv/attractions/ overview. The last sentence is remindful of Josephus's comment "here are still shown ..." (*BJ* 3.420). The perpetuation of Andromeda-tourism at Joppa is illustrated by a recent Modern Hebrew translation of Josephus's *Jewish War*, where *BJ* 3.420 is translated: ... במקום זה נראים עד היום. And in the footnote one finds: (את הסלע) אותו מראים היום ועד. See Lisa Ullman and Israel Shatzman, eds., *Yosef Ben Matityahu/[Titus] Flavius Josephus: History of the Jewish War against the Romans* (Jerusalem: Carmel, 2010).

86   The following are taken from the reviews section on "Andromeda's Rock" on *Trip Advisor*: http://www.tripadvisor.co.uk/Attraction_Review-g293984-d558632-Reviews-Andromeda _s_Rock-Tel_Aviv_District.html.

times into the concrete sea wall. Either way, the references are another point to reflect upon as one gazes out on the very ancient harbor of Old Jaffa.

Today an Israeli flag can often be seen on top of the rock of Andromeda. This in a way continues the search for links between Judaism and Greek culture known from Jewish-Hellenistic authors such as Josephus. Greek mythology is still an important topic in popular culture and widely considered an important pillar of the western heritage. And to have a Greek myth on display in one's own territory, as Tel Aviv has today, is still a powerful symbol on the map of western civilization.[87]

In the ancient reception of the Andromeda myth, Jewish and pagan interests overlapped: Josephus does not hesitate to mention the persistence of the myth at Joppa, Pausanias localizes it "in the land of the Hebrews," and traces of it were displayed both in Palestine and in Rome. In a very similar way Jewish and non-Jewish authors report on the remains of the region of Sodom. Biblical sites were used for tourism very much like sites of pagan myth (even if the sources on the latter are certainly much more numerous). Whether bones, ashes or salt formations, mythical footprints constituted contact zones between Jews and Greeks where past and present, the real and the imagined, history and myth, convened.

The texts here examined seem to suggest nothing more than informal and occasional visits rather than a prescribed itinerary. In this respect these sources are quite different from later Christian pilgrimage reports.[88] At the same time, what we can observe from them is neither simply a continuation of earlier Jewish temple pilgrimage. Rather, I suggest that in Hellenistic-Roman times a type of tourism developed which could also include Jewish sites. Jews went on sightseeing trips just as non-Jews did: in search of the truth, or maybe, rather, following Lucian, just in search of a good story.

---

87 Harvey, *The Death of Mythology* (12, 14) has the myth die in late antiquity: "'Thus did Andromeda die at Joppa.' ... Never again would Perseus or Andromeda exist as vivid figures the sites of whose exploits could be seen at first hand by Mediterranean travelers."

88 Nevertheless, this form of tourism attached to biblical sites may well have played a role in the formation of Christian pilgrimage. See Hezser, *Jewish Travel in Antiquity*, 367: "Christian pilgrimage to the 'Holy Land' may have imitated and transformed an older, pre-70 form of Jewish pilgrimage that became obsolete when the Jerusalem Temple was destroyed. While rabbis moved on to venerate Torah knowledge, Byzantine Christians revived a more ancient space-oriented form of holiness."

Bibliography

Avi-Yonah, Michael, "Perseus and Andromeda in Japho." *Yediot* 31 (1967): 213–210 (Hebr.).

Baedeker, Karl, ed., *Palästina und Syrien: Handbuch für Reisende* (Leipzig: Baedeker, 1875).

Barbu, Daniel, "Aristeas the Tourist." *Bulletin der Schweizerischen Gesellschaft für Judaistische Forschung 23* (2014): 5–12.

Begg, Christopher T., *Flavius Josephus, Judean Antiquities 5–7: Translation & Commentary*. Leiden: Brill, 2005.

Bieberstein, Klaus, *Josua–Jordan–Jericho: Archäologie, Geschichte und Theologie der Landnahmeerzählungen Josua 1–6*. Göttingen: Vandenhoeck & Ruprecht, 1995.

Bloch, René, *Antike Vorstellungen vom Judentum: Der Judenexkurs des Tacitus im Rahmen der griechisch-römischen Ethnographie*. Stuttgart: Steiner, 2002.

Bloch, René, *Moses und der Mythos: Die Auseinandersetzung mit der griechischen Mythologie bei jüdisch-hellenistischen Autoren*. Leiden: Brill, 2010.

Boardman, John, *The Archaeology of Nostalgia: How the Greeks Re-Created their Mythical Past*. London: Thames & Hudson, 2002.

Boustan, Raʿanan, "The Spoils of the Jerusalem Temple at Rome and Constantinople: Jewish Counter-Geography in a Christianizing Empire." Pages 327–372 in *Antiquity in Antiquity: Jewish and Christians Pasts in the Greco-Roman World*. Edited by Gregg Gardner and Kevin Osterloh. Tübingen: Mohr Siebeck, 2008.

Bouvier, David, "Reliques héroïques en Grèce archaïque: l'exemple de la lance d'Achille." Pages 73–93 in *Les objets de la mémoire: Pour une approche comparatiste des reliques et de leur culte*. Edited by Philippe Borgeaud and Youri Volokhine. Bern: Peter Lang, 2005.

Casson, Lionel, *Travel in the Ancient World*. Baltimore: The Johns Hopkins University Press, 1974.

Chantraine, Pierre, *Dictionnaire étymologique de la langue grecque*. Vol. 1. Paris: Klincksieck, 1968.

van Dam, Raymond, "Relics." Pages 667–668 in *Late Antiquity: A Guide to the Postclassical World*. Edited by Glen W. Bowersock, Peter Brown, and Oleg Grabar. Cambridge: Harvard University Press, 1999.

Elsner, John, "Pausanias: A Greek Pilgrim in the Roman World." *Past & Present* 135 (1992): 3–29.

Fine, Steven, "'When I went to Rome ... There I saw the Menorah ...': The Jerusalem Temple Implements during the Second Century C.E." Pages 63–86 in *Art, History, and the Historiography of Judaism in Roman Antiquity*. Leiden: Brill, 2014.

Goff, Matthew, Loren T. Stuckenbruck, and Enrico Morano, eds., *Ancient Tales of Giants from Qumran and Turfan*. Tübingen: Mohr Siebeck, 2016.

Grottanelli, Cristiano, "The Ogygian Oak at Mamre and the Holy Town of Hebron." *Vicino Oriente* 2 (1979): 39–63.

Harder, Ruth E., "Andromeda." *BNP* 1:692.

Hartmann, Andreas, *Zwischen Relikt und Reliquie: Objektbezogene Erinnerungspraktiken in antiken Gesellschaften*. Berlin: Verlag Antike, 2010.

Harvey, Jr., Paul B., "The Death of Mythology: The Case of Joppa." *JECS* 2 (1994): 1–14.

Heubner, Heinrich and Wolfgang Fauth, *P. Cornelius Tacitus: Die Historien: Kommentar*. Vol. 5. Heidelberg: C. Winter, 1982.

Heyden, Katharina, *Orientierung: Die westliche Christenheit und das Heilige Land in der Antike*. Munich: Aschendorff, 2014.

Heyden, Katharina, "Hain der Religionen: Das Abrahamsheiligtum von Mamre als Begegnungsort und locus theologicus." Pages 17–69 in *Fremdenliebe–Fremdenangst: Zwei akademische Reden zur interreligiösen Begegnung in Spätantike und Gegenwart*. Zurich: Theologischer Verlag, 2016.

Hezser, Catherine, *Jewish Travel in Antiquity*. Tübingen: Mohr Siebeck, 2011.

van der Horst, Pieter, "Die Prophetengräber im antiken Judentum." Pages 55–71 in *Interesse am Judentum: Die Franz-Delitzsch-Vorlesungen 1989–2008*. Edited by Jacobus Cornelis de Vos and Folker Siegert. Münster: LIT, 2008.

Kaizer, Ted, "Interpretations of the Myth of Andromeda at Iope." *Syria* 88 (2011): 323–339.

Keel, Othmar and Max Küchler, eds., *Orte und Landschaften der Bibel: Ein Handbuch und Studien-Reiseführer zum Heiligen Land*. Vol. 2: *Der Süden*. Göttingen: Vandenhoeck & Ruprecht, 1982.

Kerkeslager, Allen, "Jewish Pilgrimage and Jewish Identity in Hellenistic and Early Roman Egypt." Pages 99–225 in *Pilgrimage and Holy Space in Late Antique Egypt*. Edited by David Frankfurter. Leiden: Brill, 1998.

Lightfoot, Jane L., *The Sibylline Oracles: with introduction, translation, and commentary on the first and second books*. Oxford: Oxford University Press, 2008.

Lightstone, Jack N., *The Commerce of the Sacred: Mediation of the Divine among Jews in the Graeco-Roman Diaspora*. Chico, CA: Scholars Press, 1984.

Mayor, Peter, *The First Fossil Hunters: Paleontology in Greek and Roman Times*. Princeton: Princeton University Press, 2000.

Mulzer, Martin, "Andromeda und Jona in Jafo." *ZDPV* 122 (2006): 46–60.

Netzer, Ehud, *The Architecture of Herod, the Great Builder*. Tübingen: Mohr Siebeck, 2006.

Norden, Eduard, *Josephus und Tacitus über Jesus Christus und eine messianische Prophetie*. Leipzig: Teubner, 1913.

Norman, Alex and Carole M. Cusack, eds., *Religion, Pilgrimage, and Tourism*. 2 vols. London: Routledge, 2015.

Noy, David, "Rabbi Aqiba Comes to Rome: A Jewish Pilgrimage in Reverse?" Pages 373–

385 in *Pilgrimage in Graeco-Roman and Early Christian Antiquity*. Edited by Jas Elsner and Ian Rutherford. Oxford: Oxford University Press, 2007.

Perlitt, Lothar, *Riesen im Alten Testament: Ein literarisches Motiv im Wirkungsfeld des Deutoronomiums*. Göttingen: Vandenhoeck & Ruprecht, 1990.

Pfister, Friedrich, *Der Reliquienkult im Altertum*. Berlin: De Gruyter, 1974 (1909–1912).

Rauch, Michel, *Reisehandbuch (Dumont) Israel, Palästina, Sinai*. Ostfildern: Dumont, 2015.

Redfield, James, "Herodotus the Tourist." *CP* 80 (1985): 97–118.

Ronnenberg, Karsten C., *Mythos bei Hieronymus: Zur christlichen Transformation paganer Erzählungen in der Spätantike*. Stuttgart: Franz Steiner, 2015.

Stemberger, Günter, *Einleitung in Talmud und Midrasch*. Munich: C.H. Beck, 2011.

Stern, Menahem, *Greek and Latin Authors on Jews and Judaism*. 3 vols. Jerusalem: Israel Academy of Sciences and Humanities, 1974.

Stewart, Susan, *On Longing: Narratives of the Miniature, the Gigantic, the Souvenir, the Collection*. Durham, NC: Duke University Press, 1993 (1984).

Takács, Sarolta A., "Divine and Human Feet: Records of Pilgrims Honouring Isis." Pages 353–369 in *Pilgrimage in Graeco-Roman and Early Christian Antiquity*. Edited by Jas Elsner and Ian Rutherford. Oxford: Oxford University Press, 2007.

Turcan, Robert, *L'Archéologie dans l'Antiquité: Tourisme, lucre et découvertes*. Paris: Les Belles-Lettres, 2014.

Ullman, Lisa and Shatzman, Israel, eds., *Yosef Ben Matityahu/[Titus] Flavius Josephus: History of the Jewish War against the Romans*. Jerusalem: Carmel, 2010 (Hebr.).

Veyne, Paul, *Les Grecs ont-ils cru à leurs mythes? Essai sur l'imagination constituante*. Paris: Seuil, 1983.

Weeber, Karl-Wilhelm, "Reisen." *DNP* 10, 856–866.

Williamson, George, "Mucianus and a Touch of the Miraculous: Pilgrimage and Tourism in Roman Asia Minor." Pages 219–252 in *Pilgrimage in Graeco-Roman & Early Christian Antiquity: Seeing the Gods*. Edited by Jas Elsner and Ian Rutherford. Oxford: Oxford University Press, 2007.

CHAPTER 7

What If the Temple of Jerusalem Had Not Been Destroyed by the Romans?

In the summer of the year 70 CE, in the midst of the turmoil of the Jewish-Roman War, the Roman commander Titus summoned his advisors for a military council.* After persistent and heavy resistance by the Jewish rebels, the city of Jerusalem was finally about to be captured by the Roman soldiers. Jews and Romans were fighting in the immediate vicinity of the Jewish temple, which was still standing. The Roman victory was only a matter of time. But what should be done with the temple of the Jews? Together with his advisors in Jerusalem, Titus "deliberated," in the words of the late antique Christian historian Sulpicius Severus (fourth/fifth century CE).

> whether he should destroy such a mighty temple. For some thought that a consecrated shrine, which was famous beyond all other works of men, ought not to be razed, arguing that its preservation would bear witness to the moderation of Rome, while its destruction would forever brand her cruelty.[1]

The solution was not obvious. For the Romans to destroy a temple stood in opposition to their concept of piety (*pietas*), a venerable ideal that had gained renewed importance in the age of Augustus (who had built and restored a great number of temples), but was much older. When Roman leaders dared to plunder or even destroy temples and were subsequently defeated in battle, this was often understood as divine punishment.[2] In the case of Titus and the young Flavian dynasty, there was good reason to be cautious with regard to the destruction of temples. Approximately half a year earlier, the Capitol, the

---

*   I would like to thank the following for their helpful and critical remarks: Sara Bloch, Leonhard Burckhardt, Ulrich Luz, Gavriel Rosenfeld, and Seth Schwartz (naturally some reaching conclusions different from mine). An earlier version of this paper was presented as the Emil Fackenheim Lecture in the fall of 2013 in Berlin.

1   Sulpicius Severus, *Chron.* 2.30.6 (trans. LCL).

2   See the examples in Adalberto Giovannini, "Die Zerstörung Jerusalems durch Titus: Eine Strafe Gottes oder eine historische Notwendigkeit?" in *Contra quis ferat arma deos? Vier Augsburger Vorträge zur Religionsgeschichte der römischen Kaiserzeit zum 60. Geburtstag von Gunther Gottlieb*, ed. Pedro Barceló (Munich: Ernst Vögel, 1996), 24–25.

© RENÉ BLOCH, 2022 | DOI:10.1163/9789004521896_009

WHAT IF THE TEMPLE OF JERUSALEM HAD NOT BEEN DESTROYED 129

great temple of Jupiter in Rome, had burned down when Vespasian attacked the city. The Roman historian Tacitus speaks of the "saddest and most shameful crime that the Roman state had ever suffered since its foundation."[3] After taking office, Vespasian made sure to rebuild the Capitol.

Titus was not the first Roman who had the opportunity to destroy the temple of Jerusalem. When Pompey captured the city in the year 63 BCE (having been practically invited to do so by the belligerent Hasmonean brothers, Aristobulus and Hyrcanus), he famously entered the temple, but "out of piety" did not "touch" anything.[4] A decade later, Marcus Licinius Crassus, who was in charge of the province of Syria, showed less deference when he ordered the plundering of the temple. For Crassus, the treasures of the Jewish temple were a welcome means of financing his campaign against the Parthians. According to Josephus, he "took away all the gold of the temple" and stole its treasure.[5] But the temple did not fall.

So which route did Titus take towards the end of the Jewish-Roman war? We do not know for sure. According to Sulpicius Severus, he did not follow the arguments of those who pleaded for moderation:

> Yet others, including Titus himself, opposed, holding the destruction of this temple to be a prime necessity of wiping out more completely the religion of the Jews and the Christians; for they urged that these religions, although hostile to each other, nevertheless sprang from the same sources; the Christians had grown out of the Jews: if the root were destroyed, the stock would easily perish.[6]

In fact, it is unlikely that Christianity played into Titus's decision about what to do with the temple of Jerusalem. Severus probably revised his source, most likely Tacitus, and gave it a Christian reading.[7] One can assume that Severus's source only said that Titus decided to destroy the temple and bring the war to

---

3 Tacitus, *Hist.* 3.72 (trans. LCL).
4 Josephus, *BJ* 1.152–153; *AJ* 14.72. Cf. Tacitus, *Hist.* 5.9.1.
5 Josephus, *BJ* 1.179; *AJ* 14.105–109.
6 Sulpicius Severus, *Chron.* 2.30.6 (trans. LCL).
7 See the classic study by Jacob Bernays, "Über die Chronik des Sulpicius Severus, ein Beitrag zur Geschichte der classischen und biblischen Studien," in *Jacob Bernays, Gesammelte Abhandlungen.* Vol. 2, ed. Heinrich Usener (Berlin: Hertz, 1885 [1861]), 81–200 which, however, did not remain unchallenged: cf. Hugh Montefiore, "Sulpicius Severus and Titus' Council of War," *Historia* 11 (1962): 156–170, and more recently Eric Laupot, "Tacitus' Fragment 2: The Anti-Roman Movement of the Christiani and the Nazoreans," *VC* 54 (2000): 233–247.

130   CHAPTER 7

an end.[8] A very different story, by contrast, was offered by the Jewish-Roman historian Josephus, who in his *Jewish War* insisted that Titus did everything in his power to spare the temple. In Josephus's version of the military council, the accusation of impiety, which the destruction of a temple would have provoked, is also discussed. But here, in the end, Titus

> declared that, even were the Jews to mount it (the temple) and fight therefrom, he would not wreak vengeance on inanimate objects instead of men, nor under any circumstances burn down so magnificent a work; for the loss would affect the Romans, inasmuch as it would be an ornament to the empire if it stood.[9]

According to Josephus, the destruction of the temple was an accident, precipitated by a Roman soldier "awaiting no orders." Indeed, when Titus heard about the fire, he "ran to the Temple to arrest the conflagration."[10] So are we to believe Josephus or Sulpicius Severus? Both versions of the story have found their adherents.[11] It seems clear to me, however, that Josephus's report was heavily influenced by his pro-Flavian bias. As someone who relied on imperial patronage, Josephus sought to whitewash Titus and the Flavian dynasty of any responsibility for the temple's destruction. In reality, Titus probably decided to plunder and destroy the Jewish temple. After all, the edifice was the "symbol and strength of Jewish resistance."[12]

---

8   Yohanan Lewy, "Titus' Justification with regard to the Destruction of the Temple according to Tacitus," in id., *Studies in Jewish Hellenism* (Jerusalem: Bialik Institute, 1969 [1943]) (Hebr.), suspected that in Tacitus the "root" (which would be removed) referred to the temple and the "offspring" (which would easily perish) to the Jewish people (192): with the destruction of the temple, the Jews would come to an end. Orosius, a contemporary of Sulpicius Severus, also reports how Titus after deliberation concluded that the temple should be destroyed (*Chron.* 7.9.5–6).

9   Josephus,, *BJ* 6.241 (trans. LCL).

10 Josephus, *BJ* 6.252, 254 (trans. LCL). Cf. Zvi Yavetz, "Reflections on Titus and Josephus," *GRBS* 16 (1975): 411–432.

11 For Josephus see, e.g., Martin Goodman, *Rome and Jerusalem: The Clash of Ancient Civilizations* (New York: Alfred A. Knopf, 2008), 420–423; for Sulpicius Severus see, e.g., Giovannini, "Die Zerstörung Jerusalems," 32. Both versions of Titus's military council, that of Josephus as well as that of Sulpicius Severus, are of course literary constructs of what might have actually happened.

12 Hugh Montefiore, "Sulpicius Severus and Titus' Council of War," 160. Cf. on this question also the discussion in James B. Rives, "Flavian Religious Policy and the Destruction of the Jerusalem Temple," in *Flavius Josephus and Flavian Rome*, ed. Jonathan C. Edmondson, Steve Mason, and James B. Rives (Oxford: Oxford University Press, 2005), 145–166.

WHAT IF THE TEMPLE OF JERUSALEM HAD NOT BEEN DESTROYED   131

However—and this is important for the following argument—Titus *could* have decided differently, as is evident from the differing views in ancient sources and also their interpretation in modern scholarship. The counterfactual question "What if Titus had not given the order to destroy the temple of Jerusalem?" is thus a legitimate one. Exploring this provocative counterfactual question allows us to better understand the origins and consequences of what is generally considered one of the most pivotal events in Jewish history.

1   Roman Financial Policy

We need not doubt that the Romans would have brought the rebellion to an end even if they had not destroyed the temple. Maybe Titus would have merely plundered it, which would have been a less sacrilegious act than its destruction. He had good reason to seize the wealth of the Jewish temple. The young Flavian dynasty needed money. Since the great fire of 64 CE, which destroyed large parts of the city of Rome, the imperial acquisition of money had become a high priority. And with the civil war of 68/69 CE the situation did not improve.[13] There is little doubt, then, that if Titus had spared the temple of Jerusalem, he would still have made sure to profit financially from the Roman victory over the Jews, either by plundering the temple or imposing heavy taxes on the Jews— maybe both. After the temple's destruction, Jews, "wherever they were," had to pay a new tax to the Roman Capitol called the *fiscus Iudaicus*.[14] It replaced the temple tax that Jews had formerly sent to Jerusalem for generations. If the temple had not been destroyed, there would not have been such a humiliating redirection of this tax. But in one way or another, the Jews would still have suffered financially. The suppression of the rebellion and the capture of Jerusalem were unusually difficult and expensive for the Romans; indeed, it took "roughly one-seventh of the whole Imperial army … to complete the capture of the city."[15] Moreover, the Roman army would in any case have remained stationed in Judea, as it did after the destruction of the temple, when Titus left the tenth legion together with some troops of cavalry and infantry in Jerusalem.[16]

---

13   Giovannini, "Die Zerstörung Jerusalems," 21–22.
14   Josephus, *BJ* 7.218. Cf. Martin Goodman, "Nerva, The Fiscus Iudaicus and Jewish Identity," *JRS* 79 (1989): 40–44.
15   Fergus Millar, *The Roman Near East: 31 BC–AD 337* (Cambridge: Harvard University Press, 1993), 76.
16   Josephus, *BJ* 7.5.

132   CHAPTER 7

The victorious Flavian emperors, newcomers on the Roman political stage, made sure to profit from their victory as ostentatiously as possible.[17] The spoils of the Jerusalem temple were displayed in a large triumph in the year 71 CE.[18] Most famously, the spoils were later shown (and are still visible today) on the Arch of Titus, completed upon the Via Sacra in 81 CE. The vessels of gold from the temple were displayed in the newly erected temple of Peace (*templum Pacis*).[19] Similarly, the great new amphitheater, opened in the year 80 CE and later known as the Colosseum, was financed "from the spoils of war," as stated in an inscription from the site. This inscription could only refer to the Jewish-Roman War, which means that the Colosseum was financed, in part at least, by gold and other valuables taken from the Jewish temple in Jerusalem.[20] If the temple had not been destroyed (or at least plundered), the Flavians would have had to find other financial sources for the amphitheater, no easy task. Moreover, the Arch of Titus, if it had been built at all, would not have been able to flaunt its famed relief portraying the triumphal procession of the year 71 CE portraying the booty seized from the temple.

2   The End of Sacrifice

The Jewish-Roman war did not end with the fall of the Jewish temple. After destroying the temple, the Romans laid waste to almost the entire city of Jerusalem.[21] The number of Jews killed or enslaved by the Romans during the war was very high, even if Josephus's numbers are exaggerated.[22] Assuming the temple had not been destroyed, the temple cult could only have persisted if Jerusalem had remained habitable and if enough of its inhabitants had been able to stay in the city. Jews would have continued sacrificing, if at all possible. In the wake of Crassus's plundering of the temple in 54 BCE, we hear of no long-term consequences affecting ritual practice.

---

17   See Fergus Millar, "Last Year in Jerusalem: Monuments of the Jewish War in Rome," in *Flavius Josephus and Flavian Rome*, ed. Jonathan C. Edmondson, Steve Mason, and James B. Rives (Oxford: Oxford University Press, 2005), 101–128.

18   Josephus, *BJ* 7.145–150.

19   Josephus, *BJ* 7.158–162.

20   See the reconstruction of the inscription by Geza Alföldy, "Eine Bauinschrift aus dem Colosseum," *Zeitschrift für Papyrologie und Epigraphik* 109 (1995): 195–226; Millar, "Last Year in Jerusalem," 117–119.

21   Jonathan Price, *Jerusalem under Siege: The Collapse of the Jewish State 66–70 C.E.* (Leiden: Brill, 1992), 171–174.

22   Josephus, *BJ* 6.420 speaks of 97,000 prisoners and 1.1 million victims.

WHAT IF THE TEMPLE OF JERUSALEM HAD NOT BEEN DESTROYED

But for how long? For how long would Jews have offered sacrifices to their god? It may be a surprising question and, at first glance, sound like pure speculation to suggest that the Jews might have stopped performing sacrificial rites even if the temple had not been destroyed. To be sure, one needs to be aware of apologetic pitfalls.[23] In the Middle Ages, Maimonides argued in his *Guide for the Perplexed* that the fact that God restricted the sacrificial cult to one place and to one family—the temple and the Kohanim—while prayers are open to all Jews, proved the inferiority of the former to the latter.[24] What was difficult for the medieval philosopher to accept is even more problematic from the perspective of modern Western society. Few people today would consider the idea of cultic sacrifices persuasive. Jews, it has even been said, should be grateful to Titus for having released them from sacrificial rituals "before any other society."[25] The idea that Jews would have stopped sacrificing even without help from the outside, i.e. without the destruction by Titus, may be particularly attractive. It is impossible to know with any certainty what would have happened to the sacrificial cult had the temple itself survived, but there is indeed good reason to believe that Jews would have abandoned it anyway. The Jews lost their temple at a time when sacrificial rituals were being called into question. Critiques of sacrifice had been common already in ancient Israel. The prophets contrasted the superficiality of sacrificial offerings with the ideals of justice and righteousness. In the words of the prophet Isaiah:

> What to me is the multitude of your sacrifices? Says the LORD; I have had enough of burnt offerings of rams and the fat of fed beasts; I do not delight in the blood of bulls, or of lambs, or of goats ... learn to do good; seek justice, rescue the oppressed, defend the orphan, plead for the widow.[26]

To be sure, we should not assume that within Judaism sacrifices were consistently questioned. On the contrary, so long as no outside force prohibited it—as at the time of the Seleucid King Antiochus IV—the sacrificial service in the temple of Jerusalem was always upheld. Sacrifices were offered even during

---

23   See Jonathan Klawans, *Purity, Sacrifice, and the Temple. Symbolism and Supersessionism in the Study of Ancient Judaism* (Oxford: Oxford University Press, 2006).

24   Maimonides, *Guide for the Perplexed* 3.32.

25   Guy Stroumsa, *The End of Sacrifice: Religious Transformations in Late Antiquity* (Chicago: The University of Chicago Press, 2009), 63: "The Jews should no doubt pay thanks to Titus, for having destroyed their temple for the second time, for imposing on them the need to free themselves from sacrifice and its ritual violence, before any other society."

26   Isaiah 1:11, 17 NRSV.

134 CHAPTER 7

the dire conditions of the Jewish-Roman War.[27] But the old critiques of the prophets continued to linger. They can be tracked in the writings of Qumran and the New Testament. Matthew, for example, takes up an early, probably pre-70 critique of sacrifice in the Jesus-movement, citing Hosea 6:6: "I desire mercy, not sacrifice (the knowledge of God, rather than burnt offerings)."[28] Early Christian critiques of sacrifice continued and further expanded an inner-Jewish dialogue.[29]

In his now classic book, *Map is Not Territory*, Jonathan Z. Smith—in a brief afterword to his article "Earth and Gods"—offered a skeptical counterfactual claim about the survival of the temple cult. As he put it,

> Indeed, I should want to go so far as to argue that if the Temple had not been destroyed, it would have had to be neglected. For it represented a locative type of religious activity no longer perceived effective in a new, utopian religious situation with a concomitant shift from a cosmological to an anthropological view-point.[30]

Beginning in the Hellenistic period and then accelerating in late antiquity, according to Smith, a groundbreaking transition took place from sacred space

---

27 When the Roman soldiers destroyed the Antonia fortress (on the 17th of Tammuz of the year 70) the daily sacrifices were stopped: Josephus, *BJ* 6.93–94.

28 Matt 9:13; 12:7 NRSV. On the complexity of these passages cf. Ulrich Luz, *Matthew 8–20: A Commentary* (Minneapolis: Fortress, 2001), ad loc. and on rabbinic parallels citing Hosea 6:6 Hermann L. Strack and Paul Billerbeck, *Das Evangelium nach Matthäus erläutert aus Talmud und Midrasch.* Vol. 1 (Munich: C.H. Beck, 1922), 500.

29 On the difficult question as to what extent Jesus criticized the temple see Gerd Theissen, "Jesus im Judentum. Drei Versuche einer Ortsbestimmung," in *Jesus als historische Gestalt: Beiträge zur Jesusforschung zum 60. Geburtstag von Gerd Theissen*, ed. Gerd Theissen and Annette Merz (Göttingen: Vandenhoeck & Ruprecht, 2003), 35–56, 50: "Wir finden bei Jesus ebenfalls eine Opposition gegen den Tempel. Entweder wollte er den Opferhandel beenden und durch Tempelreinigung Missstände beseitigen oder er wollte die Opfer abschaffen und durch Reform den Tempel in eine Synagoge verwandeln oder er wollte als Prophet die Tempelzerstörung ankündigen." The Qumran Community distanced itself from the temple cult in Jerusalem (CD 6; Josephus, *AJ* 18.19). There is no archaeological evidence for sacrifices at the site of Qumran. According to Philo the Essenes did not offer any sacrifices (*Prob.* 75). On Qumran and the temple see Lawrence H. Schiffman, "Community Without Temple: The Qumran Community's Withdrawal from the Jerusalem Temple," in *Gemeinde ohne Tempel: Community without Temple: Zur Substituierung und Transformation des Jerusalemer Tempels und seines Kults im Alten Testament, antiken Judentum und frühen Christentum*, ed. Beate Ego et al., eds. (Tübingen: Mohr Siebeck, 1999), 267–284.

30 Jonathan Z. Smith, *Map Is Not Territory: Studies in the History of Religions* (Chicago: The University of Chicago Press, 1978), 128.

WHAT IF THE TEMPLE OF JERUSALEM HAD NOT BEEN DESTROYED   135

as a fixed center to a "relatively unfixed form" of rituals. "Rather than celebration, purification and pilgrimage," he wrote, "the new rituals will be those of conversion, of initiation into the secret society or identification with the divine man."[31] In making this argument, Smith followed Peter Brown who, writing about late antique society, declared:

> Ancient religion had revolved round great temples … their ceremonies assumed a life in which community, the city, dwarfed the individual. In the fourth and fifth centuries [CE], however, the individual, as a 'man of power', came to dwarf the traditional communities … *the emergence of the holy man at the expense of the temple marks the end of the classical world.*[32]

In late antiquity, the practice of religion withdrew more and more to the private sphere. Temples disappeared, as did animal sacrifices.[33] Sacrifice remained an important religious paradigm, but it was filled with new, symbolic meaning. Christians saw in Jesus Christ the eternal sacrifice to God, while Jews replaced the sacrifice with the study of the Torah, including the study of the sacrificial laws.[34]

Greek and Roman philosophers had also questioned the utility of sacrifice from early on. Theophrastus, a student of Aristotle, interpreted sacrifice as a substitution for cannibalism, and Varro (first century BCE) employed the same language as the biblical prophets in denying any divine demand for sacrifices, declaring: "Real gods do not wish or ask for them."[35] In late antiquity, with the

---

31   Smith, *Map is Not Territory*, 187.
32   Peter Brown, *The World of Late Antiquity: From Marcus Aurelius to Mohammed* (London: Thames & Hudson, 1971), 102–103, cited by Smith, *Map is Not Territory*, 186–187.
33   On the complexity of this shift see the critical remarks in Raʿanan S. Boustan, "Confounding Blood: Jewish Narratives of Sacrifice and Violence in Late Antiquity," in *Ancient Mediterranean Sacrifice*, ed. Jennifer Wright Knust and Zsuzsanna Várhelyi (Oxford: Oxford University Press, 2011), 265–286; cf. also Christoph Auffarth, "Le rite sacrificiel antique: la longue durée et la fin du sacrifice," (review of Maria-Zoe Petropolou, *Animal Sacrifice in ancient Greek religion, Judaism, and Christianity 100 BC-AD 200* [Oxford: Oxford University Press, 2008]), *Kernos* 25 (2012): 300–301; and for Egypt see David Frankfurter, *Religion in Roman Egypt: Assimilation and Resistance* (Princeton: Princeton University Press, 1998).
34   Late antique Christian and Jewish approaches to the sacrifice were certainly diverse. With regard to Judaism see more recently (with further literature) Boustan, "Confounding Blood" and Michael D. Swartz, "Liturgy, Poetry, and the Persistence of Sacrifice," in *Was 70 CE a Watershed in Jewish History? On Jews and Judaism before and after the Destruction of the Second Temple*, ed. Daniel R. Schwartz and Zeev Weiss (Leiden: Brill, 2012), 393–412.
35   Theophrastus, *De pietate* fr. 3 (Pötscher); Varro, Arnob. 7.1: *Dii veri ea neque desiderant neque deposcunt*; see Walter Burkert, *Homo Necans: The Anthropology of Ancient Greek Sacrificial Ritual and Myth* (Berkeley: University of California Press, 1986), 8n36.

136   CHAPTER 7

rise of Christianity, this critique was phrased in much more rigid form. An anti-
pagan law under the emperor Constantius II from the year 341 states "that the
folly of sacrifices be abolished" (*sacrificiorum aboleatur insania*).[36]

Given these trends, it is indeed reasonable to assume that Judaism—never
isolated, but always part of larger cultural contexts—would have abandoned its
sacrificial cult over the long run. Even if the temple of Jerusalem had not been
destroyed, the decline of pagan sacrificial rituals and the diminished importance of temples throughout the region make it unlikely that the Jewish sacrificial system would have survived late antiquity, a time period when more
individual and less centralized forms of religious ritual prevailed. Over time
Jews, too, would have distanced themselves from sacrificial rituals.

3   The Jewish Diaspora

While the temple had always played an important role in Jewish theological
thinking, it was not the only religious center for Jews in the ancient world. On
the contrary: when the temple fell in the year 70 CE, the majority of the Jews had
been living outside of Palestine, in the Jewish diaspora, for a long time.[37] There
is evidence of synagogues being present in Egypt as early as the third century
BCE. Jews from all over the ancient world sent their temple tax to Jerusalem, but
their religious geography was widespread and, to employ J.Z. Smith's nomen-
clature, not "locative." In Judea, too, the synagogue was not only a post-temple
phenomenon, but existed before, even in Jerusalem.[38] In the diaspora, Judaism
had, remarkably, always been "a religion without animal sacrifice."[39] The vast
majority of Jews in antiquity never personally saw the temple of Jerusalem. It

---

36   Cod. theod. 16.10.2: *cesset superstitio, sacrificiorum aboleatur insania*. See Stroumsa, *The
      End of Sacrifice*, 57. On the wider context of this passage cf. Johannes Hahn, "Gesetze als
      Waffe? Die kaiserliche Religionspolitik und die Zerstörung der Tempel," in *Spätantiker
      Staat und religiöser Konflikt: Imperiale und lokale Verwaltung und die Gewalt gegen Heilig-
      tümer*, ed. Johannes Hahn (Berlin: De Gruyter, 2011), 201–220, at 205–206.
37   See Erich S. Gruen, *Diaspora: Jews amidst Greeks and Romans* (Cambridge: Harvard Uni-
      versity Press, 2002), 3, 232–233. According to Strabo (first century BCE/CE) the people of
      the Jews had "already made its way into every city, and it is not easy to find any place in
      the habitable world which has not received this nation and in which it has not made its
      power felt" (cited by Josephus, *AJ* 14.115, trans. LCL).
38   As is indicated by the Theodotus inscription which is usually dated pre-70 CE., see Anders
      Runesson, Donald D. Binder, and Birger Olsson, *The Ancient Synagogue from its Origins
      to 200 C.E.: A Source Book* (Leiden: Brill, 2008), 52–54. Josephus reports on (pre-70) syna-
      gogues in Caesarea (*BJ* 2.285–292) and Tiberias (*Vita* 277).
39   Burkert, *Homo Necans*, 8.

WHAT IF THE TEMPLE OF JERUSALEM HAD NOT BEEN DESTROYED

is true that other Jewish temples had existed at various junctures; in the sixth and fifth century BCE, Jews on the island of Elephantine in Upper Egypt had their own temple. And in the second century BCE, the Jewish High Priest Onias built a temple in the Egyptian city of Leontopolis. But these were temporary exceptions.[40]

This is not to say that the temple was not important to diaspora Jews. To Philo of Alexandria, the great Jewish-Hellenistic philosopher of the first century CE, it was unimaginable that the temple one day would not be there any longer. In the context of the annual contribution of a half-shekel that diaspora Jews sent to Jerusalem, Philo writes:

> the revenues of the Temple are derived not only from landed estates but also from other and far greater sources which time will never destroy. For as long as the human race endures, and it will endure forever, the revenues of the Temple also will remain secure coeternal with the whole universe.[41]

Philo also mentions Jewish pilgrimage to Jerusalem, observing that

> countless multitudes from countless cities come, some over land, others over sea, from east and west and north and south at every feast. They take the Temple for their port as a general haven and safe refuge from the bustle and great turmoil of life, and there they seek to find calm weather.[42]

Jewish pilgrimage certainly constituted an important bond between the diaspora and Jerusalem. Yet Philo exaggerates its significance. Most pilgrims came from Judea, not from the wider diaspora.[43] Philo himself apparently visited Jerusalem only once. He mentions his visit to Jerusalem and the temple merely in a side remark in his tractate *On Providence*, showing more interest in the birds of the region than in the sacrifice:

---

40 At the end of the war the Romans closed the Jewish temple in Leontopolis: Josephus, *BJ* 7.420–436. I am not discussing the particular case of the Samaritans and the temple on Mount Gerizim. On recent scholarship on the Samaritans cf. Menachem Mor and Friedrich V. Reiterer, eds., *Samaritans, Past and Present: Current Studies* (Berlin: De Gruyter, 2010) and on all three temples Jörg Frey, "Temple and Rival Temple—The Cases of Elephantine, Mt. Gerizim, and Leontopolis," in Ego et al., eds., *Gemeinde ohne Tempel: Community without Temple*, 171–203.

41 Philo, *Spec.* 1.76 (trans. LCL).

42 Philo, *Spec.* 1.69 (trans. LCL).

43 Lee I. Levine, "Temple, Jerusalem," *The Eerdmans Dictionary of Early Judaism* (ed. John J. Collins and Daniel C. Harlow; Grand Rapids: Eerdmans, 2010), 1290.

138

CHAPTER 7

> While I was there (in Ashkelon) at a time when I was on my way to our ancestral temple to offer up prayers and sacrifices I observed a large number of pigeons at the cross roads and in each house.[44]

The temple was important to Philo.[45] But his interest in its rituals was also very much of a philosophical and theoretical nature.[46] Philo refers to a number of synagogues in Alexandria. This is where people went to pray and, as Philo would say, to study philosophy.[47]

Even the Jewish-Roman historian Josephus, who differed from Philo in that he spent half of his life in Jerusalem and half in the diaspora, rather quickly, or so it seems, found ways to adjust to non-sacrificial Diaspora Judaism. Josephus showed genuine emotion in mourning the Jews' defeat at the hands of the Romans and the loss of the temple.[48] Having grown up in a priestly family in Jerusalem, the historian viewed the temple as an intrinsic part of Judaism. In his apologetic treatise *Against Apion*, written towards the end of his life and about thirty years after the Roman-Jewish War, Josephus spoke of the unity of temple and God: "Judaism has one god, one temple, and one scripture."[49] But this slogan is also part of Josephus's polemic against an inconsistent paganism, with its countless temples, changing gods, and myriad books.[50] Although it is difficult to prove, Josephus probably adjusted sooner rather than later to the religious conditions of Diaspora Judaism.[51] If the sacrificial rites in the temple

---

44   Philo, *Prov.* 2.64 (trans. LCL).

45   This is very much the point of Jutta Leonhardt-Balzer, "Priests and Priesthood in Philo: Could he Have Done without Them?," in Schwartz and Weiss, *Was 70 CE a Watershed?*, 127–153.

46   See William K. Gilders, "Jewish Sacrifice: Its Nature and Function (According to Philo)," in Knust and Várhelyi, *Ancient Mediterranean Sacrifice*, 94–105.

47   Philo, *Flacc.* 41–53, 121–124; *Leg.* 132–139; *Mos.* 2.216.

48   Josephus, *BJ* 1.9–12.

49   Josephus, *CA* 2.193; 1.38–40 (on scripture). See John Barclay, *Flavius Josephus: Against Apion* (Leiden: Brill, 2007), 279. In *BJ* 5.184–237 Josephus includes a detailed ekphrasis of the temple (using the past tense); see also *BJ* 7.148–150 (spoils from the temple are presented at the Flavian triumph in Rome) and *CA* 2.102–109, 119 and on this Richard Bauckham, "Josephus' Account of the Temple in *Contra Apionem* 2.102–109," in *Josephus' Contra Apionem: Studies in its Character and Context with a Latin Concordance to the Portion Missing in Greek*, ed. Louis H. Feldman and John R. Levison (Leiden: Brill, 1996), 327–347.

50   On this see René Bloch, *Moses und der Mythos: Die Auseinandersetzung mit der griechischen Mythologie bei jüdisch-hellenistischen Autoren* (Leiden: Brill, 2011), 30–49.

51   On Josephus's Diaspora Judaism see Michael Tuval, *From Jerusalem Priest to Roman Jew: On Josephus and the Paradigms of Ancient Judaism* (Tübingen: Mohr Siebeck, 2013). Tuval observes a profound change during Josephus's tenure in Rome: "by the time he produced AJ [the Jewish Antiquities], he wanted to convey to his readers that the Temple was a mem-

WHAT IF THE TEMPLE OF JERUSALEM HAD NOT BEEN DESTROYED   139

had gradually been abandoned, Jews in the diaspora would have taken note, but their daily religious practice would not have been substantially affected. When the temple fell in the year 70 CE, the event was certainly a massive shock for Jews throughout the world. But Judaism was well prepared for such a shift, especially in the diaspora.[52]

4   Bar Kokhba and Julian

Sixty years after their defeat in the Jewish-Roman War, the Jews launched another rebellion in the form of the Bar Kokhba revolt (132–135 CE). What immediately triggered the revolt is still a matter of dispute. But the fact that coins produced by the Bar Kokhba rebels depicted both the temple of Jerusalem and the ark of the covenant indicates that the rebels wanted to restore the temple—or, at the very least, to employ it as an evocative rallying symbol.[53] The Romans' eventual suppression of the Bar Kokhba revolt had far-reaching consequences for the Jews. The province of Judea was renamed Syria Palaestina; Jews were entirely banned from Jerusalem; and on its site, a Roman colony, named Aelia Capitolina, was established. However, if the temple had not been destroyed in the year 70, if there had not been such a rupture and temple services had continued, there probably would not have been a Bar Kokhba revolt.[54]

What if the Roman emperor Julian had made good on his plan in the fourth century CE to rebuild the temple of Jerusalem? In the short period that he ruled (from 361 to 363 CE), Julian promoted the revival of pagan cults, polytheism, and sacrifice.[55] Julian embraced common anti-Jewish stereotypes, but he admired

---

ory and Torah was his present life" (12). For a different reading of Josephus's understanding of the temple see Jonathan Klawans, *Josephus and the Theologies of Ancient Judaism* (Oxford: Oxford University Press, 2012), 180–209.

52   For Judea, Nadav Sharon, "Setting the Stage: The Effects of the Roman Conquest and the Loss of Sovereignty," in Schwartz and Weiss, *Was 70 CE a Watershed?*, 415–443, notes a continuous withdrawal from the temple in Judea, starting with the loss of sovereignty in 63 BCE.

53   Cf. Werner Eck, *Rom und Judaea: Fünf Vorträge zur römischen Herrschaft in Palaestina* (Tübingen: Mohr Siebeck, 2007), 115–155; Peter Schäfer, ed., *The Bar Kokhba War Reconsidered: New Perspectives on the Second Jewish Revolt Against Rome* (Tübingen: Mohr Siebeck, 2003); and the good survey by Hanan Eshel, "Bar Kokhba Revolt," in Collins and Harlow, *Eerdmans Dictionary*, 421–425.

54   Pheme Perkins, "If Jerusalem Stood: The Destruction of Jerusalem and Christian Anti-Judaism," *Biblical Interpretation* 8 (2000): 194–204, arrives at the same conclusion.

55   On Julian and the Jews see Menaham Stern, *Greek and Latin Authors on Jews and Judaism.*

140   CHAPTER 7

ancient Judaism's sacrificial system. He believed it was similar to pagan rituals and, even more importantly, stood in stark contrast to Christianity.[56] The sources on Julian's intention to rebuild the temple are not free of polemics, to say the least, and are difficult to evaluate. The emperor's main targets were the Christians who, for their part, reacted nervously to the prospect of a new Jewish temple, whose ruins were understood as proof of the sins of the Jews. If we are to believe contemporary Christian authors, Jews answered Julian's unexpected endeavor with enthusiasm.[57] On the other hand, rabbinic responses are marked by "an almost complete silence in both Talmuds concerning Julian and his plan."[58]

In the end, Julian's plan to rebuild the Jewish temple in Jerusalem came to naught, as did his efforts to bring back traditional cults. The endeavor to rebuild the temple of Jerusalem was abandoned at an early stage and Julian died during his campaign against the Persians in 363, after having reigned for less than two years.[59] Time could not be turned back. If Julian had been able to restore the temple, this would have raised further provocative questions for Jewish history. In the words of Michael Avi-Jonah: "Would the conflict between Rome and Israel be resolved peacefully in the fourth century, as it was not in the first? ... Would there be a revival of the Jewish aspirations to complete political independence? Would there be a repetition of the tragedy of the year 70 and a third destruction?"[60] Needless to say, none of these questions would have had any

---

Vol. 2: From Tacitus to Simplicius (Jerusalem: Israel Academy of Sciences & Humanities, 1980), 502–572; Yohanan Lewy, "Julian and the Rebuilding of the Temple," in Lewy, *Studies in Jewish Hellenism*, 221–254 (Hebr.); Michael Avi-Yonah, *The Jews under Roman and Byzantine Rule: A Political History of Palestine from the Bar Kokhba War to the Arab Conquest* (Jerusalem: Magnes, 1984), 185–207; Nicole Belayche, "Sacrifice and Theory of Sacrifice During the 'Pagan Reaction': Julian the Emperor," in *Sacrifice in Religious Experience*, ed. Albert I. Baumgarten (Leiden: Brill, 2002), 101–126.

56   Julianus, *Contr. Gal.* 306B: "the Jews agree with the Gentiles, except that they believe in only one God. That is indeed peculiar to them and strange to us, since all the rest we have in a manner in common with them—temples, sanctuaries, altars, purifications, and certain precepts. For as to these we differ from one another either not at all or in trivial matters" (trans. LCL).

57   Ephrem the Syrian, *Contr. Iul.* 1.16; 2.7 and Rufinus, *Hist.* 10.38. Cf. Avi-Yonah, *Jews under Roman and Byzantine Rule*, 193–194.

58   Avi-Yonah, *Jews under Roman and Byzantine Rule*, 197; Stern, *Greek and Latin Authors*, 506, 511.

59   Ammianus Marcellinus 23.1.2–3. Cf. Johannes Hahn, "Kaiser Julian und ein dritter Tempel? Idee, Wirklichkeit und Wirkung eines gescheiterten Projektes," in *Zerstörungen des Jerusalemer Tempels: Geschehen–Wahrnehmung–Bewältigung*, ed. Johannes Hahn (Tübingen: Mohr Siebeck, 2002), 237–262.

60   Avi-Yonah, *Jews under Roman and Byzantine Rule*, 204.

WHAT IF THE TEMPLE OF JERUSALEM HAD NOT BEEN DESTROYED 141

relevance if the temple of Jerusalem had not been destroyed by the Romans in the first place. Had the temple survived, had Jewish sacrifice faded out around the same time, Julian would have taken an entirely different approach to dealing with the Jewish cult and would have had no occasion to resort to such a revolutionary and polemical project in the first place.

5   Christianity and Rabbinic Culture

The survival of the temple would have also had major consequences for early Christianity and rabbinic Judaism. According to early Christian accounts, the temple's destruction signified the end of God's affection for Israel. It became an important argument—indeed, it was seen as concrete proof—that God had decided to choose a new Israel and punish the Jews for their denial of Jesus Christ. The Gospels refer in parabolic language to Jerusalem's destruction as confirmation of God's reorientation. In Matthew, Jesus says: "The king was enraged. He sent his troops, destroyed those murderers, and burned their city. Then he said to his slaves, 'The wedding is ready, but those invited were not worthy.' "[61] And in Mark: "What then will the owner of the vineyard do? He will come and destroy the tenants and give the vineyards to others."[62] As noted above, critiques of the temple were already common before 70 CE. But with the edifice's destruction, such critiques became an anchor of early Christian thinking and an anti-Jewish argument for centuries to come.

If the temple of Jerusalem had not been destroyed, the metaphorical insistence on Jesus as the final and eternal sacrifice, replacing actual animal offerings, would have been difficult to sustain.[63] Against the backdrop of ongoing temple sacrifices, interpreting the crucifixion as the sacrifice to end all sacrifice would have been less convincing. Both theological tenets—the destruction of the temple as a sign of divine punishment and Jesus as the consummation of all sacrifices—were important elements of early Christian thought. While it may be true that "the Jerusalem temple plays no significant role in either

---

61   Matt 22:7 NRSV, cf. Ulrich Luz, *Matthew 21–28: A Commentary* (Minneapolis: Fortress, 2005), 54: "the destruction of Jerusalem is understood to be the punishment for the rejection, mistreatment, and murder of the prophets and Jesus' emissaries .... After the destruction of the city of those murderers the king seeks new guests for the wedding feast of his son."

62   Mark 12:9 NRSV, cf. Joel Marcus, *Mark 8–16: A New Translation with Introduction and Commentary* (New Haven: Yale University Press, 2009), 813–814. Cf. also Luke 19:42–44 and Perkins, "If Jerusalem Stood," 196.

63   Cf. John 2:21 NRSV: "But he [Jesus] was speaking of the temple of his body."

Paul's pre-70 letters or in the epistolary literature following him," it does in the Gospels and other early Christian texts, such as the Letter of Barnabas and the work of Justin Martyr.[64] For Christian authors, such as Origen, Eusebius, and Ps-Hegesippus, Josephus's report on the fall of the temple in the Jewish War served as a prooftext for the divine punishment of the Jews.[65] Had the temple not been destroyed, the early Christian community could not have distanced itself theologically from the Jewish religion so easily. It is probably safe to say that the development of Christianity as a world religion would not have taken flight as it did.[66]

What about rabbinic Judaism? In Jewish mythology, the destruction of the temple was a disaster of cosmic proportions. The destruction (*khurban*) marked the beginning of the exile—including the exile of God from Zion—and the introduction of chaos into the world. It signaled the removal of the people of Israel from the source of its blessing and the abandonment of its direct access to God. This view of the destruction as a cataclysmic event was most poignantly phrased by Samuel Yosef Agnon in his acceptance speech upon receiving the Nobel prize in literature in 1966 when he said: "As a result of the historic catastrophe in which Titus of Rome destroyed Jerusalem and Israel was exiled from its land, I was born in one of the cities of the Exile. But always I regarded myself as one who was born in Jerusalem."[67] Historically speaking, the significance of this rupture was greatly exaggerated in rabbinic Judaism. And Agnon was not simply born in Galicia because of Titus. The Jewish diaspora was not the result of the second temple's destruction, but was much older, extending back to the destruction of the first temple in the sixth century BCE.

---

64   Ruth A. Clements, "70 CE After 135 CE—The Making of a Watershed?" in Schwartz and Weiss, *Was 70 CE a Watershed?*, 520–521 (525–533 on Justin Martyr); Jörg Frey, "Temple and Identity in Early Christianity and in the Johannine Community: Reflections on the 'Parting of the Ways,'" in Schwartz and Weiss, *Was 70 CE a Watershed?*, 447–507; Letter of Barnabas 16 (cf. Ferdinand R. Prostmeier, *Der Barnabasbrief* [Göttingen: Vandenhoeck & Ruprecht, 1999], 501–525).

65   Cf. René Bloch, "Iosephus Flavius (Flavius Josephus), Bellum Iudaicum," in *Brill's New Pauly Supplements I—Volume 5: The Reception of Classical Literature*, ed. Christine Walde (Leiden: Brill, 2012), 191–192.

66   Cf. Perkins, "If Jerusalem Stood," 203. Would the "delocativization" of religion which we mentioned above still have happened if Christianity had developed in a different way? It probably would. The move from public to private forms of religion was not simply a Christian phenomenon, but part of a wider development. On a possible change from cult to a more interiorized form of religion in Rome see Stroumsa, *The End of Sacrifice*, 87 with further literature.

67   http://www.nobelprize.org/nobel_prizes/literature/laureates/1966/agnon-speech.html.

WHAT IF THE TEMPLE OF JERUSALEM HAD NOT BEEN DESTROYED 143

One thing that rabbinic Judaism shared with early Christianity was the fact that they both "remained sacrificial religions, but very special sacrificial religions because they functioned without blood sacrifice."[68] In rabbinic literature, temple discourse was quite distinct from early Christian interpretations. Whereas Christianity revolved around salvation through the final sacrifice of Jesus, the rabbis kept the sacrificial world alive by continuing to study and explain it. The Mishna, written down around 200 CE, is acutely aware that the second temple was gone, destroyed on the same day as its predecessor about 650 years earlier: "On the ninth of Ab ... the Temple was destroyed the first and the second time, and Beth-Tor was captured and the City was ploughed up."[69] The fall of the temple was thus turned into a mythic history of catastrophe and entered the liturgical calendar. At the same time, however, the rabbis of the Mishna were unwilling to accept the temple's fate. Ingeniously combining denial with the messianic hope for the temple's future restoration, the rabbis discussed sacrificial rites as if the holy edifice were still standing. The fifth order of the Mishna, *Qodashim*, comprises eleven tractates on issues related to the temple and sacrificial rites, thus upholding the status of sacrifice in Judaism, albeit in an intellectualized and imaginary form.[70]

If the temple had not been destroyed by the Romans, rabbinic Judaism probably would not have developed in the way it did. Commentary, scriptural arguments, and interpretations as we know them from the Mishna and the Talmud surely had precursors long before the temple's destruction. Literary and historical evidence for the earliest rabbis (the five "pairs" and the first generation of the Tannaim) is scanty, but one can also refer to Qumran, Philo of Alexandria, and also the Septuagint for pre-70 interpretive narratives.[71] The idea of engaging Scripture as a form of religious service existed before the temple fell. The rabbis had predecessors and did not simply arise in the vacuum left by the sudden cessation of sacrifice. But the Mishna's development stands in direct

---

68   Stroumsa, *The End of Sacrifice*, 63–64.

69   m. Ta'an. 4:6 (trans. Danby). Beth-Tor (Bethar) and the ploughing of the city refer to the end of the Bar Kokhba revolt. On rabbinic responses to the destruction of the temple cf. Günter Stemberger, "Reaktionen auf die Tempelzerstörung in der rabbinischen Literatur," in Hahn, *Zerstörungen des Jerusalemer Tempels*. 207–236.

70   Thus tractate *Tamid* describes the daily life in the temple, tractate *Middot* in great detail its architecture. See Shmuel Safrai, "Jerusalem and the Temple in the Tannaitic Literature of the First Generation after the Destruction of the Temple," in *Sanctity of Time and Space in Tradition and Modernity*, ed. Alberdina Houtman, Marcel J.H.M. Poorthuis, and Joshua Schwartz (Leiden: Brill, 1998), 135–152.

71   Günter Stemberger, *Einleitung in Talmud und Midrasch: Neunte, vollständig überarbeitete Auflage* (Munich: C.H. Beck, 2011), 78–84.

relation to the temple's destruction; its detailed descriptions of the temple service preserve the memory of the Second Temple Period and simultaneously serve as a "blueprint for the messianic era."[72] Had the temple survived, there would have been no Mishna—certainly not in the form in which we know it. The same would be true of the Gemara, which commented on the Mishna, and thus for the Talmud.

The rabbis later imagined a smooth transition from the destruction of the temple to the constitution of the first rabbinical school in Yavne—from temple to text, so to speak. We now know that things were more complicated and that the rabbinic movement established itself in an authoritative form only later.[73] Is the success story of the rabbinic movement imaginable without the destruction of the temple? Hardly. It was the temple's disappearance that largely triggered the paradigm change that accompanied rabbinic culture. Moreover, the temple's destruction, together with the fall of Jerusalem, played an important role in rabbinic theology as the primary rupture. The temple's fall was understood as a divine punishment for (and a warning against) moral flaws among the Jews.[74] Titus became the emblematic archenemy and paganism was convincingly presented as an anti-culture to be avoided.[75] If we prefer to think that there would have been a Talmud with the temple still standing, it would have looked quite different. If rabbinic Judaism had not emerged or had manifested itself in a much less consequential form, Judaism's long-term development would have been profoundly affected.

6   A Watershed in Jewish History?

The extent to which the Romans' destruction of the temple of Jerusalem marks a watershed in Jewish history continues to be a matter of scholarly disagreement.[76] As our counterfactual discussion has shown, there is no simple way to assess the event's significance. But there is good reason to interpret the tem-

---

72   Shaye J.D. Cohen, "The Judean Legal Tradition and the Halakhah of the Mishna," in *The Cambridge Companion to the Talmud and Rabbinic Literature*, ed. Charlotte Elisheva Fonrobert and Martin S. Jaffee (Cambridge: Cambridge University Press, 2007), 121–143, at 131.

73   See Seth Schwartz, *Imperialism and Jewish Society, 200 B.C.E. to 640 C.E.* (Princeton: Princeton University Press, 2001). According to Schwartz, "the rabbis did not have any officially recognized legal authority until the end of the fourth century" (103–104).

74   Mireille Hadas-Lebel, *Jerusalem Against Rome* (Leuven: Peeters, 2006), 152–157.

75   Günter Stemberger, *Die römische Herrschaft im Urteil der Juden* (Darmstadt: Wissenschaftliche Buchgesellschaft, 1983), 69–73.

76   Schwartz and Weiss, *Was 70 CE a Watershed?*.

ple's destruction as having profoundly affected both the history of Judaism and Christianity. The sudden loss of the cultic center of Judaism was formative not only for rabbinic culture, but became a crucial point of orientation for all subsequent periods of Judaism. In orthodox Jewish liturgy, the restoration of the temple continues to be a theme of great importance. The classic interior architecture of the synagogue—most notably, the Torah Ark (*aron haqodesh*) and the "eternal light" (*ner tamid*)—are concrete physical reminders of the temple. Without that formative event, Jewish history and Jewish myth would have looked entirely different.

In other respects, however, the events of the year 70 CE were less decisive for Judaism's subsequent development. Even if the temple had not been destroyed, Jewish sacrificial rituals would have slowly faded out of their own accord during late antiquity. Similarly, neither the Jewish diaspora nor the first synagogues were brought about by the temple's destruction. Diaspora Judaism had always been non-sacrificial (a few exceptions notwithstanding) and was certainly less affected by the temple's fall than Judaism in the land of Israel. In the end, counterfactually speculating about the temple's survival, while admittedly hypothetical, helps us understand the deeper forces that profoundly shaped Judaism in the ancient world.

Bibliography

Alföldy, Geza, "Eine Bauinschrift aus dem Colosseum." *Zeitschrift für Papyrologie und Epigraphik* 109 (1995): 195–226.

Auffarth, Christoph, "Le rite sacrificiel antique: la longue durée et la fin du sacrifice," review of *Animal Sacrifice in ancient Greek religion, Judaism, and Christianity 100 BC–AD 200*, ed. Maria-Zoe Petropolou. *Kernos* 25 (2012): 300–301.

Avi-Yonah, Michael, *The Jews under Roman and Byzantine Rule: A Political History of Palestine from the Bar Kokhba War to the Arab Conquest*. Jerusalem: Magnes, 1984.

Belayche, Nicole, "Sacrifice and Theory of Sacrifice During the 'Pagan Reaction': Julian the Emperor." Pages 101–126 in *Sacrifice in Religious Experience*. Edited by Albert I. Baumgarten. Leiden: Brill, 2002.

Barclay, John, *Flavius Josephus: Against Apion*. Leiden: Brill, 2007.

Bernays, Jacob, "Über die Chronik des Sulpicius Severus, ein Beitrag zur Geschichte der classischen und biblischen Studien." Pages 81–200 in *Jacob Bernays, Gesammelte Abhandlungen*. Vol. 2. Edited by Hermann Usener. Berlin: Hertz, 1885 (1861).

Bauckham, Richard, "Josephus' Account of the Temple in *Contra Apionem* 2.102–109." Pages 327–347 in *Josephus' Contra Apionem: Studies in its Character and Context with a Latin Concordance to the Portion Missing in Greek*. Edited by Louis Feldman and John R. Levison. Leiden: Brill, 1996.

Bloch, René, *Moses und der Mythos: Die Auseinandersetzung mit der griechischen Mythologie bei jüdisch-hellenistischen Autoren.* Leiden: Brill, 2011.

Bloch, René, "Iosephus Flavius (Flavius Josephus), Bellum Iudaicum." Pages 191–192 in *Brill's New Pauly Supplements 1—Volume 5: The Reception of Classical Literature.* Edited by Christine Walde. Leiden: Brill, 2012.

Boustan, Ra'anan S., "Confounding Blood: Jewish Narratives of Sacrifice and Violence in Late Antiquity." Pages 265–286 in *Ancient Mediterranean Sacrifice.* Edited by Jennifer Wright Knust and Zsuzsanna Várhelyi. Oxford: Oxford University Press, 2011.

Brown, Peter, *The World of Late Antiquity: From Marcus Aurelius to Mohammed.* London: Thames & Hudson, 1971.

Burkert, Walter, *Homo Necans: The Anthropology of Ancient Greek Sacrificial Ritual and Myth.* Berkeley: University of California Press, 1986.

Clements, Ruth A., "70 CE After 135 CE—The Making of a Watershed?" Pages 517–536 in *Was 70 CE a Watershed in Jewish History? On Jews and Judaism before and after the Destruction of the Second Temple.* Edited by Daniel R. Schwartz and Zeev Weiss. Leiden: Brill, 2012.

Cohen, Shaye J.D., "The Judean Legal Tradition and the Halakhah of the Mishna." Pages 121–143 in *The Cambridge Companion to the Talmud and Rabbinic Literature.* Edited by Charlotte Elisheva Fonrobert and Martin S. Jaffee. Cambridge: Cambridge University Press, 2007.

Eck, Werner, *Rom und Judaea: Fünf Vorträge zur römischen Herrschaft in Palaestina.* Tübingen: Mohr Siebeck, 2007.

Eshel, Hanan, "Bar Kokhba Revolt." Pages 421–425 in *The Eerdmans Dictionary of Early Judaism.* Edited by John J. Collins and Daniel C. Harlow. Grand Rapids: Eerdmans, 2010.

Frankfurter, David, *Religion in Roman Egypt: Assimilation and Resistance.* Princeton: Princeton University Press, 1998.

Frey, Jörg, "Temple and Rival Temple—The Cases of Elephantine, Mt. Gerizim, and Leontopolis." Pages 171–203 in *Gemeinde ohne Tempel: Community without Temple: Zur Substituierung und Transformation des Jerusalemer Tempels und seines Kults im Alten Testament, antiken Judentum und frühen Christentum.* Edited by Beate Ego et al. Tübingen: Mohr Siebeck, 1999.

Frey, Jörg, "Temple and Identity in Early Christianity and in the Johannine Community: Reflections on the 'Parting of the Ways'." Pages 447–507 in *Was 70 CE a Watershed in Jewish History? On Jews and Judaism before and after the Destruction of the Second Temple.* Edited by Daniel R. Schwartz and Zeev Weiss. Leiden: Brill, 2012.

Gilders, William K., "Jewish Sacrifice: Its Nature and Function (According to Philo)." Pages 94–105 in *Ancient Mediterranean Sacrifice.* Edited by Jennifer Wright Knust and Zsuzsanna Várhelyi. Oxford: Oxford University Press, 2011.

Giovannini, Adalberto, "Die Zerstörung Jerusalems durch Titus: Eine Strafe Gottes oder eine historische Notwendigkeit?" Pages 11–34 in *Contra quis ferat arma deos? Vier Augsburger Vorträge zur Religionsgeschichte der römischen Kaiserzeit zum 60. Geburtstag von Gunther Gottlieb.* Edited by Pedro Barceló. Munich: Ernst Vögel, 1996.

Goodman, Martin, "Nerva, The Fiscus Iudaicus and Jewish Identity." *JRS* 79 (1989): 40–44.

Goodman, Martin, *Rome and Jerusalem: The Clash of Ancient Civilizations.* New York: Alfred A. Knopf, 2008.

Gruen, Erich S., *Diaspora: Jews amidst Greeks and Romans.* Cambridge: Harvard University Press, 2002.

Hadas-Lebel, Mireille, *Jerusalem Against Rome.* Leuven: Peeters, 2006.

Hahn, Johannes, "Kaiser Julian und ein dritter Tempel? Idee, Wirklichkeit und Wirkung eines gescheiterten Projektes." Pages 237–262 in *Zerstörungen des Jerusalemer Tempels: Geschehen–Wahrnehmung–Bewältigung.* Edited by Johannes Hahn. Tübingen: Mohr Siebeck, 2002.

Hahn, Johannes, "Gesetze als Waffe? Die kaiserliche Religionspolitik und die Zerstörung der Tempel." Pages 201–220 in *Spätantiker Staat und religiöser Konflikt: Imperiale und lokale Verwaltung und die Gewalt gegen Heiligtümer.* Edited by Johannes Hahn. Berlin: de Gruyter, 2011.

Klawans, Jonathan, *Purity, Sacrifice, and the Temple. Symbolism and Supersessionism in the Study of Ancient Judaism.* Oxford: Oxford University Press, 2006.

Klawans, Jonathan, *Josephus and the Theologies of Ancient Judaism.* Oxford: Oxford University Press, 2012.

Laupot, Eric, "Tacitus' Fragment 2: The Anti-Roman Movement of the Christiani and the Nazoreans." *VC* 54 (2000): 233–247.

Leonhardt-Balzer, Jutta, "Priests and Priesthood in Philo: Could he Have Done without Them?" Pages 127-153 in *Was 70 CE a Watershed in Jewish History? On Jews and Judaism before and after the Destruction of the Second Temple.* Edited by Daniel R. Schwartz and Zeev Weiss. Leiden: Brill, 2012.

Levine, Lee I., "Temple, Jerusalem." Pages 1281–1291 in *The Eerdmans Dictionary of Early Judaism.* Edited by John J. Collins and Daniel C. Harlow. Grand Rapids: Eerdmans, 2010.

Lewy, Yohanan, "Titus' Justification with regard to the Destruction of the Temple according to Tacitus." Pages 190–194 in id., *Studies in Jewish Hellenism.* Jerusalem: Bialik Institute, 1969 (1943) (Hebr.).

Lewy, Yohanan, "Julian and the Rebuilding of the Temple." Pages 221–254 in id, *Studies in Jewish Hellenism.* Jerusalem: Bialik Institute, 1969 (1943) (Hebr.).

Luz, Ulrich, *Matthew 8–20: A Commentary.* Minneapolis: Fortress, 2001.

Luz, Ulrich, *Matthew 21–28: A Commentary.* Minneapolis: Fortress, 2005.

Marcus, Joel, *Mark 8–16: A New Translation with Introduction and Commentary.* New Haven: Yale University Press, 2009.

Millar, Fergus, *The Roman Near East: 31 BC–AD 337*. Cambridge: Harvard University Press, 1993.

Millar, Fergus, "Last Year in Jerusalem: Monuments of the Jewish War in Rome." Pages 101–128 in *Flavius Josephus and Flavian Rome*. Edited by Jonathan C. Edmondson, Steve Mason, and James B. Rives. Oxford: Oxford University Press, 2005.

Montefiore, Hugh, "Sulpicius Severus and Titus' Council of War." *Historia* 11 (1962): 156–170.

Mor, Menachem, and Friedrich V. Reiterer, eds., *Samaritans, Past and Present: Current Studies*. Berlin: de Gruyter, 2010.

Perkins, Pheme, "If Jerusalem Stood: The Destruction of Jerusalem and Christian Anti-Judaism." *Biblical Interpretation* 8 (2000): 194–204.

Price, Jonathan, *Jerusalem under Siege: The Collapse of the Jewish State 66–70 C.E.* Leiden: Brill, 1992.

Prostmeier, Ferdinand R., *Der Barnabasbrief*. Göttingen: Vandenhoeck & Ruprecht, 1999.

Rives, James B., "Flavian Religious Policy and the Destruction of the Jerusalem Temple." Pages 145–166 in *Flavius Josephus and Flavian Rome*. Edited by Jonathan C. Edmondson, Steve Mason, and James B. Rives. Oxford: Oxford University Press, 2005.

Runesson, Anders, Donald D. Binder, and Birger Olsson, *The Ancient Synagogue from its Origins to 200 C.E.: A Source Book*. Leiden: Brill, 2008.

Safrai, Shmuel, "Jerusalem and the Temple in the Tannaitic Literature of the First Generation after the Destruction of the Temple." Pages 135–152 in *Sanctity of Time and Space in Tradition and Modernity*. Edited by Alberdina Houtman, Marcel J.H.M. Poorthuis, and Joshua Schwartz. Leiden: Brill, 1998.

Schäfer, Peter, ed., *The Bar Kokhba War Reconsidered: New Perspectives on the Second Jewish Revolt Against Rome*. Tübingen: Mohr Siebeck, 2003.

Schiffman, Lawrence H., "Community Without Temple: The Qumran Community's Withdrawal from the Jerusalem Temple." Pages 267–284 in *Gemeinde ohne Tempel: Community without Temple: Zur Substituierung und Transformation des Jerusalemer Tempels und seines Kults im Alten Testament, antiken Judentum und frühen Christentum*. Edited by Beate Ego et al. Tübingen: Mohr Siebeck, 1999.

Schwartz, Seth, *Imperialism and Jewish Society, 200 B.C.E. to 640 C.E.* Princeton: Princeton University Press, 2001.

Sharon, Nadav, "Setting the Stage: The Effects of the Roman Conquest and the Loss of Sovereignty." Pages 415–443 in *Was 70 CE a Watershed in Jewish History? On Jews and Judaism before and after the Destruction of the Second Temple*. Edited by Daniel R. Schwartz and Zeev Weiss. Leiden: Brill, 2012.

Smith, Jonathan Z., *Map Is Not Territory: Studies in the History of Religions*. Chicago: The University of Chicago Press, 1978.

Stemberger, Günter, *Die römische Herrschaft im Urteil der Juden*. Darmstadt: Wissenschaftliche Buchgesellschaft, 1983.

Stemberger, Günter, "Reaktionen auf die Tempelzerstörung in der rabbinischen Literatur." Pages 207–236 in *Zerstörungen des Jerusalemer Tempels: Geschehen–Wahrnehmung–Bewältigung*. Edited by Johannes Hahn. Tübingen: Mohr Siebeck, 2002.

Stemberger, Günter, *Einleitung in Talmud und Midrasch: Neunte, vollständig überarbeitete Auflage*. Munich: C.H. Beck, 2011.

Stern, Menahem, *Greek and Latin Authors on Jews and Judaism*. Vol. 2: *From Tacitus to Simplicius*. Jerusalem: Israel Academy of Sciences & Humanities, 1980.

Strack, Hermann L. and Paul Billerbeck, eds., *Das Evangelium nach Matthäus erläutert aus Talmud und Midrasch*. Vol. 1. Munich: C.H. Beck, 1922.

Stroumsa, Guy, *The End of Sacrifice: Religious Transformations in Late Antiquity*. Chicago: The University of Chicago Press, 2009.

Swartz, Michael D., "Liturgy, Poetry, and the Persistence of Sacrifice." Pages 393–412 in *Was 70 CE a Watershed in Jewish History? On Jews and Judaism before and after the Destruction of the Second Temple*. Edited by Daniel R. Schwartz and Zeev Weiss. Leiden: Brill, 2012.

Theissen, Gerd, "Jesus im Judentum. Drei Versuche einer Ortsbestimmung." Pages 35–56 in *Jesus als historische Gestalt: Beiträge zur Jesusforschung zum 60. Geburtstag von Gerd Theissen*. Edited by Gerd Theissen and Annette Merz. Göttingen: Vandenhoeck & Ruprecht, 2003.

Tuval, Michael, *From Jerusalem Priest to Roman Jew: On Josephus and the Paradigms of Ancient Judaism*. Tübingen: Mohr Siebeck, 2013.

Yavetz, Zvi, "Reflections on Titus and Josephus." *GRBS* 16 (1975): 411–432.

PART 3

Theater and Myth

∵

CHAPTER 8

Philo's Struggle with Jewish Myth

> With all their endeavor to present Judaism to the world in an understandable and acceptable form, the Alexandrian Jewish writers never compromised with popular Greek religion or mythology or the mysteries. They never tried to present the Jewish God as any of the gods of popular religion, or Jewish tradition as myths, or Jewish religious rites as rites of mysteries .... If they ever happen to use mythological allusions, it is only as literary forms of expression and then, too, always with the proviso, sometimes expressed, that the use of a mythological allusion should not be taken as an expression of belief in the myth alluded to.[1]

In this comment on Alexandrian Jewish responses to Greek religion by Harry A. Wolfson, from his magisterial monograph *Philo* published in 1947, Wolfson shows that he sees no space for any compromise between Jewish Scripture and Greek myth in Jewish-Hellenistic literature. Philo, as Wolfson concludes his observations, "does not admit with the Greek philosophers that man-made Greek mythology contains philosophic truths which are to be discovered by the allegorical method. But what he denies to mythology he claims for the divinely read Hebrew Scripture."[2] It is not that Wolfson is unaware of nuances in Philo's discussion of myth. He admits that "despite his condemnation of popular religion, mythology, and mysteries, Philo does not hesitate to make use of the vocabulary of all these in his description of the beliefs and institutions of Judaism."[3] But in the end, according to Wolfson, for Philo myth has no meaning.

Wolfson's radical denial, finally, of any value of myth in Philo fits into the larger thesis of his history of philosophy. Wolfson's *Philo*—1000 pages of impressive learning—was part of a larger project: a history of Jewish philosophy or rather of philosophy in general. To Wolfson, Philo stands for a paradigmatic change. As a matter of fact, Wolfson does not hesitate to speak of a "Philonic revolution:"[4] by introducing scripture to philosophy and making it the most important point of reference, Philo ushered in "a fundamentally new period in

---

1 Harry A. Wolfson, *Philo: Foundations of Religious Philosophy in Judaism, Christianity, and Islam*. 2 vols. (Cambridge: Harvard University Press, 1947), 1.86.
2 Wolfson, *Philo*, 1.133.
3 Wolfson, *Philo*, 1.38.
4 Wolfson, *Philo*, 2.458.

© RENÉ BLOCH, 2022 | DOI:10.1163/9789004521896_010

154   CHAPTER 8

the history of philosophy."[5] Philo did not just become a very important source
for early Christian thought, but the predecessor or even the inventor of what
Wolfson calls the "synthetic mediaeval philosopher." That philosopher believes
"in one infallible source of truth, and that is revelation, and that revelation is
embodied in Scripture, be it Old Testament or New Testament or Koran."[6] At
the other end of Wolfson's spectrum lies Spinoza. If Philo had introduced philosophy as the handmaid of Scripture, Spinoza—in particular with his *Tractatus Theologico-Politicus*—removed Scripture from philosophy. By attacking the
Philonic belief in revelation with "his denial of revelation,"[7] Spinoza restored
the philosophical *status quo ante*. This is how Wolfson's massive study on Philo
ends: "To the question, then, what is new in Philo? the answer is that it was
he who built up that philosophy, just as the answer to the question what is
new in Spinoza? is that it was he who pulled it down."[8] Wolfson's forceful
thesis is intriguing, but in its large scale it is also courageous, and in its hes-
itance to acknowledge inconsistencies and exceptions problematic. For the
purpose of our study it is important to note that Wolfson's understanding of
Philo as a philosophical revolutionary has a great impact on his interpretation of Philo's reading of myth, whether Greek or Jewish. For Wolfson, all of
Philo is subordinate to Scripture. It is hardly by chance that Wolfson starts out
his tour d'horizon exactly with Philo's interpretation of mythology (or rather
"Polytheism, Mythology, and Mysteries"[9]). This serves as a litmus test for seeing whether the thesis that revealed Scripture becomes the overarching truth
applies throughout. Wolfson struggles with the question, but in the end his
answer is clear: "The point is that when Philo, in various ways, maintains that
some scriptural story is not like a myth, he means that it is not like a myth
because a scriptural story, whether literally true as a fact or not, always has
some underlying meaning, whereas myths neither are literally true nor have
an underlying meaning."[10]

There are indeed many passages in Philo which seem only to confirm Wolfson's conclusion that in the end for Philo there is no value in myth.[11] Nor is

---

5   Wolfson, *Philo*, 2.444.
6   Wolfson, *Philo*, 2.446.
7   Wolfson, *Philo*, 2.458.
8   Wolfson, *Philo*, 2.460.
9   Wolfson, *Philo*, 2.27–55.
10   Wolfson, *Philo*, 2.36.
11   "Myth" meant in the sense of Philo's common use of the word: legendary, fabulous tales.
        For a thorough survey of Philo's use of μῦθος see Anita Méasson, "Un aspect de la critique
        du polythéisme chez Philon d'Alexandrie: les acceptions du mot μῦθος dans son œuvre,"
        Centre Jean Palerne Mémoires 2 (1980): 75–107. In modern scholarship "myth" is understood

PHILO'S STRUGGLE WITH JEWISH MYTH   155

Wolfson by any means the only scholar to stress the incompatibility of myth and Torah in Philo.[12] In fact, right at the beginning of his tractate *On the Creation of the World* (*De opificio mundi*), a text widely considered to be at the head of the so called "Exposition of the Law" (a scholarly term, not Philo's), Philo contrasts Moses and other lawgivers (νομοθέται) presenting Jewish law as free of myth:

> Among other lawgivers some drew up the regulations that they regarded as just in an unadorned and naked fashion, while others enclothed their thoughts with a mass of verbiage and so deceived the masses by concealing the truth with mythical fictions (μυθικοῖς πλάσμασι). Moses surpassed both groups, regarding the former as lacking reflection, indolent and unphilosophical, the latter as mendacious and full of trickery (ὡς κατεψευσμένον καὶ μεστὸν γοητείας). Instead he made a splendid and awe-inspiring start to his laws. He did not immediately state what should be done and what not, nor did he, since it was necessary to form in advance the minds of those who were to make use of the laws, invent myths (μήτ', … μύθους πλασάμενος) or express approval of those composed by others.[13]

Philo's Moses is as far removed from the fabrications of myth as one can possibly imagine and his explanation for the rejection of myth is telling: myth

---

in a wider sense and much more with regard to function than with regard to content: "myth is a traditional tale with secondary, partial reference to something of collective importance" (Walter Burkert, *Structure and History in Greek Mythology and Ritual* [Berkeley: University of California Press, 1979], 23) or simply an "ideology in narrative from" (Bruce Lincoln, *Theorizing Myth: Narrative, Ideology, and Scholarship* [Chicago: The University of Chicago Press, 1999], xii). While I very much endorse this functional understanding of "myth" (also very much present in Philo's rewriting of the Bible), in the following "myth" is used in the sense of "fabulous tale." That biblical stories as they are told in the book of Genesis and elsewhere should be considered myths (very similar to Greek myths) is by now widely accepted: cf. on this Michael Fishbane, *Biblical Myth and Rabbinic Mythmaking* (Oxford: Oxford University Press, 2003).

12   Cf., e.g., Gerhard Delling, "Wunder—Allegorie—Mythus bei Philon von Alexandreia," in *Wissenschaftliche Zeitschrift der Martin-Luther-Universität Halle-Wittenberg, Gesellschafts- und Sprachwissenschaftliche Reihe* 6 (1956/57): 713–740 and note 68 below.

13   Philo, *Opif.* 1–2, translation, slightly adjusted, by David T. Runia, *Philo of Alexandria: On the Creation of the Cosmos According to Moses* (Leiden: Brill, 2001). All other translations from Philo, at times adjusted, are those of Colson (LCL). In the following I am taking up and expanding some observations made in René Bloch, *Moses und der Mythos: Die Auseinandersetzung mit der griechischen Mythologie bei jüdisch-hellenistischen Autoren* (Leiden: Brill, 2011) and, more briefly, idem, "Moses and Greek Myth in Hellenistic Judaism," in *The Construction of Moses*, ed. Thomas Römer (Paris: Gabalda, 2007), 195–208.

156   CHAPTER 8

stands in opposition to the Law, which was given for the enduring benefit
of future generations. Myths are ephemeral figures and thus the opposite of
the unchanging and true nature of the Jewish law. By making such a clear
statement right before entering the discussion of the creation of the world—
which he summarizes as "most wondrous" (ἡ δ'ἀρχὴ ... ἐστὶ θαυμασιωτάτη[14])—
Philo apologetically rejects any interpretation of the beginning of the world as
myth.[15] That there were people who accused the Torah of containing myth we
know from Philo himself,[16] but also from an author such as Celsus (second century CE, cited by Origen) who calls the Moses narrative "empty myths" (μῦθοι
κενοί), and the story about Adam, Eve, and the snake "most sinful." According
to Celsus, such myths are "old wives' fables" and "stories for young children"
and thus cannot be taken seriously.[17] Josephus, writing a generation after Philo
and thus closer to the work of Celsus, issues a similarly fierce denial of Jewish
myth at the beginning of his retelling of the book of Genesis.[18] In both cases the
preceding distancing from myth is clearly meant as a preemptive strike against
accusations of Jewish myth. But Philo's rejection of myth is by no means limited
to his discussion of the creation of the world. It is a point made repeatedly in
Philo's work: mythmaking is unsteady and unreliable (ἀβέβαιος μυθοποιία[19]). It
is symbolized by Esau, the homeless (ἄοικος) hunter and opposite of his brother
Jacob who is steady, not feigned (ἄπλαστος), and who stays in his tent.[20] Esau
is nothing other than simply "myth" (μῦθος αὐτός).[21]

But things are more complicated (and maybe also more interesting). Wolfson's view of Philo, to whom myth has no meaning, may be as simplistic as
Philo's denial of myth at the beginning of *De opificio mundi* and elsewhere.[22]
The very existence of Philo's apologetic notes points in another direction: Philo
was clearly aware of the mythological power inherent in the biblical stories.

---

14   Philo, *Opif.* 3.
15   Cf. also *Det.* 125: In God's creation there are no invented myths (ἐν δὲ τῇ τοῦ θεοῦ ποιητικῇ
      μύθου μὲν πλάσμα οὐδὲν εὑρήσεις). Philo audaciously collides divine "poetry" and pagan
      myth, cf. David Dawson, *Allegorical Readers and Cultural Revision in Ancient Alexandria*
      (Berkeley: University of California Press, 1992), 107.
16   Cf. below on Philo's treatment of Jewish critics who ridiculed the myth of the tower of
      Babel.
17   Origen, *Cels.* 1.20; 4.36,41.
18   Josephus, *AJ* 1.15–23.
19   Philo, *Sacr.* 13. On μυθοποιία see further below.
20   Philo, *Congr.* 61–62 on Gen 25:27. Esau is a companion of fiction, things made and mythical
      trash (πλάσματος καὶ ποιήματος καὶ μυθικῶν λήρων ἑταῖρος).
21   Philo, *Congr.* 62.
22   Philo is repeatedly denying the existence of myth in the Bible: cf. *Abr.* 243; *Fug.* 121 (see
      below); *Det.* 125; *Gig.* 58; *Decal.* 156; *Spec.* 1.51.

PHILO'S STRUGGLE WITH JEWISH MYTH 157

And while he often denies any kind of mythology, he can very well discuss biblical stories within mythical parameters. As a matter of fact, he can do both within the very same context. His discussion of the destruction of Sodom and the metamorphosis of Lot's wife into a pillar of salt (Gen 19) is a case in point. Philo was surely aware that the motif of a metamorphosis was a very common one in pagan mythology[23] and it thus may come as no surprise that when he introduces the story, he stresses that "Moses did not invent a myth (οὐ μυθοπλαστῶν), but indicated an actual fact (πράγματος ἰδιότητα μηνύων)."[24] Philo then reads the story of Lot's wife turning back and becoming a pillar allegorically (as he does elsewhere with regard to the destruction of Sodom[25]). The pillar is an example for those "with no desire either to find or to seek:"

> For a man who is led by innate and habitual laziness to pay no attention to his teacher neglects what lies in front of him, which would enable him to see and hear and use his other faculties for the observation of nature's facts. Instead he twists his neck and turns his face backwards, and his thoughts are all for the blind things of life, even more than for the body parts, and so he turns into a pillar and becomes like a lifeless and deaf stone.[26]

As so often it is allegory which for Philo opens up the path of exegesis:[27] the metamorphosis of Lot's wife stands for the blindness of people who disregard the potential of virtue lying in front of them. In another tractate Philo explains the etymology of Sodom as "barrenness and blindness" (στείρωσις καὶ τύφλωσις).[28] But what does Philo's allegorical reading mean for the materiality of the pillar? Does the pillar exist or is it simply a meaningful story about a pillar? Josephus in his discussion of the story leaves no doubt about this: "I have seen it (sc.

---

23   On the theme of metamorphosis in Greek mythology cf. Paul M.C. Forbes Irving, *Metamorphosis in Greek Myths* (Oxford: Clarendon, 1990).

24   Philo, *Fug.* 121.

25   Philo, *QG* 4.51.

26   Philo, *Fug.* 121–122.

27   An excellent description of Philo's use of allegory remains Jean Pépin, *Mythe et allégorie: les origines grecques et les contestations judéo-chrétiennes* (Paris: Aubier, 1976 [1958]), 231–242; cf. also idem, "Remarques sur la théorie de l'exégèse allégorique chez Philon," in *Philon d'Alexandrie, Lyon 11–15 Septembre 1966* (Paris: Éditions du Cerf, 1967), 131–168, at 143–146 and, more recently, Dawson, *Allegorical Readers*, 73–126.

28   Philo, *Ebr.* 222; *Somn.* 2.192; *QG* 2.43; 4.23; 4.31. The Hebrew etymology of which Philo makes use here is unclear: Lester L. Grabbe, *Etymology in Early Jewish Interpretation: The Hebrew Names in Philo* (Atlanta: Scholars, 1988), 208.

the stele) for it even now remains (ἱστόρησα δ’ αὐτήν, ἔτι γὰρ καὶ νῦν διαμένει)."[29] Philo does not comment on the whereabouts of the pillar, but he does comment on the remains of the larger area, that is the traces of the destroyed city of Sodom. In his *Life of Moses* he refers to the relics (μνημεῖα) of Sodom which up until his days were still being shown: "ruins and cinders and brimstone and smoke, and the dusky flame still arising as though fire were smoldering within."[30] Philo's allegorizing of the destruction of Sodom and the metamorphosis of Lot's wife does not exclude a literal understanding of the miracle and its traces. Nor does it mean that the mythical danger inherent in the story is kept under control. As a matter of fact, by pointing to the relics of Sodom that are still shown Philo participates in a "mythical" discourse that was quite common in Hellenistic and Roman times: traces of myth were shown all over the Mediterranean. Jews had mythical realia of their own.[31]

By first explicitly denying that the story about the metamorphosis of Lot's wife is a myth and then allegorizing it Philo follows an apologetic pattern that he uses repeatedly in his struggle with Jewish myth. While in the case of Lot's wife he does not explicitly explain allegory as the solution to an exegetical problem, he does so elsewhere: the snake of the biblical paradise is by no means to be understood as one of these "mythical inventions" (οὐ μύθου πλάσματα) as they are known from pagan literature. Rather, such stories are "examples of models" (δείγματα τύπων) which literally "call for allegory" (ἐπ’ ἀλληγορίαν παρακαλοῦντα).[32] Philo is even more explicit when he adds the other biblical snake, the episode of the bronze serpent (Num 21:8–9). Only when the "covert meaning" of such scenes is explained (ἐν δὲ ταῖς δι’ ὑπονοιῶν ἀποδόσεσι), "then the mythical is no longer in the way, and the truth is discovered as being manifest" (τὸ μὲν μυθῶδες ἐκποδὼν οἴχεται, τὸ δ’ ἀληθὲς ἀρίδηλον εὑρίσκεται).[33] Here Philo comes very close indeed to confirming such biblical episodes as myth. The Bible, then, is not free of myth. Such myth is, as Philo writes in the context of the story about the tower of Babel, an "impediment"—it is ἐμποδών, literally "before the feet," in one's path—which makes the interpreter stumble. In such cases it is allegory, Philo's hermeneutical panacea, which allows for a course of

---

29   Josephus, *AJ* 1.203.

30   Philo, *Mos.* 2.56.

31   On such mythical traces "still being shown" in Jewish-Hellenistic literature cf. chapter 6 in this volume.

32   Philo, *Opif.* 157.

33   Philo, *Agr.* 97. Plato, in his critique of myth in the *Politeia* (378d) uses the same term as Philo (ὑπόνοια) for the deeper sense lying at the bottom of a myth. In that passage Plato rejects myth even when it is allegorized. Plutarch, *How to study poetry* 19 explains ὑπόνοια as the older term for what in his times is called ἀλληγορία.

PHILO'S STRUGGLE WITH JEWISH MYTH 159

arguments "without stumbling" (ἄπταιστοι).[34] Then the mythical is "away from the feet," out of the way (ἐκποδών).[35] But allegory hardly makes myth disappear. Philo must have been aware that all allegory can do is domesticate myth. But to use a picture from Greek mythology: a bit like in the case of Typhon, the monster that was defeated by Zeus but continues to linger in the Tartarus,[36] myth is still there.

The spectrum of Philo's struggle with myth is thus wide: as we have seen, Philo can deny Jewish myth *tout court* (as at the beginning of *De opificio mundi* before discussing the creation of the world); he can present a story which others may understand as myth, such as the metamorphosis of Lot's wife, as an actual fact—as the so-called literalists would—and then continue anyway with an allegorical exegesis; and sometimes he more explicitly presents myth as a problem that needs to be solved in order to avoid trouble. A remarkable example of declaring a biblical story as myth if taken literally is a note at the beginning of his exegesis of the biblical story of the creation of Eve out of the side of Adam. In a simple main clause Philo, after citing Gen 2:21, states: "the literal meaning of this is mythical" (τὸ ῥητὸν ἐπὶ τούτου μυθῶδές ἐστι): "For how could anyone admit (πῶς γὰρ ἂν παραδέξαιτό τις) that a woman, or a human being at all, came into existence out of a man's side?"[37] Philo admits or accepts as true[38] that the story about the creation of Eve out of Adam is a myth—and then once more seeks refuge in allegory: the story is a metaphor for the creation of the senses which were created after the creation of the mind.[39] Somewhat different is Philo's argument earlier in the same tractate when he criticizes those who understand Eden literally as God's garden: to assume that God cultivates the land and plants gardens would be equal to "mythmaking," "fabulous invention" (μυθοποιία).[40] The story of the paradise would be mythical, if it had been intended to be understood literally. But it was not. "Mythmaking" is a fairly rare word in Greek literature.[41] Philo uses the term in another passage where he quite explicitly admits the existence of myth within Judaism. In his tractate *Quod Deus sit immutabilis* Philo struggles with the anthropomorphic descriptions of God in the Bible. That God had the same body parts as men cannot have been the intention of the text:

---

34 Philo, *Conf.* 14. Cf. on this passage below p. 168.
35 Philo, *Agr.* 97.
36 Hesiod, *Theog.* 868.
37 Philo, *Leg.* 2.19.
38 For a similar use of παραδέχομαι ("accept as correct, true") cf. *Mos.* 1.24; 2.129.
39 Philo, *Leg.* 2.24.
40 Philo, *Leg.* 1.43; cf. *QG* 1.8 where Philo also refuses to understand the biblical paradise as a real garden—an interpretation apparently defended by other (Jewish) exegetes.
41 With the exception of Strabo who uses it more regularly: 1.1.19, *passim*.

If he uses the organic parts he has feet to move from one place to another. But where will he go since he fills everything? To whom will he go, when none is his equal? And for what purpose will he walk? For it cannot be out of care for health as it is with us.[42]

God does not need to go for walks to stay fit. Nor does he have need for hands, eyes[43] or organs of nourishment:

If he has them, he eats and is filled, rests awhile and after the rest has need again, and the accompaniments of this I will not dwell upon. These are the mythical fictions of the impious (ἀσεβῶν αὗται μυθοποιίαι), who, professing to represent the deity as of human form, in reality represent him as having human passions.[44]

If God had a body which functions like that of humans, Philo continues, there would be no difference to what the "poets" say in their description of divinities.[45] However, as in some of the examples discussed above, here too Philo first cannot but admit the obvious parallels between Jewish and pagan myth. And here Philo does not deny the existence of myth in the Bible by simply fleeing into allegory. Rather he justifies the anthropomorphic language of the Bible as a didactic tool for the masses (πρὸς τὴν τῶν πολλῶν διδασκαλίαν):[46] "the Lawgiver uses such expressions, just so far as they serve for a kind of elementary lesson, to admonish those who could not otherwise be brought to their senses."[47] The verse of reference here is Deut 8:5, which parallels man and God: "as a man disciplines his child so the Lord your God disciplines you."[48] Anthropomorphic language, with all its mythical connotations, may be necessary when the targeted audience is "unable to see acutely" (ὀξὺ καθορᾶν ἀδυνατοῦντες).[49] And in such cases it is indeed Deut 8:5 and not Num 23:19—"God is not as man"—which is authoritative.[50] Philo thus admits, at least implicitly if not

---

42   Philo, *Deus* 57.

43   Philo, *Deus* 57–58.

44   Philo, *Deus* 59.

45   Philo, *Deus* 60.

46   Philo, *Deus* 54.

47   Philo, *Deus* 52: λέγεται δὲ οὐδὲν ἧττον παρὰ τῷ νομοθέτῃ μέχρι τινὸς εἰσαγωγῆς τὰ τοιαῦτα, τοῦ νουθετῆσαι χάριν τοὺς ἑτέρως μὴ δυναμένους σωφρονίζεσθαι.

48   Deut 8:5 LXX: ὡς εἴ τις παιδεύσαι ἄνθρωπος τὸν υἱὸν αὐτοῦ οὕτως κύριος ὁ θεός σου παιδεύσει σε.

49   Philo, *Deus* 63.

50   Philo, *Deus* 53. Cf. the very similar argument in *Somn.* 1.232–237 and *QG* 2.54.

PHILO'S STRUGGLE WITH JEWISH MYTH 161

explicitly, that in certain contexts "myth-making" (μυθοποιία) may be necessary. It may be myth "faute de mieux," but myth it is. As Adam Kamesar rightly
notes: "For when the literal sense is justified on the basis of its paideutic effect,
the mythical element is not healed or nullified, but rather positively affirmed
and brought to light. For it is precisely the mythical element, namely, the representation of God "as man" that is paideutic."[51] To what extent Philo's paideutic
reading of myth depends on earlier (Jewish or pagan) responses to mythology is
difficult to say.[52] But Philo certainly had predecessors: Antisthenes and Zeno in
their comments on Homeric myth distinguished in a similar way between what
people think and what is really true.[53] And Strabo explains the use of (Homeric) myth in a very similar way as Philo: to children and illiterate people myths
can convey important messages which are otherwise difficult to pass on.[54]

As far as Philo's use of *Greek* myth is concerned, it can hardly be doubted
that mythological references are meaningful in the context of his philosophical and theological arguments and interpretations.[55] Remarkably, Philo, who
elsewhere denies any kind of myth in Judaism, proves capable of drawing on
Greek myth in view of a better understanding of the Jewish law. One might
even go so far as to say that in some way mythology can serve as another body
of "scripture" for Philo: while Greek mythology is some sort of "open-end system"[56] and the Bible (for Philo, mainly the Torah) is a clearly defined canon
of revelation, both Torah and mythology can serve Philo as a source pool of
interpretation. A striking example of Philo's use of both Greek myth and Torah
is his discussion of bestiality in *Spec.* 3.43–50. Philo starts out with a remarkably detailed retelling of the Pasiphae myth (§ 44). Without declaring the story

---

51 Adam Kamesar, "Philo, the Presence of 'Paideutic' Myth in the Pentateuch, and the 'Principles' or Kephalaia of Mosaic Discourse," *SPhiloA* 10 (1998): 34–65, at 37.

52 Some suggestions in Kamsear, "Philo."

53 Cf. Pépin, *Mythe et allégorie*, 127–128, 238–239.

54 Strabo 1.2.7–8. Aristobulus, the Jewish exegete and philosopher of the second century BCE,
also feels challenged by the anthropomorphisms of the Bible. He warns "not to fall into
myth" (μὴ ἐκπίπτειν εἰς τὸ μυθῶδες) and he too already proposes allegory as the solution
without though, as far as one can tell from the excerpts, justifying myth as a paideutic tool.
He does distinguish between two groups of readers: "those who are able to think well" and
"those who have no share of power and understanding." But here the point is that only the
former are able to understand the allegorical reading, while the latter are "devoted to the
letter alone" (Eusebius, *Praep. Ev.* 8.10.2; 8.10.4–5).

55 See the various contributions to the volume in which the present essay first appeared:
Francesca Alesse and Ludovica De Luca, eds., *Philo of Alexandria and Greek Myth: Narratives, Allegories, and Arguments* (Leiden: Brill, 2019).

56 Jan Bremmer, "What is a Greek Myth?" in *Interpretations of Greek Mythology*, ed. Jan Bremmer (London: Croom Helm, 1987), 1–9, at 3.

162 CHAPTER 8

right away as myth—but rather as an old story (§ 43: φασὶ τὸ παλαιὸν)—Philo uses Pasiphae's unbridled passion for a bull as an introduction to the Jewish prohibition of bestiality (the Torah repeatedly forbids sexual relations between men and animals: Ex 22:18; Lev 18:23; 20:15–16; and Deut 27:21). Philo, of course, did not believe in the actual existence of Pasiphae (as little as a pagan author would). Such figures, Philo explicitly states (§ 45), do not exist: they are not real (ἀνύπαρκτοι), but invented (μεμυθευμένοι). However, read allegorically such myths of sexual misconduct (next to Pasiphae and the Minotaur, Philo refers to the Centaurs and the Chimeras) can serve a valid purpose. Philo's use of Greek myth is thus very similar to his way of dealing with Jewish myth. The Phasiphae-Minotaur myth cannot be taken literally, but it does have paideutic value: it served as a cautionary tale against sexual misconduct and unlimited lust. In some way Philo believed in a myth such as the one on Pasiphae: he certainly believed in the power and authority of these stories as a reference. And in this sense Greek myth can become a supporting argument of Bible interpretation. After his discussion of the Pasiphae myth Philo then returns to the "holy law" (§ 46: ἐν τοῖς ἱεροῖς νόμοις) of the Bible and first refers to Lev 19:19, which forbids the mating between different kinds of animals:

> Actually so great is the provisions made in the law to ensure that men should admit no unlawful matings, that it ordains that even cattle are not to be crossed with others of a different species. No Jewish shepherd will allow a he-goat to mount a ewe or a ram a she-goat, or a bull a mare, or if he does he will be punished as an offender against the decree of nature, who is careful to preserve the primary species without adulteration.[57]

While the Bible limits the prohibition to a simple sentence—"You shall not breed together two kinds of your cattle" (τὰ κτήνη σου οὐ κατοχεύσεις ἑτεροζύγῳ) —Philo lists concrete examples of forbidden crossbreeding between animals (besides those mentioned above also the breeding of mules: § 47). Here then Philo adds the biblical prohibition of sodomy:

> In making this provision (of cross-breeding) he considered what was in accord with decency and conformity to nature, but beyond this he gave us as from some far-off commanding height a warning to men and women alike that they should learn from these examples to abstain from unlawful forms of intercourse. Whether, then, it is the man who uses a quadruped

---

57 Philo, *Spec.* 3.46.

PHILO'S STRUGGLE WITH JEWISH MYTH

for this purpose, or the woman who allows herself to be used, the human offenders must die and the beasts also; the first because they have passed beyond the limits of licentiousness itself by evolving abnormal lusts, and because they have invented strange pleasures than which nothing could be more unpleasing, shameful even to describe; the beasts because they have ministered to such infamies, and to ensure that they do not bear or beget any monstrosity of the kind that may be expected to spring from such abominations. Besides, even people who care little for seemliness would not continue to use their aversion, disliking the very sight of them and thinking that even what they touch, that too must become unclean. And, when things serve no purpose in life, their survival, even if it can be turned to some account, is just a superfluity, "cumbering the earth," as the poet puts it.[58]

Interestingly, in his rewriting of the biblical prohibition of bestiality Philo takes up the vocabulary of his discussion of the Pasiphae myth. Transgressions of this sort lead to unnatural results (παλίμφημα): monsters and freaks (§ 45 with regard to the Minotaur: τέρατα παλίμφημα; § 49 as the result of breaking the Jewish prohibition of sodomy: ἢ τέκη ἢ γεννήσῃ παλίμφημον). Such are the results of man indulging in pleasures and lusts (ἐπιθυμίαι, ἡδοναί. Both terms are used with regard to the pagan as well as to the Jewish context: § 43, § 49). Philo thus combines Greek myth and Torah to make a point (in this case on correct sexual behavior). It is quite fitting that Philo ends his discussion of bestiality by calling the unnatural animals which spring from such abhorrence "a burden on the earth," which is a citation from Homer.[59] Philo's own simplistic dichotomy of the Jewish law as truth versus myth as invention has its limitations, and so has Wolfson's distinction between the use of divine scripture and myth in Philo. Wolfson's statement that for Philo myths "neither are literally true nor have an underlying meaning"[60] needs qualification.

Pasiphae is not the only example in Philo where Greek myth supports Bible exegesis, where Bible and myth convene, so to speak. Take Cain and Scylla (an unlikely couple at first sight): according to Philo, Cain's punishment was that he would never die (his death is not mentioned in the Bible). In Philo's allegorical reading Cain is a symbol of never vanishing evil—very much as is the case with the mythic (ἡ μεμυθευμένη) Scylla:

---

58   Philo, *Spec.* 3.48–50.
59   Homer, *Il.* 18.104; *Od.* 20.379. The exact Homeric phrase would be ἄχθος ἀρούρης. Philo uses the same Homeric reference in *Spec.* 1.74.
60   Wolfson, *Philo*, 1.36.

164   CHAPTER 8

It would seem then that just this is the sign regarding Cain that he should
not be killed, namely that on no occasion did he meet with death. For
nowhere in the Book of the Law has his death been mentioned. This
shows in a figure that, like the Scylla of fable, folly is a deathless evil, never
experiencing the end that consists in having died, but subject to all eternity to that which consists in ever dying.[61]

Philo's reference to Scylla is very brief, as are most of his references to Greek
myth. He assumes that the reader knows that Scylla as well as Charybdis are "a
deathless evil" (a phrase from Homer[62]). Here, too, Bible and Greek myth are
combined to make a point. Philo uses both biblical and mythological scripture
for his argument. The same can be said with regard to another important *theo-
logoumenon* in Philo: it is the special property of man, as created being, to suffer
(while God as the creator cannot suffer). For Philo the emblematic example of
someone who is (foolishly) unwilling to accept the human destiny of suffering is Sisyphus of Greek myth, constantly resisting his fate.[63] Even in Philo's
tractate on the Decalogue Greek myth can be a supporting argument. Here too
Philo's argument is somewhat contradictory, to say the least: on the one hand
the second commandment (the prohibition of graven images) is presented as
a Jewish warranty against myth:

> It forbids the making of images or wooden busts and idols in general pro-
> duced by the baneful craftsmanship of painting and sculpture, and also
> the acceptance of fabulous legends about the marriages and pedigrees of
> deities and the numberless and very grave scandals associated with both
> of these.[64]

With Mount Sinai and the exodus, one could say, Judaism leaves the dan-
gers of mythology behind. As Philo states elsewhere, the Egyptians were victims of mythical idolatry,[65] the sin of the golden calf was an example of a
"fable falsely invented."[66] But eight commandments later ("You shall not covet")

---

61   Philo, *Det.* 178.
62   Homer, *Od.* 12.118: ἡ δέ τοι οὐ θνητή, ἀλλ᾽ ἀθάνατον κακόν ἐστι.
63   Philo, *Cher.* 77–78. The opposite of Philo's negative picture of Sisyphus fighting the absur-
       dity of life is Albert Camus' 1942 essay *Le mythe de Sisyphe*.
64   Philo, *Decal.* 156: οὐκ ἐῶν οὐδ᾽ ὅσα μύθων πλάσματα προσίεσθαι, θεογαμίαν καὶ θεογονίαν καὶ
       τὰς ἀμφοτέραις ἑπομένας ἀμυθήτους καὶ ἀργαλεωτάτας κῆρας.
65   Philo, *Decal.* 76: ταύρους καὶ κριοὺς καὶ τράγους, ἐφ᾽ ἑκάστῳ μυθικόν τι πλάσμα τετερατευμένοι.
       Cf. *Post.* 165; *Spec.* 1.79; *Migr.* 76.
66   Philo, *Mos.* 2.271: πλάσμα μύθου κατεψευσμένον. Similarly, proselytes must leave mythology

PHILO'S STRUGGLE WITH JEWISH MYTH   165

Greek mythology is once more a welcome reference: ceaseless desire entails "Tantalus-like kind of punishment" (Ταντάλειον τιμωρίαν):

> as he (Tantalus) missed everything that he wished for just when he was about to touch it, so the person who is mastered by desire, ever thirsting for what is absent remains unsatisfied, fumbling around his baffled appetite.[67]

Once more, Philo is making use of Greek myth within Jewish theology, here even in the context of the Decalogue. This is remarkable and should not be taken lightly. According to Gerhard Delling, Philo for a brief moment did not realize that he was using Greek myth for his argument.[68] But Philo was surely aware that he recurred to Greek myth. He uses Greek myth for his own, Jewish understanding of the world. At times it almost seems less important to Philo which tradition one has in mind—the Jewish law or Greek mythology—than to interpret the story correctly: Philo can refer both to the Greek Deucalion and the biblical Noah as examples of a divine reward for human righteousness: "This person, in whose day the great deluge took place, is called by the Greeks Deucalion and by the Hebrews Noah."[69] In the case of the flood, both stories (the one on Deucalion as well as the one on Noah) convey the same message (if only interpreted correctly). Philo's identification of Noah with Deucalion is rather unusual and maybe even "unique."[70] In principle, for Philo Greek myth and Scripture are not on the same level and Judaism wins over Greek myth. As Philo notes in *That God is Unchangeable*, the divine food which God lets

---

behind, the word "proselyte" itself indicates the passage from myth to truth: cf. *Spec.* 1.51 (τούτους δὲ καλεῖ προσηλύτους ἀπὸ τοῦ προσεληλυθέναι καινῇ καὶ φιλοθέῳ πολιτείᾳ, οἳ μυθικῶν μὲν ἀλογοῦσι πλασμάτων, περιέχονται δὲ ἀκραιφνοῦς ἀληθείας) and *Virt.* 102, 178.

67   Philo, *Decal.* 149. Cf. also *Spec.* 4.81, where Philo refers to the Tantalus myth in a very similar context.

68   Delling, "Wunder–Allegorie–Mythus," 729 ("im Augenblick nicht bewußt"). On Philo's use of Greek allegory in the context of biblical motives cf. also Yehoshua Amir, "Die Übertragung griechischer Allegorien auf biblische Motive bei Philon," in *Die hellenistische Gestalt des Judentums bei Philon von Alexandrien* (Neukirchen-Vluyn: Neukirchener Verlag, 1983), 119–128; Boyancé, "Écho des exégèses de la mythologie grecque chez Philon," in *Philon d'Alexandrie, Lyon 11–15*, 169–186; John Dillon, "Ganymede as the Logos: Traces of a Forgotten Allegorization in Philo," *SPhiloA* 6 (1979/80): 37–40.

69   Philo, *Praem.* 23: τοῦτον Ἕλληνες μὲν Δευκαλίωνα, Χαλδαῖοι δὲ Νῶε ἐπονομάζουσιν ἐφ' οὗ τὸν μέγαν κατακλυσμὸν συνέβη γενέσθαι.

70   So Colson in the LCL edition, not hiding his surprise about this parallelization. But cf. also *Abr.* 54: some Greeks call Abraham, Isaak, and Jacob "with another name" (ἑτέρῳ ὀνόματι) "Charites."

166	CHAPTER 8

rain from heaven, the manna, is better than ambrosia and nectar of Greek myth.[71] Overall, there is no doubt that the Jewish god cooks better than Zeus. The Pasiphae myth in the passage cited above typically is presented as less relevant than the biblical law. But in Philo's kitchen of exegesis and philosophy Greek mythology is nevertheless an important ingredient.

It seems quite clear, then, that Philo's approach to myth is ambivalent. A passage often cited in support of his *rejection* of myth, and in particular of Jewish myth, is his paraphrase of an inner-Jewish dialogue on myth at the beginning of his tractate *De confusione linguarum*.[72] Philo here refers to Jewish critics who dislike their own tradition (δυσχεραίνοντες τῇ πατρίῳ πολιτείᾳ) and accuse the Jewish law of including mythological content.[73] The immediate context of the polemics is the biblical story about the tower of Babel in Gen 11:1–9, cited by Philo at the very beginning of the tractate (§1). He then lashes out against those fellow Jews who poke fun at what they understand as obvious parallels between Jewish and Greek mythology:

> Persons who cherish a dislike of the ancestral institution and make it their constant study to denounce and decry the Laws find in these and similar passages stepping stones as it were for their godlessness. Can you still, say these impious scoffers, speak gravely of the ordinances as containing the canons of absolute truth? For see your so-called holy books contain also myths, which you regularly deride when you hear them related by others (ἰδοὺ γὰρ αἱ ἱεραὶ λεγόμεναι βίβλοι παρ' ὑμῖν καὶ μύθους περιέχουσιν, ἐφ' οἷς εἰώθατε γελᾶν, ὅταν ἄλλων διεξιόντων ἀκούητε). And indeed, they continue, it is needless to collect the numerous examples scattered about the legislation, as we might had we leisure to spend in exposing its failings. We have but to remind you of the instances which lie at our very feet and ready to our hand. One of these we have here, which resembles the fable told of the Aloeidae, who according to Homer the greatest and most reputed of poets planned to pile the three loftiest mountains on each other in one heap, hoping that when these were raised to the height of the upper sky they would furnish an easy road to heaven for those who

---

71	Philo, *Deus* 155: ὕοντος ἡμῖν ἀνεπισχέτως οὐρανοῦ τὴν νέκταρος καὶ ἀμβροσίας τῶν μεμυθευμένων ἀμείνω τροφήν.

72	My discussion of *Conf.* 2–5 is based on Bloch, *Moses und der Mythos*, 179–182. On *Conf.* cf. also the detailed discussion in Maren Niehoff, *Jewish Exegesis and Homeric Scholarship in Alexandria* (Cambridge: Cambridge University Press, 2011), 77–94.

73	Philo clearly thinks of Jewish critics, cf. also *Conf.* 142 where he has critics of the biblical story cynically say "the lawgiver is teaching *us* something new."

PHILO'S STRUGGLE WITH JEWISH MYTH 167

wished to ascend thither. The verses on this subject run thus: "They on Olympus Ossa fain would pile, On Ossa Pelion with its quivering leaves, in hope thereby to climb the heights of heaven."[74] Olympus, Ossa and Pelion are names of mountains. For these the lawgiver substitutes a tower which he represents as being built by the men of that day who wished in their folly and insolent pride to touch the heaven. Folly indeed; surely dreadful madness! For if one should lay a small foundation and build up upon it the different parts of the whole earth, rising in the form of a single pillar, it would still be divided by vast distances from the sphere of ether, particularly if we accept the view of the philosophers who inquire into such problems, all of whom are agreed that the earth is the centre of the universe.[75]

According to these Jewish "atheists" (§ 2: τῆς ἀθεότητος αὐτῶν) Jewish law ("the so-called holy books") comprises myth, very much like the Homeric epics. As a matter of fact: Homeric myth was first, the Jewish Bible is rewritten myth (Moses replaced the mountains with a tower). In this fictitious inner-Jewish dialogue, which is nevertheless presented by Philo as realistic, myth is becoming a pitfall for pious Jews who otherwise tend to condemn pagan myth. And the story about the tower of Babel is presented by these critics as just one example, others could easily be added.[76]

The critics mentioned by Philo compare the story of the tower of Babel with the Greek myth of the Aloadae. In Greek mythology the Aloadae, sons of Aloeus or Poseidon and Iphimedeia, are giant rebels who are defeated by the gods in battle. Previously they had imprisoned Ares in a bronze urn.[77] According to the critics, nothing about the myth of the Aloadae can be true; rather, it is an example, in Philo's language, of enormous "brain damage" (§ 5: φρενοβλάβεια, a polemical term dear to Philo, but barely attested outside of his oeuvre). Thus the Jewish critics of myth also reject pagan mythology. Remarkably, Philo does not explicitly reject the comparison between the biblical story of Babel and the Greek myth of the Aloadae. It is true that at the beginning of his discussion Philo describes these Jewish critics in very negative language (§ 2), but in the subsequent paragraphs he does not really distance himself from them. As a matter of fact, it is almost impossible to draw a sharp line between the crit-

---

74 Homer, *Od.* 11.315–316.
75 Philo, *Conf.* 2–5.
76 Philo, *Conf.* 2: "in these and similar passages;" 3: "numerous examples scattered about the legislation."
77 Homer, *Il.* 5.385–387; *Od.* 11.305–316.

168 CHAPTER 8

ics' remarks and his report about them. Philo is not citing the critics, but he paraphrases them and he does so in his own language. At some point his and the critics' comments on myth merge. When in § 6 the text returns to the original topic of the tractate, the phenomenon of a shared language (ὁμοφωνία) and the loss of it, there is mention of another pagan parallel to the story of Babel. According to "mythographs," all animals had once shared one and the same language, but then lost it due to hubris (the animals had asked for immortality).[78] Compared to this myth of community of language among animals—Philo apparently comments in his own name—Moses with his story about Babel was "closer to the truth" (ἐγγυτέρω τἀληθοῦς),[79] because he attributed sameness of language only to men, not to animals. For the critics, however, to whom Philo explicitly referred only at the beginning of his discussion and to whom he now returns (ὥς γέ φασι), even that (sameness of language among men) is "mythical" (καὶ τοῦτο μυθῶδες).[80] In Philo's discussion it is indeed not easy to keep his own voice apart from that of the critics. Maren Niehoff understands all of *Conf.* 7–9, including the positive remark on Moses's more reasonable version of the story, as the analysis "offered by Philo's colleagues."[81] But this seems unlikely.[82] Rather, the argumentation wavers between Philo's own opinion and that of the critics—to the extent that at least temporarily they almost become one voice. And things do not become clearer in what follows, partly because of difficulties in the textual transmission (there is a lacuna in *Conf.* 14). As a matter of fact, one may surmise that it was exactly Philo's complex rendering of the dispute which led to some scribal confusion.[83] In *De confusione linguarum* sides repeatedly overlap. Beyond the polemics there is often no sharp line between

---

78 Philo, *Conf.* 6–8. The myth is first attested in a fragment of Callimachus (*Ia.* 2): cf. Deborah Levine Gera, *Ancient Greek Ideas on Speech, Language, and Civilization* (Oxford: Oxford University Press, 2003), 29–32; Arnd Kerkhecker, *Callimachus' Book of Iambi* (Oxford: Oxford University Press, 1999), 57–58.

79 Philo, *Conf.* 9.

80 Philo, *Conf.* 9.

81 Niehoff, *Jewish Exegesis*, 88 (and 80).

82 Also the reference to Homer as "the greatest and most reputed of poets" (*Conf.* 4) can easily be understood as Philo's own language: cf. *QG* 4.2 where Philo compares the divine visit to Abraham (Gen 18) with a Homeric comment ("the clever and considerably learned Homer") on how the gods visit humans in disguise.

83 The lacuna in *Conf.* 14 has remained a riddle and makes it difficult to understand to whom exactly Philo is referring and how he is placing himself in the discussion. It seems that he only briefly mentions the literalists' approach. In *Conf.* 15 (φαμὲν τοίνυν) Philo then speaks in his own name suggesting an allegorical reading. Cf. the discussion of the problem both in the English (Colson, LCL) and French (Kahn, *Les Œuvres de Philon d'Alexandrie*) editions as well as Niehoff, *Jewish Exegesis*, 135.

PHILO'S STRUGGLE WITH JEWISH MYTH   169

Philo, the critics of Jewish myth, and the literalists. As is to be expected, Philo
presents an allegorical interpretation of the biblical confusion of tongues: the
original state, when "the earth was all one lip and one voice" (Gen 11:1), is to
be understood as "a consonance of evil deeds great and innumerable" (§15).
Therefore the confusion of tongues is meant as a correction of and precaution
against united evil. God's decision to confuse the tongues "is equivalent to 'let
us make each part of vice mute that it may not by its separate utterance nor
yet in unison with the others be the cause of mischief'" (§189). However, right
at the end of the tractate Philo wavers once more. At least to some extent he
would be willing to give in to those who prefer a literal reading (§190):

> This is our explanation, but those who merely follow the outward and
> obvious think that we have at this point a reference to the origin of the
> Greek and barbarian languages. I would not censure such persons, for per-
> haps the truth is with them also. Still I would exhort them not to halt there.

The demarcations between the different groups or 'schools' are thus not very
clear. Typically, Philo, when he gets to the discussion of the difficult plural in
Gen 11:7 ("Come, let us go down and there confound their tongue"), he defends
biblical monotheism with the help of Homer and thus the same pagan source
which at the beginning of the tractate served as a reference for the mythical
content of the Bible. Philo underlines God's uniqueness with a citation from
the *Iliad*:

> There is only one sovereign and ruler and king, who alone may direct and
> dispose of all things. For the lines: "It is not well that many lords should
> rule; be there but one, one king" (*Il.* 2.204–205), could be said with more
> justice of the world and of God than of cities and men.[84]

Philo, the literalists, and those Jews who stressed the parallels between Jewish
and Greek myth, all tried to make sense of the dramatic story of the tower of
Babel. And they were not alone. From other Jewish-Hellenistic sources such
as the Sibylline Oracles and Josephus we know that that story was both particularly attractive and challenging.[85] Similarly, pagan philosophers, starting

---

84   Philo, *Conf.* 170. It needs to be said, though, that Philo refrains from citing the rest of the
      Homeric sentence which refers to Zeus (*Il.* 2.205–207): "one king, to whom the son of
      crooked-counselling Cronos gave the scepter and judgements, that he may give counsel
      to them."
85   *Or. Sib.* 3.97–104; Josephus, *AJ* 1.113–118. Cf. Bloch, *Moses und der Mythos*, 207–210 and

with the Presocratics, struggled with their myths: rejecting them, reinterpreting them (not the least in allegorical forms), but at times also endorsing them.[86] In his classic study *Les Grecs ont-ils cru à leurs mythes? Essai sur l'imagination constituante*, Paul Veyne describes this ambivalence about myth very pointedly:

> When filling out the contours of some legend, the writers of the Hellenistic and Roman periods seem to hesitate. They often refuse to speak in their own name. "People say ...," they write, or "according to myth." But in the next sentence they will be very definite concerning another point of the same legend. These shifts between daring and reserve owe nothing to chance. They follow three rules: state no opinion on the marvelous and the supernatural, admit a historical basis, and take exception to the details.[87]

By questioning their own mythology and by trying to come to terms with it, Jewish-Hellenistic authors, including Philo of Alexandria, did not stand out but rather were part of a common and widespread intellectual discourse. To some extent, Philo's struggle with myth can be understood as just another example of Jewish-Hellenistic adaption.[88] Maren Niehoff nicely shows how the very same myth of the Aloadae, which triggers the debate in *Conf.*, is also critically discussed in Homeric scholia.[89] And Philo's (approximate) contemporary Heraclitus, the Stoic author of a treatise on Homeric problems, uses allegory in a very similar way to Philo, as an "antidote" (ἀντιφάρμακον) against the accusation of myth.[90]

Philo's fierce denial of myth as discussed at the beginning of this chapter (and by Harry A. Wolfson at the beginning of his book) cannot be reconciled with his rather liberal use of Greek myth as well as his struggle with Jewish myth in quite a few places. But Philo's ambivalence about myth and his responses

---

Christoph Uehlinger, *Weltreich und „eine Rede": Eine neue Deutung der sogenannten Turmbauerzählung (Gen 11,1–9)* (Fribourg: Academic Press Fribourg, 1990), 134–137.

86   Cf. Luc Brisson, *Introduction à la philosophie du mythe: Tome I: Sauver les mythes* (Paris: Vrin, 2005) and, for Alexandria, Dawson, *Allegorical Readers*.

87   Paul Veyne, *Did the Greeks Believe in Their Myths? An Essay on the Constitutive Imagination* (Chicago: The University of Chicago Press, 1988 [1983]), 54.

88   Cf. also Pépin, *Mythe et allégorie*, 229–231.

89   Niehoff, *Jewish Exegesis*, 81–82.

90   Heraclitus, *Quaestiones homericae* 22.1 (Donald A. Russell and David Konstan, ed. and trans., *Heraclitus*: Homeric Problems [Atlanta: SBL, 2005]). On pagan allegory in Heraclitus as well as Cornutus, cf. Pépin, *Mythe et allégorie*, 156–167 and Dawson, *Allegorical Readers*, 23–72.

PHILO'S STRUGGLE WITH JEWISH MYTH

to what one might call the mythical challenge do not stand out in principle: whether compared to pagan or to other Jewish-Hellenistic authors.[91] As for Greek myths, Philo neither simply accepts nor rejects them: accepting myth would be to retell mythical stories, pointing out their veracity, lasting significance, and authenticity. Rejecting them would be to deny them all, i.e. claim that they are not true, not relevant, and thus not worthwhile retelling. However, as we have seen from a number of examples in Philo's oeuvre, he takes to Greek myths to look for patterns of identification and enduring symbolic wisdom. Repeatedly, Philo allows himself a remarkable "goût du comparatisme"[92] and recurs to Greek myth within theological reflections on biblical passages. Jewish myth is indeed hardly ever declared as such in Philo. But he seems to have been aware that Jewish myth is not simply an oxymoron.

Bibliography

Alesse, Francesca and Ludovica De Luca, eds., *Philo of Alexandria and Greek Myth: Narratives, Allegories, and Arguments*. Leiden: Brill, 2019.

Amir, Yehoshua, "Die Übertragung griechischer Allegorien auf biblische Motive bei Philon." Pages 119–128 in id., *Die hellenistische Gestalt des Judentums bei Philon von Alexandrien*. Neukirchen-Vluyn: Neukirchener Verlag, 1983.

Bloch, René, *Moses und der Mythos: Die Auseinandersetzung mit der griechischen Mythologie bei jüdisch-hellenistischen Autoren*. Leiden: Brill, 2011.

Bloch, René, "Moses and Greek Myth in Hellenistic Judaism." Pages 195–208 in *The Construction of Moses*. Edited by Thomas Römer. Paris: Gabalda, 2007.

Boyancé, Pierre, "Écho des exégèses de la mythologie grecque chez Philon." Pages 169–186 in *Philon d'Alexandrie, Lyon 11–15 Septembre 1966: colloques nationaux du CNRS*. Edited by Roger Arnaldez, Claude Mondésert, and Jean Pouilloux. Paris: Éditions du Cerf, 1967.

Bremmer, Jan, "What is a Greek Myth?" Pages 1–9 in *Interpretations of Greek Mythology*. Edited by Jan Bremmer. London: Croom Helm, 1987.

Brisson, Luc, *Introduction à la philosophie du mythe*. Vol. 1: *Sauver les mythes*. Paris: Vrin, 2005.

Burkert, Walter, *Structure and History in Greek Mythology and Ritual*. Berkeley: University of California Press, 1979.

Dawson, David, *Allegorical Readers and Cultural Revision in Ancient Alexandria*. Berkeley: University of California Press, 1992.

---

91   Cf. Bloch, *Moses und der Mythos*, on similar ambivalences on myth in Josephus.

92   Pépin, *Mythe et allégorie*, 237.

Delling, Gerhard, "Wunder–Allegorie–Mythus bei Philon von Alexandreia." *Wissenschaftliche Zeitschrift der Martin-Luther-Universität Halle-Wittenberg, Gesellschafts- und Sprachwissenschaftliche Reihe* 6 (1956/57): 713–740.

Dillon, John, "Ganymede as the Logos: Traces of a Forgotten Allegorization in Philo." *SPhiloA* 6 (1979/80): 37–40.

Fishbane, Michael, *Biblical Myth and Rabbinic Mythmaking*. Oxford: Oxford University Press, 2003.

Kamesar, Adam, "Philo, the Presence of 'Paideutic' Myth in the Pentateuch, and the 'Principles' or Kephalaia of Mosaic Discourse." *SPhiloA* 10 (1998): 34–65.

Kerkhecker, Arnd, *Callimachus' Book of Iambi*. Oxford: Oxford University Press, 1999.

Forbes Irving, Paul M.C., *Metamorphosis in Greek Myths*. Oxford: Clarendon, 1990.

Levine Gera, Deborah, *Ancient Greek Ideas on Speech, Language, and Civilization*. Oxford: Oxford University Press, 2003.

Lincoln, Bruce, *Theorizing Myth: Narrative, Ideology, and Scholarship*. Chicago: The University of Chicago Press, 1999.

Grabbe, Lester L., *Etymology in Early Jewish Interpretation: The Hebrew Names in Philo*. Atlanta: Scholars, 1988.

Méasson, Anita, "Un aspect de la critique du polythéisme chez Philon d'Alexandrie: les acceptions du mot μῦθος dans son œuvre." *Centre Jean Palerne Mémoires* 2 (1980): 75–107.

Niehoff, Maren, *Jewish Exegesis and Homeric Scholarship in Alexandria*. Cambridge: Cambridge University Press, 2011.

Pépin, Jean, "Remarques sur la théorie de l'exégèse allégorique chez Philon." Pages 131–168 in *Philon d'Alexandrie, Lyon 11–15 Septembre 1966: colloques nationaux du CNRS*. Edited by Roger Arnaldez, Claude Mondésert, and Jean Pouilloux. Paris: Éditions du Cerf, 1967.

Pépin, Jean, *Mythe et allégorie: les origines grecques et les contestations judéo-chrétiennes*. Paris: Aubier, 1976 (1958).

Runia, David T., *Philo of Alexandria: On the Creation of the Cosmos According to Moses*. Leiden: Brill, 2001.

Russell, Donald A. and David Konstan, ed. and trans., *Heraclitus: Homeric Problems*. Atlanta: SBL, 2005.

Uehlinger, Christoph, *Weltreich und „eine Rede": Eine neue Deutung der sogenannten Turmbauerzählung (Gen 11,1–9)*. Fribourg: Academic Press Fribourg, 1990.

Veyne, Paul, *Did the Greeks Believe in Their Myths? An Essay on the Constitutive Imagination*. Chicago: The University of Chicago Press, 1988 (1983).

Wolfson, Harry A., *Philo: Foundations of Religious Philosophy in Judaism, Christianity, and Islam*. 2 vols. Cambridge: Harvard University Press, 1947.

CHAPTER 9

Part of the Scene: Jewish Theater in Antiquity

To undertake a study on Jewish theater in antiquity is not self-evident and to the non-specialist may seem surprising.* For is it not the case that theater and Judaism for a long time had been two mutually exclusive phenomena, 'Jewish theater' being an oxymoron of sorts? Was there really a Jewish theater "scene" in antiquity? Did Jews attend the theater? Did they perform in and write for the theater? Or is the historian of theater, Shimon Lev-Ari, closer to the facts when he writes in a contribution on "The Origins of Theater in Hellenic and Judaic Culture:"

> The first civilization in world history to create the art of theater, was that of the ancient Greeks: in 534 B.C.E. Pisistratus introduced drama into the Dionysia, the state festival of Athens. The first Jew to initiate the art of theater in Judaic culture, was Abraham Goldfaden. In October 1876 in Jassi, Rumania, he performed the first professional piece of Yiddish theater. Why was there a chronological gap of more than 2400 years between these two events?[1]

According to Lev-Ari, the beginnings of Jewish theater go back to the second half of the nineteenth century, when Yiddish theater was born. Similar information about the late, or at least not ancient, origins of Jewish theater can be found in a number of lexica on theater as well as Judaism. In the *Neues Lexikon des Judentums* (1992), the entry on "Theater" begins as follows: "Jewish antiquity did not know theater."[2] In the *Oxford Handbook of Jewish Studies* (2002) we

---

* [This is a slightly revised version of an article published originally in German: René Bloch, "Von Szene zu Szene: Das jüdische Theater in der Antike," in *Juden in ihrer Umwelt: Akkulturation des Judentums in Antike und Mittelalter*, ed. Rainer C. Schwinges and Matthias Konradt (Basel: Schwabe, 2009), 57–86 and dedicated to the work of Erich S. Gruen. I would like to thank the publisher of the volume, Schwabe, for the permission to print my article in English and Eva Tyrell, Sara Kviat Bloch, and Carson Bay for their help with the translation.]

1 Shimon Lev-Ari, "The Origins of Theater in Hellenic and Judaic Cultures," in *Hellenic and Jewish Arts: The Howard Gilman International Conferences I*, ed. Asher Ovadiah (Tel Aviv: Un-Ramot, 1998), 385–392, 386.

2 Julius H. Schoeps, ed., *Neues Lexikon des Judentums* (Munich: Bertelsmann-Lexikon-Verlag, 1992), 450 ("Theater").

© RENÉ BLOCH, 2022 | DOI:10.1163/9789004521896_011

find in the chapter on Jewish theater that "Until quite recent times, the Jew has never been *homo theatralis*."[3]

Such assertions do not bear up against a more thorough analysis of ancient sources, Jewish as well as non-Jewish. As will be shown, in Greco-Roman antiquity Jews—or rather: some Jews—certainly took part in the theater "scene:" they went to see performances and read the tragic authors. There were Jewish actors and actresses. We know of at least one case where it was also conceivable for Jews to write plays themselves: fragments of a drama about the exodus of the Israelites from Egypt, written in Greek, by the Jewish tragedian Ezekiel have been transmitted by the Church fathers. "Ezekiel Tragicus," as he is called to distinguish him from the homonymous prophet, may well have written more than that one tragedy.[4]

It seems imperative, therefore, to turn the spotlight on the world of ancient Jewish theater. Its existence is not seriously cast into question in scholarship on Hellenistic Judaism;[5] outside of this field, however, it is too often denied in rather simplistic ways. At times, especially in the nineteenth century, prevail-

---

3 Ahuva Belkin and Gad Kaynar, "Jewish Theatre," in Martin Goodman, ed., *The Oxford Handbook of Jewish Studies* (Oxford: Oxford University Press, 2002), 870: "Until quite recent times, the Jew has never been *homo theatralis*. Although Jews were known as the People of the Book, and despite the very literature attached to Judaism, the dramatic genre never became an integral part of Jewish civilization, and theatre as an institution was never a part of its cultural life." For similar views, see Mendel Kohansky, *The Hebrew Theatre: Its First Fifty Years* (Jerusalem: Ktav, 1969), 2: "The historian of the Hebrew theatre cannot refer to the distant past, nor can he search for cultural roots, for there are none," and Arnold Mandel, "Les théâtres juifs," in *Histoire des spectacles*, ed. Guy Dumur (Paris: Gallimard, 1965), 1058: "Le théâtre apparaît très tardivement dans la civilisation juive." Dennis Kennedy, ed., *Oxford Encyclopedia of Theater and Performance* (Oxford: Oxford University Press, 2003) has no entry on "Jewish theater," but refers to the Argentinian *teatro judío* and the Yiddish theater. For an exception cf. the informative first section of the entry "Theater" (Origins/Post-Biblical Period) in the *Encyclopedia Judaica*. Vol. 15, first ed. (Jerusalem: Keter, 1972), 1049–1052.
4 Cf. below p. 191.
5 Cf. e.g. Louis H. Feldman, *Jew & Gentile in the Ancient World* (Princeton: Princeton University Press, 1993), 61–63; John M.G. Barclay, *Jews in the Mediterranean Diaspora: From Alexander to Trajan (323BCE–117CE)* (Edinburgh, T&T Clark 1996), *passim*; Erich S. Gruen, *Diaspora: Jews amidst Greek and Romans* (Cambridge: Harvard University Press, 2002), 194–195. For an overview on a number of important sources, see Dieter Vetter, "Juden und Schauspiel in Antike und Moderne," in *Das antike Theater: Aspekte seiner Geschichte, Rezeption und Aktualität*, ed. Gerhard Binder and Bernd Effe (Trier: WVT, 1998), 149–189. Cf. also Katherine B. Free, "Thespis and Moses: The Jews and the Ancient Greek Theater," in Shimon Levy, ed., *Theater and Holy Script* (Brighton: Sussex Academic, 1999), 149–158, and more recently Jeff Jay, "The Problem of the Theater in Early Judaism," *Journal for the Study of Judaism* 44 (2013): 218–253, and, especially, Zeev Weiss, *Public Spectacles in Roman and Late Antique Palestine* (Cambridge: Harvard University Press, 2014).

PART OF THE SCENE: JEWISH THEATER IN ANTIQUITY   175

ing prejudice about the lacking creativity of the Jews contributed to the view
that Jews could not have been involved in the theater.[6]

As will become obvious from what follows, the Jewish relationship to theater
in antiquity was complex and certainly not free of ambiguities. Nevertheless,
theater and Judaism in ancient times were not *a priori* incompatible. Jewish
theater is not, in fact, a modern invention.

1   Rabbinic Condemnations of Theater

In rabbinic literature theater is rejected in harsh terms. It is precisely these passages that are frequently cited as evidence for the alleged absence of theater in
pre-modern Judaism.[7] The most explicit texts in this respect can be found in
the tractate *Avodah Zara* of the Babylonian and the Jerusalem Talmud, which
is concerned with the Jewish prohibition of worship of idols and images (and
more generally with interactions between Jews and pagans). The Talmud first
forbids visits to Roman arenas and military camps, which apparently were also
used for performances. The reason for the prohibition of such pastimes is that
people would neglect their Torah studies.

> Our sages taught: One who goes to the stadia (איצטדינין) or an encir-
> clement, and saw there conjurers and snake charmers, *bukion* and *muki-*

---

6   How widespread this kind of thinking was becomes obvious from the following paragraph in
    Heinrich Alt's study *Theater und Kirche in ihrem gegenseitigen Verhältniß historisch dargestellt*
    (Berlin: Blahnschen, 1846), 301–302: "How then should one explain that the Jews on the one
    hand had everything whence in Greek culture dramatic poetry, dance, choir chants and
    antiphony as well as instrumental music developed and that several of their poetic works
    come as close as possible to dramatic poetry, but that on the other hand actual drama was
    unknown to them? The usual explanations such as that the Jews were generally not an artistic
    and spiritually vivid people ("kein künstlerisches und geistig regsames Volk") and that their
    whole spiritual culture was limited to a certain religious education we can assume are well
    known. However, no one will deny that these explanations are not sufficient; the reason must
    lie deeper" (trans. from the original German). Alt then goes on to explain the absence of the-
    ater in Judaism with Jewish aniconism. For the stereotype of a Jewish non-creativity (that
    some Jews internalized) see Yaacov Shavit, "Have Jews Imagination? Jews and the Creative
    Arts," in *Athens in Jerusalem: Classical Antiquity and Hellenism in the Making of the Modern
    Secular Jew* (London: Littman, 1997), 220–277. On Jewish art in antiquity, see Steven Fine, *Art
    & Judaism in the Greco-Roman World: Toward a New Jewish Archaeology* (Cambridge: Cam-
    bridge University Press, 2005).
7   Schoeps, *Neues Lexikon des Judentums*, 450 (see above n. 2): "Das jüdische Altertum kannte
    kein Theater. Der Talmud verbot den Juden die Teilnahme an heidnischen Theatervorstellun-
    gen, bei denen Götzen geopfert und die als frivol betrachtet wurden."

176   CHAPTER 9

on, and *mulion* and *lulion*, *blurin* and *salgurin*, this is a session of jesters. And of them the verse says, *Happy are those who do not follow ... but their delight is in the law of the Lord ...* (Ps 1:1–2). Hence you learn that these things lead a person to neglect of Torah.[8]

The rabbis criticized the spectacles. In late antiquity, this critique referred not so much to theater in the classical sense (tragedies, comedies) as to gladiatorial combats as well as to mimes and pantomimes.[9] In its critique, the Talmud mentions some of the stock characters of the Roman stage: the *bucco* (*bukion*) and the *maccus* (*mukion*), both roles of a simpleton. Not all of the characters listed in the passage can easily be assigned to equivalent Latin terms (and it is very possible that in Hebrew the terms are being distorted on purpose). Still, the passage shows how familiar the rabbis were with the characters of the pagan stage.[10]

Rabbinic critique of the theater identified the first two verses of the book of Psalms as an ideal biblical prooftext:

Happy are those who do not follow the advice of the wicked, or take the path that sinners tread, *or sit in the seat of scoffers*; but their delight is in the law of the Lord, and on his law they meditate day and night.[11]

Whoever watches performances sits in the seat of a blasphemer instead of, as instructed by Psalm 1, spending days and nights studying Torah. The Babylo-

---

8   b. ʿAbod. Zar. 18b. Translations of passages from the Babylonian Talmud are from the *Schottenstein* edition (2005 ff.), at times with slight revisions. On rabbinic parallels to this passage cf. Weiss, *Public Spectacles*, 126–127.

9   Cf. Klaus Sallmann, "Christen vor dem Theater," in Jürgen Blänsdorf, ed., *Theater und Gesellschaft im Imperium Romanum* (Tübingen: Francke Verlag, 1990), 244: "die Tragödie degenerierte spätestens im 2. Jh. [n.Chr.] zur Ein-Personenschau eines Pantomimus, der eine tragische Hauptrolle sang und tanzte; die Komödie wurde durch die ebenso hektischen wie erotischen Sketchs von *mimi* und *mimae* (letztere mit obligatem Striptease) ersetzt." See also Joachim Fugmann, *Römisches Theater in der Provinz: eine Einführung in das Theaterwesen im Imperium Romanum* (Stuttgart: Rombach, 1988) and Bernhard Zimmermann, "Theater," *DNP* 15.3, 397.

10   Cf. Samuel Krauss, *Griechische und lateinische Lehnwörter im Talmud, Midrasch und Targum. Teil 1* (Berlin: Calvary, 1898; repr., Hildesheim: Georg Olms, 1987), 317–322 (317–318: "Einige lustige Spaßmacher der alten Römer und ihre Schwänke waren auch den Talmudisten wohlbekannt und diese ernsten Gesetzeslehrer lassen ihrem Abscheu vor dem eitlen Treiben des weltbeherrschenden Rom auch Worte der Entrüstung folgen"). On the other stock characters mentioned in this and parallel passages from rabbinic literature cf. Krauss, ibid., and Weiss, *Public Spectacles*, 127.

11   Ps 1:1–2 NRSV (emphasis mine).

PART OF THE SCENE: JEWISH THEATER IN ANTIQUITY

nian Talmud first refers to visits in a stadium or a military camp, but soon after also bans visits to the theater or circus:

> Our sages taught: One may not go to theatres (טרטיאות) and circuses because they convene there in the interests of idolatry (מזבלין); the words of R. Meir. But the sages say: In a place where they convene in the interests of idolatry, it is prohibited to visit because of the suspicion of idolatry. And even in a place where they are not known to convene, it is prohibited because it is a seat of scoffers.[12]

The rabbis forbid visits to theaters and circuses because of the idolatry performed in these places. The reading of מזבלין ("to offer to idols") is disputed and the text should perhaps be corrected to מזבחין ("to sacrifice"), which is the reading of the parallel passage in the Tosefta.[13] From its beginnings, pagan theater had a substantial religious component: in Greece, theater performances were originally part of the cult for Dionysus;[14] and while in Roman times the religious component may have been less central at theater performances, the *ludi scaenici*, the "stage games," still began with a sacrifice.[15]

In the above-cited passage and elsewhere the Greek loanword "theaters" is rendered by *tarteiaot* (טרטיאות) instead of the more common *tiatraot* or *teatraot* (תיאטראות), which is closer to the original Greek word (θέατρα). In other rabbinic sources the word becomes *tartraot* (טרטראות). Marcus Jastrow interpreted these deviations as intended linguistic mockery, "cacophemisms."[16] Whether these deviations should really be understood as intended perversions or just as simple variations is difficult to evaluate.[17] Be that as it may, the gen-

---

12   b. ʿAbod. Zar. 18b.

13   t. ʿAbod. Zar. 2:5; cf. the discussion on the parallel in the *Yerushalmi* (y. ʿAbod. Zar. 1:7, 40a) in Gerd A. Wewers, *Avoda Zara—Götzendienst* (Tübingen: Mohr Siebeck, 1980), 28n185, and Martin Jacobs, "Theaters and Performances as Reflected in the Talmud Yerushalmi," in Peter Schäfer, ed., *The Talmud Yerushalmi and Graeco-Roman Culture I* (Tübingen: Mohr Siebeck, 1998), 327–347. On more nuanced voices on visits to the theater cited in b. ʿAbod. Zar. 18b, see below pp. 183–185.

14   Joachim Latacz, *Einführung in die griechische Tragödie* (Göttingen: Vandenhoeck & Ruprecht, 1993), 29–45.

15   John E. Stambaugh, *The Ancient Roman City* (Baltimore: Johns Hopkins University Press, 1988), 230–231; Sallmann, *Christen vor dem Theater*, 245.

16   Marcus Jastrow, *A Dictionary of the Targumim, the Talmud Babli and Yerushalmi, and the Midrashic Literature* (New York: Judaic Press, 1971), s.v. טרטיאות, טרטראות: "cacophem. perversions of תיאטראות." The corresponding passage in the *Yerushalmi* (ʿAbod. Zar. 1.7.40a) reads תיאטרון ("theatron").

17   Jastrow, s.v. איצטדין, also reads איצטדינין (stadia, see above b ʿAbod. Zar. 18b) as a caco-

178   CHAPTER 9

eral message of the rabbis seems clear: Jews must, so to speak, keep away from
the "trara" of the theater.

Passages from midrashim referring to the theater convey a very similar message. *Ruth Rabbah* (about 500 CE[18]) mentions a theater ban of sorts explicitly
addressed to Jewish women: Naomi reminds her daughter-in-law, who is about
to convert to Judaism, that after her conversion she will have to stay away from
theater and circus. This is the first rule for converts (הלכות גרים) mentioned by
Naomi:

> My daughter, it is not the way of the daughters of Israel to go to their the-
> aters and their circuses.[19]

Ruth complies with this demand with the biblical sentence, "where you go, I
will go," here neatly set in a new context.[20] As a matter of fact, the ideal of
going to the right place is a recurrent one in rabbinic comments on the theater.
Genesis Rabbah, a slightly earlier midrash (about 400 CE[21]), explains Gen 39:11
("One day, however, when he went into the house to do his work, and while no
one else was in the house") as Joseph's distancing himself from Egyptian customs:

> R. Judah said: On that day there was a fête in honour of the Nile; everyone
> went to see it, but he (Joseph) went into the house to cast up his master's
> accounts. R. Nehemiah said: It was a day of theatrical performance (יום
> תיאטירון), which all flocked to see, but he (Joseph) went into the house to
> cast up his master's accounts.[22]

---

phony, namely of the root צדה ("destroy"): "cacophemism for *theater* (a *place of destruction*)." However, Krauss, *Griechische und lateinische Lehnwörter.* Vol. 2, 119, is certainly right
to understand it as a simple loan word of the Greek στάδιον. Cf. also the critique on Jastrow
in Kaufmann Kohler, "Jastrow's Talmudic Dictionary," *Hebraica* 5 (1888): 1–6 (especially
4).

18   Günter Stemberger, *Einleitung in Talmud und Midrasch* (Munich: C.H. Beck, 2011), 351.

19   Ruth Rab. 2.22: אין דרכן של בנות ישראל לילך לבתי תיאטראות ולבתי קרקסיאות שלהם.
Translations from *Midrash Rabbah* follow (at times adjusted) the English edition edited
by Harry Freedman and Maurice Simon, *Midrash Rabbah* (10 vols.; London: Soncino, 1961).

20   Ruth 1:16: אל אשר תלכי אלך.

21   Stemberger, *Einleitung*, 309–311.

22   Gen. Rab. 87.7; cf. on this verse Maren Niehoff, *The Figure of Joseph in Post-Biblical Jewish Literature* (Leiden: Brill, 1992), 131–132. See also the parallel passages in Cant. Rab. 1.1
(cf. Samuel T. Lachs, "An Egyptian Festival in Canticles Rabbah," *JQR* 51 (1960): 47–54) and
Pesiq. Rab. 6 ("a day of theater and circus").

PART OF THE SCENE: JEWISH THEATER IN ANTIQUITY

In Rabbi Nehemiah's interpretation, Joseph stayed away from the theater on that day. He does not allow himself to be carried away by the masses but immerses himself in keeping the books of his master Potiphar. In this interpretation, Joseph not only withstands the temptations of Potiphar's wife, but also those of the theater. Joseph resists cultural as well as sexual temptations.[23] By not "going there," Joseph acts precisely the way the same midrash demands in a different passage. Because man is in control over his feet (as one is in control over one's hands and mouth, while one has no control over one's eyes, ears, or nose), man has the capacity to steer his way: either to walk to the theaters and circuses or instead to visit the houses of assembly and learning.[24] Rabbinic literature features this dichotomy between theater and synagogue repeatedly. A passage in *Pesiqta de Rab Kahana* has it that pagans celebrate their holidays by visiting theaters and circuses, whereas on their holidays, Israel attends synagogues and houses of learning.[25] Another midrash says that the ignorant, had God granted him wisdom, would sit and ponder merely on toilets, in theaters, and bathhouses; this is why God gave wisdom to the wise, for they sit and study in synagogues and study houses.[26] Finally, the ideal dichotomy of synagogue and theater (and circus) is epitomized in the passage of the *Yerushalmi* where going to the synagogue instead of the theater becomes a hymn of praise:

> And when he (R. Nehuniah b. Haqanah) exits (the study hall), what does he say? "I give thanks to you, Lord my God, God of my fathers, that you cast my lot with those who sit in the study hall and the synagogues, and you did not cast my lot with those who sit in the theaters and circuses."[27]

In these passages of rabbinic literature, the separation between synagogue and theater is depicted as absolute.[28] The theater is understood as a strict "marker

---

23 See Joshua Levinson, "An-Other Woman: Joseph and Potiphar's Wife. Staging the Body Politic," *JQR* 87 (1997): 269–301.

24 Gen. Rab. 67.3.

25 Pesiq. Rab Kah. 28.1 (on the difficulty of dating cf. Stemberger, *Einleitung*, 327–328): "they (the Gentiles) eat, drink, enjoy themselves and go to the theaters and circuses" vs. "they (Israel) eat, drink, are happy and go to synagogues and prayer houses." See also Pesiq. Rab Kah. 15.2 (also in Lam. Rab. Proem 3): R. Abba bar Kahana says with reference to Jer 15:17 ("I did not sit in the company of merrymakers, nor did I rejoice"): "The Community of Israel spoke before the Holy One, blessed be He: 'Sovereign of the Universe, never did I enter the theaters and circuses of the nations of the world and played and rejoiced with them.'"

26 Eccl. Rab. 1.7.

27 y. Ber. 4:2, 7d (trans. Tzvee Zahavy).

28 m. 'Abod. Zar. 1:7 also prohibits participation in the construction of a stadium.

of difference."[29] Theater and Judaism can only meet once the program has changed and Torah has become the content of the play, so to speak: one passage in the Babylonian Talmud refers to the theaters and circuses in Edom (i.e. Rome), "where the princes of Judah are destined to teach Torah in public."[30] For the time being, though, reality is different: God, according to a line in the Jerusalem Talmud, has to witness how theaters and circuses flourish undisturbed whereas his temple in Jerusalem lies in ruins![31]

Church fathers and early bishops argue quite similarly. Tertullian, in his *Apologeticum* (c. 200 CE), builds up a dichotomy between Christianity and theater, insisting that there is no place for theatrical performances for Christians:

> We have nothing to say, or see, or hear, in connection with the madness of the circus, the immodesty of the theater, the ferocity of the arena, the vain-glory of the gymnasium.[32]

When Gregory of Nazianzus, the fourth century archbishop of Constantinople, in one of his speeches appeals to Christian theater-goers to cease being θεατρικοί ("men of theater, theater fans") in order to become θεωρητικοί ("fond of contemplating"),[33] his exhortation to 'conversion' sounds similar to that of Naomi to Ruth in midrash *Ruth Rabbah*. Bishops and rabbis tried to talk Chris-

---

29 Levinson, "An-Other Woman," 277.

30 b. Meg. 6a (based on Zech 9:7).

31 y. Ber. 9:2, 13c, with reference to Ps 104:32 ("He looks at the earth, and it trembles; He touches the mountains, and they smoke").

32 Tertullian *Apol.* 38.4 (trans. Alexander Souter): *Nihil est nobis dictu visu auditu cum insania circi, cum impudicitia theatri, cum atrocitate arenae, cum vanitate xysti.* Cf. on this quote Richard Klein, *"Spectaculorum voluptates adimere* ... Zum Kampf der Kirchenväter gegen Circus und Theater," in *Theater, Theaterpraxis, Theaterkritik im kaiserzeitlichen Rom,* ed. Joachim Fugmann et al. (Munich/Leipzig: K.G. Saur, 2004), 155–173, 155. In his tractate *Spec.*, Tertullian deals extensively with the question of spectacles. Cf. also the polemics against the spectacles in Tatian, *Orat. ad Graec.* 23–24 (I would like to thank Carson Bay for drawing my attention to this passage). On Christian reception of ancient theater see, among others, Heiko Jürgens, *Pompa Diaboli. Die lateinischen Kirchenväter und das antike Theater* (Stuttgart: Kohlhammer, 1972); Sallmann, "Christen vor dem Theater," 242–259; Timothy D. Barnes, "Christians and the Theater," in *Roman Theater and Society: E. Togo Salmon Papers I,* ed. William J. Slater (Ann Arbor: University of Michigan Press, 1996), 161–180; and Karin Schlapbach and Markus Vinzent, eds., *New Perspectives on Late Antique* spectacula (Leuven: Peeters, 2013).

33 Gregory of Nazianzus, *Oratio* 44.9 (PG 36.617): "Yesterday you were an adherent of theater (θεατρικός), today show yourself as adherent of perception (θεωρητικός)!" The passage is cited in Klein, *"Spectaculorum voluptates adimere,"* 162.

PART OF THE SCENE: JEWISH THEATER IN ANTIQUITY

tians and Jews out of visiting the theater for the same reasons: Tertullian's keywords in the passage cited above—*insania, impudicitia, atrocitas, vanitas*—are also essential points of critique in Jewish judgments on the theater. Moreover, apart from moral and religious reservations, Christians and Jews had an additional reason to object to the theater: both Jews and Christians were mocked and ridiculed on pagan stages. The midrash *Ekha Rabbati* (*Lamentations Rabbah*, dated to the early fifth century CE[34]), commenting on Lam 3:14 ("I have become the laughingstock of all my people, the object of their taunt-songs all day long"), laments anti-Jewish sneer in theater and circus:

> *I am the subject of gossip for those who sit in the gate* (Ps 69:13). This refers to the nations of the world who sit in theaters and circuses. *And the drunkards make songs about me* (ib.): after they sit eating and drinking and become intoxicated they sit and talk of me, scoffing at me.[35]

From earlier times we know that Jews were not only laughed at in the theater: at the time of the anti-Jewish riot in Alexandria in 38 CE Jews were arrested and taken to the theater by command of the Roman prefect Flaccus.[36] In jarring language, Philo of Alexandria reports the severe abuse of Jews in the theater: they were tortured most cruelly by fire and sword and finally crucified.[37] With cynical and ironic overtones, Philo describes how the brutal murder of Jews came to be part of a theater performance, as it were:

> The spectacle was divided into acts (ἡ θέα διενενέμητο). The first shows (τὰ μὲν γὰρ πρῶτα τῶν θεαμάτων), which lasted from dawn till the third or fourth hour, were as follows: Jews were scourged, hung up, tortured on the wheel, maltreated, and led away to their death through the middle of the orchestra. The shows after this 'fine' exhibition (μετὰ τὴν καλὴν ταύτην

---

34   Stemberger, *Einleitung*, 316–317.

35   Lamentations Rabbah 3.14. It follows a list of anti-Jewish sayings that were shared on these occasions. Apparently, one of the targets for mockery was the poverty of the Jews (their simple meals, their way to dress). On the socio-historical background of derided poverty in Palestine, see Michael Avi-Jonah, *The Jews under Roman and Byzantine Rule: A Political History of Palestine from the Bar Kokhba War to the Arab Conquest* (Jerusalem: Schocken, 1984), 104–105. On the other hand, theater could also be seen as a means to calm the Gentiles down: cf. Gen. Rab. 80.1 (on Gen 34:5) and on this unusual passage Weiss, *Public Spectacles*, 211–212.

36   Philo, *Flacc.* 74: εἰς τὸ θέατρον εἰσάγει—θέαν οἰκτίστην.

37   Philo, *Flacc.* 84.

ἐπίδειξιν) included dancers, mimes, flute players, and all the other forms of amusement in theatrical competitions.[38]

On a different day, Jewish women who happened to be in the theater were dragged onto the stage:

> of which (sc. the cruelty of Flaccus and the people) even women became the victims. For they were seized like captives not only in the market place but also in the middle of the theater (ἐν μέσῳ τῷ θεάτρῳ), where they were dragged up on the stage (ἐπὶ τὴν σκηνήν) on any calumnious charge whatsoever, in an intolerably and painfully insulting way.[39]

Some thirty years later, with the beginning of the Jewish-Roman War, Flavius Josephus attests to renewed anti-Jewish excesses in Alexandria's theater.[40] In the late nineties of the first century CE, the same writer refers to tortures of Jewish prisoners in theaters almost as if it were a matter of course:

> Thus, to date many have been seen, on many occasions, as prisoners of war suffering torture and all kinds of deaths in theaters for not letting slip a single word in contravention of the laws and the records associated with them.[41]

Christians endured a similar fate. In particular, their rite of baptism was ridiculed on stage. Again we read in the orations of the late antique bishop Gregory Nazianzus:

> We have become a new spectacle (γεγόναμεν θεατρὸν καινόν) .... Nay, we have already—I can scarcely speak of it without tears—been represented on the stage, amid the laughter of the most licentious, and the most popular of all dialogues and scenes is the caricature of a Christian (Χριστιανὸς κωμῳδούμενος).[42]

---

38   Philo, *Flacc.* 85 (trans. Pieter W. van der Horst). Cf. Pieter W. van der Horst, *Philo's Flaccus. The First Pogrom* (Leiden: Brill, 2003), 177.

39   Philo, *Flacc.* 95. Note that Philo here is taking for granted the presence of Jewish women in the theater. On Jewish visitors of the theater, see below, pp. 185-190.

40   Josephus, *BJ* 2.490–492.

41   Josephus, *CA* 1.43 (trans. John M.G. Barclay).

42   Gregory Nazianzus, *Or.* 2.84 (*PG* 35, 489; trans. in *NPNF[1]* VII); on this passage see Klein, "*Spectaculorum voluptates adimere,*" 159.

PART OF THE SCENE: JEWISH THEATER IN ANTIQUITY   183

Jews and Christians were insulted on stage. It is difficult to say how regular such assaults (rhetorical or physical) were. Given the continuous flow of Jewish and Christian theater-goers—as evidenced not least indirectly by the rabbis' and bishops' criticism of the theater—we may probably infer, though, that anti-Jewish and anti-Christian performances were not the rule.[43]

2   Nuances in Rabbinic Discourse about the Theater

Despite the harsh condemnations of the theater by rabbis and bishops, there are a number of indications that in reality the Jewish and Christian discourse on theater was more nuanced. For rabbinic Judaism it is the very same tractate *Avodah Zara* which points in that direction. Right after the seemingly sweeping ban against visits to arenas and attendance at the entertaining performances that accompanied sieges (cited above), we learn about reasons that make these visits possible—under certain conditions and according to at least some rabbis:

> (To go) to stadiums is permitted because one can shout and rescue; and (to go) to an encirclement is permitted for the sake of relief for the city, so long as he is not numbered among (the besiegers). But if he is numbered among them, it is prohibited .... One may not go to stadiums because of *a seat of scoffers*; R. Nathan permits this for two reasons: One, because (the visitor) can shout and rescue, and another, because he can testify (on behalf of) the (victim's) wife (that her husband died), to allow her to marry (again).[44]

Hence, if the Jewish visitor to these sites is able to contribute to a common, just cause—to act for the benefit of a city under siege, to help someone who is in danger, or as a service to the wife left behind—then a visit is allowed. As the Tosefta formulates: if it is for the benefit of the general public (מפני צורך מדינה), then visits to theaters are allowed.[45] It seems, then, that the rabbis (or rather some rabbis) attempted to come to terms with the phenomenon

---

43   In the Middle Ages, Jews were the target of attacks in Christian passion and mystery plays: see Natascha Bremer, *Das Bild der Juden in den Passionsspielen und in der bildenden Kunst des deutschen Mittelalters* (Frankfurt: Peter Lang, 1986).

44   b. ʿAbod. Zar. 18b. Cf. y. ʿAbod. Zar. 1:7, 40a and on this Jacobs, "Theaters and Performances," 332–340.

45   t. ʿAbod. Zar. 2:7.

184   CHAPTER 9

of the theater. It was important to know what was happening in the theaters and circuses.[46] These were not only places of enjoyment but also civic centers, offering possibilities of communication and networking.[47] A complete separation from the *spectacula* was not easy. Some rabbis obviously strove for compromise. In a much earlier fictional account from the diaspora, the *Letter of Aristeas* from the second century BCE, a similar approach to theater is palpable: one of the Jewish sages who was translating the Torah into Greek, when asked by the Ptolemaic king what he recommended for recreation and distraction, answered that *decent* theater performances can indeed serve this purpose:

> To watch plays performed with propriety and to set before one's eyes scenes from life presented with decency and restraint is profitable to one's life and appropriate; for even in such things there is some edification.[48]

The Jewish sage endorses theater for a pagan king! For "even out of the slightest matters," he continues, one can learn important lessons for life.[49] The description of the plays fits that of the mime, which was understood as an "imitation of life" (μίμησις βίου).[50] What the Jewish sage suggests to the Ptolemaic king in the *Letter of Aristeas*, a Jewish pseudepigraphic text, can easily be imagined as an inner-Jewish argument in favor of theater.[51] Jews looked for strategies to make theater permissible, and so did Christians. Novatian, writing in the third century CE, in his tractate on the spectacles (*De spectaculis*) has a Christian voice defend the performances in the theater with supporting references from the Bible:

---

46   Cf. b. Ketub. 5a on going to the theater on the Sabbath to watch over the public affairs that are happening there.

47   Cf. Sallmann, "Christen vor dem Theater," 245: "Für die Gesellschaft mussten die *spectacula* den gesamten Aufgabenbereich eines heutigen Theater- und Kinobetriebes wahrnehmen, dazu von Television und Hörfunk, von Sportpalast und Zirkus, Rennbahn und Horror-show."

48   *Let. Arist.* 284 (trans. Moses Hadas): ὁ δὲ ἔφη θεωρεῖν ὅσα παίζεται μετὰ περιστολῆς καὶ πρὸ ὀφθαλμῶν τιθέναι τὰ τοῦ βίου μετ' εὐσχημοσύνης καὶ καταστολῆς γινόμενα βίῳ συμφέρον καὶ καθῆκον· ἔνεστι γὰρ καὶ ἐν τούτοις ἐπισκευή τις.

49   *Let. Arist.* 285.

50   Diomedes, *Grammatici Latini* 1.491.

51   According to *Let. Aristeas* 316 (and Josephus, *AJ* 12.114), the tragic poet Theodektes refrained from using a biblical theme for a drama because when he tried to do so he had turned blind. The context, though, does not so much suggest a critique of theater as it explains why early Greek authors are not mentioning the Jews.

PART OF THE SCENE: JEWISH THEATER IN ANTIQUITY

"Where," they ask, "are such things mentioned in Scripture? Where are they prohibited? On the contrary, not only was Elijah the charioteer of Israel, but even David danced before the ark. In Scripture, we also read of harps, lyres, timbrels, flutes, citharas, and dancing troupes .... Why then should a faithful Christian not be at liberty to be a spectator of things that the divine Writings are at liberty to mention?"[52]

3 Jews Attending the Theater

There is no doubt that in antiquity Jews attended the spectacles. Evidence for this comes mainly from the Jewish diaspora, but it is safe to assume that in Palestine also Jews did not completely shy away from the theaters and circuses. The incorporation of both prohibition and exceptions in *Avodah Zarah* (both in the *Bavli* and the *Yerushalmi*) is a fairly clear indication that at least some Jews attended the theater in Palestine as well. In a midrash, Rabbi Johanan relates the biblical line "the land was filled with them (the Hebrews)" (Exod 1:7) to Jewish visits to theater and circuses: "The theaters and circuses were filled with them."[53]

Flavius Josephus reports that at the end of the first century BCE, King Herod had theaters built in Caesarea, Jericho, and Jerusalem. At the Herodium, Herod's burial place, a theater was discovered with remarkable frescoes in one of the chambers at the top of the *cavea*.[54] These were the first theater-buildings

---

52   Novatian, *De spectaculis* 2.3 (trans. Russell J. DeSimone, adjusted): "*Ubi 'inquiunt' scripta sunt ista, ubi prohibita? Alioquin et auriga est Israel Helias, et ante arcam David ipse saltavit. Nabla, cinyras, tympana, tibias, citharas, choros legimus .... Cur ergo homini christiano fideli non liceat spectare quod licuit divinis litteris scribere?*" Cf. Sallmann, "Christen vor dem Theater," 249.

53   Tanḥ. Buber, Shemot 6: שנתמלאו בתי טרטיאות ובתי קרקסיאות מהם. The biblical reference is to the land of Egypt, but the critique can very well refer to Palestine. Cf. Levinson, "An-Other Woman," 287 who, in addition, refers to Eccl. Rab. 2.2 (on Eccl 2:2: "I said of laughter, 'It is madness,' and of pleasure, 'What does it accomplish?'"): "R. Abba bar Kahana: 'How confounded (senseless) is the laughter in which the heathen peoples indulge in their circuses and theaters! What cause can a disciple of the Sages have to enter such places (מה טיבו של תלמיד חכם להכנס שם)?'" This phrase may indeed imply that rabbis too attended the spectacles.

54   Josephus, *BJ* 1.415 (Caesarea); *AJ* 15.268 (Jerusalem), 17.161 (Jericho). Cf. Arthur Segal, *Theaters in Roman Palestine and Provincia Arabia* (Leiden: Brill, 1995), 4–5 and the map with all buildings of mass entertainment in ancient Palestine and Arabia in Weiss, *Public Spectacles*, 59. On the theater at the Herodium cf. ibid. 22–23, 34–35 and Silvia Rozenberg and David Mevorah, *Herod the Great: The King's Final Journey* (Jerusalem: The Israel Museum, 2013). Herod also had theaters built in Sidon and Damascus (*BJ* 1.422).

186   CHAPTER 9

in Palestine. In terms of its Jewish audience, the theater in Jerusalem is of special interest. Unfortunately, we have very little certain information about it.[55] Its exact location in the city is unknown. A group of theater seats and two entrance tickets, which are difficult to date and are not uncontested, are the only (possible) relics of Jerusalem's theater.[56] Nevertheless, it is indeed rather unlikely that Jews kept away from performances in Jerusalem, Caesarea, or the theaters in the Galilee (Sepphoris, Tiberias) in principle.[57]

Compelling evidence for Jewish contact with the theater in the diaspora is certainly much more numerous. Philo, who reports about the atrocious tortures of Jews in Alexandria's theater, frequently went to the theater himself. His observations about different reactions of the audience to performances can be taken to attest to regular visits at the theater:

> For example, I have often when I chanced to be in the theater noticed (ἤδη γοῦν ἐν θεάτρῳ πολλάκις παρατυχὼν εἶδον) the effect produced by some single tune sung by the actors on the stage or played by the musicians. Some of the audience are so moved, that in their excitement they cannot help raising their voices in a chorus of acclamation. Others are so unstirred that, as far as this is concerned, you might suppose them on a level of feeling with the senseless benches on which they sit. Others, again, are so repelled that they are off and away from the performance, and indeed, as they go, block their ears with both hands for fear that some echo of the music should remain to haunt them and produce a sense of discomfort to irritate and pain their souls.[58]

---

55   Cf. Josephus, *AJ* 15.268. Josephus, for one, talks about a theater, on the other hand he also mentions an amphitheater "in the plain." It seems that Josephus could well call also other buildings an "amphitheater," cf. Yosef Porath, "Why did Josephus Name the Chariot-Racing Facility at Caesarea 'Amphitheater'?," *Scripta Classica Israelica* 23 (2004): 63–67.

56   Cf. Ronny Reich and Yaakov Billig, "A Group of Theater Seats Discovered near the South-Western Corner of the Temple Mount," *IEJ* 50 (2000): 175–184.

57   Cf. Japp, *Die Baupolitik Herodes' des Großen*, 25 and Levinson, "An-Other Woman," 287; Weiss, *Public Spectacles*, 197–200. Joseph Patrich, "Herod's Theater in Jerusalem—a new proposal," *IEJ* 52 (2002): 231–239, explains the non-existent traces of Jerusalem's theater by its being a wooden structure.

58   Philo, *Ebr.* 177 (trans. LCL). Cf. also Philo, *Prob.* 141 about the enthusiastic acceptance of a piece by Euripides. I fully agree with Margaret Williams' view (*The Jews among the Greeks and Romans: A Diasporan Sourcebook* [Baltimore: Johns Hopkins University Press, 1998], 114) that there is no reason to dismiss Philo's descriptions of theater experiences as sheer rhetoric; cf. also Dorothy Sly, *Philo's Alexandria* (London: Routledge, 1996), 85–86. Cf. also more recently Jay, "The Problem of the Theater in Early Judaism," 225–232.

PART OF THE SCENE: JEWISH THEATER IN ANTIQUITY   187

In general, Philo's attitude towards the theater can be characterized as ambivalent. In many instances in his oeuvre, Philo displays resistance against Greek fiction, which stands in contradiction to Jewish truth. The "stage and the myth" are represented by Esau, who stands for paganism. Esau in Philo is opposed to Jacob, who keeps away from myth.[59] Philo condemns the brazenness of the theater.[60] His censure of the world of theater, however, is caught up by his own reality, so to speak. He knew the theater scene in Alexandria and was familiar with the classic tragedians, whom he cites on occasion.[61] Philo's ambivalent approach to theater, combining critique of and familiarity with the spectacles, becomes most obvious in *In Flaccum*, the very tractate where he reports the abuse of Jews in the theater. In presenting the pre-history of the anti-Jewish riot of 38 CE, Philo repeatedly resorts to the language of the theater: just as with Josephus later, in Philo the vocabulary of theater appears in the context of political power games, intrigues, and false characters. Flaccus's counselors pretend to be his friends like "actors do in a theater" and make him look like a "mute figure on stage."[62] As a philosopher, Philo dismisses the feigned appearances of the theater, and when he describes the abuse of Jews in the theater, he is appalled.[63] By the same token, Philo's oeuvre at times bespeaks a great familiarity with the stage. He obviously did not shun it in principle. Nor did Jews in Alexandria in later times: for late antiquity, the church historian Socrates Scholasticus reports in the context of a dispute between Christians and Jews in 415 CE that the local theater had an especially large audience on Saturdays because on this day Jews spent their time "not in listening to the law, but to indulge in the theatrical performances" (μὴ τῇ ἀκροάσει τοῦ νόμου ἀλλὰ τοῖς θεατρικοῖς σχολάζειν).[64] The

---

59 Philo, *Cong.* 62: σκηνὴ καὶ μῦθος αὐτός (Philo comments on Gen 25:27: "When the boys grew up, Esau was a skillful hunter, a man of the field, while Jacob was a quiet man, living in tents"). On Philo and myth see chapter 8 in this volume.

60 Philo, *Agr.* 35; *Legat.* 204.

61 Philo, *Aet.* 49 (Aeschylus); *Prob.* 19 (Sophocles); 99–104, 141 (Euripides); 143 (Aeschylus). Cf. Howard Jacobson, *The Exagoge of Ezekiel* (Cambridge: Cambridge University Press, 1983), 27, and David Lincicum, "An Index to Philo's Non-Biblical Citations and Allusions," *SPhiloA* 25 (2013): 139–168.

62 Philo, *Flacc.* 19 (ὥσπερ ἐν θεάτρῳ καθυποκρινόμενοι); 20 (κωφὸν ὡς ἐπὶ σκηνῆς προσωπεῖον). Flaccus in the end suffers the same anguish as the Jews previously, and Flaccus is put on stage here just as the Jews later on; cf. van der Horst, *Philo's Flaccus*, 108 and Francesca Calabi, "Theatrical Language in Philo's *In Flaccum*," in *Italian Studies on Philo of Alexandria*, ed. Francesca Calabi (Leiden: Brill, 2003), 91–116.

63 In *Legat.* 368 the denouncing of anti-Jewish actions blends into a critique of the theater; cf. Calabi, "Theatrical Language in Philo's *In Flaccum*," 104–105.

64 Socrates Scholasticus, *Historia ecclesiastica* 7.13 (on the violent conflict between Chris-

188   CHAPTER 9

rabbis were probably as unhappy with this as the roughly contemporary bishop of Constantinople, John Chrysostom, was with the many Christians who preferred the theater to the church even on the Easter holidays.[65]

In the works of Josephus, we see a similar tension between condemnations of the theater and familiarity with it. On one occasion, Josephus heavily derides the theater: in connection with Herod's theater building in Jerusalem mentioned earlier, Josephus portrays theater and Judaism as constituting an intrinsic antithesis. The splendid theaters built by Herod in Jerusalem run counter to the character (τὸ ἔθος) of the Jews:

> He (Herod) built a theater in Jerusalem, and after that a very large amphitheater in the plain, both being spectacularly lavish but foreign to Jewish custom (τοῦ δὲ κατὰ τοὺς Ἰουδαίους ἔθους ἀλλότρια), for the use of such buildings and the exhibition of such spectacles have not been traditional (with the Jews) (χρῆσίς τε γὰρ αὐτῶν καὶ θεαμάτων τοιούτων ἐπίδειξις οὐ παραδέδοται).[66]

Thus, Josephus sets up a similar dichotomy between Judaism and theater to Philo's (even if Josephus's critique here is not directed against the performance of plays but primarily against the bloody contests and the trophies at the building[67]). Unlike Philo, Josephus never mentions a visit to the theater. Yet, it can hardly be doubted that Josephus, too, knew the theater scene from his own experience (if not from Jerusalem, certainly from Rome). That he read the tragic authors can be inferred from a number of traces of Aeschylus, Sophocles, and Euripides in his work.[68] Apart from these literary allusions to the tragedians,

---

tians and Jews in Alexandria in CE 415 that originated in the theater). The passage is certainly not free from polemic, but it cannot be passed over as mere fiction either. Philo, *Mos.* 2.21, in an idealistic presentation of the Sabbath, describes the opposite of what Socrates Scholasticus observes: on their days of relaxation Jews keep themselves apart from pagan "theatromania" (θεατρομανοῦντες—this verb is not attested before Philo).

65   John Chrysostom, PG 56.264 (*Contra ludos et theatra*, a speech delivered in Constantinople on July 3, 399); cf. on this Klein, "*Spectaculorum voluptates adimere*," 164–165. On Chrysostom's attitude towards the theater see Silke-Petra Bergjan, "'Das hier ist kein Theater, und ihr sitzt nicht da, um Schauspieler zu betrachten und zu klatschen'—Theaterpolemik und Theatermetaphern bei Johannes Chrysostomos," ZAC 8 (2005): 567–592.

66   Josephus, *AJ* 15.268 (trans. LCL).

67   Josephus, *AJ* 15.274–276.

68   Cf. Louis H. Feldman, "The Influence of the Greek Tragedians on Josephus," in *Hellenic and Jewish Arts: Interaction, Tradition and Renewal*, ed. Asher Ovadiah (Jerusalem, 1998), 51–80; Honora Howell Chapman, "'By the Waters of Babylon': Josephus and Greek Poetry," in *Josephus and Jewish History in Flavian Rome and Beyond*, ed. Joseph Sievers and Gaia Lembi (Leiden: Brill, 2005), 121–124.

PART OF THE SCENE: JEWISH THEATER IN ANTIQUITY   189

there are in Josephus's oeuvre several indicators showing that Josephus was
rather familiar with the world of theater. He knows what a dramatist (δραμα-
τουργός) does,[69] and more generally what a "drama" is.[70] Josephus is familiar
with the props of the theater: in the context of the performance of a *mimos* and
another play shortly before the assassination of Gaius Caligula at the theater,
he mentions the "artificial blood" which was used on stage.[71] Josephus, just like
Philo before him, makes recourse to the vocabulary of theater to illustrate people's disguises and false pretenses. Some of the scenes in Josephus's oeuvre are
literally set "on stage," where protagonists at times wear "masks," put them on,
or take them off. Whenever people are suddenly invested with great power—as
in the case of the kings—Josephus writes, they put down their earlier righteous
disposition "like masks in a theater" (ὥσπερ ἐπὶ σκηνῆς προσωπεῖα ... ἀποθέμε-
νοι) and begin to despise both divine and human law.[72] Josephus also uses the
vocabulary of the theater when he writes about the idea of choosing priests by
lot, which had come up during the Jewish-Roman war and seemed dreadful to
Josephus, son of a priest: a man was appointed priest who had no clue himself
as to how he won such honors. The person was dressed with the holy robes of
a priest and he was given instructions what to do. The whole event was a real
spectacle: "dressing him up for his assumed part, as on the stage" (ὥσπερ ἐπὶ
σκηνῆς ἀλλοτρίῳ κατεκόσμουν προσωπείῳ).[73]

Despite his harsh condemnation of theater and myth,[74] Josephus, too, then,
did not abstain from the world of theater. Someone who can describe the geographic layout of the city of Jerusalem as "theater-like"—as Josephus does in
his *Antiquities*: "the city lay opposite to the Temple, having the form of a theater (θεατροειδής)"[75]—is unlikely to have been completely averse to the theater
(whether in Palestine or in Rome).

Finally, there are epigraphic attestations from Asia Minor that offer unequiv-
ocal evidence of regular theater visits by Jews. Inscriptions from the theater

---

69   Cf. Josephus, *BJ* 1.471 with reference to Antipater (δραματουργῶν) and 1.530. On the drama
at Herod's royal court cf. Jonathan J. Price and Lisa Ullmann, "Drama and History in Josephus' *Bellum Judaicum*," *Scripta Classica Israelica* 21 (2002): 97–111.

70   Josephus, *BJ* 1.543 ("the last act of the drama": τὸ τέλος τοῦ δράματος); *AJ* 12.113; 19.94, 199.

71   Josephus, *AJ* 19.94 (αἷμά τεχνητόν).

72   Josephus, *AJ* 6.264.

73   Josephus, *BJ* 4.156 (trans. LCL).

74   Cf. René Bloch, *Moses und der Mythos. Die Auseinandersetzung mit der griechischen Mythologie bei jüdisch-hellenistischen Autoren* (Leiden: Brill, 2011), 23–49.

75   Josephus, *AJ* 15.410 (trans. Steve Mason). As Steve Mason rightly notes (ad loc.): in the sim-
ile "the Temple is seen as the stage of the theater!" In another passage Josephus likens a
battle scene to a theater play: *BJ* 6.146: ὥσπερ τι πολέμου θέατρον.

of Miletus label certain seats as those of the Jews (and of "God-fearers"). The precise wording of the inscriptions is debated, as is their dating (second/third century CE?). Nevertheless, the inscriptions are clear evidence to the fact that Jews in the theater of Miletus had their own permanent seats.[76] Also, from the Odeon of Aphrodisias (fifth/sixth century CE) we know of seats which were designated as "seats of the Hebrews" (τόπος Ἑβρέων).[77] It is safe to assume that these were not isolated cases.[78]

4   Jewish Actors and Actresses

Jews not only visited theaters, they also acted themselves. When as a young man Josephus was sent on a mission to Rome with the task of setting Jewish priests free, he met a Jewish actor (μιμολόγος) by the name Haliturus in Puteoli, who was close to Nero and his wife Poppaea.[79] Josephus refers to this Jewish actor without any sign of astonishment. Apparently, Jewish actors were nothing extraordinary. With respect to the dichotomy of synagogue and theater in rabbinic Literature, it is noteworthy that a Jewish actor, at least according to this report by Josephus, served as a contact precisely in the attempt to free Jewish priests from captivity: in this scene of Josephus's autobiography Judaism and theater converge.[80] Another literary attestation to an actor who was presumably Jewish can be found in Martial, who mocks a circumcised comedian by the name Menophilus.[81]

---

76 Cf. Walter Ameling, *Inscriptiones Judaicae Orientis*. Vol. 2 (Tübingen: Mohr Siebeck, 2004), no. 37: τόπος Εἰουδέων τῶν καὶ θεοσεβίον ("seat of the Jews and 'God-fearers' (?)"). Other inscriptions from the theater of Miletus that mention Jews or "God-fearers" respectively are nos. 38 and 39. Cf. also Murray Baker, "Who Was Sitting in the Theater at Miletos?" *Journal for the Study of Judaism* 36 (2005): 397–416.

77 Joyce Reynolds and Robert Tannenbaum, *Jews and Godfearers at Aphrodisias* (Cambridge: Cambridge University Press, 1987), 132; Pieter W. van der Horst, "Jews and Blues in Late Antiquity," in *Des Géants à Dionysos. Mélanges offerts à F. Vian*, ed. Domenico Accorinti and Pierre Chuvin (Alessandria: Edizioni dell'Orso, 2003), 565–571; Ameling, *Inscriptiones*, nos. 15–16.

78 For other, debated evidence of Jewish theater seats cf. Weiss, *Public Spectacles*, 331.

79 Josephus, *Vita* 16. The word can also mean "writer of mimes;" cf. S. Mason, *Flavius Josephus: Life of Josephus* (Leiden: Brill, 2001), 25 and Philo, *Spec.* 4.59.

80 Cf. Hartmut Leppin, *Histrionen. Untersuchungen zur sozialen Stellung von Bühnenkünstlern im Westen des Römischen Reiches zur Zeit der Republik und des Principats* (Bonn: Rudolf Habelt, 1992), 68, 116, 247.

81 Martial, *Epigrammata* 7.82; cf. Leppin, *Histrionen*, 317; and Shaye J.D. Cohen, *The Beginnings of Jewishness: Boundaries, Varieties, Uncertainties* (Berkeley: University of California Press, 1999), 358–359.

PART OF THE SCENE: JEWISH THEATER IN ANTIQUITY

Epigraphic evidence provides more material: in a fragmentary inscription from Ostia (third century CE), Marcus Aurelius Pylades from Scythopolis (Beth Shean) in the province of Judea is presented as the "first mime of his time" (*pantomimus sui temporis primus*).[82] A Jewish sarcophagus inscription in Rome (found not far from the Via Appia), likewise from the third century CE, seems to refer to a Jewish actress named Faustina. At least the three masks next to the inscription seem to imply that Faustina was indeed an actress (although a purely aesthetic significance of the masks cannot be excluded).[83]

5 Jewish Theater Authors: Ezekiel Tragicus

Contrary to the widespread view, persistent in many reference works, there was thus indeed a Jewish involvement with theater in antiquity. Jews were part of the scene: they attended theater performances and other spectacles both in Palestine and in the diaspora. Jews read tragedies and comedies, and some Jews chose to be professional actors. And Jews also participated in the *production* of theater: Jews wrote plays for the theater. In the second century BCE (most likely), presumably in Alexandria, a certain Ezekiel wrote a drama about the biblical narrative of the exodus.[84] The play is entitled *Exagoge* ("leading out" or "evacuation") and is the only ancient Jewish drama that we know of. It can be assumed, however, that Ezekiel composed several works for the stage, since he is referred to as an author of "tragedies" or "Jewish tragedies"—at any rate as an author of more than one work.[85] There is no cogent reason

---

82 David Noy, *Jewish Inscriptions of Western Europe, Volume 1: Italy (excluding the City of Rome), Spain and Gaul* (Cambridge: Cambridge University Press, 1993), no. 15: *M(arco) Aurel[io.] f(ilio) Ter(etina) Py[ladi] A[..]sc1[...] Scythop[oli] p[an]tomim[o sui] tempor[is] primo (...) ex provincia [Iuda]e[a .... post] mortem patr[is s]ui Iud[ae; (...)*. If Noy's reading is correct and the father's name was Iuda, the mime's father was probably a Jew. See also Leppin, *Histrionen*, 251–252, 288.

83 Cf. Adia Konikoff, *Sarcophagi from the Jewish Catacombs of Ancient Rome* (Stuttgart: Franz Steiner, 1990), 41–44. The inscription is written in Greek and in Hebrew (one word); it is surrounded by the symbols typical of Jewish tomb inscriptions (Menorah, Lulav, Shofar). On actresses in late antiquity, see Ruth Webb, "Female entertainers in late antiquity," in *Greek and Roman Actors: Aspects of an Ancient Profession*, ed. Patricia Easterling and Edith Hall (Cambridge: Cambridge University Press, 2002), 282–303.

84 There exist two excellent commentaries on this text: Jacobson, *The* Exagoge *of Ezekiel*, and Pierluigi Lanfranchi, *L'Exagoge d'Ezéchiel le Tragique. Introduction, texte, traduction et commentaire* (Leiden: Brill, 2006). A good introduction to the essential questions can also be found in Barclay, *Jews in the Mediterranean Diaspora*, 132–138.

85 Clement of Alexandria, *Strom.* 1.23.155–156: ὁ τῶν Ἰουδαϊκῶν τραγῳδιῶν ποιητής. Eusebius,

192   CHAPTER 9

to doubt that this drama was written to be performed on stage (as opposed to a purely literary play).[86] Unfortunately, Ezekiel's *Exagoge* is preserved only in fragments (or rather excerpts: passages cited by Clement of Alexandria, Eusebius, and Pseudo-Eustathius). Still, the extant 269 iambic trimeters do allow for an approximate reconstruction of the overall outline of the play: as in a pagan tragedy (especially one by Euripides), here too the protagonist, Moses, first appears on the scene as a solitary figure. In a prologue Moses tells the audience—which we perhaps can imagine as partly Jewish, partly Greek/Egyptian—of the preceding events: how he came to live as a boy in the Egyptian palace after his mother had abandoned him on Pharaoh's command and how he had to flee Egypt after having killed an Egyptian. In the next scene we learn how Moses gets to meet his wife-to-be Zipporah at a well. Then Moses tells of a dream: on Mount Sinai God appeared to him and seated him on a throne which afforded him a view of the entire world. Moses's father-in-law Raguel interprets this dream for him as a vision heralding Moses's future role as a judge and leader. Then follows the biblical scene of the burning bush and the dialogue between Moses and God: Moses is prepared for his future role as leader of the Jews and the ten plagues of the Egyptians are foretold to him (they would have been difficult to stage). Later, very much in keeping with the genre of Greek tragedy, an Egyptian messenger appears on stage. He is a survivor of the dramatic dividing of the sea which brought salvation to the Israelites and death to the Egyptians. Finally, in the last known excerpt, a scout reports what the spies came upon when they explored the promised land: that is, he speaks of a strange bird (a kind of phoenix) that he discovered.

An extensive interpretation of this drama is neither possible nor necessary within the framework of this survey article.[87] Not unlike the authors of

---

Praep. Ev. 9.28.1: ὁ τῶν τραγῳδιῶν ποιητής. If the Jewish μιμολόγος mentioned by Josephus (cf. above n. 79) is meant to be a playwright, this would be additional evidence for a Jewish author writing for the theater. Moreover, there are Jewish pseudepigraphic verses (to be sure hardly intended for the stage) in the name of Greek authors of tragedy and comedy (Aeschylus, Sophocles, Euripides, Menander, Diphilos): cf. Emil Schürer, *The History of the Jewish People in the Age of Jesus Christ (175 B.C.–A.D. 135)*. Vol. 3.1 (ed. Geza Vermes, Fergus Millar, and Martin Goodman; Edinburgh: T&T Clark, 1986), 656–671.

86 Cf. Barclay, *Jews in the Mediterranean Diaspora*, 134.

87 Cf. more recently G. Anthony Keddie and Jonathan MacLellan, "Ezekiel's *Exagoge* and the Politics of Hellenistic Theater: Mosaic Hegemony on a Ptolemaic Model," *Journal of Ancient Judaism* 8 (2017): 170–187 (with further bibliography). Cf. also René Bloch, "Moses and Greek Myth in Hellenistic Judaism," in *La construction de la figure de Moïse/The Construction of the Figure of Moses*, ed. Thomas Römer (Paris: Gabalda, 2007), 195–208 (200–208 on Ezekiel).

PART OF THE SCENE: JEWISH THEATER IN ANTIQUITY

the midrashim, and at the same time following the outlines of Greek tragedy, Ezekiel rewrites the biblical exodus narrative without sidestepping its core aspects. To a large extent, he follows the storyline as told in the Septuagint, but in several instances he does deviate from it: e.g. in the scene of the bird about which the scout reports, or that of Moses's dream (Jewish tradition otherwise does not know of Moses dreaming). Apparently neither Ezekiel nor his audience found any fault with such additions and changes.

Ezekiel's *Exagoge* is a nice example of ancient Jewish "acculturation," although this expression should be used with care: for it is not the case that Jews had lived in complete isolation beforehand and then suddenly adopted elements of Greek culture. Whether in Palestine or in the diaspora, Jews were always an integral part of the ancient Mediterranean world. Ezekiel's *Exagoge* is an example of acculturation inasmuch as its author casts a Jewish story into a "pagan" vessel: a play in Greek trimeters with many elements which are reminiscent of conventional patterns of Greek tragedy (the prologue, Moses's dream, the messenger scene, and more).[88] One moment in the play symptomatically represents its symbiotic approach (which seeks to join Jewish with non-Jewish aspects). In the prologue, Moses tells the audience about his education: he first learned from his mother everything about his (Jewish) ancestors. Later, when he was brought to the Egyptian palace, he received in addition a royal (Egyptian) education (παιδεύματα):

> When my infancy had passed,
> my mother brought me to the princess' palace,
> after telling me all about
> my lineage and God's gifts.
> Accordingly, for the period of my youth, the princess
> gave me a royal upbringing and education,
> as if I were her own son.[89]

Moses receives a double education: one Jewish and one non-Jewish.[90] Both the Moses of Ezekiel the tragedian and Ezekiel himself are rooted with one

---

88 Barclay, *Jews in the Mediterranean Diaspora*, 125–180, aptly speaks of "cultural convergence" with reference to Ezekiel. On an inclusive understanding of Mediterranean religion see Fritz Graf, "What is Ancient Mediterranean Religion?" in *Religions of the Ancient World: A Guide*, ed. Sarah Iles Johnston (Cambridge: Harvard University Press, 2004), 3–16.

89 Ezekiel, *Exagoge* 32–38 (trans. Jacobson).

90 Cf. Barclay, *Jews in the Mediterranean Diaspora*, 138. Similarly, in Philo's *De vita Mosis* different teachers introduce Moses into the encyclical education: *Mos.* 1.21–24. On Moses's two mothers cf. chapter 3 in this volume.

194   CHAPTER 9

leg in Judaism and the other in Hellenism. Ezekiel does not lose his balance over this. In Ezekiel, we encounter a self-assured diaspora Jew who in Egyptian Alexandria (most likely) stages a Jewish story without being apologetic: it is an Egyptian survivor who is "entitled" to be the messenger and to tell how the Egyptians were inferior to the Israelites and their mighty God.

Howard Jacobson has compared the *Exagoge* to Aeschylus's *Persians*. There are indeed some striking parallels: just as the *Persians* is about the Greeks' crucial victory in the sea battle of Salamis (including stock elements of Greek tragedy like 'dream' and 'messenger' scenes), Ezekiel's *Exagoge* is a story about the Jewish victory over the Egyptians in the "sea battle" of the Sea of Reeds (with the same stock elements).[91] Obviously, Ezekiel did not shun engagement with the conventions of pagan tragedy. At the same time, he is deeply rooted in Jewish tradition.[92]

Greek tragedy from the Hellenistic period is poorly preserved and it is very difficult indeed to place Ezekiel's *Exagoge* within its history.[93] In spite of its peculiarities, it would be ill advised to place it too quickly outside the Greek theater tradition. The *Exagoge* is not just an "alternative entertainment to pagan Greek drama" for "the education of a Jewish audience."[94] Nor should one deny the role of Ezekiel as a poet.[95] Rather, the *Exagoge* is a Jewish play which closely follows some of the main features of Greek tragedy. It is a Jewish-Hellenistic drama.

6   Conclusion

In Greco-Roman antiquity, Jews had an ambivalent and complex relationship with theater and spectacles. Simple conclusions will not do. Some Jews certainly stayed away from the theater for religious and moral reasons: the institution of the theater was associated with idolatry, immorality, and a depar-

---

91   Jacobson, *The* Exagoge *of Ezekiel*, 95–96.
92   In the preserved excerpts, there is only one reference to Greek myth, typically in the speech given by the Egyptian messenger: in v. 217 the sun is described as "Titan Helios".
93   Cf. Agnieszka Kotlińska-Toma, *Hellenistic Tragedy: Texts, Translations and a Critical Survey* (London: Bloomsbury, 2015), with comments on Ezekiel.
94   Schürer, *The History of the Jewish People*, 565.
95   As does Meyer Araham Halévy, *Moïse dans l'histoire et dans la légende* (Paris: Rieder, 1927), 67–68: "ce drame de la Sortie d' Egypte n' etait probablement pas destiné à être joué. Et il n' a jamais pu l' être. Ezechiel le Tragique fut, comme Aristobule et comme Artapan, un apologiste du judaïsme. Ce n' est pas a un poète véritable que l' on a affaire ici, mais plutôt un commentateur du *Pentateuque*, un avocat de la cause juive."

PART OF THE SCENE: JEWISH THEATER IN ANTIQUITY   195

ture from truth in favor of illusion and hypocrisy. Moreover, the theater was at times a place where people mocked Jews or, worse, where Jews were tortured and killed. At the same time, the literary evidence from both rabbinic and Jewish-Hellenistic sources suggests that many Jews did not avoid the spectacles. Some rabbis argued in favor of the theater under certain conditions and Philo and Josephus, who otherwise declare the spectacles vane or even contrary to Judaism, knew the theater scene well. Epigraphic evidence from Asia Minor shows that some Jews had their own theater seats. Jews, perhaps the majority, did not stay clear of the theater. Since theaters were also important sites of communication and exchange, it would have been difficult to avoid them altogether. Jews certainly did not simply stay home to do book-keeping like Joseph in Potiphar's house (to take up the idealizing midrash of *Genesis Rabbah*). Judaism and theater were not necessarily incompatible: Jews watched dramas, acted on stage, and even wrote for the theater. The English word "scene" (as in theater scene) derives from the Greek word σκηνή which means tent, but also stage or stage wall.[96] In Jewish-Hellenistic literature, σκηνή often has a different meaning: the word is regularly used for the tabernacle, the portable sanctuary that the Israelites carried with them during the exodus.[97] But Jews also looked at the other σκηνή, the stage.

The origins of (western) theater lie in sixth and fifth century Greece. While some dramatic elements can also be found in the Hebrew Bible,[98] as a cultural (and cultic) institution the theater in antiquity is genuinely linked to Greece. The Jews, however, did not look the other way when theater came to be part and parcel of Greek, and later Roman, culture.[99] For Jews, too, the theater became part of their own cultural repertoire. Here (as in other examples[100]) it is manifest that Jews in Hellenistic-Roman times did not see themselves confronted

---

96   LSJ s.v.

97   Cf., e.g., LXX *passim*; Philo, *Mos.* 2.74–94; Josephus, *AJ* 3.180–181; cf. also Heb 9:2 and John 7:2 (σκηνοπηγία = Feast of Tabernacles).

98   Especially the Song of Songs and Job have repeatedly inspired readers to understand parts of the Hebrew Bible as drama texts; see for example Shimon Levy, *The Bible as Theater* (Brighton: Sussex Academic, 2000).

99   Levy's statement (*The Bible as Theater* [n. 98], 3) "While the Greeks celebrated their three-day drama festivals in the fifth century BCE, the Jews, back from their Babylonian Exile, were busy rebuilding the ruins of the Temple in Jerusalem under the leadership of Ezra and Nehemiah," is *prima facie* correct; nevertheless, it wrongly suggests the notion of two mutually exclusive alternatives.

100   Cf. the seminal studies by Erich S. Gruen, *Diaspora*, specifically, and, going beyond antiquity, the contributions in David Biale, ed., *Cultures of the Jews: A New History* (New York: Schocken, 2002).

by a choice between isolation and assimilation. They did not have to choose between the synagogue and the theater.

Bibliography

Alt, Heinrich, *Theater und Kirche in ihrem gegenseitigen Verhältniß historisch dargestellt.* Berlin: Blahnschen, 1846.

Ameling, Walter, *Inscriptiones Judaicae Orientis.* Vol. 2. Tübingen: Mohr Siebeck, 2004.

Avi-Jonah, Michael, *The Jews under Roman and Byzantine Rule: A Political History of Palestine from the Bar Kokhba War to the Arab Conquest.* Jerusalem: Schocken, 1984.

Baker, Murray, "Who Was Sitting in the Theater at Miletos?" *Journal for the Study of Judaism* 36 (2005): 397–416.

Barclay, John M.G., *Jews in the Mediterranean Diaspora: From Alexander to Trajan (323 BCE–117 CE).* Edinburgh, T&T Clark 1996.

Barnes, Timothy D., "Christians and the Theater." Pages 161–180 in *Roman Theater and Society: E. Togo Salmon Papers I.* Edited by William J. Slater. Ann Arbor: University of Michigan Press, 1996.

Belkin, Ahuva and Gad Kaynar, "Jewish Theatre." Pages 870–910 in *The Oxford Handbook of Jewish Studies.* Edited by Martin Goodman. Oxford: Oxford University Press, 2002.

Bergjan, Silke-Petra, "'Das hier ist kein Theater, und ihr sitzt nicht da, um Schauspieler zu betrachten und zu klatschen'—Theaterpolemik und Theatermetaphern bei Johannes Chrysostomos." *ZAC* 8 (2005): 567–592.

Biale, David, ed., *Cultures of the Jews: A New History.* New York: Schocken, 2002.

Bloch, René, "Moses and Greek Myth in Hellenistic Judaism." Pages 195–208 in *La construction de la figure de Moïse/The Construction of the Figure of Moses.* Edited by Thomas Römer. Paris: Gabalda, 2007.

Bloch, René, *Moses und der Mythos. Die Auseinandersetzung mit der griechischen Mythologie bei jüdisch-hellenistischen Autoren.* Leiden: Brill, 2011.

Bremer, Natascha, *Das Bild der Juden in den Passionsspielen und in der bildenden Kunst des deutschen Mittelalters.* Frankfurt: Peter Lang, 1986.

Calabi, Francesca, "Theatrical Language in Philo's *In Flaccum.*" Pages 91–116 in *Italian Studies on Philo of Alexandria.* Edited by Francesca Calabi. Leiden: Brill, 2003.

Chapman, Honora Howell, "'By the Waters of Babylon': Josephus and Greek Poetry." Pages 121–124 in *Josephus and Jewish History in Flavian Rome and Beyond.* Edited by Joseph Sievers and Gaia Lembi. Leiden: Brill, 2005.

Cohen, Shaye J.D., *The Beginnings of Jewishness: Boundaries, Varieties, Uncertainties.* Berkeley: University of California Press, 1999.

Feldman, Louis H., *Jew & Gentile in the Ancient World.* Princeton: Princeton University Press, 1993.

PART OF THE SCENE: JEWISH THEATER IN ANTIQUITY

Feldman, Louis H., "The Influence of the Greek Tragedians on Josephus." Pages 51–80 in *Hellenic and Jewish Arts: Interaction, Tradition and Renewal*. Edited by Asher Ovadiah. Tel Aviv: Un-Ramot, 1998.

Fine, Steven, *Art & Judaism in the Greco-Roman World: Toward a New Jewish Archaeology*. Cambridge: Cambridge University Press, 2005.

Free, Katherine B., "Thespis and Moses: The Jews and the Ancient Greek Theater." Pages 149–158 in *Theater and Holy Script*. Edited by Shimon Levy. Brighton: Sussex Academic, 1999.

Fugmann, Joachim, *Römisches Theater in der Provinz: eine Einführung in das Theaterwesen im Imperium Romanum*. Stuttgart: Rombach, 1988.

Graf, Fritz, "What is Ancient Mediterranean Religion?" Pages 3–16 in *Religions of the Ancient World: A Guide*. Edited by Sarah Iles Johnston. Cambridge: Harvard University Press, 2004.

Gruen, Erich S., *Diaspora: Jews amidst Greek and Romans*. Cambridge: Harvard University Press, 2002.

Halévy, Meyer Araham, *Moïse dans l'histoire et dans la légende*. Paris: Rieder, 1927.

van der Horst, Pieter W., *Philo's Flaccus. The First Pogrom*. Leiden: Brill, 2003.

van der Horst, Pieter W., "Jews and Blues in Late Antiquity." Pages 565–571 in *Des Géants à Dionysos. Mélanges offerts à F. Vian*. Edited by Domenico Accorinti and Pierre Chuvin. Alessandria: Edizioni dell'Orso, 2003.

Jacobs, Martin, "Theaters and Performances as Reflected in the Talmud Yerushalmi." Pages 327–347 in *The Talmud Yerushalmi and Graeco-Roman Culture I*. Edited by Peter Schäfer. Tübingen: Mohr Siebeck, 1998.

Jacobson, Howard, *The* Exagoge *of Ezekiel*. Cambridge: Cambridge University Press, 1983.

Jastrow, Marcus, *A Dictionary of the Targumim, the Talmud Babli and Yerushalmi, and the Midrashic Literature*. New York: Judaic Press, 1971.

Jay, Jeff, "The Problem of the Theater in Early Judaism." *Journal for the Study of Judaism* 44 (2013): 218–253.

Jürgens, Heiko, *Pompa Diaboli. Die lateinischen Kirchenväter und das antike Theater*. Stuttgart: Kohlhammer, 1972.

Keddie, G. Anthony and Jonathan MacLellan, "Ezekiel's *Exagoge* and the Politics of Hellenistic Theater: Mosaic Hegemony on a Ptolemaic Model." *Journal of Ancient Judaism* 8 (2017): 170–187.

Kennedy, Dennis, ed., *Oxford Encyclopedia of Theater and Performance*. Oxford: Oxford University Press, 2003.

Klein, Richard, "*Spectaculorum voluptates adimere* … Zum Kampf der Kirchenväter gegen Circus und Theater." Pages 155–173 in *Theater, Theaterpraxis, Theaterkritik im kaiserzeitlichen Rom*. Edited by Joachim Fugmann et al. Munich: K.G. Saur, 2004.

Kohansky, Mendel, *The Hebrew Theatre: Its First Fifty Years*. Jerusalem: Ktav, 1969.

Kohler, Kaufmann, "Jastrow's Talmudic Dictionary." *Hebraica* 5 (1888): 1–6.

Konikoff, Adia, *Sarcophagi from the Jewish Catacombs of Ancient Rome*. Stuttgart: Franz Steiner, 1990.

Kotlińska-Toma, Agnieszka, *Hellenistic Tragedy: Texts, Translations and a Critical Survey*. London: Bloomsbury, 2015.

Krauss, Samuel, *Griechische und lateinische Lehnwörter im Talmud, Midrasch und Targum. Teil 1*. Berlin: Calvary, 1898; repr., Hildesheim: Georg Olms, 1987.

Lachs, Samuel T., "An Egyptian Festival in Canticles Rabbah." *JQR* 51 (1960): 47–54.

Lanfranchi, Pierluigi, *L'Exagoge d'Ezéchiel le Tragique. Introduction, texte, traduction et commentaire*. Leiden: Brill, 2006.

Latacz, Joachim, *Einführung in die griechische Tragödie*. Göttingen: Vandenhoeck & Ruprecht, 1993.

Leppin, Hartmut, *Histrionen. Untersuchungen zur sozialen Stellung von Bühnenkünstlern im Westen des Römischen Reiches zur Zeit der Republik und des Principats*. Bonn: Rudolf Habelt, 1992.

Lev-Ari, Shimon, "The Origins of Theater in Hellenic and Judaic Cultures." Pages 385–392 in *Hellenic and Jewish Arts: The Howard Gilman International Conferences I*. Edited by Asher Ovadiah. Tel Aviv: Un-Ramot, 1998.

Levinson, Joshua, "An-Other Woman: Joseph and Potiphar's Wife. Staging the Body Politic." *JQR* 87 (1997): 269–301.

Levy, Shimon, *The Bible as Theater*. Brighton: Sussex Academic, 2000.

Lincicum, David, "An Index to Philo's Non-Biblical Citations and Allusions." *SPhiloA* 25 (2013): 139–168.

Mandel, Arnold, "Les théâtres juifs." Pages 1058–1078 in *Histoire des spectacles*, Edited by Guy Dumur. (Paris: Gallimard, 1965.

Niehoff, Maren, *The Figure of Joseph in Post-Biblical Jewish Literature*. Leiden: Brill, 1992.

Noy, David, *Jewish Inscriptions of Western Europe, Volume 1: Italy (excluding the City of Rome), Spain and Gaul*. Cambridge: Cambridge University Press, 1993.

Patrich, Joseph, "Herod's Theater in Jerusalem—a new proposal." *IEJ* 52 (2002): 231–239.

Porath, Yosef, "Why did Josephus Name the Chariot-Racing Facility at Caesarea 'Amphitheater'?" *Scripta Classica Israelica* 23 (2004): 63–67.

Price, Jonathan J. and Lisa Ullmann, "Drama and History in Josephus' *Bellum Judaicum*." *Scripta Classica Israelica* 21 (2002): 97–111.

Reich, Ronny and Yaakov Billig, "A Group of Theater Seats Discovered near the South-Western Corner of the Temple Mount." *IEJ* 50 (2000): 175–184.

Reynolds, Joyce and Robert Tannenbaum, *Jews and Godfearers at Aphrodisias*. Cambridge: Cambridge University Press, 1987.

Rozenberg, Silvia and David Mevorah, eds., *Herod the Great: The King's Final Journey*. Jerusalem: The Israel Museum, 2013.

Sallmann, Klaus, "Christen vor dem Theater." Pages 243–259 in *Theater und Gesellschaft im Imperium Romanum*. Edited by Jürgen Blänsdorf. Tübingen: Francke Verlag, 1990.

Schlapbach, Karin and Markus Vinzent, eds., *New Perspectives on Late Antique spectacula*. Leuven: Peeters, 2013.

Schoeps, Julius H., ed., *Neues Lexikon des Judentums*. Munich: Bertelsmann-Lexikon-Verlag, 1992.

Schürer, Emil, *The History of the Jewish People in the Age of Jesus Christ (175 B.C.–A.D. 135)*. Vol. 3.1. Edited by Geza Vermes, Fergus Millar, and Martin Goodman. Edinburgh: T&T Clark, 1986.

Segal, Arthur, *Theaters in Roman Palestine and Provincia Arabia*. Leiden: Brill, 1995.

Shavit, Yaacov, "Have Jews Imagination? Jews and the Creative Arts." Pages 220–277 in *Athens in Jerusalem: Classical Antiquity and Hellenism in the Making of the Modern Secular Jew*. London: Littman, 1997.

Sly, Dorothy, *Philo's Alexandria*. London: Routledge, 1996.

Sowden, Lewis, 'Theatre.' Pages 1049–1052 in *Encyclopedia Judaica*. Vol. 15. First ed. Jerusalem: Keter, 1972.

Stambaugh, John E., *The Ancient Roman City*. Baltimore: Johns Hopkins University Press, 1988.

Stemberger, Günter, *Einleitung in Talmud und Midrasch*. Munich: C.H. Beck, 2011.

Vetter, Dieter, "Juden und Schauspiel in Antike und Moderne." Pages 149–189 in *Das antike Theater: Aspekte seiner Geschichte, Rezeption und Aktualität*. Edited by Gerhard Binder and Bernd Effe. Trier: WVT, 1998.

Webb, Ruth, "Female entertainers in late antiquity." Pages 282–303 in *Greek and Roman Actors: Aspects of an Ancient Profession*. Edited by Patricia Easterling and Edith Hall. Cambridge: Cambridge University Press, 2002.

Weiss, Zeev, *Public Spectacles in Roman and Late Antique Palestine*. Cambridge: Harvard University Press, 2014.

Wewers, Gerd A., *Avoda Zara—Götzendienst*. Tübingen: Mohr Siebeck, 1980.

Williams, Margaret, *The Jews among the Greeks and Romans: A Diasporan Sourcebook*. Baltimore: Johns Hopkins University Press, 1998.

Zimmermann, Bernhard, "Theater." Pages 398–402 in *Der Neue Pauly: Enzyklopädie der Antike*. Vol. 15.3. Stuttgart: Metzler, 2003.

CHAPTER 10

Take Your Time: Conversion, Confidence and Tranquility in *Joseph and Aseneth*

Joseph and Aseneth belongs to the most controversial texts in Jewish-Hellenistic literature. Date, provenance, genre, and intention of this fascinating story are all intensely disputed.[1] The most pressing questions remain unsolved. What did our author, who to us remains anonymous, intend with this text? It has often been suggested that the author is proselytizing and seeks to call for conversion to Judaism; in this vein, *JosAs* has been called a "missionary novel." Or does the text plead at least for the *acceptance* of converts?[2] Does the text try to correct

---

1 Cf. recently B. Diane Lipsett, *Desiring Conversion: Hermas, Thecla, Aseneth* (Oxford: Oxford University Press, 2011); Christian Wetz, *Eros und Bekehrung: Anthropologische und religionsgeschichtliche Untersuchungen zu „Joseph und Aseneth"* (Göttingen: Vandenhoeck & Ruprecht, 2010), with history of scholarship (21–42); Eckart Reinmuth, ed., *Joseph und Aseneth* (Tübingen: Mohr Siebeck, 2009); Jürgen K. Zangenberg, "Josef und Asenet: Zur Pragmatik und Modellhaftigkeit der Konversion Asenets," in *Der eine Gott und die fremden Kulte: Exklusive und inklusive Tendenzen in den biblischen Gottesvorstellungen*, ed. Eberhard Bons (Neukirchen-Vluyn: Neukirchener, 2009), 95–120; the issue of *Journal for the Study of Judaism* 15 (2005); Lawrence M. Wills, *The Jewish Novel in the Ancient World* (Ithaca: Cornell University, 1995), 170–184; Nina V. Braginskaya, "'Joseph and Aseneth': A 'Midrash' before midrash and a 'Novel' before novel," *Vestnik drevnej istorii* 254 (2005): 73–96 (russ.) (*non vidi*; Nina Braginskaya kindly provided me a copy of her paper "Position of 'Joseph and Aseneth' in Greek literary history: the case of the 'first novel'," in *The Ancient Novel and Early Christian and Jewish Narrative: Fictional Intersections*, ed. Marília P. Futre Pinheiro, Judith Perkins, Richard Pervo (Groningen: Barkhuis 2016), 79–105); Sabrina Inowlocki, *Des idoles mortes et muettes au dieu vivant: Joseph, Aséneth et le fils de Pharaon dans un roman du judaïsme hellénisé* (Turnhout: Brepols, 2002); Edith M. Humphrey, *Joseph and Aseneth* (Sheffield: Sheffield Academic, 2000). In the following, the Greek text will be cited from Christoph Burchard, ed., *Joseph und Aseneth* (Leiden: Brill, 2003); a revised edition is offered by Uta Barbara Fink, *Joseph und Aseneth: Revision des griechischen Textes und Edition der zweiten lateinischen Übersetzung* (Berlin: De Gruyter, 2008). English translations of *Joseph and Aseneth* are adapted from Christoph Burchard, trans., "Joseph and Aseneth," in *The Old Testament Pseudepigrapha*. Vol. 2, ed. James H. Charlesworth (New York: Doubleday, 1985), 177–247. Translations of ancient Greek novels follow with adjustments Bryan P. Reardon, ed., *Collected Ancient Greek Novels* (Berkeley: University of California Press, 1989). Biblical citations follow NRSV.

2 Cf. the brief overview of scholarship by Manuel Vogel, "Einführung in die Schrift," in Reinmuth, *Joseph und Aseneth*, 3–31, 26–27. According to Vogel, *Joseph und Aseneth* is concerned with the legitimization of mixed marriages.

© RENÉ BLOCH, 2022 | DOI:10.1163/9789004521896_012

TAKE YOUR TIME   201

the biblical story according to which Joseph married the daughter of an Egyptian priest?[3] And linked to these questions is another: What audience did the author have in mind? A Jewish or a non-Jewish readership?[4]

Most scholars agree, as I do, that *JosAs* was written in Alexandria, or at least in Egypt—but when? And, of course, there is the question of genre: Can *JosAs* be understood as a novel? It is undisputed that it has quite a few parallels with what we usually encounter in Greco-Roman romance novels.[5] But how are these parallels to be explained?

JosAs takes up a biblical passage, or rather, an issue that the biblical text does not know as such: according to the account in the Book of Genesis, Joseph, after a difficult start in Egypt (to say the least), ends up having a remarkable career in Pharaoh's court to the point that he becomes the second man in the country and receives, at the age of thirty, an Egyptian name and an Egyptian wife from the Pharaoh: "Then Pharaoh named Joseph Zaphenath-paneah; and he gave him Asenath daughter of Potiphera, priest of On, as his wife" (Gen 41:45).

A little later in Genesis one learns that two sons were born from the union between Joseph and Aseneth (Gen 41:50, 46:20). This is all that Genesis tells us. The biblical text does not comment on the marriage between Joseph and the daughter of an Egyptian priest. It is this brief biblical passage, however, which motivates the author of *JosAs* to create quite a long text—29 chapters in Christoph Burchard's standard 2003 edition—in which Aseneth's conversion to Judaism figures prominently. A summary of the story may be useful here.

The tale of *Joseph and Aseneth* plays out as follows: there is an exceptionally beautiful 18-year-old woman named Aseneth in Heliopolis, Egypt. She is a virgin, rich, and desired by all men, not least by none other than Pharaoh's son, who will jeopardize Joseph and Aseneth's love in the second part of the tale. The story takes place during the seven years of abundance in Egypt that are reported by the biblical narrative and in which Joseph ensures that grain is collected for the seven years of famine that will follow. It is in this context, in order to collect grain, that Joseph comes to Heliopolis. Aseneth's father, Pen-

---

3   Cf. Carsten Burfeind, "Aseneth," in *Encyclopedia of the Bible and its Reception. Volume 2: Anim—Atheism*, ed. Christine Helmer et al. (Berlin: De Gruyter, 2009), 962–967, at 963: "Manifesting reservations about the marriage of Joseph to the gentile Asenath, the Hellenistic-Jewish story of Jos.Asen. shows how the idolatrous Egyptian converted to Judaism before she married Joseph."

4   Cf. the discussion of this question in Zangenberg, "Josef," 118–120.

5   Thus already Marc Philonenko, *Joseph et Aséneth: Introduction, texte critique, traduction et notes* (Leiden: Brill, 1968), 43–48.

tephres (that is the biblical Potiphar), a priest of the city, takes this opportunity to invite Joseph to his home—with the intention of marrying his daughter off to Joseph.

At the time of Joseph's arrival, Aseneth's parents are just coming home from their fields. Aseneth sees, not Joseph at first, but the "good things" which her parents bring home from the fields: grapes, dates, figs and pomegranates— "all ripe (ὡραῖα) and of good taste" (4.2). Thus in bucolic and sexually loaded language—typical of the ancient romance novel—the union of Joseph and Aseneth is prepared, just as the text continuously anticipates what happens later in the story and, in spite of the fairly simple language, impresses the reader with its sophisticated structure. The Greek word for "ripe," here in the context of fruits, is regularly used in connection with marital maturity.[6] Right at the beginning of our text, Aseneth is described as a "virgin of eighteen years of age, tall, blossoming and very beautiful" (1.4: μεγάλη καὶ ὡραία καὶ καλή). Aseneth's maturity is reflected in nature, as stated later in the text (8.5): "Her breasts were already standing upright like ripe apples."[7] The adjective ὡραῖος is used no less than six times in this story, which to some extent is a tale about Aseneth's (and also Joseph's) maturity.[8]

However, the union of Joseph and Aseneth is—as in many Greco-Roman romance novels—only possible much later in the story. Apart from Aseneth's Egyptian origin, there is an additional, fundamental issue standing in the way of Joseph and Aseneth's love: neither Aseneth nor Joseph are interested in the opposite sex:

> Καὶ ἦν Ἀσενὲθ ἐξουθενοῦσα καὶ καταπτύουσα πάντα ἄνδρα καὶ ἦν ἀλαζὼν καὶ ὑπερήφανος πρὸς πάντα ἄνθρωπον.

> And Aseneth was despising and scorning every man, and she was boastful and arrogant with everyone.
>
> *JosAs* 2.1

Aseneth lives on the top floor of a tall, inaccessible tower, surrounded by a high wall and secured by iron cast gates and eighteen "strong young men" (2.11). She sleeps in a golden bed on which "no man or any other woman ever sat" (2.9) and which looked (already, one could say) east (2.8). Later she will be able

---

6 So also Inowlocki, *Des idoles*, 64; cf. LSJ s.v. ὡραῖος III.

7 The edition by Fink, *Joseph* deletes the comparison "like ripe apples," which is not consistent among the mss.

8 *JosAs* 1.4, 5; 2.11; 4.2; 8.5; 22.7.

TAKE YOUR TIME 203

to pray from there towards Jerusalem. At this point, however, there are still Egyptian gods hanging from the walls, to which Aseneth makes daily sacrifices (2.3).

Then Aseneth hears of her father offer her in marriage to Joseph, and she is beside herself (4.9): she begins to sweat and her face turns red. Aseneth is not just angry, or even furious, as most translations suggest, but is greatly impassioned: ἐθυμώθη ἐν ὀργῇ μεγάλῃ (4.9). Aseneth looks πλαγίως at her father, the text continues: probably not just "from the side, askance," which is the basic meaning of the word, but "involving arrière-pensée, ambiguously," which πλαγίως can also mean.[9] Later, when Aseneth has fallen deeply in love with Joseph, she reacts very similarly. There again she sweats from excitement and passion: there "was continuous sweat" (ἱδρὼς συνεχής) on her (9.1).

When Aseneth catches sight of a radiantly beautiful Joseph—she clearly wants to see him despite her apparent anger, and thus watches him from the window (5.2)—she regrets her arrogance deeply and is gripped by fierce desire. However, Joseph is equally chaste, just as Aseneth had wished to be shortly before. Joseph sees Aseneth standing at her window (the window scene is one of many in this work which one can imagine being performed on a stage[10]) and is worried that she, like so many women before her, would also sexually harass him (7.2: μήποτε καὶ αὔτη ἐνοχλήσῃ με). He is relieved when he learns from Aseneth's father that she is μισοῦσα πάντα ἄνδρα, "hating all men" (7.8). Meanwhile, however, this ceases to be the case; she runs toward Joseph in order to kiss him. Joseph tries to stop her by stretching out "his right hand and put[ting] it on her chest between her two breasts" (8.5).

In the following chapters, Aseneth leaves her Egyptian religion behind her in a most dramatic way: she locks herself in her room and nearly castigates herself to death. Aseneth throws her valuables and her idols out of the window and remains seven days in sackcloth and ashes. In a long confession of sins, Aseneth asks the Jewish god for acceptance. Now Aseneth is suddenly able to pray the Jewish ritual prayer (12.1): "Lord, God of eternity, who created all things and gave the breath of life to all your creation" etc. And her prayer is instantly heard: a man (14.3, ἄνθρωπος) descends from heaven, introducing himself as the prince of angels, and asks Aseneth to dress herself again. Aseneth learns that God has accepted her. The anthropomorphic angel tells her that her name is now "City of Refuge" (πόλις καταφυγῆς) and that she shall soon marry Joseph. "City of Refuge" is a meaningful name: the angel

---

9   LSJ, s.v. πλάγιος II; cf. Plutarch, *Sayings of Romans* 2.205 (Κικέρωνα πλαγίως τι εἰπόντα).

10   In 1817 (Breslau), Süsskind Raschkow composed, in rhyme and five acts, a drama in Hebrew "Joseph und Asenath" (יוסף ואסנת‎).

204   CHAPTER 10

announces that Aseneth will not be the only one to convert to Judaism but that "many peoples" will "take refuge" in the Jewish god (καταφεύξονται ἔθνη πολλά; 15.17).

Then follows a magical interlude. Aseneth invites her heavenly guest for dinner. When he asks her for a honeycomb, which Aseneth thinks she does not have, such a honeycomb suddenly appears. Bees fly out of the honeycomb and build another one on Aseneth's mouth. As in the *bugonia* of pagan myth, according to which bees are generated from the carcass of a cow, the bees seem to symbolize a new beginning:[11] from the Egyptian corpse of Aseneth, the new Jewish "city of refuge" is born.

Now everything is set for a second attempt to get to know Joseph. Aseneth dresses like a bride and is transformed into a celestial beauty (she doesn't wash herself anymore, out of fear she may wash away her beauty: 18.10). Joseph and Aseneth embrace and kiss, but the text forgoes any voyeurism. Then, in 21.9 it is simply stated:

> Καὶ ἐγένετο μετὰ ταῦτα εἰσῆλθεν Ἰωσὴφ πρὸς Ἀσενὲθ καὶ συνέλαβεν Ἀσενὲθ ἐκ τοῦ Ἰωσὴφ καὶ ἔτεκε τὸν Μανασσῆ καὶ τὸν Ἐφραὶμ τὸν ἀδελφὸν αὐτοῦ ἐν τῷ οἴκῳ τοῦ Ἰωσήφ.

> And it happened after this, Joseph had intercourse with Aseneth and Aseneth conceived and bore Manasseh and Ephraim, his brother, in Joseph's house.[12]

The curtain could have come down at this point, but an extended drama full of jealousy and intrigue follows—as if the author, at some late hour, had realized the absence of an important motif of an ancient novel. Pharaoh's first-born, who had counted on having a chance with Aseneth, refuses to accept his bitter defeat. He tries to win over Joseph's brothers as co-conspirators. The plan nearly works, but Aseneth is able to escape. The Egyptian pursuers are held back by Joseph's youngest brother, Benjamin. The Pharaoh's son is seriously injured by Benjamin, and nearly killed. But Levi, the most confident and prudent of Joseph's brothers, stops Benjamin from striking the final deadly blow: for it is not fitting "to repay evil with evil"—an ethical ideal that Aseneth also

---

11   The *bugonia* is well known from Virgil (*Georg.* 4.287–314), but has Alexandrian-Hellenistic predecessors: cf. Manfred Erren, *P. Vergilius Maro: Georgica. Bd. 2, Kommentar* (Heidelberg: C. Winter, 2002), 897 and Wetz, *Eros*, 177–179.

12   *JosAs* 21.9. Cf. Gen 41:50 (likewise Gen 46:20): "Before the years of famine came, Joseph had two sons, whom Asenath daughter of Potiphera, priest of On, bore to him."

TAKE YOUR TIME

advocates.[13] Pharaoh's son, badly injured, ultimately dies of his wounds and out of sorrow his father follows him into death. Thus, Joseph becomes king over Egypt for forty-eight years. The throne then reverts back to the pharaonic family, to the Pharaoh's younger son, to whom Joseph had always been like a father.

This is the story. *Joseph and Aseneth* obviously has much more to say about the relationship between Joseph and the Egyptian priest's daughter than the book of Genesis. And the little that Genesis does tell us about our two protagonists is inverted. While according to the Bible (Gen 41:45) Joseph marries an Egyptian woman and is given a new Egyptian name, here he marries a Jewish woman and it is she who changes her name.

Joseph and Aseneth is no midrash: our text seeks neither to interpret the biblical episode nor to fill in its gaps. Already in the summary, an element is evident which is too often ignored in scholarship: this text obviously seeks to entertain. The story of Joseph and Aseneth, for all its linguistic limitation, is exciting and entertaining. This is ultimately a piece of popular fiction. The author, unknown to us, identified in the biblical motif of the irregular couple Joseph and Aseneth the literary potential for a romance novel.

1   Joseph and Aseneth as a Novel

It is not an easy matter to assign *Joseph and Aseneth* a particular literary genre. The most suitable, however, is certainly that of the ancient novel. Until now, we have proceeded from this assumption, but this must now be more precisely justified. Whether *Joseph and Aseneth* should be understood as a novel is a matter of some dispute.[14] As is well known, defining ancient novels is a difficult task. 'Novel' is not an ancient term for a genre; among classicists, the genre 'novel' is generally restricted to a few texts, which approximately correspond with the following definition from Niklas Holzberg:

> [B]y 'ancient novel' we mean an entirely fictitious story narrated in prose and ruled in its course by erotic motifs and a series of adventures which mostly take place during a journey and which can be differentiated into a number of specific, fixed patterns. The protagonists or protagonist live(s)

---

13   *JosAs* 23.9: καὶ οὐ προσήκει ἡμῖν ἀποδοῦναι κακὸν ἀντὶ κακοῦ; in Aseneth's words: 28.5, 7, 10, 14. Christian evidence for this maxim is found, in the same words, in Rom 12:17 (μηδενὶ κακὸν ἀντὶ κακοῦ ἀποδιδόντες). Cf. Karl-Wilhelm Niebuhr, "Ethik und Tora. Zum Toraverständnis in Joseph und Aseneth," in Reinmuth, *Joseph und Aseneth*, 187–202, at 195.

14   Christoph Burchard, *Gesammelte Studien zu Joseph und Aseneth* (Leiden: Brill, 1996), xxiii.

in a realistically portrayed world which, even when set by the author in an age long since past, essentially reflects everyday life around the Mediterranean in late Hellenistic and Imperial societies; the actual characters, however, are given idealistic or comic-realistic features.[15]

In Classics, *Joseph and Aseneth* is generally not counted among the ancient novels; at best, it is included in the not very honorable group of "fringe novels."[16] There is no doubt that the five preserved so-called ideal romances—Chariton's *Callirhoe*; Xenophon's *Ephesiaca*; Achilles Tatius's *Leucippe and Clitophon*; Longos's *Daphnis and Chloe* and Heliodorus's *Aethiopica*—have much in common. Although these five novels were written over a long period of time, they almost come across (to us at least) like a five-volume edition of the Greek novel. And there is no doubt that *Joseph and Aseneth* differs in some respects from the "big five" (as Stephan Tilg has called them):[17] once more, the Greek of *Joseph and Aseneth*, in vocabulary and syntax, is more simple, and—as has often been pointed out—is without question a text in which *religion* is of fundamental significance. However, in that respect *Joseph and Aseneth* is less unusual than has been said. The ancient novel, perhaps more than any other literary genre of antiquity, is characterized by the abundance of pagan religious elements: as Froma Zeitlin has written in her contribution to the *Cambridge Companion to the Greek and Roman Novel*, the ancient novel is a world of temples, shrines and altars, of priests, rituals, sacrifices, dreams, oracles, prophecies, epiphanies, aretalogies, and mystical language.[18] In Heliodorus's *Aethiopica*, the protagonists Theagenes and Chariclea are ordained as priests in the end (even Thyamis, the leader of the thieves in Heliodorus's *Aethiopica*, is a priest: 1.19.3),[19] and the novels of Chariton and Xenophon both begin and end in a sanctuary.[20] *Joseph and Aseneth* is thus only somewhat unusual with regard to its religious accoutrements.[21] Even the description of Joseph and Aseneth as son and daughter

---

15   Niklas Holzberg, *The Ancient Novel: An Introduction* (London: Routledge, 1995), 26–27.

16   Cf. most recently Stefan Tilg, *Chariton of Aphrodisias and the Invention of the Greek Love Novel* (Oxford: Oxford University Press, 2010), 2–3; Froma Zeitlin, "Religion," in *The Cambridge Companion to the Greek and Roman Novel*, ed. Tim Whitmarsh (Cambridge: Cambridge University Press, 2008), 91–108, at 106–107. On fringe novels cf. Grammatiki Karla, ed., *Fiction on the Fringe: Novelistic Writing in the Post-Classical Age* (Leiden: Brill, 2009).

17   Tilg, *Chariton*, 2.

18   Zeitlin, "Religion," 91.

19   Zeitlin, "Religion," 104.

20   Stephen Harrison, "Parallel Cults? Religion and Narrative in Apuleius' *Metamorphoses* and Some Greek Novels," in *The Greek and the Roman Novel: Parallel Readings*, ed. Michael Paschalis et al. (Groningen: Barkhuis, 2007), 204–218, at 208.

21   The opinion that the ancient novel was originally to be read as religious propaganda or

TAKE YOUR TIME

of God is not really unusual for the ancient novel: in Greek novels protagonists are compared with heroes of Greek myths or even gods or their statues.[22]

If we take common definitions of the ancient novel like the one by Niklas Holzberg as a benchmark, quite a few similarities between *Joseph and Aseneth* and the 'established' Greek novels come to mind: the noble descent of the eventual lovers, their virginity and beauty, the courting of the young lady by a rival as well as the 'coup de foudre,' the lovesickness, the kiss, the intrigues, the separation, the suffering, and the final reunion are inherent parts of the ancient novel. Marc Philonenko, the publisher of the now outdated French edition of *Joseph and Aseneth*, was probably the first to point out such parallels, if only briefly.[23] However, all things considered, Philonenko indicates that *Joseph and Aseneth* is *not* a typical example of an ancient novel, because he understands the protagonists' long period of chastity to be essentially different from the conventional Greek novel: "Après tant de romans libertins, c'est un roman *puritain* qui est proposé au lecteur."[24] The prudishness of the characters is also pointed to in recent research as an argument against including the work among ancient romances. In his groundbreaking survey, *The Jews in the Mediterranean Diaspora*, John Barclay points out some of the novelistic aspects in *Joseph and Aseneth*, but nevertheless speaks of a "failure of the narrative as romance" and refers to the "somewhat prudish depiction of the heroes."[25]

Already our summary showed that *Joseph and Aseneth* is not at all free of erotic moments. Moreover, one should point out that frivolous scenes in no way characterize the so-called "idealistic" ancient novel. On the contrary: the continuously threatened but constantly upheld chastity is a relevant *leitmotiv* in early novels. In Xenophon's *Ephesiaca*, the chastity of Habrocomes and Anthia is constantly threatened by others, but does not fall until the very end of the novel. In Heliodorus's *Aethiopica*, Charicleia is loyal to her beloved Theagenes for more than ten books, and even then this relationship remains very cautious

---

a mystery text is no longer represented in scholarship. Reinhold Merkelbach, *Roman und Mysterium in der Antike: Eine Untersuchung zur Religion* (Munich: C.H. Beck, 1962) understood the ancient novels as coded mystery texts, comprehensible only to the initiated of the respective cult. Merkelbach did not address *Joseph and Aseneth*, which in any case is intended to be neither a mystery nor religious propaganda.

22 Anton Bierl, "Der griechische Roman—ein Mythos?," in *Antike Mythen. Medien, Transformationen und Kontsruktionen*, ed. Christine Walde and Ueli Dill (Berlin: de Gruyter, 2009), 709–739, at 710–711.

23 Philonenko, *Joseph*, 43.

24 Philonenko, *Joseph*, 44.

25 John M.G. Barclay, *Jews in the Mediterranean Diaspora: From Alexander to Trajan (323 BCE–117 CE)* (Berkeley: University of California Press, 1996), 205.

208   CHAPTER 10

and timid. In Longus's novel *Daphnis and Chloe*, Daphnis is able to refuse Eros until almost the end of the story. In book 4, shortly before the end of the novel, he is still waiting for the right opportunity: "But he did not concede yet to Eros, but waited for the right opportunity" (4.26.4: οὔπω δὲ ὡμολόγει τὸν ἔρωτα, καιρὸν παραφυλάττων). It is not until the very end of the novel that Daphnis and Chloe kiss each other: "they embraced one another and kissed" (4.40.3: περιέβαλλον ἀλλήλους καὶ κατεφίλουν). And the mutual longing of Joseph and Aseneth ends in the same way: "they kissed each other for a long time ... and embraced each other for a long time" (*JosAs* 19.10: ἠσπάσαντο ἀλλήλους ἐπιπολύ ... καὶ περιεπλά-κησαν ἀλλήλοις ἐπιπολύ).

Joseph and Aseneth is no more puritanical than the idealistic ancient novel. In the latter, as in *Joseph and Aseneth*, love and desire—as well as strong erotic hints—run parallel to the protection of chastity. Frivolous scenes are particularly characteristic of the later *comic-realistic* novel (one thinks of Petronius's *Satyrica*), which seems to parody the idealistic novel.

In Classics scholarship, *Joseph and Aseneth* has wrongly been omitted from the canon of ancient novels. For all its differences, *Joseph and Aseneth* shares much of what is generally regarded as constituting an ancient novel. It was a classicist, Stephanie West, who in a short but incisive article "Joseph and Asenath: A Neglected Greek Romance," published in the *Classical Quarterly*, vehemently called for *Joseph and Aseneth* not to be ignored; she remained, though, within Classics at least, unheard. It is now long since time for the call to be renewed.[26]

As already mentioned, it has been argued that this text is about Aseneth's conversion, or that it is even a piece of early Jewish missionary literature. The fact that Aseneth converts to Judaism *freely* certainly is an argument against such an understanding. Aseneth's conversion is an important part of the text; the conversion, however, is above all the necessary step towards *overcoming* the obstacle standing in the way of her marriage to Joseph. Mastering difficulties that are in the way of marriage constitutes an essential motif of the ancient novel. In this case—in contrast to the regular pattern—there are no adventurous voyages that need to be overcome (although Joseph is in fact also travelling), but rather, particularly in the case of Aseneth, it is an inner voyage that needs to be pursued. And even this is not so unusual for the ancient novel:

---

26   Stephanie West, "Joseph and Asenath. A Neglected Greek Romance," *Classical Quarterly* 24 (1974): 70–81. Following this Catherine Hezser, "'Joseph and Aseneth' in the Context of Ancient Greek Erotic Novels," *Frankfurter Judaistische Beiträge* 24 (1997): 1–40 likewise located *Joseph and Aseneth* in the broader context of the Greek novel. Cf. also Wills, *The Jewish Novel in the Ancient World*.

TAKE YOUR TIME 209

Longus's *Daphnis and Chloe* is also more a journey in time than in space.[27] In fact, Aseneth shares certain similarities with Chloe, who nearly dies out of love for Daphnis.

Moreover, both Joseph and Aseneth are torn between different wishes: the sexual interest which Joseph and Aseneth show from the beginning—in different ways and without recognizing it explicitly—is in conflict with other claims, religious (in the case of Joseph) or social (in the case of Aseneth). Such "conflicted desires"[28] are indeed typical of the ancient novel.

An additional motif typical of the ancient novel concerns the initial *renunciation of love* by the protagonists. Both Joseph and Aseneth refuse the opposite sex. *Aseneth's* lack of interest in love receives particular emphasis near the story's beginning. This has been noted before (by Stephanie West). What is important, though, is that Aseneth denies both the Jewish god and love. The two denials go together. Therefore, Aseneth is to be punished for both: she falls fiercely in love and does penance by acknowledging the Jewish god. It is when God's angel (similar to Cupid in Apuleius's tale of *Cupid and Psyche*—except that the Jewish god's messenger does not fall in love himself) prepares Aseneth for her marriage, if not before, that we realize that this god guides the fated love between Joseph and Aseneth. The protagonists' initial denial of love is a familiar motif from the ancient novel: Habrocomes, the young man from Xenophon's *Ephesian Tale* who is interested in anything but love, is a *locus classicus* for this. He does not recognize Eros as a god (ἔρωτά γε μὴν οὐδὲ ἐνόμιζεν εἶναι θεόν), but banishes him and considers him to be nothing (ὡς οὐδὲν ἡγούμενος; compare ἐξουθενοῦσα in *JosAs* 2.1).[29] This is parallel to the characterization of Joseph as untouched and frightened of (at least non-Jewish) women (4.7; 7.4), but above all is seen in Aseneth: "And Aseneth regarded men as nothing and loathed each and every one" (2.1).

Charicleia in Heliodorus's *Aethiopica* is described similarly: "Virginity is her [Charicleia's] god, and she has elevated it to the level of the immortals, pronouncing it without stain, without impurity, without corruption. But Eros and Aphrodite and all nuptial revelry she curses to damnation."[30]

---

27 Bryan P. Reardon, "The Greek Novel," *Phoenix* 23 (1969): 291–309, at 301: "Daphnis and Chloë embark on a journey not in space, but in time."

28 Tim Whitmarsh, *Narrative and Identity in the Ancient Greek Novel: Returning Romance* (Cambridge: Cambridge University Press, 2011), 18–19.

29 Xenophon, *Ephesiaka* 1.1.5. West, "Joseph," 72.

30 Chariklea in Heliodorus, *Aeth.* 2:33: ἐπανατείνεται ἐκθειάζουσα μὲν παρθενίαν καὶ ἐγγὺς ἀθανάτων ἀποφαίνουσα, ἄχραντον καὶ ἀκήρατον καὶ ἀδιάφθορον ὀνομάζουσα, "Ἔρωτα δὲ καὶ Ἀφροδίτην καὶ πάντα γαμήλιον θίασον ἀποσκορακίζουσα." Cf. West, "Joseph," 72.

210   CHAPTER 10

In other words: Chariclea, too, first honored the wrong divinity, so to speak, namely virginity, before she recognized the true gods: Eros and Aphrodite. This form of hubris is well-known from the myth of Hippolytus, who worships only Artemis and is terribly punished by Aphrodite for his disdain (Euripides, *Hippolytus*). Such hubris is also a denial of god. And it is this combination of denial, of god and of love, which we find in Aseneth at the beginning of the novel. According to Niklas Holzberg, the plot of an ancient novel is often steered by the workings of one or several gods who out of anger over some misconduct of the protagonists cause their misadventures.[31] This is essentially the case in *Joseph and Aseneth*.

Again, *Joseph and Aseneth* is without question a text in which *religion* is of fundamental significance. But here too it is love which frames the story. Aseneth converts, but not out of love of Judaism, but because she is in love with Joseph: at the beginning of the story Aseneth despairs at the sight of Joseph when he arrives in Heliopolis, and towards the end of the first part of the novel she says how she feels: "I love him over my soul" (13.15: ἐγὼ ἀγαπῶ αὐτὸν ὑπὲρ τὴν ψυχήν μου).

Let me just briefly point out other novel-like characteristics in *Joseph and Aseneth*: when Aseneth stops eating and drinking out of grief and lovesickness and punishes herself nearly to death, this constitutes a well-known motif: deaths from fasting along with attempted suicide and apparent death belong firmly to the inventory of the ancient novel. Likewise, magical scenes comparable with that of the honeycomb are often found in the ancient novel. Moreover, the 'venue' in *Joseph and Aseneth* generally coincides with that of an ancient novel. A large part of the ancient novels are set in Asia Minor and the Near East. Again and again the characters in the novels end up in Egypt: this is the case in Chariton's *Callirhoe*, in Xenophon's *Ephesiaca*, in Achilles Tatius's *Leucippe and Cleitophon*, and is especially marked in Heliodorus's *Aethiopica*.[32] The biblical story of Joseph in Egypt provided an attractive setting for a novel.[33]

---

31   Holzberg, *Novel*, 10. Cf. also Heszer, "Joseph," 20–23.

32   See the maps in the appendix of Gareth L. Schmeling, *The Novel in the Ancient World* (Leiden: Brill, 2003 [1996]).

33   Cf. on this Karl Kerényi, *Die griechisch-orientalische Romanliteratur in religionsgeschichtlicher Beleuchtung: ein Versuch mit Nachbetrachtungen* (Darmstadt: Wissenschaftliche Buchgesellschaft, 1973), 74: "unsere griechischen Romane spielen gleichsam in einem Halbkreise um Aegypten, dieses als Mittelpunkt miteinbegriffen." It is not, however, necessary to conclude that the Greek novel must be of Egyptian or "oriental" origin, as John W.B. Barns, "Egypt and the Greek Romance," in *Akten des 8. Internationalen Kongresses für Papyrologie* (Wien: Rohrer, 1956), 29–36 supposed with simple dichotomies (36: "It was the *Greeks* who were peculiar in their intellectual passion for facts and reasons; the Oriental

TAKE YOUR TIME

2   Egyptian Restlesness versus Jewish Tranquility

Marc Philonenko's assertion that "Après tant de romans libertins, c'est un roman puritain qui est proposé au lecteur" misses the mark not only in its assessment of *Joseph and Aseneth* as a puritanical text, but also in the chronology: it seems to me very unlikely that *Joseph and Aseneth* was composed later than the majority of extant Hellenistic novels. It is nevertheless difficult to date. The *terminus post quem* for *JosAs* is without doubt the Septuagint, which was available to the author of *JosAs* and which was written in stages from the mid-third century BCE on. Beyond this, there is no clear evidence in the text, no realia that would allow for an accurate dating.[34] The novel is a work of fiction, after all, which is why the dating of *all* ancient novels is so difficult. For an approximate dating of *Joseph and Aseneth* it may be worthwhile to take a closer look at the characterization of the protagonists. Let us first take a quick look at Joseph: Joseph's superiority in time and space, from the beginning to the end of the novel, is striking. Joseph, too, changes over time, but only with regard to his attitude toward Aseneth.[35] Joseph is consistently presented as a confident and superior strategist.[36] He has everything under control. Right at the beginning we learn that Joseph is "touring," literally "circling" the "whole land of Egypt"—κυκλεῦσαι πᾶσαν τὴν γῆν Αἰγύπτου (1.1, following Gen 41:46)—to gather grain in the first year of the seven years of plenty. Throughout the novel Joseph comes and goes as he likes: when Joseph arrives at Heliopolis, he does not ask for Pentephres's hospitality, but tells him right away: "I will lodge with you because it is the hour of noon and the time of lunch, and the heat of the sun is great, and (I desire) that I may refresh myself under the shadow of your house" (3.2). And how does Aseneth's father Pentephres respond to this

---

world around them cared more for good stories; and of all Oriental peoples the Egyptians were second to none at telling them").

34   Cf. Erich S. Gruen, *Heritage and Hellenism: The Reinvention of Jewish Tradition* (Berkeley: University of California Press, 1998), 93. Ross S. Kraemer, in a much noted but critically received study, has placed the text in the late third or early fourth century CE: Ross S. Kraemer, *When Aseneth Met Joseph: A Late Antique Tale of the Biblical Patriarch and His Egyptian Wife, Reconsidered* (Oxford: Oxford University Press, 1998). Gideon Bohak, *Joseph and Aseneth and the Jewish Temple in Heliopolis* (Atlanta: Scholars, 1996) locates *JosAs* in the immediate context of the temple of Onias in Heliopolis: "we may read it *as a fictional history which 'foretells,' and justifies, the establishment of the Jewish temple in Heliopolis*" (102).

35   Both Joseph and Aseneth find their gender roles in the course of the novel. On the motif of such developments in the Greek novel cf. Sophie Lalanne, *Une éducation grecque: rites de passage et construction des genres dans le roman grec ancien* (Paris: Éditions La découverte, 2006) and Bierl, "Roman," 718.

36   Also noted by Gruen, *Heritage and Hellenism*, 97–98.

212 CHAPTER 10

rather direct self-invitation? By immediately praising the Jewish god: "Blessed (be) the Lord, the God of Joseph, because my lord Joseph thought me worthy to come to us" (3.3). When later in the novel Pentephres offers for Joseph to stay overnight and to rest until the next morning ("Let my lord lodge here today, and tomorrow you will go out [on] your way"), Joseph declines: "No, but I will go out today" (9.4–5). Joseph is not dependent upon Pentephres; he does not need him.

This becomes even more evident as the story further develops: when after Aseneth's conversion Pentephres is eager to organize the wedding and offers to talk to highly decorated Egyptian administrators on behalf of Joseph, Joseph ignores this kindly phrased offer. He would, so he says, go directly to the Pharaoh "because he appointed me chief of the whole land of Egypt, and I will speak about Aseneth into his ears, and he himself will give her to me for (my) wife" (20.8–9). All that Pentephres can say in response is: πορεύου μετ' εἰρήνης, "go in peace" (20.10). Joseph demonstrates confidence and sovereignty throughout—somewhat like Habrocomes in the beginning of Xenophon's *Ephesiaca*: "He [Habrocomes] was much sought after by all the Ephesians, and even all the inhabitants of Asia ... they treated the young man like a god, and some even prostrated themselves and prayed to him when they saw him" (1.1.3).

This Jewish novel, as mentioned above, was derived from a very short biblical passage: Gen 41:45 relates "Then Pharaoh named Joseph Zaphenath-paneah; and he gave him Asenath, the daughter of Potiphera, priest of On, as his wife." The author of the novel audaciously turns things around: Joseph no longer receives a new, Egyptian name but the Egyptian Aseneth is re-named and must convert to Judaism. As a symbol for her conversion, she receives the name "city of refuge." The plotline's vector has been reversed: it is no longer the Egyptians who set the rules, but the Jews. A further reversal of the biblical model is to be understood in a similar way:[37] on his first visit to Pentephres the author has Joseph sit at another table:

> because Joseph never ate with the Egyptians, for this was an abomination to him.
>
> διότι Ἰωσὴφ οὐ συνήσθιε μετὰ τῶν Αἰγυπτίων, ὅτι βδέλυγμα ἦν αὐτῷ τοῦτο.
> *JosAs* 7.1

---

37   Barclay, *Jews in the Mediterranean Diaspora*, 208.

TAKE YOUR TIME

In a similarly formulated scene in the *biblical* story of Joseph, it is the *Egyptians* who do not want to sit with the Hebrews:

> because the Egyptians could not eat with the Hebrews; for that it is an abomination to the Egyptians.
>
> Gen 43:32

In *Joseph and Aseneth*, a separate table (τράπεζαν κατ' ἰδίαν, 7.1) is brought for the Jewish Joseph in the Egyptian priest Pentephres's house. This is not just about cultic lines of demarcation, but rather expresses Jewish self-confidence: the Jews no longer eat at the side table; instead, the Egyptians serve "kosher" meals in their own land. And they depend on Joseph. If not for Joseph's critical foresight concerning the famine, all Egypt would have starved.

The early, Egyptian Aseneth is not able to see all this. First Aseneth frowned when she heard of Joseph. She calls him an "alien," a "fugitive," a "shepherd's son," and "dream interpreter," one like "the old women of the Egyptians" who "interpret (dreams)" (4.10–11). Such an effeminate Jew would be unworthy of someone like the daughter of the Egyptian priest of Heliopolis (4.10–11). Only gradually, and almost too late, does Aseneth notice how wrong she was (6.2). The end of the novel fits together with these images of Jewish superiority: the Egyptian intrigues fail, the Jews emerge victorious. The story can even afford to spare Pharaoh's son. In the end, though, he dies anyway (29.7), and thus Joseph is even able to become king of Egypt, while the biblical text and other Jewish-Hellenistic literature never promote Joseph's rank beyond second-in-command to Pharaoh.[38] Naturally, Joseph's rule is no more than a Jewish *interregnum*, else the later Egyptian-Ptolemaic rule would require an explanation.

While Joseph acts with confidence and power in time and space, Aseneth—or more accurately, Aseneth before her conversion to Judaism—is described in quite a different way: she is in a hurry. In the first part of the novel, Aseneth is presented as restless and insecure. She is constantly on the move—without getting very far. She does not leave her parents' court behind. The phrase "and Aseneth hurried (καὶ ἔσπευσεν Ἀσενέθ)" shows up not less than nine times in the novel: 3.6; 10.2; 10.10, 12; 14.14; 15.15; 16.1; 18.2; 19.2 (cf. also 4.1; 9.1; 18.5). Aseneth runs from room to room, up and down the stairs. And she is not alone. The other Egyptians, too, are in a hurry: her favorite sister, her father Pentephres, and the Pharaoh's son.[39] What eventually calms Aseneth down is her conver-

---

38   Cf. Gen 41:43; Philo, *Jos.* 148 (Joseph boards the second royal chariot as statesman behind the king).

39   *JosAs* 3.4 (Pentephres to his steward); 10.4 (Aseneth's favorite "sister"); 18.2 (Aseneth to her teacher); 25.4 (the Pharaoh's son).

sion to Judaism and union with Joseph. And this is exactly what Joseph was hoping for from the beginning. In a prayer to God Joseph says of Aseneth: "and let her enter your *rest* which you have prepared for your chosen ones" (καὶ εἰσελ-θέτω εἰς τὴν κατάπαυσίν σου ἣν ἡτοίμας τοῖς ἐκλεκτοῖς σου, 8.11). And she does. In the middle of the turbulent second part of the novel, as Joseph's spouse and partner, she is able to keep step with him: "And Aseneth went away on her way, and Joseph went away to his grain giving" (καὶ ἀπῆλθεν Ἀσενὲθ ἐπὶ τὴν ὁδὸν αὐτῆς καὶ Ἰωσὴφ ἀπῆλθεν ἐπὶ τὴν σιτοδοσίαν αὐτοῦ, 26.4). As a Jewish woman she now shows similar sovereignty, as Joseph has done from the beginning. Now she is even able to calm down others. Dan and Gad, two of Joseph's brothers who together with Pharaoh's son were planning to plot against Joseph and Aseneth, are comforted by Aseneth: "I want to ... make an end to their anger" (καταπαύσω τὴν ὀργὴν αὐτῶν, 28.7).

This idea of a Judaism which represents rest and tranquility may also lie behind Aseneth's new name: "the city of refuge" (15.7). And in a way, the metamorphosis from the daughter of the Egyptian priest constantly buzzing around into a calm Jewish wife is also symbolized by the bees "who encircled Aseneth from feet to head" (16.19; bees flew out of the honeycomb which Aseneth offered to her heavenly guest). After her confession and with her decision to follow the god of the Jews, Aseneth can now slow her pace of life down to a walk: the bees may continue to buzz around, but Aseneth no longer does.

Aseneth's initial rushing certainly also reflects the patriarchal gender discourse in this text. Aseneth—the early Aseneth at least—is imagined as a woman who dreams of being allowed to make Joseph's bed: "And you, Lord, commit me to him for a maidservant and slave. And I will make his bed and wash his feet and wait on him and be a slave for him and serve him forever (and) ever," Aseneth prays (13.15). And at times, Aseneth hurries because she is told to do so. When she is on the way to get some wine for her heavenly visitor, the latter tells her: "Hurry and bring (it) quickly" (15.15). Yet her haste is most often not ordered by someone else (except by the author, of course). Thus, I do not think that Aseneth's restlessness in the first half of the novel should be explained primarily in terms of her subordination.[40]

The novel consistently and consciously has Jews act in a calm and confident, almost stoic manner. In the last part of the novel it is Levi, one of Joseph's brothers, who, alongside Joseph and Aseneth, symbolizes this kind of tranquility. Levi never loses his countenance. Likewise for Aseneth following her

---

40   Angela Standhartinger, *Das Frauenbild im Judentum der hellenistischen Zeit. Ein Beitrag anhand von „Joseph und Aseneth"* (Leiden: Brill, 1995), 104–105.

TAKE YOUR TIME

conversion to Judaism—she exudes calm following her intimacy with Joseph. *Joseph and Aseneth* expresses a confident Diaspora Judaism that is less interested in a confrontation with the Egyptians than in highlighting Jewish presence and competence—and this is probably not directed primarily outwards, but is rather an internal dialogue with a Jewish readership. The author of *Joseph and Aseneth* is not really looking for a confrontation with the Egyptians. In fact, the novel ends with a very peaceful picture: after 48 years of Joseph's rule, the pharaonic family reclaims the scepter; in the meantime, Joseph has taken care of his Egyptian successor as a father would of his son.

Joseph's (and later also Aseneth's) sovereignty and tranquility should certainly be understood as somewhat imagined. As a matter of fact, *JosAs* shows signs not only of self-confidence, but also of caution. Jews were a minority in Ptolemaic Egypt, and it is telling how reluctantly and slowly Aseneth approaches the monotheistic faith of Judaism. The Greek verb τολμάω, "to take courage, to be bold, to dare," is used repeatedly: "I do not have the boldness to call on the Lord God of Heaven" (11.9), Aseneth first says, and then: "I will take courage too and turn to him" (11.11), and "I will take courage and cry to him" (11.14) and "I will rather take courage and open my mouth to him" (11.18). It takes courage to live a monotheistic life. When Josephus writes about Abraham as the first monotheist he uses the same language: "for he was the first who *dared* to say in public that there was but one god, the creator of the universe" (πρῶτος οὖν τολμᾷ θεὸν ἀποφήνασθαι δημιουργὸν τῶν ὅλων ἕνα; *AJ* 1.155). Jews in the ancient world knew that monotheism was an exception to the polytheistic rule.

What does this mean for the dating of *Joseph and Aseneth*? If one can assume that *Joseph and Aseneth*—as most Jewish-Hellenistic literature in Egypt—was also written in Alexandria, then an early dating is more likely than a late one. The position of the Jews in Alexandria deteriorated considerably in Roman times, and the diaspora uprisings under Emperor Trajan 115–117 CE ended, it seems, in the complete annihilation of the Jewish community. *Joseph and Aseneth* does not reflect the conflicts of the first two centuries CE. Jewish-Alexandrian literature did not, of course, come to a halt in Roman times (Philo of Alexandria after all wrote his immense oeuvre in the Roman period). But it is more likely that this Jewish novel originated in what was for Jews the more peaceful Ptolemaic period, in which similarly playful Jewish-Hellenistic literature flourished.[41] In particular, the theatrical work *Exagoge* by the Jewish

---

41   Similarly West, "Joseph," 81. On Jewish-Hellenistic recasting of biblical themes see Gruen, *Heritage and Hellenism*.

216   CHAPTER 10

tragedian Ezekiel, which revels in a confident Moses and deflated Egyptians, shares some similarities with *Joseph and Aseneth*.[42] *Joseph and Aseneth* is best understood as a Jewish-Hellenistic text of the pre-Christian era dating from the second or first century BCE.

3   The First Greek Novel?

If my interpretation so far is correct, then *Joseph and Aseneth* is a very early example of an ancient novel. Of the texts usually counted among the Greek novels the earliest are those by Chariton, Xenophon, and Achilles Tatius, all dating from the first or second century CE. In the case of the fragmentary novel of Ninos, the first century BCE is occasionally postulated. The other novels are considerably later.[43] Is *Joseph and Aseneth*, then, the first Greek novel? Is the novel a Jewish invention?

In scholarship on the beginnings of the Greek novel, *Joseph and Aseneth*, among others, is often mentioned early on—only to be disregarded for the rest of the study. Stephan Tilg, the author of a stimulating book on the beginnings of the Greek novel—*Chariton of Aphrodisias and the Invention of the Greek Love Novel* (Oxford 2010)—which seeks to clarify the actual birth of the Greek novel, states at the very beginning of his text:

> A large number of prose fictions can easily be ruled out for my pur-
> poses: historiographical writing like Xenophon's *Cyropaedia*, the *Alexan-
> der Romance*, or the *Troy Romances* by Dictys and Dares; biographies like
> the *Life of Aesop*; Jewish and Christian narrative with its transcendental
> concern—essentially all the texts that have often been subsumed under
> the heading of 'fringe novels'. This is not to say that these texts are less
> important or that they do not share any characteristics with the ideal love
> novels. They are just too different to fall within the category described
> above, or indeed to be considered "novels" at all.[44]

---

42   In *JosAs* the Pharaoh blesses the happy couple with a Jewish ritual prayer (21:6: "The Lord, God almighty, bless you ..."); in Ezekiel's *Exagoge* an Egyptian messenger reports about the superior god of the Hebrews after the miracle at the Sea of Reeds (193–242).

43   Cf. the summarizing comments in Harrison, "Parallel Cults?," 204; on the Ninos novel: Susan A. Stephens and John J. Winkler, *Ancient Greek Novels: The Fragments* (Princeton: Princeton University Press, 1995), 23; Whitmarsh, *Narrative and Identity*, 382–283.

44   Tilg, *Chariton*, 2–3; similarly Whitmarsh, *Narrative and Identity*, 25, who, however, is aware of the parallels in content between *Joseph and Aseneth* and the other pagan novels: "The Greek romance as we know it seems to have achieved its canonical form in the first cen-

TAKE YOUR TIME

It is true that *JosAs* differs in some respects from the "classic" Greek novel. In vocabulary and style *JosAs* cannot keep up with the "big five" and in *JosAs* religion plays an even more central role than in the pagan novels. And with regard to the content, too, the five so-called idealistic novels have more in common than they share with *JosAs*. The context of *JosAs* is not the pagan world with its gods, statues, and demons, but the Jewish monotheistic world. And yet, *JosAs* does share the most important characteristics of an ancient novel. *JosAs* is a Jewish example of an ancient romance novel. It is not a Jewish reaction to the literary genre of the Greek novel—which in any case cannot yet be established in the second or first century BCE. Nor do we need to assume that early pagan novels were influenced by *JosAs* (we know nothing about an early reception, Jewish or pagan, of *JosAs*). The search for dependencies is pointless and unnecessary. More important is the recognition that in the late Hellenistic and early Roman period, Jews and pagans came to write novels that have quite a bit in common. *JosAs* may in fact be the earliest Greek novel we know of, even if it differs in several respects from the pagan love novels.

Scholars have rightly pointed out parallels between *JosAs* and earlier *Jewish* texts.[45] The motif of the chaste Joseph is, of course, already present in the so-called Joseph novella in the Bible. The biblical Joseph withstands the sexual advances of the wife of his master Potiphar and is accused of raping her (a story which in turn has parallels in the pagan myth of Phaidra and Hippolytus).[46] But *JosAs* goes beyond such parallels. Other books such as Esther and Judith may, as has been stated, bear novelistic traits, but they are certainly not romances like *JosAs* or the pagan novels. As a love novel, *JosAs* stands alone in ancient Jewish literature.

In rabbinic literature one finds a rather different version of the Joseph and Aseneth motif. According to a midrash Aseneth (Asnath) was Jewish from the

---

tury of the Roman principate. For sure, Hellenistic precedents may well have existed, particularly in the 'national literature' of the subject peoples of the Greek kingdoms: one particularly important case is Joseph and Aseneth, which tells of the mutual love, marriage and tribulations of the biblical patriarch, but the dating remains controversial (estimates vary between the second century B.C.E. and the fourth century C.E.). But it remains true, on the current consensus, that the ideal, fictional romance as we know it is very much a product of the early imperial era."

45   Braginskaya, " 'Joseph and Aseneth.' "

46   Gen 39. On the Joseph novella (Gen 37–50) cf. Konrad Schmid, *Literaturgeschichte des Alten Testaments. Eine Einführung* (Darmstadt: WBG, 2008), 122–124. That the biblical story of Joseph, especially as it is reworked in Jewish-Hellenistic literature, contains parallels with the Phaedra myth is shown by Martin Braun, *History and Romance in Graeco-Oriental Literature* (Oxford: Basil Blackwell, 1938), 44–104.

beginning. She was the daughter of Dina, daughter of Jacob, who was raped by Sichem. In the midrash the angel Michael brings Asnath to Potiphar's house in Egypt, "because Asnath was destined to be Joseph's wife."[47] The motivation of this reading is obvious: the union of Joseph and Aseneth, as told in the book of Genesis, is divinely legitimized. And Asnath now has a Jewish mother.[48] The author of our novel, however, chose a completely different avenue: he used the brief biblical note in the book of Genesis to create an entertaining love story.

Bibliography

Barclay, John M.G., *Jews in the Mediterranean Diaspora: From Alexander to Trajan (323 BCE–117 CE)*. Berkeley: University of California Press, 1996.

Barns, John W.B., "Egypt and the Greek Romance." Pages 29–36 in *Akten des 8. Internationalen Kongresses für Papyrologie*. Wien: Rohrer, 1956.

Bierl, Anton, "Der griechische Roman—ein Mythos?" Pages 709–739 in *Antike Mythen. Medien, Transformationen und Konstruktionen*. Edited by Christine Walde and Ueli Dill. Berlin: De Gruyter, 2009.

Bohak, Gideon, *Joseph and Aseneth and the Jewish Temple in Heliopolis*. Atlanta: Scholars, 1996.

Braginskaya, Nina V., "'Joseph and Aseneth': A 'Midrash' before midrash and a 'Novel' before novel." *Vestnik drevnej istorii* 254 (2005): 73–96 (Russ.).

Braginskaya, Nina V., "Position of 'Joseph and Aseneth' in Greek literary history: the case of the 'first novel'." Pages 79–105 in *The Ancient Novel and Early Christian and Jewish Narrative: Fictional Intersections*. Edited by Marília P. Futre Pinheiro, Judith Perkins, Richard Pervo. Groningen: Barkhuis 2016.

Braun, Martin, *History and Romance in Graeco-Oriental Literature*. Oxford: Basil Blackwell, 1938.

Burchard, Christoph, trans., "Joseph and Aseneth." Pages 177–247 in *The Old Testament Pseudepigrapha*. Vol. 2. Edited by James H. Charlesworth. New York: Doubleday, 1985.

Burchard, Christoph, ed., *Joseph und Aseneth*. Leiden: Brill, 2003.

Burchard, Christoph, *Gesammelte Studien zu Joseph und Aseneth*. Leiden: Brill, 1996.

Burfeind, Carsten, "Aseneth." Pages 962–967 in *Encyclopedia of the Bible and its Reception*. Vol. 2: *Anim—Atheism*. Edited by Christine Helmer et al. Berlin: de Gruyter, 2009.

---

47   *Pirke R. El.*, ch. 38.

48   This is different again from the interpretation in Philo of Alexandria, who unapologetically speaks of Aseneth as the "most noble Egyptian woman," a "daughter of the priest of the Sun" (*Jos.* 121).

Erren, Manfred, *P. Vergilius Maro: Georgica. Bd. 2, Kommentar.* Heidelberg: C. Winter, 2002.

Fink, Uta Barbara, *Joseph und Aseneth: Revision des griechischen Textes und Edition der zweiten lateinischen Übersetzung.* Berlin: de Gruyter, 2008.

Gruen, Erich S., *Heritage and Hellenism: The Reinvention of Jewish Tradition.* Berkeley: University of California Press, 1998.

Harrison, Stephen, "Parallel Cults? Religion and Narrative in Apuleius' *Metamorphoses* and Some Greek Novels." Pages 204–218 in *The Greek and the Roman Novel: Parallel Readings.* Edited by Michael Paschalis et al. Groningen: Barkhuis, 2007.

Hezser, Catherine, "'Joseph and Aseneth' in the Context of Ancient Greek Erotic Novels." *Frankfurter Judaistische Beiträge* 24 (1997): 1–40.

Holzberg, Niklas, *The Ancient Novel: An Introduction.* London: Routledge, 1995.

Humphrey, Edith M., *Joseph and Aseneth.* Sheffield: Sheffield Academic, 2000.

Inowlocki, Sabrina, *Des idoles mortes et muettes au dieu vivant: Joseph, Aséneth et le fils de Pharaon dans un roman du judaïsme hellénisé.* Turnhout: Brepols, 2002.

Karla, Grammatiki, ed., *Fiction on the Fringe: Novelistic Writing in the Post-Classical Age.* Leiden: Brill, 2009.

Kerényi, Karl, *Die griechisch-orientalische Romanliteratur in religionsgeschichtlicher Beleuchtung: ein Versuch mit Nachbetrachtungen.* Darmstadt: Wissenschaftliche Buchgesellschaft, 1973.

Kraemer, Ross S., *When Aseneth Met Joseph: A Late Antique Tale of the Biblical Patriarch and His Egyptian Wife, Reconsidered.* Oxford: Oxford University Press, 1998.

Lalanne, Sophie, *Une éducation grecque: rites de passage et construction des genres dans le roman grec ancien.* Paris: Éditions La découverte, 2006.

Lipsett, B. Diane, *Desiring Conversion: Hermas, Thecla, Aseneth.* Oxford: Oxford University Press, 2011.

Merkelbach, Reinhold, *Roman und Mysterium in der Antike: Eine Untersuchung zur Religion.* Munich: C.H. Beck, 1962.

Niebuhr, Karl-Wilhelm. "Ethik und Tora. Zum Toraverständnis in Joseph und Aseneth." Pages 187–202 in *Joseph und Aseneth.* Edited by Eckart Reinmuth et al. Tübingen: Mohr Siebeck, 2009.

Philonenko, Marc, *Joseph et Aséneth: Introduction, texte critique, traduction et notes.* Leiden: Brill, 1968.

Reardon, Bryan P., "The Greek Novel." *Phoenix* 23 (1969): 291–309.

Reardon, Bryan P., ed., *Collected Ancient Greek Novels.* Berkeley: University of California Press, 1989.

Reinmuth, Eckart, ed., *Joseph und Aseneth.* Tübingen: Mohr Siebeck, 2009.

Schmid, Konrad, *Literaturgeschichte des Alten Testaments. Eine Einführung* (Darmstadt: WBG, 2008).

Standhartinger, Angela, *Das Frauenbild im Judentum der hellenistischen Zeit. Ein Beitrag anhand von „Joseph und Aseneth".* Leiden: Brill, 1995.

Stephens, Susan A. and John J. Winkler, *Ancient Greek Novels: The Fragments*. Princeton: Princeton University Press, 1995.

Tilg Stefan, *Chariton of Aphrodisias and the Invention of the Greek Love Novel*. Oxford: Oxford University Press, 2010.

Vogel, Manuel, "Einführung in die Schrift." Pages 3–30 in *Joseph und Aseneth*. Edited by Eckart Reinmuth et al. Tübingen: Mohr Siebeck, 2009.

West, Stephanie, "Joseph and Asenath. A Neglected Greek Romance." *Classical Quarterly* 24 (1974): 70–81.

Wetz, Christian, *Eros und Bekehrung: Anthropologische und religionsgeschichtliche Untersuchungen zu „Joseph und Aseneth."* Göttingen: Vandenhoeck & Ruprecht, 2010.

Whitmarsh, Tim, *Narrative and Identity in the Ancient Greek Novel: Returning Romance*. Cambridge: Cambridge University Press, 2011.

Wills, Lawrence M. *The Jewish Novel in the Ancient World*. Ithaca: Cornell University, 1995.

Zangenberg, Jürgen K., "Josef und Asenet: Zur Pragmatik und Modellhaftigkeit der Konversion Asenets." Pages 95–120 in *Der eine Gott und die fremden Kulte: Exklusive und inklusive Tendenzen in den biblischen Gottesvorstellungen*. Edited by Eberhard Bons. Neukirchen-Vluyn: Neukirchener, 2009.

Zeitlin, Froma, "Religion." Pages 91–108 in *The Cambridge Companion to the Greek and Roman Novel*. Edited by Tim Whitmarsh. Cambridge: Cambridge University Press, 2008.

PART 4

Antisemitism and Reception

∴

CHAPTER 11

Antisemitism and Early Scholarship on Ancient Antisemitism

The great German historian Theodor Mommsen, in the fifth volume of his magisterial *Römische Geschichte* (1885), framed a sentence that was soon after both endorsed and criticized by many other scholars. Mommsen stated there that "Jew-hatred and agitations against the Jews" ("Judenhass und die Judenhetzen") were as old as the Jewish diaspora itself.[1] As soon as there was Judaism—or, at least, Diaspora Judaism—there was also anti-Judaism and, thus, antisemitism. Judaism and antisemitism had a twin birth of sorts. Mommsen's comments on Judaism, both ancient and modern, are ambivalent, to say the least, and his sweeping remarks on the origins of antisemitism are problematic.[2] One could say, though, that the beginnings of the *study* of ancient antisemitism is a phenomenon contemporary with the beginnings of modern antisemitism.[3] In the last decades of the nineteenth century, ancient antisemitism became a topic of interest. It has remained so ever since.[4]

---

1 Theodor Mommsen, *Römische Geschichte: Fünfter Band, Die Provinzen von Caesar bis Diocletian* (Berlin: Weidmannsche Buchhandlung, 1921 [1885]), 519: "Der Judenhass und die Judenhetzen sind so alt wie die Diaspora selbst; diese privilegierten und autonomen orientalischen Gemeinden innerhalb der hellenischen mussten sie so nothwendig entwickeln wie der Sumpf die böse Luft."

2 Cf. the enlightening comments on Mommsen by Christhard Hoffmann, *Juden und Judentum im Werk deutscher Althistoriker des 19. und 20. Jahrhunderts* (Leiden: Brill, 1988), 87–132.

3 Rightly noted by Hoffmann, *Juden und Judentum*, 222: "Der antike Antisemitismus wurde im wesentlichen erst mit dem Aufkommen des modernen Antisemitismus ein 'Thema'." Cf. also Nicholas de Lange, "The Origins of Anti-Semitism: Ancient Evidence and Modern Interpretations," in *Anti-Semitism in Times of Crisis*, ed. S.L. Gilman and S.T. Katz (New York: New York University Press, 1991), 24 (21–37); Rainer Kampling, "Antike Judenfeindschaft," in *Handbuch des Antisemitismus: Judenfeindschaft in Geschichte und Gegenwart*. Band 3, ed. W. Benz (Berlin: De Gruyter, 2012), 14.

4 Among the recent book-length studies on the topic are: Peter Schäfer, *Judeophobia: Attitudes toward the Jews in the Ancient World* (Cambridge: Harvard University Press, 1997, with a good survey on the history of scholarship: 1–6); Zvi Yavetz, *Judenfeindschaft in der Antike: Die Münchener Vorträge. Mit einer Einleitung von Christian Meier* (München: C.H. Beck, 1997); Anton Cuffari, *Judenfeindschaft in Antike und Altem Testament: Terminologische, historische und theologische Untersuchungen* (Hamburg: Philo, 2007). Still very valuable is John G. Gager, *The Origins of Anti-Semitism: Attitudes toward Judaism in Pagan and Christian Antiquity* (Oxford: Oxford University Press, 1983). Cf. also Paula Fredriksen, *Augustine and the Jews* (New

---

© RENÉ BLOCH, 2022 | DOI:10.1163/9789004521896_013

Greco-Roman literature voices negative statements about Jews, ranging from casual mockery to overt animosity.[5] Moreover, historical sources mention various expulsions (repeatedly from the city of Rome), attacks (most specifically in Alexandria, in 38 CE), and prohibition of Jewish customs (in Jerusalem under Antiochus IV). While it would be greatly exaggerated to assume that a generalized contempt, let alone oppression, characterized Jewish life in Greco-Roman antiquity, there is no doubt that at various times Jews were the target of pagan assaults. Scholarship in the last 150 years has debated three principal questions extensively. First: Did Greeks and Romans treat Jews any differently from the ways that they treated other "barbarian" peoples? This question is further complicated by the fact that due to the Christian interest in Jewish-Hellenistic texts (including Josephus's *Contra Apionem*), pagan anti-Jewish materials assumed an outsized afterlife in our evidence. Second: Did anti-Jewish rhetoric or activities reflect circumstantial conflicts, or did these relate to some "essential" aspect of Judaism? Third: Which term—anti-Judaism, antisemitism or something else—best describes negative attitudes toward Jews in Greco-Roman antiquity?

Modern historiography, reflecting contemporary political impulses and cultural conflicts, has intensified the argument on these questions. Deliberations about the social and civil status of Jews in modern Europe (the so-called "Jewish question," beginning in the nineteenth century); German antisemitic propaganda before and during World War II; the horrors of the Holocaust and its enduring aftermath; the foundation of the state of Israel in 1948: all these factors have contributed continuingly to the proliferation of very different interpretations of what—or whether—one can identify ancient hostilities toward Jews as antisemitism. (I will discuss this problematic term below.) The literature on ancient antisemitism is vast; many questions remain controversial.

The current paper continues my earlier investigations into this topic.[6] My question, here, is specifically, What triggered scholarly interest in Greco-Roman antisemitism in the period between the late nineteenth century and World War II? Why did ancient antisemitism suddenly present such compelling ques-

---

Haven: Yale University Press, 2010), 25–102, on the origins of specifically Christian traditions *adversus Iudaeos*.

5   Here I am taking up a section from the introduction to my bibliographic entry on ancient antisemitism in *Oxford Bibliographies*, ed. Naomi Seidman (Oxford: Oxford University Press, 2016) [https://www.oxfordbibliographies.com/view/document/obo-9780199840731/obo-9780199840731-0140.xml?rskey=ZHzaoe&result=1&q=ancient+antisemitism#firstMatch]. See the entry for a detailed survey on scholarship on ancient antisemitism from the beginnings up to recent times.

6   See previous note and René S. Bloch, *Antike Vorstellungen vom Judentum: Der Judenexkurs des Tacitus im Rahmen der griechisch-römischen Ethnographie* (Stuttgart: Franz Steiner, 2002).

ANTISEMITISM AND EARLY SCHOLARSHIP ON ANCIENT ANTISEMITISM   225

tions, both to classicists and to theologians? As a matter of fact, their respective agendas often overlapped.[7] Theodor Mommsen is a case in point. In his *Roman History*, he endorses and reinterprets the distinction, quite common among Christian theologians at the time (I shall come back to this) between a putative, earlier cosmopolitan Judaism and a later, misanthropic Judaism. For Mommsen, the dividing line between these two Judaisms was demarcated not so much by the temple's destruction in 70 CE, but rather by the first Jewish revolt itself. His critique of the frozen Judaism of the rabbis, which supposedly replaced the open-minded earlier religion of Israelites, thereby acquired an added, specifically political dimension. Mommsen writes:

> The Jews had always been foreign, and wished to be so; but the feeling of estrangement mounted in horrifying fashion, both among them and towards them, and its hateful and pernicious consequences were extended starkly in both directions. From the disparaging satire of Horace against the importunate Jew from the Roman ghetto, it is quite a step to the solemn resentment which Tacitus harbours towards this scum of the earth for whom everything clean is unclean and everything unclean is clean; in between are those uprisings of the despised nation, the need to defeat it and perpetually expend money and people on keeping it down.[8]

As Christhard Hoffmann has shown, Mommsen on this point was heavily influenced by Julius Wellhausen, whose views on a Judaism in steady decline (from

---

7   In light of the main questions of this volume [*Protestant Bible Scholarship: Antisemitism, Philosemitism and Anti-Judaism*], I will focus on views by Christian scholars, referring only occasionally to Jewish scholars such as Isaak Heinemann. Towards the end of the nineteenth century Théodore Reinach's *Textes d'auteurs grecs et romains relatifs au judaïsme* (Paris: Ernest Leroux, 1895) became an important tool for the study of comments on Jews and Judaism in Greco-Roman literature, replacing earlier much less exhaustive studies. Similarly influential were the two volumes by Jean Juster, *Les Juifs dans l'Empire romain: leur condition juridique, économique et sociale* (Paris: Librairie Paul Geuthner, 1914).

8   Theodor Mommsen, *Römische Geschichte*, 551: "Fremde waren die Juden immer gewesen und hatten es sein wollen; aber das Gefühl der Entfremdung steigerte sich jetzt in ihnen selbst wie gegen sie in entsetzlicher Weise und schroff zog man nach beiden Seiten hin dessen gehässige und schädliche Consequenzen. Von dem geringschätzigen Spott des Horatius gegen den aufdringlichen Juden aus dem römischen Ghetto ist ein weiter Schritt zu dem feierlichen Groll, welchen Tacitus hegt gegen diesen Abschaum des Menschengeschlechts, dem alles Reine unrein und alles Unreine rein ist; dazwischen liegen jene Aufstände des verachteten Volkes und die Nothwendigkeit dasselbe zu besiegen und für seine Niederhaltung fortwährend Geld und Menschen aufzuwenden." English translation by David Ash from René Bloch, "Tacitus' Excursus on the Jews through the Ages: An Overview of the History of its Reception History", in *Oxford Readings in Tacitus*, ed. Rhiannon Ash (Oxford: Oxford University Press 2012), 401. Translations are mine unless otherwise indicated.

226   CHAPTER 11

the Persian period with Ezra and Nehemiah, accelerated even further by the
rabbis) he shared. Shortly after his comparison between Horace's and Tacitus's
comments on the Jews, Mommsen refers to post-70 Judaism as paralyzed to an
absurd extent.[9] Mommsen's interpretation can indeed be read as a "secularized
form of the traditional Christian template for interpretation."[10] As we shall see
shortly, Mommsen was by no means an exception among contemporary classicists, whose historiography of ancient antisemitism reflected and reaffirmed
Christian theological claims. Just how much Mommsen's reading of the Jews in
the Roman Empire was influenced by the *political* discourse on the role of the
Jews in the modern state emerges clearly from his most infamous comment on
Judaism. Commenting on the Jewish diaspora at the time of Julius Caesar in
the third volume of *Roman History*, Mommsen identified Jewish "cosmopolitanism" as an important contributing factor aiding Caesar's political goal of
"national decomposition."

> This remarkable people, yielding and yet tenacious, was in the ancient
> as in the modern world everywhere and nowhere at home, and every-
> where and nowhere powerful .... Even in the ancient world, Judaism was
> an effective leaven of cosmopolitan and national decomposition, and to
> that extent a specially privileged member in the Caesarian state, the polity
> of which was strictly speaking nothing but a citizenship of the world, and
> the nationality of which was at bottom nothing but humanity.[11]

The phrase "leaven of cosmopolitan and national decomposition" ("Ferment
des Kosmopolitismus und der nationalen Decomposition") became an antisemitic slogan later exploited by the National Socialists, including Goebbels
and Hitler.[12] Again, Mommsen's approach to Judaism and the Jews is ambivalent. He does endorse and repeat anti-Jewish stereotypes, but his understanding of the Jews' function as a ferment of decomposition for Caesar's empire,

---

9   Mommsen, *Römische Geschichte*, ibid.
10   Hoffmann, *Juden und Judentum*, 114.
11   Mommsen, *Römische Geschichte*. Vol. 3 (1856) 516–517: "Das merkwürdige nachgiebig
     zähe Volk war in der alten wie in der heutigen Welt überall und nirgends heimisch und
     überall und nirgends mächtig .... Auch in der alten Welt war das Judenthum ein wirk-
     sames Ferment des Kosmopolitismus und der nationalen Decomposition und insofern
     ein vorzugsweise berechtigtes Mitglied in dem caesarischen Staate, dessen Politie doch
     eigentlich nichts als Weltbürgerthum, dessen Volksthümlichkeit eigentlich nichts als Hu-
     manität war." English translation, William P. Dickson, *History of Rome*, 5.417–419.
12   Christhard Hoffmann, "Ancient Jewry—Modern Questions: German Historians of Antiq-
     uity on the Jewish Diaspora," *Illinois Classical Studies* 20 (1995): 191–207.

although based on the stereotype of the cosmopolitan Jew, was not meant in a necessarily negative way. During the so-called "Berliner Antisemitismus-Streit" between 1879 and 1881, Mommsen forthrightly opposed the anti-Semites gathered around historian Heinrich von Treitschke.[13] The term "Antisemitismus" as a concept and political movement was coined at this time: in September of the year 1879 the "Antisemiten-Liga," which set itself the goal of reducing a supposed Jewish influence in the German Empire, was founded in Berlin.[14] From that point on, "Antisemitismus" spread quickly and became a catchphrase.[15]

The term antisemitism is thus a problematic one. It not only, and misleadingly, uses a linguistic term—seemingly referring to Semitic languages—it also was originally a term of self-reference, coined in the late nineteenth-century by Germans who identified themselves as "anti-Semites." But it has become the term most often used, also in scholarly contexts, for any and all anti-Jewish attitudes and behaviours. Incidentally, the term "philosemitism," as Wolfram Kinzig has shown, is similarly problematic. It was created by anti-Semites as a term of derogation aimed against their opponents in the very same period: those who attacked the anti-Semites were criticized for their philosemitic fervour ("philosemitischen Eifer").[16]

But what about the ancient Greco-Roman world? Which term should be used to describe the negative treatment of Jews in Greco-Roman antiquity? In the late nineteenth century, the new term "antisemitism" was also applied to the ancient world. Konrad Zacher, a classicist based in Breslau, published

---

13 Cf. Theodor Mommsen, *Auch ein Wort über unser Judenthum* (Berlin: Weidmannsche Buchhandlung, 1880). On this debate cf. Walter Boehlich, ed., *Der Berliner Antisemitismus-streit* (Frankfurt a.M.: Insel, 1965); Jürgen Malitz, "Mommsen, Caesar und die Juden," in *Geschichte—Tradition—Reflexion: Festschrift für Martin Hengel zum 70. Geburtstag.* Vol. 2: *Griechische und Römische Religion,* ed. Hubert Cancik et al. (Tübingen: Mohr Siebeck, 1996), 371–387; Stefan Rebenich, "Eine Entzweiung: Theodor Mommsen und Heinrich von Treitschke," in *Berlins wilde Energien: Portraits aus der Geschichte der Leibnizischen Wissenschaftsakademie,* ed. Stefan Leibfried et al. (Berlin: De Gruyter, 2015), 262–285.

14 Ulrich Wyrwa, "Antisemiten-Liga," in *Handbuch des Antisemitismus: Judenfeindschaft in Geschichte und Gegenwart.* Vol. 5, ed. Wolfgang Benz (Berlin: De Gruyter, 2012), 30–33. The adjective "antisemitisch" had been used before: cf. Alex Bein, *The Jewish Question: Biography of a World Problem* (Rutherford, NJ: Fairleigh Dickinson University Press, 1990), 594.

15 Werner Bergmann, "Antisemitische Bewegung," in *Handbuch des Antisemitismus: Judenfeindschaft in Geschichte und Gegenwart.* Vol. 5, ed. Wolfgang Benz (Berlin: De Gruyter, 2012), 34–39.

16 Wolfram Kinzig, "Philosemitismus—was ist das?: Eine kritische Begriffsanalyse," in *Geliebter Feind—gehasster Freund: Antisemitismus und Philosemitismus in Geschichte und Gegenwart, Festschrift zum 65. Geburtstag von Julius H. Schoeps,* ed. Irene Diekmann and Elke-Vera Kotowski (Berlin: vbn-Verlag, 2009), 25–60.

an article in 1898 entitled "Antisemitismus und Philosemitismus im klassischen Alterthum." The article appeared in the *Preußische Jahrbücher*, the same monthly in which von Treitschke had published his anti-Jewish contributions twenty years earlier.[17] Zacher, who otherwise had a keen interest in Greek linguistics as well as in Greek comedy, may indeed have been the very first scholar to use the term "antisemitism" ("Antisemitismus") for the ancient world.[18] In this essay, Zacher, whose academic career was not very successful,[19] does not hide his antipathy towards the Jews of his own day, complaining of their "national characteristics that emerge unpleasantly, such as the tendency to arrogance, doctrinarism and scepticism."[20]

Very much like Mommsen, Zacher begins his article by stating that antisemitism was as old as Judaism.[21] While Zacher stresses from the beginning that antisemitism has not always been the same in all times and places; and that in Greco-Roman antiquity, unlike in nineteenth-century Germany, Jews were not capitalists, he does refer to some "very interesting parallels" to antisemitism of his own time. Zacher's study obviously mirrors the debates of the days in which it was written. Towards the end of this article, Zacher explains ancient antisemitism as a consequence of Jewish, that is "Pharisaic" torpidity which, originating in Jerusalem with the Maccabees in the aftermath of the anti-Jewish edict of Antiochus IV Epiphanes, had then spread throughout the diaspora. Antisemitism is a reaction to the religious stubbornness of the Jews, as well as (in Egypt) to their contempt of the Egyptian religion.[22] The first encounters of Jews and Greeks, at the time of Alexander, had been fruitful and

---

17   Konrad Zacher, "Antisemitismus und Philosemitismus im klassischen Alterthum," *Preußische Jahrbücher* 94 (1898): 1–24.

18   Hoffmann, *Juden und Judentum*, 222.

19   Ulrich von Wilamowitz-Moellendorff argued strongly against Zacher's promotion, cf. William M. Calder III, Alexander Košenina, ed., *Berufungspolitik innerhalb der Altertumswissenschaft im wilhelminischen Preußen* (Frankfurt a.M.: Klostermann, 1989), 71, 160.

20   Zacher, "Antisemitismus und Philosemitismus," 2–3 ("unangenehm hervortretende nationale Eigenschaften, wie die Neigung zur Ueberhebung, zum Doktrinarismus und Skeptizismus"). Zacher's stereotypical picture of modern Judaism is not only negative: he also refers to the Jews' "intelligence," "ambition," and "diligence" (2: "Intelligenz," "Ehrgeiz," "Fleiß") which leads to their success and then to envy and antipathy (2: "Neid und Mißgunst").

21   Zacher, "Antisemitismus und Philosemitismus," 1: "Der Antisemitismus, im weitesten Sinne gefaßt als feindliche Gesinnung oder Bethätigung gegen jüdische Mitbürger, ist so alt wie das Judenthum selbst und die jüdische Diaspora; aber seine Erscheinungsformen und Motive sind sehr verschieden nach Zeiten und Völkern." Later in the article, Zacher criticizes Mommsen's interpretation of the Jewish *privilegia*. These were not introduced by Caesar, Zacher argues, but must already have existed before in the Greek East (13–14).

22   Zacher, "Antisemitismus und Philosemitismus," 20–21.

ANTISEMITISM AND EARLY SCHOLARSHIP ON ANCIENT ANTISEMITISM   229

positive, Zacher claimed: Greek authors interpreted Judaism as a philosophy.[23] What Mommsen noticed for the time of Julius Caesar, Zacher then suggests, was already true for the period of Alexander the Great: the Jews served both men as a means to implement their respective political agendas. The Jews, adapting and adopting Hellenistic ideas, were the perfect "oriental element" facilitating the merging of Hellenism with the East.[24] But later on, after the Maccabean revolt and the success of the Pharisees (sic), Jewish self-confidence and exclusive presumptuousness contrasted sharply with tolerant, open Hellenism.[25] Thus, Greek philo-Semitism yielded to Greco-Roman antisemitism. Zacher ends his article with the very dichotomy that stands at the core of his argument, the same one common among theologians at the time, but clearly shared by Christian classicists: Judaism had started off well but, in its orthodox, Pharisaic form, it deteriorated into torpor ("erstarrte"). In Rome, Judaism served for some time as a "stimulating leaven" ("anregender Sauerteig")—this language recalls Mommsen's picture of Judaism as a "ferment"—but eventually it was replaced by Christianity, the emerging world power, which was "new," "fresh," and "vital."[26] Zacher's article begins with antisemitism and culminates in "das Christentum."

A few years after Zacher's article, in 1905, Felix Stähelin—later to become professor of ancient history at the University of Basel—published the first (if brief) monograph on ancient antisemitism, like Zacher using that very term: *Der Antisemitismus des Altertums in seiner Entstehung und Entwicklung*.[27] Stä-

---

23   Interestingly Zacher uses the word "Philosemitismus" only in the title of his article, but this is what is meant by the term: the early Greek sympathy for the Jews.

24   Zacher, "Antisemitismus und Philosemitismus," 18: "Seine Absicht war ja eine Verschmelzung von Griechenthum und Orient; welches orientalische Element konnte für die Förderung dieses Planes geeigneter erscheinen als die Juden, die sich dem aufgeklärten Hellenenthum so wesentlich näher zu stellen schienen als die übrigen Orientalen?"

25   Zacher, "Antisemitismus und Philosemitismus," 23: "Es (sc. das Judentum) wurde orthodoxer, starrer, gegen alles Andere abgeschlossener. Das hochmüthig zur Schau getragene Selbstbewusstsein, im Besitz der allein wahren Religion zu sein, mußte das tolerante Griechenthum mehr und mehr abstoßen." 20: "Unter der Führung der Makkabäer sammelte sich das altgläubige Judenthum und errang Freiheit des Glaubens nicht nur, sondern auch des Landes. Die Folge war denn auch im Innern der völlige Sieg der pharisäischen Richtung ...."

26   Zacher, "Antisemitismus und Philosemitismus," 24: "sein Erbe übernahm die neue, frische, lebendige welterobernde Macht—das Christentum." Overall, Zacher's article is not unbalanced throughout. He denounces the absurdity of some of the antisemitic accusations and calls the riot in Alexandria of 38 CE a "furchtbaren Ausbruch" (22).

27   Felix Stähelin, *Der Antisemitismus des Altertums in seiner Entstehung und Entwicklung* (Basel: C.F. Lendorff, 1905). In its original form Stähelin published his study first in 1901

helin's study is a mostly descriptive history of political conflicts involving Jews and negative statements on the Jews. Stähelin, who had just filed his dissertation on the history of the Galatians, was also influenced by current theological discourse on Jews, as is clear from the beginning and the end of his book. On page one he refers to Julius Wellhausen's *Israelitische und jüdische Geschichte* to recount that Jewish separatism and legalism had replaced the "fresh, religious life" of ancient Israel.[28] Concluding, Stähelin states that Christianity should not be accused of having invented antisemitism since antisemitism predated Christianity by centuries. It is "a pagan instinct that erupts now and then" ("ein heidnischer Instinkt, der von Zeit zu Zeit wieder hervorbricht").[29]

The relation of pagan, Christian, medieval and modern animosity towards Jews is much debated in scholarship. Many scholars try to avoid using "antisemitism" as a term of historical description for the ancient and medieval periods. The main argument in this instance is that modern antisemitism encompasses a racialist component seemingly foreign to the earlier periods, Greco-Roman, Roman Christian, and medieval. Prominent alternative suggestions for pagan antiquity are "anti-Judaism" and "Judeophobia."[30] Each of these labels, however, is problematic in its own way. "Judeophobia" (used most prominently by Zvi Yavetz and Peter Schäfer)[31] seemingly implies psychological issues (more so than the broader term "xenophobia"). Pagans indeed mocked Jews and occasionally targeted them with violence, but "phobia" scarcely seems descriptively correct.

As for "anti-Judaism," many scholars avoid using it for pagan contexts, reserving it rather for Christianity. The study of ancient antisemitism regularly and from its beginnings revolved around the question whether or to what extent pagan polemics against the Jews should be distinguished from Christian ones. Zacher and Stähelin exemplify this issue. At times, an apologetic agenda is quite

---

in the conservative Swiss newspaper *Allgemeine Schweizer Zeitung* (Nr. 17–19) which was printed in Basel.

28 Stähelin, *Der Antisemitismus des Altertums*, 2: "den endgiltigen Triumph jener geisttötenden, peinlichen Gesetzlichkeit, zu dem sich kaum ein grellerer Gegensatz läßt als das frische religiöse Leben, das im alten Israel geherrscht, und der Geist, der einst die Propheten getrieben hatte."

29 Stähelin, *Der Antisemitismus des Altertums*, 54.

30 An extensive survey on the use of different terms in Cuffari, *Judenfeindschaft in Antike und Altem Testament*, 21–56.

31 Peter Schäfer, *Judeophobia: Attitudes toward the Jews in the Ancient* World (Cambridge: Harvard University Press, 1997); Zvi Yavetz, "Judeophobia in Classical Antiquity: A Different Approach," *Journal of Jewish Studies* 44 (1993): 1–22.

tangible: if antisemitism was already virulent in pagan antiquity, it can hardly be called a Christian invention. Or the other way around: by stressing the origins of *Christian* antisemitism, Greco-Roman antiquity can be freed from the ugliness of Jew-hatred. The question of the extent to which pagan antisemitism differs from Christian antisemitism is central in practically all wide-ranging studies on the topic. Jules Isaac, in *Genèse de l'antisémitisme*, published in 1956 and written with great passion (and under the direct impact of the Holocaust), concludes that pagan antisemitism remained a temporary and fragmentary phenomenon, while Christian antisemitism was much more virulent and more fundamental to Christian identity.[32] Some thirty years later, John Gager, in his *The Origins of Anti-Semitism: Attitudes toward Judaism in Pagan and Christian Antiquity*, also compared pagan and Christian antisemitism, stressing the differences between the two.[33] According to Gager, neither paganism nor early Christianity knew some kind of pervasive antisemitism. However, Gager argues, the various contributions of early Christian contribution to modern antisemitism should not be minimized by referring to selected anti-Jewish passages in Greco-Roman literature.[34]

Being aware of the apologetic risks inherent in this discussion, I tend to agree in principle with both Isaac and Gager. Early Christianity, at least from the time of the church fathers on, brought a new dimension to earlier pagan polemics against the Jews. Quite enlightening is a comparison between Roman historian Tacitus, in the early second century CE, and Christian writer Sulpicius Severus some three centuries later. Sulpicius Severus (ca. 363–420 CE) seems to have used a lost part of Tacitus's *Histories* to describe the Roman destruction of Jerusalem.[35] Whether or not he did so,[36] the differences between the two authors are telling. Tacitus indeed disparages Jews and Jewish customs in *Histories* 5; but outside of his long digression on Judea and Judaism, he has

---

32   Jules Isaac, *Genèse de l'antisémitisme: Essai historique* (Paris: Calmann-Lévy, 1956). Also James Parkes, *The Conflict of the Church and the Synagogue: A Study in the Origins of Antisemitism* (London: Soncino Press, 1934), draws a sharp line between pagan polemics and Christian antisemitism: "the advent of Christianity perpetuated their (the Jews') tragedy. The reasons for this have nothing to do with the old enmities. They are to be found only in the conflict of Christianity with its parent religion" (26).

33   Gager, *The Origins of Anti-Semitism*.

34   Gager, *The Origins of Anti-Semitism*, 268.

35   Jacob Bernays, "Über die Chronik des Sulpicius Severus, ein Beitrag zur Geschichte der classischen und biblischen Studien," in id., *Gesammelte Abhandlungen*. Vol. 2, ed. Hermann Usener (Berlin: Hertz, 1885 [1861]), 81–200.

36   Cf. the critical remarks by Eric Laupot, "Tacitus' Fragment 2: the Anti-Roman Movement of the Christiani and the Nazoreans," *VChr* 54 (2000): 233–247.

232   CHAPTER 11

little else to say about the Jews. He nowhere comments on the Jewish origins of figures like Tiberius Julius Alexander, King Agrippa II, or his sister Berenice. Tacitus may not have liked Jews, but they were of no major concern to him.[37] He hardly "feared" them.

Christian authors like Sulpicius Severus, however, had much more at stake. The destruction of the temple in Jerusalem for him is of fundamental theological importance:

> Thus, according to the divine will, the minds of all being inflamed, the temple was destroyed, three hundred and thirty-one years ago. And this last overthrow of the temple, and final captivity of the Jews (*haec ultima templi eversio et postrema Iudaeorum captivitas*), by which, being exiles from their native land, they are beheld scattered through the whole world (*per orbem terrarum dispersi*), furnish a daily demonstration to the world, that they have been punished on no other account than for the impious hands which they laid upon Christ (*cotidie mundo testimonio sunt, non ob aliud eos quam ob illatas Christo impias manus fuisse punitos*).[38]

More than Christian vocabulary distinguishes Sulpicius Severus from Tacitus. Striking, for our concerns, is his deployment of *cotidie*, "daily." For authors such as Sulpicius Severus—as centuries earlier, with Ignatius, Justin, and Tertullian—"the Jews" had become a fundamental theological category framing Christian claims to Jewish scriptures (the church's Old Testament), thus a daily issue, so to speak.[39] The terms *Iudaeus* and *Iudaicus* appear fewer than a hundred times in all of pagan Roman literature (not counting the toponym *Iudaea*). Tertullian alone (who writes three generations after Tacitus, whom he read) uses *Iudaeus* and *Iudaicus* 270 times.[40] To the Romans, the Jews were a strange people, often viewed as foreign, but only one ethnic group among many. It is only with the arrival of Christianity that the *Iudaei* become an essential topic—

---

37   Bloch, *Antike Vorstellungen vom Judentum*.
38   Sulpicius Severus, *Chron.* 2.30.8 (trans. A. Roberts).
39   Cf. Hubert Cancik, "Der antike Antisemitismus und seine Rezeption," in *Das 'bewegliche' Vorurteil'. Aspekte des internationalen Antisemitismus*, ed. Christina von Braun and Eva-Maria Ziege (Würzburg: Königshausen & Neumann, 2004), 63–79, who also refers to the differences between Tacitus and Sulpicius Severus stating that with the latter "ist das Unglück der Juden zum festen Bestandteil der christlichen Heilsgeschichte und zu einem handgreiflichen Beweisstück geworden" (76).
40   Cf. René Bloch, "Jew or Judean: The Latin Evidence," in *Torah, Temple, Land: Constructions of Judaism in Antiquity*, ed. Markus Witte, Jens Schröter, and Verena M. Lepper (Tübingen: Mohr Siebeck, 2021), 231–242.

although also in the case of early Christian literature there were of course nuances with regard to each individual author's relation to the Jews.[41]

Christian animosity towards the Jews is thus different *in kind* from its pagan predecessor. And this seems to be a good reason to use different terms, "anti-Judaism" for Christianity and something else for the pagan phenomenon. But matters are, alas, more complicated. If anti-Judaism is a phenomenon specific to Christian antiquity (if not also already to some late first-century texts gathered in the New Testament), when does that period end? Medieval polemics against the Jews are no less theologically charged and, as is clear from our observations on Mommsen, Zacher, and Stähelin, confessional Christian agendas continued to shape modern academic discourses.

The beginnings of racialist anti-Jewish discourse in the nineteenth century did not exclude the influence of long-lived Christian tropes. And scholars debate whether some kind of proto-racism shaped such discourse in the Middle Ages or even in Greco-Roman antiquity.[42] Alas, we lack a simple answer to the question what the appropriate term(s) are for which times. In my earlier research, I had avoided using "antisemitism" for those centuries before the term itself was coined in the late nineteenth century. Today, I hesitate less. The distinctions between the different periods that have been suggested are in my view inaccurate and rather artificial. It is true, as Nicholas de Lange wrote, that "Anti-Semitism, in the strict sense of the term, cannot be detached from the racial theories which exercised such an important influence on the ethos of Western politics and thought from the middle of the nineteenth century to the middle of the twentieth."[43] The term "antisemitism" with its antisemitic origins is problematic and there were different forms and degrees of this phenomenon over time. Still, "antisemitism" has become the general denominator for any kind of anti-Jewish hostility or agitation. According to the *Oxford English Dictio-*

---

41   As de Lange, "The Origins of Anti-Semitism," 30, rightly notes it would indeed be "an exaggeration to claim that early Christianity was uniformly hostile to the Jews and Judaism."

42   Cf. Benjamin Isaac, *The Invention of Racism in Classical Antiquity* (Princeton: Princeton University Press, 2004). Rather sophisticated is Gavin I. Langmuir's distinction between anti-Judaism and antisemitism in *Toward a Definition of Anti-semitism* (Berkeley: University of California Press, 1990). According to Langmuir anti-Judaism is a theologically framed precursor ("the necessary preparation") of antisemitism which is more irrational, but the two terms are not simply to be understood in a chronological way. Thus for Langmuir, e.g. the medieval blood libel should also be considered antisemitic. On Langmuir (and on Jules Isaac) cf. the helpful comments by Robert Chazan, *From Anti-Judaism to Anti-Semitism: Ancient and Medieval Christian Constructions of Jewish History* (Cambridge: Cambridge University Press 2016), vi–xvi.

43   De Lange, "The Origins of Anti-Semitism," 22.

nary, it denotes "prejudice, hostility, or discrimination towards Jewish people on religious, cultural, or ethnic grounds; (also) the theory, action, or practice resulting from this."[44] This is a good working definition. Adjectives such as "religious," "racist," as well as "ancient," "Christian," "medieval," and "modern" can help clarify further what kind of antisemitism we mean. This is why I think it is legitimate to talk about ancient antisemitism, knowing that it was, then, often simply a species of Greco-Roman ethnographies that denigrated exotic "others" and in which ancient Jews also engaged. But the fact that there are no specific modern terms for animosity against the Egyptians, Phoenicians and other ethnic groups insulted by classical authors must not preclude the historian from using a specific term for ancient anti-Jewish animosity. Finally, it hardly needs to be brought to mind that research on antisemitism post-Holocaust is haunted by that unprecedented catastrophe. Research into pre-Holocaust anti-Jewish hostility—but also into contemporary, post-Holocaust animosity—risks being belittled by comparison. In sum: ancient antisemitism was often more circumstantial than essential and the suffix -ism, often indicating some kind of greater movement or ideology, may be somewhat misleading. Ancient antisemitism does differ from later Christian and still later racial antisemitism; but Greek and Roman animosity towards Jews could be quite substantial. *Faute de mieux*, even for antiquity, antisemitism seems the most appropriate term.

Let us now return to the late nineteenth century's stirrings of scholarship on ancient antisemitism. A variety of causes triggered interest in the topic. Of fundamental importance, as Christhard Hoffmann writes, was

> the political debate on the 'Jewish question', i.e. on the position of the Jewish minority in modern society. Against the thesis of the liberal proponents of emancipation, according to which hatred of the Jews is nothing more than a Christian religious prejudice that must be overcome, the nationalistic opponents of Jewish equality (such as Friedrich Rühs) and the intellectual sympathisers with modern anti-Semitism (such as Heinrich von Treitschke), which was forming in the 1870s, offered the arguments of the supposedly universal ancient anti-Semitism .... The persuasive function of this interpretation in the contemporary discussion of the 'Jewish question' is clear: If Jews have been the object of contempt,

---

44　*Oxford English Dictionary*, third edition (2019), s.v. (the second edition (1989) had: "Theory, action, or practice directed against the Jews. Hence anti-Semite, one who is hostile or opposed to the Jews").

ANTISEMITISM AND EARLY SCHOLARSHIP ON ANCIENT ANTISEMITISM   235

hatred and persecution wherever they appeared in world history, then the reason must lie within themselves and not in Christian religious prejudice.[45]

In midst of the modern debates on the Jews' place in civic society, ancient antisemitism could serve to exemplify a seemingly eternal problem. At times, and especially in the period of National Socialism, scholars looked for historical steppingstones to their own antisemitic agendas. A very explicit example for this is the volume *Das antike Weltjudentum*, co-authored by Gerhard Kittel (professor of New Testament at the University of Tübingen) and Eugen Fischer (professor of medicine and promotor of eugenics in Nazi Germany). The book was published in 1943 as volume 7 of the *Forschungen zur Judenfrage* (FzJ). The two authors attempt to show that Jews, "whether in the first or the 20th century," had always striven for absolute world domination.[46] The first part of the book ends with a brief chapter on ancient antisemitism ("Antike Judengegnerschaft") which serves to validate its modern iterations.[47] The second and third parts of the book, mainly by Fischer, provide a racist discussion of supposedly Jewish portraits on Egyptian mummies and of terracotta figures with crooked noses, explained as anti-Jewish caricatures.[48] Religion is not at the core of the volume, but Kittel, a Lutheran theologian, had already expanded his often antisemitic views on ancient Judaism in a number of earlier publications.[49] In the late nineteenth century up to the time of National Socialism, ancient anti-

---

45   Christhard Hoffmann, "Judaism," in *Brill's New Pauly, Antiquity volumes*, ed. Hubert Cancik and Helmuth Schneider, English Edition by: Christine F. Salazar, Classical Tradition volumes edited by: Manfred Landfester, English Edition by: Francis G. Gentry. http://dx.doi .org/10.1163/1574--9347_bnp_e1407860. Jewish scholars, especially Isaak Heinemann and Elias Bickermann, responded to the view that ancient antisemitism was a natural precursor of the Jewish problem by putting ancient hostility towards the Jews in a historical context: cf. Hoffmann, ibid. and Bloch, "Ancient Antisemitism." Heinemann explicitly rejects Mommsen's view that antisemitism is as old as the Jewish diaspora: Isaak Heinemann, "Antisemitismus," in *Paulys Realencyclopädie der classischen Altertumswissenschaft*, Supplement 5, Agamennon bis Statilius, ed. G. Wissowa (Stuttgart: Metzler, 1931), 3–43 (19).

46   Eugen Fischer, Gerhard Kittel, *Das antike Weltjudentum: Tatsachen, Texte, Bilder*. Forschungen zur Judenfrage 7 (Hamburg: Hanseatische Verlagsanstalt, 1943), 11 ("ob im Ersten oder im Zwanzigsten Jahrhundert"). Cf. Hoffmann, *Juden und Judentum*, 254–259.

47   Fischer, Kittel, *Das antike Weltjudentum*, 89–92. Interestingly the two authors avoid the term "Antisemitismus," but speak instead of "Judengegnerschaft."

48   Fischer, Kittel, *Das antike Weltjudentum*, 95–219.

49   Cf. the extensive discussion on Kittel in Anders Gerdmar, *Roots of Theological Anti-Semitism: German Biblical Interpretation and the Jews, from Herder and Semler to Kittel and Bultmann* (Leiden: Brill, 2009), 417–530.

semitism could serve as "a historical legitimization" for modern antisemitism.[50] Particularly attractive to early interpreters of ancient antisemitism, it seems to me, was a seemingly clear development of the phenomenon in Greco-Roman (that is, non-Christian) texts. As Zacher's work especially demonstrates, many scholars stressed the differences between a positive view on the Jews in Hellenistic texts ("Jews as philosophers" and "cosmopolitan citizens") on the one hand, and the very negative depictions of the misanthropic Jews in later Roman literature (with Tacitus in a starring role). More recently, some scholars—Erich S. Gruen, Nicholas de Lange and I, for example—have pointed out that things may be quite a bit more complicated. After all, the accusation of Jewish misanthropy shows up for the first time as early as the late 4th century BCE, with Hecataeus of Abdera.[51] Even when one puts the Roman evidence aside and only looks at the Greek, one arrives at the conclusion, with Bezalel Bar-Kochva, that there is no "logical, coherent line from admiration at the time of first contacts between Greeks and Jews through a cooling-off period as Greeks learned more about the Jews to extreme hostility with the rupture between Jews and the Greek world following the religious persecutions by Antiochus Epiphanes."[52] In short, no simple and straight development from philosemitism to antisemitism can be supported by our ancient evidence. To interpreters in the late nineteenth century and early twentieth century, however, such a reading easily accommodated the Christian theological interpretation of a Judaism that had had a good start (and thus was praised), but that fell into depravity (and thus became the object of hatred). It was no coincidence that this developmental timeline traced an arc from the heights of Israelite prophecy to the moribund depths of "rabbinic legalism" (itself also a trope of Reformation anti-Catholic polemic, with rabbis as stand-ins for Papists). Moreover, two prominent pagan authors—one Greek, the other Latin—could be pressed into service of such an interpretation. The geographer Strabo and the Roman historian Publius Cornelius Tacitus report on a dichotomy between an early, positive period of Judaism and a later time when Judaism fell into decadence.[53] It comes as no surprise that some scholars made use of these ancient sources to strengthen their general understanding of Judaism as a history of decline.

---

50   Hoffmann, "Judaism."

51   Erich S. Gruen, *Diaspora: Jews Amidst Greeks and Romans* (Cambridge: Harvard University Press, 2002), 41–53; de Lange, "The Origins of Anti-Semitism," 31–33; René Bloch, "Misanthropia," *RAC* 24: 828–845; Bloch, *Antike Vorstellungen vom Judentum*.

52   Bezalel Bar-Kochva, *The Image of the Jews in Greek Literature: The Hellenistic Period* (Berkeley: University of California Press, 2010), 517.

53   Strabo 16.2.35–37; Tacitus, *Hist.* 5.4–5.

A particularly interesting and telling exemplar of such historiography is Johannes Leipoldt. Leipoldt authored two important contributions to the study of ancient antisemitism: a 50 page article, "Antisemitismus in der alten Welt" (1933), and the entry on antisemitism in the very first volume of the *Reallexikon für Antike und Christentum* (1950).[54] Leipoldt, who lived from 1880 to 1965, studied Theology and *Orientalistik* in Berlin and Leipzig. His academic work ranges widely from Coptic Christianity to the historical Jesus to late Roman patristics. From 1916 until his retirement in 1959 he taught New Testament in Leipzig.[55] During World War II, Leipoldt was involved with the "Institute for the Study and Eradication of Jewish Influence on German Church Life," a Protestant pro-Nazi institute that worked to "dejudaize" Christianity.[56] His 1933 study on antisemitism in the ancient world mixes sound scholarly assessments of ancient sources with imaginary conjurings of ancient anti-Judaism, thoroughly influenced by contemporary antisemitic discourse. Ten years before Kittel and Fischer, Leipoldt (who became Kittel's doctoral advisor in Kiel[57]) refers to Egyptian mummy portraits that he claims have a Jewish look, thus proving that Jewish physiognomy had not changed since ancient times. This extraordinary stability was especially instantiated by "what appears to us today as the most striking physical peculiarity of the Jew: the curved nose."[58] But it was not Jewish noses that triggered ancient antisemitism,[59] Leipoldt urged, but the Jews' religion.[60] On this point Leipoldt enlists Strabo's comments on Moses and his successors. Leipoldt writes:

---

54 Johannes Leipoldt, *Antisemitismus in der alten Welt*. Leipzig: Dörffling & Franke, 1933; id. "Antisemitismus," *RAC* 1: 469–476.

55 Klaus-Gunther Wesseling, "Johannes Leipoldt," *Biographisch-Bibliographisches Kirchenlexikon* 4, 1391–1395.

56 Susannah Heschel, *The Aryan Jesus: Christian Theologians and the Bible in Nazi Germany* (Princeton: Princeton University Press, 2008), 178: "Within the Institute Leipoldt was a constant presence, lecturing frequently at its conferences, including at its final meeting in March of 1944. The Institute gave him the opportunity to incorporate racial theory in his academic work, explaining the rise of Christianity in antiquity as an Aryan triumph that incorporated Teutonic ideas, as he argued in a paper on "The History of the Ancient Church in Racial Illumination," presented at an Institute conference in November 1941."

57 Gerdmar, *Roots of Theological Anti-Semitism*, 419.

58 Leipoldt, *Antisemitismus in der alten Welt*, 17–18: "was uns heute als die auffälligste körperliche Besonderheit des Juden erscheint: die gebogene Nase .... Die körperliche Art des Juden hat sich also von der alten Zeit bis heute ziemlich unverändert erhalten."

59 Leipoldt, *Antisemitismus in der alten Welt*, 20: "Der Rassengegensatz reicht nicht aus, um den Antisemitismus der alten Welt zu erklären."

60 Ibid.: "Mir scheint der religiöse Grund des Antisemitismus der wichtigste zu sein." Two years before, Heinemann, "Antisemitismus," argued the opposite (10: "Gegen die jüdische

Perhaps the average judgment of the educated is best rendered by the carefully weighing geographer Strabo (d. 19 CE). He does not hesitate to recognize the greatness of Moses. According to Strabo Moses rightly said that the divine being should not be thought of in animal or human form. Strabo takes antisemitism into account by portraying the later successors of Moses as superstitious and tyrannical: it was they who first introduced the dietary laws, circumcision and the like.[61]

In his long description of Judea and the Jews in Book 16 of his *Geography*, Strabo indeed speaks of Judaism's gradual decline. Moses was an Egyptian priest who had left Egypt because he was "displeased with the state of affairs there."[62] Moses particularly disliked the Egyptian way of worshipping gods, their theriomorphic representations of divine being, since he rejected any production of an "image of God resembling any creature amongst us." Moses, Strabo continues, persuaded many reasonable men and led them to Jerusalem, where he installed "a kind of worship and kind of ritual which would not oppress those who adopted them either with expenses or with divine obsessions or with other absurd troubles."[63] But this ideal form of Mosaic Judaism eventually degenerated once Moses was gone. Strabo continues:

> His successors for some time abided by the same course, acting righteously and being truly pious toward God; but afterwards, in the first place, superstitious men were appointed to the priesthood, and then tyrannical people; and from superstition arose abstinence from flesh, from which it is their custom to abstain even today, and circumcisions and excisions and other observances of the kind. And from the tyrannies arose the bands of robbers.[64]

Religion als solche hat man nichts einzuwenden." 18: "Überblicken wir nunmehr die politischen Verwicklungen zwischen den Juden und ihrer Umwelt im Altertum, so erkennen wir, daß es sich in der Hauptsache nicht um Religionskriege, sondern um Machtkämpfe handelt.").

61 Leipoldt, *Antisemitismus in der alten Welt*, 14: "Vielleicht wird das Durchschnittsurteil des Gebildeten am besten von dem vorsichtig abwägenden Geographen Strabon wiedergegeben (gest. 19 nach Christus). Er ist ohne weiteres bereit, die Größe des Moses anzuerkennen. Mit Recht sage Moses, das göttliche Wesen dürfe nicht in Tier- oder Menschengestalt gedacht werden. Dem Antisemitismus trägt Strabon dadurch Rechnung, daß er die späteren Nachfolger des Moses als abergläubisch und tyrannisch hinstellt: sie erst hätten die Speisegebote, die Beschneidung und dergleichen Dinge eingeführt."

62 Strabo 16.2.35: δυσχεράνας τὰ κατεσθῶτα (English translation of Strabo from LCL).

63 Strabo 16.2.36.

64 Strabo 16.2.37.

ANTISEMITISM AND EARLY SCHOLARSHIP ON ANCIENT ANTISEMITISM 239

According to Strabo, who seems to have drawn from Posidonius (for whom the pattern of decline is essential), Mosaic piety (*theosebeia*) was later replaced by superstitious ritual (*deisidaimonia*) such as dietary laws and circumcision. With the religious decline came political depravation: tyrannies and robber bands.[65] Leipoldt does not explicitly draw a line from Strabo's description of Judaism's deterioration to his own version of such a history, but he seems to both share and endorse the geographer's antitheses, praising Strabo's astute assessment of the evidence.[66] Towards the end of his study on ancient antisemitism, Leipoldt discusses Christianity, very much as historians Zacher and Stähelin had done. Here Leipoldt stresses the differences between Christianity and Judaism. In these differences lay the root reason for antisemitism:

There must be significant differences between Judaism and Christianity: otherwise the mutual countercurrents would not have had such a different fate. The differences lie first and foremost in religion. Christianity does not shut itself off. It knows no ceremonial law. Jesus already disregards the Sabbath commandments when there is a need. He absolutely ignores the purity regulations. Paul coined sharp formulas. For this Christian freedom of law. Its ultimate reason is the new relationship with God that Jesus introduces. ... the Christian feels driven and called to love his neighbor without limit and without restriction; and with this charity he can be a blessing in any economic system. Christianity has remained true to this social character to this day.[67]

---

65   Among the first who argued for Posidonius as Strabo's source was Isaak Heinemann, "Poseidonios über die Entwicklung der jüdischen Religion," *Monatsschrift für Geschichte und Wissenschaft des Judentums* 63 (1919): 113–121. On Strabo on the Jews, including the question whether the argument might go back to Posidonius, cf. more recently Bar-Kochva, *The Image of the Jews*, 355–398; René Bloch, "Posidonian thoughts-ancient and modern," *Journal for the Study of Judaism* 35 (2004): 284–292. On Strabo's reference to female circumcision (ἐκτομαί), unique in Greco-Roman ethnography on the Jews, cf. Shaye J.D. Cohen, "Why aren't Jewish Women Circumcised?" in *Gender and the Body in the Ancient Mediterranean*, ed. Maria Wyke (Malden: Wiley-Blackwell, 1998), 139–141.

66   As for Tacitus's distinction (*Hist.* 5.5) between ancient Jewish rituals that can be justified because of their antiquity (*antiquitate defenduntur*) and other customs that prevail because of their depravity (*pravitate valuere*), which in its origins may go back to Strabo/Posidonius, it similarly went along with commentators' thoughts on a Jewish decline: cf. Bloch, "Posidonian Thoughts," 288–294.

67   Leipoldt, *Antisemitismus in der alten Welt*, 52–53: "Es muß bedeutende Unterschiede geben zwischen Judentum und Christentum: sonst hätten nicht die beiderseitigen Gegenströmungen ein so verschiedenes Schicksal. Die Unterschiede liegen zunächst und hauptsächlich auf religiösem Gebiete. Das Christentum sperrt sich nicht ab. Es kennt kein

Leipoldt's tractate on ancient antisemitism ends with this paean to Christian love of neighbour (evidently innocent of its source, Leviticus 19). In Strabo's (Posidonius') language one could thus say that, for Leipoldt, Moses leaving Egypt, peacefully entering Jerusalem and piously worshiping God, represents the last Christian before Judaism's fall into depravity.[68] In his entry "Antisemitismus" for the *Reallexikon für Antike und Christentum*—published in 1950 but written during World War II[69]—Leipoldt stresses once more the religious causes of ancient antisemitism. It was Jewish separatism which led to anti-Jewish hostility. As in his earlier work on the topic, Leipoldt combines sound historical observation with standard antisemitic stereotypes, as when he writes of a "financial dominance of the Jews" (nodding to Cicero's *Flacc.*), as well as of their political and economic power (as contrasted to the early Christians, who lived in poverty).[70]

To conclude. The beginnings of scholarship on ancient antisemitism coincided with the invention of the term itself and with the development of a new form, modern racial antisemitism. As we have seen, the discourses of theolo-

---

Zeremonialgesetz. Schon Jesus setzt sich über die Sabbatgebote hinweg, wenn es Not tut. Von den Reinheitsordnungen will er überhaupt nichts wissen. Paulus prägt scharfe Formeln. Für diese christliche Gesetzesfreiheit. Ihr letzter Grund ist das neue Verhältnis zu Gott, in das Jesus einführt. ... der Christ fühlt sich zur Nächstenliebe getrieben und berufen, ohne Grenze und ohne Einschränkung; und mit dieser Nächstenliebe kann er in jeder Wirtschaftsordnung ein Segen sein. Diesem sozialen Zuge ist das Christentum treu geblieben bis auf den heutigen Tag."

68   Isaak Heinemann once noted that "Posidonius has, in a certain sense, become a predecessor of the interpretation of the development of the Israelite religion, today usually named after Wellhausen," cf. Heinemann, "Poseidonios über die Entwicklung der jüdischen Religion" (121: "[Poseidonios ist] in gewissem Sinne zum Vorläufer der heute meist nach Wellhausen genannten Vorstellung von der Entwicklung der israelitischen Religion geworden."). In his 1940 article "The Attitude of the Ancient World towards Judaism," *The Review of Religion* 4 (1940): 385–400, Heinemann argues very much against the view, shared by Leipoldt and others, that it was "ritual difference which gave anti-Semitism its special stamp" (394). According to Heinemann it was "the exclusiveness of Jewish monotheism" (397) which attracted the proselytes and repelled the anti-Semites: "the roots of hate and love were the same" (398). Remarkably, Heinemann gives Leipoldt credit for taking some Talmudic literature in consideration (385n1) and otherwise does not mention him by name in his critique.

69   Cf. Theodor Klauser's introduction to the first volume of the RAC, published in 1950.

70   Johannes Leipoldt, "Antisemitismus," 472: "finanzielles Übergewicht der Juden;" 473–474: "daß die Juden nach politischer Macht streben und bei erster Gelegenheit sich an den Vertretern des Antisemitismus rächen .... So war zu befürchten, daß man die Christen als Juden ansah und mit den Waffen des Antisemitismus bekämpfte. Aber das geschah selten. Wer die Christen kannte, stellte leicht fest, daß die Vorwürfe des Antisemitismus auf sie nicht zutrafen." ... "waren so arm, daß sie keine wirtschaftliche Macht darstellten."

gians and (Christian) classicists writing on the topic could overlap: ancient Judaism, from the beginnings to the rabbinic period, is regularly viewed as a Wellhausian tale of decline. The argument is not always overtly theological, but very often it is teleological, Christianity serving as Judaism's soteriological corrective. Does the history of antisemitism have articulated inflection-points? A number have been proposed but, as current scholarship has shown, all are problematic. Anti-Jewish hostility is neither specific to the Hasmonean period nor to that following the temple's destruction in 70 CE; neither was there a development from Greek philosemitism to Roman antisemitism. The view, widespread in early scholarship, that ancient antisemitism was the result of some kind of deterioration (whether religious or political) within Judaism mirrors the Christian conviction that Judaism was in decline. Pagan sources describing an earlier, pious form of Judaism and a later, superstitious, ritually overladen one were happily pressed into service. At times, the study of ancient antisemitism served simply to legitimate modern antisemitism.

Can a history of antisemitism in Greco-Roman antiquity be written? Difficult to say, and hard to imagine. It would have to be a history with many twists and turns and location-specific hotspots. Nonetheless, substantial differences mark pagan antisemitism off from that of Christian tradition. Greco-Roman hostility towards the Jews could indeed wax ferocious at times; but religiously, Jews could never occupy in paganism the central role they were forced into by Christian discourse, which was on a fundamentally different scale. Antisemitism may remain a problematic term. For the ancient world, it may require some qualifications. Nevertheless, its heuristic value abides.

Bibliography

Bar-Kochva, Bezalel, *The Image of the Jews in Greek Literature: The Hellenistic Period.* Berkeley: University of California Press, 2010.

Bautz, Friedrich Wilhelm, *Biographisch-Bibliographisches Kirchenlexikon.* 14 Vols. Nordhausen: Verlag Traugott Bautz, 1975–1998.

Bein, Alex, *The Jewish Question: Biography of a World Problem.* Rutherford: Fairleigh Dickinson University Press, 1990.

Bergmann, Werner, "Antisemitische Bewegung." Pages 34–39 in *Handbuch des Antisemitismus. Judenfeindschaft in Geschichte und Gegenwart.* Vol. 5. Edited by Wolfgang Benz. Berlin: De Gruyter, 2012.

Bernays, Jacob, "Über die Chronik des Sulpicius Severus, ein Beitrag zur Geschichte der classischen und biblischen Studien." Pages 81–200 in *Gesammelte Abhandlungen.* Vol. 2. Edited by Herman Usener. Berlin: Hertz, 1885.

Bloch, René, *Antike Vorstellungen vom Judentum: Der Judenexkurs des Tacitus im Rahmen der griechisch-römischen Ethnographie*. Stuttgart: Franz Steiner, 2002.

Bloch, René, "Posidonian thoughts-ancient and modern." *Journal for the Study of Judaism* 35 (2004): 284–292.

Bloch, René, "Misanthropia." *RAC* 24: 828–845.

Bloch, René, "Tacitus' Excursus on the Jews through the Ages: An Overview of the History of its Reception History." Pages 377–409 in *Oxford Readings in Tacitus*. Edited by Rhiannon Ash. Oxford: Oxford University Press, 2012.

Bloch, René, "Ancient Anti-Semitism." In *Oxford Bibliographies in Jewish Studies*. Edited by Naomi Seidman, 2016. https://www.oxfordbibliographies.com/view/document/obo-9780199840731/obo-9780199840731-0140.xml?rskey=ZHzaoe&result=1&q=ancient+antisemitism#firstMatch.

Bloch, René, "Jew or Judean: The Latin Evidence." Pages 229–240 in *Torah, Temple, Land: Constructions of Judaism in Antiquity*. Edited by Markus Witte, Jens Schröter, and Verena Lepper. Tübingen: Mohr Siebeck, 2021.

Boehlich, Walter, ed., *Der Berliner Antisemitismusstreit*. Frankfurt am Main: Insel, 1965.

Calder III, William M., and Alexander Košenina, eds., *Berufungspolitik innerhalb der Altertumswissenschaft im wilhelminischen Preußen*. Frankfurt am Main: Klostermann, 1989.

Cancik, Hubert, "Der antike Antisemitismus und seine Rezeption." Pages 63–79 in *Das 'bewegliche' Vorurteil'. Aspekte des internationalen Antisemitismus*. Edited by Christina von Braun and Eva M. Ziege. Würzburg: Königshausen & Neumann, 2004.

Cuffari, Anton, *Judenfeindschaft in Antike und Altem Testament: Terminologische, historische und theologische Untersuchungen*. Hamburg: Philo, 2007.

Cohen, Shaye J.D., "Why aren't Jewish Women Circumcised?" Pages 136–154 in *Gender and the Body in the Ancient Mediterranean*. Edited by Maria Wyke. Malden: Wiley-Blackwell, 1998.

De Lange, Nicholas, "The Origins of Anti-Semitism: Ancient Evidence and Modern Interpretations." Pages 21–37 in *Anti-Semitism in Times of Crisis*. Edited by Sander L. Gilman and Steven T. Katz. New York: New York University Press, 1991.

Fischer, Eugen, and Gerhard Kittel, *Das antike Weltjudentum. Tatsachen, Texte, Bilder*. Hamburg: Hanseatische Verlagsanstalt, 1943.

Gager, John G., *The Origins of Anti-Semitism: Attitudes toward Judaism in Pagan and Christian Antiquity*. Oxford: Oxford University Press, 1983.

Gerdmar, Anders, *Roots of Theological Anti-Semitism. German Biblical Interpretation and the Jews, from Herder and Semler to Kittel and Bultmann*. Leiden: Brill, 2009.

Gruen, Erich S., *Diaspora: Jews Amidst Greeks and Romans*. Cambridge: Harvard, 2002.

Heinemann, Isaak, "Antisemitismus." Pages 3–43 in *Paulys Realencyclopädie der classischen Altertumswissenschaft*, Supplement 5. Edited by Georg Wissowa and Wilhelm Kroll. Stuttgart: Metzler, 1931.

Heinemann, Isaak, "Poseidonios über die Entwicklung der jüdischen Religion." *Monatsschrift für Geschichte und Wissenschaft des Judentums* 63 (1919): 113–121.

Hoffmann, Christhard, *Juden und Judentum im Werk deutscher Althistoriker des 19. und 20. Jahrhunderts.* Leiden: Brill, 1988.

Hoffmann, Christhard, "Ancient Jewry—Modern Questions: German Historians of Antiquity on the Jewish Diaspora." *Illinois Classical Studies* 20 (1995): 191–207.

Hoffmann, Christhard, "Judaism." In *Brill's New Pauly*. Edited by Hubert Cancik and Helmuth Schneider, and Francis G. Gentry. http://dx.doi.org/10.1163/1574--9347_bnp _e1407860.

Isaac, Benjamin, *The Invention of Racism in Classical Antiquity.* Princeton: Princeton University Press, 2004.

Isaac, Jules, *Genèse de l'antisémitisme: Essai historique.* Paris: Calmann-Lévy, 1956.

Kampling, Rainer, "Antike Judenfeindschaft." Pages 14–16 in *Handbuch des Antisemitismus. Judenfeindschaft in Geschichte und Gegenwart.* Vol 3. Edited by Wolfgang Benz. Berlin: De Gruyter, 2012.

Kinzig, Wolfram, "Philosemitismus—was ist das?: Eine kritische Begriffsanalyse." Pages 25–60 in *Geliebter Feind—gehasster Freund. Antisemitismus und Philosemitismus in Geschichte und Gegenwart. Festschrift zum 65. Geburtstag von Julius H. Schoeps.* Edited by Irene Diekmann and Elke-Vera Kotowski. Berlin: VBN-Verlag, 2009.

Klauser, Theodor et al., *Reallexikon für Antike und Christentum. Sachwörterbuch zur Auseinandersetzung des Christentums mit der antiken Welt.* Vol. 1. Stuttgart: Hiersemann, 1950.

Langmuir, Gavin I., *Toward a Definition of Anti-semitism.* Berkeley: University of California Press, 1990.

Laupot, Eric, "Tacitus' Fragment 2: the Anti-Roman Movement of the Christiani and the Nazoreans." *VC* 54 (2000): 233–247.

Leipoldt, Johannes, *Antisemitismus in der alten Welt.* Leipzig: Dörffling & Franke, 1933.

Malitz, Jürgen, "Mommsen, Caesar und die Juden." Pages 371–387 in *Geschichte–Tradition–Reflexion. Festschrift für Martin Hengel zum 70. Geburtstag. Vol. 2. Griechische und Römische Religion.* Edited by Hubert Cancik, Hermann Lichtenberger and Peter Schäfer. Tübingen: Mohr Siebeck, 1996.

Mommsen, Theodor, *Römische Geschichte. Fünfter Band. Die Provinzen von Caesar bis Diocletian.* Berlin: Weidmannsche Buchhandlung, 1921.

Mommsen, Theodor, *History of Rome.* Vol. 3, Translated by William P. Dickson. London: Richard Bentley, 1863.

Mommsen, Theodor, *Auch ein Wort über unser Judenthum.* Berlin: Weidmannsche Buchhandlung, 1880.

Parkes, James, *The Conflict of the Church and the Synagogue: A Study in the Origins of Anti-semitism.* London: Soncino Press, 1934.

Rebenich, Stefan, "Eine Entzweiung. Theodor Mommsen und Heinrich von Treitschke."

Pages 262–285 in *Berlins wilde Energien. Portraits aus der Geschichte der Leibnizi-schen Wissenschaftsakademie*. Edited by Stephan Leibfried et al. Berlin: De Gruyter, 2015.

Sevenster, Jan Nicolaas, *The Roots of Pagan Anti-Semitism in the Ancient World*. Leiden: Brill, 1975.

Schäfer, Peter, *Judeophobia: Attitudes toward the Jews in the Ancient World*. Cambridge: Harvard University Press, 1997.

Stähelin, Felix, *Der Antisemitismus des Altertums in seiner Entstehung und Entwicklung*. Basel: C.F. Lendorff, 1905.

Wyrwa, Ulrich, "Antisemiten-Liga." Pages 30–33 in *Handbuch des Antisemitismus. Judenfeindschaft in Geschichte und Gegenwart*. Vol. 5. Edited by Wolfgang Benz. Berlin: De Gruyter, 2012.

Yavetz, Zvi, "Judeophobia in Classical Antiquity: A Different Approach." *Journal of Jewish Studies* 44 (1993): 1–22.

Yavetz, Zvi, *Judenfeindschaft in der Antike: Die Münchener Vorträge*. München: C.H. Beck, 1997.

Zacher, Konrad, "Antisemitismus und Philosemitismus im klassischen Alterthum." *Preußische Jahrbücher* 94 (1898): 1–24.

CHAPTER 12

A Leap into the Void: The *Philo-Lexikon* and Jewish-German Hellenism

Philo of Alexandria, born c. 20 BCE (in c. 40 CE presented an embassy of the Alexandrian Jews before Caligula), theologian and philosopher, classic representative of Jewish Hellenism, master of allegorical interpretation, marries the language and ideas of Greek philosophy (Plato) with those of Jewish, revelation-based faith; for a long time unique within the Jewish context, his influence is visible in the first place on the Christian Church Fathers. His extant corpus comprises about 70 writings (in Greek), explanations of the Pentateuch (especially the Greek text), monographs on the forefathers, an explanation of the Mosaic legislation, and others.
(Dt. Übers., L. Cohn u. I. Heinemann, 1909 ff.).
L: Heinemann, P.'s griech. u. j. Bildung 1932.

Thus reads the entry for "Philo of Alexandria" in the *Philo-Lexikon*, which appeared for the first time in 1935 and for a fourth and last time in 1937.[1] This one-volume, eventually 832-column *Handlexikon* was designed to provide a quick overview of everything "which Judaism contains: religion and history, practice and way of life."[2] It is therefore by no means a lexicon of the Jewish-Hellenistic theologian and philosopher Philo of Alexandria or even one especially concerned with ancient Judaism. However, Philo and Hellenistic Judaism generally could well function as both a starting point and a point of contention for describing Jewish self-understanding in Germany in the 1920s and 1930s.

---

1 Emanuel Bin Gorion, Alfred Loewenberg, Otto Neuburger, and Hans Oppenheimer, eds., *Philo-Lexikon: Handbuch des jüdischen Wissens*. Mit 250 Abbildungen, zahlreichen Plänen, Tabellen und Übersichten sowie 40 zum Teil mehrfarbigen Tafeln und Karten. Vierte vermehrte und verbesserte Auflage (Berlin: Philo-Verlag, 1937), 558. The German original reads: "Philo von Alexandria, geb. um 20 v. (40 n. Führer einer j.-alexandrin. Gesandtschaft bei Caligula), Theologe u. Philosoph, klassischer Vertreter d. j. Hellenismus, Meister d. allegor. Schriftauslegung, vereinigt Sprach- u. Gedankengut d. griech. Philosophie (Plato) mit j. Offenbarungsglauben; im j. Bereich für lange Zeit singulär, wirkt er sichtbar zunächst auf d. christl. Kirchenväter. Erhaltene W etwa 70 Schriften (griech.), Erklärungen zum Pent. (insbes. zu G), Monographien über d. Urväter, Darstellung d. mosaischen Gesetzgebung u. a."
2 "was das Judentum umschließt: Religion und Geschichte, Leistung und Leben;" *Philo-Lexikon*, iv.

© RENÉ BLOCH, 2022 | DOI:10.1163/9789004521896_014

246   CHAPTER 12

In this paper I would like to elucidate this phenomenon with reference to the *Philo-Lexikon* and its reception.[3]

For the author of the entry on Philo of Alexandria, it was certainly no easy task to present the life and work of such a complex author in such a small space (just ninety-one words!). The entry's many abbreviations and the bibliography, limited to one title, indicates that contributors to the *Lexikon* were called to make their entries as short as possible. It is impossible to tell for sure who wrote the article, as entries contain no shortened author's names. However, from the list of around one hundred contributors' names in the *Lexikon's* front matter, it is reasonable to assume that the entry came from the pen of the great Philo expert Isaak Heinemann (1876–1957). Not only the characterization of Philo as theologian, not self-evident, but also the striking terminology of 'Jewish Hellenism' (instead of 'Hellenistic Judaism') point to Heinemann as the author.[4] Heinemann, who came from an orthodox Jewish home in Frankfurt, was until 1938 a Lecturer in Jewish Philosophy of Religion at the Jewish Theological Seminary of Breslau. From 1930 to 1933 he was also Honorary Professor of the Intellectual History of Hellenism at the University of Wroclaw. In 1939 he emigrated to Palestine and became a professor at the Hebrew University of Jerusalem.[5] In 1897 Heinemann had completed his doctorate in Berlin under Hermann Diels, having written his PhD thesis on Solon before submitting two volumes on Posidonius. The centerpoint of his academic interests, however, became Jewish Hellenism. Heinemann became co-editor and co-translator of the German edition of Philo put out by Leopold Cohn. His translation of the long treatise *On the Special Laws* (*De specialibus legibus*), completed in 1910, led to his lengthy comparative study, *Philons griechische und jüdische Bildung: Kulturvergleichende Untersuchungen zu Philons Darstellung der jüdischen Gesetze* (published in Breslau 1929–1932). Along with his dual interest in Jewish and Greek culture, there was always the question of their dissociation as well. Thus, Heine-

---

3 The widespread Jewish reception of Hellenism in 1920s–1930s Germany has received little scholarly attention to date. For literature on the Philo-Verlag, see note 9; on the interpretation of Jewish antiquity by Jewish scholars of antiquity, see Christhard Hoffmann, *Juden und Judentum im Werk deutscher Althistoriker des 19. und 20. Jahrhunderts* (Leiden: Brill, 1988), 200–245.

4 In his comparative study of Philo's Greek and Jewish educations, listed in the *Lexikon* article as the sole bibliographic reference, Heinemann calls Philo a theologian and speaks of Jewish Hellenism (pp. 3, 5). Heinemann also wrote a more detailed article on Philo in Georg Herlitz and Bruno Kirschner, eds., *Jüdisches Lexikon: Ein enzyklopaedisches Handbuch des jüdischen Wissens.* Volume IV.1 (Berlin: Jüdischer Verlag, 1927), 907–910.

5 Renate Heuer, comp., *Archiv Bibliographia Judaica: Lexikon deutsch-jüdischer Autoren, Band 11: Hein-Hirs* (München: K.G. Saur, 2002), 30–37.

A LEAP INTO THE VOID   247

mann repeatedly and intensively dealt with ancient antisemitism.[6] He understood antisemitism to have appeared primarily in isolated conflicts (rather than
being normative); on the other hand, Heinemann had as a student earlier in
his own life already noticed parallels between ancient anti-Jewish hostility and
modern antisemitism. When, during his time of study in Göttingen, he was
denied access to the "philologischer Verein" because he was a Jew, he wrote a
letter of complaint as a nineteen-year-old student to the great Hellenist Ulrich
von Wilamowitz-Moellendorf, whom he worshipped. Heinemann maintained
that Jews were confronted by antisemitism regardless of their religious affilia-
tion, drawing a parallel to the ancient Jewish experience in Hellenistic Alexandria: "And yet I have often had the personal experience that today a more liberal
practice protects against opposition as little as it did in ancient Alexandria."[7]

Whith his work, which combines the Jewish with the non-Jewish, his struggle for an adequate understanding of Jewish Hellenism, but also his biography,
which ends in persecution and exile, Isaac Heinemann in a way embodies that
which is symptomatic of the *Philo-Lexikon*.[8] The name of the lexicon is derived
from that of its publisher of the same name, the Philo-Verlag.[9] The Philo-Verlag
was founded by the Central-Verein deutscher Staatsbürger jüdischen Glaubens
e.V. (abbreviated: C.V.) and published—as per the entry for "Buchhandel" in the
Philo-Lexikon—mostly "apologetic literature," but also "scientific works" and
"popular literature."[10] The press's first publisher was the lawyer Ludwig Hollän-

---

6   See, especially, Isaak Heinemann, "Antisemitismus," in Georg Wissowa and Wilhelm Kroll,
     eds. *Paulys Realencyclopädie der Classischen Altertumswissenschaft*, Supplementband 5
     (Stuttgart: Metzler, 1931), 3–43.

7   Christhard Hoffmann, "Antiker Völkerhass und moderner Rassenhass: Heinemann an Wil-
     amowitz," in *Quaderni di Storia* 25 (1987): 145–157, at 151 ("Und doch habe ich schon häufig
     die persönliche Erfahrung gemacht, daß heute sowenig, wie einst in Alexandrien, freiere
     Praxis vor Zurücksetzung schützt."). On a later correspondence, see Christhard Hoffmann
     and Adam Kamesar, "Wilamowitz and Heinemann II: Three Letters from the 1920s," *Illinois
     Classical Studies* 31/32 (2006–2007): 130–144.

8   Incidentally, the *Philo-Lexikon* contains short entries for Isaac Heinemann and Leopold
     Cohn: see p. 138 and p. 286.

9   On the publisher's history, see Helmuth F. Braun, "Der Philo Verlag (1919–1938): Ein Ber-
     liner Verlag für jüdische Abwehr- und Aufklärungsliteratur," in *Berlinische Notizen: Zeit-
     schrift des Vereins der Freunde und Förderer des Berliner Museums e.V.* 4 (1987): 90–103 and
     Susanne Urban-Fahr, *Der Philo-Verlag 1919–1938: Abwehr und Selbstbehauptung* (Hildes-
     heim: Georg Olms, 2001). Further on the Philo-Verlag see Volker Dahm, *Das jüdische Buch
     im Dritten Reich: Zweite, überarbeitete Auflage* (München: C.H. Beck, 1993) and Jan-Pieter
     Barbian, *Literaturpolitik im NS-Staat: Von der "Gleichschaltung" bis zum Ruin* (Frankfurt am
     Main: Fischer, 2010).

10   "apologetische Literatur … wissenschaftliche Werke … Unterhaltungsliteratur." *Philo-
     Lexikon*, 113.

der. The name "Philo-Verlag" was only his second choice: for its first few months it was called the "Gabriel Riesser-Verlag" after the Jewish judge and politician Gabriel Riesser (1806–1863), who vehemently advocated for the equality of the Jews and for a Jewish-German self-image.[11] The publisher's original name was therefore quite fitting. However, Jacob Riesser, a (baptized) nephew of Gabriel Riesser, filed an objection, whereupon the courts forced the publisher to find a new name; it found one in the great Jewish philosopher Philo of Alexandria.[12]

One can readily understand Philo as a kind of Hellenistic alternative to Gabriel Riesser: Philo joined Jewish and Greek ideas, sometimes corrected prejudices in the course of his exegesis, and acted as a politician when, following the anti-Jewish riot in Alexandria (38 CE), he led a Jewish delegation to the Roman imperial court.[13] Opposition also arose against this new name of the publishing house, this time in the form of an inner-Jewish critique: Jewish nationalists protested that the publisher had founded itself upon an 'assimilant.' Thus did the newspaper *Das Jüdische Echo* polemicize in a note to the effect that Philo was "without any effect on his immediate family" inasmuch as "his nephew Alexander even fell away from Judaism."[14] The reference to Tiberius Julius Alexander who, according to Flavius Josephus, "did not remain faithful to the practices of his people,"[15] was countered on the side of the C.V. via a reference to Moses Mendelssohn: although Mendelssohn was also "without effect on his immediate family," saying so does not do justice to his enormous significance in general.[16] In a reply entitled "Kann uns Philo Vorbild sein?" in the C.V.'s print outlet, the *C.V.-Zeitung*, Max Mayer, co-editor of *Der Jude*, rebuffed the apparently ongoing criticism of the name of the publishing house

---

11   Renate Heuer, comp., *Archiv Bibliographia Judaica: Lexikon deutsch-jüdischer Autoren, Band 18: Phil—Samu* (Berlin: De Gruyter, 2010), 269–279.

12   The new Philo-Verlag proclaimed in an announcement: "Von Seiten der Familie Riesser ist Einspruch erhoben worden gegen die Führung des Namens 'Gabriel Riesser Verlag.' Wir nennen den Verlag nunmehr in Erinnerung an den großen jüdischen Philosophen 'Philo' Philo-Verlag." Cf. *Im Deutschen Reich: Zeitschrift des Centralvereins Deutscher Staatsbürger Jüdischen Glaubens*, 1 January 1920, 19.

13   Behind *Philo*'s work one can assume a kind of *imitatio Mosis*: the biblical Moses had previously reacted to the oppression of the Jews in Egypt by protesting to the authorities (i.e., Pharaoh); see chapter 1 in this volume.

14   "ohne Wirkung auf seine nächste Familie ... sein Neffe Tiberius Alexander fiel sogar vom Judentum ab." So cited in the reply in *Im Deutschen Reich: Zeitschrift des Centralvereins Deutscher Staatsbürger Jüdischen Glaubens*, 5 May 1920, 173.

15   Josephus, *AJ* 20.100: τοῖς γὰρ πατρίοις οὐκ ἐνέμεινεν οὗτος ἔθεσιν. In Philo's tractates *De animalibus* and *De providentia*, Tiberius Julius Alexander is his philosophical conversation partner.

16   "ohne Wirkung auf seine nächste Familie geblieben." *Im Deutschen Reich*, 5 May 1920, 173.

A LEAP INTO THE VOID   249

within Jewish nationalist circles ("nationaljüdischen Kreisen"): Philo was by
no means an assimilant. In any case, he had not "rid himself uncritically and
shamefully of his Jewish values and given in to the cultural influences of his
Alexandrian context."[17] Rather, Philo embodies the successful combination of
Jewish morality with the "worldview of Hellenism" ("Weltbild des Hellenen-
tums").

In Mayer's plea for Philo, his own Jewish-German sensitivities clearly res-
onate. He expresses his respect for Philo by means of an explicit reference to
the situation of German Jewry: "We have it easier, since there is no contradiction between our fundamental morality and that of our non-Jewish com-
patriots, insofar as they are true Christians. That which constituted work for
Philo, which he did, is for us a conceptual given."[18] Philo had it harder in the
Hellenistic world than Jews in Christian Germany. And yet Philo prevailed. In
connection with antisemitism aimed at the Jews, Mayer once again suggests a
parallel to his contemporary situation: "Just as today's Jew-haters, so also the
pagans of that time sought to portray Judaism as misanthropic."[19] To this Philo
resisted. Likewise, it was he who defended Jewish civic virtue ("Bürgertugend")
and Jewish citizenship before the Roman emperor—with the knowledge that
the political accusations aimed at the Jews were designed to "destabilize the
equality of the Jews within the Roman Empire."[20] As in the letter sent by the
young Isaac Heinemann to Ulrich von Wilamowitz, ancient Alexandria under
the Roman Empire serves as a cipher for the challenges facing Jews living
within the Weimar Republic. Philo therefore provided a twofold orientation:
he successfully combined the Jewish and the non-Jewish under difficult conditions, and he fought boldly against anti-Jewish slander. Therefore, "he is and
remains a shining example of our efforts in his struggle for honor, justice, and
truth."[21]

The *Philo-Lexikon* was a booming success right from the start. It printed
31,000 copies in four editions between 1935 and 1937.[22] In retrospect, the under-

---

17   "(sich nicht) kritik- und würdelos seiner jüdischen Werte entäußert und den kulturellen
      Einflüssen seiner alexandrinischen Umwelt hingegeben."
18   "Wir haben es leichter, denn kein Gegensatz besteht zwischen unserer sittlichen Grund-
      auffassung und der unserer nichtjüdischen Volksgenossen, soweit sie wahre Christen sind.
      Was für Philo Aufgabe war, die er vollendete, ist für uns seelische Gegebenheit."
19   "Wie unsere heutigen Judenhetzer suchten auch die Heiden der damaligen Zeit das Juden-
      tum als menschenfeindlich hinzustellen."
20   "die Gleichstellung der Juden im römischen Reiche zu erschüttern."
21   "ist und bleibt er in seinem Kampf um Ehre, Recht und Wahrheit ein leuchtendes Vorbild
      für unsere Arbeit." *c.v.-Zeitung*, 19 July 1923, 236–237.
22   Urban-Fahr, *Philo-Verlag*, 241.

250   CHAPTER 12

taking almost appears like an apocalyptic attempt to collect Jewish knowledge shortly before its imminent decline and to secure it for posterity. However, the impetus given by the publishers at the time was different: they wanted to satisfy the interests of the time by providing a comprehensive, but at the same time manageable and affordable, lexicon.[23] However, the venture was not free in its operation: the *Philo-Lexikon* developed under National Socalist censorship. Thus the article on "Aryan and Jewish Legislation" ("Arier- und Judengesetzgebung"), which was forced upon the lexicon,[24] grew in size from two columns in the first edition of 1935 to almost seven in the fourth edition of 1937. "Gentiles" ("Nichtjuden"), people of Jewish descent ("jüdischer Abstammung"), and "Anti-Semites" ("Antisemiten") are all identified in the *Lexikon* with their own abbreviations. Thus, e.g., Alexander the Great, Boccaccio, and Dante are marked as non-Jews. The fact that the editors included entries like these also reflects on the self-understanding of the *Lexikon*: Jews are presented as an integral component of *Weltkultur*. The empire of Alexander the Great encompassed "the majority of Judaism at that time," Boccaccio "in the *Decameron* (1.3) explains the parable of the ring known from Lessing," and Dante Alighieri is said to be "imitated several times in Hebrew literature."[25] Even more important to the *Lexikon* is the Jewish contribution to science, culture, and politics. This is underlined with long lists of names, for example in the entries on "Inventors and Discoverers" ("Erfinder und Entdecker"), "Nobel Laureates" ("Nobelpreisträger"), or "Translators" ("Übersetzer"). The latter article demonstrates how, regarding many classics of world literature, Jews "den Weg zum deutschen

---

23   Otto Neuburger, "Rund um ein Lexikon," in *Der Morgen: Monatsschrift der Juden in Deutschland*, December 1934, 414–417: "Fragt man nach den Gründen, so liegt die Antwort auf der Hand: Unsere Zeit ist jüdischem Wissen so aufgeschlossen wie kaum eine andere zuvor [sic!]. Eine Unzahl von Menschen drängt danach, sich über Gebiete, die ihr bisher mehr oder weniger fremd und uninteressant waren, rasch und zuverlässig zu orientieren. Auf der Suche nach einem Hilfsmittel standen ihr bisher nur umfangreiche Werke zur Verfügung: einmal die 'Encyclopaedia Judaica,' von der die Buchstaben A bis L bisher in 10 Bänden vorliegen, und dann das fünf bändige 'Jüdische Lexikon;' beides sind große, doch auch teure und anspruchsvolle Werke, die weder zur Massenverbreitung bestimmt noch zur Massenwirkung geeignet waren" (414). The seizure of power by National Socialism was not the reason behind the enterprise: "Es wäre aber falsch zu glauben, daß die an sich naheliegende Idee eines jüdischen „Knaur" ihr Entstehen erst den Ereignissen des Jahres 1933 zu verdanken habe" (414–415).

24   See the foreword by Susanne Urban-Fahr, *Philo-Atlas: Handbuch für die jüdische Auswanderung: Reprint der Ausgabe von 1938 mit einem Vorwort* (Bodenheim b. Mainz: Philo-Verlag, 1998), 28–29; Braun, *Philo Verlag*, 100.

25   "den größten Teil der damaligen Judenheit ... [Boccaccio] erzählt im Dekameron (1, 3) die durch Lessing bekannte Ringparabel ... [Dante] in der hebräischen Literatur mehrfach nachgeahmt." *Philo-Lexikon*, 14, 102, 143.

A LEAP INTO THE VOID 251

Leser vermittelt haben."[26] The Jewish nation is described as a nation of culture; it is said that Jewish illiterates hardly ever existed:

> Illiterates: those unable to read and write, are and were rare among the Jews; just as knowledge of the Holy Scripture was taken for granted in Jewish antiquity, so also later on was knowledge of the national language and script.[27]

Jewish antiquity is well-represented in the *Philo-Lexikon*. In spite of the *Lexikon*'s conciseness, marginal themes are included, for which one would look in some later encyclopedias in vain: attention is given to the Jewish-Hellenistic Ezekiel the Tragedian, author of an exodus tragedy, as well as numerous aspects of ancient Jewish magic (one finds entries on "Abracadabera," "Abraxas," "Amulett," "Aschmedai," "Dämonen").[28] At the time when the *Lexikon* was being drafted, the surprising discovery of the synagogue frescoes at Dura Europos in Syria (1932), which challenged the idea of an aniconic Judaism, was still fresh. With two pictures, the articles on "Dura Europos" and "wall painting" ("Wandmalerei") refer to the "recently discovered frescoes" ("vor kurzem entdeckten Fresken"), whose art historical evaluation ("kunstgeschichtliche Auswertung") has yet to be completed.[29] Bold, but representative of the self-understanding of the *Philo-Lexikon*, is the short entry on Athens ("Athen"), which "as the spiritual centerpoint of the ancient world" is said to have had "connections with Palestinian Judaism already in antiquity."[30] In reality, the contact suggested here between classical Athens and Jerusalem hardly existed. Such entries sometimes sound like a desperate cry in difficult times and the reminder of a long-standing Jewish-German synthesis. The entry on "Hellenismus," quite detailed for the brevity of the *Lexikon*, first mentions the heterogeneity of Hellenistic influence and, for Palestine, its negative consequences. Towards the end of the article, however, it emphasizes the cultural enrichment that Hellenism brought to the Jewish diaspora. The entry concludes with the name of Philo. As alphabetic luck would have it, the entry on "Hellenismus" is separated from that on "Heinemann, Isaak" only by that on "Heirat" (marriage):

---

26   *Philo-Lexikon*, 179–180, 512, 771.
27   "Analphabeten: Schreibens und Lesens Unkundige, sind und waren unter Juden selten; wie Kenntnis der heiligen Schrift im jüdischen Altertum selbstverständlich war, so später Kenntnis der Landessprache und -schrift." *Philo-Lexikon*, 24–25.
28   *Philo-Lexikon*, 3–4, 24, 51, 142.
29   *Philo-Lexikon*, 163–164, 793.
30   "als geistiger Mittelpunkt der antiken Welt ... schon im Altertum Beziehungen zum palästinischen Judentum." *Philo-Lexikon*, 55.

252   CHAPTER 12

Hellenism. Designation for the particular cultural mixture influenced by
Greece and certain oriental influences which took hold in the Mediterranean since around the time of Alexander the Great; predominated until
the triumph of Christianity and had an equalizing, often destructive and
very often (at least artistically) enriching effect on popular cultures. At
first, the destructive effects won out within Palestinian Judaism .... But
there also exists a self-confident, enthusiastically promotional "Hellenistic Judaism." It applies Greek literary forms (drama, epic, rhetoric, historiography) to Jewish history and seeks a synthesis between a biblical
worldview and a Greek worldview by allegorizing teachings and commandments (circumcision = the curtailing of living by base instincts) and
by scientifically undergirding and formulating the ethical monotheism of
the Bible (Philo).[31]

In addition to the *Philo-Lexikon*, the Philo Verlag published two other lexica:
the *Philo Zitaten-Lexikon* in 1936 (with the subtitle *Worte von Juden—Worte für
Juden*) and the *Philo-Atlas: Handbuch für die jüdische Auswanderung* in 1938.[32]
The former exhibits a self-understanding similar to that of the *Philo-Lexikon*:
there, in a generic context more edifying than that of a lexicon, Jewish cultural achievement is brought to light. The first clause of the subtitle—"Jewish
Words" ("Worte von Juden")—signals the intention of the collection: namely,
to present the Jewish contribution to the common German vocabulary.[33] The
collection was likewise understood as a supplement to Georg Büchmann's vol-

---

31   "Hellenismus. Bezeichnung der durch das Griechentum, daneben durch orientalische
      Einflüsse bestimmten Mischkultur, die etwa seit Alexander dem Großen die Mittelmeer-
      länder ergriff, sich bis zum Sieg des Christentums behauptete und auf die Volkskul-
      turen nivellierend, oft zerstörend, vielfach (zumal künstlerisch) bereichernd gewirkt hat.
      Im palästinischen Judentum überwogen anfangs die zerstörenden Wirkungen .... Aber
      es entsteht auch ein selbstsicheres, werbefreudiges „hellenistisches Judentum". Es wen-
      det griechische Literatur-Formen (Drama, Epos, Rhetorik, Geschichtsschreibung) auf die
      jüdische Geschichte an und sucht eine Synthese zwischen biblischer und griechischer
      Weltanschauung, indem es Erzählungen und Gebote allegorisiert (Beschneidung = Ein-
      schränkung des Trieblebens) und den ethischen Monotheismus der Bibel wissenschaft-
      lich unterbaut und formuliert (Philo)." *Philo-Lexikon*, 286–287.
32   Ernst Fränkel, *Philo Zitaten-Lexikon: Worte von Juden—Worte für Juden* (Berlin: Philo Ver-
      lag, 1936). The historian Ernst Fränkel (1891–1971) completed the work begun by Eugen
      Tannenbaum (1890–1936) after the latter's death. Ernst G. Löwenthal and Hans Oppen-
      heimer, eds., *Philo-Atlas: Handbuch für die jüdische Auswanderung* (Berlin: Philo Verlag,
      1938).
33   See Fränkel, *Philo Zitaten-Lexikon*, 7: "Manches dieser Worte gehört zum Bestand des all-
      gemeinen Sprachgutes."

A LEAP INTO THE VOID 253

ume on "winged words," *Geflügelte Worte*; this work, which was published in
many editions, receives explicit mention in the *Philo-Zitaten-Lexikon*. Most
recently, however, Büchmann's book had appeared without cited Jewish quotations.[34] Remarkably, the *Philo Zitaten-Lexikon* also contains a section "Aus
der jüdisch-hellenistischen Literatur" containing eleven quotations from the
oeuvre of Philo of Alexandria: four from his treatise *On the Virtues* (*De vir-
tutibus* 147, 177, 187, 194), three from that *On the Special Laws* (*De specialibus
legibus* 2.69, 259; 4.73), and one each from his tractates *On the Creation of the
World* (*De opificio mundi* 146), *On the Sacrifices of Cain and Abel* (*De sacrificiis
Abelis et Caini* 41), *On Allegorical Interpretation* (*Legum allegoriae* 3.137), and
On the Decalogue (*De decalogo* 5). This selection of quotations appears somewhat arbitrary, and none of the passages cited are likely to have been known
to the broader reading public. But they do provide a brief insight into Philonic
thinking, from that which concerns the spiritual relationship of man with God
(*Opif.* 146: "Every man, in respect of his mind, is allied to the divine Reason")
to the fundamental freedom of human beings (*Spec.* 2.69: "no man is naturally
a slave"). Philo of Alexandria apparently had some place within the German
Jewry of the 1930s, not only as a namesake and reference, but also as a Jewish-
Hellenistic author.

The *Philo-Atlas*, published two years after the *Philo Zitaten-Lexikon*, was the
last book to be published by a Jewish publisher in Germany. It had only one
goal: to be a guidepost out of Germany toward a better world. By 1938, the legal
situation of German Jews had worsened. The assumption of a German-Jewish
symbiosis, still present in the *Philo-Lexikon*, now seemed very far off. Jewish-
German Hellenism was nearing the ends of its course. Symptomatic of this was
an article on the history of the Jewish diaspora which appeared in two parts
in the October 27 and November 3 issues of the *c.v.-Zeitung*.[35] The author of
this article, entitled "Sprungbretter der Diaspora" ("Springboards of the Diaspora"), was journalist and teacher Fritz Friedländer (1901–1980), who had also
contributed to the *Philo-Lexikon*. Based on the "current diaspora" ("aktuellen
Diaspora") of his time, Friedländer identified a link to the Jewish-Hellenistic
diaspora: the world-change of Hellenism had also been a blessing for the Jews.
In that context an equally enlightened Judaism, allegorically reading its own
tradition, was able to develop: "the Grecizing sentiments of a seemingly 'modern' reformed Judaism were a springboard for the existence of the diaspora

---

34   Fränkel, *Philo Zitaten-Lexikon*, 11: "Die Auflage von 1935 konnte nicht herangezogen wer-
     den, da sie die Namen jüdischer Autoren im Textteil nicht mehr enthält."
35   *c.v.-Zeitung*, 27 October 1938, 1; *c.v.-Zeitung*, 3 November 1938, 2.

within a unified Hellenistic culture."[36] And Philo of Alexandria was "in thought and personality the characteristic paradigm of this diaspora."[37] This (modern, ancient) Judaism was also attractive to the non-Jewish world. Proselytes found their way into the upper echelons of the imperial court. While Friedländer's presentation is not per se wrong, it is clearly influenced by his own Jewish-German self-image. Alexandria appears to the Jews like an ancient version of Berlin. At both places the diaspora came to a standstill because the Jews had found their place in society. However, this happened only just for some time, both in Berlin and in Alexandria. After all, according to Friedländer, the Jewish diaspora of antiquity had become "a victim of its allegiance to Judaism" ("ein Opfer ihrer Treue zum Judentum"). Refusal to participate in the imperial cult and an attachment to "Anders-sein"—ultimately the "inability to give to Hellenism what Hellenism demands"—led to conflict.[38] At the time when Friedländer wrote his article, the "quiet rest of emancipation ("Ruhepause der Emanzipation")[39] in Germany had come to an end"—emigration remained as the only option for Jews. Jewish Hellenism failed in the same way: "Hellenism was certainly a springboard for the diaspora; but as soon as convergence with an alien world threatened to make it abandon itself, it became a leap into the void."[40] What looked at first to be an exciting leap turned out to be just another example of movement within an intermittent diasporic trajectory, "a leap into the void." And this, the recurrent transience of the Jewish diaspora, was—as Friedländer pointed out—the "common thread" ("der rote Faden") of Jewish history.[41] Friedländer's article was supposed to have continued in later editions of the newspaper: further installments were planned to deal with the Jewish diaspora on the Iberian Peninsula, in the Slavic east, and finally its new form overseas.[42] But that did not happen. The November 3, 1938 issue of the *c.v.-Zeitung* was the last ever to appear. A week later, on November 10, 1938, the Gestapo also closed the Philo-Verlag. Fritz Friedländer, after a temporary deten-

---

36 "Die gräzisierenden Stimmungen eines sich 'modern' dünkenden Reformjudentums waren ein Sprungbrett zu der Diaspora-Existenz in der hellenistischen Einheitskultur."

37 "als Denker und Persönlichkeit das charakteristische Paradigma dieser Diaspora." *c.v.-Zeitung*, 3 November 1938, 2.

38 "Unmöglichkeit, dem Hellenismus zu geben, was des Hellenismus ist." *c.v.-Zeitung*, 3 November 1938, 2.

39 *c.v.-Zeitung*, 27 October 1938, 1.

40 "Der Hellenismus war gewiß ein Sprungbrett zur Diaspora; aber es war, sobald durch die Annäherung an die fremde Welt eine Preisgabe der eigenen drohte, ein Sprung ins Leere." *c.v.-Zeitung*, 3 November 1938, 2.

41 *c.v.-Zeitung*, 27 October 1938, 1.

42 *c.v.-Zeitung*, 3 November 1938, 2.

A LEAP INTO THE VOID   255

tion in the Sachsenhausen Concentration Camp in 1939, managed to emigrate to China (Shanghai) and then to Australia in 1946.[43]

Thirty years after the fourth edition of the *Philo-Lexikon*, under the direction of one of its former publishers, John F. (Hans) Oppenheimer, the *Lexikon des Judentums* appeared.[44] Its goal was "following the former paradigm in the form of one compendious volume yet without intellectual censorship, to instruct the modern reader anew, in the German language, about Judaism."[45] The new *Lexikon* was significantly more extensive than the *Philo-Lexikon*, while integrating many entries from its predecessor. The entry on "Philo of Alexandria" appeared again, unchanged, in the 1967 edition.[46] However, the optimistic vision of a Jewish-German Hellenism, represented by that entry, had long since lost its context.

Bibliography

Barbian, Jan-Pieter, *Literaturpolitik im NS-Staat: Von der "Gleichschaltung" bis zum Ruin*. Frankfurt am Main: Fischer, 2010.

Braun, Helmuth F., "Der Philo Verlag (1919–1938): Ein Berliner Verlag für jüdische Abwehr- und Aufklärungsliteratur." *Berlinische Notizen: Zeitschrift des Vereins der Freunde und Förderer des Berliner Museums e.V.* 4 (1987): 90–103.

Dahm, Volker, *Das jüdische Buch im Dritten Reich: Zweite, überarbeitete Auflage*. München: C.H. Beck, 1993.

Fränkel, Ernst, *Philo Zitaten-Lexikon: Worte von Juden—Worte für Juden*. Berlin: Philo Verlag, 1936.

Gorion, Emanuel Bin, Alfred Loewenberg, Otto Neuburger, and Hans Oppenheimer, eds., *Philo-Lexikon: Handbuch des jüdischen Wissens: Mit 250 Abbildungen, zahlreichen Plänen, Tabellen und Übersichten sowie 40 zum Teil mehrfarbigen Tafeln und Karten—Vierte vermehrte und verbesserte Auflage*. Berlin: Philo-Verlag, 1937.

---

43   See the "Fritz Friedländer Collection" at the Leo Baeck Institute: http://findingaids.cjh.org/ ?pID=403515.

44   John F. Oppenheimer et al., eds., *Lexikon des Judentums* (Gütersloh: C. Bertelsmann, 1967).

45   "nach dem damaligen Vorbild in der durch Beschränkung auf einen Band gedrängten Form, aber ohne geistige Zensurfesseln, den heutigen Lesern in deutscher Sprache aufs neue über das Judentum zu unterrichten." *Lexikon des Judentums*, preface.

46   *Lexikon des Judentums*, 623. The name of what is today the "Philo Fine Arts" Publisher, based in Hamburg, goes back to the Berlin-based Judaica Publisher "Philo," which is not a formal successor to the former Philo-Verlag: see http://www.philo-fine-arts.de/verlag .html.

Heinemann, Isaak, "Philo." Pages 907–910 in *Jüdisches Lexikon: Ein enzyklopaedisches Handbuch des jüdischen Wissens*. Volume 4.1. Edited by Georg Herlitz and Bruno Kirschner. Berlin: Jüdischer Verlag, 1927.

Heinemann, Isaak, *Philons griechische und jüdische Bildung: Kulturvergleichende Untersuchungen zu Philons Darstellung der jüdischen Gesetze*. Breslau 1929–1932.

Heinemann, Isaak, "Antisemitismus." Pages 3–43 in *Paulys Realencyclopädie der Classischen Altertumswissenschaft* (RE). Supplementband 5. Edited by Georg Wissowa and Wilhelm Kroll. Stuttgart: Metzler, 1931.

Heuer, Renate, comp., *Archiv Bibliographia Judaica: Lexikon deutsch-jüdischer Autoren, Band 11: Hein-Hirs*. München: K.G. Saur, 2002.

Heuer, Renate, comp., *Archiv Bibliographia Judaica: Lexikon deutsch-jüdischer Autoren, Band 18: Phil—Samu*. Berlin: De Gruyter, 2010.

Hoffmann, Christhard, "Antiker Völkerhass und moderner Rassenhass: Heinemann an Wilamowitz." *Quaderni di Storia* 25 (1987): 145–157.

Hoffmann, Christhard, *Juden und Judentum im Werk deutscher Althistoriker des 19. und 20. Jahrhunderts*. Leiden: Brill 1988.

Hoffmann, Christhard and Adam Kamesar, "Wilamowitz and Heinemann II: Three Letters from the 1920s." *Illinois Classical Studies* 31/32 (2006–2007): 130–144.

Löwenthal, Ernst G. and Hans Oppenheimer, eds., *Philo-Atlas: Handbuch für die jüdische Auswanderung*. Berlin: Philo Verlag, 1938.

Neuburger, Otto, "Rund um ein Lexikon." *Der Morgen: Monatsschrift der Juden in Deutschland*, December 1934: 414–417.

Oppenheimer, John F., et al., eds., *Lexikon des Judentums*. Gütersloh: C. Bertelsmann, 1967.

Urban-Fahr, Susanne, *Philo-Atlas: Handbuch für die jüdische Auswanderung: Reprint der Ausgabe von 1938 mit einem Vorwort*. Bodenheim b. Mainz: Philo-Verlag, 1998.

Urban-Fahr, Susanne, *Der Philo-Verlag 1919–1938: Abwehr und Selbstbehauptung*. Hildesheim: Georg Olms, 2001.

CHAPTER 13

Tacitus's Excursus on the Jews through the Ages: An Overview of its Reception History

Auguror (nec me fallit augurium) historias tuas immortalis futuras
PLINY, *Ep.* 7.33.1

∴

The complete works of the Roman historian Publius Cornelius Tacitus have, in recent decades, been repeatedly examined for the process of their reception at particular times and in particular places and Stefan Borzsák's 'research call' on this topic, issued a good 30 years ago, is probably now somewhat behind the times.*[1] So far, however, no examination has been forthcoming of the reception of the Jewish excursus.[2] These twelve chapters have had enormous influence

---

* [The editor (Rhiannon Ash) comments: I am extremely grateful to David Ash for translating this extract from Bloch's book. Some of the longer quotations in French, German, and Italian have been cut from Bloch's original footnotes, but where quotations have been retained, they have generally been translated into English.]

1 Stefan Borzsák, "Tacitus," in *RE Supplementband* 11: 373–512, at 509: "The need to investigate the survival record of Tacitus—as well as of Virgil, Horace, etc.—should rank high on the list of *desiderata*." Among the more important recent studies may be mentioned Kenneth C. Schellhase, *Tacitus in Renaissance Political Thought* (Chicago: The University of Chicago Press, 1976); Catherine Volpilhac-Auger, *Tacite et Montesquieu* (Oxford: Oxford University Press, 1985); Raymond Chevallier and Rémy Poignault, eds., *Actes du colloque Présence de Tacite: Hommage à G. Radke* (Tours: University of Tours, 1992); Catherine Volpilhac-Auger, *Tacite en France de Montesquieu à Chateaubriand* (Oxford: Oxford University Press, 1993); Torrey J. Luce and Anthony J. Woodman, eds., *Tacitus and the Tacitean Tradition* (Princeton: Princeton University Press, 1993); Ronald Mellor, *Tacitus: The Classical Heritage* (New York: Garland, 1995). Lastly, on the reception of the *Germania*, see Allan A. Lund, *Germanenideologie im Nationalsozialismus: zur Rezeption der 'Germania' des Tacitus im 'Dritten Reich'* (Heidelberg: Winter, 1995).

2 Walter Schmitthenner, "Kennt die hellenistisch-römische Antike eine 'Judenfrage'?" in Bernd Martin and Ernst Schulin, eds., *Die Juden als Minderheit in der Geschichte* (Munich: Deutscher Taschenbuch-Verlag, 1981), 9–29, at 27 has already drawn attention to this *desideratum*: "The profound effect produced by this portrayal of the Jews by Tacitus in particular and by other

---

© RENÉ BLOCH, 2022 | DOI:10.1163/9789004521896_015

258   CHAPTER 13

ever since the late classical period, are consistently referred to, and have even
had something of a collateral effect on the reception of the entire Tacitean
oeuvre. The entire palette of reception possibilities has been deployed in the
process: sober commentaries alongside militant pamphlets, protests about the
Tacitean portrayal of the Jews, attempted rebuttal or even enthusiastic appropriation of its sometimes invidious propositions. In the following study, these
kinds of reactions and (where possible) their background in intellectual history
will be traced in broadly chronological order. As with all studies of the reception of ancient authors, completeness can never be the aim.

1   Pagan Reception and Tertullian's Critique

A pagan reception of Tacitus's works is discernible only with difficulty.[3] Certainly, the work of Senator Tacitus must have found an interested readership in
senatorial circles, and his correspondence with his younger contemporary and
friend Pliny the Younger indicates that Tacitus's work indeed enjoyed reception during his lifetime.[4] But his difficult Latin acted even in ancient times as
a barrier to wider reception, and for that reason Tacitus "in no way [took] the
place to which he might have laid claim."[5] In the few and sometimes heavily
disputed Greek and Roman responses to Tacitus, no trace of the Jewish excursus can be detected. Ammianus Marcellinus seems to have allowed himself to
be inspired stylistically and intellectually by Tacitus, but in the four passages
of his historical work in which he deals with Judea and the Jews, no Tacitean
influence can be established.[6] So all that may be said about this first phase of

---

  classical authors since the revival of classical antiquity has not to my knowledge been studied
  in any cohesive fashion."

3 For Tacitus's reception in ancient times, cf. the early studies by Emmerich Cornelius, *Quomodo Tacitus, Historiarum Scriptor, in Hominum Memoria Versatus Sit ad Renascentes Litteras
  Saeculis XIV et XV* (Wetzlar: Nabu, 1888), Philippe Fabia, *Les sources de Tacite dans les Histoires
  et les Annales* (Paris: Imprimerie Nationale, 1895), and Francis Haverfield, "Tacitus during the
  Late Roman Period and the Middle Ages," *JRS* 6 (1916): 196–201.

4 Fabia, *Les sources de Tacite*, 2. Cf. Pliny, *Ep.* 1.6; 6.16, 20; 7.20.

5 Martin Schanz and Carl Hosius, *Geschichte der römischen Literatur bis zum Gesetzgebungswerk des Kaisers Justinian* (Munich: C.H. Beck, 1935), 639. Fabia, *Les sources de Tacite*, 10: "If
  we maintain that the fashion for Tacitus was considerable, we acknowledge that it was brief."

6 Ammianus 14.8.11–12; 22.5.4–5; 23.1.2–3; 24.4.1–2. Conspicuously absent from Ammianus's
  description of Judea (14.8.11–12) are lists of the distinguishing features of Judaic geography
  such as balsam, the Dead Sea, etc. Nor is Ammianus referring back to Tacitus when he
  describes in polemical tones Marcus Aurelius's alleged aversion to the Jews in: 22.5.5: *Ille* [sc.

TACITUS'S EXCURSUS ON THE JEWS THROUGH THE AGES 259

Tacitus's reception, among pagan authors, is that few traces can be found, none of them involves the Jewish excursus.

The oldest and most significant reference to Tacitus's Jewish excursus is that by Tertullian in his *Apologeticus* (197 CE). Tertullian alludes to Tacitus's description of the exodus, especially the episode of the wild asses which were said to have led Moses to abundant sources of water (*Hist.* 5.3.2), and the corresponding worship by the Jews of the image of an ass (*Hist.* 5.4.2). Tertullian reckons that with this story Tacitus opened up the Christians, through their relationship to the Jews (*Iudaicae religionis propinquos*, "associates of the Jewish religion," *Apol.* 16.3), to the suspicion that they worshipped an ass's head. Tertullian argues, moreover, that Tacitus directly contradicts himself on this point, because in the same historical work (*Hist.* 5.9.1) he reports that Pompey on entering the temple found *no* images of gods.[7] On the strength of this contradiction, Tertullian derides Tacitus as *sane ille mendaciorum loquacissimus* ("to be sure, that most eloquent of liars," *Apol.* 16.3).[8]

The (indirect) reception of Tacitus's Jewish excursus has been strongly influenced by this critique of Tertullian's. His derisive comment has echoed down the centuries. His critique is above all a Christian one: besides the contradictory information about the Jews' form of worship, Tacitus's work could have offered up many another contradiction for criticism. On just the same topic—religious ceremony without images—Tacitus reports in the *Germania* that the Germanic tribes did not model their gods on the human form (*Germ.* 9.2). This statement

---

Marcus Aurelius] *enim cum Palaestinam transiret Aegyptum petens, Iudaeorum faetentium et tumultuantium saepe taedio percitus*, "For Marcus Aurelius, as he was passing through Palestine heading for Egypt, often being disgusted with the foul-smelling and troublesome Jews."

7   Tertullian, *Apol.* 16.1–3 (cf. also the parallel passage, Tertullian, *Nat.* 1.11.2; the two passages are completely identical in content and virtually so in their language). Surprisingly, Tertullian shows no interest at all in the passage where Tacitus, in his discussion of Jewish monotheism, states that there were no images of gods in Jewish temples (*Hist.* 5.5.4). This passage would have bolstered Tertullian's argument by making the contradiction even more apparent.

8   Tertullian does not quote Tacitus accurately; in particular he misses the fact that Tacitus does not speak of an ass's *head*, but refers less specifically to an *image* of an ass (*Hist.* 5.4.2: *effigiem animalis, quo monstrante errorem sitimque depulerant, penetrali sacravere*, "In the innermost part of the temple, they dedicated an image of the animal who had guided them and ended their wandering and thirst"). Such imprecision is found in many later recipients, directly or indirectly linked to Tertullian. There are two probable reasons for Tertullian's lack of precision: firstly, he is thinking predominantly of reproaches made against the *Christians* of worshipping the *head* of an ass (cf. Tertullian, *Nat.* 1.14–15; Minucius Felix, *Oct.* 9.3 [Caecilius' criticism of Christianity]). Secondly, there does exist a reproach of *Jewish* worship of an ass's head: Flavius Josephus mentions an assertion by Apion that the Jews had worshipped an ass's head at the time of Antiochus Epiphanes (Josephus, *CA* 2.80). Tertullian may have known this passage from Josephus (*Apol.* 19.6 quotes Josephus's *CA*).

260   CHAPTER 13

stands in contradiction to the description of the Nerthus festival, involving the washing of this goddess (*Germ.* 40). It is clear from this just how decisive it was for the early reception of this chapter of Tacitus that he had expressed himself on the Jews and thus—in the eyes of Christian authors such as Tertullian— on the Christians also. The Christian reception, as will become even clearer in what follows, played a large role in determining the effect made by the Jewish excursus.[9]

Tertullian's comments are significant in another respect. Beatus Rhenanus noticed that Tertullian referred to the fifth book of the *Histories*, whereas the numbering at that time listed the Jewish excursus as the twenty-first book of Tacitus's work. It also occurred to Rhenanus that there was a gap between Books 16 and 17. From this, Justus Lipsius drew the conclusion that the text must constitute two different works: sixteen books of *Annals* and five books of *Histories*.[10] So this allocation of the books arose from an observation of Tertullian's comment about the relevant passage on the Jewish excursus. Also important in this regard is a passage in Jerome's commentary on Zachariah, which refers to Tacitus's account of the fall of Jerusalem and gives the size of Tacitus's complete historical work (*Annals* and *Histories*) as thirty books.[11] Here too it is apparent that the reception of the Jewish excursus played an important role in the manuscript tradition of Tacitus's collected output.

2   Sulpicius Severus, Orosius, and Pseudo-Hegesippus

Tacitus's account of the Jewish-Roman War was accorded its first more or less detailed reception by the Christian historiographers Pseudo-Hegesippus, Sulpicius Severus and Orosius, for whom Tacitus was a welcome source for their

---

9   Tertullian makes use of the Jewish excursus in other places also. In his discussion of the Roman god Saturn (*Nat.* 2.12), he refers to Tacitus's mention of this god at *Hist.* 5.4.4 in the context of his remarks about the Sabbath. Elsewhere Tertullian describes the burnt region of Sodom and Gomorrah in terms which recall those of Tacitus: compare Tertullian, *Apol.* 40.7 with Tacitus, *Hist.* 5.7.1. It is noteworthy that Tertullian, in his *Adversus Iudaeos*, does not appear to refer to the aggressive language of Tacitus's Jewish excursus.

10   Else-Lilly Etter, *Tacitus in der Geistesgeschichte des 16. und 17. Jahrhunderts* (Basel: Helbing & Lichtenhahn, 1966), 29–30.

11   Jerome, *Comm. in Zach.* 3.14: *Cornelius quoque Tacitus, qui post Augustum usque ad mortem Domitiani Vitas Caesarum triginta uoluminibus exaravit* ("Cornelius Tacitus, who set down in thirty books the Lives of the Caesars after Augustus all the way to Domitian's death"). Whether Jerome actually read Tacitus is questionable: cf. Timothy D. Barnes, *Tertullian: A Historical and Literary Study* (Oxford: Oxford University Press, 1985), 200.

TACITUS'S EXCURSUS ON THE JEWS THROUGH THE AGES 261

literary retelling of the war. I have previously treated Severus and Orosius more fully in connection with the reconstruction of the lost narrative of Tacitus.[12] It is highly important for the reception of Tacitus in general and the Jewish excursus in particular that Orosius was so commonly read in the Middle Ages, at a time when Tacitus's reception seems to have been largely at a standstill. Thus the Jewish excursus remained known even in the 'dark' years of Tacitus's reception.

Pseudo-Hegesippus, the (unknown) author of a work called *On the Destruction of Jerusalem* (*De Excidio Hierosolymitano*), written around 370 CE, produced a Latin history of the Jewish War in five books. Even if it is not an actual translation of the *Bellum Judaicum* of Flavius Josephus, Hegesippus quite clearly followed the Flavian historian. Josephus was not his only source, however: he also used pagan Roman authors, including Tacitus. In particular he draws on the geographical chapters of Tacitus's Jewish excursus (*Hist.* 5.6–7).[13] The passages which depend on Tacitus are not always paraphrased consistently: Pseudo-Hegesippus's description of the burnt-out region of Sodom and Gomorrah owes much to Tacitus, but in contrast to Tacitus, who gives a rational interpretation of the region's destruction, Pseudo-Hegesippus adopts the biblical explanation.[14] Like Sulpicius Severus and Orosius (and also Jerome[15]), Pseudo-Hegesippus supplements the information he takes from Josephus with material from the *Histories* of Tacitus.[16] Pseudo-Hegesippus distances himself from Josephus in that he interprets the destruction of the temple of Jerusalem, in an anti-Jewish reversal of Josephus's critical Jewish insider's account, as a punishment for the perfidy of the Jews and the killing of Jesus.[17] It is worth noting that this undisguised anti-Jewish sentiment is not fuelled by any Tacitean arguments or expressions. Striking and explicit evidence of the early reception

---

12   See René Bloch, *Antike Vorstellungen vom Judentum: Der Judenexkurs des Tacitus im Rahmen der griechisch-römischen Ethnographie* (Stuttgart: Franz Steiner, 2002), 116–119.

13   Tacitus, *Hist.* 5.6.1: *septemtrionem e latere Syriae longe prospectant*; Ps-Heg. 3.6: *septentrionalia eius a dextero latere Tyrus claudit.*

14   Ps-Hegesippus 4.18 (on Sodom and Gomorrah): *haec propter impiorum supplicia de Sodomitano territorio conperta silentio obducere non oportuit* ("just because of the punishments inflicted on the wicked, one should not conceal in silence these things which have been discovered about the territory of Sodom"). Cf. Tacitus, *Hist.* 5.7.2.

15   Cf. note 11 above.

16   Cornelius, *Quomodo Tacitus*, 26: "Besides, in several places Hegesippus adds various words drawn from the books of Tacitus to the words of Josephus." This is especially clear at Ps-Hegesippus 4.18, where he combines Josephus, *BJ* 4.476 with Tacitus, *Hist.* 5.6.2.

17   Cf. Esther Sorscher, "A Comparison of Three Texts: The Wars, the Hegesippus, and the Yosippon" (MA Thesis, Yeshiva University, New York, NY, 1973) on this point.

262 CHAPTER 13

of Tacitus is provided by a *scholion* on Juvenal (ca. 400 CE?).[18] It relates to an extended section of *Satire* 14.96–106, which mentions amongst other things Jewish law said to have been handed down by Moses in some kind of secret book.[19] At the word "Moses" the scholiast has noted that this may be a priest or king of the Jews, or—and here he relies on Tacitus's Jewish excursus—the "founder of their religion" (*inventor religionis*).[20] So here the Jewish excursus is used as an aid to understanding (who was Moses?).[21]

Summing up, one can say that the early Christian reception of Tacitus is in a large part a reception of the Jewish excursus. The perspective of this reception is a distinctly Christian one: for Tertullian, the contradiction which he detected in Tacitus's presentation of Jewish monotheism is a convenient example of the false ideas spread by the heathens about the Christians. Similarly, Orosius refers repeatedly to Tacitus in order to illustrate, on the basis of his handling of Israelite history, the arbitrariness with which pagan historians presented biblical history. Sulpicius Severus, on the other hand, uses Tacitus in accordance with his purpose of convincing 'unbelievers' of Christianity also by taking pagan sources into account.[22] For Jerome, finally, Tacitus's description of the capture of Jerusalem is an illustration of the veracity of Zachariah's prophesy. These authors name or use Tacitus 'on the coat-tails,' so to speak, of Josephus: Tacitus is used as an ancillary (and occasionally contradictory) source for what in the first instance is reported by Josephus. In none of the authors covered can any recourse be demonstrated to the sometimes invidious language of the Jewish excursus (*Hist.* 5.4–5). Tacitus's anti-Jewish formulations in these passages are neither adopted nor criticized by their recipients. Tertul-

---

18   Paul Wessner, ed., *Scholia in Iuvenalem Vetustiora* (Leipzig: Teubner, 1931), 215 on Juvenal, *Sat.* 14.102: [*Volumine*] *Moyses: sacerdos vel rex eius gentis. aut ipsius quidem religionis inventor, cuius Cornelius etiam Tacitus* (*Hist.* 5.3) *meminit* ("[In a book] Moses: priest or king of that people; or indeed the founder of that religion itself, as Cornelius Tacitus also says").

19   Juvenal, *Sat.* 14.102.

20   The scholiast therefore can be connected with Tacitus, *Hist.* 5.4.1: *Moyses quo sibi in posterum gentem firmaret, novos ritus contrariosque ceteris mortalibus indidit* ("In order to strengthen the bond with his people in the future, Moses prescribed for them novel religious rites which were quite different from those practiced by other mortals").

21   It has been mooted that the Juvenal scholiast knew Tacitus only indirectly, via Orosius; see Gavin B. Townend, "The Earliest Scholiast on Juvenal," *ClQ* 22 (1972): 376–387. The Juvenal scholion then cannot have been written before 400 CE. Militating against any earlier dating are, among other things, the many obvious factual errors which no contemporary of Juvenal would have made; cf. Wessner, *Scholia*, xxxviii and Theodor Mommsen, "Cornelius Tacitus und Cluvius Rufus," *Hermes* 4 (1870): 295–325.

22   Cf. Bloch, *Antike Vorstellungen*, 116–117.

lian's harsh critique is concerned with Tacitus's inconsistency and the reproach made (by others) against the *Christians* of worshipping an ass's head.

For the wider reception history of the Jewish excursus it is significant that, through the use made of it by Christian authors, parts of it became accessible even to readers who did not read Tacitus, especially in the Middle Ages.

3   Budé's Reproach and the First Commentaries on the *Histories*

During the Middle Ages, the reception of Tacitus's writings can be brought to light only with great difficulty.[23] Tacitus seems to have fallen almost entirely into obscurity, so that from the seventh to the fourteenth centuries only isolated traces of his reception can be shown. Of course, parts of the Jewish excursus did remain known, thanks to the rejoinders of Tertullian, Pseudo-Hegesippus and Orosius. Alongside the actual reception of Tacitus, there emerged quite early on an indirect one which, given the strong resonance of the works of these Christian authors, is not to be underestimated.[24]

The fifteenth and sixteenth centuries finally saw the rediscovery of Tacitus, and gradually even a veritable Tacitus renaissance.[25] In completely different contexts, the Jewish excursus was now being referred to once more.[26] However, this renaissance was soon to be faced with a new derogatory judgment

---

23   See on this point Francis Haverfield, "Tacitus during the Late Roman Period and the Middle Ages," *JRS* 6 (1916): 196–201 and Mary F. Tenney, "Tacitus in the Middle Ages and in England to about 1650," (PhD Dissertation, Cornell University, Ithaca, NY, 1931).

24   So in the ninth century, the chronicler Freculph, Bishop of Lisieux, is seemingly able to quote Tacitus's version of the Exodus in his own description. In fact, he is citing Orosius, *Hist.* 1.10.3!

25   Cf. here Etter, *Tacitus in der Geistesgeschichte* and Schellhase, *Tacitus in Renaissance Political Thought*.

26   The Florentine Leon Battista Alberti in his work *On the Art of Building* (1452) refers at one point to Tacitus's description of the strong and impregnable walls of Jerusalem (Tacitus, *Hist.* 5.11): *ceterum, quod alibi diximus, omnium erit capacissima urbs, quae sit rotunda; tutissima, quae sinuosis amfractibus murorum obvalletur, qualem fuisse Hierosolimam scribit Tacitus* ("yet as I have said elsewhere, the most capacious city will be one which is round, but the safest will be one which is fortified with curving sinuous walls, just like the city of Jerusalem about which Tacitus writes"); Leon Battista Alberti, *De Re Aedificatoria* 4.3, [ed. G. Orlandi; Milan: Edizioni il Polifilo, 1966]. In the *Liber Chronicarum* of Hartmann Schedel (1493) the etymology of Jerusalem, probably following Tacitus, is clarified in the following way: "The Solymi were people living in the land of Lycia in the mountains, who named Hierosolima after themselves" (*Die Schedelsche Weltchronik von 1483* [fourth ed.; Dortmund: Harenberg, 1988], folio XVII); cf. Tacitus, *Hist.* 5.2.3, *clara alii Iudaeorum initia, Solymos, carminibus Homeri celebratam gentem, conditae urbi Hierosol-*

of Tacitus. The French humanist Guillaume Budé reproached Tacitus with having taken up Nero's scapegoating of the Christians for the fire in Rome in order to please his patron Domitian. Budé called Tacitus in this regard a "nefarious man," his stylus "smeared with the poison of falsehood."[27] This attack by Budé had devastating consequences and was "more than a mere repetition of Tertullian's harsh judgment of Tacitus."[28] Budé's critique would rumble on in the same far-reaching way as Tertullian's.

Yet in Jean Bodin, Michel de Montaigne, and Marc-Antoine Muret, Tacitus found eloquent defenders against the reproaches of the likes of Tertullian and Budé.[29] In a letter written in 1572 Muret, newly installed as professor of rhetoric, reacted against reservations which the Church had raised concerning a proposed lecture on Tacitus. It was put to Muret that Tacitus had somewhere said bad things about the Christians and the Jews.[30] The French humanist did not allow himself to be deterred from his lecture plans, but he did feel obliged to justify his liking for Tacitus.[31] This polemic indicates what a heavy burden Tacitus's chapters about the Jews and the Christians were now charged with.

---

    ma nomen e suo fecisse ("Others posit a famous ancestry for the Jews in the Solymi, a tribe celebrated by Homer in his poems: these people allegedly founded Jerusalem and named it after themselves").

27   G. Budé, *De Asse et Partibus Eius* (Basel 1556 [Paris 1514]), 192–193.

28   Jürgen von Stackelberg, *Tacitus in der Romania: Studien zur literarischen Rezeption des Tacitus in Italien und Frankreich* (Tübingen: Max Niemeyer, 1960), 160.

29   Reacting to Budé's judgment, Bodin attempts to place Tacitus's remarks on the Jews in a historical context. See Jean Bodin, *Methodus ad facilem historiarum cognitionem* (Paris, 1572), 96. In this piece, Bodin recognizes Tacitus's accomplishments as historian, politician and stylist. For the reactions to Bodin, cf. Arnaldo Momigliano, "The First Political Commentary on Tacitus," *JRS* 37 (1947): 91–101, at 91n8. See Michel de Montaigne, *Essais*, book 3, chapter 8 in Robert Barral, ed., *Œuvres complètes* (Paris: Éditions du Seuil, 1967 [1586]), 380: "He [sc. Tacitus] needs no excuse for agreeing with the religion of his own times, in accordance with the laws which governed him, and for being ignorant of the true religion. This is his misfortune, not his failing." On the reception of Tacitus by Montaigne, cf. von Stackelberg, *Tacitus in der Romania*, 164–186, Etter, *Tacitus in der Geistesgeschichte*, 65–69 and Alain Malissard, "Montaigne lecteur de Tacite," in Rémy Poignault, Raymond Chevallier, eds., *Présence de Tacite, Hommage au professeur G. Radke, Actes du colloque de l'ENS (Paris, octobre 1991)* (Tours: l'Université de Tours, 1992), 157–164. On Muret, see the following notes.

30   See Pierre de Nolhac, ed., *Lettres inédites de Muret*. Mélanges Charles Graux (Paris: Ernest Thorin, 1884), 381–403, at 389, cited by von Stackelberg, *Tacitus in der Romania*, 107. Muret also defends Tacitus against the then widespread reproach that he was a poor stylist. For Muret and Tacitus in detail see von Stackelberg, *Tacitus in der Romania*, 106–118.

31   He did this in a somewhat sarcastic tone: "If we think that at this time nothing should be read except that which agrees with the Christian religion, of course we should lay aside

TACITUS'S EXCURSUS ON THE JEWS THROUGH THE AGES   265

A key reason for Tacitus's advancing at this time to become one of the most widely-read ancient authors was that his work could serve as a substitute for one placed on the Index of prohibited books: Machiavelli's *The Prince*. In this intensive phase of his reception ('Tacitism,' c. 1580–1680), Tacitus was called into evidence by both supporters and opponents of absolutism.[32] 'Tacitism' also meant that the old critiques of the Jewish excursus and the chapter on the Christians could now also be deployed against Machiavelli. Religious criticism was sometimes just a cover for political criticism.[33]

After the *editio princeps* of 1470 (Vindolino de Spira, Venice), Tacitus's work over the next two centuries saw a regular flurry of new editions and commentaries.[34] While the first commentators, self-evidently great admirers of the rediscovered Tacitus, expressed their astonishment at the malicious tone and false allegations in the Jewish excursus, they nonetheless strove visibly and sometimes touchingly to comment on these chapters of the *Histories* in a sober manner. Even so, Andrea Alciato (1517) is put off by Tacitus's *impietas* in questioning divine power.[35] Marcus Vertranius Maurus (1565) believes that despite the audaciousness with which Tacitus speaks of the Jews, one cannot help laughing; Tacitus has clearly carried his inaccuracies across from his sources.[36] Justus Lipsius (1585) rallies to Tacitus's defense and repudiates in relatively

---

all those ancient Greek and Latin writers. Or is any one of us so weak as to be in danger of starting to waver in the Christian faith if he recognizes that Tacitus was not a Christian?" (M.A. Muret, *Orationes, epistulae, hymnique sacri*. editio nova [Leipzig 1629 (1604)], 2.14).

32   Von Stackelberg, *Tacitus in der Romania*, 63–93; Etter, *Tacitus in der Geistesgeschichte*, 15–26; Peter Burke, "Tacitism," in *Tacitus* (ed. Thomas A. Dorey; London: Routledge, 1969), 149–171; Volpilhac-Auger, *Tacite et Montesquieu*, 23–26.

33   Cf. Etter, *Tacitus in der Geistesgeschichte*, 62.

34   Between 1580 and 1700 there appeared more than 100 commentaries on Tacitus (Burke, "Tacitism," 150). It would of course have been impossible for me to consult all the commentaries on the *Histories*. However, those summarized in the following pages must be representative. The extraordinarily large collection of commentaries on Tacitus in Basel University Library was very useful to me. Joannes Gronovius's publication *C. Cornelii Taciti Opera quae exstant* (Utrecht 1721 [1672]) includes, alongside his own commentary, notes on many earlier commentaries (by among others, Beatus Rhenanus, Marc-Antoine Muret, and Hugo Grotius). In the following discussion, for the sake of simplicity, quotations will be taken from this publication of Gronovius. An overview of editions, commentaries, and translations of the fifteenth to seventeenth centuries is given by Etter, *Tacitus in der Geistesgeschichte*, 213–215.

35   Alciato, in Gronovius, *Opera*, 355 on Tacitus, *Hist*. 5.5.5. On Alciato, cf. Etter, *Tacitus in der Geistesgeschichte*, 27–28.

36   Marcus Vertranius Maurus, in Gronovius, *Opera*, 349 on Tacitus, *Hist*. 5.2.1. On Vetranius, cf. Etter, *Tacitus in der Geistegeschichte*, 32–33.

strong terms the Tertullianic polemic against Tacitus's assertion that Jews worshipped an ass's head; he points to even more absurd passages in other pagan authors.[37] Tacitus's unpolemical handling of Jewish monotheism is accordingly noted with relief by Lipsius.[38] In similar vein to Lipsius, the Frenchman Julianus Pichon (1686) a hundred years later attempted to relativize Tacitus's errors. For him there is no question in the excursus of onolatry by the Jews; they may, as Tacitus declared, have consecrated an image of an ass, but they did not worship it.[39]

Generally Tacitus received only restrained criticism from the early historical commentators for his apparent errors, and his standing as a historian was not called into question. It was pointed out that Tacitus was, after all, only a heathen (*ethnicus*), and as such could not understand Judaism and hence Christianity.[40] The outcry raised by Tertullian and Budé did not in the end stand in the way of sober-minded commentaries.

In none of the recognized commentaries can there be seen any anti-Jewish attitude such as might seek to endorse or 'contemporize' reproaches of Tacitus, though this would scarcely have been surprising against the background of the heavy burden of Tertullian and Budé with which the commentators had to contend. But even the openly anti-Jewish polemics in sixteenth and seventeenth century literature seem not to have resorted to Tacitus's diatribes against the Jews.[41] Also after the rediscovery of Tacitus, the Jewish excursus did not serve as a source for antisemitic observations.

Not all of the commentators were so lenient with Tacitus's errors as the aforementioned sixteenth and seventeenth century interpreters. The two earliest essays (probably) to deal extensively with the Jewish excursus in isolation

---

37   Justus Lipsius, *C. Cornelii Taciti Opera quae exstant* (Antwerp 1585), on Tacitus, *Hist.* 5.4.2.

38   Lipsius, *Opera* on Tacitus, *Hist.* 5.5.4.

39   Julianus Pichon, *C. Cornelii Taciti Opera* (Paris 1682–1687; *Histories*: 1686) on *Hist.* 5.4.2.

40   The chapter on the Christians (*Ann.* 15.44) receives similar comments. Cf. for example Beatus Rhenanus in Gronovius, *Opera*, 662 on Tacitus, *Ann.* 15.44: "He calls Christian piety a 'deadly superstition,' but he speaks as a heathen, and one ignorant of the mysteries of our religion."

41   Abraham Melamed, "Simone Luzzatto on Tacitus: Apologetica and Ragione di Stato," in Isadore Twersky, ed., *Studies in Medieval Jewish History* (Cambridge: Harvard University Press, 1984), 143–170 examined anti-Jewish polemics of the sixteenth and seventeenth centuries for echoes of Tacitus and reaches the conclusion that Tacitus is not referred to anywhere (147: "In all the anti-Jewish literature consulted, Tacitus is not mentioned"). Melamed suggests that this is because Tacitus expressly describes the Christians as stemming from the Jews (Tacitus, *Ann.* 15.44: Judea as *origo eius mali*, "the source of that wickedness"), so that using Tacitus as "raw material for anti-Jewish literature" could also be interpreted as anti-Christian (149).

TACITUS'S EXCURSUS ON THE JEWS THROUGH THE AGES   267

from the *Histories*, by Georg Caspar Kirchmaier (1676 and 1679) and Christian Worm (1694), were distinctly harder on Tacitus.[42] Worm was not concerned exclusively with Tacitus, but also with erroneous reporting on the Jews by other ancient authors. Kirchmaier's commentary, on the other hand, is probably the oldest specialized essay on the Jewish excursus. Both authors assail Tacitus's observations with other pagan authors' statements about the Jews and with relevant passages from the Bible and the Talmud. Their commentaries thus become miniature treatises on ancient Judaism. For Worm it is ultimately inexplicable that Tacitus can report on the origin of the Jews in the way he does. Rather than such self-contradiction, he would have done better to remain silent.[43] Kirchmaier, for his part, believes Tacitus's Jewish excursus has scarcely anything to do with historiography; Tacitus did not know what he intended, and his opinions jump first this way then that.[44]

The difference could not have been greater between these commentaries drawn up on more firmly theological lines and the first philological-historical (not to say political) commentaries. Worm and Kirchmaier are not afraid to pillory Tacitus for his errors. For them, what stands pre-eminent is the biblical truth which they consider to have been disparaged by Tacitus's misconstructions. Thus both commentaries turn into Christian *apologiae* against Tacitus's

---

42   Georg C. Kirchmaier, *Exercitatio academica ad C.C. Taciti Histor. Lib. v. Capita aliquot priora de rebus moribusque Judaeorum* (Wittenberg 1676); Christian Worm, *De corruptis antiquitatum Hebraearum apud Tacitum et Martialem vestigiis libri duo* (Copenhagen 1694). Both in Blasius Ugolinus, *Thesaurus Antiquitatum Sacrarum complectens selectissima clarissimorum virorum opuscula, in quibus veterum Hebraeorum mores, leges, instituta, ritus sacri et civiles illustrantur*. Vol. 2 (Venice 1744), 1–300 (Worm), 301–328 (Kirchmaier). Kirchmaier also wrote a separate commentary on the historical section (Tacitus, *Hist*. 5.1, 8–13): *De obsidione Hierosolymitana, ex v. Hist. C.C. Taciti* (Wittenberg 1679).

43   See Worm, *De corruptis antiquitatum*, 21. Worm attempts in somewhat sophistical fashion to explain Tacitus's statements through false conclusions from Jewish sources—as though Tacitus had consulted these himself. On the first account of the *origo*, that the Jews came from Crete, Worm remarks that he rates this theory as completely unfounded (*tanta & vesana hallucinatio*, "an enormous and mad delusion"), but that it may have arisen through confusion with the Philistines, whose homeland is described in the Old Testament (Jer 47:4; 1 Sam 30:14) as "the south of Crete" (30–31).

44   In the short introduction to his commentary, *Exercitatio*, 301 Kirchmaier writes, "There is more ignorance and malice apparent here than historical truth." On Tacitus, *Hist*. 5.2.1 (Cretan origin of the Jews; Jews driven out at same time as Saturn; the *Ida-Iudaei* etymology): "Tacitus begins from traditions which are false and derive from fables," "These matters should be ascribed to the mythology of poets, not to a chronological account," "a most wretched proof, sought from name-play" (Kirchmaier, *Exercitatio*, 301–303). On Tacitus, *Hist*. 5.2.3 (Assyrian origin of the Jews): "Tacitus hurtles this way and that, uncertain about his thoughts" (Kirchmaier, *Exercitatio*, 305).

268   CHAPTER 13

portrayals. Concerning the prodigies described at Tacitus, *Hist.* 5.13, Kirchmaier remarks that neither Roman nor Jew had recognized the true prodigy, Jesus Christ.[45]

4   Jewish Reactions in the Seventeenth Century

What reactions were there from the Jewish side to Tacitus's ethnography? Here there are three significant Jewish authors of the seventeenth century to be noted, who either received or made use of Tacitus's Jewish excursus: the Venetian rabbi Simone Luzzatto, the Spanish Marrano[46] emigré to Italy Isaac Cardoso, and the Dutch philosopher Baruch (Benedictus) de Spinoza. Prior to Luzzato, Tacitus's Jewish excursus was addressed only very marginally in Jewish writings.[47]

---

45   Kirchmaier, *De obsidione*, 24: "But indeed neither Jews nor Romans were willing or had the power to discern the prophecy (Micah 5) about the leader of Israel and heavenly king of the Jews, Jesus of Nazareth." Julianus Pichon, *C. Cornelii Taciti Opera* (Paris 1682–1687, *Histories*: 1686), in his note on *Hist.* 5.5.3 (*hinc generandi amor*), relates the "passion for propagation" to the expectation of Christ: "There was some more forceful explanation, without doubt because they were expecting Christ."

46   A Marrano was an Iberian 'crypto-Jew' legally obliged to convert, but doing so only nominally.

47   Azariah de Rossi, in his Hebrew work *Light of the Eyes* (Berlin 1794 [second edition], Mantua 1573–1575), refers repeatedly to Greek and Roman authors, among them Tacitus. In chapter 26, drawing specifically on Tacitus, he points out that until Pompey no Roman had harmed the Jews. Rossi here relies on the analogous statement in the Jewish excursus: *Romanorum primus Cn. Pompeius Iudaeos domuit* ("Gnaeus Pompey was the first of the Romans to conquer the Jews"), citing Tacitus, *Hist.* 5.9.1; Rossi's Hebrew translation of this passage also evokes a biblical verse: cf. Lamentations 4:6. Rossi does not cite Tacitus directly but—as he himself states—via Juan L. Vives' commentary on Augustine (Basel 1543). Thus Rossi, whose work combines Jewish tradition and Italian Renaissance culture (Yosef Hayim Yerushalmi, *Zakhor: Jewish History and Jewish Memory* [Seattle: University of Washington Press, 1982], 69), uses Tacitus as a historical source; on this, cf. also the introduction to the English translation by Joanna Weinberg, trans., *Azariah de'Rossi: The Light of the Eyes* (New Haven: Yale University Press, 2001), xli–xlii. A first (albeit very brief) Jewish rebuttal of Tacitus's depiction of Judaism appears in Menasseh (Manasseh) ben Israel. In his *Conciliador* (Amsterdam 1632, *non vidi*), in the course of a discussion of imageless worship, he examines how this topic is dealt with in Tacitus: "We ... clearly see the falsehood recorded by Tacitus to vilify the Jews, stating that they worshipped the head of a wild ass in the wilderness, when they were in want of water, until they came to a fountain at which he drank; which tale not only shows his ignorance of Holy Writ, but also his hatred and evil disposition" (from the English translation by Elias H. Lindo, *The Conciliator of R. Manesseh ben Israel* (New York: Hermon, 1972 [1842]), 157). On the reception of Tacitus by Rossi and Manesseh ben Israel, cf. Melamed "Simone Luzzatto," 151–152.

TACITUS'S EXCURSUS ON THE JEWS THROUGH THE AGES 269

5   Simone Luzzatto

Simone Luzzatto's annotations on the Jewish excursus of Tacitus, the "famoso Historico Romano" as he called him, form the longest chapter of his *Discorso circa il stato degl'Hebrei et in particolàr dimoranti nell'inclita Città di Venetia*.[48] Among a number of reasons for these being of interest is the fact that, in contrast to many other commentators, Luzzato's focus is expressly not on the six different accounts of Jewish origins offered by Tacitus, but on those points which relate to Jewish everyday life.[49] Just how far he links Tacitus's polemic, between the lines, to his own milieu in Venice is not easy to judge. It has certainly been demonstrated that Luzzatto's essay is not exclusively apologetic in character. Luzzatto shows himself, rather, to be a Tacitist and a Machiavellist.[50]

Luzzatto takes seven anti-Jewish "slanders" ("diffamationi"), which he explains in turn and refutes with quotations from the Bible. The slanders comprise: the worship of an ass's head, immorality, misanthropy, contrast between the Jewish god and the Roman Bacchus, renunciation of pork, prodigies of Jerusalem, and the Sabbath. The fact that here, too, the first item on the list is the worship of asses is no coincidence. Luzzatto was aware of the numerous reactions regarding this issue.[51] Just like the Christian commentators of Tacitus, Luzzatto also finds himself torn between, on the one hand, his intellectual affinity with Tacitus, and, on the other, the polemical excursus on the Jews. Luzzatto tries to show that Judaism too is based on meaningful *political* principles. Judaism and Rome are not two different worlds. Rather, the banning of pork, for example, should be understood as a political matter—precisely in the Tacitean

---

48   Simone Luzzatto, *Discorso circa il stato degl'Hebrei et in particolàr dimoranti nell'inclita Città di Venetia* (Venice 1638), 58–73 on Tacitus. The following citations refer to this publication, though its pagination is not always consistent. On Luzzatto and Tacitus, see at length Melamed, "Simone Luzzatto." At the start of his treatise Luzzatto pays tribute to Tacitus the historian: "The famous Roman historian Cornelius Tacitus, through his learning and experience of political affairs deservedly numbered amongst the leading masters of civil government" (*Discorso*, 58).

49   See *Discorso*, 58.

50   Melamed, "Simone Luzzatto," 157: "Luzzato does not use Tacitus only in order to attack Christian anti-Semitism. He uses him also since he accepted him, like many other contemporary thinkers, as a supreme authority on political thought .... In the Jewish context he uses him as a secure means of presenting the Macchiavellian position. Christian anti-Semitism, on the one hand, and Machiavellism, on the other, thus appear in Tacitean disguise." Melamed demonstrates (161–164) that Luzzatto in part uses the language of Macchiavelli.

51   *Discorso*, 60: "A lie which has already been refuted by many learned men, and in particular by Tertullian."

sense. Such laws serve to bind the faithful to their authorities.[52] Likewise, Luzzatto defends the Sabbath with political and social arguments and draws connections to parallel Roman institutions. However, whereas the Jewish day of rest served to bring spiritual relaxation and greater dedication to commercial matters on the remaining days of the week, Roman rest days were mainly to do with licentiousness.[53] Luzzatto goes on to explain the political background to the sabbatical year: it benefits efficient farming, makes enough food for everyone after seven years, and gives land workers the chance, every seventh year, to devote themselves to military training. The sabbatical year makes it possible to have a civilian army without economic hardship.[54]

6 Isaac Cardoso

Isaac Cardoso is the author of the important Spanish apology *Excelencias* (1679), a work shaped by Cardoso's recollections of antisemitism in Spain.[55] Cardoso has quite frequent recourse to Tacitus's Jewish excursus, and he seems to assume that the educated of his time were familiar with Tacitus's *Histories* and therefore also the Jewish excursus.[56] Cardoso defends Judaism against antisemitic slanders, among others that the Jews are misanthropic. As his prime evidence for this reproach he names Tacitus's Jewish excursus, and refutes it with numerous biblical references—and also with Tacitus's own statement that the Jews did not kill posthumously-born babies (*Hist.* 5.5.3: *nam et necare quemquam ex agnatis nefas*, "for it is a sin to kill any surplus children"), which in Cardoso's view is proof of humanity.[57]

Like many a Christian recipient of Tacitus (Worm for instance), Cardoso is surprised that such a critical and truthful historian as Tacitus should have uncritically adopted such far-fetched tales as that of Moses leading the way to water with the help of a herd of asses, and that he relied on Apion rather than

---

52 See *Discorso*, 66.
53 See *Discorso*, 71.
54 See *Discorso*, 73. Cf. Melamed, "Simone Luzzatto," 167–170.
55 Isaac Cardoso, *Las excelencias de los Hebreos* (Amsterdam 1679, *non vidi*). I cite from the Hebrew translation by Joseph Kaplan, trans., *Isaac Cardoso: Las Excelencias de los Hebreos* (Jerusalem: Bialik, 1971). For a discussion of Cardoso's work at length, see Yosef Hayim Yerushalmi, *From Spanish Court to Italian Ghetto: Isaac Cardoso—A Study in Seventeenth-Century Marranism and Jewish Apologetics* (New York: Columbia University Press, 1971).
56 Yerushalmi, *Spanish Court*, 418.
57 *Excelencias* (trans. Kaplan), 109–111.

on either Josephus, the Septuagint, or direct information from Roman Jews.[58] Cardoso's respect for Tacitus is reflected in his resolution of Tacitus's contradictory portrayals of the Jewish concept of God (worship of asses [*Hist.* 5.4.2] vs. aniconic worship [5.5.4]): his explanation is that Tacitus corrected his original view at a later stage, having either acquired better information or, perhaps through pure impulse, realized that the Jews had an imageless God.[59] Cardoso uses a Tacitean reference to counter the antisemitic stereotype that Jews smell bad, arguing that if even an author such as Tacitus says of the Jews that they have healthy and resilient bodies (*Hist.* 5.6.1: *corpora hominum salubria et ferentia laborum*, "the bodies of these people are healthy and tolerant of hard work"), then this reproach must be absurd, for how can a healthy body smell bad?[60]

7 Baruch de Spinoza

Baruch de Spinoza quotes Tacitus with some frequency.[61] When, for example, in chapter 17 of his *Tractatus Theologico-Politicus*, which deals with the Jewish state, he introduces the topic of a government endangered by its own citizens, he refers his readers to Tacitus's description of civil war turmoil during the Year of the Four Emperors.[62] In his historical contextualization of the Jewish theocracy—proposing that after the exodus from Egypt the Jews handed their natural right to self-government over to God—Spinoza poses the question of how far this kind of constitution was capable of keeping both governors and governed in check. Fundamental to this, he suggests, had been a patriotic love of country expressing itself on the one hand as religious piety

---

58 *Excelencias* (trans. Kaplan), 41. Cf. Yerushalmi, *Spanish Court*, 419.

59 *Excelencias* (trans. Kaplan), 44. In connection with his defense against the reproach of onolatry, Cardoso argues that this belief may have had a real basis insofar as it might be related to Samson's heroic deeds—Samson slew 1,000 Philistines with the jawbone of an ass (Judg 15:14–20) (*Excelencias* [trans. Kaplan], 48). Luzzatto had earlier argued in similar fashion: objects associated with biblical miracles—the manna vase, Aaron's rod, etc.,— were kept in holy places (*Discorso*, 60).

60 *Excelencias* (trans. Kaplan), 55.

61 Baruch de Spinoza, *Tractatus Theologico-Politicus* (Amsterdam 1670), abbreviated in subsequent notes as *TThP*; my citations are from the edition by Carl Gebhardt, *Spinoza Opera*. Vol. 3 (Heidelberg: Carl Winter, 1972 [1925]). On Spinoza and Tacitus, cf. Chaim Wirszubski, *Libertas as a Political Idea at Rome during the Late Republic and Early Principate* (Cambridge: Cambridge University Press, 1955).

62 *TThP*, 204: "Concerning this matter, see Tacitus at the start of *Histories* 4, where he depicts the utterly wretched appearance of the city."

272 CHAPTER 13

and on the other—and here Spinoza begins to echo the Tacitus of the Jewish excursus—as hatred of other nations.[63] Nonetheless Spinoza makes no explicit reference here to the Jewish excursus. When giving an example of the strength of this double-sided Jewish 'policy' (strengthening inwardly, exclusion outwardly) and the associated difficulties for others in prevailing over the Jews, Spinoza does then explicitly reference Tacitus, who in the second book of the *Histories* (Spinoza does not explicitly refer to the fifth!) alludes to the difficulties anticipated by the Flavians in conquering Jerusalem.[64] Finally, in the same chapter Spinoza asks why it is that the Jews had so often fallen away from the law. He considers the fault to lie not with the Jews but with their laws and customs. These, Spinoza declares with astonishment, were given by God not as laws but as a punishment for their disobedience. At this, Spinoza feels compelled, as he himself states, to repeat Tacitus's words: "*quae mutatio* (that as a punishment for worshipping the golden calf, the firstborn should be cast aside and the Levites chosen in their stead) *quo eam magis ac magis considero, in uerba Taciti me cogit erumpere, illo tempore non fuisse Deo curae securitatem illorum, fuisse ultionem*" ("the more and more I ponder that exchange, I feel compelled to blurt out the words of Tacitus, that at that time God cared not for their peace of mind, but only for vengeance").[65] The gods, wrote Tacitus in his general description of the period to be covered in the *Histories*, were concerned with punishment, not with a carefree existence.[66] This remarkable transfer of a statement coined by Tacitus about Rome and its relationship with its gods to the relationship of the Jews with theirs serves, therefore, as an illustration of God as punitive authority.

---

63   *TThP*, 215, where Spinoza's use of *odium, separati*, and *contrarius* recalls Tacitus's Latin: *hostile odium* (*Hist.* 5.5.1), *separati epulis* (5.5.2), and *novos ritus contrariosque* (5.4.1).

64   *TThP*, 215: "as Tacitus himself attests in the following words from *Histories* 2: *profligaverat bellum Iudaicum Vespasianus, oppugnatione Hierosolymorum reliqua, duro magis et arduo opere ob ingenium gentis et pervicaciam superstitionis, quam quod satis virium obsessis ad tolerandas necessitates superesset*" ("Vespasian had already given the decisive turn to the Jewish war, although the siege of Jerusalem still remained. This was a difficult and uphill task, more because of the peculiar characteristics of the people and the bigotry of its inhabitants than because the besieged had enough strength left to endure a desperate struggle."). It appears from this quotation from Tacitus (*Hist.* 2.4.3) that Spinoza used the edition of Lipsius. Lipsius has *ob ingenium gentis*, whereas the *Codex Mediceus* has *ob ingenium montis*, as noted by Wirszubski, *Libertas*, 180.

65   *TThP*, 218.

66   Tacitus, *Hist.* 1.3.2: *nec enim umquam atrocioribus populi Romani cladibus magisve iustis indiciis adprobatum est non esse curae deis securitatem nostram, esse ultionem* ("For it has never been verified by more terrible disasters for the Roman people or by fuller portents that the gods care not for our peace of mind, but only for vengeance").

TACITUS'S EXCURSUS ON THE JEWS THROUGH THE AGES   273

In the third chapter of his *Tractatus*, which deals with the vocation of the Hebrews and their gift of prophesy, Spinoza relies on Tacitean formulations from the Jewish excursus. He attributes the phenomenon of Jewish continuity to the peculiarity of Jewish customs and the consequent hatred among other nations which holds the Jews together.[67] Here again, however, Spinoza dispenses with a specific reference to Tacitus's Jewish excursus. Finally, an almost literal echo of Tacitus is to be found in the *Praefatio* of the *Tractatus*. Spinoza is discussing in general terms—not specifically applying to the Jews—the phenomenon of superstition, to which people in their fear and insecurity constantly cling. Once again without expressly quoting Tacitus, he makes his borrowing from the Jewish excursus quite apparent: "*Si quid porro insolitum magna cum admiratione uident, id prodigium esse credunt, quod Deorum aut summi Numinis iram indicat, quodque adeo hostiis, et votis non piare, nefas habent homines superstitioni obnoxii, et religioni aduersi*" ("If moreover they see with great astonishment anything unusual, they believe that this is a prodigy indicating the anger of the Gods or of the highest power, and men steeped in superstition and hostile to proper religious practice regard it as wrong not to atone for it by sacrifices and vows").[68]

Although Spinoza frequently credits Tacitus as a source (five times altogether in chapter 17 of the *Tractatus Theologico-Politicus*), in his allusions to the Jewish excursus he expressly chose not to refer to it. Despite his high regard for Tacitus as a historian, Spinoza evidently baulks at declaring him as his source—not just in words but content—for his account of Jewish concepts of law: it may be that Tacitus's strongly anti-Jewish propositions ruled out any reference to these chapters on Spinoza's part. Yet there, among Tacitus's observations on Jewish separatism, Spinoza found some very acceptable formulations for his critique of Jewish law.[69] It is striking that Spinoza, in setting out his philosophy

---

67   *TThP*, 256. Spinoza's use of *separaverunt | odium | ritibus caeterarum nationum | contrariis | circumcisionis* recalls Tacitus's *ritus contrariosque ceteris* (*Hist.* 5.4.1), *odium* (5.5.1), *separati epulis* (5.5.2), *circumcidere* (5.5.2). Wirszubski, *Libertas*, 183–184 points out that Spinoza here speaks only of *ritus*, whereas elsewhere he uses *caerimonia* or *cultus*.

68   *TThP*, 5 (*Praefatio*). Cf. Tacitus *Hist.* 5.13.1: *Evenerant **prodigia**, quae neque **hostiis** neque votis piare fas habet gens **superstitioni obnoxia**, religionibus **adversa*** ("Various prodigies had occurred, but a nation steeped in superstition and hostile to proper religious practices considered it unlawful to atone for them by offering victims or solemn vows"). Cf. Wirszubski, *Libertas*, 181–182. Admittedly, Tacitus is saying the exact opposite of what Spinoza here expresses: according to Tacitus, *superstitio* caused the Jews (in contrast to the Romans) to refrain from expiating the omens with vows and sacrifice, whereas for Spinoza, who already saw belief in omens as in itself a superstition, vows and sacrifice were marks of *superstitio*.

69   Also in his description of the Israelites' rebellion against Moses Spinoza echoes a Tacitean

274   CHAPTER 13

of religion, makes use of the partially hostile Jewish excursus, and in the preface to his *Tractatus* even employs a phrase from Tacitus that is clearly directed against the Jews as a general critique of religion, which he broadens into a general anthropological observation.

It does, however, appear that in the end, Spinoza distances himself from Tacitus's polemic. In this same chapter 17 of the *Tractatus Theologico-Politicus*, Spinoza criticizes those who view the end of the Jewish state as a consequence of the closed-mindedness of the Jews (*gentis contumacia*, "the stubbornness of the people"). For Spinoza it is Jewish laws, not the Jews themselves that are narrow-minded. Nature creates only individuals, not nations.[70] It seems possible that Spinoza is including Tacitus in this criticism. For Tacitus's ethnographical account of the Jews culminates in precisely the Jewish obsessiveness which Spinoza repudiates: *obstinatio viris feminisque par; ac si transferre sedis cogerentur, maior vitae metus quam mortis* ("The women were no less determined than the men, and the thought that they might be forced to leave their homes made them fear life more than death;" Tacitus, *Hist.* 5.13.3). If Spinoza's criticism is indeed directed against Tacitus, or at least includes him, it is worth noting that Spinoza does not name him. Spinoza's handling of Tacitus's Jewish excursus is the reception-history equivalent of shadow-boxing.

Reviewing these three examples of the first Jewish reception, it can be seen that Luzzatto and Cardoso pursued mainly apologetic goals, with the former author's *apologia* for Tacitus involving Tacitist ideas. Spinoza, on the other hand, uses Tacitus for a quite different purpose: Tacitus's statements are for him convenient arguments in bringing out his own concepts of tolerance as he weans his critical writing away from his own Jewish tradition. Detectable in all three authors is a certain uneasiness with the great Roman historian's anti-Jewish polemic. Luzzatto and Cardoso, like the Christian recipients before them, struggle to find explanations for Tacitus's errors. As to whether Spinoza also shared this uneasiness, circumstances appear to suggest that in his several linguistic allusions to Tacitus's Jewish excursus—in contrast to other passages in Tacitus—he never explicitly names the source and at one point, moreover, even seems to repudiate it. Ultimately, however, it is apparent what an important author Tacitus was for the political discourse of the seventeenth century.

---

formulation, again without explicitly citing Tacitus; cf. *TThP*, 219, "*quare tunc temporis seditio magis desierat quam concordia coeperat*" ("Accordingly, it was more that the revolt of that time had stopped rather than that a state of harmony had begun") with Tacitus, *Hist.* 4.1.1: *Interfecto Vitellio bellum magis desierat quam pax coeperat* ("After the murder of Vitellius, it was more that the war had stopped than that peace had begun").

70   See *TThP*, 203.

TACITUS'S EXCURSUS ON THE JEWS THROUGH THE AGES

8 The Eighteenth Century and the Age of Enlightenment

Following in the tradition of Spinoza are the French philosophers of the Enlightenment.[71] For many of them, Tacitus was an 'esprit critique' and thus, even if not unconditionally, one of their own.[72] It is important for the reception of the Jewish excursus that during the Enlightenment Judaism was often the target of freethinking and anti-clerical polemics,[73] and that Tacitus's Jewish excursus was turned to in the process. In Voltaire, "Jewish misanthropy," very much as Tacitus described it, is a negative example of his own concept of tolerance.[74] In another context, Voltaire refers to the myth of the Jews worshipping an ass's head and attempts to place this 'error' in a historical context and make it understandable. In the article "Idole, idolâtre, idolâtrie" from his *Dictionnaire philosophique*, Voltaire writes that Judaism was full of images representing God, and that his messengers, the cherubim, also had physical form, with human bodies and animal heads. No wonder, then, that ancient authors such as Tacitus had mistakenly reproached the Jews for worshipping an ass's head.[75] Like other authors of his time,[76] Voltaire endeavoured to see meaning behind Tacitus's errors with the aid of (dubious) attempts at reconstructing historical reality.

Linked to Voltaire through his Enlightenment views, Edward Gibbon, a great admirer of Tacitus, makes conspicuous use of phrases from the Jewish excursus in his *Decline and Fall of the Roman Empire*.[77] When Gibbon describes the successful expansion of Christianity as something which would have been alien to the misanthropic Jews, he too makes use of the corresponding Tacitean charge

---

71 Arthur Hertzberg, *The French Enlightenment and the Jews* (New York: Columbia University Press, 1968), 39–45.

72 For readings of Tacitus in the eighteenth century, cf. the works of Volpilhac-Auger, *Tacite et Montesquieu*, eadem, "Tacite du XVIIIe au XIXe siècle: les causes d'une révolution," in *Présence de Tacite, Hommage au professeur G. Radke, Actes du colloque de l'ENS (Paris, octobre 1991), Caesarodunum*, ed. Rémy Poignault and Raymond Chevallier (Tours: l'Université de Tours, 1992), 281–289, and eadem, *Tacite en France*, 215–229: "L'esprit critique de Tacite."

73 Cf. Christhard Hoffmann, "Das Judentum als Antithese: Zur Tradition eines kulturellen Wertungsmusters," in *Antisemitismus in Deutschland: Zur Aktualität eines Vorurteils*, ed. Wolfgang Benz (Munich: Deutscher Taschenbuch Verlag, 1990), 25–46.

74 Cf. Hertzberg, *French Enlightenment*, 304–305.

75 See Voltaire, *Dictionnaire philosophique, Les Œuvres Complètes de Voltaire*, ed. Ula Kölving (Oxford: Oxford University Press, 1994 [1764]), "Idole, Idolâtre, Idolâtrie," at 219.

76 For Voltaire and other examples, cf. Volpilhac-Auger, *Tacite en France*, 210–214.

77 Edward Gibbon, *The History of the Decline and Fall of the Roman Empire* (1776), with an introduction by Christopher Dawson (London: Allen Lane, 1910), 1.430–441 (chapter 15).

276   CHAPTER 13

of misanthropy.[78] Ultimately however the Jewish excursus serves Gibbon more as an indirect argument against Christianity, which he saw as retrograde, than as a polemic against Judaism.[79]

The reproaches of Tertullian and Budé, albeit less widespread, continued to have their effect in the eighteenth century. Of particular interest here are the two editions of Tacitus by Gabriel Brotier (1771) and Jean Henri Dotteville (1772).[80] Both commentators attempt to do justice to two irreconcilable claims. They wanted to bolster Tacitus's credibility without making any concessions to their own religious stances (Brotier was a Jesuit priest, Dotteville an Oratarian).[81]

Brotier does his level best to defend Tacitus. In the introduction to his lengthy commentary on the Jewish excursus, he strives to find explanations for Tacitus's gaffes: his lack of interest in religion (his own as well as that of

---

78   Gibbon, *Decline and Fall*, 1.432: "who boldly professed, or who faintly disguised, their implacable hatred to the rest of humankind," cf. Tacitus, *Hist.* 5.5.1: *sed adversus omnes alios hostile odium* ("but against all others a hatred reserved for enemies," though Gibbon may have in mind the *odium humani generis*, "hatred of the human race" from Tacitus, *Ann.* 15.44, referring to the Christians). Other apparent allusions to the Jewish excursus are: Gibbon, *Decline and Fall*, 1.431: "The Jews, who under the Assyrian and Persian monarchies, had languished for many ages as the most despised portion of their slaves." Cf. Tacitus, *Hist.* 5.8.2: *dum Assyrios penes Medosque et Persas Oriens fuit, despectissima pars servientium* ("While the Assyrian, Median and Persian empires dominated the East, the Jews were considered to be the lowliest element of those enslaved"); Gibbon, *Decline and Fall*, 1.433: "The mad attempt of Caligula to place his own statue in the temple of Jerusalem was defeated by the unanimous resolution of a people who dreaded death much less than such an idolatrous profanation." Cf. Tacitus, *Hist.* 5.9.2, *dein iussi a C. Caesare effigiem eius in templo locare arma potius sumpsere, quem motum Caesaris mors diremit* ("Then, after being ordered to put up a statue of Gaius Caesar in the Temple, the Jews chose to fight instead, although the rebellion came to nothing since the emperor was assassinated").

79   However, Gibbon's antipathy towards the Jews was genuine (cf. chapter 23, on Julian, in his *History*), and he followed Tacitus's account of Jewish history out of conviction. He defended his close adherence to Tacitus's arguments in "A Vindication of Some Passages in the Fifteenth and Sixteenth Chapters of the History of the Decline and Fall of the Roman Empire" (London 1779), in Patricia B. Craddock, ed., *The English Essays of Edward Gibbon* (Oxford: Oxford University Press, 1972), 229–313 (240–248 on Tacitus). Cf. Christhard Hoffmann, *Juden und Judentum im Werk deutscher Althistoriker des 19. und 20. Jahrhunderts* (Leiden: Brill, 1988), 16.

80   *C. Cornelii Taciti Opera. Recognovit, emendavit, supplementis explevit, notis, dissertationibus, tabulis geographicis illustravit Gabriel Brotier*. Vol. 3 (Paris 1771). To his already extensive footnotes on the Jewish excursus, Brotier adds further detailed notes at the end of the volume (537–580). See too Jean Henri Dotteville, *Tacite, Oeuvres complètes en latin et en français* (Paris: Librairie des Augustins, 1780). On Brotier and Dotteville, cf. Volpilhac-Auger, *Tacite en France*, 210–214.

81   Volpilhac-Auger, *Tacite en France*, 213.

TACITUS'S EXCURSUS ON THE JEWS THROUGH THE AGES

foreigners), the already unsavory reputation of the Jews in Greco-Roman literature, and the exacerbation of this in the wake of the Judaeo-Roman war, are all enlisted to explain Tacitus's curious portrait of the Jews. Nonetheless Tacitus did get many things right; it is possible to extract truth from error— Brotier's cue for a very detailed commentary.[82] Brotier does in fact criticize Tacitus's charge of misanthropy, for example,[83] but commends the sections on proselytes and monotheism.[84] Even Tacitus's closing swipes at Judaism (Jewish ritual is *absurdus sordidusque*, "discordant and degrading," whereas Bacchus instituted *festos laetosque ritus*, "festive and joyous rites") are not completely unfounded in Brotier's view.[85] And finally Brotier aligns himself with those commentators who see the fall of Jerusalem as God's punishment for the Jews' non-recognition of Jesus Christ.[86] Thus Brotier interprets the section on prodigies in the same way as Kirchmaier had a hundred years earlier.

The balancing act between admiration for Tacitus and his own religious beliefs also causes Dotteville some strains in his line of argument. On the one hand, like Bodin, Montaigne, and Lipsius before him, he adopts the position that Tacitus should not be held responsible for the evident errors in the Jewish excursus as he is basically not interested in Judaism (he refers to the phrase *hi ritus quoquo modo inducti*, "these observances, whatever their origin" [*Hist.* 5.5.1]) and has merely echoed the judgments on the Jews which were circulating at that time.[87] On the other hand Dotteville wishes to detect Tacitus's own handwriting in his description of the Jews' imageless and monotheistic form of worship.[88] These examples show very clearly the tensions under which

---

82 See Brotier, *Opera*, 537. As with Kirchmaier's commentary, Tacitus's Jewish excursus also triggers in Brotier a detailed discussion of biblical and early Jewish history.

83 See Brotier, *Opera*, on Tacitus, *Hist.* 5.5.1.

84 Brotier, *Opera*, on Tacitus, *Hist.* 5.5.2 (proselytes): "most carefully spoken" and "still true;" on *Hist.* 5.5.4 (monotheism): "truly and excellently spoken."

85 See Brotier, *Opera*, on Tacitus, *Hist.* 5.5.5.

86 Both Jews and Flavians misinterpreted the prodigies; Brotier, *Opera*, on Tacitus, *Hist.* 5.13.1: "Yet it is utterly certain and clear to anyone thinking back over the course of eras and events that the kingdom of Jesus Christ was foretold by this oracle and by several other ones."

87 Dotteville, *Tacite*, on Tacitus, *Hist.* 5.5.1: "It is clear from these words that Tacitus relates these explanations without adopting them." In contrast to those commentaries which assiduously refute Tacitus's errors, Dotteville prefers to dispense with proof of the individual statements: "Tacitus relates these explanations without adopting them, so I will not waste time refuting them," he writes in introducing his notes on the Jewish excursus.

88 Dotteville, *Tacite*, on Tacitus, *Hist.* 5.4.4: "Tacitus speaks here of the Jews based on his own experiences and not on the evidence of other authors. Must he not have been struck by the sublimity of an idea which he expresses with so much justness and accuracy?"

278   CHAPTER 13

Dotteville was writing his commentary. Dotteville's purpose, to portray Tacitus as a credible historian, does sometimes involve antisemitic stereotypes,[89] and draws the line at Tacitus's interpretation of the Jerusalem prodigies (*Hist.* 5.13). In Dotteville's view, too, these are not portents of Vespasian's successful campaign in the East, but of the emergence of Christianity which occurred in the same period.[90]

9   The Nineteenth Century

During the nineteenth century, when the role of Jews in society became a subject for heated debate, a whole series of scholarly works on the ancient Jews began to emerge.[91] In 1843 there appeared the first scholarly treatise on the Jewish excursus in the German language. Its author, the theologian Johann G. Müller, confined his discussion to the six different accounts of Jewish origins provided by Tacitus.[92] Müller's introductory remarks are typical of a whole range of authors of his time, who, though they might denounce Tacitus's falsehoods, nonetheless share his view that the Jewish religion is depraved. Müller writes:

> while he (Tacitus) and other contemporaries sometimes unjustly ascribed to them (the Jews) many strange characteristics, and sometimes mistook defective outgrowths for the whole, can anybody really take him to task for the overall impression given, the scant affection shown; anybody, that is, who knows from purer sources not accessible to Tacitus with what ossified conformity this prejudiced people so disdainfully thrust off the Salvation of the World which the German people would soon so fervently

---

89   Already, in the introduction to his notes on the Jewish excursus, Dotteville (*Tacite*) observes: "[The Jews] rendered themselves too contemptible for Tacitus to be willing to take the trouble to examine the facts." At one point he calls the Jews a "coarse and carnal people" (on Tacitus, *Hist.* 5.4.4). On Tacitus's polemical comparison of Jewish and Roman festivals (*Hist.* 5.5.5), Dotteville remarks: "*dies festus* amongst the Romans signified a day dedicated to enjoyment, spectacles, banquets. There is none of that in a Jewish holiday. Even the sacrifice of the paschal lamb, their greatest ritual, had something depressing about it: doors daubed with blood, a modest meal eaten in haste, the apparel of a traveller ready to depart." Cf. similar arguments in Brotier, *Opera*.

90   See Dotteville, *Tacite*, on Tacitus, *Hist.* 5.13.1.

91   Cf. the bibliographical data in Theobald Labhardt, "Quae de Iudaeorum Origine Iudicaverint Veteres" (PhD Dissertation University of Augsburg, 1881).

92   Johann G. Müller, "Kritische Untersuchung der taciteischen Berichte über den Ursprung der Juden, Hist. 5.2 ff.," *Theologische Studien und Kritiken* 16 (1843): 893–958.

espouse and cherish? However, with the knowledge we now possess we can scarcely avoid some sense of how the great man was able to pass down such strange views concerning the origins and characteristics of the Jews.[93]

Behind this attitude, where Germanophilia goes hand in hand with hatred of the Jews, lies the widely-held nineteenth-century view that the first century CE marked the beginning of so-called 'Late Judaism.' This concept holds that with the fall of the temple the historical role of Judaism is lost: Judaism, now frozen in the legalistic orthodoxies of 'Late Judaism,' was supplanted by Christianity.

A few years after Müller, another essayist on Tacitus's Jewish excursus, Franz X. Leonhard, argued along very similar lines: "Circumstances decreed that the greatest historian of Rome, at a time when that city's approaching doom too was making itself strongly felt, should set forth the origins and character of another nation which had fulfilled its world-historical significance, and in which all that had refused to follow spiritually the principle newly arisen in its midst was now about to lose the visible symbol of its outmoded way of life."[94]

A similar line can already be observed in the early work of the historian Heinrich Leo, particularly in his Berlin lecture "On the history of the Jewish state," delivered from 1828 onwards.[95] Despite his assurances to the contrary,[96] his arguments are steeped in antisemitic polemic and wholly focused on the break-up of the Jewish state.[97] For Leo this was a direct consequence of the Jew-

---

93   Müller, "Kritische Untersuchung," 895–896. Müller elsewhere tries to come to Tacitus's defense (899): "For him to have achieved the path of critical truth would have been an almost superhuman step beyond that stage of human development."

94   Franz X. Leonhard, *Über den Bericht des Tacitus über die Juden, Hist. 5,2–6* (Ellwangen: Kaupert, 1852), 4. Leonhard's work (apart from the generalized introduction) also deals mainly with the alternative theories of Jewish origin. Leonard also sees the Jews of the first century CE as a kind of 'discontinued model' and thus can just as readily accept Tacitus's theory of depravation (*Hist.* 5.4–5) as denounce "his blatant misjudgment" concerning individual Jewish customs (6).

95   Heinrich Leo, *Vorlesungen über die Geschichte des Jüdischen Staates: gehalten an der Universität zu Berlin* (Reutlingen: Duncker & Humblot, 1829). On Leo's treatment of Judaism, see at length Hoffmann, *Juden und Judentum*, 42–73. According to Hoffmann (p. 43n8), Leo first delivered this lecture in 1828.

96   In his preface (*Vorlesungen*, v), Leo asserts that he is writing "impersonally and dispassionately."

97   Leo's portrayal of Judaism has clear antisemitic undertones from the very first lecture (*Vorlesungen*, first lecture, 8): "As far as the characteristics of the Jewish people are concerned, what distinguishes them from all other peoples in the world is that they possess a truly corrosive and destructive mind."

280   CHAPTER 13

ish revolt against the Romans. The severity with which the Romans suppressed
the Jews was a reaction to their religious and political fanaticism. In this connection Leo, invoking Tacitus, writes: "It is understandable, therefore, that the
Romans regarded the Jews as the most degraded race on earth, as Tacitus said
of them: *Profana illic omnia quae apud nos sacra, rursum concessa apud illos
quae nobis incesta*—and even more understandable that he could add *apud
ipsos fides obstinata, misericordia in promptu, sed adversus omnis alios hostile
odium*."[98] Leo, who was later to distance himself from some of his rhetoric,[99]
is here quite simply projecting Tacitus's words onto Roman opinion in general, and using the Jewish excursus for his own antisemitic interpretation of
the Jewish-Roman war. Leo follows Tacitus in depicting a Judea which is not
only fanatical in its religion but obdurate in its politics. "The once proud and
self-contained Israelites," writes Leo, "had been turned by the fate which had
befallen them into a misanthropic nation which snuggled up to superior powers yet took revenge on its enemies with deceit and dagger, and had cast aside
all morality."[100] To the eighteenth-century Enlightenment's religious criticisms
is now added a political dimension.[101]

In 1885 the fifth volume of Theodor Mommsen's *Roman History* appeared,
with a long chapter tackling the subject of "Judea and the Jews." In it, Mommsen distinguishes between two radically different philosophies of Judaism. The
dividing line is once again the destruction of the temple of Jerusalem: the earlier cosmopolitan, proselytizing Judaism and, set against it, the frozen, misanthropic Judaism of the "rabbi state" which succeeded this event. To illustrate
the two periods, Mommsen makes reference to Horace and Tacitus:

> The Jews had always been foreign, and wished to be so; but the feel-
> ing of estrangement mounted in horrifying fashion, both among them
> and towards them, and its hateful and pernicious consequences were
> extended starkly in both directions. From the disparaging satire of Horace

---

98   Leo, *Vorlesungen*, 24th lecture, 250 quotes from Tacitus, *Hist.* 5.4.1 ("Among the Jews every-
      thing that we hold sacred is regarded as sacrilegious; on the other hand, they allow things
      which we consider immoral") and 5.5.1 ("amongst themselves there is stubborn loyalty and
      a ready benevolence, but they confront all others with a hatred reserved for enemies"). Leo
      then refers to the passage in the *Annals* which tells of the expulsion of the Jews to Sardinia
      (*Ann.* 2.85): "[It then becomes understandable], how, in another passage, he (Tacitus) was
      able to cast them away in a manner which barely allows them to appear human (this is
      followed by the quotation from *Ann.* 2.85)."
99   Hoffmann, *Juden und Judentum*, 63–67.
100   Leo, *Vorlesungen*, end of the 24th lecture, 250.
101   According to Hoffmann, *Juden und Judentum*, 73.

against the importunate Jew from the Roman ghetto, it is quite a step to the solemn resentment which Tacitus harbours towards this scum of the earth for whom everything clean is unclean and everything unclean is clean; in between are those uprisings of the despised nation, the need to defeat it and perpetually expend money and people on keeping it down.[102]

Thus for Mommsen the aggressive tone of Tacitus's Jewish excursus is a reaction to the Jewish revolts and their consequences. The dichotomy yet again expressed here between a "cosmopolitan" and a "frozen" Judaism is distinguished from that evoked by the theologian Johann G. Müller forty years earlier only by the fact that for the latter, the counterpoint to "rabbi state" was not assimilation but Christianity.[103]

Mommsen's argument, which incidentally resembles Gibbon's in reflecting a more general anti-clerical polemic, is a typical nineteenth-century political judgment of Judaism, which in the age of the nation-state was viewed as the prototype of particularism and unwillingness to integrate—"the importunate Jew from the Roman ghetto."[104]

When the so-called 'antisemitic dispute' was raging in Berlin in 1879–1880, Tacitus was brought into the ring. In an article in the *Preußische Jahrbücher*

---

102 Theodor Mommsen, *Römische Geschichte*. Vol. 5 (Berlin: Weidmanns, 1885), 551. On Mommsen's relations with the Jews, cf. the commentary of Täubler in Theodor Mommsen, *Judaea und die Juden—Mit einem Nachwort von Eugen Täubler* (Berlin: Schocken, 1936), and also Hoffmann, *Juden und Judentum*, 87–132 and idem, "Ancient Jewry—Modern Questions: German Historians of Antiquity on the Jewish Diaspora," *Illinois Classical Studies* 20 (1995): 191–207, at 195–201 and Jürgen Malitz, "Mommsen, Caesar, und die Juden," in *Geschichte—Tradition—Reflexion. Festschrift für Martin Hengel zum 70. Geburtstag, Band II: Griechische und Römische Religion*, ed. Hubert Cancik, Hermann Lichtenberger, and Peter Schäfer (Tübingen: Mohr Siebeck, 1996), 371–387.

103 Applicable here is Hoffmann, *Juden und Judentum*, 114: "Mommsen's account could be seen as a secularised form of the traditional Christian interpretation."

104 Elsewhere, in connection with the role of the Jewish diaspora at the time of Caesar, Mommsen sees Jewish "cosmopolitanism" as an important aid (or "ferment") for the "national decomposition" that was an important part of Caesar's politics. Mommsen ascribes an important political role to the Jews in this development. His assessments of diasporic Judaism are ambivalent but viewed overall are scarcely antisemitic; the fact that the phrase "ferment of cosmopolitanism and national decomposition" soon became an antisemitic slogan and would later be exploited by the National Socialists (including Goebbels and Hitler) is not Mommsen's fault. When the "Berlin antisemitic dispute" broke out at the end of the 1870s, Mommsen opposed the anti-Semites in plain terms: see Theodor Mommsen, *Auch ein Wort über unser Judenthum* (Berlin: Weidmanns, 1880). Cf. Hoffmann, *Juden und Judentum*, 92–103.

282 CHAPTER 13

the historian Heinrich von Treitschke denounces the alleged particularism of the Jews and mentions Tacitus's reproach against them for their *odium generis humani*, "hatred of humankind" (*Ann.* 15.44.4): "A gulf between western and Semitic natures has existed through the ages, since Tacitus complained of the *odium generis humani*; there will always be Jews who are nothing but German-speaking Orientals."[105] In polemical tones, von Treitschke called for the total assimilation of the Jews. Whereupon, in reply to this article, the Jewish historian Heinrich Graetz points out that the Tacitus quotation in question comes from the chapter in the *Annals* concerning the Christians: "In support of your anti-Jewish position you quote Tacitus's phrase against the Jews' *odium generis humani*: you should be aware, however, that this one-sided aristocratic Roman historian uses this phrase only about the Christians, when describing their persecution by Nero: *correpti (Christiani) qui fatebantur, deinde indicio eorum multitudo ingens haud proinde in crimine incendii quam odio humani generis convicti sunt*."[106] This exchange of blows was followed by another, with von Treitschke arguing that Tacitus made no distinction between Christians and Jews, and Graetz remaining unimpressed by these "interpretative arts."[107] What is strik-

---

105 Heinrich von Treitschke, "Unsere Aussichten," *Preußische Jahrbücher* (November 1879), quoted in Walter Boehlich, *Der Berliner Antisemitismusstreit* (Frankfurt: Insel-Verlag, 1965), 14.

106 Heinrich Graetz, "Erwiderung an Herrn von Treitschke," *Schlesische Presse* (7 December 1879), quoted in Boehlich, *Antisemitismusstreit*, 28. Cf. Tacitus, *Ann.* 15.44.4: *igitur primum correpti qui fatebantur, deinde indicio eorum multitudo ingens haud proinde in crimine incendii quam odio humani generis convicti sunt* ("The first then to be seized were those who confessed, then, on their information, a mighty number was convicted, not so much on the charge of the conflagration as for their hatred of the human race").

107 H. von Treitschke, "Herr Graetz und sein Judenthum," *Preußische Jahrbücher* (December 1879), quoted in Boehlich, *Antisemitismusstreit*, 38–39: "In the course of this I mentioned Tacitus's well-known phrase *odium generis humani*. Then along comes Herr Graetz and cites the phrase, which refers to the Christians, and of course in the eyes of unscholarly readers he is right. But every historian knows—and Herr Graetz better than anyone—that the Christians were regarded as a Jewish sect until the time of Trajan. In the days of Nero about which Tacitus is speaking, the Christians were still frequently called *Judaei*, and the charge of 'hatred for humanity' was levelled equally against the Old Jews and the New Jews, the Christians .... That passage of Tacitus has never been understood otherwise, and cannot be understood otherwise, than as bearing witness both to the citizens' repugnance for the new religion and to the hatred of the Jews that prevailed in the Eastern lands. Almost all the authors of the late Classical period agreed about this hatred: Pliny, Quintilian, Tacitus, Juvenal and many others." To which Heinrich Graetz replied, in "Mein letztes Wort an Professor von Treitschke," *Schlesische Presse* (28 December 1879), quoted by Boehlich, *Antisemitismusstreit*, 49: "No amount of interpretive art will extricate you from your blunder over *odium generis humani*. Tacitus is speaking only of the Christians and

TACITUS'S EXCURSUS ON THE JEWS THROUGH THE AGES 283

ing about this dispute between the two historians is that it involves only the *Annals* and not the Jewish excursus in the *Histories*. When replying to Graetz's correction, von Treischke does not even mention Tacitus's formulation from the Jewish excursus *adversus omnes alios hostile odium*, "against all others a hatred reserved for enemies" (*Hist.* 5.5.1).[108]

As has been seen, in the view of many nineteenth-century authors Tacitus, with his distinction between Jewish customs that are sanctioned by their age (*antiquitas*) and those that are perverted (*pravitas*), brings handy evidence of Jewish depravation.[109] In nineteenth-century commentary editions of the *Histories*, however, attempts at this kind of interpretation do not appear. During this period there is a discrepancy between commentaries and essays on the Jewish excursus. The commentaries of Theophil Kiessling (1840) and Johann G. Orellius (1848) describe the Jewish excursus with restraint, and tend to criticise the more invidious sections.[110] The same can be said of the

---

    not the Jews. Only the Christians were accused by Nero of starting the fire and brutally tortured by him, not the Jews."

108   The phrase *odium humani generis* from the chapter on the Christians (Tacitus, *Ann.* 15.44) had already been applied to the Jews by Hegel. According to Hegel, the Jews' hate-filled relationship with those around them is a direct result of their self-segregation: the "soul of Jewish nationality" is "*odium generis humani.*" Cf. Georg W.F. Hegel, *Frühe Schriften, Werke in 20 Bänden.* Vol. 1 (Frankfurt am Main: Suhrkamp, 1971), 293. Cf. Hoffmann, *Juden und Judentum*, 17–18.

109   This one-sided depiction of the ancient Jews was redressed by various Jewish authors (such as Moritz Güdemann, Eugen Täubler, Isaak Heinemann, and Elias Bickermann). On this, cf. the observations and references in Hoffmann, *Juden und Judentum*, 287, *passim*. It seems that Posidonius lies behind Tacitus's account of the depravation of Judaism. Isaac Heinemann, "Poseidonios über die Entwicklung der jüdischen Religion," *Monatszeitschrift für Geschichte und Wissenschaft des Judentums* 63 (1919): 113–121, at 121 remarks very aptly and perhaps not without irony that Posidonius, with his theory of a gradual ritualization of Judaism, "has become in a certain sense the precursor of the concept of the development of the Israelite religion which today is usually attributed to Wellhausen."

110   Theophil Kiessling, *C. Cornelii Taciti Historiarum libri quinque* (Leipzig: Teubner, 1840); Johann G. Orellius, *C. Cornelii Taciti Opera quae supersunt.* Vol. 2 (Zürich 1848). Orellius provides a special appendix on the Jewish excursus (323–329). On the reproach of misanthropy on the part of the Jews (Tacitus, *Hist.* 5.5.1), Kiessling notes: "By law there was no hostile hatred .... The same charge of hatred is cast at Christians jumbled together with Jews." In their *Breviaria* on Book 5 of the *Histories*, Kiessling and Orellius reject Tacitus's representation of Judaism as "spiteful opinions of the ignorant." To redress this Orellius repeatedly points to passages in the Bible. On the other hand, just as Lipsius before him, he explicitly praises Tacitus's description of Jewish monotheism as distinct from the less accurate one by Diodorus. Orellius, *Opera*, 327–328 (on *Hist.* 5.5.4): "Tacitus has examined much more subtly and truthfully than Diodorus (40 p. 543) the innermost power and special source of the Jewish religion."

284

CHAPTER 13

commentaries of Wilhelm Heraeus (1884), and later those of Eduard Wolff and Georg Andresen (1886).[111]

An indication meanwhile of the momentum acquired by the reception history of the Jewish excursus is provided by a remark by Friedrich Nietzsche. Nietzsche, in *Beyond Good and Evil*, evokes Tacitus in connection with his religious criticism, which here again is aimed mostly at Christianity: "The Jews—'a people born to slavery' as Tacitus and the whole world say, 'the chosen people out of all people' as they themselves say and believe."[112] Nietzsche is of course wrong to attribute this quotation to Tacitus; it comes in fact from a speech by Cicero.[113]

10   The National Socialist Period

Tacitus certainly provided the anti-Jewish rhetoric of some recipients as a convenient peg for antisemitic polemics. This is particularly so in the period of National Socialism (1933–1945). At this time an extensive literature on the ancient Jews appeared in Germany. This is for the most part vehemently anti-Jewish in tone.[114] Here just one representative work will be considered, by the 'race researcher' Eugen Fischer and the New Testament scholar Gerhard Kittel; its tendentious title *World Jewry in Antiquity* already hints at the use (or misuse and distortion) of ancient records to bolster National Socialist conspiracy theories concerning the Jews. This will be clear from the following extract, in which the two authors seek backing from Tacitus:

---

111   Wilhelm Heraeus, *Cornelii Taciti Historiarum libri qui supersunt* (Leipzig and Berlin: Teubner, 1899 [1884]); Eduard Wolff and Georg Andresen (second ed.; Berlin 1926 [1886]; second edition by Georg Andresen). Heraeus comments unequivocally on Tacitus's malicious observations, speaking of "absurdity," "the wrong end of the stick," "prejudice and libel." On *Hist.* 5.13.1 (*gens supersitioni obnoxia, religionibus adversa,* "a nation steeped in superstition and hostile to proper religious practices"), Heraeus notes: "Viewed from an unbiased position, one would expect the opposite judgment." Wolff and Andresen make a similar comment, speaking of "Tacitus's narrative, riddled with mistakes" and "distorted by elements of fable." In questioning the reproach of misanthropy (*Hist.* 5.5.1), Wolff and Andresen respond that "the law was different" and cite Exod 22:20.

112   Friedrich Nietzsche, *Jenseits von Gut und Böse* (Leipzig: C.G. Naumann, 1886), No. 195. Cf. Schmitthenner, "eine 'Judenfrage,'" 127.

113   Cicero, *Prov.* 5.10: *iam vero publicanos miseros … tradidit in servitutem Iudaeis et Syris, nationibus natis servituti* ("Then too he has handed over the wretched revenue farmers to servitude under the Jews and Syrians, peoples born to slavery").

114   On the "Image of Judaism in German scholarship of antiquity under the Nazis," cf. Hoffmann, *Juden und Judentum*, 246–279.

As far back as Tacitus the emergence of the Jewish community is closely analogous to modern Zionism: international World Jewry artificially creates and sustains a central point which does nothing to impede World Jewry but serves to maintain and strengthen its role as a destructive element throughout the world. At the same time this increased concentration quite obviously facilitates proselytism: the proselyte is completely freed from his traditional ties to become a factor in the power ranking of World Jewry: 'Also they stick firmly together, and among themselves display ungrudging generosity, while hating the rest of mankind as enemies' (Tacitus).[115]

Here Tacitus is patently misused in the service of the National Socialist racial theory. Neither the literary nor the historical context is taken into account. The authors wish to demonstrate that "always, at all times, whether in the first or the twentieth century ... World Jewry dreams of absolute world domination in this world and the life hereafter."[116] But even such a plainly antisemitic book as that of Fischer and Kittel may still find itself surprised by Tacitus's somewhat abstruse passages. In the chapter "Ancient Antagonism Towards the Jews," which again was intended to appear fully researched, they write: "This antagonism towards the Jews sometimes took the form of fanciful stories; (for instance that of) the ass's head they were said to worship as a god, which was taken up by Tacitus."[117]

11   Conclusion

How is it that Tacitus's ethnographical study of the Jews can have had such a strong effect? Various moments appear to have been decisive in securing the Jewish excursus its intensive reception.

1) The sparse early reception of Tacitus's collected works cannot be explained by the anti-Jewish and anti-Christian propositions in the *Histories* and the *Annals*. On the contrary, it would appear that Tacitus's reception

---

115   Eugen Fischer and Gerhard Kittel, *Das antike Weltjudentum: Forschungen zur Judenfrage*. Vol. 7 (Hamburg: Hanseatische Verlagsanstalt, 1943), 79–80 (cf. Tacitus, *Hist*. 5.5.1, *et quia apud ipsos fides obstinata, misericordia in promptu, sed adversus omnes alios hostile odium*). On Kittel, cf. Hoffmann, *Juden und Judentum*, 254–259. The book of Fischer and Kittel is part of an eight-volume series, "Forschungen zur Judenfrage."
116   Fischer and Kittel, *Das antike Weltjudentum*, 11.
117   Fischer and Kittel, *Das antike Weltjudentum*, 90.

286 CHAPTER 13

was boosted by the chapters on the Christians and the Jews, as these passages were of particular interest to Christian authors and commentators. Right from the start, ever since Tertullian's polemic, the Jewish excursus has held a special place in the reception of Tacitus. Tertullian's critique gained further impetus in the sixteenth century through Budé. Thereafter the religious components of the reception became somewhat secondary, but still found a place in the work of commentators.

2) Tacitus presents the Jewish religion as being in complete antithesis to that of the Romans'. Jewish customs are part of a negative and perverted world. Hence Tacitus became the emblem of an antithetical mindset which runs like a red thread through subsequent periods of anti-Jewish rhetoric. Tacitus's richly detailed polemic provided numerous opportunities for this.[118]

3) In addition to this antithetical mindset there was another moment of considerable importance for the reception: the chronological dividing line Tacitus draws between "customs that were sanctioned by their age (*antiquitas*)" and those that "owed their value to their perverted nature (*pravitas*)." In this way Tacitus gave the antithetical position a chronological cloak which was particularly to the taste of nineteenth-century authors.

This survey of the reception history has made it clear how large was the effect of Tacitus's little chapters. On the other hand the potential significance of the excursus for hatred and antisemitism has by and large been kept within bounds. With the exception of the anti-Jewish polemics of nineteenth-century authors mentioned above, and those of National Socialist literature, Tacitus's description of the Jews has very seldom been used to launch or justify anti-Jewish rhetoric. This may be related to the complexity and difficulty of the excursus, but also to the fact that Tacitus's criticism of Christianity was a complicating factor for Christian authors contemplating the adoption of his arguments.

Moreover, the 'reputation' of the great Roman historian has scarcely been dented by the old criticisms of Tertullian, Budé, and a few later commentators. Certainly a great many authors, both Christian and Jewish, found them-

---

118 Cf. Hoffmann, *Juden und Judentum*, 285–286 and idem, "Das Judentum als Antithese." Hoffmann sets out a list of various dualities for gauging the anti-Jewish polemics of ancient historians of the nineteenth and twentieth centuries: "universal spirit religion" vs. "particular law religion," "enlightened free scientific culture" vs. "clerical dogmatism," "secular national state" vs. "theocracy/church," "popular national consciousness" vs. "homeland-lacking cosmopolitanism." Judaism at that time represented the negative, and Tacitus could be called into evidence for all of this.

TACITUS'S EXCURSUS ON THE JEWS THROUGH THE AGES 287

selves struggling to preserve their high regard for Tacitus over questions of *ira et studium* in the Jewish excursus. But usually the historiographical brilliance of Tacitus caused critics to exercise restraint. Occasionally there are signs of wishing to separate the character of anti-Jewish polemicist from that of far-sighted historian. A final example may help to make this clear: the *Josephus* trilogy by the German-Jewish novelist Lion Feuchtwanger, written between 1932 and 1940.[119] The first part of the trilogy features a Roman captain who will later attack the temple of Jerusalem with fire. Feuchtwanger gives this character lines of anti-Jewish dialogue which are almost literally (somewhat beefed up) drawn from Tacitus's Jewish excursus:

Vol. 1, p. 376: "You hate and despise all others. You circumcise yourself only as a mark of difference." (cf. Tacitus, *Hist.* 5.5.1: *sed adversus omnis alios hostile odium.* 5.5.2: *circumcidere genitalia instituerunt ut diversitate noscantur*).

Vol. 1, p. 376: "These stupid people believe that the souls of those who keep their squalid commandments will be preserved for eternity by their God." (cf. Tacitus, *Hist.* 5.5.3: *animosque proelio aut suppliciis peremptorum aeternos putant*).

Vol. 1, p. 377: "and some even say they worshipped an ass in their holy of holies." (cf. Tacitus, *Hist.* 5.4.2: *effigiem animalis ... penetrali sacravere*).

Vol. 1, p. 377: "But that's not right, these lunatics and criminals believe in a god you can't see or taste, a god as shameless as themselves existing only in their minds." (cf. Tacitus, *Hist.* 5.4.4: *Iudaei mente sola unumque numen intellegunt*).

Feuchtwanger is obviously drawing on Tacitus here, but does not name his source. Later in the book Feuchtwanger actually brings Tacitus the historian into the action. Feuchtwanger presents him—doubtless autobiographically—as an intelligent and eloquent man standing up for freedom under the tyrant Domitian (somewhat Hitleresque in Feuchtwanger's portrayal), but who sees himself for the time being as condemned to silence. Feuchtwanger depicts Tacitus as a cool-headed champion of freedom who reads people and politics with

---

119   Lion Feuchtwanger, *Josephus Trilogie*. Vol. 1: *Der jüdische Krieg* (1932, English translation published as *Josephus*); Vol. 2: *Die Söhne* (1935, English translation published as *The Jews of Rome*); Vol. 3: *Der Tag wird kommen*, also published as *Das gelobte Land* (1942, English translation published as *The Day will Come* or *Josephus and the Emperor*). I cite from the edition of the *Aufbau Taschenbuch* press (Berlin 1994).

the utmost care.[120] The anti-Jewish statements quoted above—derived from Tacitus's Jewish excursus!—are placed by Feuchtwanger into the mouth of a fierce Roman captain. However, Feuchtwanger allows other authors such as Quintilian to express explicit anti-Jewish views.[121]

Feuchtwanger's disparate handling of the polemical sections of the Jewish excursus on the one hand and the serious-minded figure of Tacitus on the other does not square with the fact that Tacitus is the author of this polemic, and is in the end a further example of the unease felt by many recipients that the great historian Tacitus should have written so negatively about the Jews.

Bibliography

Alberti, Leon Battista, *De Re Aedificatoria*. Edited by Giovanni Orlandi. Milan: Edizioni il Polifilo, 1966.

Barnes, Timothy D., *Tertullian: A Historical and Literary Study*. Oxford: Oxford University Press, 1985.

Barral, Robert, ed., *Michel de Montaigne. Œuvres complètes*. Paris: Éditions du Seuil, 1967 (1586).

Ben Israel, Menasseh (Manasseh), *Conciliador*. Amsterdam 1632.

Bloch, René, *Antike Vorstellungen vom Judentum: Der Judenexkurs des Tacitus im Rahmen der griechisch-römischen Ethnographie*. Stuttgart: Franz Steiner, 2002.

Boehlich, Walter, *Der Berliner Antisemitismusstreit*. Frankfurt: Insel-Verlag, 1965.

---

120   For Feuchtwanger's depiction of the historian Tacitus, cf. e.g. vol. 3, 61: "I (Tacitus) am here to write down what happens under the tyrants. If I didn't constantly tell myself that, then I wouldn't know how I could bear this life either;" 201: "And Cornelius could no longer restrain himself, and in his dark, grave, threatening voice he added, 'Freedom is no prejudice, my dear Regin, freedom is something very definite and palpable. If I have to reflect whether I'm allowed to say what I have to say, then my life becomes narrower, I become poorer, I can no longer think without constraint, I oblige myself against my will to think only the 'permissible', I deteriorate, I hem myself in with a thousand paltry reflections and hesitations, instead of looking out to the wide horizons my brain grows fat. In servitude one merely breathes: only in freedom can one live;'" 377: "In dark and mighty sentences which piled up like boulders he set out the crimes and terrors of the Palatine, and found words as wide and as bright as an early summer's day for the heroism of his friends."

121   Feuchtwanger, vol. 2, 208: "Quintilian was never fond of the Jews, and the influence of the 'Jewish Venus' (meaning Berenice) on Roman politics always made him uneasy." Cf. Quintillian 3.7.21: *et parentes malorum odimus et est conditoribus urbium infame contraxisse aliquam perniciosam ceteris gentem qualis est primus Iudaicae supersitionis auctor* ... ("We tend to hate the parents of evil children, and founders of cities have a bad reputation for having brought together a people destructive to others, such as the man who was the founder of the Jewish superstition").

Borzsák, Stephanus, "Tacitus." *RE Supplementband* 11: 373–512.

Brotier, Gabriel, *C. Cornelii Taciti Opera. Recognovit, emendavit, supplementis explevit, notis, dissertationibus, tabulis geographicis illustravit Gabriel Brotier*. Vol. 3. Paris 1771.

Budé, Guillaume, *De Asse et Partibus Eius*. Basel 1556 (Paris 1514).

Burke, Peter, "Tacitism." Pages 149–171 in *Tacitus*. Edited by Thomas A. Dorey. London: Routledge, 1969.

Cardoso, Isaac, *Las excelencias de los Hebreos*. Amsterdam 1679.

Chevallier, Raymond, and Rémy Poignault, eds., *Actes du colloque Présence de Tacite: Hommage à G. Radke*. Tours: University of Tours, 1992.

Cornelius, Emmerich, *Quomodo Tacitus, Historiarum Scriptor, in Hominum Memoria Versatus Sit ad Renascentes Litteras Saeculis XIV et XV*. Wetzlar: Nabu, 1888.

Craddock, Patricia B., ed., *The English Essays of Edward Gibbon*. Oxford: Oxford University Press, 1972.

Etter, Else-Lilly, *Tacitus in der Geistesgeschichte des 16. und 17. Jahrhunderts*. Basel: Helbing & Lichtenhahn, 1966.

Fabia, Philippe, *Les sources de Tacite dans les Histoires et les Annales*. Paris: Imprimerie Nationale, 1895.

Feuchtwanger, Lion, *Josephus Trilogie*. 3 vol. Berlin: Aufbau Taschenbuch 1994.

Fischer, Eugen and Gerhard Kittel, *Das antike Weltjudentum: Forschungen zur Judenfrage*. Vol. 7. Hamburg: Hanseatische Verlagsanstalt, 1943.

Gebhardt, Carl, *Spinoza Opera*. Vol. 3. Heidelberg: Carl Winter, 1972 (1925).

Gibbon, Edward, *The History of the Decline and Fall of the Roman Empire* (1776), with an introduction by Christopher Dawson. London: Allen Lane, 1910.

Gronovius, Joannes, *C. Cornelii Taciti Opera quae exstant*. Utrecht 1721 (1672).

Haverfield, Francis, "Tacitus during the Late Roman Period and the Middle Ages." *JRS* 6 (1916): 196–201.

Hegel, Georg W.F., *Frühe Schriften, Werke in 20 Bänden*. Vol. 1. Frankfurt am Main: Suhrkamp, 1971.

Heinemann, Isaac, "Poseidonios über die Entwicklung der jüdischen Religion." *Monatszeitschrift für Geschichte und Wissenschaft des Judentums* 63 (1919): 113–121.

Heraeus, Wilhelm, *Cornelii Taciti Historiarum libri qui supersunt*. Leipzig and Berlin: Teubner, 1899 (1884).

Hertzberg, Arthur, *The French Enlightenment and the Jews*. New York: Columbia University Press, 1968.

Hoffmann, Christhard, *Juden und Judentum im Werk deutscher Althistoriker des 19. und 20. Jahrhunderts*. Leiden: Brill, 1988.

Hoffmann, Christhard, "Das Iudentum als Antithese: Zur Tradition eines kulturellen Wertungsmusters." Pages 25–46 in *Antisemitismus in Deutschland: Zur Aktualität eines Vorurteils*. Edited by Wolfgang Benz. Munich: Deutscher Taschenbuch Verlag, 1990.

Hoffmann, Christhard, "Ancient Jewry—Modern Questions: German Historians of Antiquity on the Jewish Diaspora." *Illinois Classical Studies* 20 (1995): 191–207.

Kaplan, Joseph, trans., *Isaac Cardoso: Las Excelencias de los Hebreos*. Jerusalem: Bialik, 1971.

Kiessling, Theophil, *C. Cornelii Taciti Historiarum libri quinque*. Leipzig: Teubner, 1840.

Kirchmaier, Georg C., *Exercitatio academica ad C.C. Taciti Histor. Lib. V. Capita aliquot priora de rebus moribusque Judaeorum*. Wittenberg 1676.

Kirchmaier, Georg C., *De obsidione Hierosolymitana, ex V. Hist. C.C. Taciti*. Wittenberg 1679.

Labhardt, Theobald, *Quae de Iudaeorum Origine Iudicaverint Veteres*. PhD Dissertation University of Augsburg, 1881.

Leo, Heinrich, *Vorlesungen über die Geschichte des Jüdischen Staates: gehalten an der Universität zu Berlin*. Reutlingen: Duncker & Humblot, 1829.

Leonhard, Franz X., *Über den Bericht des Tacitus über die Juden, Hist. 5,2–6*. Ellwangen: Kaupert, 1852.

Lindo, Elias H., *The Conciliator of R. Manesseh ben Israel*. New York: Hermon, 1972 [1842].

Lipsius, Justus, *C. Cornelii Taciti Opera quae exstant*. Antwerp 1585.

Luce, Torrey J., and Anthony J. Woodman, eds., *Tacitus and the Tacitean Tradition*. Princeton: Princeton University Press, 1993.

Lund, Allan A., *Germanenideologie im Nationalsozializmus: zur Rezeption der 'Germania' des Tacitus im 'Dritten Reich'*. Heidelberg: Winter, 1995.

Luzzatto, Simone, *Discorso circa il stato degl'Hebrei et in particolàr dimoranti nell'inclita Città di Venetia*. Venice 1638.

Malissard, Alain, "Montaigne lecteur de Tacite." Pages 157–164 in *Présence de Tacite, Hommage au professeur G. Radke, Actes du colloque de l'ENS (Paris, octobre 1991)*. Edited by Rémy Poignault and Raymond Chevallier. Tours: l'Université de Tours, 1992.

Malitz, Jürgen, "Mommsen, Caesar, und die Juden." Pages 371–387 in *Geschichte–Tradition–Reflexion. Festschrift für Martin Hengel zum 70. Geburtstag, Band II: Griechische und Römische Religion*. Edited by Hubert Cancik, Hermann Lichtenberger, and Peter Schäfer. Tübingen: Mohr Siebeck, 1996.

Melamed, Abraham, "Simone Luzzatto on Tacitus: Apologetica and Ragione di Stato." Pages 143–170 in *Studies in Medieval Jewish History*. Edited by Isadore Twersky. Cambridge: Harvard University Press, 1984.

Mellor, Ronald, *Tacitus: The Classical Heritage*. New York: Garland, 1995.

Momigliano, Arnaldo, "The First Political Commentary on Tacitus." *JRS* 37 (1947): 91–101.

Mommsen, Theodor, "Cornelius Tacitus und Cluvius Rufus." *Hermes* 4 (1870): 295–325.

Mommsen, Theodor, *Auch ein Wort über unser Judenthum*. Berlin: Weidmanns, 1880.

Mommsen, Theodor, *Römische Geschichte*. Vol. 5. Berlin: Weidmanns, 1885.

Mommsen, Theodor, *Judaea und die Juden—Mit einem Nachwort von Eugen Täubler*. Berlin: Schocken, 1936.

Müller, Johann G., "Kritische Untersuchung der taciteischen Berichte über den Ursprung der Juden, Hist. 5.2 ff." *Theologische Studien und Kritiken* 16 (1843): 893–958.

Muret, M. Antonius, *Orationes, epistulae, hymnique sacri*. *Editio nova*. Leipzig 1629 (1604).

Nietzsche, Friedrich, *Jenseits von Gut und Böse*. Leipzig: C.G. Naumann, 1886.

de Nolhac, Pierre, ed., *Lettres inédites de Muret*. Mélanges Charles Graux. Paris: Ernest Thorin, 1884.

Orellius, Johann G., *C. Cornelii Taciti Opera quae supersunt*. Vol. 2. Zürich 1848.

Pichon, Julianus, *C. Cornelii Taciti Opera*. Paris 1682–1687; *Histories*: 1686.

de Rossi, Azariah, *Light of the Eyes*. Berlin 1794, second edition. Mantua 1573–1575.

Schanz, Martin, and Carl Hosius, *Geschichte der römischen Literatur bis zum Gesetzgebungswerk des Kaisers Justinian*. Munich: C.H. Beck, 1935.

Schedel, Hartmann, *Die Schedelsche Weltchronik von 1493*, fourth edition. Dortmund: Harenberg, 1988.

Schellhase, Kenneth C., *Tacitus in Renaissance Political Thought*. Chicago: The University of Chicago Press, 1976.

Schmitthenner, Walter, "Kennt die hellenistisch-römische Antike eine 'Judenfrage'?" Pages 9–29 in *Die Juden als Minderheit in der Geschichte*. Edited by Bernd Martin and Ernst Schulin. Munich: Deutscher Taschenbuch-Verlag, 1981.

Sorscher, Esther, "A Comparison of Three Texts: The Wars, the Hegesippus, and the Yosippon." MA Thesis, Yeshiva University, New York, NY, 1973.

de Spinoza, Baruch, *Tractatus Theologico-Politicus*. Amsterdam 1670.

von Stackelberg, Jürgen, *Tacitus in der Romania: Studien zur literarischen Rezeption des Tacitus in Italien und Frankreich*. Tübingen: Max Niemeyer, 1960.

Tenney, Mary F., "Tacitus in the Middle Ages and in England to about 1650." PhD Dissertation, Cornell University, Ithaca, NY, 1931.

Townend, Gavin B., "The Earliest Scholiast on Juvenal." *ClQ* 22 (1972): 376–387.

Ugolinus, Blasius, *Thesaurus Antiquitatum Sacrarum complectens selectissima clarissimorum virorum opuscula, in quibus veterum Hebraeorum mores, leges, instituta, ritus sacri et civiles illustrantur*. Volume 2. Venice 1744.

Volpilhac-Auger, Catherine, *Tacite et Montesquieu*. Oxford: Oxford University Press, 1985.

Volpilhac-Auger, Catherine, *Tacite en France de Montesquieu à Chateaubriand*. Oxford: Oxford University Press, 1993.

Voltaire, *Dictionnaire philosophique, Les Œuvres Complètes de Voltaire*. Edited by Ula Kölving. Oxford: Oxford University Press, 1994 (1764).

Weinberg, Joanna, trans., *Azariah de' Rossi: The Light of the Eyes*. New Haven: Yale University Press, 2001.

Wessner, Paul, ed., *Scholia in Iuvenalem Vetustiora*. Leipzig: Teubner, 1931.

Wirszubski, Chaim, *Libertas as a Political Idea at Rome during the Late Republic and Early Principate*. Cambridge: Cambridge University Press, 1955.

Worm, Chrisitan, *De corruptis antiquitatum Hebraearum apud Tacitum et Martialem vestigiis libri duo*. Copenhagen 1694.

Yerushalmi, Yosef Hayim, *From Spanish Court to Italian Ghetto: Isaac Cardoso—A Study in Seventeenth-Century Marranism and Jewish Apologetics*. New York: Columbia University Press, 1971.

Yerushalmi, Yosef Hayim, *Zakhor: Jewish History and Jewish Memory*. Seattle: University of Washington Press, 1982.

CHAPTER 14

Polytheism and Monotheism in Antiquity: On Jan Assmann's Critique of Monotheism

The ancient Greco-Roman world was, in general, not an environment of political correctness. Those familiar with the invectives of Cicero, the ethnographic representations of various peoples by the Greek and Roman historians, or some of the more aggressive ancient poetry quickly recognize the often limitless possibilities of rhetorical abuse in Greco-Roman antiquity. Authors attacked and were attacked. A later, with regard to transmission complicated, yet still very telling text provides us with a snapshot of this rhetorical battlefield, in which, at times, everyone took up arms against everyone else: in 248 CE, the Christian author Origen produced an apologetic work aimed at the pagan philosopher Celsus (second century CE). We know of Celsus only by means of Origen's eight books *Against Celsus* (*Contra Celsum*): in his apology, Origen cites and paraphrases at length the arguments which had appeared in a tractate published by Celsus entitled Ἀληθὴς λόγος ("The True Teaching"). In this tractate, Celsus had attacked Christianity in particular, but also Judaism. Since Celsus allowed a Jew to appear in his invective as well, in Origen's subsequent response we find a verbal exchange between a Jew (who remains nameless), a pagan (Celsus), and a Christian (Origen).

An example of how all three sides polemicized with no holds barred comes with their arguments over myth: pagans, Jews, and Christians all accuse the other(s) of believing in 'myths' (in the sense of fictional stories). Celsus dubs the accounts and laws of Moses "empty myths" and "children's stories:" the stories in Genesis concerning Adam and Eve are examples of "old wives' tales" (so much the more because the Greek author Hesiod had dealt with these things much earlier). Origen fires back, dismissing the myths of the Greeks as arbitrary inventions.[1] The Jewish interlocutor comes to Origen's aid, criticizing those figures in Greek myth who disappear temporarily into Hades, such as Orpheus, Heracles, and Theseus, as "swindlers."[2] Yet this Jewish support against pagan accusation then turns in a different, anti-Christian direction and puts forward a polemic against Jesus: Celsus, according to Origen, has his Jewish

---

1 Origen, *Cels.* 1.23.
2 Origen, *Cels.* 2.56.

© RENÉ BLOCH, 2022 | DOI:10.1163/9789004521896_016

representative claim that at least the *old* myths (οἱ μὲν παλαιοὶ μῦθοι), which ascribe to Perseus or to Minos a divine lineage (though the Jews do not accept these either) depict their characters' actions as "great, marvelous, and genuinely superhuman, so that they do not appear unworthy of credence."[3] But not so with the accounts of Jesus.

Within ancient polemics, depending upon one's perspective such 'false ideas' could signal either monotheism or polytheism. In the following, I would like to take a closer look at this issue and thereby deal in more detail with a modern polemical exchange which, as will be shown, follows in the tradition of an older one: namely, the controversial theses of the Heidelberg Egyptologist Jan Assmann regarding monotheism, which have appeared in a series of publications on this topic over the last ten years.[4]

Polytheism-vs-monotheism also constitutes a theme within Origen's *Contra Celsum*: the pagan Celsus had said that at one time a hoard of goat- and sheepherders had, in their "uncultivated credulity" (ἀγροίκοις ἀπάταις), allowed themselves to be "misled" (ψυχαγωγηθέντες) by their leader Moses into believing that there was only one God.[5] They had "without any rational cause" (ἀλόγως) turned their back on belief in multiple gods and had followed Moses in the belief that there was only one God. This God was called "the Most High," "Adonai," "Ouranios" ("the Heavenly One"), or "Sabaoth." They would recognize no other deity than this (καὶ πλεῖον οὐδὲν ἔγνωσαν).[6] Celsus' pagan critique of monotheism exudes disgust: the belief in only one God is the irrational thinking of the peasant.[7]

Celsus's portrayal of the Jews' ancestors as naïve shepherds following Moses, who convinced them of the truth of monotheism, had a forerunner around 110 CE in the Roman historian Publius Cornelius Tacitus: Tacitus reported that, after the Jews had been expelled from Egypt—the Egyptian oracle had cited the Jews as the cause for a nasty plague—they did not really know what to do (they had just stood there, crying); then Moses had shaken them out of their stupor and given them new laws. Tacitus has nothing positive to say about the Jews

---

3 Origen, *Cels.* 1.67.

4 First in Jan Assmann, *Moses the Egyptian: The Memory of Egypt in Western Monotheism* (Cambridge: Harvard University Press, 1998), also published as *Moses der Ägypter: Entzifferung einer Gedächtnisspur* (Munich: Carl Hanser Verlag, 1998). Citations from Assmann's work follow English translations where available. In all other cases, the original German has been translated into English for this article.

5 Origen, *Cels.* 1.23.

6 Origen, *Cels.* 1.24.

7 The verb ψυχαγωγεῖν here stands for the seduction of people into a delusion: LSJ ad loc.

POLYTHEISM AND MONOTHEISM IN ANTIQUITY   295

in his depiction of the Jewish way of life: he calls them a *taeterrima gens*, "the most abominable people;" Jewish customs are "preposterous and mean" (*absurdus sordidusque*). They are presented as running absolutely counter to Roman culture. Jewish monotheism and aniconism are part of this negative portrait:[8] the monotheistic Jews worship no images, not even in their synagogues. Tacitus says pejoratively that they did not offer such "groveling" (*adulatio*) to kings or Caesars.[9] Here Jewish monotheism is understood from the pagan-polytheistic perspective to represent a departure from proper, natural worship of the gods. The *polytheistic* "distinction," if one wants to call it that (vs. Assmann's "Mosaic distinction"), here maintains that the Greco-Roman idea of a polytheistic realm of the gods is the right one; the other idea, of a realm in which there is only one god, is wrong.

In Greco-Roman antiquity, pagan attacks on the Jews were primarily politically motivated. But it could happen that 'pagans' would ridicule the Jewish belief in a single, formless God. When an anti-Jewish campaign emerged in the year 38 CE in Alexandria, the Jews tried in vain to save their synagogues by arguing that the synagogues—which had not infrequently been dedicated to the royal family since Ptolemaic times—were a reasonable Jewish alternative to the imperial cult, which monotheism disallowed. The Jewish philosopher-theologian Philo of Alexandria said in his tractate *Against Flaccus*:

> everywhere in the habitable world the religious veneration of the Jews for the Augustan house has its basis as all may see in the meeting-houses, and if we have these destroyed no place, no method is left to us for paying this homage.[10]

The supplication was made in vain. Around the same time (40/41 CE), the Emperor Caligula tried to have a statue erected in the Jerusalem temple,[11] where only the one God of the Jews was worshipped; this contributed significantly to the deterioration of the political situation, which later erupted into the Jewish-Roman war.

---

8   René Bloch, *Antike Vorstellungen vom Judentum: Der Judenexkurs des Tacitus im Rahmen der griechisch-römischen Ethnographie* (Stuttgart: Franz Steiner Verlag, 2002), 95–96.

9   Tacitus, *Hist.* 5.3. The other use of *adulatio* in Tacitus demonstrates that "groveling" rather than "worship" is meant here; see Arnold Gerber and Adolf Greef, *Lexicon Taciteum* (Hildesheim: Georg Olms, 1962 [1877–1890]), 47–48.

10   Philo, *Flacc.* 49 (trans. LCL).

11   Tacitus, *Hist.* 5.9.2.

296 CHAPTER 14

Perhaps the most violent example of pagan polemic against Judaism comes in a text by Diodorus, probably adopted from Posidonius,[12] which records a conversation between Antiochus VII Sidetes, who besieged Jerusalem in 135 BCE, and his advisors. When the king was unsure whether or not to attack Jerusalem, his friends advised him to do so and referred to the earlier anti-Jewish actions of Antiochus IV Epiphanes:

> When King Antiochus (VII Sidetes), says Diodorus, was laying siege to Jerusalem, the Jews held out for a time, but when all their supplies were exhausted they found themselves compelled to make overtures for a cessation of hostilities. Now the majority of his friends advised the king to take the city by storm and to wipe out completely the race of Jews, since they alone of all nations avoided dealings with any other people and looked upon all men as their enemies. They pointed out, too, that the ancestors of the Jews had been driven out of all Egypt as men who were impious and detested by the gods. For by way of purging the country all persons who had white or leprous marks on their bodies had been assembled and driven across the border, as being under a curse; the refugees had occupied the territory round about Jerusalem, and having organized the nation of the Jews had made their hatred of mankind into a tradition, and on this account had introduced utterly outlandish laws: not to break bread with any other race, nor to show them any good will at all. His friends reminded Antiochus also of the enmity that in times past his ancestors had felt for this people. Antiochus, called Epiphanes, on defeating the Jews had entered the innermost sanctuary of the god's temple, where it was lawful for the priest alone to enter. Finding there a marble statue of a heavily bearded man seated on an ass, with a book in his hands, he supposed it to be an image of Moses, the founder of Jerusalem and organizer of the nation, the man, moreover, who had ordained for the Jews their misanthropic and lawless customs. And since Epiphanes was shocked by such hatred directed against all mankind, he had set himself to break down their traditional practices. Accordingly, he sacrificed before the image of the founder and the open-air altar of the god a great sow, and poured its blood over them. Then, having prepared its flesh, he ordered that their holy books, containing the xenophobic laws, should be sprinkled with the broth of the meat; that the lamp, which they call undy-

---

12 Menahem Stern, *Greek and Latin Authors on Jews and Judaism*. 3 vols. (Jerusalem: Israel Academy of Sciences and Humanities, 1974), 1.184.

ing and which burns continually in the temple, should be extinguished; and that the high priest and the rest of the Jews should be compelled to partake of the meat.[13]

Here too, as later on with Tacitus and Celsus (according to Origen), we find circulating the 'version' of exodus, apparently well-known in antiquity, according to which the Jews had to leave Egypt due to a plague and then, guided by Moses, founded their own religion in Judea. Here this story is rehashed by the advisors of Antiochus VII in their attempt to convince him to destroy Jerusalem and obliterate the Jews. The report goes on to relate that Antiochus did not follow the advice of his friends and did not initiate any anti-Jewish initiative,[14] in contrast to his predecessor Antiochus IV, whose religious persecution is well-known. That persecution was politically motivated and to some extent fostered by inner-Jewish intrigue,[15] although it had undeniable religious connotations as well.

To say that there could be no violence "in connection with the question of God" within the pagan religions, as Jan Assmann claims, is a bold statement.[16] Polytheism could indeed be "exclusive" and, in connection with political motivations, "violently implemented." Polytheism could lapse into "the language of violence," even into violent actions. *Stricto sensu*, polytheism is the *exclusive* belief in many gods; monotheism is the opposite, the exclusive belief in one god.

In the ancient ethnographic representations of Judaism, the Jewish religion often appears as a counter-religion to the polytheistic system described by Greeks and Romans (from Hecataeus of Abdera [ca. 300 BCE] and Diodorus [first century BCE] to Tacitus [first/second century CE]). One may well doubt that the "criterion of incompatibility is missing"[17] with any consistency in the context of ancient polytheism. That it exists on the side of monotheism—at

---

13 Diodorus 34/35.1.1–4 (trans. LCL). See Bloch, *Antike Vorstellungen*, 44–45.

14 Diodorus, 34/35.1.5.

15 See the summary of the discussion in Ernst Haag, *Das hellenistische Zeitalter: Israel und die Bibel im 4. bis 1. Jahrhundert v.Chr.* (Stuttgart: Kohlhammer, 2003), 56–73.

16 Jan Assmann, *Monotheismus und die Sprache der Gewalt* (Vienna: Picus, 2004), 23: "There [in 'pagan' religions] one finds violence in the context of the political principle of government, but not in the context of the question of God. Violence is a question of power, not of truth" ("Dort gibt es Gewalt im Zusammenhang mit dem politischen Prinzip der Herrschaft, aber nicht im Zusammebnhang mit der Gottesfrage. Gewalt ist eine Frage der Macht, nicht der Wahrheit.").

17 Jan Assmann, *The Price of Monotheism* (Stanford: Stanford University Press, 2009), 18.

least in principle—is obvious (even if there do exist for almost all eras coun-terexamples in the form of integrative monotheism).[18]

Assmann refers to biblical satire and polemical religious constructions of the other, such as in Psalm 115, where the invisibility of the biblical God is juxta-posed to the visibility of pagan images. Here, as Assmann writes, a "deliberately uncomprehending glance" is cast upon the "religious practices of others" which "exposes them to ridicule in the harsh and alienating light of satiric descrip-tion: the genre of religious satire."[19] That such a rhetoric also appears contra monotheism may be seen in several polytheistic representations of monotheis-tic Judaism. This back and forth continued and found its way into late antiquity. Nor does Assmann doubt that there existed "mutual hatred" between the two sides.[20] But Assmann's interest lies first of all in what he sees as the particularly pronounced potential for violence inherent within monotheism. At the same time, Assmann portrays a pacifistic, storybook polytheism, the excluding side of which receives little emphasis from him.[21]

Hostility towards Jews in the Greco-Roman period was formed to a large extent in Egypt. Egyptian authors like Lysimachus, Chairemon, and Apion reproached the Jews for being misanthropic and godless. Anti-Jewish stereo-types thus came in large part from Hellenistic Egypt, were preserved by Roman authors (Seneca, Quintilian, Tacitus, Juvenal), and were then adopted by later Christian authors. Therefore, much of the anti-Jewish thought and Jewish

---

18   See Ekkehard W. Stegemann, "Wieder einmal Unbehagen am Monotheismus," *Reforma-tio: Zeitschrift für Kultur, Politik und Religion* 56 (2007): 20–27, at 20: "Sein (Jan Assmann's) Referent ist ein Konstrukt bzw. ein Abstraktum, nämlich jener Eingottglaube, der in der Wirklichkeit als solcher realexistierend nicht vorkommt." For a brief critique of Assmann's monotheism discussion, see also Walter Dietrich, "Israel und die Völker in der Hebräischen Bibel," in *Juden in ihrer Umwelt: Akkulturation des Judentums in Antike und Mittelalter*, ed. Matthias Konradt and Rainer C. Schwinges (Basel: Schwabe, 2009), 7–27, at 8–9.

19   Assmann, *Price of Monotheism*, 24. Ps 115 is responding, by the way, to a pagan polemic against the Israelite idea of God (vv. 2–3: "Why should the people say, 'Where is their God?' Our God is in the heavens, he does whatever he pleases." NRSV). Thereafter, in vv. 4–8, fol-lows the "satirical description" of polytheism and image worship.

20   Assmann, *Moses the Egyptian*, 4: "This hatred was mutual and the ⟨idolaters⟩ did not fail to retaliate." Of course, this formulation ("retaliate") results in the conclusion that the hatred began with the monotheists.

21   Walter Burkert uses the phrase "Bilderbuch-Polytheismus" independent of the question under discussion here, in reference to classical Greek polytheism with its gods, statues, and temples: Walter Burkert, "Mythen—Tempel—Götterbilder: Von der Nahöstlichen Koiné zur griechischen Gestaltung," in *Götterbilder, Gottesbilder, Weltbilder: Polytheismus und Monotheismus in der Welt der Antike, Band II: Griechenland und Rom, Judentum, Chris-tentum und Islam*, ed. Reinhard G. Kratz and Hermann Spieckermann (Tübingen: Mohr Siebeck, 2006), 3–20, at 19–20.

apologetic in antiquity constitutes an exchange between Jews and Egyptians. When the Jewish-Roman historian Flavius Josephus, writing in Rome near the end of the first century CE, polemicizes against anti-Jewish sentiment in his own time, he responds first of all to Egyptian authors (and indirectly to Roman anti-Judaism). The story that an Egyptian oracle arranged for the expulsion of the Jews as a remedy for a plague is an Egyptian story.[22]

I do not want to lose the thread of the controversy about monotheism, and therefore only briefly refer to this particular Egyptian polemic. Yet one cannot avoid the impression that Assmann's critique of monotheism ultimately stands somewhat within the tradition of this ancient Egyptian-Jewish competition. Egyptian and Jewish authors of Hellenistic and Roman times stressed the originality and brilliance of their own respective religions. Some of Assmann's comments read like a continuation in that ancient exchange: Assmann writes that the biblical punishments for adultery are, for example, "a cruelty that sharply contrasts with the Jurisprudence of Egypt."[23] Or, elsewhere, "the monotheism of Akhenaten of Amarna was a monotheism of knowledge. Behind it stands a new worldview that makes everything that exists, the sum total of reality, depend on the effects of the sun, which produces light and heat through its rays and time through its motion." This is "something completely different from the Mosaic project."[24] Referring to biblical passages that deal with a God of Israel who demands justice instead of sacrifice (Isa 1:11–17; Am 5:21–24; Mic 6:6–8; Ps 50), Assmann asks: "Did the Egyptian religion amount to nothing more than magic and sacrificial ritual? Ethical demands for a rational way of life were also proffered by it, only in a different context, in a different place, outside the limits of that which pertained to the 'appeasement of the gods.'"[25] Justice likewise need not be a biblical construct: "Justice has been in the world since time immemorial,"[26] only in Egypt it was understood as justice between man and man, rather than between man and God. Assmann comes to this conclusion: "Monotheism did not usher law and justice into the world; these had long been

---

22 The idea that the authors of this story wanted to challenge the biblical version of the Exodus, as often maintained previously, has rightly been questioned by Erich Gruen, *Heritage and Hellenism: The Reinvention of Jewish Tradition* (Berkeley: University of California Press, 1998), 41–72. The position that Manetho and authors after him formed an anti-Jewish "counterhistory," appears first in Amos Funkenstein, *Perceptions of Jewish History* (Berkeley: University of California Press, 1993), 36–39.

23 Assmann, *Monotheismus und die Sprache der Gewalt*, 36.

24 Assmann, *Price of Monotheism*, 38.

25 Jan Assmann, *Politische Theologie zwischen Ägypten und Israel* (Bonn: Carl Friedrich von Siemens Stiftung, 1992), 69.

26 Assmann, *Price of Monotheism*, 50.

300   CHAPTER 14

in existence."[27] This is the language of *presbyteron kreitton*, of 'greater antiquity,' regarding who recognized these truths "earlier, more determinedly, and
more clearly."[28] According to Assmann, Egypt regularly has the upper hand.[29]
This becomes particularly evident in his comparison of the 'Hebrew' and the
'Egyptian' Moses.[30] Assmann writes:

> Moses—in the biblical sense—stands for the step made in human his-
> tory at this point, the Exodus out of Egypt, out of a symbiotic relation-
> ship to the external world, and out of unity in civic and religious order,
> and he embodies this step in the manner of a violent, iconoclastic cult
> via estrangement and exclusion. But for what does "Moses the Egyptian"
> stand? ... Moses the Egyptian stands for the same step, but not in the
> exclusion and destruction of polytheism labelled as paganism, but in the
> sense of an integration, or, to pick up the felicitous language used in Jür-
> gen Habermas's Peace Award speech, of a "redeeming" transformation.
> Moses the Egyptian is the cosmotheist initiated into the Egyptian mys-

---

27   Assmann, *Price of Monotheism*, 52. See also idem, "Monotheism and Polytheism," in *Reli-
      gions of the Ancient World: A Guide*, ed. Sarah Iles Johnston (Cambridge: Harvard Univer-
      sity Press, 2004), 17–31, at 30, and idem, *Politische Theologie*, 69–70: "In addition, it should
      not be forgotten that already in an Egyptian text from the Middle Kingdom the astonish-
      ing sentence is written: *the good behavior of the righteous is sooner accepted than the ox of
      the wrongdoer*. This phrase could be in the Bible. The Egyptian text, however, addressed to
      a king, continues: *act for God, that he may do the same to you, through great sacrifice that
      adorn the altar generously, through inscriptions*. Although 'justice' is just as important as
      'ritual,' the latter is worthless without the former and they are bound together, and yet no
      change is made here: cultic ritual is in no way seen as unimportant in favor of justice."
      See also idem, "Gerechtigkeit und Monotheismus," in *Freiheit und Recht: Festschrift Frank
      Crüsemann zum 65. Geburtstag*, ed. Christof Hardmeier et al. (Gütersloh: Gütersloher Ver-
      lagshaus, 2003), 78–95 (at 82: "However, it is not right to say that pagan societies had no
      advanced moral systems, but rather developed only within monotheistic religions. To say
      so is a serious error, if not deliberate slander; the "pagans and idolators", e.g. the Babylo-
      nians and old Egyptians, also had highly developed concepts of morality." At 88: "Ethics
      already existed before monotheism ... monotheism did not invent it, but it has theologized
      it, i.e. made it a matter of God").
28   So says Assmann himself regarding this *Tendenz* in Jewish and Christian apologetics; see
      Jan Assmann, *Monotheismus und Kosmotheismus: Ägyptische Formen eines "Denkens des
      Einen" und ihre europäische Rezeptionsgeschichte* (Heidelberg: Winter, 1993), 12.
29   Here it is not my purpose to question or confirm the aforementioned examples, brought
      forth by Assmann. I only wish to demonstrate Assmann's *Tendenz* to juxtapose the Jewish
      with the Egyptian.
30   Jan Assmann, "Der hebräische und der ägyptische Mose—Bilder und Gegenbilder," in *Das
      Alte Testament und die Kultur der Moderne*, ed. Manfred Oeming et al. (Münster: LIT, 2004),
      147–155.

POLYTHEISM AND MONOTHEISM IN ANTIQUITY

teries who attempts to cast the Egyptian secret of the divine unity of the cosmos into the form of a public religion and to replace the long path of initiation, only possible for a few, with the form of revelation, and thus knowledge with faith. Moses the Egyptian stands for the idea of a higher wisdom beyond the distinction between nature and revelation and thus beyond the 'Mosaic' distinction between true and false religion.[31]

The violent, iconoclastic Moses of the Hebrews is compared to the integrating, higher-wisdom-seeking Egyptians (underlined, as it were, by referring to the "felicitous" [*glücklichen*] language of redemption [*rettend*] used in Jürgen Habermas's Peace Prize speech). Thus does Assmann's discussion of monotheism often sound like an Egyptian (and likewise Egyptological)[32] apology which, with an opposite valence, recalls the Jewish apologetic of Flavius Josephus. One may read the present chapter as a reply from the perspective of Jewish Studies.

A central thesis of Assman's first book on the theme, which first appeared in English in 1998 under the title *Moses the Egyptian: The Memory of Egypt in Western Monotheism*, runs thus:

> anti-Semitism was anti-monotheism in its earliest, Egyptian origins. Monotheism, for its part, was originally anti-cosmotheism.[33]

According to Assmann, "the Egyptians reacted with excessive hostility to the monotheism they encountered in the form of the Jews because it came up against an anti-monotheistic disposition."[34] According to Assmann's thesis, the Egyptians held in their memory a kind of phobia towards the Amarna Period of the fourteenth century BCE, i.e. Akhenaten's monotheistic and iconoclastic revolution, which had once underminded the Egyptian polytheistic system and allowed no other cult than that of the God of Sun and Light: "In the encounter with Jewish monotheism, the Egyptians experienced a return of the repressed, to which they reacted by resorting to violent repudiatory mechanisms."[35] This

---

31   Assmann, "Der hebräische und der ägyptische Mose," 153.
32   Assmann occasionally emphasizes his explicitly Egyptological perspective; see, e.g., Assmann, "Gerechtigkeit und Monotheismus," 93: "When I am attempting to deconstruct these stereotypes from the perspective of Egyptology, I do not think that I am offending or correcting monotheism. It would be bad for monotheism if it should stand and fall on ideas that cannot be historically maintained."
33   Assmann, *Price of Monotheism*, 57, summarizing these twin theses together.
34   Assmann, *Price of Monotheism*, 58.
35   Assmann, *Price of Monotheism*, 61.

302   CHAPTER 14

déjà vu experience is supposed to have effectively forced hostility toward the
Jews out of the Egyptians.

Assmann tries to show that this trauma of monotheism is tangible in the
report of the Egyptian author Manetho, a priest of the third century BCE:
there we find an account concerning lepers which is quite common in ancient
sources concerning the Jews. Flavius Josephus, who cites Manetho, explicitly
associates the story with the Jews.[36] According to Manetho, an Egyptian priest
named Osarsiph had been appointed leader of a group of lepers. The Egyptian
king Amenophis, who wanted to cleanse the land of lepers so as to be able to
see the gods, shrewdly made these lepers work in stone quarries (εἰς τὰς λιθο-
τομίας), separated from the rest of the Egyptian population.[37] The leader of
the lepers, Manetho's account goes on to relate, had as a first order of busi-
ness commanded that they not worship the gods (this scene reappears later in
Celsus), and the lepers then destroyed the images of the gods and burned the
temple.

> By his first law he (Osarsiph) ordained that they should not worship the
> gods nor abstain from the flesh of any of the animals held in special rever-
> ence in Egypt, but should kill and consume them all, and that they should
> have no connection with any save members of their own confederacy.
> After laying down these and a multitude of other laws, absolutely opposed
> to Egyptian custom .... It is said that the priest who gave them a constitu-
> tion and code of laws was a native of Heliopolis, named Osarsiph after
> the Heliopolitan god Osiris, and that when he went over to this people he
> changed his name and was called Moses.[38]

Only at the end of Manetho's story does Josephus make explicit that these lepers are Jews and that Osarsiph is Moses. Whether or not Manetho really referred
to the Jews in this vein is debated and does not allow for a definite answer.[39]

---

36   The history of research on Manetho in Josephus is well summarized by John Barclay, *Flav-
      ius Josephus, Translation & Commentary: Volume 10. Against Apion* (Leiden: Brill, 2007),
      335–337. See also Dagmar Labow, *Flavius Josephus: Contra Apionem, Buch 1. Einleitung,
      Text, Textkritischer Apparat, Übersetzung und Kommentar* (Stuttgart: Kohlhammer, 2005),
      58–72, 245–252.

37   Josephus, *CA* 1.235.

38   Josephus, *CA* 1.235, 250 (trans. LCL).

39   See the summary and history of scholarship in Barclay, *Against Apion*, 336. A balanced
      discussion of the problem appears in Peter Schäfer, "The Exodus Tradition," in *The Jews
      in the Hellenistic-Roman World: Studies in Memory of Menahem Stern*, ed. Isaiah M. Gafni
      et al. (Jerusalem: Graphit Press, 1996), 13–17. See also Gruen, *Heritage and Hellenism*,

POLYTHEISM AND MONOTHEISM IN ANTIQUITY 303

The final sentence of the quotation, in which Osarsiph is revealed to be Moses, may have been added after the fact. On the other hand, the story contains some notable parallels to aspects of the Egyptian exodus narrative (displacement, leprosy, antisocial legislation).

According to Assmann, Manetho's story reflects Akhenaten's monotheistic revolution in the Amarna Period. He speaks of "vague recollections in the official records of the covered-over Amarna religion" which were "later intermixed with what had been learned and experienced of the Jewish religion."[40] Manetho himself knew nothing of the monotheism of the Amarna Period, which nevertheless shines through the text.[41] Whether there are in Manetho (or Josephus's version of Manetho) traces of reception of the Amarna Period, I cannot tell.[42] But I find problematic Assmann's conclusions regarding ancient hostility towards the Jews. For Assmann allows himself to use Manetho's text as an example of monotheism's traumatic impact upon Egypt to demonstrate that the encounter with Jewish monotheism was destined to have negative consequences. That Egyptian anti-Judaism should be explained as merely the logical response to an anti-cosmotheistic monotheism seems to me a rather simplistic conclusion.[43]

The possibility that Manetho might not have been talking about the Jews (i.e., that his report reproduces an inner-Egyptian argument) should not lead

---

    63–64, who sees behind part of the history a Jewish author with an interest in maintaining Jewish superiority over the Egyptian cult.

40   Assmann, *Monotheismus und Kosmotheismus*, 24–25.

41   Assmann, *Monotheismus und Kosmotheismus*, 48: "In Hellenistic antiquity, as Hecataeus of Abdera travelled to Egypt and Manetho of Sebennytos wrote his *Aigyptiaka*, no one any longer knew anything of an episode of revolutionary monotheism which had occurred more than 1,000 years before and whose traces had been erased from the official annals and any accessible monuments."

42   Assmann understands the desire of the king to see the gods as trace evidence of the Amarna Period: "Behind the wish of the king must be a situation of deprivation: the gods are apparently hiding and refusing to show themselves, the cult images have disappeared, and the usual cultic production and institutionalization of sighting the gods is blocked," Jan Assmann, "Exodus und Amarna: Der Mythos der 'Aussätzigen' als verdrängte Errinerung der Aton-Religion," in *Ägypten-Bilder: Akten des "Symposions zur Ägypten-Rezeption", Augst bei Basel, vom 9.–11. September 1993*, ed. Elisabeth Staehelin and Bertrand Jaeger (Freiburg: Universitätsverlag Freiburg Schweiz, 1997), 11–34, at 23.

43   See also Stegemann, "Wieder einmal Unbehagen am Monotheismus," 21: "The representatives of monotheism are supposed to 'have brought a new form of hatred into the world,' namely towards those who differ from them, the common people or pagans and heretics or apostates. But these also answered with an anti-monotheistic form of hatred, eventually in the form of anti-Judaism. But it was the others, the monotheists, who started it, because the cosmotheists had preceded them."

304   CHAPTER 14

us to the conclusion that the anti-Jewish stereotypes attributed to him are simply a Jewish projection of inner-Egyptian polemic:

> This complex [i.e. 'the mass-psychology' complex of a violent polemic against those who think or act differently "which ultimately originated with the trauma of the Amarna Period"] reveals not only xenophobic, but also explicitly antisemitic (i.e. anti-Jewish) strains. These arise as a result of the Jews' own identification of the Egyptian myth of the expulsion of lepers, which probably grew out of the experiences made during the Amarna period, with the Jewish Exodus tradition. This is what creates the hideous image of the Jew as sacrilegious malefactor, as devil's ally, as ritual murderer, and as foreign body which must be eliminated for a holy, pure, and divinely-attended mode of life to be possible. Many features of modern anti-Semitism are already visible here as well as the political *Angstmotive* of the 'fifth column' and the 'state within the state.' Therefore it seems particularly important for us to deconstruct this complex by elucidating its genesis.[44]

Assmann refers to a passage in tractate *Shabbat* of the Babylonian Talmud in which he reads a Jewish concession of sorts to the fact that anti-Judaism is a consequence of the giving of the monotheistic Law at Sinai. The passage records arguments regarding the etymological meaning of Mount "Sinai," also called "Horeb:"

> One of the Rabbis asked R. Kahana: Hast thou heard what the mountain of Sinai [connotes]? ... For R. Hisda and Rabbah the son of R. Huna both said, What is [the meaning of] Mount Sinai? The mountain whereon there descended hostility [*sin'ah*] toward idolaters. And thus R. Jose son of R. Hanina said: It has five names:[45] The Wilderness of Zin, [meaning] that Israel were given commandments there; the Wilderness of Kadesh, where the Israelites were sanctified [*kadosh*], the Wilderness of Kedemoth, because a priority [*kedumah*] was conferred there; the Wilderness of Paran, because Israel was fruitful [*paru*] and multiplied there; and the Wilderness of Sinai, because hostility toward idolaters descended thereon. Whilst what was its [real] name? Its name was Horeb. Now they disagree with R. Abbahu, For R. Abbahu said: its name was Mount

---

44   Assmann, "Exodus und Amarna," 34.

45   The text suggests etymologies for the five names.

POLYTHEISM AND MONOTHEISM IN ANTIQUITY

Sinai, and why was it called Mount Horeb? Because desolation to idolaters descended thereon.[46]

In a play on words, some of the rabbis connect "Sinai" (סיני) with the Hebrew
word *sin'ah* (שנאה; "hate") and "Horeb" (חרב) with the Hebrew word *ḥorbah*
(חרבה; "devastation"). What does "Mount Sinai" signify? *The mountain whereon
there descended hostility toward idolaters.* Assmann reads this as a Jewish real-
ization that what happened upon Sinai—the giving of the Law, and with it
monotheism—brought with it hatred toward the Jews, thus anti-Judaism. He
writes:

> The Jews themselves ... knew that "on Mount Sinai hate came down to the
> peoples of the world," and they took up the burden of this hate for love
> of the Torah. That gave them the certainty that their sufferings were not
> in vain, and that there was more to them than the blind contingencies of
> history.[47]

Is this really what is being discussed in this passage of the Talmud? The
wordplay—one of many in the Talmud from which one is *a priori* prevented
from drawing conclusions that are too far-reaching—does not state that anti-
Judaism resulted from Sinai, but simply that at Sinai all that was left for the idolaters was hatred (whereby *sin'ah*, "hatred," offers itself to etymological wordplay; other options might have been "delusion" or, as proposed by one of the
rabbinic parties, of "devastation"). Anti-Judaism as a consequence of the giving
of the Law at Sinai is not in view here. The Talmud does not ask, as Assmann
insinuates (as he does elsewhere in connection to Sigmund Freud),[48] whether
or how the Jews wrought hatred upon themselves.

It is certainly true that the Hebrew Bible, Jewish-Hellenistic literature, and
rabbinic texts often strongly condemn polytheism from a monotheistic perspective. Thus does Flavius Josephus write of pagan polytheism in a manner
full of ridicule:

---

46   b. Šhab. 89a–b (trans. Epstein, Soncino).
47   Assmann, *Price of Monotheism*, 59.
48   Assmann, *Moses the Egyptian*, 5: "When Sigmund Freud felt the rising tide of German
     anti-Semitism outgrowing the traditional dimensions of persecution and oppression and
     turning into a murderous attack, he—remarkably enough—did not ask the obvious ques-
     tion of 'how the Germans came to murder the Jews,' instead he asked 'how the Jews came
     to attract this undying hatred.'"

306   CHAPTER 14

> They (the Greeks) represent them (the gods) to be as numerous as they
> choose, born of one another and engendered in all manner of ways. They
> assign them different localities and habits, like animal species, some liv-
> ing under ground, others in the sea, the oldest of all being chained in
> Tartarus. Those to whom they have allotted heaven have set over them
> one who is nominally Father, but in reality a tyrant and despot; with the
> result that his wife and brother and the daughter, whom he begot from
> his own head, conspire against him, to arrest and imprison him, just as he
> himself had treated his own father. Justly do these tales merit the severe
> censure which they receive from their intellectual leaders. Moreover, they
> ridicule the belief that some gods are beardless striplings, others old and
> bearded; that some are appointed to trades, this one being a smith, that
> goddess a weaver, a third a warrior who fights along with men, others lute-
> players or devoted to archery; and again that they are divided into factions
> and quarrel about men, in so much that they not only come to blows with
> each other, but actually lament over and suffer from wounds inflicted by
> mortals.[49]

Here the monotheist, in a rather sneering fashion, makes light of the absurdity of the 'other,' just as polytheists elsewhere do in regard to monotheists: the
same charges that Celsus brings against monotheists—stupidity and naivety—
are those that Josephus levels at polytheists. Yet there does exist—and this
seems to me not an insignificant point—a critical difference between the two
sides of this combative cultural exchange: the Jews were a minority in Greco-
Roman antiquity (as the Israelites were in earlier times). Up until the proliferation of Christianity in late antiquity, monotheism was the exception, not
the rule. The Jews were self-conscious of the uniqueness of their monotheistic position in the midst of a polytheistic society. Thus does Flavius Josephus
in his *Jewish Antiquities*, written toward the end of the first century CE, refer
to the patriarch Abraham's monotheism explicitly as a risk: "He was thus the
first boldly (τολμᾷ) to declare that God, the creator of the universe, is one."[50]
The Jewish monotheists of antiquity generally lacked political leverage; accordingly, Jewish polemics against pagan religions in the Greco-Roman world did
not result in political action, as the reverse sometimes did.

This aspect—the aspect of power—is given too little attention in modern
discussions of the culture wars between monotheism and polytheism in antiq-

---

49   Josephus, *CA* 2.240–243 (trans. LCL).
50   Josephus, *AJ* 1.155: πρῶτος οὖν τολμᾷ θεὸν ἀποφήνασθαι δημιουργὸν τῶν ὅλων ἕνα (trans. LCL).

uity. For Assmann, the monotheistic semantics of the Bible is inherently violent. At the same time, Assmann distinguishes Jewish monotheism from Christian and Muslim, as only Christians and Muslims in the name of "the power of their God" exercised force against others. Assmann grants that the Jews never converted the violent potential of their monotheism into action. For Judaism only ever marginalized itself.[51] Jewish "self-exclusion" (*Selbstausgrenzung*) protects the Jews from violence against others, as it were. A more fruitful question, then, would be under what form of power relations in antiquity the adherents of monotheistic religion, or alternatively of polytheistic religion, employ or could employ force. Assmann is probably correct to write (and with reference to Othmar Keel) that behind the idea of a jealous and angry god there exist "political impulses, which have their origins in empire."[52] But ancient Judaism rarely faced the seduction of political power—on the contrary, it repeatedly suffered under non-Jewish, polytheistic authorities.[53]

---

51   Jan Assmann, "Monotheismus," in *Monotheismus: Jahrbuch für Politische Theologie 4*, ed. Jürgen Manemann (Münster: LIT, 2003), 122–132, at 131: "Still, even if the violence of biblical semantics can in no way be denied, it can be clearly stated that of the three Abrahamic religions which are heir to this semantics, never the Jews, but only Christians and Muslims have implemented this violence in action. Judaism is a culture of difference. For Judaism it is completely self-evident that monotheism constitutes a border and that the Jews must maintain this border. The border between Israel and the people is not the border between friend and enemy. Only those who ignore these borders become enemies. Thus Judaism draws and guards this border in the manner of self-preservation. No violence is required for self-exclusion. Christianity and Islam have not recognized the nature of this border and for this reason have been violent throughout their histories. The might of their God exercised against other gods gives them the right to exercise violence against other peoples who in their eyes are attached to other gods. Behind this stands the distinction between truth and falsehood, which is characteristic of monotheistic religion."

52   Jan Assmann, "Gesetz, Gewalt und Monotheismus," *TLZ* 62 (2006): 475–486, at 480. See Othmar Keel, "Monotheismus—ein göttlicher Makel? Über eine allzu bequeme Anklage," *Neue Zürcher Zeitung*, 30 October 2004, 68: "At the end of the seventh century BCE the Assyrian Empire broke down. A power vacuum replaced it. Jewish theologians had the original idea to fill that vacuum by allowing the demands made by the Assyrian King to come from the God of Israel, from Yahweh. Thus they filled the power vacuum, thus they rendered Israel internally independent of all despots, while at the same time ascribing to Yahweh the properties of a despot of the highest order." Keel then adds: "One can invoke the cited text (Deut 13:7–11) as evidence of the intolerance, aggression, and brutality of monotheism. But one might overlook that here one is not dealing with a monotheistic text. This text accounts for other gods, who can pose a danger to the exclusive covenant with the one God; true monotheism is based on the assumption that there only exists one God, and thus provides no grounds for jealousy."

53   "Violence is a question of power, not of truth," Assmann admits elsewhere: *Monotheismus und die Sprache der Gewalt*, 23.

There is no doubt that much of Jan Assmann's treatment of monotheism is correct. It cannot be denied that the idea of a (strict) monotheism may be, at its source, prohibitive of other beliefs. Likewise the idea of a certain aggressiveness implicit within monotheism—actualized internally, but also externally toward others—is not to be doubted. But Assmann erects too great a theoretical construct of monotheism, one which—as Assmann well knows—was hardly ever implemented in reality and whose aggressive potential was almost never realized in the polytheistic world of antiquity. A related question one would have to ask is whether the 'distinction' fundamental to the reality of the ancient world—between Greek/Roman on the one hand and barbarian on the other—is not much more important than the monotheist/polytheist distinction (and one that became, beyond ancient times, much more serious). Further, the development of a concept of absolute truth should not necessarily be specifically associated with monotheism. Monotheism was a quiet idea in antiquity, one that was rarely 'risked' (to pick up Josephus's language) so as to appear prominent, let alone to reach for the sword. Jewish Hellenistic literature dreams of the great figures of pagan culture—e.g., Orpheus, or the Classical tragedians Aeschylus, Sophocles, and Euripides—coming to the insight of monotheism on their own initiative. These are peaceful literary-theological contrivances.[54] Even where the tone of monotheism becomes thoroughly polemical (e.g., in the Sibylline Oracles),[55] the text is always aware of limitations in reality.

Assmann takes care to emphasize that monotheism did not become violent within Judaism, but only at the hands of Christianity and Islam.[56] But the original monotheistic distinction (*Ur-Unterscheidung*)—that is, the distinction between what is true and false "in religion"—is for Assmann a "Mosaic distinction."[57] So ultimately, the Jews are to blame for this. Thus one may wonder about Assmann's motivations in levelling his harsh critique of monotheism. At the beginning of his *Moses the Egyptian*, Assmann reflects on his personal experiences which undergird that study:

---

54 See Nikolaus Walter, "Pseudepigraphische jüdisch-hellenistische Dichtung: Pseudo-Phokylides, Pseudo-Orpheus, Gefälschte Verse auf Namen griechischer Dichter," in *Jüdische Schriften aus hellenistisch-römischer Zeit 4.3: Poetische Schriften*, ed. W. Georg Kümmel (Gütersloh: Gerd Mohn, 1983), 217–243.

55 Cf. Sib. Or. 2.15–19: "Then indeed the tenth generation of men will also appear after these things, when the earth-shaking lightning-giver will break the glory of idols and shake the people of seven-hilled Rome. Great wealth will perish, burned in a great fire by the flame of Hephaestus" (trans. Collins, *The Old Testament Pseudepigrapha*).

56 Cf. note 51 above.

57 Assmann, *Moses the Egyptian*, 1: "Let us call the distinction between true and false in religion the 'Mosaic distinction' because tradition ascribes it to Moses."

POLYTHEISM AND MONOTHEISM IN ANTIQUITY   309

The present text reflects my situations as a German Egyptologist writing fifty years after the catastrophe which Freud saw approaching, knowing the full extent of the genocide which was still unthinkable in Freud's time, and having turned to ancient Egypt thirty-five years ago with questions that are all too easily forgotten as soon as one enters an academic discipline.[58]

Assmann (born 1938) writes as a post-war German academic, and in the shadow of the Holocaust, about the figure of Moses. On the other hand, Assmann approaches Jewish monotheism as an Egyptologist by training. I have already mentioned the *Tendenz* toward Egyptological apologetic in Assmann's scholarship. Assmann often writes as if in the name of the Egyptians concerning their relationship to Israel in antiquity. Moreover, in Assmann one finds traces of what is a hardly intentional but ultimately apologetic discourse on the Holocaust. Several times in his work Assmann projects images of the Second World War onto the ancient world. In his engagement with 'the Mosaic distinction,' Assmann routinely depicts an ancient world in which there exists totalitarianism, forced labor, concentration camps, even a "premonition of Auschwitz" (*Vorahnung von Auschwitz*). Assmann runs the risk of trivializing these terms by projecting them back onto antiquity, partially in contexts in which the Jews appear as the culprits. Just so when, for Assmann, exclusive monotheism embodies a "totalitarian state:"

The revolutionary thing about exclusive monotheism is that it is not just a matter of cult and perhaps also of one's general orientation toward the world, but like a state—yes, one hesitates to say it—like a totalitarian state, it wants to direct the entire course of life, from feast days to everyday life, right down to the smallest detail.[59]

In regard to the above-mentioned account of Manetho, where the leprous Egyptian followers of the priest and revolutionary Osarsiph (who, for Assmann, is not the same as Moses) are forced by the king to work in "stone quarries,"[60]

---

58   Assmann, *Moses the Egyptian*, 6. Further: "I had always felt the challenge that Freud's book posed for both Egyptology and Comparative Religion .... It is in a rather personal attempt to 'come to terms with,' similar to Freud's, that I embark on the writing of this study about Moses the Egyptian."

59   Assmann, "Gesetz, Gewalt und Monotheismus," 484.

60   Josephus, *CA* 1.235.

Assmann speaks of "concentration camps." Likewise in the description of the land of Goshen in the biblical history of exodus:

> The king had interned these lepers in concentration camps and consigned them to forced labor.[61]

> The colony first appears as the settlement of the children of Israel in Goshen, that is, as in Manetho, it takes the harsher form of a work- and concentration camp (*Arbeits- und Konzentrationslagers*), and then appears as the establishment of a people (*Volksgründung*) in the wake of the giving of the Law at Sinai and the Mosaic legislation.[62]

In his more recently published Vienna lecture, "Monotheismus und die Sprache der Gewalt," Assmann connects the future punishments threatened in Deuteronomy 28 to Auschwitz:

> These almost sadistic descriptions of the annihilation, destruction, and extermination of the unfaithful people read like a premonition of Auschwitz and come to be cited by, e.g., Primo Levi in this context.[63]

Here Assmann is referring to Primo Levi's poem at the beginning of *Se questo è un uomo* (1947). In this poem, Levi asks whether it is still a human being who experiences the grisliest of realities like those experienced by the prisoners of Auschwitz. Levi calls for the constant remembrance of the horror of Auschwitz and in this context paraphrases (and partially cites) the Shema prayer of Deuteronomy 6:6–7 as follows: "I commend these words to you. / Carve them in your hearts / At home, in the street, / Going to bed, rising; / Repeat them to your children, / Or may your house fall apart, / May illness impede you, / May your children turn their faces from you."[64]

These last three verses are reminiscent of the biblical threats. But Levi does not connect the crimes committed by human hands at Auschwitz with the images of divine punishment communicated in Deuteronomy (as though

---

61 Assmann, *Price of Monotheism*, 59. Likewise in idem, "Exodus und Amarna," 17: "Konzentration und Zwangsarbeit."

62 Assmann, "Exodus und Amarna," 24.

63 Assmann, *Monotheismus und die Sprache der Gewalt*, 28.

64 "Scolpitele nel Vostro cuore / Stando in casa andanda per via, / Coricandovi alzandovi; / Ripetetele ai vostri figli. / O vi si sfaccia la casa, / La malattia vi impedisca, / I vostri nati torcano il viso da voi" (trans. Stuart Woolf; New York: Collier, 1959).

the crimes of Auschwitz existed long before in the mind of God and the ancient Jewish text respectively), but rather threatens those who might forget Auschwitz, using the vocabulary of biblical threats to do so. It is not so that, as Assmann thinks, in Levi's poem the divine threats of biblical punishment are compared with the horrors of Auschwitz. The ancient world knew of no concentration camps, no Auschwitz, and no totalitarian states. Such diffuse retrojections, as one finds several times in Assmann, run the risk of trivialisation (even though this is not Assmann's intention).[65]

Bibliography

Assmann, Jan, *Politische Theologie zwischen Ägypten und Israel.* Bonn: Carl Friedrich von Siemens Stiftung, 1992.

Assmann, Jan, "Exodus und Amarna: Der Mythos der "Aussätzigen" als verdrängte Erinnerung der Aton-Religion." Pages 11–34 in *Ägypten-Bilder: Akten des "Symposions zur Ägypten-Rezeption," Augst bei Basel, vom 9.–11. September 1993.* Edited by Elisabeth Staehelin and Bertrand Jaeger. Freiburg: Universitätsverlag Freiburg Schweiz, 1997.

Assmann, Jan, "Re-membering—Konnektives Gedächtnis und jüdisches Erinnerungsgebot." Pages 23–46 in *Die Gegenwart des Holocaust—"Erinnerung" als religionspädagogische Herausforderung.* Edited by Michael Wermke. Münster: LIT, 1997.

Assmann, Jan, *Moses the Egyptian: The Memory of Egypt in Western Monotheism.* Cambridge: Harvard University Press, 1998.

Assmann, Jan, *Moses der Ägypter: Entzifferung einer Gedächtnisspur.* Munich: Carl Hanser Verlag, 1998.

Assmann, Jan, "Gerechtigkeit und Monotheismus." Pages 78–95 in *Freiheit und Recht:*

---

65 See Jan Assmann, "Re-membering—Konnektives Gedächtnis und jüdisches Erinnerungsgebot," in *Die Gegenwart des Holocaust—"Erinnerung" als religionspädagogische Herausforderung,* ed. Michael Wermke (Münster: LIT, 1997), 23–46, at 45: "One cannot speak of forgiveness, finality, and atonement, because the dead are dead and there is no one that can settle accounts in their name and release the culprits and their descendants of their guilt. The important thing is to acknowledge this guilt and to construct a culture of remembrance which articulates this recollection clearly, permanently, and authoritatively. Nothing like this had ever before existed in history, and there are no models or recipes how that most terrible experience of collective guilt can be implemented in the lived form of connective memory." Assmann's theses were combined into one tendentious essay in the weekly magazine *Der Spiegel* 52 (22 December 2006). Assmann distances himself from this essay in an open letter (at spiegelkritik.de on 5 January 2007) and in an interview with the daily publication *Die Welt* on 13 January 2007.

Festschrift Frank Crüsemann zum 65. Geburtstag. Edited by Christof Hardmeier et al. Gütersloh: Gütersloher Verlagshaus, 2003.

Assmann, Jan, "Monotheismus," in Jürgen Manemann, ed., *Monotheismus: Jahrbuch für Politische Theologie 4* (Münster: LIT, 2003): 122–132.

Assmann, Jan, *Monotheismus und die Sprache der Gewalt.* Vienna: Picus, 2004.

Assmann, Jan, "Monotheism and Polytheism." Pages 17–31 in *Religions of the Ancient World: A Guide.* Edited by Sarah Iles Johnston. Cambridge: Harvard University Press, 2004.

Assmann, Jan, "Der hebräische und der ägyptische Mose—Bilder und Gegenbilder." Pages 147–155 in *Das Alte Testament und die Kultur der Moderne.* Edited by Manfred Oeming et al. Münster: LIT, 2004.

Assmann, Jan, "Gesetz, Gewalt und Monotheismus." *TLZ* 62 (2006): 475–486.

Assmann, Jan, *The Price of Monotheism.* Stanford: Stanford University Press, 2009.

Barclay, John, *Flavius Josephus, Translation & Commentary.* Vol. 10. *Against Apion.* Leiden: Brill, 2007.

Bloch, René, *Antike Vorstellungen vom Judentum: Der Judenexkurs des Tacitus im Rahmen der griechisch-römischen Ethnographie.* Stuttgart: Franz Steiner Verlag, 2002.

Burkert, Walter, "Mythen–Tempel–Götterbilder: Von der Nahöstlichen Koiné zur griechischen Gestaltung." Pages 3–20 in *Götterbilder, Gottesbilder, Weltbilder: Polytheismus und Monotheismus in der Welt der Antike.* Vol. 2: *Griechenland und Rom, Judentum, Christentum und Islam.* Edited by Reinhard G. Kratz and Hermann Spieckermann. Tübingen: Mohr Siebeck, 2006.

Dietrich, Walter, "Israel und die Völker in der Hebräischen Bibel." Pages 7–27 in *Juden in ihrer Umwelt: Akkulturation des Judentums in Antike und Mittelalter.* Edited by Matthias Konradt and Rainer C. Schwinges. Basel: Schwabe, 2009.

Funkenstein, Amos, *Perceptions of Jewish History.* Berkeley: University of California Press, 1993.

Gerber, Arnold and Adolf Greef, *Lexicon Taciteum.* Hildesheim: Georg Olms, 1962 (1877–1890).

Gruen, Erich S., *Heritage and Hellenism: The Reinvention of Jewish Tradition* Berkeley: University of California Press, 1998.

Haag, Ernst, *Das hellenistische Zeitalter: Israel und die Bibel im 4. bis 1. Jahrhundert v.Chr.* Stuttgart: Kohlhammer, 2003.

Keel, Othmar, "Monotheismus—ein göttlicher Makel? Über eine allzu bequeme Anklage." *Neue Zürcher Zeitung,* 30 October 2004.

Labow, Dagmar, *Flavius Josephus: Contra Apionem, Buch 1—Einleitung, Text, Textkritischer Apparat, Übersetzung und Kommentar.* Stuttgart: Kohlhammer, 2005.

Schäfer, Peter, "The Exodus Tradition." Pages 13–17 in *The Jews in the Hellenistic-Roman World: Studies in Memory of Menahem Stern.* Edited by Isaiah M. Gafni et al. Jerusalem: Graphit Press, 1996.

Stegemann, Ekkehard W., "Wieder einmal Unbehagen am Monotheismus." *Reformatio: Zeitschrift für Kultur, Politik und Religion* 56 (2007): 20–27.

Stern, Menahem, *Greek and Latin Authors on Jews and Judaism*. 3 volumes. Jerusalem: Israel Academy of Sciences and Humanities, 1974.

Walter, Nikolaus, "Pseudepigraphische jüdisch-hellenistische Dichtung: Pseudo-Phokylides, Pseudo-Orpheus, Gefälschte Verse auf Namen griechischer Dichter." Pages 217–243 in *Jüdische Schriften aus hellenistisch-römischer Zeit 4.3: Poetische Schriften*. Edited by W. Georg Kümmel. Gütersloh: Gerd Mohn, 1983.

CHAPTER 15

Testa incognita: The History of the Pseudo-Josephus Bust in Copenhagen

In room 13 of the Ny Carlsberg Glyptotek in Copenhagen there is an impressive variety of busts from the time of Vespasian to Trajan on show: when you enter the room, you are welcomed on the right by Vespasian, the bust of a very determined looking man from around 70 CE. This is how one might imagine Vespasian when Tacitus writes about him that he was *acer militiae anteire agmen*: "an energetic soldier marching at the head of his troops." Now his bust first welcomes the visitor at the entrance of the room. This is the man who "had completed the war in Judea with only the siege of Jerusalem remaining" (*profligaverat bellum Iudaicum Vespasianus, oppugnatione Hiersolymorum reliqua*).[1] On the left side of the room is a much larger bust of Titus which in spite of its size lacks the energy of Vespasian across the hall (there is also a smaller bust of Titus on show). But Titus finished the job. He destroyed Jerusalem and the Jewish temple. For a scholar of ancient Jewish history, room 13 at the Glyptotek presents in a nutshell some of the most dramatic events of antiquity: chronologically it starts with Vitellius, one of the four emperors of 69 CE (as usual not hiding his rather fleshy face), and ends with the emperor Trajan under whose reign the diaspora riots broke out. Not all portraits in the room can be attributed with certainty to known figures. The severe looking face of a woman's bust with an impressive coiffure seems to be Domitia Longina, who was married to Domitian. On the other side of the room is a portrait that very likely renders Julia, the daughter of Titus and Domitian's lover. There is thus

---

1   Tacitus, *Hist.* 2.4–5. For a detailed description of all Roman portraits from the Flavian period up to Trajan at the Glyptotek see Flemming Johansen, *Catalogue: Roman Portraits II. Ny Carlsberg Glyptotek* (Copenhagen: Ny Carlsberg Glyptotek, 1995), 24–143. I would like to thank Anne Marie Nielsen, Museumsinspektør of the Antik Samling at the Ny Carlsberg Glyptotek in Copenhagen for her precious help at the museum. Selma Balsiger, University of Bern, patiently helped me track down a number of sources in different places. My wife Sara, originally from Copenhagen, gave me many opportunities to visit Ny Carlsberg Glyptotek and assisted me with the Danish sources. This article was written during a research stay at the Sorbonne in the winter 2019/2020 where I also presented an earlier version. I would like to thank my colleagues, Prof. Olivier Munnich and Prof. Sébastien Morlet, for their great hospitality and their helpful inputs. I would also like to thank the librarians of the École Normale Supérieure for giving me access to their splendid library.

© RENÉ BLOCH, 2022 | DOI:10.1163/9789004521896_017

FIGURE 1 Ny Carlsberg Glyptotek, room 13 (from right to left): Vespasian, A Roman lady, Vitellius, A Roman man, Domitia Longina (?)
COURTESY NY CARLSBERG GLYPTOTEK. PHOTO: ANDERS SUNE BERG

FIGURE 2–3   A Roman. I.N. 770
COURTESY NY CARLSBERG GLYPTOTEK. PHOTO: OLE HAUPT

some tension in the room. And then there is, somewhat hidden between the massive Vitellius and the fairly tall bust of what has been interpreted as Marcia Furnilla, Titus's second wife,[2] a small bust of an unnamed man. The bust, which has no inscription, is dated by the museum to ca. 69–96 CE and its height measures 44 centimeters. This is the bust which has mistakenly become known to many as portraying the Jewish-Roman general and author Flavius Josephus.[3]

---

2 Johansen, *Catalogue*, 54. In the exhibition she is presented as "a Roman lady."
3 The history of the "Josephus" bust in Copenhagen has been only briefly touched upon: cf. Magen Broshi, *Bread, Wine, Walls, and Scrolls* (Sheffield: Sheffield Academic Press, 2001), 46–49 and Steven Fine, "How Do You Know a Jew When You See One? Reflections on Jewish Costume in the Roman World," in *Fashioning Jews: Clothing, Culture, and Commerce*, ed. Leonard Greenspoon (West Lafayette: Purdue University Press, 2013), 19–20. The various catalogues of the Ny Carlsberg Glyptotek proved to be very valuable in tracking down the history of the bust (see details in notes below).

FIGURE 4   Nasothek in the Ny Carlsberg Glyptotek
PHOTO: WIKIMEDIA COMMONS

The bust is of white marble. It shows the face of a man who is perhaps in his twenties, with curly hair and a beard. "The rims of the ears are battered .... A section of the hair over the forehead is missing. Both corners of the sternum section have been repaired."[4] But overall, the bust is in an excellent condition.

The nose has some scratches but it is complete, which is not self-evident for busts from the Greco-Roman period. Often noses of busts and statues fell off or were violently removed.[5] Thus, in this room the noses of Vitellius, Vespasian and Titus are missing or broken. In the past museums often restored such portraits with new noses. In the case of the Ny Carlsberg Glyptotek these reconstructed noses were later removed from the busts and placed together in a "nasothek" (fig. 4) which is on display in room 14 (next to the Flavian room). "Josephus's" nose, on the other hand, is complete and authentic. In light of the "nasothek" next door it is somewhat ironic that it was notably the crooked

---

4   Johansen, *Catalogue*, 68.
5   Cf. Mark Bradley and Eric Varner, "Missing noses", in *Smell and the Ancient Senses*, ed. Mark Bradley (London, New York: Routledge, 2015), 171–180.

318 CHAPTER 15

shape of the nose of this bust which 90 years ago led to the assumption that it portrayed Flavius Josephus.

1 Robert Eisler

It was Robert Eisler, an Austrian art historian, who in an article published in 1930 in the French journal *Aréthuse* with the title "Deux sculptures de l'antiquité classique représentant des Juifs" identified the bust as one of Josephus.[6] In the article—which is highly problematic, as we shall see—Eisler looks for archaeological evidence of portrayals of Jews in Greco-Roman antiquity. In order to understand the circumstances of this article we need first to look at Robert Eisler's life and work. Eisler was a prolific polymath who lived from 1882 to 1949. He was of Jewish origin, but already as a young man (1903) converted to Catholicism.[7] Eisler submitted two dissertations to the University of Vienna, one in economics and one in art history. During his career he taught at a number of universities, including Oxford, Cambridge and the Sorbonne. However, he never held a tenured position in academia. While some scholars showed great respect for his work, most thought poorly of his manifold publications. In 1925, Eisler came to Paris and took up the position of assistant director at the "Institut International de Coopération Intellectuelle" (the executive body of the "Commission Internationale de Coopération Intellectuelle," the predecessor organization of the UNESCO). His assumption of office became a scandal, though, since apparently Eisler had not been officially appointed by the Austrian government. We get some insight into Eisler's time in Paris from Gershom Scholem's memoirs. This was the Paris of the 1920s, with a great number of intellectuals arriving from different places in Europe. In his book on his friendship with Walter Benjamin, Scholem describes how the two of them visited Robert Eisler in his huge apartment on the Rue de Lille, just across from the Gare d'Orsay. It is worth citing Scholem's memories about his encounter with Eisler in Paris:

> I took Benjamin to see Robert Eisler, an astonishing figure in the world of scholarship. I had already introduced them in Munich, where I saw Eisler on a number of occasions. Eisler was one of the most imagina-

---

6 Robert Eisler, "Deux sculptures de l'antiquité classique représentant des Juifs," *Aréthuse* 26 (1930): 29–38.

7 Cf. "Eisler, Robert," in *Lexikon deutsch-jüdischer Autoren*. Vol. 6, ed. Renate Heuer et al. (München: Saur, 1998), 193–201.

TESTA INCOGNITA 319

tive and—if one looked at the inconceivably erudite store of quotations in his books without checking them—of the most learned historians of religion. For all unsolved problems he had in readiness brilliantly false solutions of the most surprising kind. He was a man of unbridled ambition, ceaseless diligence, but rather unstable character. Benjamin was interested in him for a long time, and I often reported to him on Eisler's quotation-laden leaps into scholarly adventurism, with enterprises that at various times were as sensational as they were unsuccessful. Around 1925, through the good offices of the great English philologist Gilbert Murray, Eisler was named head of the League of Nations' Section de Coopération Intellectuelle, headquartered in Paris; he had accepted that appointment without first consulting with the government of Austria (whose citizen he was). When I arrived in Paris, Benjamin told me about the scandal this appointment had caused. The Austrian government had lodged an official protest, while Eisler, confident of future official duties, had taken an enormous apartment on the rue de Lille. The visit we paid Eisler in the deserted rooms of his luxury apartment—the "official people" already had dissociated themselves from him—was a depressing experience for us. Eisler, however, cheerfully discussed his great discoveries about the person and role of Jesus as the leader of a political revolt, the subject of the *cours libre* he was then giving at the Sorbonne. At that time he was developing the ideas he later wrote down in his voluminous work *Jesus Basileus ou Basileusas*. It was an eerie scene. Benjamin, who had a special feeling for situations of that kind, was spellbound. We also attended a session of Eisler's course, which was taken by Salomon Reinach's pupils and friends. The highly un-Christian hypothesis with which Eisler took up Kautsky's theories on the origin of Christianity (in an uncommonly ingenious, self-assured manner), supporting them with unexpected interpretations of equally unexpected sources, was received with considerable acclaim by the freethinkers of the Cercle Ernest Renan. But we realized that we were witnessing a sad turning point in the life of an unusual human being.[8]

Scholem's portrait of Eisler is a mixture of admiration, wonder, and—especially—pity. Elsewhere he calls him a "juggler of scholarship."[9] I will return shortly to the "adventurous" research Eisler conducted on early Christianity

---

8 Gershom Scholem, *Walter Benjamin: The Story of a Friendship* (Philadelphia: The Jewish Publication Society of America 1981), 159–160.

9 Gershom Scholem, *From Berlin to Jerusalem: Memories of My Youth* (New York: Schocken, 1980), 130.

320   CHAPTER 15

at the time and its link to the bust in Copenhagen. But Scholem is also a valuable—if not necessarily objective—source for Eisler's views on Judaism. As a matter of fact, it was Martin Buber who introduced Eisler to Scholem. In 1918 Buber informed Scholem about an enigmatic society promoting the study of Kabbalah called "Johann Albert Widmanstetter-Gesellschaft zur Erforschung der Kabbala e.V." which "owed its existence to Dr. Robert Eisler, its 'secretary' and actually its only active member."[10] It was around this time that Scholem became very interested in the study of Kabbalah. Apparently, the society had no impact of any kind besides the fact that it (that is, Robert Eisler) figures as the editor of Scholem's first two books—as he somewhat shamefully admits.[11] Eisler's own work, which included a study on the book *Yezirah*, Scholem found disgraceful.[12] Eisler's relationship to his Jewish origins remained complicated and was not free of constraints. In spite of his early conversion to Christianity, Scholem experienced him as "completely Jewish. His store of Jewish jokes and anecdotes was virtually inexhaustible, and it was understandable that he was able to pour out his Jewish heart, which he held back rightly when dealing with non-Jews, freely to someone like me."[13] With regard to Eisler's failed academic career, Scholem explains it in part as a result of antisemitism: "He had had himself baptized out of love for the daugh-

---

10   Scholem, *From Berlin to Jerusalem*, 126. Scholem is paraphrasing Buber.

11   Scholem, *From Berlin to Jerusalem*, 132: "However, my first two books, which were published in Germany in 1923 and 1927, managed to appear as volumes 1 and 2 in the series *Quellen und Forschungen zur Geschichte der jüdischen Mystik, im Auftrag der Johann Albert Widmanstetter-Gesellschaft herausgegeben von Robert Eisler* [Sources and Studies in the History of Jewish Mysticism. Edited for the Johann Albert Widmanstetter Society by Robert Eisler]. These were the only signs of life ever shown by this fictitious society."

12   Scholem, *From Berlin to Jerusalem*, 129: "The substance of that research was so frivolous that it only drew a skeptical shudder from me, since I was now subjecting myself to serious philological discipline." When Scholem together with Benjamin, both bored with their studies at the University of Bern, set up an imaginative University ("Universität Muri") with a fictitious course catalogue, he made sure to also poke fun at one of Eisler's books: Eisler's monograph *Weltenmantel und Himmelszelt* became "Damenmantel und Badezelt in religionsgeschichtlicher Bedeutung" ("Ladies' Coats and Beach Cabanas in the Light of the History of Religion"), cf. ibid. 128–129. On Scholem's and Benjamin's fictitious University outside of Bern cf. Oliver Lubrich and Michael Stolz, *Die Universität von Muri. Benjamins Berner Anfänge* (Bern: Walter Benjamin Kolleg, 2019).

13   Scholem, *From Berlin to Jerusalem*, 131. Scholem also reports that Eisler had tried to place an article in the journal *Der Jude* edited by Martin Buber, who, however, was not willing to publish a piece by a "converted Jew." Eisler then apparently signaled to Buber his plan to reconvert to Judaism (128: "Eisler had replied that he had long since decided to return to Judaism and was just about to take this step under the aegis of the Jewish Community Council in Munich."). Eisler does not seem to have followed up on this.

FIGURE 5   Robert Eisler
PHOTO: ABRAHAM SCHWADRON
COLLECTION OF THE NATIONAL
LIBRARY OF ISRAEL (WIKIMEDIA
COMMONS)

ter of a well-known Austrian painter, but despite this, his various attempts to obtain *Habilitation* had been blocked by distrust on the part of the departments involved. The Gentiles were made uneasy by his markedly Jewish appearance, and the Jews by his apostasy."[14] To what extent Eisler's "Jewish appearance" is part of Scholem's interpretation, or whether it (also) reflected Eisler's own impression, is not clear. Eisler's interest in ancient Jewish physiognomy was certainly not unrelated to contemporary discourses, and it may also mirror painful experiences he had himself. Later Eisler fell victim to the Nazi persecution of the Jews: in 1938 he was deported to Dachau and Buchenwald, where he suffered greatly.[15] After his release from Buchenwald in 1939 he managed to emigrate to England. In Oxford he became a lecturer and taught on a variety of topics. Eisler was married to Lili von Pausinger, an Austrian Catholic. He died in 1949 in Oxted, Surrey, south of London.

---

14   Scholem, *From Berlin to Jerusalem*, 127.
15   Scholem, *From Berlin to Jerusalem*, 131.

322   CHAPTER 15

Among the many topics that interested Eisler was the work of Flavius Josephus and in particular his value as a source for the history of early Christianity. This was also the topic of Eisler's lectures at the Sorbonne in 1926 entitled "Political Messianism and the Origins of Christianity," which eventually led to a massive monograph: *Iēsous basileus ou basileusas: die messianische Unabhängigkeitsbewegung vom Auftreten des Johannes des Täufers bis zum Untergang Jakobs des Gerechten nach der neuerschlossenen Eroberung von Jerusalem des Flavius Josephus und den christlichen Quellen*. Volume 1 was published in 1929, volume 2 in 1930.[16] In this book, Eisler tries to show that Jewish and pagan authors discussed the beginnings of Christianity much more extensively than the surviving sources would have us believe. These sources, including Josephus's "Testimonium Flavianum," were altered by Christian censors. In their original version, they presented Jesus as a political rebel who wanted to become king. This eventually led to his conviction and execution. In 1931, the book was published in an English version.[17] It was widely reviewed, mostly rather negatively (by scholars such as Solomon Zeitlin, who differed greatly with Eisler on the interpretation of the Slavonic Josephus, and Rudolf Bultmann; we have already pointed out Gershom Scholem's radical critique).[18] An exception is H.St. John Thackeray who endorsed Eisler in his 1929 monograph on Josephus.[19] The overall response to Eisler's book, though, was very negative. Pierre Vidal Naquet summarized the quality of the book as follows: "un énorme et souvent insane ouvrage."[20] It was around the publication of this "insane" book that Eisler developed his thesis that the Roman bust from the Glyptotek in Copenhagen is in fact a portrait of Flavius Josephus. The book includes a biography of

---

16   Robert Eisler, *Iesous basileus ou basileusas. Die messianische Unabhängigkeitsbewegung vom Auftreten Johannes des Täufers bis zum Untergang Jakobs des Gerechten. Nach der neuerschlossenen Eroberung von Jerusalem des Flavius Josephus und den christlichen Quellen dargestellt*. 2 vols. (Heidelberg: Winter 1929/30). On page v Eisler refers to the course at the Sorbonne.

17   Robert Eisler, *The Messiah Jesus and John the Baptist according to Flavius Josephus' Recently Rediscovered 'Capture of Jerusalem' and the Other Jewish and Christian Sources* (New York: Lincoln Macveagh, 1931).

18   Solomon Zeitlin, "Josephus on Jesus," *JQR* 21 (1931): 377–417. Rudolf Bultmann, *Literaturblatt der Frankfurter Zeitung*, 24 January 1932: "Kurz, alle angeblich echten Texte, die Eisler rekonstruiert, halte ich für Phantasien." ("In short, I consider all seemingly original texts which Eisler reconstructed to be fantasies.").

19   Henry St. John Thackeray, *Josephus: The Man and the Historian* (New York: Jewish Institute of Religion, 1929). Thackeray translated a substantial part of Eisler's book into English (cf. p. xv of the English edition of Eisler's *The Messiah Jesus*).

20   Pierre Vidal Naquet, "Flavius Josèphe où du bon usage de la trahison." Préface à la *Guerre des Juifs*, traduit par Pierre Savinel (Paris: Editions de minuit, 1977), 19n49.

TESTA INCOGNITA

Josephus in which Eisler refers to Eusebius's and Jerome's mentioning a statue that was erected in Rome.[21] In the first volume of the original German edition, published in 1929, Eisler wonders where the bust might be: maybe one day, he writes, by a lucky coincidence, the statue will be discovered in Rome—if it is not already in some collection, undetected.[22] Here Eisler seems to be dreaming that the Josephus statue known from the church fathers may one day show up. Or maybe he is already reacting to a visit he made to the Glyptotek in Copenhagen in the same year the first volume of his *Iēsous basileus ou basileusas* was published. It was indeed in 1929 that Robert Eisler discovered Josephus in Copenhagen. Eisler was on his way to Lund in Sweden to attend the fifth international meeting on the history of religions which took place from August 27 to 29. Eisler describes how during his visit to the Roman portraits at the Glyptotek, he "was deeply struck at first glance by the head Number 646 which undeniably seemed to me a portrait of a Jewish type and especially of Jewish expression."[23] At the time of Eisler's visit to the museum, he was actively looking for Roman portraits of Jews and in particular the statue of Josephus: in light of the literary evidence, he thought that it would make sense to "search systematically" among the portraits from that time period for a "head of the Jewish type."[24] In the second volume of *Iēsous basileus ou basileusas* Eisler included a photograph of the Copenhagen bust, calling it the "mutmaßlicher Kopf des römischen Standbildes des Flavius Josephus" ("presumed head of the Roman bust of Flavius Josephus"). With this caption, Eisler's identification of the bust from Copenhagen with Josephus reached a large audience. And it did even more so when the English version of the book appeared a year later, in 1931, now with a photograph of the Josephus bust on the very first page of the book (fig. 6).

---

21   Eusebius, *Hist. eccl.* 3.9.2; Jerome, *Vir. ill.* 13. On these passages see below, p. 329.

22   Eisler, *Iesous basileus ou basileusas*, XLII: "das (das Standbild) vielleicht ein glücklicher Zufall noch einmal aus dem Schutt des kaiserlichen Rom ans Tageslicht fördern wird, wenn es nicht etwa heute schon, durch einen Zufall seiner Inschriftbasis beraubt, unerkannt in irgendeiner Sammlung steht."

23   Eisler, "Deux sculptures," 33: "En parcourant la salle des portraits romains, je fus vivement frappé au premier coup d'œil par la tête N° 646, qui me sembla indéniablement un portrait de type et surtout d'expression juifs."

24   Eisler, "Deux sculptures," 33: "de faire une recherche systématique parmi les reproductions qu'on possède des portraits de ce temps pour chercher à découvrir une tête de type juif, et du style de l'époque flavienne." At the congress in Lund Eisler presented a paper on the statue of Jesus mentioned by Eusebius (*Hist. eccl.* 7.18.1–2), cf. *Actes du ve congrès*, 24. In *Iesous basileus ou basileusas* 2, 375–387 Eisler reconstructs (in a most imaginative way) Josephus's supposed description of Jesus's physiognomy.

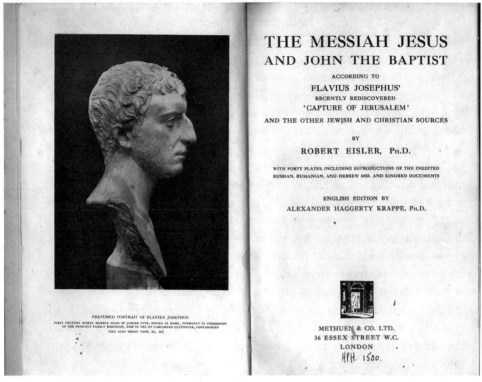

FIGURE 6 Picture from page 1 of the English version of Robert Eisler's *The Messiah Jesus and John the Baptist* (1931)

As already mentioned, Eisler made his point that the Roman man from the Glyptotek in Copenhagen represents Josephus in an article entitled "Deux sculptures de l'antiquité classique représentant des Juifs," published in 1930 in the French journal *Aréthuse*. In this article, Eisler first stresses a well-known fact which, with nuances, remains true until today: there are very few portraits of Jews from Greco-Roman antiquity (Eisler wrote the article shortly before the discovery of the synagogue paintings from Dura Europos). A rare exception in this regard are presentations on coins of the heads of King Agrippa I and of King Agrippa II.[25] Eisler prints a drawing of a coin from Caesarea showing the head of Agrippa I, calling it "très caractéristique" of the king who persecuted the Jerusalem church (Acts 12). For the coin Eisler refers to the "Cabinet des Médailles de Paris" and Frederic W. Madden's *Coins of the Jews* which has a

---

25 Yaakov Meshorer, *Ancient Jewish Coinage. Vol. II: Herod the Great through Bar Cochba* (New York: Amphora Book, 1982), 51–64.

FIGURE 7-8 Coin of Agrippa I in Eisler, "Deux sculptures de l'antiquité," 32 (left) and in Madden, *Coins of the Jews*, 133 (right)

drawing of the same coin.[26] However, in Eisler's drawing Agrippa I now has a crooked nose and a generally less attractive face (fig. 7-8).[27]

But for Eisler another portrait was much more significant in his search for a Jewish physiognomy in Roman antiquity. In a statue from the Naples Archeological Museum which was found in Pompeii and which had become known as Drusus (and sometimes as Marcellus), Eisler saw a portrait of Agrippa III, son of Drusilla (daughter of Agrippa I) and M. Antonius Felix, procurator of Judea. According to Josephus, this Agrippa died in the eruption of Vesuvius in 79 CE,[28] thus in the region of Naples. This and a likeness with Agrippa I and II were sufficient reasons for Eisler to identify the statue as one of Agrippa III.[29] Eisler was not the first scholar, however, to see a Jew in "Drusus." Already Frederik Poulsen, the director of the Glyptotek who showed Eisler the bust in Copenhagen, compared it with the statue in Naples as presented in Bernoulli's *Römische Ikonographie* (fig. 9).[30] And as in the case of the bust in Copenhagen, whose subject was already identified as a Jew by Poulsen (see below), Eisler went a step further and identified the statue with a specific Jew: the Jewish bust in the Glyptotek shows Josephus, the Jewish statue from Naples Agrippa III.

---

26 Eisler, "Deux sculptures," 37; Madden, *Coins of the Jews*, 133.
27 Eisler may have seen the intaglio showing Agrippa at the Cabinet des Médailles de Paris. Cf. Marie-Louise Vollenweider and Mathilde Avisseau-Broustet, *Les portraits romains du Cabinet des Médailles* (Paris: Bibliothèque nationale de France, 2003), II, 67–68, n°72. On the intaglio Agrippa has if anything "un nez long et plongeant" (p. 68) as he does on the coins in Meshorer, *Ancient Jewish Coinage*, pl. 9–10.
28 Josephus, *Ant.* 20.143–144.
29 Eisler, "Deux sculptures," 35–36.
30 Frederik Poulsen, *Tillæg til katalog over Ny Carlsberg Glyptoteks antike kunstværker* (Copenhagen: Nielsen & Lydiche, 1925), 191 ("ligner noget den saakaldte Drusus in Neapel" ["looks somewhat like the so-called Drusus in Naples"], referring to Bernoulli, *Römische Ikonographie II.1*, plate 8).

FIGURE 9   "Statue des sog. Drusus von Pompeji, in Neapel", from Bernoulli, *Römische Ikonographie* (1886). Eisler shows the statue in his 1930 article (plate 6) and reinterprets it as Agrippa III ("Agrippa Ier" on the plate, but Eisler means Agrippa III as is obvious from his argument).

TESTA INCOGNITA

For Eisler the statue from Naples—with its melancholic look, almond-shaped eyes and long, curved nose—represents even more than the bust from Copenhagen the "Jewish type" ("type juif").[31] What in Eisler's view makes "Agrippa III" look more Jewish than "Josephus" is the former's blackness. While according to Eisler the bust from Copenhagen seems to have blond or red hair and light-colored eyes, the statue from Naples "was certainly of very dark complexion and had black hair with bluish reflections."[32] With this distinction Eisler follows a stereotype which, as Sander Gilman has shown, was widespread in the nineteenth century but certainly also continued into the twentieth century: "The general consensus of the ethnological literature of the late nineteenth century was that the Jews were 'black' or, at least, 'swarthy.' This view had a long history in European science .... For the eighteenth-and nineteenth-century scientist the 'blackness' of the Jew was not only a mark of racial inferiority, but also an indicator of the diseased nature of the Jew." Skin color is, as Gilman notes, "one of the most salient markers for the construction of race in the West over time."[33] This is indeed what Eisler is doing here. And this is what makes "Agrippa III" look (even) more Jewish than "Josephus." Eisler constructs and invents a Jewish body that was unknown to the ancient Romans.[34] Such constructions are by no means harmless, because they tend to imply social boundaries. As, again, Sander Gilman writes, here following Mary Douglas: "Where and how a society defines the body reflects how those in society define themselves. This is especially true in terms of the 'scientific' or pseudo-scientific categories such as race which have had such an extraordinary importance in shaping how we all understand ourselves and each other."[35] The imagined Jewish body (with regard to the nose, to hair color or to other bodily aspects) helps foster social differences. At the time of the Nazis, caricatures

---

31   Eisler, "Deux sculptures," 35: "Il me semble qu'on ne peut s'y méprendre en observant le regard mélancolique ... des yeux en forme d'amande, ce nez long et courbe, cette bouche aux lèvres longues et saillantes, les grandes oreilles en forme d'anses, ces joues maigres et ce menton pointu, couverts d'un léger duvet."

32   Eisler, "Deux sculptures," 35: "Tandis que le présumé Flavius Josèphe fait l'impression d'un blond ou d'un roux aux yeux clairs, ce personnage héroïsé ... était certainement de teint très foncé et d'une chevelure noire aux reflets bleuâtres."

33   Gilman, The Jew's Body, 171–172.

34   In Greco-Roman ethnography, the body of the Jews is not discussed (with the sole exception of male circumcision). One may also note that even Tacitus, who has some very negative things to say about the Jews (Hist. 5.4–5), does not identify Jewish figures, such as Agrippa I and II, as Jews. Cf. Bloch, Antike Vorstellungen vom Judentum, 126–127, 149–150. In Hist. 5.6 Tacitus describes the bodies of the inhabitants of Judea as "healthy and hardy" (salubria et ferentia laborum).

35   Sander L. Gilman, The Jew's Body (New York: Routledge, 1991), 170.

328   CHAPTER 15

of Jews marked the beginning of their total exclusion from society.[36] It is note-worthy that Eisler was aware of at least some of the problematics involved in his approach. In a footnote at the end of his 1930 article, he assures the reader that he knows that there are "several types of Jews" and that "no isolated body characteristic is peculiar to the Jews." Nevertheless, Eisler adds, Jews are recognizable and if Jews deny this it is a sign of missing self-confidence and pride.[37] Overall, Eisler was not willing to question the physical stereotypes he used.

With the construction of the other comes a judgement on esthetics. Before the bust from Copenhagen was interpreted as the portrait of a Jew, it could be referred to as a beautiful head (see below). But when seen as representing a Jew, the bust was described in negative terms. In his description of the bust Eisler points out "the hooked or 'broken' nose" which is "quite large in its lower part and very different in this from the aquiline nose which one finds so often among the Romans." The eyes have a "slightly shady expression," they are "at the same time sad, worried and vigilant." The bust has a "thin beard," the hair is "curly and uncut at the temples (*peath r'ōš*)." Eisler's Josephus is the opposite of a Roman: "all these features are certainly not those of a Roman."[38] This gloomy picture of Josephus goes hand in hand with Eisler's interpretation of the Jewish military and the author: Josephus is a "base and hypocrite character" as is obvious from the contradictions in his books.[39] The bust shows the cheerless portrait of a suspect man. In a publication from 1933 the German archaeologist Robert West refers to the "ugly facial features" ("unschönen Gesichtszüge") of the bust.[40] And in 1951 Frederik Poulsen in a new catalogue of the Ny Carlsberg Glyptotek can still write about the "fine, excellently preserved bust" that

---

36   Eugen Fischer and Gerhard Kittel in their notorious *Das antike Weltjudentum*, published in 1943, compare what they consider to be typical Jewish looks from their time with portraits on Egyptian sarcophagi. For Fischer and Kittel the most characteristic feature of the Jewish body, both in antiquity and in modern times, is the nose (p. 112). The book also includes a long list of what the authors interpret as ancient Jewish caricatures. Neither the bust from Copenhagen nor the statue from Naples is mentioned in the book.

37   Eisler, "Deux sculptures," 38 (n. 44: "qu'il n'y a pas un, mais plusieurs types juifs et qu'aucun caractère somatique isolé n'est particulier aux Juifs").

38   Eisler, "Deux sculptures," 34: "Le nez crochu ou "cassé" est assez gros dans sa partie inférieure et très différent en ceci du nez aquilin qu'on trouve si souvent chez les Romains. Le front bombé au-dessus des sourcils dont la partie supérieure fuyante se cache sous les cheveux bouclés, l'expression un peu ombrageuse des yeux à la fois tristes, inquiets et vigilants, de la bouche un peu maussade, surtout de la lèvre inférieure légèrement allongée, les boucles de cheveux frisées, non coupées aux tempes (*peath r'ōš*), la barbe maigre qui forme une espèce de duvet, tous ces traits ne sont certes pas ceux d'un Romain."

39   Eisler, "Deux sculptures," 34 ("caractère vil et hypocrite").

40   Robert West, *Römische Porträt-Plastik* (München: Bruckmann, 1933), 40.

TESTA INCOGNITA   329

it "doubtless represents a young Jew .... It is a wise, melancholy face, and both
race and individuality are well characterized."[41]

2   The Origins of the Bust

Robert Eisler's idea that the Copenhagen bust might represent Josephus did not
come out of nowhere. Eusebius speaks of a statue that was erected in Rome
in honor of Josephus (ὡς αὐτὸν μὲν ἀναθέσει ἀνδριάντος ἐπὶ τῆς Ῥωμαίων τιμη-
θῆναι πόλεως) and Jerome takes this up (*ob ingenii gloriam statuam quoque
meruit Romae*).[42] There is no mention of such a statue in Josephus or in any
pagan source, but this does not necessarily mean that Eusebius cannot be
trusted on this. Christian readers of late antiquity had a great interest in Josephus, both as a source of the first century CE and as witness to the Jews'
punishment for not recognizing Christ,[43] but there would have been no reason to make him greater by inventing a statue in his honor. One can assume
that the statue existed. Eisler incidentally assumes that the bust in Copenhagen was originally the head of a statue and not just a bust.[44] But this seems
unlikely.[45]

The earliest traces of the bust at the Glyptotek in Copenhagen reach back
to the early nineteenth century. In 1832 the bust was on display in the Villa
Borghese in Rome. Since the seventeenth century the family Borghese had
assembled a large collection of sculptures and paintings. It is unclear when the
bust was added to the Borghese collection and whence it came. The bust is
labeled as "unknown head" ("testa incognita") in Antonio Nibby's catalogue of
the Villa Borghese. The drawing in Nibby's catalogue (fig. 10, without commentary) seems to be the earliest representation of the bust.[46]

---

41   Frederik Poulsen, *Catalogue of Ancient Sculpture in the Ny Carlsberg Glyptotek* (Copen-
      hagen: Ny Carlsberg Glyptotek, 1951), 451.
42   Eusebius, *Hist. eccl.* 3.9.2; Jerome, *Vir. ill.* 13.
43   Cf. René Bloch, "Flavius Josephus, Bellum Judaicum," in *The Reception of Classical Litera-
      ture. Brill's New Pauly.* Supplements, ed. Christine Walde (Leiden: Brill 2012), 190–194. On
      Eusebius as reader of Josephus see Sabrina Inowlocki, *Eusebius and the Jewish Authors: His
      Citation Technique in an Apologetic Context* (Leiden: Brill, 2006).
44   Eisler, "Deux sculptures," 34: "la tête faisait jadis partie d'une statue."
45   I would like to thank Anne Marie Nielsen, Ny Carlsberg Glyptotek, for her advice on this
      question.
46   Vagn Poulsen, *Les portraits romains.* Vol. II (Copenhagen: Ny Carlsberg Glyptotek, 1974),
      54–55.

FIGURE 10
Antonio Nibby, *Monumenti Scelti della Villa Borghese*, Rome 1832, pl. 31

The bust did not stay anonymous for very long. It became associated with Domitius Corbulo, who in the first century CE held different offices (including consul and governor of Asia Minor). This proposition was rejected in 1882 by the Swiss archaeologist Johann Jacob Bernoulli who described the bust as "vortrefflichen Kopf mit der höckerigen Nase" ("a splendid head with the bumpy nose") but lingered for some time.[47] In the nineteenth century the Borghese family repeatedly had to sell parts of its collection because of financial constraints.[48] At the beginning of the century Napoleon I purchased a substantial part of the collection and brought it to Paris. If our bust was already on show at the Villa Borghese it did not end up on Napoleon's list (and in the Louvre). Towards the end of the nineteenth century the Danish brewer and art collector Carl Jacobsen, son of the founder of the Carlsberg brewery and art collector, showed strong interest in the Villa Borghese. It was Jacobsen's private collection which eventually became the foundation of the Ny Carlsberg Glyptotek. In Rome Jacobsen was represented by the German archaeologist and art dealer Wolfang Helbig. When in 1889 Marcantonio Borghese signaled that he was ready to relinquish a substantial part of the collection, the bust was evaluated by two

---

47   Johann Jacob Bernoulli, *Die Bildnisse berühmter Römer mit Ausschluss der Kaiser und ihrer Angehörigen* (Stuttgart: Spemann, 1882), 276. According to Bernoulli the bust stood in room 13, "im Zimmer des Hermaphroditen," of the Villa Borghese.
48   Cf. Mette Moltesen, "From the Princely Collections of the Borghese Family to the Glyptotek of Carl Jacobsen," *Analecta Romana* 16 (1987): 187–203.

TESTA INCOGNITA

assessors. One (Michel Tyszkiewicz) assessed the "Busto di Corbulone" for the price of 5000 francs, while another one (Francesco Martinetti) as "Corbulo? (buona, perfetta conservazione)" assessed it for 2500 francs.[49] Negotiations turned out to be lengthy, though, partly because of different interests within the Borghese family. There was also some attachment to the bust because of a likeness with the Borghese family: as a matter of fact, the bust had stood for some time in the study of Marcantonio Borghese (which, again, indicates the esthetic value the bust could exhibit before it "became" a Jew).[50] In any event, the bust was not sold directly to Wolfang Helbig and Carl Jacobsen. In 1890 it first came by lot to Agnese Boncompagni Ludovisi, Princess of Piombino and born Borghese. In the summer of the same year Michel Tyszkiewicz, art collector and one of the previous assessors, wrote to Carl Jacobsen, praising the bust as "un très beau buste de Corbulon." He noted that it was currently in the possession of a member of the family (presumably Agnese Boncompagni Ludovisi) who was willing to sell it ("vous n' aurez qu' à m' écrire un mot, et le buste sera à Votre disposition").[51] In 1891 the deal was finally struck: Carl Jacobsen bought the bust for the price of 4400 Francs for the Carlsberg Glyptotek (which would become the Ny Carlsberg Glyptotek in 1897). In 1892 the bust is mentioned in a catalogue of the museum edited by Carl Jacobsen. It is no longer identified with Corbulo, but cautiously labeled "A Roman man" ("en romer"). It is dated to the first century CE. In his brief description of the bust Jacobsen stresses its "outstanding execution and almost complete preservation." As for esthetic values, Jacobsen depicted the bust in a remarkably negative light: "He carries a light down-like beard. As a true realist, the artist has not wanted to flatter. The large nose is presented in all its ugliness."[52] The bust will only be identified with a Jew some 30 years later. Jacobson's comment on its "ugly nose" may to some extent have facilitated such an attribution. In 1907, in a new catalogue of the museum edited by Frederik Poulsen, the bust is still listed, with a photograph,

---

49   Moltesen, "From the Princely Collections," 189, 197–198.
50   Mette Moltesen, *Perfect partners. The Collaboration between Carl Jacobsen and his Agent in Rome Wolfgang Helbig in the Formation of the Ny Carlsberg Glyptotek 1887–1914* (Copenhagen: Ny Carlsberg Glyptotek, 2012) (Danish original 1987), 177.
51   Letter from Michel Tyszkiewicz to Carl Jacobsen (Neuilly sur Seine, July 12 1890). The letter is in the *Carl Jacobsens Brevarkiv* [https://brevarkivet.ny-carlsbergfondet.dk/d/GuPD?q= Borghese].
52   Carl Jacobsen, *Carlsberg Glyptotek. Nyt Tillæg til fortegnelse over kunstværkerne* (Copenhagen: Nielsen & Lydiche, 1892), 229: "Fortrinligt udført og næsten fuldstændig bevaret. Han bærer et let dunagtigt Skjæg. Som ægte Realist har Kunstneren ikke villet flattere. Den store Næse er fremstillet i al dens Grimhed. Tidligere i Villa Borghese."

332   CHAPTER 15

as "a Roman" ("Romer").[53] Things changed with the museum's catalogue of 1925, edited once more by Frederik Poulsen (who became the museum's director the year after). Poulsen sees in the bust a young Jew: "surely a young Jew" ("Sikkert en ung Jøde"), he writes. As already mentioned, Poulsen notes parallels with the statue of "Drusus" in Naples as presented by Bernoulli (which Eisler then transforms into Agrippa III).[54] Poulsen's 1925 entry on the bust seems to be the first reference to the portrait as a Jew. The "testa incognita" of the Villa Borghese, for some time identified as Corbulo, has now become a Jew. Four years later, in 1929, Eisler visited the Ny Carlsberg Glyptotek in Copenhagen and identified the subject of the bust as Josephus.[55] In 1929 and 1930 Eisler published, as we have seen, his large book *Iēsous basileus ou basileusas* including, in the second volume, the bust of "Flavius Josephus" from Copenhagen. In 1930 his article "Deux sculptures de l'antiquité classique représentant des Juifs" was published in Paris and the following year, in 1931, the English version of *Iēsous basileus ou basileusas* appeared with a picture of the bust from the Glyptotek on the first page.

Until then the identification of the bust had changed several times, but its date had not been questioned. It was interpreted as a portrait of the first century CE. Eisler, incidentally, dared to suggest a more precise dating: according to him it was Josephus himself who after the successful publication of his *Jewish War*, after 76–80 CE, commissioned the bust.[56] But in 1932 the German archaeologist Ludwig Curtius questioned the first-century-CE-dating of the bust. In an article published in *Römische Mitteilungen*, Curtius dated it to the end of the Republic and the beginnings of the Augustan age.[57] Curtius rejected Poulsen's parallelization of the bust with the statue in Naples ("Drusus," also interpreted

---

53   Frederik Poulsen, *Ny Carlsberg Glyptotek. Billedtavler til Kataloget over antike kunstværker* (Copenhagen: Ny Carlsberg Glyptotek, 1907), LII.

54   Poulsen, *Tillæg til katalog*, 191.

55   In his 1930 article Robert Eisler mentions that Frederik Poulsen had already for a long time labeled the statue as a Jew: "En effet, le directeur de la fameuse collection fondée par le généreux mécène Jacobsen, le Dr Frederic (sic) Poulsen, dont on connaît la grande compétence en matière d'iconographie, l'avait déjà signalée depuis longtemps comme: *Jøde, romersk Portraet fra c. 50 E. KR*, c'est-à-dire 'Juif, portrait romain du milieu du 1er siècle'" (Eisler, "Deux sculptures," 33). Unfortunately, Eisler does not say where exactly Poulsen made that statement. The description cited above is a bit different.

56   Eisler, "Deux sculptures," 34–35: "... après 76–80. Ce serait donc au moment où il eut la satisfaction de publier la seconde édition de sa *Guerre Juive*, que l'auteur, grisé de ce succès qu'il attribuait certainement plutôt à son génie littéraire qu'à la protection de ses hauts et puissants patrons, aurait cédé à la tentation de se faire sculpter."

57   Ludwig Curtius, *Mitteilungen des Deutschen Archäologischen Instituts. Römische Abteilung*. Vol. 47 (München: Bruckmann, 1932), 208–210.

FIGURE 11
Carnelian by Agathangelos, first century BCE, from Ludwig Curtius, *Mitteilungen des Deutschen Archäologischen Instituts*, 209. Curtius sees close parallels between the gem and the bust in the Glyptotek.

as "Marcellus," Eisler's "Agrippa III"). According to Curtius, that statue shows a Roman, while the bust from Copenhagen is some "personality from the Greek East" ("eine Persönlichkeit des griechischen Ostens"). According to Curtius, the only feature the faces have in common is the "large crooked nose" ("die große gebogene Nase"). Curtius preferred to compare the bust from Copenhagen with a carnelian from Berlin signed by Agathangelos from the first century BCE (fig. 11).

Curtius's dating of the bust to the first century BCE did not find any followers. Robert West dated the bust to the early Flavian period.[58] In 1939 Frederik Poulsen reacted to Curtius' interpretation, upholding a dating in the first century CE, more specifically in the period of the Flavians. At the same time, Poulsen found Eisler's identification of the bust with Flavius Josephus unconvincing ("bedenklich") in the absence of replicas. What continued to be clear to Poulsen was that the bust shows a Jew. He called it the "Kopenhagener Judenbüste."[59] From then on, the dating of the bust was no longer questioned. The interpretation of the bust as showing Flavius Josephus, however, proved persistent (in spite of Poulsen's critique). Eisler's thesis, unscientific and based on racist stereotypes, was widely adopted. The desire to have a real portrait of Flavius Josephus, possibly even the one mentioned by Eusebius, may have been too strong simply to reject Eisler's interpretation. And the stereotypes of a Jewish physiognomy as outlined by Eisler may have been shared or internalized by some. Eisler's arguments from his 1930 article, published in French, were

---

58 West, *Römische Porträt-Plastik*, 40.
59 Poulsen, *Römische Privatporträts und Prinzenbildnisse*, 3–5.

334 CHAPTER 15

hardly ever discussed, but his interpretation of the bust as one of Josephus developed considerable momentum. In Abraham Schalit's Hebrew translation of the *Jewish Antiquities*, published in Jerusalem in 1944, the bust is printed at the beginning of the edition, with a reference to Robert Eisler's article.[60]

It seems that at the Ny Carlsberg Glyptotek the bust was never displayed as "Flavius Josephus." In 1974 Vagn Poulsen, Frederik Poulsen's successor as director of the Ny Carlsberg Glyptotek (no relation), in a new catalogue on the Roman portraits in the museum, situated the bust with its "southern physiognomy" in the early Flavian period, but left its identity explicitly open. The bust was no longer described as the portrait of a Jew.[61] The brief Museum Guide, edited by Vagn Poulsen and reprinted several times, makes no mention of the bust in its description of room 13.[62] While at the museum the bust remained known as "the Jew" until the seventies,[63] with Vagn Poulsen's correction the attribution gradually faded. The most recent catalogue published by Ny Carlsberg Glyptotek, the one by Flemming Johansen, stresses once more that a "reasonable identification does not seem to be possible."[64] The bust has definitely become what it had been when it was first on show at the Villa Borghese in Rome: una testa incognita. Outside of the museum, however, the myth of the portrait of Flavius Josephus continued. In 1986, the *Abguss-Sammlung Antiker Plastik* of the Institute for Classical Archaeology at the Freie Universität Berlin acquired a copy of the bust from the Ny Carlsberg Glyptotek and listed it as a portrait of "Josephus Flavius" (in quotation marks).[65]

---

60   Abraham Schalit (translator), *Flavius Josephus: Antiquities of the Jews. Translated into Hebrew with an Introduction and Notes* (Jerusalem: Bialik Foundation, 1944) [Hebrew]. On Schalit see Daniel R. Schwartz, "Herod, Josephus, the Holocaust, Horst R. Moehring, and the Study of Ancient Jewish History," in *Jewish History* 2 (1987): 9–28.

61   Poulsen, *Les portraits romains*. Vol. 2, 55: "A en juger par le style, ce portrait semble bien appartenir aux premiers temps des Flaviens, mais l'auteur du présent catalogue ne se sent pas en mesure de localiser de façon plus précise une physionomie méridionale telle que celle-là. Certes, une courte barbe est quelque chose d'insolite dans l'art du portrait du Ier siècle, mais le cas n'est pas unique. On n'a guère l'impression qu'il soit possible de trouver une base solide permettant d'aboutir à la dénomination exacte du sujet représenté par notre buste."

62   Vagn Poulsen, *Führer durch die Sammlungen* (Copenhagen; Ny Carlsberg Glyptitek, 1969/ 1977). Room 13 is described on page 53.

63   Anne Marie Nielsen (Museumsinspektør, Antik Samling, Ny Carlsberg Glyptotek) in an oral information.

64   Johansen, *Catalogue*, 68.

65   Friederike Fless, Katja Moede, Klaus Stemmer, eds., *Schau mir in die Augen ... Das antike Porträt* (Berlin: Freie Universität Berlin, 2006), 150, Kat.Nr. 394. The editors do note that "eine begründbare Identifizierung ist jedoch nicht möglich."

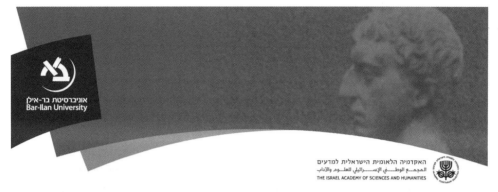

FIGURE 12   Program of a colloquium on Josephus organized by Bar Ilan University in 2019

The museum's corrections notwithstanding, Robert Eisler's identification of the Copenhagen bust as one of Flavius Josephus was widely disseminated. Editors of Josephus's oeuvre did not hesitate to print a photograph of the bust.[66] Robert Eisenman in his widely read (and criticized) book *James the Brother of Jesus*, published in 1997, reprinted the "presumed bust of the Jewish historian Josephus" and facilitated further dissemination of the attribution.[67] And today, 90 years after the publication of Robert Eisler's article in *Aréthuse*? Even Josephus himself might have felt somewhat uncomfortable if he saw how widely his (Pseudo-)portrait is shared and distributed. The Wikipedia article on Josephus includes in many languages a picture of the bust from the Ny Carlsberg Glyptotek. One finds the bust in contributions on Josephus on Youtube, Twitter, and in blogs—but also at academic conferences. At a very recent colloquium on "Josephus between the Bible and the Mishna" organized by Bar Ilan University the bust was prominently printed at the top of the program (fig. 12). Most scholars are of course aware that the bust has precious little to do with Josephus. It somehow has become a conventional placeholder for a vacuum which seems difficult to accept. However, in light of the problematic history of this bust, the attribution to Josephus should be laid to rest for good.

---

66   We have already referred to the Hebrew edition by Schalit. A French example with a photograph of the bust is the 1968 edition by Arnauld D'Andilly and Jean A.C. Buchon (translators), *Flavius Josèphe. Histoire ancienne des Juifs & la guerre des Juifs contre les Romains 66–70 ap. J.-C. Autobiographie* (Paris: Lidis, 1968) with a preface by Valentin Nikiprowetzky.
67   Robert Eisenman, *James the Brother of Jesus* (London: Faber and Faber, 1997), fig. 18.

Bibliography

Actes du ve congrès international d'histoire des religions à Lund, 27–29 août 1929. Lund: C.W.K. Gleerup, 1929.

Bernoulli, Johann Jacob, *Die Bildnisse berühmter Römer mit Ausschluss der Kaiser und ihrer Angehörigen*. Stuttgart: Spemann, 1882.

Bernoulli, Johann Jakob, *Römische Ikonographie II.1*. Berlin: Spemann, 1886.

Bloch, René, *Antike Vorstellungen vom Judentum: Der Judenexkurs des Tacitus im Rahmen der griechisch-römischen Ethnographie*. Stuttgart: Franz Steiner, 2002.

Bloch, René, "Flavius Josephus, Bellum Judaicum." Pages 190–194 in *The Reception of Classical Literature. Brill's New Pauly*. Supplements 5. Edited by Christine Walde. Leiden: Brill 2012.

Bradley, Mark and Eric Varner, "Missing noses." Pages 171–180 in *Smell and the Ancient Senses*, ed. Mark Bradley. London: Routledge, 2015.

Broshi, Magen, *Bread, Wine, Walls, and Scrolls*. Sheffield: Sheffield Academic Press, 2001.

Bultmann, Rudolf. Review of Eisler, *The Messiah Jesus. Literaturblatt der Frankfurter Zeitung*, January 24, 1932.

Curtius, Ludwig, *Mitteilungen des Deutschen Archäologischen Instituts. Römische Abteilung*. Vol. 47. München: Bruckmann, 1932.

D'Andilly, Arnauld, and Jean A.C. Buchon (translators), *Flavius Josèphe. Histoire ancienne des Juifs & la guerre des Juifs contre les Romains 66–80 ap. J.-C. Autobiographie*. Paris: Lidis, 1968.

Eisenman, Robert, *James the Brother of Jesus*. London: Faber and Faber, 1997.

Eisler, Robert, "Deux sculptures de l'antiquité classique représentant des Juifs." *Aréthuse* 26 (1930): 29–38.

Eisler, Robert, *Iesous basileus ou basileusas. Die messianische Unabhängigkeitsbewegung vom Auftreten Johannes des Täufers bis zum Untergang Jakobs des Gerechten. Nach der neuerschlossenen Eroberung von Jerusalem des Flavius Josephus und den christlichen Quellen dargestellt*. 2 vols. Heidelberg: Winter 1929/30.

Eisler, Robert, *The Messiah Jesus and John the Baptist according to Flavius Josephus' Rediscovered 'Capture of Jerusalem' and the Other Jewish and Christian Sources*. New York: Lincoln Macveagh, 1931.

Eisler, Robert, *Weltenmantel und Himmelszelt. Religionsgeschichtliche Untersuchungen zur Urgeschichte des antiken Weltbildes*. München: C.H. Beck, 1910.

Fine, Steven, "How Do You Know a Jew When You See One? Reflections on Jewish Costume in the Roman World." Pages 19–28 in *Fashioning Jews: Clothing, Culture, and Commerce*. Edited by Leonard Greenspoon. West Lafayette: Purdue University Press, 2013.

Fischer, Eugen, Gerhard Kittel, *Das antike Weltjudentum: Tatsachen, Texte, Bilder*. Hamburg: Hanseatische Verlagsanstalt, 1943.

Fless, Friederike, Katja Moede, Klaus Stemmer, eds., *Schau mir in die Augen ... Das antike Porträt*. Berlin: Freie Universität Berlin, 2006.

Gilman, Sander L., *The Jew's Body*. New York: Routledge, 1991.

Heuer, Renate et al., eds., *Lexikon deutsch-jüdischer Autoren*. Vol. 6. München: Saur, 1998.

Inowlocki, Sabrina, *Eusebius and the Jewish Authors: His Citation Technique in an Apologetic Context*. Leiden: Brill, 2006.

Jacobsen, Carl, *Carlsberg Glyptotek. Nyt Tillæg til fortegnelse over kunstværkerne*. Copenhagen: Nielsen & Lydiche, 1892.

Johansen, Flemming, *Catalogue: Roman Portraits II. Ny Carlsberg Glyptotek*. Copenhagen: Ny Carlsberg Glyptotek, 1995.

Lubrich, Oliver, Michael Stolz, eds., *Die Universität von Muri. Benjamins Berner Anfänge*. Bern: Walter Benjamin Kolleg, 2019.

Madden, Frederic W., *Coins of the Jews*. London: Trübner & Co., 1881.

Meshorer, Yaakov, *Ancient Jewish Coinage*. Vol. 2. *Herod the Great through Bar Cochba*. New York: Amphora Book, 1982.

Moltesen, Mette, "From the Princely Collections of the Borghese Family to the Glyptotek of Carl Jacobsen." *Analecta Romana* 16 (1987): 187–203.

Moltesen, Mette, *Perfect partners. The Collaboration between Carl Jacobsen and his Agent in Rome Wolfgang Helbig in the Formation of the Ny Carlsberg Glyptotek 1887–1914*. Copenhagen: Ny Carlsberg Glyptotek, 2012 (Danish original 1987).

Poulsen, Frederik, *Ny Carlsberg Glyptotek. Billedtavler til Kataloget over antike kunstværker*. Copenhagen: Ny Carlsberg Glyptotek, 1907.

Poulsen, Frederik, *Tillæg til katalog over Ny Carlsberg Glyptoteks antike kunstværker*. Copenhagen: Nielsen & Lydiche, 1925.

Poulsen, Frederik, *Römische Privatporträts und Prinzenbildnisse*. Kopenhagen: Munksgaard, 1939.

Poulsen, Frederik, *Catalogue of Ancient Sculpture in the Ny Carlsberg Glyptotek*. Copenhagen: Ny Carlsberg Glyptotek, 1951.

Poulsen, Vagn, *Führer durch die Sammlungen*. Copenhagen; Ny Carlsberg Glyptotek, 1969/1977.

Poulsen, Vagn, *Les portraits romains*. Vol. II. Copenhagen: Ny Carlsberg Glyptotek, 1974.

Schalit, Abraham (translator), *Flavius Josephus: Antiquities of the Jews. Translated into Hebrew with an Introduction and Notes*. Jerusalem: Bialik Foundation, 1944 (Hebrew).

Scholem, Gershom, *From Berlin to Jerusalem: Memories of My Youth*. New York: Schocken, 1980.

Scholem, Gershom, *Walter Benjamin: The Story of a Friendship*. Philadelphia: The Jewish Publication Society of America 1981.

Schwartz, Daniel R., "Herod, Josephus, the Holocaust, Horst R. Moehring, and the Study of Ancient Jewish History." *Jewish History* 2 (1987): 9–28.

Thackeray, Henry St. John, *Josephus: The Man and the Historian*. New York: Jewish Institute of Religion, 1929.

Vidal-Naquet, Pierre, "Flavius Josèphe où du bon usage de la trahison". Préface à la *Guerre des Juifs*, traduit par Pierre Savinel. Paris: Editions de minuit, 1977, 7–115.

Vollenweider, Marie-Louise and Mathilde Avisseau-Broustet, eds., *Camées et intailles, II, Les portraits romains du Cabinet des Médailles*. Paris: Bibliothèque nationale de France, 2003.

West, Robert, *Römische Porträt-Plastik*. München: Bruckmann, 1933.

Zeitlin, Solomon, "Josephus on Jesus." *JQR* 21 (1931): 377–417.

Index of Cited Passages

Hebrew Bible

Gen

2:21	159
3:16	67
6	113
6:1–4	112
8:4	118
10:8	113
11:1	169
11:1–9	166
11:7	169
13:18	112
15:18	75
16	32
18	168
19	101, 104, 157
19:17	101
19:17–26	101
19:26	101
20:12	62, 63
23:19	112
25:9	112
25:27	156, 187
26:2	74
34:5	181
37–50	217
39	217
39:11	178
41:43	213
41:45	205, 212
41:46	211
41:50	204
43:32	213
46:20	204
49:29–32	112
50:12–13	112

Exod

1:7	185
1:8–10	26
1:15–21	56
1:22	58
2:1	57, 58, 59
2:2	59
2:2–10	56
2:10	59
2:10–11	55
2:11–12	55
3	69
3–4	23
3:5	69
3:8	69
3:17	69
4:14	35
4:16	55
4:24–26	56
6:20	57
7:1	55
7:1–13	51
7:8–15	45, 46, 47, 50
7:11	45
12–28	75
14:5	46
22:17	47
22:18	162
22:20	284
23:20	75

Lev

18:23	162
19	240
19:19	162
20:15–16	162

Num

13:22	111
13:28	113
13:33	113
21:8–9	158
23:19	160
26:59	57

Deut

3:11	106
6:6–7	310
13:7–11	307
18:10–11	47
27:21	162
28	310

INDEX OF CITED PASSAGES

Deut (*cont.*)

34:6	73
34:10	55

Josh

4:9	106
7:26	106

Judg

15:14–20	271

Ruth

1:16	178

1 Sam

30:14	267

2 Sam

21:16	113

1 Chr

4:18	66

Job

22:28	58

Ps

1	176
1:1–2	176
50	299
69:13	181
104:32	180
115	298
115:2–8	298

Eccl

2:2	185

Isa

1:11	133
1:11–17	299
1:17	133

Jer

15:17	179
47:4	267

Lam

3:14	181
4:6	268

Hos

6:6	134

Amos

5:21–24	299

Jonah

1:3	122
2:1	122

Mic

5	268
6:6–8	299

Zech

9:7	180

New Testament

Matt

9:13	134
12:7	134
22:7	141

Mark

12:9	141

Luke

19:42–44	141

John

2:21	141
7:2	195

Acts

7:22	44
13:4–12	47

Rom

1:14	95
12:17	205

INDEX OF CITED PASSAGES

Gal

1:18	102

LXX

Exod

7:11	45

Deut

8:5	160
28:64	5

Wis

10:7	102
11:5	77

Dead Sea Scrolls

CD

6	134

Ancient Jewish Writers

Aristobulus

See Eus. Praep. ev. 8.10.2

Artapanus

See Eus. Praep. ev. 9.27.4 and Hist. eccl.
9.18.1

Ezekiel Tragicus

v. 1–6	78
v. 32–38	66, 193
v. 35	35
v. 37	35
v. 109–112	78
v. 167	78
v. 193–242	216
v. 236	79
Fr. 1–2	60

Joseph and Aseneth

1.1	211
1.4	202
1.5	202
2.1	202, 209

Heb

9:2	195
11:15–16	77
19:22	77

2 Macc

2:21	94, 95
12:24	52

2.3	203
2.8	202
2.9	202
2.11	202
3–31	200
3.2	211
3.3	212
3.4	213
3.6	213
4.1	213
4.2	202
4.7	209
4.9	203
4.10–11	213
5.2	203
6.2	213
7.1	212, 213
7.2	203
7.4	209
7.8	203
8.5	202, 203
8.11	214
9.1	203, 213

INDEX OF CITED PASSAGES

Joseph and Aseneth (*cont.*)

9.4–5	212
10.2	213
10.4	213
10.10	213
10.12	213
11.9	215
11.11	215
11.14	215
11.18	215
12.1	203
13.15	210, 214
14.3	203
14.14	213
15.7	214
15.15	213, 214
15.17	204
16.1	213
16.19	214
18.2	213
18.5	213
18.10	204
19.2	213
19.10	208
20.8–9	212
20.10	212
21.6	216
21.9	204
22.7	202
23.9	205
25.4	214
26–27	200
26.4	214
28.5	205
28.7	205, 214
28.10	205
28.14	205
29.7	213

Josephus

BJ

1.9–12	138
1.152–153	129
1.179	129
1.415	185
1.422	185
1.471	189
1.530	189
1.543	189

2.254–265	41, 48
2.261	41
2.285–292	136
2.490–492	182
2.565	52
3.419–420	119
4.45	95
4.84–120	48
4.85	48
4.103	48
4.156	189
4.476	261
4.483–485	102, 109
4.530–533	111
5.17	95
5.184–237	138
5.317–330	48
5.318	48
5.329	48
6.93–94	134
6.146	189
6.241	130
6.252	130
6.254	130
6.420	132
7.5	131
7.145–150	132
7.148–150	138
7.158–162	117, 132
7.160	118
7.218	131
7.420–436	137

AJ

1.15–23	104, 156
1.73	113
1.93	118
1.113–114	113
1.113–118	169
1.155	215, 306
1.186	111
1.203	101, 102, 158
1.240	104
2.148	94
2.284–287	45, 50, 51
2.286	45, 46
2.320	46
3.180–181	195
3.305	114
3.420	123

INDEX OF CITED PASSAGES

4.12	95
5.125	114
6.264	189
8.45	47
8.46	47, 102
10.195–238	42
11.327–328	2
11.329	2
11.329–332	1
11.336–339	2
11.338	3
12.113	189
12.114	184
14.72	129
14.105–109	129
14.115	98, 136
15.268	185, 186, 188
15.274–276	188
15.410	189
17.161	185
18.19	134
18.257	21
18.257–260	21, 71
18.259	21, 22
19.94	189
19.199	189
20.25	118
20.97–98	49
20.97–99	49
20.100	22
20.141–144	42, 47
20.142	47
20.143–144	325
20.160	40
20.167	40, 41
20.167–168	40
20.167–172	48
20.169	41
20.169–172	40
20.188	49

Vita

16	190
40	22, 52
277	136

CA

1.38–40	138
1.43	182
1.235	302, 309
1.250	302
1.309	51
2.42	3
2.80	259
2.102–109	138
2.119	138
2.123	98
2.145	8, 39, 41, 44, 50, 51, 52, 53
2.145–286	39
2.146	48
2.148	43
2.156	50
2.158	50
2.160	50
2.161	8, 39, 41, 44, 48, 50, 51, 52, 53
2.193	138
2.236	52
2.236–256	104
2.239	104
2.240–243	306
2.257	61
2.282	95, 98

Jub.

10:10–15	44

Let. Arist.

83–120	107
284	184
285	184
316	184

Philo

Abr.

54	165
65	22, 71
134–141	105
243	156

Aet.

49	187

Agr.

35	187
97	158, 159

Cher.

50	63
77–78	164

Conf.

1	166

INDEX OF CITED PASSAGES

Conf. (*cont.*)

2	167
2–5	166, 167
3	167
4	168
5	167
6	168
6–8	168
7–9	168
9	168
14	159, 168
15	168, 169
142	166
170	169
189	169
190	169

Congr.

61–62	156
62	156, 187
73	32
74–76	32, 33, 76
79	32, 33

Decal.

5	253
76	164
149	165
156	156, 164

Det.

125	156
178	164

Deus

52	160
53	160
54	160
57	160
57–58	160
59	160
60	160
63	160
155	166

Ebr.

61	62, 67
122	105
177	74, 186
222	157

Flacc.

19	187
20	187

41–53	138
46	25, 71, 72
49	70, 295
74	181
84	181
85	182
95	182
121–124	138

Fug.

121	105, 156, 157
121–122	104, 157
122	105

Gig.

58	156

Her.

62	62
214	36
216	61
272–274	34

Hypoth.

See Eus. Praep. ev. 8.6.2

Jos.

30	86
119–121	26
121	218
148	213

Leg.

1.15	62
1.43	159
2.19	159
2.24	159
3.137	253
3.213	105

Legat.

1	21
33	25
121	25
132–139	138
142	25
143–147	25
147	25
150	65, 72
182	26
190	25
196	26
204	187
368	187
370	21

INDEX OF CITED PASSAGES

Migr.

76	164
77	73
151	73
154	73

Mos.

1.4	106
1.7	63
1.9	63
1.10–12	63
1.14–15	64
1.17	64
1.19	65
1.20	33
1.20–26	30
1.21	33, 34
1.21–23	31, 64
1.21–24	31, 74, 76, 193
1.22	34
1.23	26, 31, 33
1.23–24	33
1.24	34, 159
1.25	33
1.30–31	27
1.32	33, 65
1.33	65
1.36	24
1.43	25
1.44	25
1.45	25
1.48	23
1.65–70	28
1.65–84	70
1.67	70
1.68	70
1.69	70
1.71	70
1.73	70
1.88	26
1.150–154	72
1.157	72
1.158	67
1.158–159	24
1.163	73
1.180	26
2.18–20	95
2.21	188
2.27	95
2.29	106

2.43	28
2.56	102, 105, 158
2.74–94	195
2.129	159
2.192	23
2.103	61
2.204	24
2.209–210	61
2.210	62, 67
2.212	30
2.215	30
2.216	30, 138
2.271	164
2.288	73

Mut.

90	73
167–168	35

Opif.

1–2	104, 155
3	73, 156
100	62
118	61
146	253
157	158

Post.

165	164
174	24

Praem.

23	165
53	28

Prob.

19	187
57	36
73–75	95
75	134
99–104	187
141	186, 187
143	187

Prov.

2.64	22, 71, 105, 138
2.107 (arm.)	22, 71, 105

QE

2.13	75

QG

1.8	159
2.43	157
2.54	160
4.2	168
4.23	157

INDEX OF CITED PASSAGES

QG (*cont.*)

4.31	157
4.51	157
4.177	74

Sacr.

13	156
41	253
50	24

Som.

1.232–237	160
2.192	157
2.255	75

Spec.

1.51	156, 165
1.69	137
1.74	163
1.76	137
1.79	164
1.315	45
2.69	253
2.259	253
3.3	23
3.4	33
3.43	162, 163
3.43–50	161
3.44	161
3.45	162, 163
3.46	162

3.47	162
3.48–50	163
3.49	163
4.59	190
4.73	253
4.81	165

Virt.

51	24
52	28
102	165
147	253
177	253
178	165
187	253
194	253

Ps.-Eupolemus

See Eus. Praep ev. 9.26.1 and Hist. eccl.
9.17.8

Ps.-Philo, LAB

9.2–9	58
9.15–16	60

Sibylline Oracles

2.15–19	308
3.97–104	169

Rabbinic Literature

Mishnah

'Abod. Zar.

1:7	179

Ber.

9:1	115

Ta'an.

4:6	143

Jerusalem Talmud

'Abod. Zar.

1:7, 40a	177, 183

Ber.

4:2, 7d	179
9:2, 13c	180

Babylonian Talmud

'Abod. Zar.

18b	176, 177, 183

Ber.

54a	102, 116
54a–b	116

Joma

57a	117

Ketub.

5a	184

Meg.

6a	180
13a	66

Šabb.

63b	117
89a–b	305

INDEX OF CITED PASSAGES

Sotah

12a	58, 67
12a–13a	57
13a	67

Sukkah

5a	117

Tosefta

'Abod. Zar.

2.5	177
2:7	183

Kippurim

2:16	117

Midrashim

Bet Ha-Midrash

6, 112–113	67

Cant. Rab.

1.1	178

Eccl. Rab.

1.7	179
2.2	185

Ex. Rab.

1.13	58
1.26	55

Gen. Rab.

67.3	179
80.1	181
87.7	178

Lam. Rab.

Proem 3	179
3.14	181

Pesiq. Rab Kah.

15.2	179
28.1	179

Pirqe R. El.

25	101, 102
38	218

Ruth Rab.

1.16	178
2.22	178

Sifre Zuta

be-haalotekha 8.2	
	117

Tanḥ. Buber

Shemot 6	185

Yal.

Parashat Wayera	101

Early Christian Writings

Arnobius

Adv. nat.

7.1	135

Augustine

Civ.

6.11	98
10.9	42

Clement of Alexandria

Strom.

1.23.150.4	29
1.23.155–156	191

Codex Theodosianus

16.10.2	136

Egeria

Itin. 12.7	102

Ephrem

Contr. Iul.

1.16	140
2.7	140

Eusebius

Hist. eccl.

3.9.2	323, 329
7.18.1–2	323
9.7.1	43
9.17.8	44
9.18.1	44

Praep. ev.

8.6.2	44
8.10.2	104, 161
8.10.4–5	161
9.26.1	29
9.27.4	29, 61
9.28.1	192
13.12.3–4	29

INDEX OF CITED PASSAGES

Gregory of Nazianzus
Or.

2.84	182

Jerome
Comm. in Zach.

3.14	260

In Ion.

1.3b	122

Ep.

108.8.2	122

On.

11.2.22	106

Vir. ill.

13	323, 329

John Chrysostom

PG 35.489	182
PG 36.617	180
PG 44.9	180
PG 56.264	188

Minucius Felix
Oct.

9.3	259

Novatian

Spec. 2.3	185

Origen
Cels.

1.20	156
1.23	293, 294
1.24	294
1.26	43
1.67	294
2.56	293
4.36	156
4.41	156

Orosius
Hist.

1.10.3	263

Ps.-Hegesippus

3.6	261
4.18	261

Rufinus
Hist.

10.38	140

Socrates Scholasticus
Hist. eccl.

7.13	187

Sulpicius Severus
Chron.

2.30.6	128, 129
2.30.8	232
7.9.5–6	130

Tatian
Orat. ad Graec.

23–24	180

Tertullian
Apol.

16.1–3	259
16.3	259
19.6	259
38.4	180
40.7	260

Nat.

1.11.2	259
1.14–15	259
2.12	260

Greco-Roman Literature

Aeschylus

Prom. 442–506	29

Ammianus Marcellinus

14.8.11–12	258
22.5.4–5	258
22.5.5	258
23.1.2–3	140, 258
24.4.1–2	258

Apuleius

Apol. 90	44

INDEX OF CITED PASSAGES

349

Arrian
Epict.

2.9.19–20	98

Callimachus
Ia.

2	168

Cassius Dio

73.24.1–2	117

Cicero
Flacc.

66	98
67	94
66–69	96

Prov.

5.10	284

Verr.

2.4.132	107

Curtius

8.9.20	85

Diodorus

2.48.7	88, 94
4.20.1	85
19.98	88
19.99.3	94
34/35.1.1–4	297
34/35.1.5	297

Diogenes Laertius

1.9	43

Diomedes
Grammatici Latini

1.491	184

Euripides

Fr. 115	122

Herodotus

1.30	102
2.35	85
4.11	86
4.82	118
4.105	42
7.61	120

8.55	112
9.122	85

Heliodorus
Aeth.

1.19.3	206
2.33	209

Heraclitus
All.

22.1	170

Hesiod
Theog.

868	159

Homer
Il.

2.204–205	169
2.205–207	169
5.385–387	167
18.104	163

Od.

11.305–316	167
11.315–316	167
12.118	164
20.379	163

Julian
C. Gal.

306B	140

Justin

See Pompeius Trogus 36.2.7.11

Juvenal

6.542–546	43
14.96–106	96, 262
14.102	262

Longus

4.26.4	208
4.40.3	208

Lucan

6.107	89

Lucian

Alex.

13	43

Philops.

4	107
16	43

Trag.

171–173	43

Martial

Epigr.

7.82	190

Mela (Pomponius Mela)

1.64	121

Numenius of Apamea

See Euseb. Hist. eccl. 9.7.1

Pausanias

1.21.3	103
1.35.3	116
4.35.9	121
5.10.7	107

Philostratus

Her.

8.14–17	114

Plato

Men.

80a–b	42

Nom.

649a	42
909b	43

Resp.

364b	43
378d	158
380d	42
383a	42
413b–d	42
526–530d	31
531d	33
572e	42

Symp.

203d	52

Theaet.

183d	34

Pliny the Older

Nat.

5.71	88
5.69	121
9.5.11	121
12.111	89
30.2	47
30.11	44

Pliny the Younger

Ep.

1.6	258
6.16	258
6.20	258
7.20	258
7.33.1	257

Plutarch

Adul. poet. aud.

19	158

Alex.

9	112

Apoph. Rom.

2.205	203

De Pyth.

2	107

Quaest. conv.

4.5.3	94
4.6.2	94

Superst.

3.166	98

Pol.

4.21.1	85

Pompeius Trogus (Justinus)

36.2.1–3.9	94
36.2.7.11	44

Ptolemy

Tetr.

2.3.65–66 (29–31)	
	86

Quintilian

3.7.21	288

Sallust

Jug.

17.6	93

INDEX OF CITED PASSAGES
351

Seneca

De Superst. See Aug. Civ. 6.11

Strabo

1.1.19	159
1.2.7–8	161
1.35	120
6.3.5	108, 110
14.2.28	94
15.1.13	85
16.2.28	121
16.2.35	238
16.2.36	238
16.2.37	238
16.2.39	44
16.2.43	43
16.2.44	107, 108
17.1.29	108

Suetonius

Aug.

72	114

Tacitus

Agr.

10.1	97
10.2	97
10.3	97
10.5	89
11.1	97
11.2	87, 92

Ann.

2.60	108
2.85	280
2.85.4	97
15.44	266, 276, 283
15.44.4	282

Germ.

5.1	87
9.2	259
16–17	92
29.1	92
29.3	87
30.2–3	92
32	92
36.1	89
40	260
45.1	89

Hist.

1.3.2	272
1.10.3	97
1.22.1	44
1.46.3	89
2.4–5	314
2.4.3	272
2.74	22
2.79	22, 97
3.54	109
3.72	129
4.1.1	274
5.1.8–13	267
5.2–13	86
5.2–3	91
5.2.1	91, 95, 265, 267
5.2.3	263, 267
5.3	262, 295
5.3.1	51
5.3.2	259
5.4–5	262, 279, 327
5.4.1	91, 262, 272, 273, 280
5.4.2	91, 259, 266, 271, 287
5.4.3	89, 91
5.4.4	260, 277, 278, 287
5.5	91, 239
5.5–8	90
5.5.1	91, 272, 273, 276, 277, 280, 283, 284, 285, 287
5.5.2	43, 91, 272, 273, 277
5.5.3	91, 268, 270, 287
5.5.4	91, 259, 266, 271, 277, 283
5.5.5	91, 265, 277, 278
5.6–7	88, 261
5.6	327
5.6.1	89, 91, 93, 261, 271
5.6.2	88, 89, 91, 261
5.6.4	89
5.7	109
5.7.1	88, 89, 260
5.7.2	261
5.8–10	88
5.8.2	91, 276
5.8.3	91
5.9.1	129, 259, 268
5.9.2	276, 295
5.11	263
5.13	91, 268, 278

INDEX OF CITED PASSAGES

Hist. (*cont.*)

5.13.1	273, 277, 278, 284
5.13.3	91, 274

Theophrastus

Hist. plant.

9.6.1–4	89

De pietate

fr. 3	135

Varro *See Arnob. Adv. nat. 7.1*

	135

Virgil

Aen.

6.440–441	88, 110

Georg.

4.287–314	204
4.490–491	101

Xen. Eph.

1.1.3	212
1.1.5	209

Inscriptions

IJO (Inscriptiones Judaicae Orientis)

15–16	190
37	190
38	190
39	190

JIWE (Jewish Inscriptions of Western Europe)

15	191

Index of Names and Places

Aaron   23, 45–46, 58, 271
Abimelech   62
Abraham   22, 24, 32, 44, 62–63, 71, 101, 104,
    111–112, 165, 168, 215, 306
Abraham Schalit   334–335
Abram   75
Achilles Tatius   206, 210, 216
Acropolis   112
Adam   12, 156, 159, 293
Adam Kamesar   161
Aelia Capitolina   139
Aeneas   8, 57, 66
Africa, Africans   93
Agathangelos   333
Agnese Boncompagni Ludovisi   331
Agrippa I   324–325
Agrippa II   232, 324
Agrippa III   325, 327, 332–333
Ajax   116
Akhenaten   15, 301
Alan Mendelson   32
Albert Camus   164
Albert Socin   122
Alexander (Philo's brother)   21
Alexander the Great   1–3, 6, 112, 228–229,
    250
Alexandria   3, 7–8, 22–29, 31, 34, 65–66, 71–
    72, 74, 76–77, 79, 138, 180, 182, 186–187,
    191, 194, 201, 215, 224, 229, 247, 249, 254,
    295
    See also Alexandria, anti-Jewish riot
Aloadae   167, 170
Aloeus   167
Amenophis   302
Amram   57–59, 63
Andrea Alciato   265
Andromeda   10, 104, 119–124
Angelos Chaniotis   7
Anthia   207
Antiochus IV Epiphanes   133, 224, 228, 236,
    259, 296–297
Antiochus VII Sidetes   296–297
Antisthenes   161
Antonio Nibby   329
Aphrodisias   190
Aphrodite   209–210

Apion   3, 250, 270, 298
Apollonius Molon   8, 39–40, 44, 50–52, 94
Apuleius   44
Arcadia, Arcadians   85
Ares   167
Aristobulus (philosopher)   29, 104, 161
Aristobulus II (Hasmonean)   129
Armenia, Armenians   94, 118
Artapanus   29, 35, 44, 60
Artemis   210
Aseneth   12–13, 200–218
Asia   85, 96
Asia Minor   189, 195, 210, 330
Athena   57, 62–63, 112
Athens   112, 251
Augustus   25, 114, 128
Auschwitz   15, 309–311
Australia   255
Azariah de Rossi   268

Babel, tower of   12, 158, 166–169
Bacchus   269
Baruch (Benedictus) de Spinoza   14, 154,
    268, 271–274
Batavians   87
Beatus Rhenanus   260
Benjamin   204
Berenice   47, 232
Berlin   227, 246, 254, 279, 281, 333
Bern   320
Berossus   118
Beth Shean
    See Scythopolis
Beth-Tor (Bethar)   143
Bezalel Bar-Kochva   87–88, 236
Bitjah   66
Boccaccio   250
Breslau   227, 246
Britannia, Britons   9–10, 87, 89, 92, 94, 97
Buchenwald   321

Caesarea   185–186, 324
Caiaphas   102
Cain   163–164
Caligula   8, 21–22, 25–26, 71, 189, 295
Callimachus   3

354 INDEX OF NAMES AND PLACES

Cambridge 318
Canaan 75, 78, 113
Capitol 128–129, 131
Capri 114
Carl Jacobsen 330–331
Carlsberg brewery 330
Cassiopeia 119
Castor 48–49
Celsus 43–44, 156, 293–294, 297, 302, 306
Celts 94
Centaurs 162
Cepheus 119, 121
Chairemon 298
Chaldea, Chaldeans 1, 86
Chariclea 206–207, 209–210
Charites 165
Chariton 206, 210, 216
Charybdis 164
Chatti 92
Chimeras 162
China 255
Chloe 208–209
Christhard Hoffmann 225, 234
Christian Worm 14, 267, 270
Christoph Burchard 201
Colosseum 132
Constantinople 180, 188
Constantius II 136
Copenhagen 15, 314–335
Crassus (Marcus Linius) 129, 132
Cremona 109
Cupid 209
Cyrenaica 96
Cyrus 85

Dachau 321
Dan 214
Dante 250
Daphnis 208–209
Dead Sea 43, 88–89, 94, 105–106, 109, 258
Deucalion 165
Dina 218
Dionysus 177
Domitia Longina 314
Domitian 264, 287, 314
Domitius Corbulo 330, 332
Dositheus 52
Drusilla 47, 325
Drusus 325, 332

Dura Europos 251, 324

Eden 159
Edith 101
Edom 180
Eduard Norden 87
Eduard Wolff 284
Edward Gibbon 275–276, 281
Egeria 102
Egypt, Egyptians 2–4, 6, 8–9, 13, 15, 23, 25–
 27, 33–34, 40–41, 44–46, 51, 64, 67,
 69–79, 85, 96, 107, 137, 164, 192, 201,
 205, 210, 212–216, 218, 228, 234, 238,
 240, 294, 297–303
Ekaterina Matusova 34
Eleazar (exorcist) 47, 102
Eleazar (high priest) 107
Eleazar (son of Simon) 52
Eleazar ben Rabbi Jose 117
Elephantine 137
Elias Bickermann 235, 283
England 321
Erich S. Gruen 5, 93, 236
Eros 209–210
Esau 156, 187
Ethiopia 119
Eugen Fischer 235, 237, 284, 328
Eugen Täubler 283
Eurydice 101
Eve 11, 156, 159, 293
Ezra 226

Fadus 49
Faustina 191
Felix Stähelin 13, 229–230, 233, 239
Felix, procurator of Judea 40, 47, 49
Flaccus 181, 187
Frankfurt 246
Franz X. Leonhard 279
Frederik Poulsen 15, 325, 328, 331–334
Friedrich Nietzsche 284
Fritz Friedländer 253
Fritz Graf 39, 41–42
Froma Zeitlin 206

Gabriel Brotier 276
Gabriel Riesser 248
Gad 214
Galicia 142

INDEX OF NAMES AND PLACES

Galilee   48, 186
Gaza   2
Georg Andresen   284
Georg Büchmann   252–253
Georg Caspar Kirchmaier   14, 267
Gerhard Delling   165
Gerhard Kittel   235, 237, 284, 328
Germania, Germani   10, 87, 92, 94, 259
Germany   14, 228, 235, 245–246, 249, 253–254, 284
Gershom Scholem   318–322
Goebbels   226, 281
Gomorrah   88–89, 101, 260–261
Goshen   310
Göttingen   247
Greece   107, 177, 195
    See also Hellenism
Guillaume Budé   14, 264, 266, 276, 286

H. St. John Thackeray   322
Habrocomes   207, 209, 212
Hades   101, 293
Hagar   32–33
Haliturus   190
Harry A. Wolfson   12, 153–154, 156, 163, 170
Hebron   10, 111–114, 118
Hecataeus of Abdera   51, 86, 236, 297
Hegel   283
Heidelberg   294
Heinrich Graetz   282–283
Heinrich Leo   15, 279–280
Heinrich von Treitschke   227–228, 282–283
Heliodorus   206–207, 210
Heliopolis   201, 210–211, 213
Heracles   104, 118, 293
Heraclitus   35
Hermann Diels   246
Herod the Great   112, 185, 188
Herodium   185
Hippolytus   210
Hitler   226, 281
Horeb   69, 304–305
Howard Jacobson   194
Hyrcanus II   129

India, Indians   85
Iphimedeia   167
Isaac Cardoso   268, 270, 274
Isaak   165

Isaak Heinemann   235, 240, 246–247, 249, 251, 283
Israel (ancient)   5–6, 11, 43, 55, 70, 133, 141–142, 145, 179, 230, 268, 299, 307, 309
Israel, state of   123–124, 224
Israelites   8, 23–26, 28, 34–35, 45, 51, 67, 69, 72–79, 106, 113, 174, 192, 194–195, 225, 236, 240, 262, 273, 280, 283, 304, 306

Jacob   78, 165, 187, 218
Jacob Riesser   248
Jaddus   1
Jan Assmann   15, 293–311
Japho
    See Joppa
Jean Bodin   14, 264, 277
Jean Henri Dotteville   276–278
Jericho   116, 185
Jerusalem   1–3, 10–11, 22, 25, 41, 43, 48, 71–72, 86–91, 102–103, 105, 107, 117, 120, 128–129, 131–133, 136–142, 144, 185–186, 188–189, 195, 203, 224, 228, 231–232, 238, 240, 251, 260–264, 269, 272, 277–278, 280, 287, 295–297, 314, 324
Jesus   11, 134–135, 141, 143, 237, 240, 261, 268, 277, 293–294, 319, 322
Jethro   69, 78
    See also Raguel
Jocasta   66
Johann G. Müller   278, 281
Johann G. Orellius   15, 283
Johann Gustav Droysen   6–7
Johann Jacob Bernoulli   325, 330
Johannes Leipoldt   13, 237, 239–240
John Barclay   5, 207
John F. (Hans) Oppenheimer   255
John Gager   231
John of Gischala   8, 48–50
Jonah   122
Jonathan Z. Smith   11, 84, 96, 134, 136
Joppa/Japho/Jaffa   10, 104, 119–122, 124
Jordan River   49, 106
Joseph   13, 25, 44, 67, 178–179, 195, 200–218
Joseph and Aseneth   200–218
Judea   6–7, 9–11, 14, 40, 51, 84, 86–90, 95–97, 103, 105–107, 121, 131, 136–137, 139, 191, 231, 238, 258, 280, 297, 314, 325, 327
    See also Palestine
Jules Isaac   231

INDEX OF NAMES AND PLACES

Julia 314
Julian (emperor) 139–141
Julianus Pichon 266
Julius Caesar 226, 229, 281
Julius Wellhausen 225, 230
Jupiter 129
Jürgen Habermas 301
Justus Lipsius 260, 265–266, 277
Justus of Tiberias 22

Karl Trüdinger 90
Konrad Zacher 13, 227–230, 236, 239

Laios 66
Leonard Cohen 58
Leon Battista Alberti 263
Leontopolis 137
Leopold Cohn 28, 246
Leuca 108, 110
Levi 204, 214
Ligurians 85
Lion Feuchtwanger 287–288
London 321
Longus 206, 208–209
Lot 101
Lot's wife 11, 101–104, 116, 157–159
Louis Feldman 28
Ludwig Curtius 332–333
Ludwig Holländer 247
Lund 323
Lysimachus 8, 39–40, 44, 50–53, 298

Machiavelli 265
Machpelah, Cave of 112
Maimonides 133
Mamre 111–112
Manetho 302–303
Marc Philonenko 207, 211
Marc-Antoine Muret 14, 264
Marcantonio Borghese 330–331
Marcel Mauss 83
Marcel Simon 43
Marcellus 325, 333
Marcia Furnilla 316
Marcus Antonius Felix 325
Marcus Aurelius Pylades 191
Marcus Jastrow 177
Marcus Vertranius Maurus 265
Maren Niehoff 168, 170

Martin Buber 320
Mattiaci 87
Max Mayer 248–249
Menophilus 190
Merope 66
Mesopotamia 111
Michael (angel) 218
Michael Avi-Jonah 140
Michel de Montaigne 264, 277
Michel Tyszkiewicz 330–331
Miletus 190
Minos 294
Minotaur 162–163
Miriam 56–59, 63
Moab 73
Moritz Güdemann 283
Moses Mendelssohn 248
Moses 7–9, 22–27, 35, 55, 69–79, 105–106,
    116, 155–157, 167–168, 192–193, 216,
    237–238, 240, 259, 262, 270, 293–294,
    296–297, 300–303, 309
  as inventor 29, 61
  as magician 39–54
  as philosopher 29–36
  before Pharaoh 23, 45–47
  his death 73
  his education 30–34, 64–66, 74, 193–194
  his mothers 8–9, 55–67
  his name 60, 64
Mount Gerizim 137
Mount of Olives 40
Mount Scopus (Saphein) 1
Mount Sinai 45–46, 164, 192, 304–305
Muri 320

Naomi 178, 180
Naples 325, 327, 332
Napoleon I 330
Near East 210
Nehemiah 179, 226
Nereids 119
Nero 190, 264, 282–283
Nerthus 260
Nicholas de Lange 233, 236
Nike 62
Niklas Holzberg 205, 207, 210
Nile 8, 63
Nimrod 113
Ninos 216

INDEX OF NAMES AND PLACES

357

Niobe   102
Noah   44, 118, 165
Numidians   94
Ny Carlsberg Glyptotek   15, 314–335

Odysseus   8, 57
Oedipus   66
Og   106
Ogyges   111
Onias   137
Orpheus   101, 293, 308
Osarsiph   302–303, 309
Ostia   191
Othmar Keel   307
Otto Bauernfeind   48
Otto Michel   48
Oxford   318, 321
Oxted   321

Palestine   10, 55, 75, 73, 75, 84, 95, 103, 106,
   119–122, 124, 136, 185–186, 189, 191,193,
   251
   See also Judea
Pannonians   94
Parthians   94, 129
Persians   1–2, 94, 120, 140, 276
Paris   318, 330
Pasiphae   12, 161–163, 166
Paul   71, 102, 141, 239–240
Paul Veyne   170
Penelope   33
Pentephres   202, 211–213
Perses   120
Perseus   10, 120–121, 294
Persians   1–2
Peter Brown   135
Peter Schäfer   230
Pharaoh   8, 23, 25–26, 35, 45–46, 51, 53, 56,
   58–60, 66, 72, 76, 79, 192, 201, 212–213,
   216, 248
Pharaoh's daughter   8, 35, 56, 58–60, 63–64,
   66, 78
Pharaoh's son   201, 204–205, 213–214
Phineas   121
Phoenicia, Phoenicians   1–2, 73, 86, 97, 123,
   234
Pierre Vidal Naquet   322
Pompeii   325
Pompey   129, 259, 268

Pontos   94
Poppaea   190
Poseidon   119, 167
Posidonius   13, 43, 51, 86, 239–240, 246, 296
Potiphar   179, 195, 202, 218
Potiphar's wife   179
Primo Levi   310–311
Prometheus   29
Puah   56
Puteoli   190
Pythagoras   29, 62

Raguel   78, 192
   See also Jethro
Remus   57
Robert Eisenman   335
Robert Eisler   15–16, 318–334
Robert West   328, 333
Rome, Romans   3, 9–11, 21, 26, 48–49, 76,
   84–88, 92–98, 114, 117, 119, 121–122, 124,
   128–132, 139, 143–144, 177, 180, 188–191,
   224, 231–232, 236, 241, 249, 270, 279–
   280, 297–299, 306, 323, 329–330
Romulus   57
Rudolf Bultmann   322
Ruth   178, 180

Sachsenhausen   255
Salamis   116, 194
Samson   271
Samuel Yosef Agnon   142
Sander Gilman   327
Sarah   62–63, 67, 112
   See also Sarai
Sarai   32
   See also Sarah
Scylla   12, 163–164
Scythia, Scythians   86, 118
Scythopolis   191
Sea of Reeds   77, 79, 216
Seleucids   7
Sepphoris   186
Serah bat Asher   67
Shanghai   255
Shaye Cohen   92
Shimon Lev-Ari   173
Shiphrah   56
Sigmund Freud   59, 305
Simone Luzzatto   14, 268–269, 271, 274

INDEX OF NAMES AND PLACES

Sisyphus 164
Socrates 29, 34
Sodom 10, 88–89, 101–102, 104–105, 107–112, 114, 118–119, 124, 157–158
Solomon 47, 76
Solomon Zeitlin 322
Sorbonne 318, 322
Sosipater 52
Spaniards 94
Stefan Borzsák 257
Stephan Tilg 216
Stephanie West 208–209
Suiones 89
Sweden 323
Syria, Syrians (ancient) 1, 96, 105, 122, 129, 139

Tantalus 165
Tartarus 159
Telamon 116
Tel-Aviv 123–124
Tencteri 92
Teucer 116
Theagenes 206–207
Theodor Klauser 240
Theodor Mommsen 13, 223, 225–226, 228–229, 233, 280–281
Théodore Reinach 225
Theodotus 136
Theophil Kiessling 15, 283
Theseus 293
Theudas 49–50
Thracia, Thracians 94
Thyamis 206
Tiberias 186
Tiberius 25
Tiberius Julius Alexander 22, 232, 248
Timothy 52

Titus 48, 117, 128–131, 133, 142, 144, 314, 316–317
Trajan 15, 215, 314
Troy 116
Typhon 159
Tyre 2

Ulrich von Wilamowitz-Moellendorf 247, 249
Ur 22, 71

Vagn Poulsen 334
Venice 269
Venus 57, 66
Vespasian 15, 93, 95, 102, 117, 129, 278, 314, 317
Vesuvius 325
Via Appia 191
Via Sacra 132
Vienna 318
Villa Borghese 329, 334
Vindolino de Spira 265
Vitellius 314, 316–317
Voltaire 15, 275

Walter Benjamin 318
Walter Burkert 42
Wilhelm Heraeus 284
Wolfgang Helbig 330–331
Wolfram Kinzig 227

Yavne 144
Yochebed 8, 56–59, 63, 67

Zeno 35–36, 161
Zeus 62, 166, 159, 169
Zipporah 56–57, 192
Zvi Yavetz 230

Index of Subjects

Acculturation, Jewish   2, 93
Actors and actresses, Jewish   174, 190–191
Alabarch   22
Alexandria, anti-Jewish riot   8, 24, 26, 28, 76, 181, 187, 229, 248, 295
Alexandrian citizenship, Jews   3, 249
Allegory   9, 33, 75, 104–105, 157–161, 169–170
Amarna Period   299, 301, 303
Angels   44, 203, 209, 218
Aniconism   2, 26, 175, 251, 259, 271, 295
Anthropogeography   10, 84–90, 93, 95
Anthropomorphism   159–161, 203
Anti-Judaism   13, 223–224, 230, 233, 237, 303–305
Antisemiten-Liga   227
Antisemitism   8, 13, 15, 89, 223–241, 247, 249, 270, 274, 279, 286, 320
Antisemitismus-Streit, Berliner   227
Apologetics   27–28, 32, 158, 230–231, 247, 269, 293, 299–301, 309
Arch of Titus   117, 132
Atheism   167
Autochthony   86

Bar Kokhba Revolt   139–141, 143
Barbarians   10, 25, 34, 84, 93–98, 224, 308
Bees   204, 214
Bestiality   161–163
Body   9, 61, 63, 73–75, 84, 87, 91–93, 97, 159–160, 271, 327–328
Burning bush   9, 28, 69–70, 72–73, 78, 192
Bugonia   204

Cherubim   275
Christianity   6, 11, 129, 140–142, 145, 229–233, 237, 239, 241, 275–276, 278–279, 281, 284, 286, 293, 306, 308, 319–320, 322
Christians   11–12, 135, 140, 180–184, 187–188, 240, 249, 259–266, 282–283, 286, 293, 307
Circumcision   57, 93, 96, 239, 273, 327
Classics   4, 206, 208
Climatic theories   85, 87, 92
Conversion   12, 178, 180, 200–218

Cosmopolitanism   7, 10, 72–73, 225–227, 236, 280–281, 286
Creation of the world   61, 72, 111, 156, 159

Decalogue   164–165
Diaspora   3, 5–6, 9–11, 71, 83–84, 95–98, 104, 107, 117, 136–139, 142, 145, 184–186, 191, 193, 215, 223, 226, 228, 251, 253–254
Diaspora revolts   215, 314
Dietary laws   213, 239, 269

Embassy to Caligula   21–22, 26, 71
Enlightenment   14, 85, 275, 280
enkyklios paideia   31–34, 64, 74
Essenes   134
Ethnography   10, 14–15, 44, 83–98, 239, 297, 327
Exile, Jewish   142, 247
Exodus   4, 8–9, 26, 51, 53, 69–79, 164, 193, 271, 297, 303, 310
Exorcism   47
Expulsion, of Jews   97, 224, 280

fiscus Iudaicus   131
Flavians   86, 132, 272, 277, 333
Frühchristentum   5
Frühjudentum   5

Gabriel Riesser-Verlag   248
Giants   10, 103, 106, 108, 112–115, 119, 167
Globalization   7
Gospels   141–142
Greek tragedy   78, 192–194
Hellenism   3–4, 6–7, 35, 251–252
    Jewish Hellenism   2–4, 7, 9–10, 12–14, 35, 246–255
Hellenistic drama   4, 173–199
Hieroglyphs   33
Holocaust   224, 231, 234, 309

Idolatry   12, 66, 164, 177, 194
IUDAEA CAPTA, coins   93
Ioudaios/Iudaeus, meaning of   5, 97
Islam   307–308

Jewish diaspora
   See diaspora
Jewish Hellenism
   See Hellenism
Jewish magic
   See magic
Jewish novel
   See novel
Jewish polemic, anti-pagan   305–306
Jewish-Roman War   11, 96, 119, 122, 128–129,
     132, 134, 139, 182, 189, 260, 280, 295, 299
Jews, body of
   See body
Jews, German   14, 253
Judeophobia   230

Koine Greek   3

Late Judaism   5, 279
Law of nature   73
Levites   272

Maccabees/Maccabean revolt   7, 11, 228–229
Magic   204, 210
   anti-Jewish accusation   1, 42–44
   erotic   47
   Jewish   1, 8, 39–53, 251
   papyri   44
Manna   166, 271
Menorah   61, 117, 191
Messianic age   11, 143–144
Middle Ages   2, 133, 183, 233, 261, 263
Misanthropy   50, 89, 225, 236, 269, 275–277,
     282–284, 298
Mission, Jewish   12, 200, 208
Monotheism   2, 13, 15, 169, 215, 266, 294–295,
     297–299, 302–303, 306–308
Mysticism   207
Myth   10–11, 103, 108, 112, 116, 120, 161, 189,
     204, 293
   biblical   107, 118
   Greek (pagan)   11–12, 62, 66, 104, 110,
     112–115, 118–122, 124, 161–171, 204, 210,
     217
   Jewish   11–12, 103–104, 112, 114, 119, 142,
     145, 153–171
   Jewish critique of   105, 166–170, 187, 189
   modern meaning of   154–155
   paideutic   161

trees   111–112
mythological hero   8, 55–56, 66

National Socialism   14–15, 226, 235, 250, 281,
     284–286, 321
Nectar   166
Novel, Greek/Jewish   4, 7, 12–13, 200–218
Numbers, symbolic meaning   61–62

Pharisees   228–229
Philo Verlag   14, 247–248
Philo-Lexikon   13, 245–255
Philosemitism   227–229, 236, 241
Philosophy   22, 29–36, 61, 64, 74–75, 138,
     153–154, 166, 222, 246, 274
Pilgrimage   10, 102–103, 106, 108, 112, 115, 117,
     124, 135, 137
Polytheism   15, 139, 215, 294, 297–298, 305–
     306
Pork, abstinence from eating   96, 269
Postcolonialism   6, 35
Privileges (*privilegia*)   3

Qumran   134, 143

Rabbis
   condemning theater   175–183
   travelling to Rome   117–118
Race, Racism   15, 327, 333
Reallexikon für Antike und Christentum
     237, 240
Relics   102, 109–110, 115, 117–118, 158
Renaissance   14

Sabbath   30, 48, 61, 89, 96, 184, 188, 239, 260,
     269–270
Sabbatical year   89, 270
Sacrifice   1, 91, 119, 139, 177, 203, 206, 273
   Christian   11, 135–136, 141–143
   Jewish   70, 115, 132–137, 141, 143, 278, 299
Samaritans   137
Septuagint   5, 28, 76, 122, 143, 193, 211, 271
Sophists   52
Souvenirs   115
Spätjudentum
   See Late Judaism
Synagogue(s)   55, 136, 138, 145, 179, 190, 196,
     251, 295, 324
Tacitism   14, 265, 274

INDEX OF SUBJECTS

Temple of Jerusalem
  see Jerusalem
Temple of Pax (Peace) 117, 132
Temple tax 131, 136–137
Testimonium Flavianum 322
Theater 12, 74, 132, 177
  Christian 180–185
  Jewish 12, 173–196

Topoi, ethnographic 10, 44, 84, 90–93, 95
Tourism 10, 102–124

Weimar Republic 249
World War II 15, 224, 237, 240, 309

Xenophobia 230